SECOND EDITION

# The Joy of Children's Literature

## DENISE JOHNSON
College of William and Mary

**WADSWORTH**
CENGAGE Learning™

Australia • Brazil • Japan • Korea • Mexico • Singapore • Spain • United Kingdom • United States

To all teachers and caring adults who give the joy of literature to children every day.

**The Joy of Children's Literature,**
**Second Edition**
Denise Johnson

Executive Publisher: Linda Schreiber-Ganster

Executive Editor: Mark D. Kerr

Assistant Editor: Beckie Dashiell

Editorial Assistant: Genevieve Allen

Marketing Manager: Kara Kindstrom

Marketing Assistant: Dimitri Hagnéré

Marketing Communications Manager: Tami Strang

Content Project Manager: Samen Iqbal

Design Director: Rob Hugel

Art Director: Jennifer Wahi

Print Buyer: Rebecca Cross

Rights Acquisitions Specialist: Don Schlotman

Production Service: Andrea Clemente, Cadmus
Communications

Text Designer: Marsha Cohen

Photo Researcher: Megan Lessard

Text Researcher: Christie Barros

Copy Editor: Kim Bernard

Cover Designer: Jeff Bane

Cover Image: © Getty Images/56586199

Compositor: Cadmus Communications

For product information and technology assistance, contact us at
**Cengage Learning Customer & Sales Support, 1-800-354-9706.**
For permission to use material from this text or product,
submit all requests online at **www.cengage.com/permissions**.
Further permissions questions can be e-mailed to
**permissionrequest@cengage.com.**

Library of Congress Control Number: 2010934547

ISBN-13: 978-1-111-29836-4
ISBN-10: 1-111-29836-X

**Wadsworth**
20 Davis Drive
Belmont, CA 94002-3098
USA

Cengage Learning is a leading provider of customized learning solutions with office locations around the globe, including Singapore, the United Kingdom, Australia, Mexico, Brazil, and Japan. Locate your local office at **www.cengage.com/global.**

Cengage Learning products are represented in Canada by Nelson Education, Ltd.
To learn more about Wadsworth, visit **www.cengage.com/wadsworth**.
Purchase any of our products at your local college store or at our preferred online store **www.CengageBrain.com.**

Printed in the United States of America
1 2 3 4 5 6 7 14 13 12 11 10

# BRIEF CONTENTS

# CONTENTS

## 3    Literacy: How Children Become Good Readers / 38

## VISUAL DISCUSSION 1:

Children's Literature in Action:
The Book, the Child, and Literacy

## VISUAL DISCUSSION 3:

### How to Use Children's Literature in the Classroom

As educators, we seek to "pay it forward," to return the discovery of the delights of learning in the same coin to a new generation. Many of us who have moved from one side of the teacher's desk to the other still hold in our hearts the happy memories of a teacher reading aloud, or maybe we remember the special pleasure of choosing books from a classroom library based on our own interests, having the minutes slip away while under the magical spell of a story, recommending books to friends, or the distinct connection of recognizing parts of ourselves reflected back from the pages. We may also remember *not* seeing ourselves reflected, nervously waiting for our turn during a reading "round robin," seeing the rolled eyes of our classmates as we sounded out words slowly or suffered the indignity of being in the "guppy" reading group. These experiences have lasting power. They can demarcate the difference between a lifelong learner and a lifelong test-taker. The more we know about children's books, the more we can individualize instruction to make sure our practice builds the confidence, capability, and enthusiasm of the children we serve.

What really stood out to me in Denise Johnson's text is her recognition of the delicate balance that must be struck by the modern educator between policy and practice. Teachers are under increasing pressures to meet mandates, but even in the face of stresses and challenges, integration of great children's literature into the curriculum offers the opportunity for critical thinking, creativity, community, and as Johnson so aptly puts it, *joy*. Positivity permeates Johnson's unique text; I use the term "positivity" not only in the sense of optimism but in the certainty that integration of children's literature benefits students and fortifies teacher satisfaction and retention to boot. Readers will discover within these pages an ambitious overview of children's literature in its many flavors, but this book also undertakes a broad range of pragmatic topics of special interest to educators, such as comprehension strategies, applying criteria, developing classroom libraries, and a wealth of digital resources. Rather than a heavy-handed intrusion to the actual reading experience, this text is a highly accessible companion to discovery, an open door to the beginning of a professional expertise. Whoever walks through will be better equipped to create far-reaching positive experiences for the children and reinvigorate their own practice.

Excellent children's literature has always had the capacity to create a profound impact on the educational experience, and this will continue into the new millennium, as long as teachers recognize its power and have the knowledge to use it. To this end, I am one of many readers grateful for the resource Denise Johnson has created.

Enjoy!

Esmé Raji Codell
*http://www.planetesme.com*

## Why I Wrote This Book

Why, you might ask, is the title of this book *The Joy of Children's Literature*? Why choose the word *joy* to describe children's literature when it can evoke sadness or reflection or a range of other emotions? Joy is a very small, yet very intense word. Pat Mora coined the term *bookjoy* to describe the "intense private pleasure readers experience when they savor a book. Delicious text" (Prichard, 2006, p. 24). The goal of this book is to assist teachers with understanding how to instill bookjoy—the intense pleasure of reading—in their students and thus develop lifelong readers.

To serve children well, teachers must become insightful and observant readers and knowledgeable purveyors of children's literature. Without a teacher who has insight and experience with children's literature, what can the young child in the classroom expect to learn about reading? Much is missed if preservice teachers are not well-versed in the literary works their students will be reading. Yet teachers must also be cognizant of the direct connection of children's literature to reading development and instruction. The second edition of *The Joy of Children's Literature* provides in-depth coverage of children's literature, usually available only in larger texts, while also integrating reading methods in a brief, accessible format.

The brevity of this text allows time to read and experience numerous children's books. Reading, writing, discussing, comparing, criticizing, evaluating, and finding pleasure in children's books is essential to the ability to recognize and recommend literature and ultimately to share with children the joy of children's literature.

*The Joy of Children's Literature*, second edition, is designed for undergraduate or graduate children's literature courses in teacher preparatory programs or English literature programs. This text may also be used as a supporting text for Reading and Language Arts courses in teacher education programs not having a separate children's literature course. Reading specialists, practicing teachers, counselors, or parent volunteers wanting more information on children's literature will also find valuable information here.

## What Makes This Book Unique

There is a void in children's literature texts. The brief children's literature books that are available may offer outstanding color illustrations but skimp on the coverage of genres. Or a text might cover genres but offer few illustrations, no color, and limited pedagogy. Some texts are merely shortened versions of the bigger texts, the tomes of children's literature—in which hundreds of books are mentioned, but little is done to teach readers how to evaluate good children's literature on their own. It has been my mission to bridge this gap.

*The Joy of Children's Literature*, second edition, offers complete genre coverage, color illustrations, and more pedagogical features. Most important, there is full coverage of genres, theories, reader response, controversial issues, and the art of writing and illustration. Such full coverage can be accomplished in a brief book partially because material such as evaluation criteria and categories of genres are formatted into tables—which is space-saving and provides an easy-to-find reference for the reader.

But the depth of the coverage in this brief book is what I hope will stand out most about this text. Children's literature is examined in detail for each genre. The narrative goes beyond the brief facts of each genre or a list of titles. I "teach the reader to fish" by giving the reader the tools to discern quality children's literature. The connection to reading methods is integrated throughout the genres and at the beginning and end of the book.

Here is more about what makes this book unique:

- A separate chapter for each of nine genres
- A chapter dedicated to digital texts and information technology
- In-depth analysis of two children's books: one analysis of the visual content and another analysis of cultural content and authenticity
- A companion website where you can listen to a book online while reading about it in the text and where you can link to a blog site dedicated to *The Joy of Children's Literature*
- Extensive pedagogy and special features including categories of genre books, evaluation criteria, booklists, and professional development activities that challenge the reader to think critically about children's literature, to bring children's literature into the classroom, and to investigate authors and illustrators

## A Walk Through the Content

*The Joy of Children's Literature* is organized into three parts. Part 1 emphasizes the foundations of children's literature. Part 2 is the body of the text with nine chapters, each devoted to a genre of children's literature. Part 3 provides instructional methods for using children's literature in the classroom.

### PART 1: AN INTRODUCTION TO LITERATURE, CHILDREN, AND LITERACY

- **Chapter 1** focuses on the foundations of children's literature—literary elements and a brief history of children's literature.
- **Chapter 2** addresses the child—how children respond to literature, including cultural influences.
- **Chapter 3** examines literacy—how to involve children in reading and how to create a classroom environment that supports the use of children's literature throughout the curriculum.
- Pulling It All Together: Children's Literature, Child Development, and Literacy for Preschool Through Grade 6 is a reference tool that teachers will refer to again and again when they are searching for the best children's literature to use with children at each stage of development.
- "Children's Literature in Action: The Book, the Child, and Literacy" is a vivid color section that uses the visual impact of classroom photos and captions to highlight effective instructional practices to engage children in children's literature across the day.

## PART 2: THE GOOD BOOKS THEMSELVES

**Chapters 4 through 12** investigate each of the major genres of children's literature:

- Picturebooks and illustrations
- Traditional literature
- Modern fantasy
- Realistic fiction
- Historical fiction
- Poetry
- Nonfiction: biographies and informational books
- Multicultural and international literature
- Digital books and information communication technology

Each genre chapter follows a consistent organization and offers significant coverage to involve the reader in a thorough understanding of the distinctions of that genre. The narrative includes definition of the genre, categories of the genre, benefits and considerations, evaluation and selection criteria, the role of the genre in literacy development, opportunities for reader response, and making the connections to children's literature across the curriculum.

Part 2 concludes with a color section entitled "The Art of Children's Books: A Visual Discussion of Genre and Illustration." The captions identify the media and visual techniques and serve as a learning tool to increase the reader's visual literacy.

## PART 3: CHILDREN'S LITERATURE IN THE CLASSROOM

Part 3 presents methods for using children's literature in the classroom—independent reading, read alouds, and literature circles.

- Part 3 begins with a special chart, "Instructional Framework: Optimal Learning Model Across the Curriculum," which provides a practical way for teachers to organize instruction with children's literature.
- **Chapter 13** addresses methods for reading aloud and reading with children (read-alouds, shared reading, and guided reading).
- **Chapter 14** examines classroom methods for children reading on their own— independent reading and literature circles.
- Part 3 closes with a color feature, "How to Use Children's Literature in the Classroom," which presents color classroom photos to show how children engage with literature in the classroom.

# New to This Edition

Users of the first edition of *The Joy of Children's Literature* will find several important changes in the second edition. The most apparent change is in the attractive and inviting new exterior cover and interior design. The cover art and accompanying interior design serve to remind readers that the ultimate goal of this book is to invite children to enter the joyous world of children's literature.

Each chapter of this edition has been revised and updated with new research, book titles, Read/Watch/Listen icons and websites, censorship issues, and end-of-chapter resources, including Top 10 Read Alouds, Activities for Professional Development, Print

and Online Resources, Creating Your Classroom Library, and References.
Other new features of this edition include the following:

- Updated Chapter 12, *The New Literacies: The World of Online Children's Literature*, which includes the NCTE Framework for 21st Century Curriculum and Assessment and new online resources and tools for assisting students in learning about, responding to, and engaging critically with children's literature.
- A new special topic, *Perspectives on Censorship*, at the end of Chapter 7, *Realistic Fiction*, includes new challenge information from the American Library Association for 2010 and the previous decade and resources and strategies for responding to challenges to children's books.
- New reflection questions accompany the Child's Voice and the Teacher's Voice features to help students engage in the material.
- A new *Joy of Children's Literature* Ning site (social networking site) that will allow college classes as well as individual readers to come together to discuss books, topics, and issues in children's literature.

# Special Features

The tantalizing array of features includes real voices of teachers and young readers and a look at the inner workings of two extraordinary children's books. There are opportunities to investigate authors and illustrators, to think critically about literature, and to listen and view children's literature online. Here is what you'll find:

### "THE CHILD'S VOICE" AND "THE TEACHER'S VOICE"

These features are authentic responses to prominent children's books that provide real-life examples of how children and teachers respond to children's literature.

### "A CLOSER LOOK"

Unique to *The Joy of Children's Literature* are two in-depth analyses of children's books that are seamlessly woven into the narrative. This feature provides an unprecedented depth of discussion in an easy-to-read format. In Chapter 4, *The Man Who Walked Between the Towers* is a source for discussion of the elements of picturebooks and a walk through the steps to obtaining visual literacy.

In Chapter 5, "A Closer Look" features *Yeh-Shen: A Cinderella Story from China* and is accompanied by an explanation of authenticity and accuracy in the portrayal of culture.

### SPECIAL "HOT" TOPIC SECTIONS

Throughout the text, there are specially designed sections that highlight "hot" topics in children's literature: graphic novels (Chapter 4), censorship issues (Chapter 7), sharing "risky" books (Chapter 11), digital literacy in the classroom (Chapter 12), and online literature discussions (Chapter 13).

 ### WEBSITE CONNECTIONS: LISTEN, WATCH, READ

The narrative in each chapter becomes a multimedia experience when margin notes alert the reader to discover more about a children's book by going to this text's website. There, the reader will find links to "Listen" to audio recordings of a children's book, to "Watch" an online video interview with an author or illustrator, or to "Read" the complete children's book online.

## BOOKLISTS AND PROFESSIONAL DEVELOPMENT ACTIVITIES

Each chapter concludes with booklists, activities, and resources:

- *Top 10 Read Alouds* highlight current and classic titles in each genre.
- *Activities for Professional Development* fall under three categories: Thinking Critically About Children's Literature, Bring Children's Literature into the Classroom, and Learn About Authors and Illustrators. These activities offer the preservice teacher an opportunity to actively engage with children's literature and the concepts they've discovered in the chapter.
- *Print and Online Resources* provide annotated recommendations for print sources and websites related to chapter content. All online resources are also linked on this text's website.
- *Creating Your Classroom Library* presents the reader with additional lists of quality children's literature, including books for younger readers, older readers, and multicultural books.

## END-OF-BOOK RESOURCES

At the end of the book, readers will find two useful listings: one for selecting children's literature and the other for the winners of all the major awards for children's books.

# Accompanying Teaching and Learning Support

An extensive online support program, for both students and instructors, accompanies this text.

## WEBSITE FOR *THE JOY OF CHILDREN'S LITERATURE*

*The Joy of Children's Literature* companion website features extensive links to online resources. Website resources include those developed by prominent educators, professional organizations, book companies, journals and magazines, teachers, parents, authors, illustrators, and libraries with resources on children's literature. Finding these resources on the vast landscape of the Internet can be extremely time-consuming. The dedicated website for this text is easy to navigate, searchable, and contains dependable, quality content. Remember that this text's website is keyed to the text with symbols identifying children's books to "Listen," "Watch," or "Read" online. Also, you will find the following:

- Chapter objectives
- Reflection questions for each chapter
- A list of the children's literature cited in each chapter of the text
- Extension questions and activities for out-of-classroom assignments
- A bonus list of read-alouds for each chapter
- Additional web resources for more information on particular topics in children's literature
- A list of additional notable authors and illustrators
- A list of children's literature awards
- Easy access to the blog, Ning, and WebQuest for keeping readers updated and connected

The website can be accessed at www.cengage.com/education/johnson and through the author's website at www.thejoyofchildrensliterature.com.

## ONLINE INSTRUCTOR'S MANUAL AND TEST BANK

An online instructor's manual accompanies this book. The instructor's manual contains information to assist the instructor in designing the course, including a sample syllabus, learning objectives, teaching and learning activities, and additional print and online resources. In addition, for assessment support, there is a test bank with multiple-choice, short-answer, and essay questions for each chapter.

# Acknowledgments

When I was pregnant with my son, many of my friends and colleagues shared their stories of what it was like to give birth. They offered well-intentioned advice, but nothing could prepare me for the experience, because it is unique to each woman. Writing the first edition of *The Joy of Children's Literature* was like giving birth (except much longer). It was a process for which no one could prepare me—full of ups and downs—but a true labor of love. When it was finally delivered, I was so proud. Since the publication of the first edition of *The Joy of Children's Literature* I have received invaluable feedback from adopters, reviewers, and friends that has informed the second edition. Thank you to each of them and to Cengage for this opportunity.

The person who has had the greatest influence on my understanding, insight, and love of children's literature is my son, Derek. Though I read children's literature, took graduate courses on children's literature, and shared books with my elementary students for many years before he came into my life, it was not until I read books with him and saw children's literature through his eyes that I truly understood the joy and value of children's literature. Derek, thank you for being the giver of light.

This book would not have been possible without Sue Pulvermacher-Alt. She saw in me a dream and the potential of this book for which I will be forever grateful. Sue, even though I do not understand your faith in the Packers, I'm glad you had faith in me (Go Cowboys!).

Beside the word "dedicated" in the dictionary should be the name Ann Greenberger, the development editor for the first edition. Ann's unwavering commitment to excellence went beyond commendable during the writing of this book. Ann's editorial brilliance made *The Joy of Children's Literature* the best it could be. Ann, thank you for always being there, for seeing something in me that I could not always see in myself, and for pushing me to "come out from behind a tree and become the center of all beauty." I would also like to thank Beckie Dashiell, the development editor for the second edition, who embraced *The Joy of Children's Literature* with the care and enthusiasm needed to bring fresh ideas and changes.

Thank you to the original Houghton Mifflin editorial, production, and marketing teams—Lisa Mafrici, Mary Finch, Shani Fisher, Amy Whitaker, Nancy Benjamin, Amanda Nietzel—and the new team at Cengage—Lisa Mafrici, Lisa Schreiber-Ganster, Kara Parsons, Andrea Clemente—for their wisdom, guidance, and dedication throughout the writing, editing, and publication of *The Joy of Children's Literature*. You are true professionals.

I have taught with many wonderful teachers throughout my career, all of whom have stretched and extended my knowledge of children's literature. Vicki Altland stands tall among those teachers. Vicki is the consummate teacher, the teacher I hope to inspire my students to become. Vicki's knowledge of children and the joy children's literature brings to them is admirable. Her willingness and desire to share her knowledge with other teachers shows her passion and devotion to children and to the profession. Vicki, I'm so glad you brought your Kansas State cup to that first balanced literacy inservice training session. I can't imagine my life without you in it.

Throughout the process of writing this book, the students in my children's literature courses have been an invaluable source of strength, insight, and joy. Thank you for your enthusiasm and support. I would especially like to thank Elisabeth. I still keep your note on my desk which begins, "Smile, I believe in you!"

I owe a huge debt of gratitude to my graduate assistants, Sarah Coccoli and Tricia Berry, for whom the word "library" took on a whole new meaning. "Wow, that's just about all I can say. Wow!"

I am grateful to many of my colleagues for their criticisms and suggestions during the writing and revision of this text. I would especially like to thank John Moore, a brilliant author, teacher, musician, and friend. I would also like to thank the reviewers of the first edition of *The Joy of Children's Literature* along with the following reviewers of the second edition for their critical comments and ideas, which helped shape and improve the book's presentation.

L. N. Calhoun, Florida Atlantic University
John B. French, Cape Cod Community College
Kathleen Hickey, Ed.D., Dominican College
Jessica Kahn, Chestnut Hill College
Dr. J. Michael King, Pikeville College
Prisca Martens, Towson University
Roxanne Owens, DePaul University
Karen Sands-O'Connor, Buffalo State College
Jayne H. Wolfskill, Chowan University

I saved the best for last. I thank my husband, Travis, for being who he is and who he has always been throughout our twenty-two years of marriage—my anchor and my biggest fan. Travis, God smiled on me when he brought you into my life. Thank you for loving me.

*Denise Johnson*

## Reference

Pritchard, G. (2006). An interview with Pat Mora: The reader and writer. *Journal of Children's Literature, 32*(2), 23–26.

# Part I

# An Introduction to Literature, Children, and Literacy

# 1 The Books: Children's Literature

> She laughed and she cried as she read, and she exclaimed aloud in the high and echoing room: "Wow!"
> —*Jerry Spinelli, 1997, p. 74*

A book can be a magic ticket to a faraway or in imaginary place. In *The Library Card*, Jerry Spinelli tells the story of a magic library card that provides exactly what each of the young characters in the book needs most. This fantastic story illustrates how a good book can have a significant influence on the mind of the reader—what children's book author Pat Mora calls "bookjoy": the "intense personal pleasure readers experience when they savor a book—delicious text."

## The Joy and Value of Children's Literature

*Most of us can remember* a favorite book from our childhood that left a lasting impression. Do you remember the silly antics and language of a Dr. Seuss book such as *Green Eggs and Ham* or *The Cat in the Hat?* Maybe you preferred the comfort and security of Margaret Wise Brown's *Goodnight Moon* or the rhyme and rhythm of the *Mother Goose Tales*. Did you read about the beautiful friendship between Wilbur and Charlotte in E. B. White's *Charlotte's Web,* or did you become captivated by the mystery and intrigue of Frances Hodgson Burnett's *The Secret Garden*, or the fanciful, imaginary world of Lewis Carroll's *Alice's Adventures in Wonderland?* These books still bring joy to our lives today, and they will continue to do that as long as adults help children to experience this joy.

*Read* 

*Read* Charlotte's Web.

### THE PERSONAL BENEFITS OF CHILDREN'S LITERATURE

Children are drawn to books because of the enchantment and delight they bring. Yet, entertainment is only one of the many personal benefits that children gain from literature. Good literature allows children to enter into the vicarious experiences full of mystery, excitement, turmoil, and friendship with other people, places, and times. It not only expands their life experiences and perceptions of the world, but good literature also does the following:

- It gives children a point of reference for understanding their own life experiences, as well as provides a broader view of their world.
- It develops their imagination, piques their curiosity, and stimulates their problem-solving abilities.
- It helps children develop insight into human behaviors, such as morality, relationships, empathy, and compassion, and the universality of these emotions and into experiences among diverse peoples all over the world.
- It provides a way to hand down our literary and cultural heritage to the next generation and both validate the child's own culture and introduce other cultures.

Although it may not be possible to measure the impact of literature on children's lives, we can still see how it helps children develop personal values and better understand both themselves and those around them.

## THE EDUCATIONAL BENEFITS OF CHILDREN'S LITERATURE

In addition to personal benefits, children's literature is pertinent to children's language and literacy development. Reading books at an early age increases language acquisition, reading comprehension, vocabulary, story patterns, fluency, writing skills, and a positive attitude toward reading (Krashen, 2004; Sulzby & Teale, 2003; Wells, 1986). Once children are in school, the benefits of children's literature continue to inform and influence language and literacy development. The content and availability of books on specific topics gives children the opportunity to think critically and creatively, to solve problems, to make judgments, and to discuss literature with other children. The plethora of topics in fiction, poetry, and nonfiction children's literature also allows for a natural connection to other curriculum areas. For example, the picturebook *Peppe the Lamplighter,* written by Elisa Bartone and illustrated by Ted Lewin, portrays the immigrant experience of one Italian family in America while accurately depicting American history at the turn of the twentieth century.

Literature's personal and educational contributions to a child's development should be enough to ensure that books have a prominent place in every child's life. But children do not come into the world with a natural affinity for books, so it is up to adults to introduce the joys of literature. Children are more likely to internalize the pleasure of reading if they have a caring adult in their life who shares an enthusiasm about books with them. Unfortunately, many children never have a book read to them and never develop the desire to read on their own. But it is *never* too late! Whether we are parents, grandparents, teachers, librarians, volunteers, or friends, as children come into our lives, we have the opportunity to share the wonder of books with them often. The enjoyment and delight of books are perhaps the greatest gifts we can give a child.

Teachers understand the importance of children's literature in their students' lives. Their classrooms are usually full of books and often they spend their own money to buy more. Yet, good teachers also realize how the appropriate selection and use of children's books can impact instruction.

As you read the following chapters, you will discover ways to evaluate, select, and share quality literature with children. Many factors must be considered when choosing books that will be read aloud to children or read by children. Part 1 of this book explores the meaning of quality in childrens' literature, the importance of understanding child development and effective literacy instructional methods. With this foundation, Part 2 examines each of the genres of children's literature in more

**FIGURE 1.1**

The Elements of Teaching with Children's Literature. Important concepts foundational to the effective selection, evaluation, and utilization of children's literature in the classroom. These concepts are also critical to the establishment of effective structures and contexts represented *In the Classroom* that enable students to become good readers and lovers of literature.

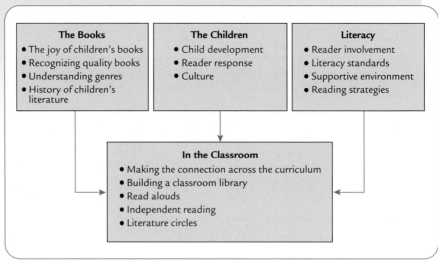

Each of the elements in the top set of boxes, *The Books, The Children, and Literacy,* represent

**The Books**
- The joy of children's books
- Recognizing quality books
- Understanding genres
- History of children's literature

**The Children**
- Child development
- Reader response
- Culture

**Literacy**
- Reader involvement
- Literacy standards
- Supportive environment
- Reading strategies

**In the Classroom**
- Making the connection across the curriculum
- Building a classroom library
- Read alouds
- Independent reading
- Literature circles

detail and how to incorporate children's books into literacy learning. Part 3 covers in more depth how to use literature in the classroom: reading aloud to children, independent reading, and literature circles. Figure 1.1 shows the structure of this book and how children's literature, the child, and literacy instruction interconnect in the classroom. Now, let's find out what exactly *good* children's literature is.

## Defining Quality Children's Literature

The term *quality* is generally used when a book both possesses literary merit and appeals to the reader. Well known author and children's literature expert Charlotte Huck (1976) explains that quality literature consists of "good writing or effective use of language that will help the reader to experience the delight of beauty, wonder, and humor. . . . He will be challenged to dream dreams, to ponder, and to ask questions to himself" (p. 4). Quality literature connects with us emotionally; increases our awareness, compassion, and humanity; teaches us; and delights us with interesting language and stories.

### LITERARY ELEMENTS

Literary merit for narratives is measured by evaluating the different literary elements, including style, setting, character, plot, and theme (see Table 1.1).

When the elements of literature are effectively woven together by a skillful author, then a book can be said to possess *quality.* Additionally, there are a few conditions for looking at the literary features of children's books that can serve as guidelines for selecting quality literature for children (Table 1.2).

**TABLE 1.1**

# Elements of Children's Literature

| Element | Description | Example |
|---|---|---|
| Style | *Style* refers to the author's distinctive way of writing. The author's word choice and arrangement, and sentence construction come together in a unique way that makes the characters, setting, and plot come alive. The author's writing style also creates the mood or atmosphere of the story, the tone, and the pacing of the story. *Point of view* is also an aspect of style and is the position the narrator takes while telling the story. | The writing style in *Sarah, Plain and Tall* by P. MacLachlan reflects the straightforward manner of the main character, Sarah, a mail-order bride who has come to live on the prairie. Summer, the main character in *Missing May* by C. Rylant, reflects the language of a child and the natural sound of dialogue. *Bull Run* by P. Fleischman presents many points of view from different participants in the Civil War. *Encounter* by J. Yolen is the story of Christopher Columbus's arrival in the New World told from a Taino child's point of view. |
| Setting | The *setting* is when and where the story takes place. The story can be set in the past, present, or future. When and where a story takes place affects the plot, characters, and theme of the story. | *Julie of the Wolves* by J. George is set in Alaska's harsh wilderness, which serves as the antagonist, as the main character, Miyax, struggles to survive. *Midwife's Apprentice* by K. Cushman is set in medieval England and reflects the historical accuracy of the era, which plays a prominent role in the story. |
| Character | It is important for the *characters* in a story to be well developed and believable. Authors must create characters in such a way that we become involved with them and care about them. | Stuart Little, Wilbur, Madeline, Olivia, Ramona, Amelia Bedelia, Peter Rabbit, Cassie Logan, Gilly Hopkins, and Bilbo Baggins are just a few characters from children's books that have left an indelible impression on us. |

*(continued)*

TABLE 1.1

(*continued*)

| Element | Description | Example |
|---------|-------------|---------|
| Plot | *Plot* is the action of the story, usually consisting of a beginning, rising action, climax, and falling action or resolution. The plot must have a conflict, and the resolution of that conflict carries through to the conclusion. The *pacing* of the plot, or how quickly the action moves, can be steady throughout the story or move faster or more slowly at times. *Suspense* and *tension* create interest in the plot. | *Holes* by L. Sachar employs dual plots: the story of Stanley Yelnat's crime and punishment at Camp Green Lake, a juvenile detention facility, and the other experienced by the reader through flashbacks when Stanley reflects on the story of his no-good-dirty-rotten-pig-stealing-great-great-grandfather. The two plots come together in the end to reveal how the past comes to fruition in the present. |
| Theme | *Theme* is the central idea of the entire story that lies beneath the story's surface. Enduring themes of friendship, growing up, overcoming fear, and acceptance of self do not overpower the characters or plot and are not didactic or preachy. | *Bridge to Terabithia* by K. Paterson includes themes of friendship and death. In *Heart of a Chief* by J. Bruchac, the theme is "growing up." *Project Mulberry* by L. Park has the themes of friendship and finding oneself. |

Another element that determines quality literature is its appeal to the reader. This is discussed in detail in Chapter 2.

## Genres of Children's Literature

*Looking back together, telling our stories to one another, we learn how to be on our own.*

Lois Lowry, 1998, p. 174

Literature for children encompasses a wide range of ages and topics, from nursery rhymes and concept books to novels and informational books. Books can be categorized according to different criteria—for example, narratives that tell a story and nonnarratives that present concepts and information. Literature can also be categorized by *genre*, which is defined by a set of characteristics such as characters, setting, action, and overall form or structure.

**TABLE 1.2**

# Guidelines for Selecting Children's Literature

- The target audience should be able to identify with the protagonist, who may share similar characteristics such as age.

- The theme appropriately reflects the emotions and experiences of children today.

- The language is not convoluted but rather specific and clear.

- The literary elements consist of a believable plot and characters, an engaging writing style, and a theme that unite into a satisfying whole.

- The book doesn't blatantly teach or moralize and tells the truth about the human experience.

- The book broadens understanding and perspective on the world that open up new possibilities and the capacity for empathy.

- Books for younger children include engaging pictures, fast-paced action that is presented in a straightforward manner, a single setting, and a satisfying ending.

- Books for older readers may not include pictures and therefore may include more descriptions to assist readers with visualizing the characters, setting, and dialogue to provide insight into characters' motives and intentions. The stories convey ideas that are important and meaningful and have a satisfying ending.

## DEFINING AND CATEGORIZING GENRES

*Watch* an interview with Lois Lowry.

In *Looking Back: A Book of Memories,* Newbery medalist Lois Lowry states that her autobiography is about the "moments, memories, fragments, falsehoods, and fantasies" that shaped her life and inspired her writing. Eventually, Lowry's experiences with storytelling developed into rich and wonderful books, such as *The Giver* and *Number the Stars.* Lowry's stories fall within certain genres. For example, *The Giver* is considered science fiction because it is set in a futuristic world that does not really exist, and *Number the Stars* is considered historical fiction because it is set at the time of the Holocaust. As shown in Table 1.3, the genres of children's literature include traditional literature, poetry, fantasy and science fiction, realistic fiction, historical fiction, nonfiction, and digital texts.

## THE ROLE OF GENRE IN LITERACY

Each genre has its own defining qualities of excellence that help us recognize the organization of the discipline of literature, provide a framework for talking about books, and guide our selection. In his book *Time for Meaning,* Bomer (1995) explains:

> Every piece of writing, every text we read, comes to us both as a text—the piece it is— and as a *kind* of text—an instance of genre. And what kind of thing it is puts some limits as to what we expect to find there. Genre, an often overlooked cueing system in reading, constrains our prediction, and lays down a track for our reading. (p. 8)

**TABLE 1.3**

# Genres of Children's Literature

| Genre | Categories Within the Genre | Selected Examples of This Genre |
|---|---|---|
| **Traditional Literature** Oral and literary heritage of humankind—no known author. | Folktales Fairy tales Myths and legends Tall tales Fables | *The Rough-Faced Girl* retold by R. Martin *Little Red Riding Hood* retold by Grimm Brothers *The First Strawberries: A Cherokee Story* retold by J. Bruchac *Swamp Angel* by A. Isaacs *The Ant and the Grasshopper* retold by Aesop |
| **Fantasy** Imaginative worlds; make-believe story settings, people and creatures, or events that could not happen. **Science Fiction** Stories about what might occur in the future based on extending physical laws and scientific principles. | Animal fantasy Toys and objects Miniature worlds Time warps Unreal worlds Magic Preposterous characters or situations Quest tales Science fiction | *The Tale of Despereaux* by K. DiCamillo *Winnie the Pooh* by A. A. Milne *The Family Under the Bridge* by N. Carlson *Devil's Arithmetic* by J. Yolen *The Phantom Tollbooth* by N. Juster *Tuck Everlasting* by N. Babbitt *James and the Giant Peach* by R. Dahl *The Sea of Trolls* by N. Farmer *The Giver* by L. Lowry |
| **Realistic Fiction** "What if" stories, illusion of reality; characters seem real; contemporary setting. | Adventure stories Mysteries Animal stories Stories about growing up Families Sports | *Hatchet* by G. Paulsen *From the Mixed-Up Files of Mrs. Basil E. Frankweiler* by E. Konigsburg *Shiloh* by P. Naylor *Yolanda's Genius* by C. Fenner *Kira Kira* by C. Kadohata *Taking Sides* by G. Soto |
| **Historical Fiction** Set in the past, could have happened, story reconstructs events of past age, things that could have or did occur. | Fictionalized memoir Fictionalized family history Fiction based on research | *The Upstairs Room* by J. Reiss *Roll of Thunder, Hear My Cry* by M. Taylor *A Single Shard* by L. Park |

*(continued)*

**TABLE 1.3**

(*continued*)

| Genre | Categories Within the Genre | Selected Examples of This Genre |
|---|---|---|
| **Poetry** Condensed language, imagery, expression of imaginative thoughts and perceptions. | Mother Goose Nursery rhymes Lyric Narrative Limericks Haiku Free verse Concrete Sonnet Ballad | *The Random House Book of Mother Goose* by A. Lobel *A Child's Garden of Verses* by R. Stevenson *Stopping by Woods on a Snowy Evening* by R. Frost *Paul Revere's Ride* by H. Longfellow *The Book of Pigericks* by A. Lobel *If Not for the Cat* by J. Prelutsky *A Light in the Attic* by S. Silverstein *A Poke in the I* by P. Janeczko *A Wreath for Emmet Till* by M. Nelson *On Top of Old Smoky* by Anonymous |
| **Nonfiction Biography** An account of a person's life or part of a life history. Informational Facts about the real world. | Authentic biography Memoir Autobiography Informational | *The Voice That Challenged a Nation: Marian Anderson and the Struggle for Equal Rights* by R. Freedman *The Lost Garden* by L. Yep *Knots in My Yo-Yo String: The Autobiography of Jerry Spinelli* |
| | | *Sea Turtles* by G. Gibbons *What Do You Do with a Tail Like This?* by S. Jenkins and R. Page *The Tarantula Scientist* by S. Montgomery |
| **Digital Texts** Narrative or nonnarrative information that has been digitized for access by a computer, a PDA, an e-book, or another digital reading device. | CD-ROM books Internet and World Wide Web sites Electronic texts (e-books) | *Arthur's Teacher Trouble CD* by M. Brown Children's Digital Library *The Watsons Go to Birmingham—1963: Digital* by C. P. Curtis |

The process and structure an author uses to describe events or ideas can vary considerably, depending on the writer's purpose and the genre he or she uses. Each genre is unique and requires certain strategies for reading, so it is not safe to assume that students who are competent in one genre will have no problem mastering others. Also, it is not a good idea to concentrate on one genre to the exclusion of others because of personal preferences or biases. Children learn about different genres by reading independently, discussing literature with peers, and observing the teacher's modeling, demonstrations, and explicit instructions.

Part 2 discusses each of these genres in more detail and provides information and criteria for evaluating and selecting quality children's books. Picturebooks, multicultural literature, and digital texts cross all genres but are discussed in separate chapters so the unique characteristics of each can be closely examined. Lists of picturebooks, multicultural books, and digital books are provided as they apply to each of the genre chapters and the entire text. A section on literacy development and children's responses to literature in each chapter provides instructional strategies specific to each genre. Additionally, each genre chapter includes a section on integrating literature across the curriculum.

Identifying good books also requires a sense of where children's books have come from. The abundance of beautiful books written expressly for children that are so easily obtainable today have only been available within the last century. A brief history of children's literature is presented in the next section. It highlights the dramatic changes in social and cultural values, economic factors, and attitudes toward children and childhood since the fifteenth century.

# A Brief History of Children's Books

*He'll be famous—a legend—I wouldn't be surprised if today was known as Harry Potter day in the future—there will be books written about Harry—every child in our world will know his name!*

J. K. ROWLING, 1997, P. 13

This excerpt from the first book in the Harry Potter series, *Harry Potter and the Sorcerer's Stone*, written by J. K. Rowling, couldn't have been more foretelling. Today, Harry Potter is a household name throughout the world, and the Harry Potter phenomenon is proof of the current popularity and widespread publication of children's literature. The first three books in the series—*Harry Potter and the Sorcerer's Stone* (1997), *Harry Potter and the Chamber of Secrets* (1999), and *Harry Potter and the Prisoner of Azkaban* (1999)—topped the *New York Times* best-seller list for 82 weeks before the newspaper finally instituted a separate list for best-selling children's literature on July 23, 2001.

Children's literature consists of an immense collection of prose and poetry written over the past 250 years for children from birth to adolescence. Children's book sales have grown at such a rapid rate over the past few years that the publication of children's books now accounts for the majority of many book publishers' releases. Currently, there are 250,151 books available from 18,437 U.S. publishers (Bowker, 2008). This, however, has not always been the case.

Before there were books, there were oral stories. Prior to the invention of Gutenberg's printing press in Germany in 1452, only a few wealthy individuals or monastery teachers were able to purchase books. Stories were told in cottages and castles as the primary means of sharing daily events, information, inspiration, and entertainment. Children of that time were treated the same as adults: The food they ate, the language they spoke, the clothes they wore, the work they did, and the stories they heard were all of an adult nature. For generations, the village storyteller or castle minstrel delighted listeners with tales and legends about heroes such as Beowulf and King Arthur, which still have a place in children's literature today. Storytelling is still a valued part of classrooms and family gatherings everywhere.

### THE PRINTING PRESS, CHAPBOOKS, AND HORNBOOKS

In 1476, William Caxton brought the first printing press to England. Three of Caxton's books, although not intended to be read by children, are now considered children's classics: *Reynart the Foxe, The Fables of Aesop,* and *Le Morte d'Arthur (The Death of Arthur)*. Caxton's books were very beautiful but too expensive for the commoner. The introduction of the printing press led to the production of cheaper books, called chapbooks, which were sold for pennies by peddlers, or "chaps." They were extremely popular. Chapbooks were made of cheap paper that was folded into quarters, and they included popular narrative stories such as *Robin Hood* and *Jack and the Giant Killer,* as well as religious instruction, supernatural tales, legends, and ballads.

Hornbooks (Figure 1.2) consisted of a wooden paddle with parchment attached to one side on which was printed the alphabet, vowels, and the Lord's Prayer and were covered with a thin layer of cow's horn. Hornbooks were still available into the 1700s in both Europe and America, and peddlers sold them to teach reading and numbers to children.

**FIGURE 1.2**

Hornbooks were used to teach reading and numbers to children. A hornbook was a wooden paddle with printed parchment on one side beneath a transparent layer of cow's horn.

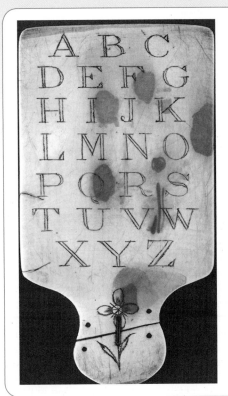

## PURITAN BELIEFS

During the seventeenth century, books were dominated by the uncompromising spiritual beliefs of the Puritans. Puritans considered children to be miniature adults and thus subject to original sin and eternal damnation. Because the mortality rate of infants and young children was extremely high, books for children were primarily concerned with morality. The first book written and printed for children in the American colonies was *Spiritual Milk for Boston Babes in Either England, Drawn from the Breast of Both Testaments for Their Souls' Nourishment*. It was written by John Cotton in 1646 and revised for children in 1656. Another popular title, *A Token for Children of New England, or Some Examples of Children in Whom the Fear of God Was Remarkable Budding Before They Died* was written by Cotton Mather in 1700. One of the most influential pieces of literature of the time, *Pilgrim's Progress,* written by John Bunyan in England in 1678, offered children and adults an adventure as well as moral improvement. Today, many adults still believe that children's literature should serve to instill morality in children.

Toward the end of the seventeenth century, English philosopher John Locke proposed the tabula rasa, or "blank tablet," view of children. He argued that children were not innately bad but acquired their characteristics through experience. He advised parents to spend a lot of time with their children and help them become contributing members of society.

*Read* Spiritual Milk for Boston Babes in Either England.

## THE EIGHTEENTH AND NINETEENTH CENTURIES

The eighteenth century brought books such as *Tales of Mother Goose,* retold from the French oral tradition by Charles Perrault, *Robinson Crusoe* written by Daniel Defoe, and *Gulliver's Travels* written by Jonathan Swift.

These books often were written for adults but read by children because they conveyed ideal moral values of hard work and self sufficiency. In 1744, John Newbery, a London publisher, writer, and advocate of a gentler way of treating children, was among the first to publish a book for children titled, *A Little Pretty Pocket Book.*

This book was written explicitly for children, and it attempted to teach the alphabet with games, fables, and rhymes. During his long, successful career, Newbery published 20 books for children, all with the primary purpose of entertaining children. In 1922, the John Newbery Medal for outstanding children's literature was established and is awarded annually by the American Library Association. It is a highly prestigious award given for children's literature published in the United States. You'll find a complete list of Newbery Medal winners at the end of this book.

The nineteenth century saw the spread of industry and the need for a more educated workforce to address increasingly complex technological industrial operations. Laws were passed that restricted child labor and made schooling compulsory. John Newbery's success opened the door for other publishers of literature specifically for children. The nineteenth century saw a firm establishment of literature for children and produced many classics; some of these classic stories are listed in Table 1.4.

Although several of the books in Table 1.4, such as *Treasure Island*, were originally written for adults, children read them because so few books written expressly for them existed at the time. Yet, these books have stood the test of time—the true sign of a classic—and are still read and adored by both children and adults today.

Until the nineteenth century, pictures in children's books were mostly rough woodcuts printed in black and white, but in the 1800s, a color printing press was invented and made it possible to print high-quality color illustrations. Randolph Caldecott's illustrations conveyed action, joy, and humor. Caldecott, one of the best-known illustrators

*Read* Robinson Crusoe *and* Gulliver's Travels.

*Read* A Little Pretty Pocket Book.

**TABLE 1.4**

*Read*

*Read many of these books online.*

# Nineteenth-Century Classic Children's Literature

- Hans Christian Andersen's *The Ugly Duckling* and *The Little Mermaid*
- Jacob and Whelm Grimm's folktale collection, including *Snow White* and *Rumpelstiltskin*
- Lewis Carroll's *Alice's Adventures in Wonderland*
- Robert Louis Stevenson's *Treasure Island* and *Kidnapped*
- Louisa May Alcott's *Little Women*
- Mark Twain's *The Adventures of Tom Sawyer* and *The Adventures of Huckleberry Finn*

*Read*

*Read the complete collection of Randolph Caldecott's works.*

of the nineteenth century, illustrated such picturebooks as *The Diverting History of John Gilpin, The Fox Jumps Over the Parson's Gate,* and *Hey Diddle Diddle Picture Book.*

In 1938, the coveted Randolph Caldecott Medal for outstanding illustration in a children's picturebook was established and is awarded annually by the American Library Association. A complete list of Caldecott Medal winners is at the end of this book.

## THE TWENTIETH CENTURY TO THE PRESENT

During the mid-nineteenth and twentieth centuries, childhood was no longer viewed as an inconvenient "waiting" period during which adults must suffer the incompetencies of the young. Today, childhood is valued as a special time of growth and change, and great resources are invested in caring for and educating children (Santrock, 2008). The twentieth century brought technological advances that allowed mass production of quality children's books at a lower price, making books more affordable for school and public libraries as well as the home. Book publishers established separate departments and editors for children's literature.

The American Bookseller's Association, a not-for-profit organization founded in 1900 to represent members of independently owned bookstores, established a Children's Book Week. Schools, libraries, and bookstores celebrated children's books and the love of reading with storytelling, parties, author and illustrator appearances, and other book-related events the week before Thanksgiving. In 1944, Children's Book Week was taken over by the Association of Children's Book Editors, who created the Children's Book Council to oversee the project and to serve as a year-round promotion and information center about children's books and children's book publishing.

*The Horn Book Magazine,* dedicated solely to children's literature, was first published in 1924, and the same year, the *New York Herald Tribune* introduced critical reviews of children's literature. The dedication of these resources created a rising interest in and the increased publication and distribution of children's books. For more information on the history of children's literature, see the Print and Online Resources at the end of this chapter.

Many of today's beloved books for children were published in the early to mid-twentieth century, including the following:

- Beatrix Potter's *The Tale of Peter Rabbit*
- Frances Hodgson Burnett's *The Little Princess* and *The Secret Garden*
- A. A. Milne's *Winnie the Pooh* and *When We Were Very Young*
- Laura Ingalls Wilder's *Little House in the Big Woods*
- J. R. R. Tolkien's *The Hobbit*
- Robert McCloskey's *Make Way for Ducklings* and *Homer Price*
- E. B. White's *Charlotte's Web*

Poetry and nonfiction were also produced expressly for children. For example, children were delighted with author/illustrator Shel Silverstein's silly and fun poetry in *Where the Sidewalk Ends* (1974) and with the fantastic discoveries in author/illustrator Joanna Cole's *Magic School Bus* series (1986). Author/illustrators such as Eric Carle, Theodor Geisel (Dr. Seuss), and Maurice Sendak also were much admired. As we move into the twenty-first century, these authors continue to bring joy to children all over the world. Advances in technology make it possible for authors and illustrators to be more creative in conception, design, and distribution of their work.

**Issues and Perspectives in Children's Literature.** Although children's literature has experienced an explosion in both publication and popularity, until the 1960s the subjects of children's books didn't include controversial or sensitive issues, and the characters were mostly European-American. The emergence of contemporary authors such as Judy Blume, Eve Bunting, Katherine Patterson, and Betsy Byars introduced important issues such as divorce, death, abuse, and homelessness. Their books are highly praised by critics and continue to be popular with children, although maybe not as well received by parents, librarians, and teachers. These books did not immediately become assigned readings. Many adults believe it's important to protect children from influences they perceive as evil or harmful. Religion, sex, and obesity, to name a few, are not topics that educators and some parents feel comfortable discussing with children, but that is probably the reason that children found them helpful.

Mark Oppenheimer (1997) writes the following about Judy Blume's books:

We learned about puberty from *Are You There, God? It's Me, Margaret* and *Then Again, Maybe I Won't*; about sex from *Forever*; about divorce from *It's Not the End of the World*. And everybody had read about the sibling rivalry between Fudge and Peter, made famous in *Tales of a Fourth Grade Nothing* and its sequel *Superfudge*. (Online document)

Thanks to the efforts of organizations such as The American Library Association and the Council on Interracial Books for Children, literature for children has become more multiethnic and multicultural. Authors such as Mildred Taylor, Virginia Hamilton, Gary Soto, and Laurence Yep and author/illustrators such as Ezra Jack Keats, Paul Goble, and Allen Say have written books that feature African Americans, Latinos, Asian Americans, and American Indians.

- *Roll of Thunder, Hear My Cry* by Mildred Taylor
- *Zeely* by Virginia Hamilton
- *Too Many Tamales* by Gary Soto
- *Dragonwings* by Laurence Yep
- *Grandfather's Journey* by Allen Say
- *The Girl Who Loved Wild Horses* by Paul Goble

Today, parents and teachers may choose from a rich variety of multicultural books to share with children. Chapter 11 focuses on multicultural children's literature.

*Listen*

Listen to The Tale of Peter Rabbit.

*Read*

Read The Secret Garden.

*Watch*

Watch an interview with Judy Blume.

*Watch*

Watch interviews with many of these authors.

*Allen Say is an accomplished illustrator of picturebooks highlighting characters from Asian culture.*

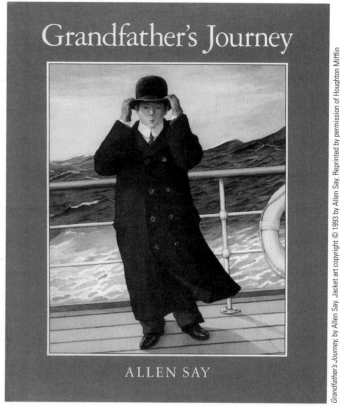

As we embark upon the twenty-first century, the history of children's literature continues to be written. New authors and illustrators will continue to amuse, delight, and entertain; address contemporary and controversial issues; introduce different perspectives; and document the lives of individuals and the expansion of knowledge. The brief and linear presentation of the history of children's literature presented here, however, runs a risk: It obscures the reality that there exist many who would use children's literature as a means of moralizing and socializing children and who work to censor or restrict what children are permitted to read. Although censorship is an issue that should concern us all, a larger problem may be that even though more books are available to children today than ever before, many homes throughout the world lack them. In the United States, many children start school without ever having read a book or having one read to them.

### Technology

> *The world of story is changing in important ways, just as it has always changed in the past and will continue to change in the future.*
>
> D. Leu, T. Grace, & J. Bevans, 2000, p. 1

Since the advent of the printing press, technology has had a profound effect on the creation, publication, and distribution of children's books. Leu, Grace, and Bevans (2000) believe that not only has literature changed lives, but the advancement of technology in publishing has changed literature. Printing processes, for example, have transformed the production of picturebooks in much the same way as authors and illustrators have transformed stories through the way they present them. Lewis (2001) states, "Pictures and words can now be combined in more or less any way that a book's designer might wish, and that in turn raises all sorts of possibilities and challenges for the reader" (p. 144). The Internet and other new forms of information and communication technology make it possible for us to broaden our definition of *story.* These resources help us appreciate stories in new and powerful ways.

The Internet allows teachers to literally bring a whole world of e-literature into the classroom. The Internet provides access to powerful resources that can enrich children's understanding of both authors and their stories and provides new opportunities for expanding their responses to literature.

The Internet, CD-ROM books, e-books, and other digital texts comprise a different genre, and we use different strategies to read them. With the widespread use of computer and multimedia technologies has come a change in the skills necessary to be a competent reader. "We are faced with an urgent need to expand our understanding of . . . digital text, which is nonlinear, multimodal with a heavy visual orientation, interactive, unbounded in time and space, with murky conveyance of authorship and authority" (Dalton & Proctor, 2008, p. 297). Mary Leonhardt (1998) says the following:

> The sophisticated skills demanded by high-level academic or professional work— the ability to understand multiple plots or complex issues, a sensitivity to tone, the expertise to know immediately what is crucial to a text and what can be skimmed— can be acquired only through years of avid reading. (p. 30)

Just as it is essential that children understand the unique structure and expectations of the traditional genres of fiction and nonfiction, children must also become familiar with the genre of digital texts if they are to live, learn, and work successfully in today's world. It is vital that students have opportunities to use technology in meaningful ways that support the literacy and literature goals of mindful, knowledgeable teachers. Chapter 12 is dedicated to strategies for the effective and meaningful use of digital texts and technology in the literacy curriculum. In addition, the website icon alerts you to online content, such as children's books, that you can listen to online, author and illustrator interviews, and other features. Remember to check out the Online Resources at the end of each chapter.

# Top 10 Read Alouds

## THE JOY OF READING

1. **A Story for Bear** by Dennis Haseley, illustrated by Jim LaMarche (2002, Harcourt). A young bear who is fascinated by the mysterious marks he sees on paper finds a friend when a kind woman reads to him.

2. **The Library** by Sarah Stewart, illustrated by David Small (1995, Farrar, Straus and Giroux). Elizabeth Brown loves to read more than anything else, but when her collection of books grows and grows, she must make a change in her life.

3. **Library Lil** by Suzanne Williams, illustrated by Steven Kellogg (1997, Dial). A formidable librarian turns not only the stubborn residents of her small town but a tough-talking, television-watching motorcycle gang into book lovers as well.

4. **Miss Smith's Incredible Storybook** by Michael Garland (2003, Dutton). When the new teacher, Miss Smith, reads to her class, Zack and his classmates are amazed to find that the storybook characters come to life.

5. **More Than Anything Else** by Marie Bradby, illustrated by Chris Soentpiet (1995, Orchard). Nine-year-old Booker works with his father and brother at the saltworks, but he dreams of the day when he'll be able to read.

6. **Miss Brooks Loves Books (And I Don't)** by Barbara Bottner, illustrated by Michael Emberley (2010, Knof). A first-grade girl who does not like to read stubbornly resists her school librarian's efforts to convince her to love books until she finds one that might change her mind.

7. **Tomás and the Library Lady** by Pat Mora, illustrated by Raúl Colón (1997, Random House). While helping his family in their work as migrant laborers far from their home, Tomás finds an entire world to explore in the books at the local public library.

8. **The Wednesday Surprise** by Eve Bunting, illustrated by Donald Carrick (1989, Houghton Mifflin). When Grandma stays with Anna on Wednesday nights, everyone thinks she is teaching Anna to read.

9. **Wild About Books** by Judy Sierra, illustrated by Marc Brown (2004, Knopf). Mavis McGrew, a librarian, introduces the animals in the zoo to the joy of reading after she drives her bookmobile to the zoo by mistake.

10. **Wolf!** by Becky Bloom, illustrated by Pascal Biet (1999, Orchard). A wolf learns to read to impress a group of farmyard animals.

# Activities for Professional Development

## Bring Children's Literature into the Classroom

**1.** What was your favorite book as a child? Why was it your favorite? Write your answers in a reading journal. If possible, read the book aloud to a small group of children. Describe their reaction to the book in your reading journal. Comment on how your own enthusiasm for the book affects the children's reaction to the book.

## Think Critically About Children's Literature

**2.** Choose one book from each of the last three centuries (e.g., *Little Women* (nineteenth), *Are You There God? It's Me, Margaret* (twentieth), and *Criss Cross* (twenty-first). Read and compare them to one another. What differences and similarities do you see?

**3.** Identify several children's books that you believe appeal to adults (e.g., *Love You Forever, The Giving Tree*). What themes are represented in the books? Are they appropriate for children? Why or why not?

**4.** Throughout the centuries, children's books have reflected the social issues of the time. What social issues do you see reflected in books published in the twenty-first century (e.g., gay or lesbian parents, divorce, and drug abuse)? What issues do you predict will be included in the future?

## Learn About Authors and Illustrators

**5.** Watch a video interview with author Eve Bunting. Use the *Reading Rockets* website (http://www.readingrockets.org) for the following activities: Click on the "books & authors" tab on the left side of the web page, and then click on "video interviews." View the video interview with author Eve Bunting, specifically the clip titled "Books that Heal the World." Then view the interview by Katherine Paterson, specifically the clip titled "A Writer Deals with Tragedy." If possible, read several of the picturebooks Eve Bunting mentions as "heal the world books" in the interview and Katherine Paterson's *Bridge to Terabithia*.

- Why do you think these books have received such acclaim from children and teachers?
- What did you find to be particularly meaningful about the interviews?
- How could you use these videos (and others) in the classroom?

ACTIVITY: Search by theme (under the Children's Books & Authors tab on the left side of the web page) to compile a list of books that would be part of a study on a particular culture or time period. Compile a list that is appropriate for a particular grade level.

# Print and Online Resources

## Print Resources

Graves, D. (1990). *Discover your own literacy*. Portsmouth, NH: Heinemann.

Hunt, P. (1995). *Children's literature: An illustrated history*. New York: Oxford University Press.

Lerer, S. (2009). *Children's literature: A reader's history from Aesop to Harry Potter*. University of Chicago Press.

Marcus, L. (2008). *Minders of make-believe: Idealists, entrepreneurs, and the shaping of American children's literature*. New York: Houghton Mifflin Harcourt.

Nodelman, P. (2008). *The hidden adult: Defining children's literature*. Baltimore, MD: The Johns Hopkins University Press.

Pennac, D. (1999). *Better than life*. York, ME: Stenhouse.

Silvey, A. (2004). *100 best books for children*. New York: Houghton Mifflin.

Yokota, J. (2001). *Kaleidoscope: A multicultural booklist for grades K–8*, 3rd ed. Urbana, IL: National Council of Teachers of English.

## Online Resources

### The Children's Book Council
**http://www.cbcbooks.org**
The Children's Book Council is the national non-profit trade association for children's trade book publishers. The CBC website provides links to resources such as Building a Home Library Bibliographies, Children's Book Week, and The National Ambassador for Young People's Literature.

### The Cooperative Children's Book Center (CCBC)
**http://www.education.wisc.edu/ccbc/links/links.asp?idLinksCategory=2**
Sponsored by the University of Wisconsin-Madison, the CCBC website houses a rich collection of resources on children's and young adult literature including bibliographies and book lists, annual awards and distinctions, resources for information on authors and illustrators, intellectual freedom, multicultural literature, professional organizations, review journals, and much more.

### The History of Children's Literature: A Pathfinder by Ellen Decker and Ruffin Priest
**http://www.ils.unc.edu/~prier/KidLit**
This website provides an annotated list of resources for the history of children's literature, including books and the Internet. Included in this website are a timeline of major trends in the history of children's literature, journals, and articles that are relevant to children's literature and its history.

### Landmarks in the History of Children's Literature by San Antonio College
**http://www.accd.edu/sac/english/bailey/childlit.htm**
This website outlines the landmarks in the history of children's literature with a chronological list of books for children as well as books that are sources of material suitable for young readers.

### World of the Child: Two Hundred Years of Children's Books by the University of Delaware's Special Collections Department
**http://www.lib.udel.edu/ud/spec/exhibits/child**
This website, designed by the University of Delaware, explores two hundred years of children's books. Included within the website are fables, fairy tales, books of instruction, primers, poetry, and pop-up or movable books.

## CHILDREN'S BOOK AWARDS ONLINE

### Database of Award Winning Children's Literature
**http://www.dawcl.com**
The DAWCL is a searchable database compiled by Lisa Bartle, a reference librarian at California State University, San Bernardino. Users can search thousands of award winning titles by 14 different criteria including readers' age, genre, award, publication year, gender, ethnicity, and language.

### The American Library Association's website
**http://www.ala.org**
The American Library Association's website includes pages for the John Newbery Medal, the Randolph Caldecott Medal, the Coretta Scott King Award, the Pura Belpre Award, and many more.

### National Book Award
**http://www.nationalbook.org**
This website provides information on the National Book Awards, which recognize literary excellence in four categories: Fiction, Nonfiction, Poetry, and Young People's Literature.

### Orbis Pictus Nonfiction Award
**http://www.ncte.org/awards/orbispictus**
The Orbis Pictus award, given by the National Council of Teachers of English, is an annual award for promoting and recognizing excellence in the writing of nonfiction for children. The name *Orbis Pictus* commemorates the work of Johannes Amos Comenius, *Orbis Pictus—The World in Pictures* (1657), considered to be the first book actually planned for children.

Visit the companion website at **www.cengage.com/education/johnson** to find links related to the Read/Watch/Listen icons noted throughout the chapter, as well as additional resources.

# References

Bomer, R. (1995). *Time for meaning.* Portsmouth, NH: Heinemann.

*Bowker's children's books in print* (40th ed.). (2008). New Providence, NJ: R. R. Bowker.

Dalton, B., & Proctor, C. (2008). The changing landscape of text and comprehension in the age of new literacies. In J. Coiro, M. Knobel, C. Lankshear, & D. Leu (Eds), *Handbook of research on new literacies* (pp. 297–324). New York: Erlbaum.

Huck, C. (1976). *Children's literature in the elementary school* (3rd ed.). New York: Holt, Rinehart and Winston.

Krashen, S. (2004). *The power of reading* (2nd ed.). Portsmouth, NH: Heinemann.

Leonhardt, M. (1998). How to sweeten your school's climate for reading. *School Library Journal, 44*(11), 28–31.

Leu, D., Grace, T., & Bevans, J. (2000). Hidden treasures: Discovering new experiences with story on the Internet. *The Dragon Lode, 19*(1), 1–5.

Lewis, D. (2001). *Reading contemporary picturebooks: Picturing text.* New York: RoutledgeFalmer.

Lowry, L. (1998). *Looking back: A book of memories.* Boston: Houghton Mifflin.

Oppenheimer, M. (1997, November 16). Why Judy Blume endures. *The New York Times Book Review, 147*(50978), 44–5.

Rowling, J. K. (1997). *Harry Potter and the sorcerer's stone.* New York: Scholastic.

Santrock, J. W. (2008). *Life-span development* (12th ed.). Boston: McGraw-Hill.

Spinelli, J. (1997). *The library card.* New York: Scholastic.

Sulzby, E., & Teale, W. (2003). The development of the young child and emergent literacy. In J. Flood, J. Jensen, D. Lapp, & J. Squire (Eds.), *Handbook of research on teaching the English language arts,* pp. 300–313. New York: Erlbaum.

Wells, G. (1986). *The meaning makers.* Portsmouth, NH: Heinemann.

# How Children Respond to Literature

Our images of children-as-learners are reflected inevitably, in our definition of what it means to teach.
—*David Wood, 1998, p. 1*

Recently, I visited my friend Diane who has a three-year-old daughter, Rachel. We were sitting in her living room talking when Rachel came running into the room with her favorite book, *Brown Bear, Brown Bear, What Do You See?,* by Bill Martin Jr. and illustrated by Eric Carle. On each page of the book a different tissue-paper collage animal is introduced that gives clues, with a repeated, rhyming text, about which creature will appear on the next page. Rachel crawled onto Diane's lap, opened the book, and began to recite the text, pointing and commenting on the pictures.

*I realized that Rachel* has been read to many times and that she finds great joy in the experience. If we examine this ritual more closely, we can see how it helps Rachel's development:

> Positive emotions are created from an established lap-reading routine that generates an intimate closeness and feeling of security (emotional development).
>
> Interactive social dialogues between Rachel and her mother build on prior knowledge and provide immediate feedback as they discuss each animal they encounter as the story progresses (linguistic and social development).
>
> The language used to label, compare, explain, and classify creates a foundation for thinking and concept formation (cognitive development).

Linguistic, cognitive, social, and emotional factors all come into play and all contribute to Rachel's development. Although each of these four factors comprises an entire theoretical approach to child development, no single theory can explain the complex, dynamic, reciprocal, and personal aspects of development (Santrock, 2009).

*Children's literature supports children's development as they talk, share, and think about books.*

Listen to
an interview
with Eric Carle.

*Brown Bear, Brown Bear, What Do You See?* Text by Bill Martin Jr. Illustrated by Eric Carle. Cover illustration ©1992 by Eric Carle. Reprinted by permission of Henry Holt and Company, LLC.

## Learning and Child Development

The joy that children experience from literature is naturally entwined with their development. Research by cognitive psychologists during the past few decades (most notably Swiss psychologist Jean Piaget) has revealed new information about how children develop and learn. Each child has unique needs, interests, and capabilities. A child is born with the ability to organize, classify, and impose order on the environment, which is the foundation for the child's unique theory about the world around her (Piaget, 1926; Wood, 1998). Very little of the content and order of such theories comes from direct instruction. Rather, the interaction of biological, cultural, and life experiences is the basis of our theories and the way we organize experiences.

As children encounter new experiences, already existing memory structures in the brain or schema are reshaped, impacting the child's linguistic, cognitive, social, and emotional development. According to Ryan and Cooper (2010), "Knowledge cannot be *given* directly from the teacher to the learner, but must be *constructed by the learner* and *reconstructed* as new information becomes available." Learning is not a *result of* development but development itself. From this perspective, a child's potential for learning is revealed and even realized through interactions with those who possess greater knowledge.

## READING AND CHILD DEVELOPMENT

Lev Vygotsky (1978), a twentieth-century Russian psychologist, believed that linguistic, social, emotional, and cognitive development are complementary processes that work together to shape a child's literacy growth. He theorized that social interaction shapes intellectual development, and he stressed the importance of language in the development of thought. Sociocognitive theory posits that social interaction is the primary means by which children arrive at new understanding. For example, Rachel learns a lot about the act of reading from the book experiences she shares with her mother. Diane is a powerful role model for Rachel by demonstrating many concepts about the printed word (see Table 2.1).

Rachel is also becoming familiar with story structures and story language, which improves her comprehension by helping her to predict the language and content of new stories. Vocabulary and concept development are also affected as Diane and Rachel work together to construct a meaningful experience around a common literacy event. From the first time Diane read *Brown Bear, Brown Bear, What Do You See?* to Rachel, she scaffolded, or adjusted her support based on the feedback she received from Rachel. As Rachel began to internalize the actions and language of her mother, she used those tools to guide and monitor her own processing behavior until she was able to assume much of the responsibility for reading the book, as we saw when she climbed onto her mother's lap.

In the classroom, cognitive development is advanced by interactions such as discussions with adults and peers about a book read to, with, or by the child. Leading children to label, compare, explain, and classify new information or exposing children to other points of view and to conflicting ideas may encourage them to rethink or review their ideas. This interaction also promotes social development as children learn to value and appreciate the opinions of others. Such discussions also promote language development as the child is immersed in the conventions and pronunciations of language during literature response exchanges. These conversations must take place in a supportive environment where children feel safe and know their comments will be respected.

There are, however, exceptions. A preservice teacher read the very humorous book *Piggie Pie!*, written by Margie Palatini and illustrated by Howard Fine, aloud to a group of preschoolers with unexpected results. To her dismay, the children did not find the book nearly as funny as she did. In the story, a witch who has a hankering for piggie pie visits a farm to get the main ingredient: pigs! The clever pigs disguise themselves as other farm animals and successfully fool the witch into thinking that the farm has no pigs. At the end of the story, a wolf (presumably the big, bad wolf), who also was unable to find any pigs, consoles the witch, and they go off together to "have lunch" (or eat each other!).

**TABLE 2.1**

# Concepts About Print

- How Diane holds a book (which end is up and which side is the front cover)

- How Diane turns the pages, reading the left page before the right page and starting at the top of the page and moving down

- How Diane reads with tone, inflection, and enthusiasm, and expresses excitement and joy

- How Diane points out the pictures and words as she reads and pauses to discuss what she is thinking

- How Diane responds appropriately to Rachel's comments or questions

Why didn't the children think this book was funny? It is not uncommon for children and adults to have different ideas about humor, mostly because of the vast developmental gap between children and adults. Jalongo (1985) maintains, "Often when humorous books fail to amuse children, it is indicative of a poor match between children's cognitive-developmental level and the reading material" (p. 109). Jalongo's research identifies characteristics of children's humor such as "cognitive challenge," or the intellectual ability required to understand a particular joke, and "novelty," or surprise, which is really the cornerstone of humor. If a child doesn't have the appropriate set of expectations, the unexpected is not surprising. *Piggie Pie!* draws much of its humor from references to other stories and songs such as *The Wizard of Oz, The Three Little Pigs, Old MacDonald's Farm, To Grandmother's House We Go,* and an advertising campaign for the Yellow Pages, "Let your fingers do the walking." So preschoolers who were not familiar with these references would not find humor in *Piggie Pie!*

The preschoolers did consider some parts of the story funny, especially when the pigs dressed up like other farm animals. Jalongo (1985) explains, "Because young children are learning to distinguish between fantasy and reality, events that are incongruous with their expectations are considered to be funny" (p. 110). In this case, the teacher would have to provide a considerable amount of scaffolding to help the children appreciate the references on which much of the humor in the book depended. As a result, this literature experience was not as beneficial for the majority of these preschoolers as another book selection might have been.

Humor is just one example of how child development plays an important role in book selection for children. Books that adults find emotionally and psychologically appealing, such as Robert Munsch's *Love You Forever* and Shel Silverstein's *The Giving Tree,* are also beyond most children's comprehension. The book *Brown Bear, Brown Bear, What Do You See?* is within Rachel's developmental level, and she enjoys it a great deal, whereas the textual references from which *Piggie Pie!* draws its humor are outside the preschool children's realm of development. A child who is not developmentally ready for a particular book will gain less pleasure and meaning from it and will respond to it differently. If children are to receive the maximum benefits from experiences with literature, teachers must recognize children as individuals—their level of development, their rate of development, and their varying interests.

*Read*

*Read more about developmentally appropriate practice.*

## How Does a Child Make Meaning from a Book? Influences on Children's Responses to Literature

The reading process is much more complex than just decoding the words, or even understanding the words on the page. Karolides (1997) explains as follows:

> The central premise of the reading process is that the literary work exists in the transaction between a reader and a text. The active participatory role of readers encompasses—in conjunction with comprehension—discovering meaning, responding emotionally, developing interpretation. Readers are not passive spectators *of* the text but are active performers *with* the text. (p. 8)

The "transaction" Karolides speaks of is the key to Louise Rosenblatt's (1978) theory of reader response and should be at the heart of literacy and literature instruction. When we read, we are connected to the text in a unique way, one that will not be experienced in exactly the same way by another reader. (See "The Child's Voice" below.) Readers bring to a text their own backgrounds and experiences, which influence how they interpret the text and what they take away from it. Yet, a transaction with the text is not necessarily guaranteed. If a reader has difficulty reading the text, does not find it interesting, or is distracted,

A First Grader's Response
to *Thank You, Mr. Falker*,
Written and Illustrated
by Patricia Polacco

My favrite Patricia Polacco book is Thank you Mr. Falker because Mr. Falker helped Patricia with reading and writing and Mrs. Altland my teacher helped me with the things I have trouble with. Patricia was a good artist in school and I love art and I draw alot. I think the message in this book is it doesn't matter if you are diffrent you always can do something good.

—*How does this child's response reflect her developmental level and unique background and experiences?*

*Watch*

*Watch* Thank You,
Mr. Falker *read aloud.*

or if the situations, issues, or characters are beyond his experiences or development, then he cannot actively participate with the text. This is true for both adults and children.

Teachers, however, can ensure that children will be able to actively participate with texts if they consider the reader, the text, and the context. Based on the knowledge of each child, teachers can select texts that are interesting, engaging, and accessible; build background knowledge and experiences through teacher-led and student-led discussions; and provide instruction and support as needed.

## CHILDREN RESPOND BASED ON THEIR BACKGROUND AND EXPERIENCES

Ask any child what he or she considers a "good" book, and you will probably get answers like these:

"A good book makes me happy, and it sometimes makes me and my mom cry."
"A really good book is about dinosaurs!"
"I think a good book can make pictures in your head."

These children are telling you exactly what a "good" book is—*to them*. But what one child likes may not be acceptable to another; it depends on the child's interests, age, background experiences, and culture. Each reader, in the process of experiencing a literary work, brings meaning to and takes meaning away from that book (Rosenblatt, 1978). Philip Pullman (2006) writes, "Every reader brings to every text his or her own preconceptions, assumptions, habits, knowledge, expectations, assiduity, openness of mind (or the reverse), temperament, and intelligence; and every reader has the perfect right to think that my text, like any other, means whatever they take it to mean." The meanings derived from a book are personal and idiosyncratic and depend on the reader's experiences *outside* the book. So the quality of a book from an adult's viewpoint will be quite different from that of a child.

Yet, as Chatton (2004) reminds us, "Adults who write, edit, publish, market, select, purchase, honor, critique, analyze, and teach books for the young, consciously or unconsciously, suggest to children what they need to value in their readings" (p. 31). Some children's books were originally written for adults but became popular children's literature, including Jonathan Swift's *Gulliver's Travels* and Daniel Defoe's *Robinson Crusoe*. Many books that were written for children appeal to adults—for example, A. A. Milne's *Winnie the Pooh* and J. R. R. Tolkien's

*The Hobbit.* Some books written *about* children may not be *for* them, such as Tony Earley's *Jim the Boy* and Harper Lee's *To Kill a Mockingbird*. How a book is written affects its suitability for children. Stories about children that are written in nostalgic or overly sentimental terms reflect adult themes and should not figure prominently in a child's book. Robert Munsch's *Love You Forever* (about the assumption of responsibility for an aging parent) and Shel Silverstein's *The Giving Tree* (about the passing of childhood) are both beyond the psychological and emotional realm of children. Cynicism and despair are also inappropriate content for children's books. Another popular author, Theodor S. Geisel (Dr. Seuss), wrote many books early in his career that have delighted children for years, but later titles such as *The Lorax, The Butter Battle Book,* and *Yertle the Turtle* reflect adult themes of pollution, war, and ambition.

The goodness of a book lies in the eye of the reader. Children's books that you now enjoy as an adult may not have been your favorites as a child. Therefore, choosing books for children requires knowledge of child development, the children for whom you are selecting literature, and an in-depth knowledge of children's literature.

## HOW CHILDREN RESPOND TO BOOKS

The characteristics of different genres also influence how readers respond to a particular book. Typically, we approach the reading of nonfiction, such as Gail Gibbons's *Giant Pandas,* with the purpose of learning about giant pandas, such as where they live and what they eat. A child's experience with reading nonfiction and her level of interest in the subject of giant pandas will affect her response to the book. The structure of the expository text in *Giant Pandas* is very different from the structure of narrative text. There is a color-coded picture of China with a legend and labeled diagrams of giant pandas and their habitats throughout the book. Children who have not read much expository text may find this book challenging. Children typically have more experience with narrative text and approach it with the expectation of becoming emotionally involved with characters, events, or themes. In Pat Hutchins's *Rosie's Walk,* children cheer for Rosie, a chicken who decides to take a walk across a farm, and laugh at the antics of the bumbling fox that follows her. But this doesn't guarantee that some children will not have difficulty reading or becoming engaged in the text. Children who are not familiar with farms may not be able to relate to the setting, so the fox's predicaments might not be very interesting.

Another factor that impacts a child's reading experience is whether the child chose to read the book or the book was assigned reading. Reading a book to complete an assignment is very different from reading for pleasure. Think about how you felt when you were reading a college textbook compared to how you felt when you were reading the latest book by your favorite author. To be academically successful, children must learn to read and respond thoughtfully to assigned literature, but to become lifelong readers, children must be given the opportunity to choose their own books.

## HOW CHILDREN RESPOND TO
## TEACHERS AND PEERS

Teachers play a vital role in encouraging, nurturing, and deepening their students' responses to books. One way to do this is to give children ample opportunity to discuss the books they are reading with other children. Research has shown that through conversations with peers, children become involved in understanding and negotiating ideas and perspectives that promote reflection and insight (Allington & Johnston, 2002; Knapp, 1995; Möller, 2005). Peers can also have an enormous impact on one another.

Recently, while working in a third-grade classroom, I noticed a few of the students were reading *The Bad Beginning,* the first book in *A Series of Unfortunate Events* by Lemony Snicket. Each time I returned to the classroom, more and more of the children were reading books in the series. The popularity of the books spread as the children were given the

*Listen*

Listen to
Dr. Philip Nel, an
authority on Dr. Seuss,
discuss his insights
into Dr. Seuss' writing.

*Watch*

Watch an interview
with Gail Gibbons.

*Listen*

Listen to an interview
with Lemony Snicket
(Daniel Handler) about
the publication of The
End, *the last book in* A
Series of Unfortunate
Events.

opportunity to share their excitement and interest with one another during daily book talks. As more children began reading the same books, several book clubs were formed to discuss them exclusively. In one book club, a child reported his theory that Lemony Snicket was the father of the three orphaned Baudelaire children. This idea intrigued the other children, and they asked their classmate thoughtful questions about how he came up with his theory and what evidence he had from the stories that would support it. The ensuing conversation was authentic, rich, and engaging in a way that expanded and deepened the children's thinking about this series.

# Cultural Influences

*At a time when so many children are now proud of their ethnic heritages, I'm ashamed to say that when I was a child, I didn't want to be Chinese. It took me years to realize that I was Chinese whether I wanted to be or not. And it was something I had to learn to accept: to know its strengths and understand its weaknesses. It's something that is a part of me from the deepest levels of my soul to my most common, everyday actions.*

LAURENCE YEP, 1991, P. 43

*Watch*

*Watch an interview with Laurence Yep.*

Along with the elements of reader, text, and context, reading is also influenced by the child's culture, cultural allusions in the text, and the classroom's culture. The combination of these cultural influences shapes the reader's response.

In his memoir *The Lost Garden* (1991), Laurence Yep looks back on his childhood in the 1950s:

I would never care to go back. It was as if everyone in America was in one giant parade; and we were all expected to march in the same direction and at the same pace. . . . There were immense pressures on white children to conform—to be like all the other children in their school and neighborhood instead of themselves; and the pressures were even greater on the minorities to be like the whites. (p. 42)

During the nineteenth and early twentieth centuries, schools contributed to the concept of the "melting pot" by socializing and acculturating immigrant children to American ways while discouraging them from maintaining their own culture.

## CULTURE AND EDUCATION

*Culture* is the ways of knowing, believing, valuing, and thinking among a group of people. The concept of the melting pot has generally been replaced by the notion of cultural pluralism, which calls for an understanding and appreciation of the cultural differences and languages among the nation's citizens. In their book *Those Who Can, Teach,* Ryan and Cooper state the following:

Cultural pluralism rejects both assimilation and separatism. Instead, it seeks a healthy interaction among the diverse groups in our society; that is, each subculture maintains its own individuality while contributing to our society as a whole. (p. 102)

Multicultural education values cultural pluralism and seeks to enrich the cultural perspectives of *all* students, not just members of minority racial or ethnic groups. Rather than a surface-level study of cultures, such as Black History Month, multicultural education weaves multiple perspectives and viewpoints throughout the curriculum to help students understand how events and facts can be interpreted differently by various groups. This book integrates a discussion of multicultural children's literature and issues throughout every genre chapter, with more in-depth coverage in Chapter 11.

## CULTURAL FACTORS

Cultural context has a significant impact on book sharing and literacy acquisition. Van Kleeck, Stahl, and Bauer (2003) note the following:

> Family book sharing with young preliterate and early literate children is by no means a universal practice across cultural, linguistic, and social lines. Where it is practiced, it may be negotiated in a variety of ways, many of which are quite different from those favored in middle-class White families. As such, interventions based on research among middle-class White families may be inappropriate, and hence less effective, for families from other backgrounds. (pp. vii–viii)

The National Center for Education Statistics (2003) reports the following:

- Eighty-four percent of public elementary and secondary classroom teachers are European American.
- Forty percent of elementary and secondary students are African American, American Indian, Asian American, or Hispanic American.
- Five percent of these students are English language learners.

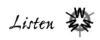

*Listen*

*Listen to Kathy Au discuss culturally responsive instruction.*

Children's difficulties in achieving adequate literacy can emanate from the mismatch between the teacher's narrow view of literacy and the reality of multiple literacies in today's society. Au (1998) states, "To overcome barriers of exclusion proposed by conventional literacy instructional practices, educators must work with an expanded vision of literacy strategies and concepts in school, so that school definitions of literacy are transformed" (p. 308).

Teachers relay, sometimes unwittingly, vast amounts of cultural information through their own implicit and explicit actions. For example, when selecting children's books to read aloud, a teacher may consciously or unconsciously choose books that reflect his or her own culture and values. If a child's culture matches the culture of the teacher, then the child is more likely to get positive feedback about his ideas and comments. Educators' recognition of these inequalities depends on an understanding of their own cultural identities as well as the cultural identities of their students. Cross-cultural understanding can help to identify ways cultures and school settings interact effectively or ineffectively in bringing students of diverse backgrounds to high levels of literacy (Au, 1998).

## MULTICULTURAL AND INTERNATIONAL LITERATURE

This focus on multicultural literature developed from the need to find a place in both literature and education for the historically marginalized social groups, thus promoting equality and the goals of multicultural education (Cai, 2002). Cai defines *multicultural literature* in terms of the role it plays in education as "a group of works used to break the monopoly of the mainstream culture and make the curriculum pluralistic" (p. 4). At the heart of this definition is the term *culture,* which has been interpreted differently according to the parameters placed by the number of social groups included, ultimately leading to multiple definitions of multicultural literature. At one end of the wide range of definitions, multicultural literature is characterized as books about those most excluded and marginalized: people of color (Harris, 1992; Kruse & Horning, 1990; Sims Bishop, 1994). This multiethnic definition ensures that children from underrepresented socioeconomic backgrounds, religions, genders, and exceptionalities will not be included. At the other end of the definition spectrum is the belief that *all* literature is multicultural and that separating multicultural children's literature from other children's literature could make it more conspicuous (Fishman, 1995; Shannon, 1994).

*Read*

*Read more about gender and culture in children's literature.*

However, emphasizing that all literature is multicultural because to do otherwise sets up a dissolution between "them" and "us" could cause a significant decrease in the publication of multicultural literature (Cai, 2002). The debate over the definition of *multicultural children's literature* is multifaceted, complex, and ongoing. Yet, your perception as an educator will inform your choice and use of multicultural literature. This book maintains that multicultural children's literature must be inclusive of all underrepresented cultures and deserves special attention.

Multicultural and international literature can enhance children's education and have a profound effect on individual beliefs and respect for others' beliefs. Research has shown that reading and discussing multicultural books can help students embrace diversity (Wham, Barnhart, & Cook, 1996). According to Dowd (1992), children learn that although people may be very different in ways, "from reading, hearing, and using culturally diverse materials, young people learn that beneath surface differences of color, culture or ethnicity, all people experience universal feelings of love, sadness, self-worth, justice and kindness" (p. 220).

International literature is literature that comes from countries outside the United States. These books may be originally written in English, such as *Koala Lou,* written by Australian author Mem Fox, or originally written in a language other than English and subsequently translated, such as *The Dragon Rider,* written by German author Cornelia Funke. International books must adhere to standards of literary quality, accuracy, and authenticity, just as any other children's book. International literature can give us insights into the thoughts and lives of our global neighbors and provide cultural knowledge that reflects the culture and language diversity found in our own classrooms—helping children see themselves as citizens of the world (see Chapter 11 for more on multicultural and international children's literature).

## THE TEACHER'S ROLE

*Stories* do *matter, particularly in this troubling time when the constraints of scripted reading programs, mandated high-stakes testing, and monocultural standards often relegate literature and multicultural concerns to the fringes of classroom life.*

D. Fox and K. Short, 2003, p. 22

Teachers must investigate the sociocultural process of learning to discover meaningful classroom learning interactions for students who are not members of the mainstream community. Adults can use books to promote "ownership of literacy" by children from diverse cultures (Au, 1998). They must recognize *each* child's path of development and provide opportunities for scaffolded learning and shared activities designed to accommodate each child's strengths. Au (1998) states the following:

Educators who wish to make literacy personally meaningful to students consistently draw on students' interests and experiences. By making literacy activities rewarding in an immediate sense, they provide students with the situational rationales for staying in school and engaging in literacy learning. (p. 309)

Educators must also ensure that children have regular, meaningful engagements with high-quality children's books that are culturally authentic and accurate. Authenticity is very important in the selection of literature that depicts the values, beliefs, and cultural backgrounds of various groups. According to Barrera, Liguori, and Salas (1993), this is important "because inauthentic representation subverts the very cultural awareness and understanding that such literature can build" (p. 212). Critical evaluation of multicultural literature for authenticity and literary quality is essential to effective book selection. This book (particularly Chapter 11) shows you how to apply evaluative criteria for selecting authentic, quality multicultural children's literature.

# Selecting "Just Right" Literature

The selection of literature is key to providing an experience that promotes literacy development. If the literature is not appropriate, what the child takes from the book and how he or she responds to it will be limited, or even nonexistent. For example, the book *Brown Bear, Brown Bear, What Do You See?* is perfect for Rachel because of the layout, repeated and rhyming patterned text format, and simple concepts that promote cognitive development. Rachel also engaged in conversations with her mother about the animals. Because Rachel is from a European-American, middle-class family, her use of language, thinking, feeling, believing, valuing, and acting will be similar to those she experiences in school.

Bauer (2003), however, writes about the literature response of Elena, a four-year-old English-German bilingual, when she read the same book with her mother. Bauer reports that although the rhyming words and simple language made it easy for Elena to memorize the book, she never mentioned the animals in the story or made connections to animals she had interacted with. When presented with a different book—Marguerite Davol's *Black, White, Just Right*—Elena took an active role in seeking opportunities to discuss the story. The story is about a girl whose parents have different skin colors and different tastes in art, food, and pets. The girl in the story is different, too, but she is "just right"! Bauer noted that Davol's book was better at helping Elena make connections between the family in the book and her own family. Consequently, Elena discussed the book more and responded to it more enthusiastically.

Although books can and should be read to, with, or by children for a variety of reasons and levels, books that are within a child's *zone of proximal development* (ZPD) are more likely to be intellectually stimulating. According to Vygotsky (1978), the zone of proximal development is "the distance between the actual developmental level as determined through problem-solving under adult guidance or in collaboration with more capable peers" (p. 86). Figure 2.1 shows the conceptual framework for the ZPD in the

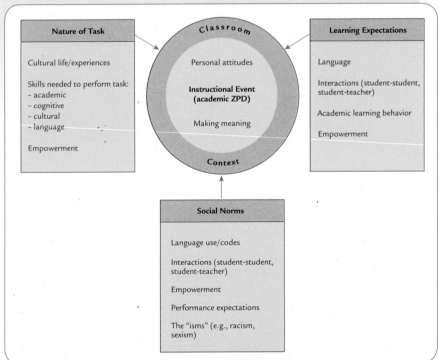

**FIGURE 2.1**

Zone of Proximal Development in the Teaching/Learning Process: A Conceptual Framework

K. Pansky & F. Bailey (Dec. 2002/Jan. 2003). To meet your students where they are, first you have to find them: Working with culturally and linguistically diverse at-risk students. *The Reading Teacher, 56*(4), 370–383. Reprinted with permission of the International Reading Association.

teaching and learning process. The inner circle is the adult's academic focus, and the outer circle represents the sociocultural context of the classroom. The classroom context is impacted by the nature of the task, the learning expectations, and the social norms set by the adult. When adults understand that learning is a sociocultural process in which students make meaning based on their life experiences, cultural knowledge, and language, they make instructional decisions based on those dynamics.

Barbara Rogoff (1990) considers children to be apprentices as they acquire a diverse repertoire of skills and knowledge under the guidance and support of those more knowledgeable. In an apprenticeship setting, adults model the significance of written language as an important tool for documenting and communicating information. In an apprenticeship role, the teacher models, scaffolds, and demonstrates during a literacy event when the child is unable to complete a task on her own or when she needs a model of expertise. If the child is not engaged in the literacy event, he or she is not likely to learn from the experience. As adults and children engage in discussions about books, children gain important "tools of the mind" for literacy acquisition (Bodrova & Leong, 1996).

## Discovering Your Own Literacy

> *Time spent reading, like time spent loving, increases our lifetime.*
>
> D. PENNAC, 1999, P. 146

In *Discover Your Own Literacy,* Donald Graves (1990) points out that before we can encourage children's literacy, we must consider teachers' literacy. Thus, the best way to determine which books are good for children is to read the books ourselves.

Although in today's hectic world, it is difficult to find the time to read, the issue is not whether we have the time but whether we allow ourselves the joy of reading. So rather than finding time, we *make* time—we steal a little time here and there from life's obligations: We read the newspaper in the morning while drinking that first cup of coffee, we read on the subway, or we listen to an audiobook as we drive to work. We read to our children before they go to bed, and we read a good book to help us fall asleep. All of these stolen moments contribute to our joy of being a reader. Reading, discussing, and analyzing books increases our ability to recognize and recommend excellent literature for children in a way that simply reading a textbook about children's literature cannot. In *Through the Eyes of a Child,* Norton (2007) explains as follows:

> Those of us who work with students of children's literature are rewarded when for the first time people see literature with a new awareness, discover the techniques that an author uses to create a believable plot or memorable characters, and discover that they can provide rationales for why a book is excellent, mediocre, or poor. (p. 76)

Often, there is an observable progression in the development of this "new awareness" over time. Vandergrift (1990) identifies the following seven stages in the development of understanding literary theory:

1.  The reader experiences a unique work of art: an internal act ordinarily not "visible either to the reader or to an outside observer."
2.  There is some precritical response ("I like it."): How do I feel about this work or in response to it?
3.  The reader takes the first steps in critical response with some theory at least implicit ("I like it because . . . . "): What in the work evoked these personal reactions? What questions are suggested by the work?
4.  There is a comparison and contrast among works and among various responses to a particular work: How is this work like and unlike other works? How is my experience of this work like and unlike my experiences of other works?

5. The reader develops some general notions applicable to all literary works (a general theory): How does this work relate to other works? Are there some things that seem to be true of all literature, or at least of all works similar to this one? Rephrase specific questions to become general questions. Relate them to each other in an organized system.

6. There is a testing of that general theory in relation to specific works: Is each additional work examined and illuminated in some way by the developing theory?

7. The reader revises the theory in response to that testing: What new knowledge or understandings of literature will I bring to subsequent reading?

*Watch*

*Watch an interview with Christopher Paul Curtis.*

Writing can help us become more conscious of our own interaction with texts and progression in the development of our analysis and interpretation of children's literature. Consider keeping a reading response journal to write down your thoughts about the books you read. Graves (1990) insightfully proclaims, "Writing is learning to listen to yourself and your own voice, to watch for the sense of self that emerges, and to trust what you see coming" (p. 26). In the following sample journal entry (see "The Teacher's Voice" below), a middle school teacher responded to *Bud, Not Buddy*, by Christopher Paul Curtis.

## THE · TEACHER'S · VOICE

> Journal Response to *Bud, Not Buddy* by Christopher Paul Curtis

I have turned into a huge Christopher Paul Curtis fan. He is such a compassionate and thoughtful writer. He trusts me, the reader, to have some intelligence and insight. I picked up Bud, Not Buddy because I had to read all of Curtis's books. I consumed Bud in two sittings.

I've always been fascinated with the time of the Great Depression. Maybe it's an Oklahoma thing, maybe it's from spending so much time with a grandmother who lost her husband and raised my father alone in the midst of it. I think it's because of the human element—the stories of such resiliency. I'm fascinated with the pictures of Dorothea Lange.

In any event, I was immediately drawn in by the character Bud. Here is where my latent maternal instincts start coming out. I wanted to bring Bud home—clean him up, feed him, give him a warm place to stay where he was safe. I got so caught up with Bud, I actually caught myself thinking, "We could convert the office. . . ."

I was thrilled for Buddy that the band and Miss Thomas were kind to him. I wanted to shake Herman E. Calloway. He'd already run off one child. I was surprised that he turned out to be Buddy's grandfather. I want a sequel. I want to know how their relationship developed.

In Curtis's style, the language, pacing, and tone were dead on. He made jazz come alive without having a musical medium in which to do it. His words are music though, as they wrap the reader in another place, another time, and a strong story.

Now, I have also gotten hooked on Newbery acceptance speeches, so I read Curtis's speech to accept his award for this novel. With self-deprecating humor and a tone of humility, he accepted the award while remaining grateful to all the people and all the experiences that made his book possible.

As a person who likes to write, I found it comforting and fascinating that this book ended up being about something quite different than its original intended subject. I think it is better for its focus on Bud, not a strike during the Depression. Again, whether he intended to or not, Curtis focuses on people and families with the events of history providing the backdrop. I didn't get the sense of characters and events colliding as in Watson's, but I did understand his exploration of suffering. There are many ways to suffer, and Curtis explores that without beating the reader over the head.

When compared to <u>The Truth About Sparrows</u>, Curtis's concern with characters over events becomes evident. I thought Marian Hale did an amazing job with the characters in her novel. Those characters, however, just can't reach the level of Curtis's. Interestingly, when I look back at what I wrote, I said, "Sadie and her family are as real as people I know." That seems to be the highest compliment one could give an author about her characters. Yet, Curtis is somehow better. It's like seeing a master painting; somehow you know a masterpiece when you see it. I am so grateful to Curtis's wife who gave him the opportunity to share his gift with the rest of us.

*—How does this teacher's response reflect her personal connection to the story, to other stories she has read, to the author's writing style, and to a general theory about characterization in a story?*

Reading, writing, and critiquing children's literature reflects what we should encourage children to do. As Ray (1999) reminds us, actions speak louder than words:

> Children have a remarkable sixth sense that tells them when we adults aren't what we seem to be. They're on to us so fast when we try to give them medicine disguised as candy. And they'll know if we are sharing words with them more out of duty than out of love, more to cover curriculum than to really sigh with them over words. And when that fundamental trust in us is broken, learning all but shuts down. The engagement is no longer about readers and writers sharing wondrous words—it's just about "doing more school." (p. 79)

By continually reading a variety of genres and staying abreast of current titles, teachers not only epitomize a lifelong reader but can recommend titles that will motivate, enhance, and extend their students' reading lives.

# Top 10 Read Alouds

## ACCEPTING YOURSELF AND OTHERS

*Watch* A Bad Case of
Stripes *as it is read
aloud.*

1. **A Bad Case of Stripes** by David Shannon (1998, Blue Sky). To ensure her popularity, Camilla Cream always does what people expect of her, until the day arrives when she no longer recognizes herself.

2. **Ella Sarah Gets Dressed** by Margaret Chodos-Irvine (2003, Harcourt). Against the advice of her family, Ella Sarah insists on wearing a striking and unusual outfit.

3. **The Important Book** by Margaret Wise Brown, illustrated by Leonard Weisgard (1949, Harper). What is most important about many familiar things, like rain and wind, apples and daisies, is suggested in rhythmic words and vivid pictures.

4. **Ira Sleeps Over** by Bernard Waber (1972, Houghton Mifflin). A little boy is excited at the prospect of spending the night at his friend's house but worries how he'll get along without his teddy bear.

5. **Jazzy Miz Mozetta** by Brenda Roberts, illustrated by Frank Morrison (2004, Farrar, Straus and Giroux). On a beautiful evening, Miz Mozetta puts on her red dress and blue shoes and dances the jitterbug just like she did many years before.

6. **Pinduli** by Janell Cannon (2004, Harcourt). Pinduli, a young striped hyena, is hurt by the unkind words of Dog, Lion, and Zebra, but her clever trick ensures her clan's survival and spreads harmony throughout the savannah.

7. **Pumpkinhead** by Eric Rohmann (2003, Knopf). A boy with a pumpkin for a head has a perilous adventure and learns a valuable lesson about what it means to be different.

8. **The Dunderheads** by Paul Fleischman, illustrated by David Roberts (2009, Candlewick). Junkyard, Einstein, Wheels, Pencil, Spider, Hollywood, Spitball, Clips, and Google-Eyes team up to try to outwit their teacher, Miss Breakbone.

9. **Apple Pie Fourth of July** by Janet Wong, illustrated by Margaret Chodos-Irvine (2002, Harcourt). A Chinese-American child fears that the food her parents are preparing to sell on the Fourth of July will not be eaten.

10. **Yo! Yes?** by Chris Raschka (1993, Orchard). Two lonely characters, one black and one white, meet on the street and become friends.

# Activities for Professional Development

## Think Critically About Children's Literature

1. Create a literacy timeline of your own reading history. What books influenced you at different points in your life? Think about why certain books have remained a part of your memory since childhood. Why do certain books appeal to you today? Which books did you think were funny? Compare your answers with your classmates'.

2. Join a social networking site for readers such as Goodreads (http://www.goodreads.com), LibraryThing (http://www.librarything.com), or Shelfari (http://www.shelfari.com). These sites make it easy to compile a list of children's books you would like to read and to add new books over time, write reviews, and recommend books to your classmates, teachers, or friends.

3. One of the first encounters young children have with literature is often the Mother Goose rhymes. Although Mother Goose is most commonly associated with the nursery, her power extends beyond babies and toddlers to many aspects of adult life. Scholars study the literary history of Mother Goose as well as social and historical referents in these nursery rhymes. The instantaneous recognition of characters and events leads to allusions in other literary works, in popular culture, and in advertising. Visit the website for Project ECLIPSE: Exemplary Children's Literature Interface for Scholarly Education (http://eclipse.rutgers.edu) and click on Mother Goose: A Scholarly Exploration. This website builds on the familiarity, the popularity, and the potential of multiple levels of learning inherent in Mother Goose and traces both verbal and visual variants of Mother Goose rhymes over time and across cultures.

   • Click on What Makes a Mother Goose a Mother Goose on the menu to the left. Read and explore this and the many other links to literary, social, and historical aspects of the Mother Goose rhymes illuminated on the site.
   • Be sure to read some of the nursery rhymes and view some of the many digitized versions of early Mother Goose editions
   • After thoroughly exploring the Mother Goose site, describe how versions and variants of Mother Goose have changed over time. Explain how your understanding and perspective of Mother Goose has changed after this exploration. How will you use this information to inform your work with children?

## Bring Children's Literature into the Classroom

4. Select several children's books that you believe will appeal to preschool children. If possible, share your selections with the children and note their responses. Did they respond as you anticipated? Why or why not?

## Learn About Authors and Illustrators

5. View video interviews with authors Laurence Yep and Nikki Grimes. Go to the *Reading Rockets* website (http://www.readingrockets.org). Click on "books & authors," and then click on "video interviews." View the video interviews with author Laurence Yep titled "Adapting to Different Realities" and "A Cultural Outsider." Then view the video clips by Nikki Grimes titled "Invisible Reader" and "Marginalizing Multicultural Books."

   • According to these two authors, what are the benefits of multicultural literature?
   • What did you find to be particularly meaningful about the interviews?
   • How could you use these videos (and others) in the classroom?

# Print and Online Resources

## Print Resources

Cai, M. (2002). *Multicultural literature for children and young adults: Reflections on critical issues.* Westport, CT: Greenwood.

Dixon-Krauss, L. (1996). *Vygotsky in the classroom.* White Plains, NY: Longman.

Sipe, L. (2008). *Storytime: Young children's literary understanding in the classroom.* New York: Teachers College Press.

Wood, D. (1998). *How children think and learn* (2nd ed.). Cambridge, MA: Blackwell.

 **Online Resources**

*Reading Is Fundamental*
**http://www.rif.org/parents**

*Reading Rockets*
**http://www.readingrockets.org/audience/parents**
Both of these sites offer extensive resources for parents and child care providers on selecting developmentally appropriate books for young children, reading together, creating literacy rich homes, early literacy, and connecting with schools.

*Gender and Culture in Children's Literature*
**http://comminfo.rutgers.edu/professional-development/childlit/index.html**

Click on "Gender and Culture in Picturebooks." This invaluable site is hosted by Kay Vandergrift, Professor Emerita in the School of Communication, Information and Library Studies at Rutgers University. Vandergrift has included sources on gender and culture in children's picturebooks, translations, links to other gender and culture websites, booklists, and other professional sources.

*Making Meaning in Literature—Grades 6–8*
**http://www.learner.org/resources/series170.html**

Hosted by the Annenburg Foundation, this video library provides the philosophy and techniques that can be used to help all students make meaning from the literature they read to become lifelong readers, thinkers, and talkers.

*Research on Children's Literature by Lee Galda, Gwynne Ash, and Bernice Cullinan*
**http://www.readingonline.org/articles/art_index.asp?HREF=/articles/handbook/galda/index.html**

This article looks into the research in children's literature and the developing interests and literary understandings of its readers and the implications of literary study in classrooms.

Visit the companion website at **www.cengage.com/education/johnson** to find links related to the Read/Watch/Listen icons noted throughout the chapter, as well as additional resources.

# References

Allington, R., & Johnston, P. (2002). *Reading to learn: Lessons from exemplary fourth-grade classrooms.* New York: Guilford.

Au, K. (1998). Social constructivism and the school literacy learning of students of diverse backgrounds. *Journal of Literacy Research, 30*(2), 297–319.

Barrera, R., Liguori, O., & Salas, L. (1993). Ideas a literature can grow on: Key insights for enriching and expanding children's literature about the Mexican-American experience. In V. J. Harris (Ed.), *Teaching multicultural literature in grades K–8* (pp. 203–241). Norwood, MA: Christopher-Gordon.

Bauer, E. (2003). Finding Esmerelda's shoes: A case study of a young bilingual child's responses to literature. In A. Willis, G. Garcia, R. Barrera, & V. Harris (Eds.), *Multicultural issues in literacy research and practice* (pp. 11–27). Mahwah, NJ: Erlbaum.

Bodrova, E., & Leong, D. (1996). *Tools of the mind: The Vygotskian approach to early childhood education.* Englewood Cliffs, NJ: Merrill.

Cai, M. (2002). *Multicultural literature for children and young adults: Reflections on critical issues.* Westport, CT: Greenwood.

Chatton, B. (2004). Critiquing the critics: Adult values, children's responses, postmodern picture books, and Arlene Sardine. *Journal of Children's Literature, 30*(1), 31–37.

Dowd, F. (1992). Evaluating children's books portraying Native American and Asian cultures. *Childhood Education, 68*(4), 219–224.

Fishman, A. (1995). Finding ways in: Redefining multicultural literature. *English Journal, 84*(6), 73–79.

Fox, D., & Short, K. (2003). *Stories matter.* Urbana, IL: National Council of Teachers of English.

Graves, D. (1990). *Discover your own literacy.* Portsmouth, NH: Heinemann.

Harris, V. (1992). (Ed.). *Teaching multicultural literature: In grades K–8.* Norwood, MA: Christopher-Gordon.

Jalongo, M. (1985). Children's literature: There's some sense to its humor. *Childhood Education, 2,* 109–114.

Karolides, N. J. (1997). Transactional theory and literature-based teaching. In N. J. Karolides (Ed.), *Reader response in elementary classrooms* (pp. 3–28). Mahwah, NJ: Erlbaum.

Knapp, M. (1995). *Teaching for meaning in high-poverty classrooms.* New York: Teachers College Press.

Kruse, G., & Horning, K. (1990). Looking into the mirror: Considerations behind the reflections. In M. V. Lindgren (Ed.), *The multicolored mirror: Cultural substance in literature for children and young adults.* Fort Atkinson, WI: Highsmith.

Möller, K. (2005). Creating zones of possibility for struggling readers: A study of one fourth grader's shifting roles in literature discussions. *Journal of Literacy Research, 36*(4), 419–460.

National Center for Education Statistics. (2003). *Digest of education statistics 2003.* Available: http://nces.ed.gov/programs/digest/.

Norton, D. (2007). *Through the eyes of a child* (7th ed.). Upper Saddle River, NJ: Merrill/Prentice Hall.

Pansky, K., & Bailey, F. (2003). To meet your students where they are, first you have to find them: Working with culturally and linguistically diverse at-risk students. *The Reading Teacher, 56*(4), 370–383

Pennac, D. (1999). *Better than life.* Portland, ME: Stenhouse.

Piaget, J. (1926). *Language and thought of the child.* New York: Kegan Paul, Trench, and Trubner.

Pullman, P. (2006, August 5). Help finding "stuff" on religious references in HDM. Message posted to Child lit electronic mailing list, archived at http://email.rutgers.edu/pipermail/child_lit.

Ray, K. (1999). *Wondrous words.* Urbana, IL: National Council of Teachers of English.

Rogoff, B. (1990). *Apprenticeship in thinking: Cognitive development in social contexts.* New York: Oxford University Press.

Rosenblatt, L. (1978). *The reader, the text, the poem: The transactional theory of the literary work.* Carbondale: Southern Illinois University Press.

Ryan, K., & Cooper, J. (2010). *Those who can, teach* (12th ed.). Boston: Houghton Mifflin.

Santrock, J. W. (2009). *Life-span development* (12th ed.). Boston: McGraw-Hill.

Shannon, P. (1994). I am the cannon: Finding ourselves in multiculturalism. *Journal of Children's Literature, 20*(1), 1–5.

Sims Bishop, R. (1994). (Ed.). *Kaleidoscope: A multicultural booklist for grades K–8.* Urbana, IL: National Council of Teachers of English.

Vandergrift, K. (1990). *Children's literature: Theory, research, and teaching.* Englewood, CO: Libraries Unlimited, Inc.

van Kleeck, A., Stahl, S., & Bauer, E. (2003). Preface. In van Kleeck, A., Stahl, S., & Bauer, E. (Eds.), *On reading books to children: Parents and teachers.* Mahwah, NJ: Erlbaum.

Vygotsky, L. (1978). *Mind in society.* Cambridge, MA: Harvard University Press.

Wham, M., Barnhart, J., & Cook, G. (1996). Enhancing multicultural awareness through the story book reading experience. *Journal of Research and Development in Education, 30,* 1–9.

Wood, D. (1998). *How children think and learn* (2nd ed.). Cambridge, MA: Blackwell.

Yep, L. (1991). The secret garden. Englewood Cliffs, NJ: Messner.

# 3 Literacy: How Children Become Good Readers

> A simple principle—children differ—explains why there can be no one best method, material, or program. This simple principle has been reaffirmed so repeatedly in education research that one would think folks would have noted it by now.
> —*Richard Allington, 2006, p. 34*

Every day, teachers welcome into their classrooms children from a wide range of cultural, linguistic, and economic diversity. For some of these children, reading acquisition will be very easy, but for others, it will be more difficult. But the needs of *all* children influence the teaching and learning of literacy in the classroom. Effective teaching requires good teaching decisions regarding individuals and groups of children, especially those children who depend primarily on school for most of their literacy learning (Bandura, 1997). Reading achievement for children of poverty and urban minorities has continued to decline exponentially. While 68 percent of all 4th grade public school students scored below proficient levels on 2009 reading tests administered through the National Assessment of Educational Progress, in low-income schools, 85 percent of fourth-graders scored below proficient. Eighty-three percent of poor black students in schools with moderate to low levels of poverty and 90 percent of poor black students in schools with high concentrations of poverty failed to hit the grade-level reading target. Eighty-eight percent of economically disadvantaged Hispanic students fell short of proficiency (Annie E. Casey Foundation, 2010). Children who do not learn to read well early in school are more likely to fail subjects later in school, drop out of high school, abuse alcohol and drugs, engage in criminal behavior, and serve jail time (Fielding, Kerr, & Rosier, 1998). This widening achievement gap for America's schoolchildren has prompted an unprecedented national focus on ways to improve reading instruction.

# Expectations for Literacy

*The No Child Left Behind Act* of 2001 (NCLB) was designed to ensure that all children read fluently by third grade and to help close the gap in literacy achievement between the rich and the poor. The Act provides federal funding through the Reading First program to schools that comply with specific requirements for teaching reading based on a report by the National Reading Panel (NRP) (NICHD, 2000), which was appointed by the U.S. Congress to analyze the field of literature and is considered to be "scientifically based" research on reading instruction. Based on this research, the panel concluded that there are five essential components of reading instruction: phonemic awareness, phonics, fluency, vocabulary, and comprehension. Although the NRP report received some adverse criticism by the literacy community for selecting scientifically based research studies that consisted of "quantitative, positivistic research often conducted in laboratory settings removed from the rigors of class-room practice" (Lapp, Flood, Brock, & Fisher, 2007), the findings from the report became the basis for reading instruction in NCLB (Allington, 2002; Cunningham, 2001; Garan, 2002) and the result has been a federal push for one-size-fits-all instructional materials and methods.

## ACCOUNTABILITY

Under NCLB, the federal government mandated a single test-based accountability system for all states, annual testing, and disaggregation of test scores by students' racial and socio-economic backgrounds. To remain accredited, schools must demonstrate adequate yearly progress. Some states have restricted the curriculum and teaching materials to emphasize only those subjects on the state-mandated test. Moreover, some teachers are responding to the accountability policy in ways that widen the achievement gap by spending hours of class time completing isolated test preparation exercises instead of engaging in more sub-stantive work, which emphasizes critical thinking skills and further widens the gap rather than closing it (Watanabe, 2008).

In *The Shame of the Nation: The Restoration of Apartheid Schooling in America,* respected educator and activist Jonathan Kozol (2005) recounts his visits to 60 public schools in 11 states over a five-year period. He found, despite the promise of No Child Left Behind, that many inner-city schools serving black and Hispanic children are spiraling backward. In many districts, Kozol found a restricted curriculum, rote drill-and-practice teaching meth-ods, and test-mandated retention policies. Former New York City principal Deborah Meier states, "Every time we hold a child over, we are substantially reducing the odds of that child graduating anytime in the future—and when a child is held back twice, the likelihood that he or she will never graduate increases by 90 percent" (Kozol, 2005, p. 117). In the nation's 100 largest districts, less than half the entering ninth graders graduate in four years.

Although it might be expected that stricter accountability standards and a stronger emphasis on reading would substantially improve student achievement, this is not the case. A study from the National Bureau of Educational Research (Dee & Jacob, 2009) looked at whether NCLB has influenced student achievement based on an analysis of state-level panel data on student test scores from the National Assessment of Educa-tional Progress (NAEP) and found no evidence that NCLB increased reading achieve-ment in either 4th or 8th grade.

## NEW RESEARCH CONTINUOUSLY INFORMS LITERACY INSTRUCTION

It is important to note that in the decade since the NRP report, significant studies such as the National Early Literacy Panel (2008) (focused on PreK-K literacy), the National

*Watch*

*Watch a video of Jonathan Kozol as he delivers a speech concerning the decrepit state of health and education.*

Literacy Panel for Language Minority Children and Youth (August & Shanahan, 2006) (focused on literacy for English language learners), and the Reading First Impact Study (Gamse, et al., 2008) have significantly contributed to the existing knowledge base about effective reading instruction. For example, studies from the NRP report indicate the significance of phonemic awareness instruction but the National Early Literacy Panel report found that it was more important for young children to learn phonological awareness or larger sound units than phonemes. Additionally, though the NRP report found phonics instruction important, the National Literacy Panel for Language Minority Children and Youth study found that English learners have often already developed adequate phonics knowledge so that phonics instruction has a smaller effect size with English language learners. Finally, The Reading First Impact Report found that Reading First did not have statistically significant impacts on student reading comprehension test scores in grades 1-3.

As we move into the next decade, new research will continue to provide insight to our existing knowledge base about the best instructional practices for reading instruction. New initiatives such as the Common Core Standards may influence what is taught in classrooms across the country. However, as Richard Allington asserts in the opening quote, there is no single best instructional approach that will meet the needs of all students all of the time. Effective teachers of reading use what they know about best instructional practices and their knowledge of the students they teach to make decisions for instruction that meet all students' needs.

It is a tribute to the nation's teachers and administrators that, despite the limitations placed on them, they are working hard to implement it and make it work. No teacher wants to see a single child left behind. Kozol considers teachers to be our greatest hope:

> Teachers in these schools must work, and know that they must work, within "the box" of segregated demographics and extreme inequities; but in their temperaments and in their moral disposition many also stand *outside* that box, because they are aware of this existence, and this sense of double-vision, being part of something and aware of what it is at the same time, regenerates the energy they bring with them each morning to the very little place (one room, one set of chairs) in which they use what gifts they have to make the school day good and whole and sometimes beautiful for children. (p. 287)

In all schools, the teacher is the most important contributor to student achievement. In high-poverty schools, teachers do not wallow in the demographics associated with their students; rather, they identify and extend the personal and academic potential within each student.

## GOOD TEACHERS MAKE THE DIFFERENCE

The way teachers think about, understand, and value instruction influences their practice. As a way to get teachers to reflect on what they think, understand, and value about reading instruction, I begin each semester by asking preservice and inservice teachers to reflect on their own early reading experiences by responding to three questions about their early memories of learning to read (see Table 3.1).

No teacher wants a child to leave a classroom with the negative, counterproductive feelings that the college students quoted in Table 3.1 still hold in their twenties and thirties. Ability grouping and round-robin reading, unfortunately, are common practices that

**TABLE 3.1**

# What Were Your Early Experiences with Reading?

- Think about your early experiences in learning to read, both at home and at school. What specifically do you remember?

- What were the experiences like?

- How did you feel?

*The following written responses are typical of the positive experiences with reading that most preservice teachers had at home and at school:*

"I remember mostly my dad reading me endless book after book. I loved it! Both of my parents read me stories before I went to sleep and I would beg them to read to me all the time."

"My mom was really good about reading to me. My earliest memory of being read to is sitting in a big comfortable recliner, on my mom's lap, listening to her read to me."

"I remember the first thing my kindergarten teacher did was to read stories to us."

"During fifth grade I remember my teacher reading to us every day after lunch. I really enjoyed this particular book, and to this day I can remember it as if I had watched a movie of it."

*But these preservice teachers did not always have positive responses when it came to their reading experiences in school:*

"Every day we would read a book together as a class. My teacher would read some, and then she would randomly call on us to read some. I didn't want to read because reading aloud always made me feel nervous. Sometimes I would stutter as I read because I was concentrating too much on what everyone else would be thinking about me."

"My teacher would work with us in small groups and have each student read one line all around the semicircle. Let me tell you, this is the cruelest thing you can do to a child like me who was anxious and shy. I would count ahead to the sentence I was supposed to read and practice the line over and over without paying attention to what the other sentences were, because I was so afraid I would mess up or be criticized by my classmates."

"I was in the lowest group. I sat in the circle and waited for my turn to read, and I often felt as though I would rather run away and hide. Reading aloud was the worst. I hated when I got to a word that I didn't recognize and I couldn't figure out. It always seemed as though every eye was on me at this point and it made me feel stupid."

are not supported by research and leave children with an indelible, negative impression of reading that can last a lifetime. Teachers have a powerful influence on their students and the instructional practices they employ must encourage children to become lifelong readers. The Standards for the English Language Arts can provide valuable guidelines as to the best practices for helping children become good readers.

## USING STANDARDS AS GUIDELINES

With each stage of development, children exhibit certain behaviors, strategies, and skills that move them closer to becoming good readers. The National Council of Teachers of English and the International Reading Association have established the *Standards for the English Language Arts* (1996) that are based on current research and theory about how students learn language. In many instances, these guidelines reflect the stages of literacy development (Cooper & Kiger, 2005), and can provide teachers with guidelines for both assessment and instruction. The standards (Table 3.2) constitute a broad framework that is meant to be suggestive, not exhaustive or prescriptive. If implemented effectively and with consideration of each educator's unique range of purpose, development, and context of language learning, the English Language Arts (ELA) standards can also help teachers plan for instruction.

*Read*

*Read more about the NCTE/IRA Standards for the English Arts*

Often, the ELA national standards serve as guidelines for state and local school districts in developing specific standards or benchmarks at each grade level. As such, this set of standards "is a powerful tool for guiding discussion about the connection between evaluation and learning that is applicable across a wide spectrum, including

**TABLE 3.2**

# Standards for the English Language Arts

The vision guiding these standards is that all students must have the opportunities and resources to develop the language skills they need to pursue life's goals and to participate fully as informed productive members of society. These standards assume that literacy growth begins before children enter school as they experience and experiment with literacy activities—reading and writing, and associating spoken words with their graphic representations. Recognizing this fact, these standards encourage the development of curriculum and instruction that make productive use of the emerging literacy abilities that children bring to school. Furthermore, the standards provide ample room for the innovation and creativity essential to teaching and learning. They are not prescriptions for particular curriculum or instruction. Although we present these standards as a list, we want to emphasize that they are not distinct and separable; they are, in fact, interrelated and should be considered as a whole.

1. Students read a wide range of print and nonprint texts to build on understanding of texts, of themselves, and of the cultures of the United States and the world; to acquire new information; to respond to the needs and demands of society and the workplace; and for personal fulfillment. Among these texts are fiction and nonfiction, classic and contemporary works.

2. Students conduct research on issues and interests by generating ideas and questions, and by posing problems. They gather, evaluate, and synthesize data from a variety of sources (e.g., print and nonprint texts, artifacts, people) to communicate their discoveries in ways that suit their purpose and audience.

*(continued)*

**TABLE 3.2**

(*continued*)

# Standards for the English Language Arts

| | |
|---|---|
| **3.** Students read a wide range of literature from many periods and many genres to build an understanding of the many dimensions (e.g., philosophical, ethical, aesthetic) of human experience. | **4.** Students use a variety of technological and information resources (e.g., libraries, databases, computer networks, video) to gather and synthesize information and to create and communicate knowledge. |
| **5.** Students apply a wide range of strategies to comprehend, interpret, evaluate, and appreciate texts. They draw on their prior experience, their interactions with other readers and writers, their knowledge of word meaning and of other texts, their word identification strategies, and their understanding of textual features (e.g., sound-letter correspondence, sentence structure, context, graphics). | **6.** Students develop an understanding of and a respect for diversity in language use, patterns, and dialects across cultures, ethnic groups, geographic regions, and social roles. |
| **7.** Students adjust their use of spoken, written, and visual language (e.g., conventions, style, vocabulary) to communicate effectively with a variety of audiences and for different purposes. | **8.** Students whose first language is not English make use of their first language to develop competency in the English language arts and to develop understanding of content across the curriculum. |
| **9.** Students employ a wide range of strategies as they write and use different writing process elements appropriately to communicate with different audiences for a variety of purposes. | **10.** Students participate as knowledgeable, reflective, creative, and critical members of a variety of literacy communities. |
| **11.** Students apply knowledge of language structure, language conventions (e.g., spelling and punctuation), media techniques, figurative language, and genre to create, critique, and discuss print and nonprint texts. | **12.** Students use spoken, written, and visual language to accomplish their own purposes (e.g., for learning enjoyment, persuasion, and the exchange of information). |

*Standards for the English Language Arts* (1996), by the National Council of Teachers of English and the International Reading Association.

policy making, curriculum development, and classroom practice" (Faust & Kieffer, 1998, p. 540).

## INTEGRATING THE LANGUAGE ARTS

According to the ELA national standards, instruction should produce competency in speaking, listening, reading, writing, viewing, and visually representing. These six language systems are interrelated and therefore should be taught in tandem, not in

**TABLE 3.3**

# Integrated Language Arts

| | Written Language | Spoken Communication | Visual Literacy |
|---|---|---|---|
| Receptive Language Process | **Reading** A cognitive process whereby individuals engage with written text, decode it, and gain meaning from it. | **Listening** Listening requires us to receive and make sense of the oral language of others. | **Viewing** Viewing and interpreting pictures, signs, commercial logos, computer graphics, TV, movies, video, and websites. |
| Expressive Language Process | **Writing** The reciprocal of reading, writing requires us to encode and produce written language. | **Speaking** When we talk, we produce language. Speaking is the reciprocal of listening. | **Visually Representing** Making meaning from visual information conveyed through images such as art, web pages, movies, drawings, and paintings. |

separate lessons. Table 3.3 shows how the language arts support one another. Research has shown that exemplary teachers integrate language learning among the language arts, content area learning, and literature study (Allington & Johnston, 2002; Pressley et al., 2001; Wharton-McDonald, Pressley, & Hampston, 1998).

## Enchanted Hunters: Supporting Children's Comprehension of Text

***Watch***

*Watch an interview with Maria Tartar.*

In her book, *Enchanted Hunters: The Power of Stories in Childhood* (2009), Maria Tartar uses the term *enchanted hunters* to describe what happens to children through the transformative power of reading books. Tarter writes, "Curious, energetic, and enthralled, those bookworms have earned the right to a metamorphosis, one that captures the magic and drama of what happens to them when they read powerful, breathtaking books" (p. 27).

Reading is thinking (Smith, 2005) and the *metamorphosis* to which Tartar refers can only happen if the child is a good reader who comprehends text.

### DEFINING COMPREHENSION

***Read***

*Read the full report of the RAND study: Reading for Understanding.*

Comprehension is "the process of simultaneously extracting and constructing meaning through interaction and involvement with written language" (RAND Study Group, 2002, p. 12). The "extracting and constructing" process corresponds to the transactional process of reading response discussed in Chapter 2. The unique exchange among the reader, the text, and the activity occurs within a larger sociocultural context that shapes and is shaped by the reader. Ruddell (2002) states, "Comprehension reflects who people are, how they relate to the world and others in it, their accumulated store of factual and intuitive knowledge, the social environment in which they are reading, and even how they feel on a given day" (p. 105). Therefore, comprehension instruction must take into consideration the teacher's knowledge of the child as a reader. To assist children in becoming "curious, energetic, and enthralled" readers, teachers should consider what good readers *do* when they read.

### CHARACTERISTICS OF GOOD READERS

In a review of research, Duke and Pearson (2002) found that, in particular, good readers are *active* readers. Table 3.4 shows that good readers do quite a bit more than simply decode words and comprehend text. The dynamic interaction among the reader, the text, and the social context, as discussed in Chapter 2, affects the construction of meaning

---

**TABLE 3.4**

# Characteristics of Good Readers

- They have clear goals in mind for their reading. They constantly *evaluate* whether the text, and their reading of it, is meeting their goals.

- They *look over* the text before they read, noting such things as the *structure* of the text and text sections that might be most relevant to their reading goals.

- They frequently *make predictions* about what is to come.

- They read *selectively*, continually making decisions about their reading—what to read carefully, what to read quickly, what not to read, what to reread, and so on.

- They *construct, revise*, and *question* the meaning they make as they read.

- They try to determine the meaning of *unfamiliar words* and *concepts* in the text, and they deal with inconsistencies or gaps as needed.

- They draw from, compare, and *integrate their prior knowledge* with material in the text.

- They think about the *authors* of the text, their style, beliefs, intentions, historical milieu, and so on.

- They *monitor their understanding* of the text, making adjustments in their reading as necessary.

- They *evaluate the text's quality and value,* and react to the text in a range of ways, both intellectually and emotionally.

- They read different kinds of text differently.

- They attend closely to the setting and characters when reading narrative.

- They construct and revise summaries of what they have read, when reading expository text.

- They understand that text processing occurs not only during "reading" as we have traditionally defined it, but also during short breaks taken during reading, even after the "reading" itself has commenced, even after the "reading" has ceased.

- They experience comprehension as a consuming, continuous, and complex activity that is both *satisfying* and *productive*.

N. Duke & P. D. Pearson (2002). Effective practices for developing reading comprehension. In A. Farstrup & S. J. Samuels (Eds.), *What research has to say about reading instruction* (3rd ed., p 206). Newark, NJ: International Reading Association. Reprinted with permission of the International Reading Association.

and requires that instruction take into consideration the ways children learn, the types of interaction in which they participate, and the texts they read.

The next section of this book will discuss ways effective teachers can support the development of children's comprehension as they journey to becoming enchanted hunters.

# Characteristics of Highly Effective Reading Teachers

How can teachers assist children in becoming good readers—what supports matter? A synthesis of several studies of exemplary reading teachers (Allington & Johnson, 2002; Block, 2001; Morrow, Tracey, Woo, & Pressley, 1999; Pressley et al., 2001; Taylor, Pearson, Clark, & Walpole, 1999) found that effective reading teachers share several important characteristics. These characteristics are supported by the research on effective reading comprehension instruction (Duke & Pearson, 2002; RAND Study Group, 2002).

- Create a supportive, encouraging, and nurturing environment that includes using various genres of text to enhance students' knowledge of text structures and giving students choices, challenging tasks, and collaborative learning structures to increase students' motivation to read and comprehend text.
- Provide clear explanations and model how to perform a repertoire of strategies to promote comprehension monitoring and foster comprehension.
- Engage students in constructive conversations with teachers and with other students.
- Providing comprehension strategy instruction that is deeply connected throughout the curriculum.
- Create print-rich environments with a variety of literacy materials that support instruction readily accessible.

Each of these characteristics will be discussed in the next sections. Additional characteristics that include understanding effective strategies for grouping, assessment, management, and making connections with families are discussed in Chapters 13 and 14.

## CREATE A SUPPORTIVE ENVIRONMENT

*The truly literate are not those who know how to read, but those who read: independently, responsively, critically, and because they want to. The first real business of reading instruction is to make children want to read.*

G. SLOAN, 2003, p. 4

Teachers can create supportive, nurturing environments that promote the development of good readers. Encouraging children to become *engaged* in reading is an important step in literacy. Teachers can create a more positive attitude toward reading by engaging children in reading not only in school but at home as well. Children also become more involved with reading when they select their own reading material. This section examines the factors that actively involve children in reading.

**A Positive Attitude.** Children come to school with many different attitudes toward reading. Many children will have been read to at home by parents or caregivers who are important models for reading. Others will come from homes where reading is practiced differently or where books are unavailable. Attitude, or desire, is everything. Children's attitude toward reading will determine how much effort, motivation, and engagement they will invest in it. According to Krashen (2004), "Those who 'hate to read' simply do not have access to books" (p. 61).

**Engagement.** Reading is more than a cognitive process of decoding the words, reading fluently, or comprehending the text. It is becoming deeply involved, captivated, absorbed, and immersed in a text—in other words, *engaged*. Reading engagement integrates the cognitive, motivational, and social dimensions of reading and reading instruction (Baker, Dreher, & Guthrie, 2000). Engaged reading can occur at all levels of development. In fact, engagement at a younger age predicts achievement at an older age. Baker, Dreher, and Guthrie state the following:

> Students are engaged readers when they read frequently for interest, enjoyment, and learning. The heart of engagement is the desire to gain new knowledge of a topic, to follow the excitement of a narrative, to expand one's experience through print. Engaged readers draw on knowledge gained from previous experiences to construct new understandings, and they use cognitive strategies to regulate comprehension so that goals are met and interests are satisfied. (p. 2)

A child who is engaged in reading employs both his mind and his heart and is well on his way to becoming a lifelong reader. Developing lifelong readers should be the goal of every teacher, and, therefore, providing an instructional environment that promotes reading engagement should be at the top of the priority list. The engaged reader is capable of overcoming obstacles of low parental education and income, as well as preferences and abilities associated with gender. Unfortunately, in an effort to ensure that students are decoding and comprehending, many teachers promote unengaged reading.

Educators must focus their attention not only on *how* students read but *why*. Guthrie and Anderson (1999) explain, "Motivations and social interactions are equal to cognitions as foundations for reading," and the "engaged readers not only have acquired reading skills, but use them for their own purposes in many contexts" (p. 17). When children can make a connection between what they read and their personal lives, they are more likely to be involved, interested, and constantly learning from their books.

**Motivation.** Motivation is a critical part of engagement. As motivation increases, students want to spend more time reading. Therefore, motivation plays a dual role: It becomes a part of both the process and the product of engagement. Engaged children read widely for a variety of purposes and create situations that extend opportunities for literacy. In the classroom, promoting reading engagement requires a coordinated emphasis on competence and motivation in reading instruction.

Motivation is a primary concern of many teachers because lack of motivation is at the heart of many of the problems they face in teaching. Yet, research has found that many teachers have little knowledge of practices that facilitate motivation and interest (Pressley, Wharton-McDonald, Mistretta-Hampston, & Echevarria, 1998). To this end, Edmunds and Bauserman (2006) conducted interviews with 831 K–5 students to find out what motivated them to read. The interviews revealed five main factors:

1. Self-selection of books
2. Access to a variety of fiction and nonfiction books
3. Books that are personally interesting

**4.** Access to lots of books
**5.** Being read to by teachers and family members and when peers shared what they were reading with them

The result of this study is very encouraging. Rather than extrinsic rewards or punishment, children are motivated to read by reading. When read to by adults and given the opportunity to self-select books of interest from a variety of fiction and nonfiction texts and to share books with each other, children read because they *want* to and not because they *have* to. Ruddell's (2004) research found that influential teachers positively affect students' attitudes toward reading by tapping their internal motivation as they encourage children to enter into and transact with the text. Ruddell (2004) states, "Influential teachers are highly effective in taking an instructional stance that uses internal reader motivations and incorporates children's prior knowledge, experiences, and beliefs in the meaning-negotiation and construction process" (p. 993).

**Self-Selected Literature.** When he was in fourth grade, my son Derek became enamored with Thomas Jefferson while studying the Declaration of Independence at school. I took Derek to the library, and he selected several books about Thomas Jefferson; one of them was *Thomas Jefferson: Man with a Vision,* by Ruth Crisman. The book was 152 pages long, and, after flipping through it, I felt it was too long and too detailed to hold Derek's attention. But every night, Derek curled up in bed with *Thomas Jefferson: Man with a Vision,* and he often discussed with me certain points of interest or fascinating facts. Despite my doubts, he read the book from cover to cover. Derek self-selected the book, was motivated to read the book, and was completely engaged in reading the book—all without my guidance.

Children are self-regulating individuals and as such, will seek and select experiences that are consistent with their developmental level (Vygotsky, 1978). Enjoyment of a book cannot be forced on a child; it must come about naturally. Even with a teacher's caring guidance and a parent's well-intended recommendation, children will always choose books that reflect *their* interests and preferences. Many adults believe that children will be shortchanged or cannot learn if they do not always read what adults consider "quality" literature. But an adult's interests often differ from a child's (Chatton, 2004; Worthy, Moorman, & Turner, 1999). When given the option, children will make positive selections based on their individual interests and abilities. Research suggests that students can, and do, make choices that increase their awareness and extend their growing knowledge of literacy (Fresch, 1995; McLaughlin & Allen, 2002; Schlager, 1978; Worthy, 1996).

In addition to fostering internal or intrinsic motivation, self-selection of literature allows students to make choices and gives them control. When real-world readers choose a text, they are reading to learn and to enjoy. They accomplish these tasks by selecting a text that fulfills their needs. Selecting what to read is a major part of becoming a reader (Ollman, 1993). According to Darigan, Tunnel, and Jacobs (2002), self-selecting literature is so essential to the reading process that without its inclusion into a reading program, reading development will not occur. For students to engage with a text, they must feel that they have control over which materials they read.

**Authenticity of Texts.** Authentic texts are hardcover or paperback books, magazines, or newspapers (such as you find in a library or bookstore); they are not specially constructed materials or short workbook passages created with controlled, unnatural vocabulary for the purpose of teaching a vowel sound. Although commercial programs are used in approximately 90 percent of classrooms across the United States (Reutzel & Cooter, 2002), Allington's (2002) review of research indicates that the expert and engaging teacher doesn't really need a basal or packaged program: "The expert teacher will reject it or tailor it until it no longer is recognizable" (p. 18). This seems to parallel the "sense of double-vision" referred to by Kozol (2005). Expert teachers produce readers regardless of the reading series they are mandated to use by altering and modifying reading programs and simply ignoring mandates in order to better meet the needs of their students (Hibbert & Iannacci, 2005; Kozol, 2005; Pressley, Allington, Wharton-McDonald, Collins-Block, & Morrow, 2001). During my many years of teaching, I have never had a preservice or an inservice teacher tell me that her favorite story was from a basal, that she fondly remembers reading from a basal, or that a basal made her love to read. Basal series also typically follow a "one story a week" format in which students read and do activities around only one story for the entire week. One story a week is simply not enough. The most critical factor in fostering reading achievement is the opportunity to read.

Charlotte Huck (1989) observes, "We don't achieve literacy and then give children literature; we achieve literacy through literature" (p. 258). Children enjoy reading in school more when their classrooms use authentic books for instruction and not basals, worksheets, and workbooks (Duke & Pearson, 2002; Thames & Reeves, 1994). Experience reading real texts for real purposes will increase the likelihood that students will transfer the use of strategies to their independent reading.

**Range of Genre.** For all children to become good readers, teachers must accommodate their students' different interests and reading abilities by using a range of authentic texts, such as picturebooks, easy readers, chapter books, informational books, poetry, magazines, newspapers, and biographies. Including a range of literary selections not only meets each child's interests and abilities, but it exposes children to other genres, topics, cultures, characters, minorities, and people with disabilities.

Giving children the opportunity to engage in a range of genres also helps them understand their structures or how different genres are organized. This helps children anticipate what to expect and make inferences based on those expectations, so reading is easier.

**Time for Reading.** Ample time for reading is defined as "more time to read than the combined total allocated for *learning* about reading and *talking or writing* about what has been read" (Fielding & Pearson, 1994, p. 63), allowing students the opportunity to orchestrate the skills and strategies that are important to skillful reading. It also allows for the acquisition of new knowledge. Students should also be given the chance to choose their own books within their level of difficulty, reread texts for fluency, and read and discuss books with peers. Routman (2003) suggests that teachers use the 20/80 rule, where approximately 20 percent of the time allocated for reading each day is dedicated to explicit strategy instruction and 80 percent for applying that instruction during actual reading.

In his book *The Power of Reading: Insights from the Research*, Stephen Krashen (2004) reviews extensive research on free voluntary reading (FVR), which he defines as "reading because you want to . . . no book report, no questions at the end of the chapter, and no looking up every vocabulary word. . . . It is the kind of reading highly literate people do all the time" (p. x). Table 3.5 lists the benefits from free voluntary reading from Krashen's review of research.

Krashen's review of research provides insights into the benefits of independent reading and powerful evidence of why teachers must provide time for children to read every day. The most important thing a teacher can do is to make available a wide variety of books, model herself as a reader and lover of literature, and give students the *time* to read real books in class every day.

**TABLE 3.5**

# Benefits of Free Voluntary Reading

- Those who say they read more read and write better.
- Those who recognize more authors' names have read more and have superior literacy development.
- In school, FVR results in better reading comprehension, writing style, vocabulary, spelling, and grammatical development.
- FVR is nearly always superior to direct instruction on tests of reading, vocabulary, writing, and grammar.
- The richer the print environment, the better the literacy development.
- Children who are read to at school or at home read more and show better literacy development.
- Reading itself promotes reading.
- Children read more when they see other people reading and when they have time to read.
- Children who are readers will develop at least acceptable levels of literacy. Without a reading habit, children simply do not have a chance.

**Decoding.** The ability to quickly and accurately decode words facilitates comprehension because automatic decoding permits readers to focus their attention on the text's meaning and on their own response (Pressley, 2000; Snow, Burns, & Griffin, 1998). Specific instruction on decoding such as developing phonemic awareness and phonics is beyond the scope of this text. However, good literature engages young readers with books that they *want* to read over and over, and repeated readings allow children to discover many important elements of decoding knowledge, such as letter–sound relationships, sight–word recognition, and context clues.

**Vocabulary and Concept Development.** Prior knowledge is an important factor in text comprehension. Certainly field trips, discussions about texts, hands-on activities, and other instructional experiences can assist in building concept and vocabulary knowledge (Duke & Pearson, 2002). Nagy (1988) states the following:

> Most growth in vocabulary knowledge must necessarily come though reading. There is no way that vocabulary instruction alone can provide students with enough experiences with enough words to produce both the depth and breadth of vocabulary knowledge that they need to attain. Increasing the volume of students' reading is the single most important thing a teacher can do to promote large-scale vocabulary growth. (p. 32)

Good literature can take children to places that classroom experiences cannot: a visit to the land of Narnia, a trip inside the human body on *The Magic School Bus,* time travel back to Nazi-occupied Germany in *Anne Frank: The Diary of a Young Girl.* These vicarious experiences provide a powerful way to learn word meanings. Teachers can directly scaffold students' vocabulary development by using graphic organizers such as word webs or concept maps to help them make connections to existing words or concepts. For example, terms such as *allies, deportation,* and *dissent* are important for understanding *Anne Frank*. Providing students with the definition, characteristics, and relevant examples of these words will help them activate prior knowledge, make connections to existing schema, and organize knowledge into categories.

**Writing.** Like reading, writing *is* thinking because it helps students interpret the structure of the genres in which they are writing, especially when a strong connection is made between reading and writing. When students analyze the structure of a text, determine the conventions of a genre, and recognize how authors use and adapt these conventions to fit their purposes, they can use this knowledge to gather ideas, outline, draft, edit, revise, and publish their own writing.

Writing is also reconstructing meaning from reading. A recent report from the Carnegie Foundation, *Writing to Read* (2010), summarizes the findings of a meta-analysis of high-quality research in writing instruction. The analysis found that students' comprehension of science, social studies, and language arts texts is improved when they write about what they read. When children write personal reflections, question, analyze, or interpret text through literature response activities such as journal entries, summaries, or notes, they reconstruct their understanding of the story with their own words and express their own ideas and perspectives.

Electronic discussion via e-mail, discussion forums, listservs, and weblogs (blogs) are another way to foster authentic conversation. Electronic discussion not only enables interaction and collaboration, but it also promotes reflection. Reading and responding to peers' comments make us think about and form ideas in a meaningful way. Reading peers' thoughts urges us to compare them with our own and, in turn, to examine our own understandings and interpretations.

*Read*

*Read about the use of blogs in the classroom.*

### PROVIDE CLEAR EXPLANATIONS AND MODELING OF COMPREHENSION STRATEGIES

The publication of Delores Durkin's (1978–1979) now-classic study of reading comprehension instruction rocked the literacy community. Durkin's research revealed that less than one percent of the time spent during reading was devoted to comprehension instruction. The vast majority of time was spent assessing comprehension through recitation—the teacher asking questions about what students had been assigned to read. This finding resulted in great attention to research in comprehension instruction over the next three decades.

In 1999, the Office of Educational Research and Improvement of the U.S. Department of Education charged the RAND Reading Study Group (RRSG) with developing a research agenda to address the most-pressing issues in literacy. The RRSG decided to focus on reading comprehension, and the subsequent report (2002) found that typical classrooms across the primary and upper elementary grades still do not devote adequate time and attention to comprehension instruction.

Additionally, the group's extensive review found the research on reading comprehension to be "sizeable but sketchy, unfocused, and inadequate as a basis for reform in reading comprehension instruction" (p. xii). However, the group did find that comprehension instruction can be effective in providing students with a repertoire of strategies that promote comprehension monitoring and that the explicitness with which teachers teach comprehension strategies makes a difference in learner outcomes, especially for low-achieving students.

**A Model for Comprehension Strategy Instruction.** Duke and Pearson (2002) propose a model of comprehension instruction that includes the following five phases (see Figure 3.1):

1. An explicit description of the strategy and when and how it should be used.
2. Teacher and/or student modeling of the strategy in action.
3. Collaborative use of the strategy in action.
4. Guided practice using the strategy with gradual release of responsibility.
5. Independent use of the strategy.

In Figure 3.1, as you move diagonally from the upper left to the lower right, you can see that students assume more, and teachers less, responsibility for task completion. In the upper left corner, the teacher is primarily responsible for performing the task, providing modeling, demonstrations, and guided practice. As the teacher gradually releases responsibility, in the lower right corner, students begin to take over the task through guided participation and then assume independence. While students are participating in guided practice, the teacher facilitates and provides scaffolding when necessary. The gradual release of responsibility for a task may take place over a few days, weeks, or even months, depending on the task and students, and it should be flexible and dynamic. For example, after the teacher has modeled a task and then engages the students in guided practice, he or she may decide that more modeling is necessary (see Chapters 13 and 14 for more information on the gradual release of responsibility).

With this in mind, five comprehension strategies, shown in Table 3.6, have been found to be effective in improving children's comprehension of text (Snow et al., 1998; NICHD, 2000). Using short texts, such as picturebooks, for explicit teaching of strategies during anchor lessons and with the support of anchor charts (described below) is an effective way to introduce strategies that can be referred to later during discussions about texts students are reading independently or in small groups (McKeown, Beck, & Blake, 2009).

**FIGURE 3.1**

A Model for Teaching Comprehension: Gradual Release of Responsibility

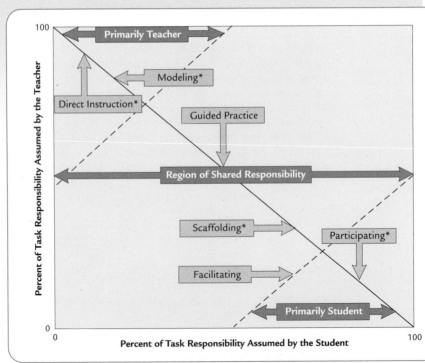

N. Duke & P. D. Pearson (2002). Effective practices for developing reading comprehension. In A. Farstrup & S. J. Samuels (Eds.), *What research has to say about reading instruction* (3rd ed., p. 10). Reprinted with permission of the International Reading Association.

**TABLE 3.6**

# Strategies to Improve Comprehension

| Comprehension Strategy | Definition | Texts for Modeling Strategies |
|---|---|---|
| Prediction | When readers speculate on what will be discussed next in the text based on relevant prior knowledge so they can connect what they are reading with what they already know. | *The Name Jar* by Yangsook Choi<br>*Up North at the Cabin* by Marsha Chall, illustrated by Steve Johnson<br>*Firefly Mountain* by Patricia Thomas, illustrated by Peter Sylvada<br>*Scaredy Squirrel Makes a Friend* by Mélanie Watt |
| Monitoring Comprehension | When readers apply strategies to "fix-up" comprehension when they do not understand or lose track of the story. For example: rereading to make sense or going back to an earlier part of the text to check for understanding. | *The Magic School Bus and the Science Fair Expedition* by Joanna Cole<br>*The Sweetest Fig* by Chris Van Allsburg<br>*Alexander Who Used to Be Rich Last Sunday* by Judith Viorst |
| Making Inferences | When the reader uses the information from the author and combines it with his or her own knowledge to "read between the lines" to reach a deeper understanding of the text. | *Tight Times* by Barbara Hazen, illustrated by Trina Hyman<br>*Now One Foot, Now the Other* by Tomie dePaola<br>*Officer Buckle and Gloria* by Peggy Rathmann |
| Summarization | When readers restate the most important ideas of what they have read. Initially, their summaries may be of sentences or paragraphs but later summarizing should focus on larger units of text. | *Hana's Suitcase: A True Story* by Karen Levine<br>*Hatchet* by Gary Paulsen<br>*Let's Talk About Race* by Julius Lester |
| Questions/ questioning | There is much research to support the need for teachers to ask students higher level—inferential and evaluative—questions that require them to connect information in the text to their own knowledge base to improve students' comprehension. Additionally, students must learn to ask questions themselves as they are reading. | *Brave Irene* by William Steig<br>*Chicken Sunday* by Patricia Polacco<br>*Coming On Home Soon* by Jacqueline Woodson, illustrated by E. B. Lewis<br>*Miz Berlin Walks* by Jane Yolen, illustrated by Floyd Cooper |

*Watch comprehension strategy instruction in action.*

It is also important to note that comprehension strategies are not used in isolation, but instead, several strategies are used as needed and when appropriate. For example, we do not start to read a new book and *only* make predictions. Rather, we make predictions based on our *background knowledge* and our understanding of the *text structure of the story*, and *then* we formulate *questions* about what might happen next. If the story starts with "Once upon a time…," then our knowledge of the fairy tale *story structure* takes us to a time long ago, and we might *predict* there will be a princess, a witch, and a happily-ever-after ending. If it is a "fractured fairy tale," then this story will have a unique twist on an original tale, and then we might *wonder* what the author will do differently as the story unfolds. Although teachers may find it necessary to model and demonstrate a particular strategy at a particular time, other strategies should also be suggested, modeled, and integrated throughout the process (Dorn & Soffas, 2005; Duke & Pearson, 2002).

**Anchor Lessons and Anchor Charts.** Providing anchor lessons when delivering instruction in reading comprehension can help students remember what they learn and understand it. An anchor lesson is selected by the teacher as the most effective lesson for teaching a particular comprehension strategy and serves as an anchor or foundation for scaffolding student learning. For example, a fourth-grade teacher read aloud *Thunder Cake* by Patricia Polacco in which a grandma finds a way to dispel her grandchild's fear of thunderstorms. While reading the book, the teacher made personal connections to her own childhood growing up on a farm in Michigan. After modeling her own personal connections, she gave students time to write their own connections and share them with each other. Later, when the teacher referred to making personal connections to the text, she referred to *Thunder Cake* as a way to activate their prior knowledge and promote independence.

*Watch an interview with Patricia Polacco.*

Anchor charts can also be an effective scaffold for students' learning during instruction. Anchor charts, which are created by the teacher and children, highlight specific guidelines or behaviors for performing a particular literacy strategy, or they can serve as a concrete representation of students' thinking. For instance, after giving an explicit description of fairy tales and exposing children to many examples of fairy tales, the teacher could create an anchor chart documenting what the students noticed about how the genre works—for example, fairy tales often start with "Once upon a time"; end with "happily ever after"; have magic; have characters such as kings and queens; take place in foreign lands; have good characters and bad characters; have animals that can talk; and teach a lesson (see example in Chapter 5 on page XX). As children read fairy tales independently, new entries can be added to the chart. It should be posted in a prominent place in the room and serve as a temporary scaffold for children's learning over time. The use of anchor charts as a scaffold to support children's understanding of genre structures is discussed in each of the genre chapters. Examples of how anchor charts can be used to support students' literacy learning can be found in many of the genre chapters.

**Technology and Reading Comprehension.** Reading comprehension on the Internet and other informational communication technologies (ICT) requires an expanded definition of *comprehension*. The RAND Study Group (2002) found that using the Internet requires new literacy skills and new methods to teach those skills (Chapter 12 discusses this issue in more detail).

## ENGAGE CHILDREN IN CONSTRUCTIVE CONVERSATIONS

Through peer and collaborative learning, equity, community, and access to other students' thinking processes can be achieved. During teacher–student dialogues about text, the teacher should allow for student input and control and accept multiple interpretations of texts. Teachers must resist approaches that stress the "real" meaning of the story. Students should be given the opportunity to discuss with classmates and teachers the meaning of the text. Allington's (2006) description of the differences between real-world literacy interactions and in-school literacy interactions highlights why providing an environment for genuine classroom talk is so important:

> When you consider the richness of the talk about texts that occurs outside of school, the typical pattern of school talk about texts seems shallow and barren. Outside school we rely on the richness of a person's conversation about texts to judge how well they understood it. Their literateness. In school we typically rely on the flat recitation of events or information to make that same judgment. Outside of school settings we engage in conversations about the adequacy of texts and authors to inform, engage, and entertain us. In school we engage in interrogations about what was "in the text." (p. 111)

It is important for children to engage in authentic talk about texts before and after reading, but it is also important for these conversations to take place during reading.

**Engage children in active processing during reading.** Active processing is when the reader actively builds meaning while reading in ways that promote attending to important ideas and establishing connections between them (McKeown, Beck, & Blake, 2009). One way to promote active reading is to alternate reading with discussion while students are actively reading texts. Recent research by McKeown, Beck and Blake (2009), found the value of this practice to be three-fold:

- enables students with poor decoding skills to have access to the text, providing an external model of the comprehension process,
- allows students to have access to their peers' thinking, assisting students in building meaning that may be provided by collaboration, and
- allows an expert other—the teacher—to support students' meaning building (p. 245).

The teacher also gains a three-fold benefit from this format by

- being able to observe confusion as it occurs and consider what the source of confusion might be,
- gaining understanding of the complexity of the comprehension process and students' individual differences in engaging in that process, and
- providing a basis for deciding how to intervene to support students (p. 245).

**Questioning Approaches.** The questioning approach employed to activate comprehension processing during reading is important. Two approaches that bring about active student engagement with reading are the strategies and content approaches (see Table 3.7). In strategies instruction, students are taught to use specific procedures to guide their access to text during reading. At stopping points, the teacher uses a strategy to prompt discussion and remind students how to apply the strategy. Content instruction focuses student attention on the content of the text though general, meaning-based questions about the text. At stopping points, the teacher provides an initiating question designed to make public the important ideas in a text.

In a study comparing the two approaches, McKeown, Beck, and Blake (2009) found a significant difference in favor of the content approach. Findings from the study indicated that, "Focusing on strategies during reading may leave students less aware of the overall process of interacting with text, especially in terms of the need to connect ideas

**TABLE 3.7**

# Questioning Approaches to Activate Comprehension Processing During Reading

| | Strategy Instruction | Content Instruction |
|---|---|---|
| Theoretical Foundation | Developed from models of thinking and learning processes | Developed from models of text processing |
| Description | Encourages students to think about their mental processes and on that basis, to execute specific strategies with which to interact with text | Attempts to engage students in the process of attending to text ideas and building a mental representation of the ideas, with no direction to consider specific mental processes (strategies) |
| Instructional approaches | • Reciprocal teaching (Palincsar & Brown, 1984)<br><br>• Transactional instruction (Pressley et al., 1992)<br><br>• Informed strategies for learning (Paris, Cross, and Lipson, 1984)<br><br>• Duffy & Roehler (1989) | • Questioning the Author (QtA; Beck & McKeown, 2006)<br><br>• Construction-integration model (Kintsch, 1998)<br><br>• Collaborative conversations (Saunders & Goldenberg, 1999)<br><br>• Collaborative reasoning (Chinn, Anderson, & Waggoner, 2001)<br><br>• Dialogic instruction (Nystrand, 1997)<br><br>• Junior Great Books (Dennis & Moldof, 1983) |
| Features of instruction | Direct explanation of strategies, explicit modeling of strategies, use of strategies to guide dialog about text | Open questions, student control of interpretive authority, more student than teacher talk, and teacher responses that are based on students' responses |

Adapted from McKeown, M., Beck, I., & Blake, R. (2009). Rethinking reading comprehension instruction: A comparison of instruction for strategies and content approaches. *Reading Research Quarterly, 44*(3), 218–253.

they encounter and integrate those ideas into a coherent whole" (p. 246). Active processing does not necessitate students' knowledge of and focus on specific strategies. Rather, directly prompting for meaning promotes attending to important ideas and establishing connections between them.

This is not to say that students should not be taught comprehension strategies. However, strategy instruction need not "lead the process of building understanding of a text" (p. 246). As suggested in the section on comprehension strategy instruction, short texts such as picturebooks can be used to introduce and reinforce strategies and then those terms can be used to talk about such interactions as the occur during meaningful discussions about texts.

## CHILDREN'S LITERATURE ACROSS THE CURRICULUM

I am always pleased when a preservice or inservice teacher in my class discovers that he really loves a particular genre that he didn't expect to like at all. Students often feel strongly about genres, reporting things like "I never really liked historical fiction" or "My favorite genre is realistic fiction."

**Discovering Genres.** In most cases, it has been a very long time since these students have read anything besides a college textbook, so it is interesting to watch students' reactions after they have had the opportunity to explore different genres. After reading Karen Cushman's Newbery award–winning *The Midwife's Apprentice* (1995; a nameless, homeless girl in medieval England is taken in by a shrewish midwife and, despite obstacles and hardships, forges an identity for herself and learns some timeless truths), students usually change their minds about disliking historical fiction. They are surprised to find themselves captivated by a time period they thought was excruciatingly boring in history class (and it probably was). Textbooks are intended to be neutral. Trade books have interesting perspectives, details, and characters. The author pulls us into the plot, and, before we know it, we actually care about the characters and the outcome of the story. After reading *Midwife's Apprentice,* one student signed up for a medieval literature course, another looked up author Karen Cushman's Newbery acceptance speech to find out how she researched the book, and several others went on to read *Catherine, Called Birdy* (1994), another book by Cushman that is set in approximately the same time period.

*Good historical fiction provides opportunities for young people to live vicariously in times and places they cannot experience any other way.*

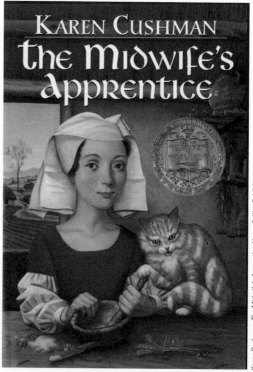

Karen Cushman, *The Midwife's Apprentice*, HarperCollins Publishers.

**Moving Beyond Textbooks.** Subject area textbooks are a useful and necessary resource for the classroom. They provide the content set by the district curriculum and state and national standards, and they serve as a resource to the classroom teacher. But textbooks are limited in the depth and perspective they take on any subject. For example, if history textbooks were to include in-depth coverage and multiple perspectives of the topics covered in the curriculum for any grade level, a student would need a wagon to get it to class. The result: two pages on slavery, one paragraph on Hiroshima or Einstein's theory of relativity. Roseman, Kulm, and Shuttleworth (2003) said the following:

> Today's textbooks cover too many topics without developing any of them well. Central concepts are not covered in enough depth to give students a chance to truly understand them. While many textbooks present the key ideas described in national and state standards documents, few books help students learn the ideas or help teachers teach them well.

In the now classic *Independence in Reading,* Don Holdaway (1980) asserts, "It is difficult to provide natural motivation for reading in an environment where books are things you work through rather than things you come to depend on for special pleasure and enlightenment" (p. 25). A nonfiction or fiction trade book has the potential to be a magnifying glass that enlarges and enhances the reader's personal interaction with a subject. Teachers can supplement textbooks with fiction and nonfiction trade books that can provide motivation, enthusiasm, caring, and insight into just about any aspect of the curriculum and inspire children to do their own research or further reading to learn more. Each genre chapter in this text includes a section "Making the Connection Across the Curriculum," where you will find teaching strategies and children's book selections that are perfect for including in content area study in history, math, English, art, and science.

## THE CLASSROOM LIBRARY

Most of us remember the weekly trips to the library when we were in school. Many times the librarian would read a book aloud to us, and then we would have time to browse the shelves and check out one or two books to read for the week. School libraries and librarians continue to play an important role in children's lives, but as research has repeatedly shown, there is a high correlation between the amount students read and their reading achievement. One or two books a week just isn't enough. Children must have access to a large number of books and other media every day in their classrooms, along with instruction on how to select, read, write, and talk about books with other children. Therefore, it is critical for teachers to have a classroom library (Neuman, 1999). Table 3.8 shows Reutzel and Fawson's (2002) five major functions of the classroom library.

*Read*

*Read more resources on classroom libraries.*

The classroom library plays an integral role in children's literacy development if the collection is well stocked and organized and the space facilitates easy access, selection, and student interaction. Incorporated into this text are many ways for you to begin building your own classroom library:

- "Creating Your Classroom Library" at the end of each genre chapter in Part 2.
- The genre chapters of Part 2 provide abundant ideas for books, magazines, and Internet sites to include in your classroom library.
- Chapters 13 and 14 give specific details and information on organizing a classroom library for instruction.
- Links to the Newbery and Caldecott award winners along with other book awards are listed in the Print and Online Resources section at the end of each chapter, at the back of this book, and on the student website.

**TABLE 3.8**

# How the Classroom Library Supports Literacy Success

| Classroom Libraries . . . | |
|---|---|
| **1.** Support literacy instruction. | Build an adequate collection of fiction and nonfiction materials at enough different levels to accommodate the many interests, cultures, and abilities of students desiring to check out books for take-home reading. |
| **2.** Help students to learn about books. | The small size of the classroom library is ideal for teaching children how to select just right books and how to take care of books. |
| **3.** Provide a central location for classroom resources. | The classroom library can be used as a central storage location for instructional resources such as science equipment, CDs, tape players, VHS/DVDs, computers, games, magazines, and other materials. |
| **4.** Provide opportunities for independent reading and curricular extensions. | Every good reading program provides students daily time to read independently. The classroom library is typically the resource that supports children's daily independent reading of self-selected books that meet their personal, recreational reading interests. |
| **5.** Serve as a place for students to talk and interact with books. | The classroom library also provides a place for students to have book discussions with peers or the teacher. It is an area that makes books exciting and that kids can't wait to get to so they can talk about their reactions to books. |

*Read*

*Read the IRA's book awards chosen by children, young adults, and teachers.*

The International Reading Association's Children's, Young Adult, and Teacher's Choices awards are also a great source for book recommendations because these books are chosen by children, young adults, and teachers themselves. These books are voted on annually and the winners are listed in *The Reading Teacher* and online at http://www.reading.org.

Unfortunately, teachers often must spend their own money to buy books and other media for their classrooms. Other sources for obtaining books for your classroom library include book clubs such as Scholastic, yard sales, donations from parents, contributions from the school's Parent Teacher Organization, and local grants.

## A Framework for Planning Literature Experiences: Children's Literature, Child Development, and Literacy

The following chart, "Children's Literature, Child Development, and Literacy for Preschool Through Grade 6," is a framework for understanding the interrelated nature of the cognitive, social, emotional, linguistic, and literacy development of children and adult/peer social interaction and literature selection in preschool through grade 6. This chart is a general guide for the appropriate selection of books that takes into consideration the importance of child development and the social interaction of adults and other children. It details a child's developmental skills in each age group, what teachers can do to encourage literacy at this stage of development, and books that are appropriate for these skills and developmental level.

- The first column gives an overview of the general developmental characteristics of children in the areas of cognitive, language, and social and emotional development.
- The second column gives examples of important experiences adults can provide when interacting with children and books based on the implications from the developmental characteristics for each grade level.
- The third column provides a list of suggested books appropriate for each stage of development. These books are compiled from recommendations from teachers, children, parents, and professional literature resources such as children's literature journals and books.

*Watch* ✴

*Visit the student website for a list of the children's literature cited in* LITERACY DEVELOPMENT and BOOK CHOICES for PRESCHOOL THROUGH GRADE 6.

The information in the chart should be informed by ongoing observational information acquired about individual children. With this in mind, the framework can assist in planning appropriate literature experiences and in understanding children's responses to books and book preferences at different levels of development. Additionally, each genre chapter in this text presents strategies for literacy development. Additionally, each genre chapter in this text presents strategies for literacy development, reader response, and content area connections.

## Pulling It All Together

### Children's Literature, Child Development, and Literacy for Preschool Through Grade 6

#### Preschool—Kindergarten (Ages 5–6)

Readers seek out and enjoy experiences with books and print; become familiar with the language of literature and the patterns of stories; understand and follow the sequence of stories read to them; begin to acquire specific understandings about the nature, purpose, and function of print; experiment with reading and writing independently, through approximation; and see themselves as developing readers and writers.

| How the Child Responds to Literature | Literacy: Involving Children in Becoming Good Readers | Children's Literature Selections |
|---|---|---|
| **Cognitive Development**<br>• Begins to understand spatial, perceptual, and attributional relationships<br>• Can retell a short story; has a vague concept of time; can count to ten and knows primary colors | • Read simple picture books with easily identifiable characters and poetry aloud several times a day at school and at home<br>• Actively involve children in shared reading in which they can participate in the reading process | • *Ten, Nine, Eight* (Bang)<br>• *The Bus for Us* (Bloom)<br>• *Red Light, Green Light* (Brown)<br>• *From Head to Toe* (Carle)<br>• *ABC I Like Me!* (Carlson) |

# Pulling It All Together

## Children's Literature, Child Development, and Literacy for Preschool Through Grade 6

### Preschool—Kindergarten (Ages 5–6)

Readers seek out and enjoy experiences with books and print; become familiar with the language of literature and the patterns of stories; understand and follow the sequence of stories read to them; begin to acquire specific understandings about the nature, purpose, and function of print; experiment with reading and writing independently, through approximation; and see themselves as developing readers and writers

| How the Child Responds to Literature | Literacy: Involving Children in Becoming Good Readers | Children's Literature Selections |
|---|---|---|
| **Language Development**<br>• Rapid vocabulary growth and speech development; use of correct verb and pronoun tense; use of language to explore the environment; enjoys playing with sound and rhythm in language<br>• Enjoys dramatic/role/creative play<br>• Understands that there is a connection between language and print<br><br>**Social and Emotional Development**<br>• Begins to develop relationships with other children and enjoys participating in group activities and games that use imagination<br>• Understands that others have feelings, too, and expresses those feelings through facial expressions<br>• Wants to help around the house and with younger siblings; takes pride in accomplishments; exhibits anxiety or fears (i.e., dark); likes to go to new and familiar places and play with favorite toys | • Select literature about everyday experiences, yet also expands language and concept development, encourages curiosity about the world and engages the imagination<br>• Provide opportunities to respond to literature with peers and the teacher and also through writing/drawing<br>• Provide opportunities for students to self-select fiction and nonfiction books, including alphabet, number, and concept books and books that include environmental print with guidance | • *The Princess and the Pea* (Child)<br>• *Five Little Monkeys Play Hide-and-Seek* (Christelow)<br>• *Today I Feel Silly* (Curtis)v<br>• *Growing Vegetable Soup* (Ehlert)<br>• *Feast for 10* (Falwell)<br>• *Owls* (Gibbons)<br>• *Kitten's First Full Moon* (Henkes)<br>• *You Read to Me and I'll Read to You: Very Short Stories to Read Together* (Hoberman)<br>• *What Do You Do with a Tail Like This?* (Jenkins)<br>• *The Hello, Goodbye Window* (Juster)<br>• *Peter's Chair* (Keats)<br>• *Mary Had a Little Jam and Other Silly Rhymes* (Lansky)<br>• *A Color of His Own* (Lionni)<br>• *Chicka Chicka Boom Boom* (Martin)<br>• *Brown Bear, Brown Bear, What Do You See?* (Martin)<br>• *Here Comes Mother Goose* (Opie)<br>• *The Tale of Peter Rabbit* (Potter)<br>• *Bashi, Baby Elephant* (Radcliffe)<br>• *Encyclopedia Prehistorica Dinosaurs: The Definitive Pop-Up* (Sabuda)<br>• *Mommy?* (Sendak)<br>• *Trucks, Trucks, Trucks* (Sis)<br>• *Hop on Pop* (Suess)<br>• *Knuffe Bunny* (Willems)<br>• *September Roses* (Winter) |

*(continued)*

# Pulling It All Together
## (continued)

## First and Second Grades (Ages 6–8)

Readers understand that reading is a meaning-making process; acquire sight vocabulary; make balanced use of the cueing systems in written language (syntax, semantics, and graphophonemics) to identify words not known at sight; and see themselves as readers and writers.

| How the Child Responds to Literature | Literacy: Involving Children in Becoming Good Readers | Children's Literature Selections |
|---|---|---|
| **Cognitive Development**<br>• Enjoys listening to stories read aloud and can listen to longer stories due to an increased attention span; still needs concrete experiences to learn<br>• Understands relationships among categories<br>• Vague understanding of time<br>• Beginning to understand the difference between fantasy and reality<br><br>**Language Development**<br>• Continues to add words to their vocabularies and use increasingly complex sentences<br><br>**Social and Emotional Development**<br>• Begins to develop a sense of humor<br>• Has definite, inflexible ideas of right and wrong<br>• May occasionally challenge parents and argue with siblings but continues to need the security of family relationships<br>• Continues to take pride in accomplishments, sometimes showing assertiveness and initiative<br>• Seeks teachers' praise<br>• Curious about gender differences | • Read picturebooks and poetry aloud several times a day at school and at home<br>• Read aloud short chapter books in which each chapter contains independent episodes<br>• Provide small group and whole group opportunities to respond to literature with peers and the teacher and through writing/ drawing—becoming more sustained over time<br>• Actively involve children in shared reading in which they observe the teacher demonstrate concepts about print and model using appropriate reading strategies with both fiction and nonfiction texts and involve student participation<br>• Initial reading experiences should be enjoyable using books with familiar concepts and experiences with predictable, repeated patterned text and then moving into longer texts with more complex structure<br>• Give ample opportunities to select books on their own from a wide variety of topics in both fiction and nonfiction books and to recommend books through book talks to other children with guidance | • *When Sophie Gets Angry— Really, Really Angry* (Bang)<br>• *Ramona* books (Cleary)<br>• *Mercy Watson to the Rescue* (DiCamillo)<br>• *My Little Sister Ate One Hare* (Grossman)<br>• *Lilly's Purple Plastic Purse* (Henkes)<br>• *Jitterbug Jam* (Hicks)<br>• *Julius* (Johnson)<br>• *Prehistoric Actual Size* (Jenkins)<br>• *Please Bury Me in the Library* (Lewis)<br>• *Frog and Toad* books (Lobel)<br>• *Gooney Bird Green* (Lowry)<br>• *The Three Silly Billies* (Palatini)<br>• *Peggony-Po* (Pinkney)<br>• *Hot Air: The (Mostly) True Story of the First Hot-Air Balloon Ride* (Priceman)<br>• *10 Minutes Till Bedtime* (Rathmann)<br>• *My Name Is Yoon* (Recorvits)<br>• *Henry and Mudge* books (Rylant)<br>• *The Journey: Stories of Migration* (Rylant)<br>• *Where the Wild Things Are* (Sendak)<br>• *Meow Ruff* (Sidman)<br>• *Runny Babbit* (Silverstein)<br>• *Oceans* (Simon)<br>• *Too Many Tamales* (Soto)<br>• *The Talking Eggs: A Folktale from the American South* (Souci)<br>• *Pete's Pizza* (Steig)<br>• *The Terrible, Horrible, No Good Very Bad Day* (Viorst)<br>• *A Chair for My Mother* (Williams)<br>• *The Librarian of Basara* (Winters) |

*(continued)*

# Pulling It All Together
*(continued)*

## Third and Fourth Grades (Ages 8–10)

Readers increase fluency in reading and writing; increase motivation to read and write; and focus on meaning in reading and writing.

| How the Child Responds to Literature | Literacy: Involving Children in Becoming Good Readers | Children's Literature Selections |
|---|---|---|
| **Cognitive Development**<br><br>• Beginning to exhibit independence in reading, but a wide range of reading abilities and interests prevail<br>• Concept of time and space continue to develop<br>• Memory improves with increased attention span<br>• Begins to connect ideas and concepts as thoughts become flexible and reversible increasing capacity for problem solving, categorizing, and classifying<br><br>**Language Development**<br><br>• Vocabulary continues to increase<br>• Increased use of connectors such as *meanwhile, unless,* and *although*<br><br>**Social and Emotional Development**<br><br>• Begins to be influenced by social situations and peers<br>• Sports and hobbies become more important<br>• Searching for values; influenced by models other than their own family: TV, movies, music, sports, books<br>• Beginning to develop empathy for others as concepts of right and wrong become more flexible | • Provide children with opportunities for storytelling and dramatization of stories<br>• Read more sophisticated picturebooks and poetry aloud every day<br>• Read aloud longer chapter books with more variety, perspectives, and issues to promote interest and appreciation for a variety of genres<br>• Sustain small group and whole group opportunities to respond to literature with peers and the teacher and through writing<br>• Actively involve children in small group and whole group shared reading in which the teacher engages students in discussion/modeling/demonstrations of more complex reading strategies that promote understanding of literary devices, vocabulary development, connections to text, and graphic aids in fiction and nonfiction texts<br>• Provide opportunities for students to self-select fiction and nonfiction books, including series books, biographies, how-to books, riddles, comics, and magazines with guidance<br>• Provide children with opportunities for storytelling and dramatization of stories, reader's theater, and choral reading | • *Cam Jansen and the Snowy Day Mystery* (Adler)<br>• *A Bear for Miguel* (Alphin)<br>• *The Penderwicks* (Birdsall)<br>• *Tales of a Fourth-Grade Nothing* (Blume)<br>• *The Magic School Bus* books (Cole)<br>• *Bud, Not Buddy* (Curtis)<br>• *Because of Winn-Dixie* (DiCamillo)<br>• *The Miraculous Journey of Edward Tulane* (DiCamillo)<br>• *Joey Pigza Loses Control* (Gantos)<br>• *Stone Fox* (Gardner)<br>• *Rosa* (Giovanni)<br>• *The Girl Who Loved Wild Horses* (Goble)<br>• *Finding Out About Whales* (Kelsey)<br>• *Wilma Unlimited: How Wilma Rudolph Became the World's Fastest Woman* (Krull)<br>• *The Boy Who Drew Cats: A Japanese Folktale* (Levine)<br>• *The Lion, the Witch and the Wardrobe* (Lewis)<br>• *The Problem with Chickens* (McMillan)<br>• *Jazz* (Myers)<br>• *Sitti's Secrets* (Nye)<br>• *Martin's Big Words* (Rappaport)<br>• *When Marian Sang* (Ryan)<br>• *Time Warp Trio* books (Scieszka)<br>• *Nate the Great* (Sharmat)<br>• *The Song of the Water Boatman* (Sidman)<br>• *Worlds Apart: Fernie and Me* (Soto)<br>• *Mufaro's Beautiful Daughters: An African Tale* (Steptoe)<br>• *Just a Dream* (Van Allsburg)<br>• *Show Way* (Woodson) |

*(continued)*

# Pulling It All Together
## *(continued)*

### Fifth and Sixth Grades (Ages 10–12)

Readers expand their experience in reading, comprehend increasingly complex reading material, and extend meaning vocabulary.

| How the Child Responds to Literature | Literacy: Involving Children in Becoming Good Readers | Children's Literature Selections |
|---|---|---|
| **Cognitive Development**<br>• Development of the concept of chronological order of past or historical events<br>• Development of the ability to apply reasoning and formal operations to abstract ideas<br><br>**Language Development**<br>• Continued vocabulary development<br>• Continued use of complex sentences and sentence connectors<br><br>**Social and Emotional Development**<br>• Peer groups become more influential and exert pressure to conform and belong<br>• Parents' authority may be challenged as children seek independence and adopt other role models such as sports and TV/movie stars.<br>• Some children express attitudes of racial prejudice<br>• Developing sense of justice and interest in values and world problems<br>• Interested in activities, hobbies, and future occupations<br>• Developing sense of gender expectations and the role it plays in identity and society | • Read aloud to students from a variety of formats and genres, especially more abstract and analytical forms of prose and poetry with opportunities for questioning and discussion<br>• Provide opportunities to respond to literature with peers and the teacher through a variety of literature extension activities<br>• Provide children with the opportunity to engage with historical fiction, biography, and nonfiction depicting historical changes with differing perspectives on historical events<br>• Give children the opportunity to engage in higher-level questioning and critical thinking through literature discussions<br>• Provide instruction in reading strategies that promote understanding of complex plot structures in mysteries, science fiction, and high fantasy<br>• Give students opportunities for self-selection of books that are of interest to them from a variety of genres<br>• Provide access to a variety of books reflecting multicultural values, gender roles, family structures and values, the development of relationships, and role models | • *The True Confessions of Charlotte Doyle* (Avi)<br>• *Tuck Everlasting* (Babbitt)<br>• *Ruby Holler* (Creech)<br>• *Matilda* (Dahl)<br>• *One Grain of Rice* (Demi)<br>• *Speak to Me and I Will Listen Between the Lines* (English)<br>• *The Birchbark House* (Erdrich)<br>• *House of the Scorpion* (Farmer)<br>• *The Lotus Seed* (Garland)<br>• *Pictures of Hollis Woods* (Giff)<br>• *1621: A New Look at Thanksgiving* (Grace and Bruchac)<br>• *Out of the Dust* (Hesse)<br>• *Penny from Heaven* (Holm)<br>• *Hidden Worlds* (Kramer)<br>• *A Wrinkle in Time* (L'Engle)<br>• *Bound* (Napoli)<br>• *Hatchet* (Paulsen)<br>• *The Legend of Bass Reeves* (Paulsen)<br>• *If Not for the Cat* (Prelutsky)<br>• *Becoming Naomi Leon* (Ryan)<br>• *Missing May* (Rylant)<br>• *Holes* (Sachar)<br>• *Lizzie Bright and the Buckminster Boy* (Schmidt)<br>• *Destination: Space* (Simon)<br>• *Maniac Magee* (Spinelli)<br>• *The Fairies of Nutfolk Wood* (Ullman)<br>• *Brothers in Hope* (Williams)<br>• *Flotsam* (Wisner)<br>• *Favorite Folktales from Around the World* (Yolen) |

# Top 10 Read Alouds

## BUILDING COMMUNITY AND MAKING FRIENDS

1. **A Splendid Friend, Indeed** by Suzanne Bloom (2005, Boyds Mills). When a studious polar bear meets an inquisitive goose, they learn to be friends.

2. **Danitra Brown, Class Clown** by Nikki Grimes, illustrated by E. B. Lewis (2005, HarperCollins). In this story, told in a series of rhyming poems, Zuri faces her fears about starting a new school year with the help of free-spirited best friend Danitra.

3. **Hot Day on Abbott Avenue** by Karen English (2004, Houghton Mifflin). After having a fight, two friends spend the day ignoring each other, until the lure of a game of jump rope helps them to forget about being mad.

4. **The Hundred Dresses** by Eleanor Estes, illustrated by Louis Slobodkin (1944, Harcourt). Wanda Petronski, a Polish girl in an American school, is laughed at because she always wears a faded blue dress, until her classmates learn a lesson.

5. **Miz Berlin Walks** by Jane Yolen, illustrated by Floyd Cooper (1997, Philomel). Mary Louise gradually gets to know and love her elderly neighbor lady, who tells wonderful stories as she walks around the block of her Virginia home.

6. **My Best Friend** by Mary Ann Rodman, illustrated by E. B. Lewis (2005, Viking). Six-year-old Lily has a best friend all picked out for play group day, but unfortunately the differences between first graders and second graders are sometimes very large.

7. **My Friend Rabbit** by Eric Rohmann (2002, Roaring Brook Press). Something always seems to go wrong when Rabbit is around, but Mouse lets him play with his toy plane anyway because he is a good friend.

8. **Officer Buckle and Gloria** by Peggy Rathmann (1995, Putnam). The children at Napville Elementary School always ignore Officer Buckle's safety tips, until a police dog named Gloria accompanies him when he gives his safety speeches.

9. **Otis** by Loren Long (2009, Philomel). When a big new yellow tractor arrives, Otis the friendly little tractor is cast away behind the barn, but when trouble occurs Otis is the only one who can help.

10. **The Other Side** by Jacqueline Woodson, illustrated by E. B. Lewis (2001, Putnam). Two girls, one white and one black, gradually get to know each other as they sit on the fence that divides their town.

# Activities For Professional Development

## Think Critically About Children's Literature

1. The Standards for the English Language Arts are included in a book defining the standards and providing examples of what the standards look like in classrooms. Visit the website for the National Council of Teachers of English (http://www.ncte.org). Locate the IRA/NCTE Standards, and then find the excerpt from Chapter 3, the preface to the standards. In your own words, describe how the standards work together rather than individually.

2. Examine two basal readers published by different publishing companies. Note the philosophy, content, organization, and activities. Are the stories from trade books or are they created by writers of the textbook series? Is there a variety of genre and readability levels? How could you use these materials flexibly to meet all students' needs?

3. View real classroom lessons in *Teaching Reading 3–5 Workshop*. This site hosts workshop video programs featuring K–12 classrooms that exemplify excellent teaching across the curriculum. This series is produced by Annenberg Media to advance excellent teaching in the schools.

4. Several video series are on reading and literature discussions. One of these series, *Teaching Reading 3–5 Workshop,* features leading experts who discuss current research on learning to read and teaching a diverse range of students. The research is illustrated by clips from real classroom lessons, allowing teachers to better understand and apply the research in their own classes. This series will be referenced in activities throughout this book. Go to the student website for a link to the website: http://www. learner.org/resources/series204.html#.

5. Read the description of the *Teaching Reading 3–5 Workshop,* then click on "enter the series website." Click on the third video in the series, "building comprehension," featuring Dr. Nell Duke, a leading researcher in the field of comprehension and referenced in this chapter. Click on "session preparation," review the terms listed, and explore the other resources available, such as the printable charts and articles. Return to the previous page and watch the video. After watching the video, click on the link "what did you learn" under "reflect on your learning" and respond to the questions listed.

# Print and Online Resources

## Print Resources

Baker, L., Dreher, M., & Guthrie, J. (2000). *Engaging young readers.* New York: Guilford Press.

Daniels, H., & Zemelman, S. (2004). *Subjects matter: Every teacher's guide to content-area reading.* Portsmouth, NH: Heinemann.

Kamil, M., Pearson, P., Moje, E., Afflerbach, P., Mosenthal, P., & Barr, R. (Eds.). (2010). *Handbook of reading research* (Vol. 4). New York: Routledge.

National Council of Teachers of English and International Reading Association (1996). *Standards for the English language arts.* Urbana, IL, and Newark, DE: NCTE and IRA.

Reutzel, R., & Fawson, P. (2002). *Your classroom library: New ways to give it more teaching power.* New York: Scholastic.

Tarter, M. (2009). *Enchanted hunters: The power of stories in childhood.* New York: Norton.

## Online Resources

*Contexts for Engagement and Motivation in Reading* by John T. Guthrie

**http://www.readingonline.org/articles/handbook/guthrie/**

This article focuses on the instructional contexts that promote student motivation and engaged reading and the consequences that exist as a result of students being engaged in what they are reading.

*International Reading Association's Teacher's, Children's, and Young Adult's Choices Lists*

**http://www.reading.org/resources/tools/choices.html**

Free download of book lists chosen by teachers, children, and young adults.

*LibraryThing*

**http://www.librarything.com**

As you collect books for your classroom library, LibraryThing will help you keep track of your books and share with others. LibraryThing is an online service to help people catalog their books easily. The catalog can be accessed from anywhere, and users can check out other people's libraries and swap reading suggestions. LibraryThing also comes up with suggestions for what to read next. Up to 200 books can be cataloged free of charge.

*Reading Rockets: Comprehension 101*
**http://www.readingrockets.org/teaching/ reading101/comprehension**

The Reading Rockets site offers several excellent articles on text comprehension including Questioning the Author, which encourages students to reflect on what the author of a selection is trying to say so as to build a mental representation from that information, and a short video clip on Reciprocal Teaching, a teaching routine that assists children in orchestrating the use of comprehension strategies when reading.

Visit the companion website at **www.cengage.com/education/johnson** to find

links related to the Read/Watch/Listen icons noted throughout the chapter, as well as additional resources.

# References

Annie E. Casey Foundation. (2010*). Early Warning!: Why reading by the end of third grade matters.* Retrieved from the Annie E. Casey Foundation's website: http://datacenter.kidscount.org/ reports/readingmatters.aspx.

Allington, R. (Ed.). (2002). *Big brother and the national reading curriculum: How ideology trumped evidence.* Portsmouth, NH: Heinemann.

Allington, R. (2006). *What really matters for struggling readers* (2nd ed.). New York: Longman.

Allington, R., & Johnston, P. (2002). *Reading to learn: Lessons from exemplary fourth-grade classrooms.* New York: Guilford.

August, D., & Shanahan, T. (2006). *Developing literacy in second-language learners.* Report of the National Literacy Panel on Language-Minority Children and Youth. Retrieved from Center for Applied Linguistics website: http://www.cal.org/projects/archive/ nlpreports/Executive_Summary.pdf.

Baker, L., Dreher, M. J., & Guthrie, J. T. (2000). Why teachers should promote reading engagement (pp. 1–16). In L. Baker, M. J. Dreher, & J. T. Guthrie (Eds.), *Engaging young readers.* New York: Guilford.

Bandura, A. (1997). Self-efficacy: Toward a unifying theory of behavioral change. *Psychological Review,* (84, 191–215).

Beck, I., McKeown, M. (1998). *Improving comprehension with Questioning the Author: A fresh and expanded view of a powerful approach.* New York: Scholastic.

Block, C. (2001). *Distinctions between the expertise of literacy teachers preschool through grade 5.* Paper presented at the National Reading Conference, San Antonio, TX.

Chatton, B. (2004). Critiquing the critics: Adult values, children's responses, postmodern picture books, and Arlene Sardine. *Journal of Children's Literature, 30*(1), 31–37.

Chinn, C., Anderson, R., & Wagggoner, M. (2001). Patterns of discourse in two kinds of literature discussion. *Reading Research Quarterly, 36*(4), 378–411.

Cooper, J., & Kiger, N. (2005). *Literacy assessment: Helping teachers plan instruction* (2nd ed.). Boston: Houghton Mifflin.

Cunningham, J. (2001). The national reading panel report. *Reading Research Quarterly, 36*(3), 326–335.

Cushman, K. (1995). *Catherine, called Birdy.* New York: Houghton Mifflin.

Darigan, D., Tunnel, M., & Jacobs, J. (2002). *Children's literature: Engaging teachers and children in good books.* Upper Saddle River, NJ: Merrill/ Prentice Hall.

Dee, T., & Jacob, B. (2009). *The impact of No Child Left Behind on student achievement* (Report No. 15531). Report of the National Bureau of Educational Research. Retrieved from the National Bureau of Educational Research website: http:// www.nber.org/papers/w15531.

Dennis, R., & Moldof, E. (1983). *A handbook on interpretive reading and discussion.* Chicago: Great Books Foundation.

Dorn, L., & Soffas, C. (2005). *Teaching for deep comprehension*. Portland, ME: Stenhouse.

Duffy, G., & Roehler, L. (1989). Why strategy instruction is so difficult and what we need to do about it. In C. B. McCormick, G. E. Miller, & M. Pressley (Eds.), *Cognitive strategy research: From basic research to educational applications* (pp. 133–157). New York: Springer-Verlag.

Duke, N., & Pearson, P. D. (2002). Effective practices for developing reading comprehension. In A. Farstrup & S. J. Samuels (Eds.), *What research has to say about reading instruction* (3rd ed.). Newark, NJ: International Reading Association.

Edmunds, K., & Bauserman, K. (2006). What teachers can learn about reading motivation through conversations with children. *The Reading Teacher, 59*(5), 414–424.

Faust, M., & Kieffer, R. (1998). Challenging expectations: Why we ought to stand by the IRA/NCTE *Standards for the English Language Arts*. *Journal of Adolescent & Adult Literacy, 41*(7), 540–547.

Fielding, L., Kerr., N., & Rosier, P. (1998*). The 90% reading goal*. Kennewick, WA: National Reading Foundation.

Fielding, L., & Pearson, P. (1994). Reading comprehension: What works. *Educational Leadership, 51*(5), 62–68.

Fresch, M. (1995). Self-selection of early literacy learners. *The Reading Teacher, 49*(3), 220–227.

Gamse, B., Bloom, H., Kemple, J., Jacob, R. Boulay, B., Bozzi, L., et al. (2008). *Reading first impact study: Interim report* (NCEE 20084016), Retrieved from Institute of Educational Sciences website: http://ies.ed.gov/ncee/pdf/20084016.pdf.

Garan, E. (2002). *Resisting reading mandates*. Portsmouth, NH: Heinemann.

Graham, S., & Hebert, M. (2010). *Writing to read: Evidence for how writing can improve reading*. Retrieved from the Carnegie Corporation's website: http://www.all4ed.org/files/WritingToRead.pdf.

Guthrie, J. T., & Anderson, E. (1999). Engagement in reading: Processes of motivated strategic, knowledgeable, social readers. In J. T. Guthrie & D. E. Alvermann (Eds.), *Engaged reading*. New York: Teachers College Press.

Hibbert, K., & Iannacci, L. (2005). From dissemination to discernment: The commodification of literacy instruction and the fostering of "good teacher consumerism." *The Reading Teacher, 58*(8), 716–727.

Holdaway, D. (1980). *Independence in reading*. New York: Scholastic.

Huck, C. (1989). No wider than the heart is wide. In J. Hickman & B. Cullinan (Eds.), *Children's literature in the classroom: Weaving "Charlotte's Web"* (pp. 252–262). Needham Heights, MA: Christopher-Gordon.

International Reading Association and National Council of Teachers of English (1996). *Standards for the English language arts*. Newark, DE: International Reading Association.

Kintsch, W. (1998). *Comprehension: A paradigm for cognition*. New York: Cambridge University Press.

Kozol, J. (2005). *The shame of the nation: The restoration of apartheid schooling in America*. New York: Crown.

Krashen, S. (2004). *The power of reading: Insights from the research* (2nd ed). Portsmouth, NH: Heinemann/Libraries Unlimited.

Lapp, D., Flood, J., Brock, C., & Fisher, D. (2007). *Teaching reading to every child*. Mahwah, NJ: Erlbaum.

McLaughlin, M., & Allen, M. (2002). *Guided comprehension: A teaching model for grades 3–8*. Newark, DE: International Reading Association.

Morrow, L., Tracey, D., Woo, D., & Pressley, M. (1999). Characteristics of exemplary first grade literacy instruction. *The Reading Teacher, 52*(5), 462–476.

Nagy, W. (1988). *Teaching vocabulary to improve reading comprehension*. Urbana, IL: National Council of Teachers of English.

National Institute of Child Health and Human Development. (2000). *Report of the National Reading Panel. Teaching children to read: an evidence-based assessment of the scientific research literature on reading and its implications for reading instruction*. Retrieved from http://www.nichd.nih.gov/publications/nrp/smallbook.htm.

National Literacy Panel. (2008). *Developing early literacy: A Scientific Synthesis of Early Literacy Development and Implications for Intervention*. Retrieved from the National Institute for Literacy website: http://www.nifl.gov/publications/pdf/NELPReport09.pdf.

Neuman, S. (1999). Books make a difference: A study of access to literacy. *Reading Research Quarterly, 34,* 286–311.

Nystrand, M. (with Gamoran, A., Kachur, R., & Prendergast, C.). (1997). *Opening dialogue: Understanding the dynamics of language and learning in the English classroom*. New York: Teachers College Press.

Ollman, H. (1993). Choosing literature wisely: Students speak out. *Journal of Reading, 36*(8), 648–653.

Palincsar, A., & Brown. A. (1984). Reciprocal teaching of comprehension-fostering and comprehension-monitoring activities. *Cognition and Instruction, 1*(2), 117–175.

Paris, S., Cross, D., & Lipson, M. (1984). Informed strategies for learning: A program to improve children's reading awareness and comprehension. *Journal of Educational Psychology, 76*(6), 1239–1252.

Pressley, M. (2000). What should comprehension instruction be the instruction of? In M. Kamil, P. Mosenthal, P. Pearson, & R. Barr (Eds.), *Handbook of reading research* (Vol. 3, pp. 545–561). Mahwah, NJ: Erlbaum.

Pressley, M., Allington, R., Wharton-McDonald, R., Collins-Block, C., & Morrow, L. (2001). *Learning to read: Lessons from exemplary first-grade classrooms.* New York: Guilford.

Pressley, M., El-Dinary, P., Gaskins, I., Schuder, T., Bergman, J., Almasi, J., et al. (1992). Beyond direct explanation: Transactional instruction of reading comprehsnion strategies. The Elementary School Journal, 92(3), 513–555.

Pressley, M., Wharton-McDonald, R., Mistretta-Hampston, J., & Echevarria, M. (1998). Literacy instruction in 10 fourth- and fifth-grade classrooms in upstate New York. *Scientific Studies of Reading, 2,* 159–194.

RAND Study Group. (2002). *Reading for understanding: Toward an R&D program in reading comprehension.* Arlington, VA: RAND Corporation.

Reutzel, R., & Cooter, R. (2002). *Teaching children to read: From basals to books.* Upper Saddle River, NJ: Merrill/Prentice Hall.

Reutzel, R., & Fawson, P. (2002). *Your classroom library: New ways to give it more teaching power.* New York: Scholastic.

Roseman, J., Kulm, G., & Shuttleworth, S. (2003). *Putting textbooks to the test.* Project 2061: American Association for the Advancement of Science. http://www.project2061.org/research/articles/enc.htm. Accessed May 20, 2005.

Routman, R. (2003). *Reading essentials.* Portsmouth, NH: Heinemann.

Ruddell, R. (2002). *Teaching children to read and write.* Boston: Allyn & Bacon.

Ruddell, R. (2004). Researching the influential literacy teacher: Characteristics, beliefs, strategies, and new research directions. In R. Ruddell & N. Unrau (Eds.), *Theoretical models and processes of reading* (5th ed., pp. 979–997). Newark, DE: International Reading Association.

Saunders, W., & Goldenberg, C. (1999). Effects of instructional conversations and literature logs on limited- and fluent-English-proficient students; story comprehension and thematic understanding. *The Elementary Journal, 99*(4), 277–301.

Schlager, N. (1978). Predicting children's choices in literature: A developmental approach. *Children's Literature in Education, 9*(3), 136–142.

Sloan, G. (2003). *The child as critic: Developing literacy through literature, K–8* (4th ed). New York: Teachers College Press.

Smith, F. (2005). *Reading without nonsense* (4th ed.). New York: Teachers College Press.

Snow, C., Burns, M., & Griffin, P. (Eds.). (1998). *Preventing reading difficulties in young children.* Washington, DC: National Academy Press.

Tartar, M. (2009). *Enchanted hunters: The power of stories in childhood.* New York: W. W. Norton & Company.

Taylor, B., Pearson, P., Clark, K., & Walpole, S. (1999). *Beating the odds in teaching all children to read* (CIERA Report no. 2-006). Ann Arbor, MI: Center for the Improvement of Early Reading Achievement.

Thames, D., & Reeves, C. (1994). Poor reader's attitudes: Effects of using interests and trade books in an integrated language arts approach. *Reading Research and Instruction, 33*(4), 293–308.

Vygotsky, L. (1978). *Mind in society: The development of higher psychological processes.* Cambridge, MA: Harvard University Press.

Watanabe, M. (2008). *Tracking in the era of high stakes state accountability reform. Teachers College Record, 110*(3), 489-534.

Wharton-McDonald, R., Pressley, M., & Hampston, J. (1998). Outstanding literacy instruction in first grade: Teacher practices and student achievement. *Elementary School Journal, 99,* 101–128.

Worthy, J. (1996). Removing barriers to voluntary reading for reluctant readers: The role of school and classroom libraries. *Language Arts, 73*(7), 483–492.

Worthy, J., Moorman, M., & Turner, M. (1999). What Johnny likes to read is hard to find in school. *Reading Research Quarterly, 34*(1), 12–27.

# Children's Literature in Action:
# The Book, The Child, and Literacy

*Courtesy of Denise Johnson.*

*Teachers develop their own literacy by continually reading children's books. Then teachers can authentically support children's literacy by recommending titles that motivate, enhance, and extend their students' reading lives.*

*Courtesy of Denise Johnson.*

*These third grade students learn implicitly about genres through reading independently and discussing literature with peers.*

Courtesy of Denise Johnson.

*These first graders are reading independently books of their choice. Reading is more than decoding the words, reading fluently, or comprehending the text. It is becoming deeply involved, captivated, absorbed, and immersed, which happens when books are self-selected.*

*This third grader is writing in her reader's response journal. She is reconstructing her understanding of the story with her own words and perspectives. Her culture and experiences, the book itself (including the cultural context of the book), and the social context of teachers and peers will impact how she responds to the book.*

Courtesy of Denise Johnson.

*These fourth graders are enjoying the time they are given to talk about this book. Good literature develops the imagination, piques curiosity, and stimulates problem solving. Allocate 20 percent of the day's reading time to explicit instruction and 80 percent to actual reading time.*

Courtesy of Denise Johnson.

Courtesy of Denise Johnson.

*These first graders are buddy reading* A House for Hermit Crab *by Eric Carle.*

These fourth-grade students are reading on the Internet. They will use different strategies to read on the Internet than to read from a print book. To be a competent reader students will learn these important new skills: navigating a webpage for the most useful information, evaluating the information, bookmarking to organize and save information, and communicating it with an email or weblog.

© Susie Fitzhugh.

This fifth-grade teacher includes children's literature across the curriculum. A nonfiction or fiction trade book is a magnifying glass that enlarges and enhances the reader's personal interaction with a subject. Teachers can supplement textbooks with children's literature that provides motivation, enthusiasm, caring, and insight into just about any aspect of the curriculum.

© Ellen B. Sensi/The Image Works.

# The Good Books Themselves

# 4 Picturebooks: Beyond Words and Illustrations

> Once or twice she had peeped into the book her sister was reading, but it had no pictures . . . in it, "and what is the use of a book," thought Alice, "without pictures?"
> —*Alice's Adventures in Wonderland*

One of my favorite things to do when discussing picturebooks with prospective teachers is to bring in a cartload, spread them out, and step back to observe. I frequently see expressions of joy as some remember favorites from their childhood, looks of astonishment as others find the beauty and sophistication in picturebooks, and thoughtful contemplation as still others consider the potential for personal and curriculum connections. Inevitably, adults and children alike come to find that picturebooks hold a special place in their hearts. Author and illustrator Mordicai Gerstein (2004) reflects, "I've found that the books I loved then, I still loved when I later read them to my children; they were still important, still meaningful to me as an adult" (p. 406). It may have been a long time since you have read a picturebook. The only way to discover or rediscover this "provocative, sophisticated, cultural product" (Schwarcz, 1982, p. 10) is to read and experience many, many picturebooks. Prepare to be fascinated, mesmerized, and moved by what you encounter.

## Defining the Picturebook

*Maurice Sendak, noted illustrator/author* and winner of the 1964 Caldecott Medal for *Where the Wild Things Are,* describes a picturebook as a "juxtaposition of picture and word, a counterpoint. Words are left out and the picture says it. Pictures are left out and the word says it" (Lanes, 1980, p. 110).

Picturebooks have a unique format that is defined by words and illustrations rather than genre. Marantz (1977) elaborates: "A picturebook, unlike an illustrated book, is properly conceived of as a unit, a totality that integrates all the designated parts in a sequence in which the relationships among them—the cover, endpapers, typography, pictures—are crucial to understanding the book" (p. 3). This description makes clear the interconnected relationship between all aspects of a picturebook and denotes the importance of viewing the picturebook as a unified whole. Even the word picturebook (rather than *picture book* or *picture-book*) is preferred by many to "reflect the compound nature of the artifact itself . . ." (Lewis, 2001, p. xiv).

Picturebooks come in many forms, shapes, and sizes, such as board books, toy books, pop-up books, and storybooks (see "Categories of Picturebooks" on pages 73–74). Some picturebooks contain stories of fiction—realistic, historical, and fantasy. Others consist of poetry and folktales, and some present biographies, information, and concepts. No other type of literature works in the same way. Given this proviso, the picturebook has limitless potential. Each aspect of a picturebook serves as a visual

## Categories of Picturebooks

*Watch/ Listen/ Read*

Watch/Listen/Read interviews/books by many of the authors/ illustrators listed in the Categories of Picturebooks.

| Category | Selected Examples |
|---|---|
| **Mother Goose Stories** teach a lesson or moral to young readers. | *Here Comes Mother Goose* edited by Iona Opie, illustrated by Rosemary Wells *The Arnold Lobel Book of Mother Goose* edited and illustrated by Arnold Lobel *James Marshall's Mother Goose* edited and illustrated by James Marshall |
| **Concept books** tell a story about a specific concept primarily through illustrations. They may also be called informational picture books. Concept books help children think about ideas such as colors and numbers. | *Black? White! Day? Night!* by Laura Seeger *The Reason for Seasons* by Gail Gibbons *Is It Red? Is It Yellow? Is It Blue?* by Tana Hoban *I Stink!* by Kate and Jim McMullan |
| **Alphabet books** engage students in connecting letters with objects that begin with the letter and creates stories using the letters of the alphabet in addition to teaching the alphabet. There are books explicitly about the alphabet and books that use the alphabet as an organizational device for conveying concepts or content. | *AlphaOops!: The Day Z Went First* by Alethea Kontis, illustrated by Bob Kolar *Tomorrow's Alphabet* by George Shannon, illustrated by Donald Crews *Eating the Alphabet* by Lois Ehlert *Illuminations* by Jonathan Hunt *D Is for Drinking Gourd: An African-American Alphabet* by Nancy Sanders, illustrated by E. B. Lewis *Gathering the Sun: An Alphabet in Spanish and English* by Alma Ada, illustrated by Simon Silva |
| **Counting books** introduce the concept of numbers, the calendar, and the seasons through a story. These books are usually simple in appearance, giving the reader an obvious opportunity to learn how to count. | *Anno's Counting Book* by Mitsumasa Anno *A Million Dots* by Andrew Clements *Mouse Count* by Ellen Stoll Walsh *The Water Hole* by Graeme Base |

*(continued)*

# Categories of Picturebooks *(continued)*

| Category | Selected Examples |
|---|---|
| **Wordless picturebooks** use illustrations to tell the story. This provides children with an opportunity to explore how stories work. Children may also discover their creativity by producing their own written stories based on the illustrations. | *Frog Goes to Dinner* by Mercer Mayer<br>*The Red Book* by Barbara Lehman<br>*Flotsam* by David Weisner<br>*Anno's Journey* by Mitsumasa Anno<br>*Once Upon a Banana* by Jennifer Armstrong, illustrated by David Small |
| **Toy books** physically engage the reader in the story through the use of pop-ups, pull tabs, or flaps. These books may also include textured pages to allow the reader to sense what the story feels like. | *Pat the Bunny* by Dorothy Kunhardt<br>*Fuzzy Yellow Ducklings* by Matthew Van Fleet<br>*Color Zoo* by Lois Ehlert<br>*Joseph Had a Little Overcoat* by Simms Taback |
| **Pop-up books** contain one or more pages in which a three-dimensional structure rises up when a page is opened. | *600 Black Dots* by David Carter<br>*Encyclopedia Prehistorica: Dinosaurs* by Robert Sabuda and Matthew Reinhart<br>*Dragons: A Pop-Up Book of Fantastic Adventures* by Keith Moseley, illustrated by M. Robertson |
| **Easy-to-read books** contain stories that have strong characterization, themes related to the reader, and engaging plots with simple sentences and direct dialogue. | *The Cat in the Hat* by Dr. Seuss<br>*Frog and Toad Are Friends* by Arnold Lobel<br>*Today I Will Fly!* by Mo Willems<br>*Mercy Watson to the Rescue* by Kate DiCamillo, illustrated by Chris Van Dusen |
| **Picture storybooks** integrate words and illustration on each page to tell a story. | *The Tale of Peter Rabbit* by Beatrix Potter<br>*The Hello, Goodbye Window* by Norton Juster, illustrated by Chris Raschka<br>*The Other Side* by Jacqueline Woodson, illustrated by E. B. Lewis<br>*Lilly's Purple Plastic Purse* by Kevin Henkes |
| **Postmodern picturebooks** employ multiple perspectives and/or narrators within a nonlinear story structure. These books use multiple colors with complex lines and images that move in and out of page space. The tone may be sarcastic or cynical. Postmodern picturebooks actively invite the reader to coauthor the text (Goldstone, 2002). | *Black and White* by David Macaulay<br>*The Stinky Cheese Man and Other Fairly Stupid Tales* by Jon Scieszka and Lane Smith<br>*Yo! Yes?* by Chris Raschka<br>*Three Pigs* by David Wiesner |

cue or sign that affects the way readers construct meaning from the text. These signs help readers form a type of framework that informs their interpretation of the text and helps them shape their construction of the story (Nodelman, 1988). For example, the front cover of a book serves as an invitation to readers as they select a book and predict the story content. Illustrations depict characters' actions, expressions, and dispositions and create and capture emotions such as humor, happiness, or sadness. Illustrations establish setting (both time and place), convey story plots, and show whether a story is realism or fantasy. They also contribute different points of view and interesting asides to the story. Additional information after the story is sometimes included, such as biographical information or how to find more information about the subject of the book. As you will see through the many examples in this chapter and in the illustrations in the color insert, book design elements can extend a book's message or theme, therefore allowing more insight into its meaning. See the Part 2 Visual Discussion.

Several studies support the belief that reading is a meaning-making process that is supported and facilitated by children's ability to respond to visual cues with text (Elster, 1998; Golden & Gerber, 1990). The interdependence of all aspects of the picturebook—from cover to endpaper—is critical to the meaning-making process and is central to evaluating the picturebook.

## Illustrations in Picturebooks

Has a striking work of art ever made you stop in your tracks and stare and then look some more? With picturebooks, it is important to look and then look again, to take a more analytical view to find the source of our pleasure. "The ultimate purpose of analysis and criticism should be to assist us in returning to any given picturebook with the power of seeing and feeling more intensely, thereby increasing our pleasure and capacity for wonder" (Sipe, 2001, p. 39). Engaging in analysis and criticism of picturebooks means we have a greater depth of understanding and can share our knowledge with children, thereby spreading the capacity for wonder.

How does one analyze a picturebook? Sipe (2001) sets forth a framework for picturebook criticism that focuses on the formal aspects and elements of the picturebook as a way of evaluating the visual aspects of picturebooks:

- Physical characteristics of picturebooks
- Elements of illustrations in isolation
- Elements of illustrations in the picturebook context

### *A Closer Look*

#### The Man Who Walked Between the Towers

In the next section, we follow the Sipe framework while taking a close look at one particular picturebook: *The Man Who Walked Between the Towers*, written and illustrated by Mordicai Gerstein, recipient of the 2004 Caldecott Medal, the most prestigious award for children's book illustration in the United States.

This is a factual story about Philippe Petit, a French street performer and aerialist, who danced across a tightrope between the unfinished World Trade Center Towers in Manhattan on August 7, 1974.

This touchstone book will be referred to frequently throughout this chapter as a model for how to "read" a picturebook—as a context for making clear the relationship between all the parts of a picturebook that create a meaningful whole.

Although we will examine other picturebooks, concentrating on a particular book will help us discover what can be found in and taken from a picturebook, and a careful scrutiny of one particular book will aid in the analysis of others. So go to the library or bookstore and find a copy of this wonderful book. Read it while you are reading this chapter, and it will open up a whole new world for you. If you don't have a copy of the book, then the photo on page 77 will be your guide to the discussion.

*Read* 

*Preview* The Man Who Walked Between the Towers.

## PHYSICAL CHARACTERISTICS OF THE PICTUREBOOK

A conventional sequence of book design elements is obvious to anyone who is familiar with books. The contents are contained in an exterior casing that may be covered by a dust jacket. The interior pages are formed from large sheets of paper that are printed on both sides, cut, and folded to form sections called signatures. The pages of each signature are sewn together down the folded side and the signatures are sewn or glued together. The first page and the last page of the bound signatures, known as the endpapers, are affixed to the casing. The text itself is preceded by a title page and, occasionally, by a half-title page, which has a title in smaller print and/or a small illustration. Extra pages, called blank leaves, sometimes precede the title page and/or follow the last page of the text.

A carefully planned picturebook will effectively employ design elements to entice us into a book—from the front cover, endpages, title page, and dedication to a satisfying close. Your heightened awareness and appreciation for these essential elements will result in a richer, more meaningful experience for you and the children with whom you share picturebooks.

**Size and Shape.** The first thing we notice about a book is its physical size and shape. Some books, such as *Grandmother Bryant's Pocket,* written by Jacqueline Briggs Martin and illustrated by Petra Mathers, are small and fit nicely in little hands, giving them an intimate feeling. Most of the time, the size of the book conveys the theme of the book. *Grandmother Bryant's Pocket* is set in the eighteenth century when women wore pockets (purses) tied around their waists under long skirts. In the story, after eight-year-old Sarah loses her dog in a fire, her nightmares begin. The special herbs and other things in Grandmother Bryant's pocket turn out to be just the cure for Sarah's bad dreams. The small size of the book parallels the size of grandmother's pocket. Books of this size are often understated and more complex (Nodelman, 1988).

> Most books, like *The Man Who Walked Between the Towers,* are around the size and shape of a standard sheet of paper. The excitement and determination of the infamous walk between the towers is effectively captured through the detailed characterization of Philippe Petit.

Other books are oversized, like *The Story of the Nile,* written by Anne Millard and illustrated by Steve Noon, which is 14 inches wide. The width of the book parallels the 4,350-mile path of the Nile River from its source to the Mediterranean Sea and allows for the comprehensive, detailed illustrations of life and civilization along the Nile.

*The Man Who Walked Between the Towers, written and illustrated by Mordicai Gerstein, is referred to throughout this chapter to provide a meaningful context for understanding the semiotic relationship between the parts of a picturebook.*

*Reprinted by permission of Mordicai Gerstein and his agents, Raines and Raines. Copyright © 2003 by Mordicai Gerstein.*

**Cover.** The cover of a book serves as a window into the content of the book. It gives us clues as to mood and subject matter of the book and is used to a great extent by children and adults when looking for a book to read.

> The cover of *The Man Who Walked Between the Towers* shows a close-up illustration of a foot balanced on a wire that is breathtakingly high above tall buildings and streets filled with traffic. When the cover is opened fully so that both the front and back are visible, we see that the picture continues to the back as the other foot of the tightrope walker comes into view along with an extension of the cityscape below.

The fact that the cover gives away the climactic event that the plot builds toward suggests how little Gerstein is interested in suspense and how much he wants to tell the amazing story of Philippe Petit's walk between the towers. The cover immediately grabs the viewer's attention, promising an exciting story inside.

The trade book versions of most picturebooks have a dust jacket, a removable paper cover used to protect the cover of a book. A trade book is a book published for distribution to the general public through booksellers, as distinguished from library editions, which have a more durable cover and do not have a dust jacket. The dust jacket of *The Man Who Walked Between the Towers* is identical to the cover of the book; the dust jacket of *Grandmother Bryant's Pocket* is not the same as the cover of the book. The background of the dust jacket of *Grandmother Bryant's Pocket* looks like printed fabric from which a dress might be made. In the middle of the front of the dust jacket is a small, oval, framed illustration of Grandmother Bryant sewing a pocket while Sarah leans lovingly against her with the countryside in the background. The back of the dust jacket continues with the same background but with a circular framed illustration of a water pitcher filled with flowers and herbs. Both front and back effectively convey the loving relationship between Grandmother Bryant and Sarah, the time period, and a hint as to the role medicinal herbs will have in the story. The cover under the dust jacket has the texture of cloth and is the color of the dirt in Grandmother Bryant's garden. There is a small triangular design in gold lettering that is similar to the print design on the dust jacket. The cover of this book adds another layer of meaning to that of the dust jacket.

**Endpapers.** Endpapers or endpages are the pages affixed to the inside of the front and back cover. Endpapers can serve as a transition between the exterior and interior of the book, setting the mood of the story. "They provide a visual framing device that serves the same purpose as 'once upon a time' and 'they lived happily ever after,' the classic signals of narrative structure" (Hearne & Sutton, 1992, p. 84).

Endpapers may be a solid color or illustrated as they are in *Smoky Night,* written by Eve Bunting and illustrated by David Diaz, winner of the 1995 Caldecott Medal. The endpapers in this book about a young boy and his mother who experience urban violence display mixed-media collages of symbolic materials—from scraps of paper, cardboard, and cloth to burned matches—all of which are significant throughout the story. The endpapers of the nonfiction picturebook *Hidden Worlds: Looking Through a Scientist's Microscope* by Stephen Kramer consist of photos by Dennis Kunkel of insects as they would appear through a microscope. (See illustration 3 in the Part 2 Visual Discussion.)

**Frontmatter.** The pages of a book that lie between the endpapers and the text are called frontmatter and consist of the blank leaves before the title page, title page, dedication, and copyright information (Figure 4.1).

> The blank pages in *The Man Who Walked Between the Towers* are beige, and the title page has an illustration of the towers as they were being built. It appears to be winter because snow is falling and the trees are brown and bare. The title page sets the stage for the story, which begins in the spring when the towers are nearly complete and has an important connection to the ending.

Authors and illustrators frequently show their appreciation to relatives, friends, and colleagues by dedicating their works to them.

> Mordicai Gerstein appropriately dedicates *The Man Who Walked Between the Towers* "To Philippe Petit for the gifts of his courage, his impeccable art, and his mythic sense of mischief."

**FIGURE 4.1**

The Parts of a Book

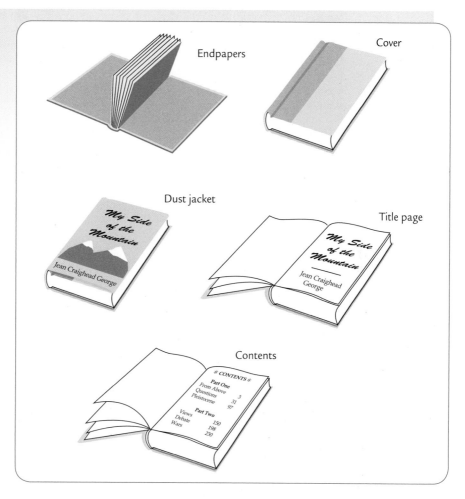

*Watch*

*Watch an interview with Toni Morrison.*

Authors will occasionally reveal their humor, cleverness, or values in a dedication statement. In Toni Morrison's *Remember: The Journey to School Integration*, the dedication page is at the end of the book:

"This book is dedicated to Denise McNair, Carole Robertson, Addie Mae Collins, and Cynthia Wesley, who died in the racist bombing of their Birmingham church on September 15, 1963. Things are better now. Much, much better. But remember why and please remember us."

At the end of *Remember: The Journey to School Integration* is a list of the key events in civil rights and school integration history. Also included are photo notes with a thumbnail copy of the photographs from the book with the place, time, and event for each. Many nonfiction picturebooks include further information about the topic of the book so children can do research on their own to find out more about the topic. Another feature, also distinctive to nonfiction picturebooks, is a table of contents, as in the biography *To Fly: The Story of the Wright Brothers,* written by Wendie Old and illustrated by Robert Parker.

**Paper.** Our response to events depicted in picturebooks is also influenced by the choice of paper on which they are printed. Nodelman (1988) points out, "Glossy paper gives colors a glistening clarity, but it is distancing, partially because the light shines equally through all the colors and creates an overall sheen that attracts attention to the surface of a picture and therefore makes it more difficult for us to focus on specific objects depicted" (p. 47). This distancing can convey a sense of staidness, serenity, or stillness.

> In books like *The Man Who Walked Between the Towers,* which is printed on glossy paper, a paradoxical relationship is established between the serene evenness of the surface and the complex tensions of the pictures. The improbability of a man walking between the Twin Towers is contrasted not only by the evenness of the shiny surface but by the serene effect of a limited range of colors.

This paradoxical tension is also apparent in Chris Van Allsburg's *Wreck of the Zephyr* and Maurice Sendak's *Outside Over There,* in which both illustrators create worlds of magical reality.

According to Nodelman (1988), "More roughly textured paper seems to invite our touch and in that way supports an atmosphere of involvement and intimacy" (p. 48). *Jumanji* and *The Garden of Abdul Gasazi*, both written and illustrated by Chris Van Allsburg, are books in black and white on matte or roughly textured paper. The surface of the paper allows for varying levels of light and darkness, which permits a heightened focus on specific objects, creating a sense of direct communication to the viewer (Nodelman, 1988; Sipe, 2001).

## ELEMENTS OF ILLUSTRATIONS USED IN ISOLATION

Traditional elements of design include color, line, shape, and texture. Artists use these elements to communicate meaning suggested in the text. Artists must use their talents with color, line, shape, and texture to reach readers and help them enjoy illustrated books.

**Color.** Color—or lack of color—is used by artists to convey character, mood, and emotion. Artists are able to achieve these visual effects by manipulating the aspects of color: hue, value, and saturation in order to tap into our associations with color as it occurs in our culture and in nature.

- *Hue* is the color itself, such as red, blue, or yellow. These colors are often categorized as cool (blue, green, violet) or warm (red, yellow, orange).
- *Value*, or *tone*, is the lightness or darkness of the color (dark blue, light green), achieved by adding black or white to the hue.
- *Saturation* is the brightness or dullness of a color. Color can range over the full spectrum, or it can be limited to a defined range.

> The colors in *The Man Who Walked Between the Towers* are predominately shades of blue and green of low intensity and light tone. Gerstein's choice of color is based on his illustrating a story that takes place almost completely outside in the park or high in the sky above the ocean during the summer or early fall. The color choices reflect the mood—happy, light, and fun. There are several night scenes in which the color and tones become darker.

When the tone changes, so does the mood of the story. Robinson (2003) comments, "When Philippe and his co-conspirators, disguised as construction workers, toil through the night setting up the wire, the area between the illustrations' borders and the edge of the page fills with a gray-blue wash, providing the visual equivalent of foreboding background music" (p. 763).

In *Where the Wild Things Are*, Maurice Sendak uses a color palate much like that of Gerstein: low-intensity shades of blue. The colors are used with a dark tone to create a dream world taking place at night. Both illustrators have used hue, value, and saturation in a way that creates a setting and mood appropriate to the story.

Chris Van Allsburg communicates meaning by manipulating the value of color in many of his books, including his two Caldecott award–winning titles, *Jumanji* (see page 82) and *The Garden of Abdul Gasazi*. In both books, Van Allsburg uses varying values of black, white, and gray to create a surreal quality that crosses between reality and fantasy. Van Allsburg, trained as a sculptor, also uses the technique of chiaroscuro—dramatic lighting and shading—in his illustrations. On the dust jacket for *Probuditi!*, Van Allsburg is able to achieve an illusory three-dimensionality of Trudy, who is stuck in a trance after becoming hypnotized by her brother Calvin, by applying value to a two-dimensional figure and using shading and shadows. In *Ben's Dream*, when the children are awake, the shading created by parallel lines is sustained and consistent. But when the children are in the dream world, instability is implied by the clash of the individual lines.

*Listen*

*Listen to an interview with Chris Van Allsburg.*

**Line.** Line is considered to be the most common and expressive element in picturebooks (Hearne & Sutton, 1992). Artists use line to direct our attention or to focus our eye. Line can be straight or curved, thick or thin, smooth or rough, depending on the meaning the artist wishes to communicate. Here are some examples:

- Horizontal lines suggest order and tranquility.
- Vertical lines create a sense of stability.
- Diagonal lines evoke a sense of motion or tension.

From the first illustrated page to the last, Gerstein effectively uses line in *The Man Who Walked Between the Towers*.

> The long horizontal and vertical lines of the Twin Towers on the first page and successive pages up to the night scenes suggest stability as we see Petit and the buildings from the ground. But, when Petit and cohorts reach the top of the towers, we see them from a new perspective created by diagonal lines, giving us a sense of instability and uneasiness. When Petit crawls down the side of the tower to retrieve the undershot arrow, the diagonal lines of Petit's body, the scaffolding, the towers, and the surrounding buildings converge to create an overwhelming sense of vertigo as our eyes are directed to the street far below.

When Petit steps out on the wire in the first double gate-fold spread, a reviewer writes, "Unparalleled use of perspective and line—architectural verticals opposed to the curve of wires and earth—underscore disequilibrium and freedom" (*Kirkus Reviews*, 2003, p. 1017). Line can also be the predominate form for illustrations, as with many of Shel Silverstein's poetry books, such as *A Light in the Attic* and *Runny Babbit*.

*Jumanji, written and illustrated by Chris Van Allsburg, is about two bored children who, left on their own one afternoon, find more excitement than they bargained for in a mysterious and mystical jungle adventure board game. Chris Van Allsburg masterfully walks the line between fantasy and reality through his use of chiaroscuro to create dramatic lighting and shading in the illustrations.*

**Shape.** Shape is the two-dimensional form representing an object.

Horizontal shapes give us a sense of stability and calm, as we experience in the first illustrations of the Twin Towers in *The Man Who Walked Between the Towers*. Vertical shapes are more exciting and suggest energy, as with the wire and balancing pole Petit uses. Diagonal shapes, like diagonal lines, create a dynamic sense of motion or tension as we encounter in the scenes of Petit preparing for and actually walking between the towers.

The placement of shape on the page—top, center, bottom, left, or right—can also suggest meaning. According to Bang (1991), shape placement in the upper half of a picture implies freedom, happiness, triumph, or spirituality. Center stage in an illustration is associated with greater importance.

On the double-page spread (when two pages create a continuous scene when opened out) in which Petit is laying on the wire "to rest," we see a seagull in the upper right corner of the right page, wings spread. From our perspective, which is slightly above Petit, the seagull appears large and strong. Below the bird in the center of the page, Petit is laying on the wire, arms spread. Bird and man mirror each other, both experiencing freedom and happiness; Petit obviously triumphant in his quest.

Moebius (1986) explains, "A character shown on the left page is likely to be in a more secure, albeit potentially confined space than one shown on the right, who is likely to be moving into a situation of risk or adventure" (p. 149). This is true of several scenes in *The Man Who Walked Between the Towers*.

> As we witness Petit standing on the railing preparing to take his first step, he is in the left corner of the left page. Though high above the city, he appears to be stable. The next scene on the right page shows his foot as he steps onto the wire. When we turn the page to the next double-page spread, we see Petit on the far right. Not only has he taken the first step, he is half way across. Petit has definitely moved into a position of greater risk. But, when we open up the gate-fold page, Petit is even farther to the right as he approaches the opposite tower thus; our sense of disequilibrium and peril is even greater.

In *Show Way*, Jacqueline Woodson shares her family history of making "show ways," or quilts that once served as maps for freedom-seeking slaves that passed from mother to daughter in the Woodson family. (See illustration 7 in the Part 2 Visual Discussion.) The story starts with the author's great-grandmother, Soonie passing the show way to the author's grandmother, Georgia, who passed it to her twin daughters, the author's mother, Ann, and Aunt Caroline. At this point in the story, illustrator Hudson Talbott shows how the twins, as young girls in the 1950s and 1960s, would sometimes feel surrounded by hate and would use the show way as a source of comfort. The young girls are depicted on the far right of the page looking wide-eyed as they are surrounded by newspaper clippings and photos illustrating the racial prejudice of the time. We can feel the sense of jeopardy and risk that the girls faced at that time in their lives. On the following page, a picture of Ann and Caroline at their graduation is in the center of the page. They are not only safe but successful and proud.

**Texture.** The illusion of texture is created by an artist to communicate the sensation of roughness, smoothness, hardness, softness, and so forth. Artists use various techniques such as line, mixed media, or scratchboard (see Table 4.1) to create the look of texture.

> The crosshatched lines on Philippe Petit's clothing create a sense of texture as well as energy and motion.

David Diaz's collages of mixed media—from scraps of paper and shards of broken glass to spilled rice and plastic dry-cleaner bags—for *Smoky Night* convey the turmoil, fear, and anxiety caused by riots. Beth Krommes's captivating rounded scratchboard art in Jacqueline Briggs Martin's *The Lamp, the Ice, and the Boat Called Fish* captures the strength and grace of Iñupiaq culture (a group of Eskimos who inhabit northern Alaska). The scratchboard illustrations highlight the details within the centuries-old crafts and skills of sewing boots from caribou legs and ugruk skin, of quickly cutting snow houses, and of wearing wooden goggles to ward off snow blindness.

**Style.** Unlike the other elements of illustration discussed earlier (color, line, shape, and texture), style is not a separate element but the impact of all of the elements together. Just as an author's style is a distinctive way of writing—use of words, figures of speech, sentences, and other language constructions to make the characters, setting, and action come alive—an illustrator's artistic style is also distinctive. According to Nodelman (1988), "'Style,' then, refers to that which is distinct about a work of art—that which transcends the implications of its specific codes and makes it out as different from other works" (p. 77). Style is a reflection of the artist's personality and individuality because it encompasses the conscious and unconscious choices an artist makes. Style influences meaning in subtle yet powerful ways. Artists sometimes vary their style according to the content and mood of the text and by the intended audience (Table 4.1). Gerstein (Silvey, 2004) reflects on this process:

> With many of my books, like *The Mountains of Tibet,* I studied Tibetan art, and then I took on that stylistic persona. With *The Seal Mother,* it was like putting on an opera, designing costumes and sets. I enjoyed approaching each book in a different way. But *The Wild Boy* was so liberating, so direct, because it came from within me. So I began to work more that way, approaching things head on, finding the material internally. (p. 57)

**TABLE 4.1**

## Styles of Illustration in Picturebooks

| Illustrative Style | Definition | Example |
|---|---|---|
| Representational | Displays people, nature, and objects as they actually appear. | *Rapunzel* by Paul Zelinsky *Alexander and the Terrible, Horrible, No Good, Very Bad Day* by Judith Viorst |
| Surrealistic | Creates a dreamlike state to attempt to represent the workings of the unconscious mind. | *The Voice of the Wood* by Andrew Clement *Amanda, Dreaming* by Barbara Wersba |
| Impressionistic | Emphasizes light, movement, and color over detail. | *Freedom Summer* by Deborah Wiles *Mr. Rabbit and the Lovely Present* by Charlotte Zolotow |
| Cartoon | Tells the story in the form of a series of illustrations followed by captions. | *Don't Let the Pigeon Drive the Bus* by Mo Willems *The Amazing Bone* by William Steig |
| Expressionistic | Give objective expression to inner experience; bright colors and figures are a bit disproportionate. | *A Chair for My Mother* by Vera Williams *Hiroshima No Pika* by Toshi Maruki |
| Naive/Folk Art | Gives the appearance of being childlike, at times lacking perspective or sense of proportion. | *Ox-Cart Man* by Donald Hall *The Apple Pie That Papa Baked* by Lauren Thompson |

Ultimately, the style of illustration an artist chooses must be appropriate and supportive of the meaning in the text. An example of illustration that is not appropriate or supportive to the story is Jim Edmiston's *Little Eagle, Lots of Owls*. In the story, an American Indian boy, Little Eagle Lots of Owls, is puzzled by his grandfather's gift of a strange animal that will not wake up, until he discovers that the creature represents part of his name. Whatever one might think about the text, illustrator Jane Ross's batik illustrations do little to accurately depict the American Indian characters, culture, and traditions. One reviewer wrote, "The images seem to be drawn exclusively from spaghetti westerns and outdated calendar art" (Polese, 1993, p. 73). Ross's silk painting technique resembling stained glass lack facial detail that gives a two-dimensional quality to the characters. Whereas Peter Parnell's illustrations for Miska Miles's *Annie and the Old One,* the story of a Navajo girl who believes the completion of the weaving of a rug will mean the death of her grandmother, is executed in bold pen and ink and muted earth tones that capture the character, individuality, and pride of the American Indian people.

Table 4.1 provides definitions and examples of the styles of illustrations in picturebooks. For visual examples of some of these styles, see the Part 2 Visual Discussion.

**Point of View.** Illustrators use a variety of perspectives to give readers different vantage points from which to view the events in a story.

> The climactic scenes of Petit's daredevil feat in *The Man Who Walked Between the Towers* actually fold out, creating an even larger expanse of the scene. These gate-folds contain two different perspectives: one from Petit's point of view and the other from the bystanders' point of view.

Without the illustrations, it would be hard to imagine such a scene, especially from different perspectives. Gerstein (2004) states, "I wanted this book to cause real vertigo, to put the reader, child or adult—and of course myself—on the wire" (p. 408). The gate-folds allow readers to actually experience the incredibly dangerous heights Petit faced.

Chris Van Allsburg is an undisputed master of perspective. He creates the impression of "magic realism—a realism more real than real" (Neumeyer, 1990, p. 4) by frequently changing the viewer's point of view or perspective. Neumeyer (1990) writes, "In *Ben's Dream,* once Ben has fallen asleep, the angles from which the famous landmarks are seen change at a dizzying pace from page to page. We have lost our stability, our spatial locus, in the illustrations, and they take on a sense of hallucinatory rudderlessness in space" (p. 4).

**Distance.** Distance refers to how close or far the viewer is from the scene in the illustration. According to Sipe (2001), "The closer we seem to the action, the more empathy and emotion we may feel; whereas a long view tends to make us more objective and detached, viewing the action from a safe distance" (p. 32).

> The two gate-fold scenes in *The Man Who Walked Between the Towers* not only provide us with two different perspectives, but they also bring us close to Petit in the first gate-fold and position us far away from him in the second gate-fold. When we are close to Petit, we experience a range of emotions from fear to freedom. When we look up at Petit as a spectator from the bottom of the towers, we feel safe and disconnected.

David Shannon's use of distance in several illustrations in *Encounter,* Jane Yolen's interpretation of how things might have been when Columbus first met the indigenous peoples of San Salvador (the Taino), provides the viewer with a sense of the shifting and changing realities between the two cultures. Columbus and his men looked and sounded very different from the Taino people, thus leaving them to wonder if the strangers were "true men." One illustration shows a close-up picture of a Taino boy's small hand pinching one of the Spanish men's hands. The text reads, "The hand felt like flesh and blood, but the skin was moon to my sun." The close-up highlights the emotion of the boy who recognizes the stark contrast between the size and skin tones of the two hands, along with the fact that the man's hand is hanging in front of his sword, brings a disquieting reality to their differences.

*Watch*

*Watch an interview with David Weisner.*

In David Wiesner's humorous contemporary rendition of *Three Pigs* (see illustration 6 in the Part 2 Visual Discussion), as the pigs break free of the traditional story and are about to enter other stories, we get a close-up illustration of one of the pigs looking at us in a confiding way as the speech bubble reads, "I think . . . someone's out there."

**Media.** Picturebook illustrators use a variety of media to create their artwork. There are basically two categories of media: painterly and graphic (Table 4.2). Many of these types of media are represented in the Part 2 Visual Discussion.

It may be difficult to the untrained eye to determine the type of media used, especially since some are not easy to distinguish, though recently this information has been included on the copyright page or the back page of picturebooks. The choice of media must be appropriate to convey the meaning of the story.

Gerstein's choice of "dramatic ink-and-oil paintings capture the exhilarating feats, the mischief, and the daring of the astonishing young acrobat" (Rochman, 2003, p. 498).

---

**TABLE 4.2**

# Media Used in Illustrations

*Watch/ Listen/ Read*

*Watch/Listen/Read interviews with many of the authors/illustrators listed in Media used in Illustrations.*

| Painterly Media | Example |
|---|---|
| Acrylic or oil creates an opaque layering of colors, plastic paints. | *Rapunzel* by Paul Zelinsky<br>*The Librarian of Basra* by Jeanette Winter<br>*Sky Boys: How They Built the Empire State Building* by Deborah Hopkinson, illustrated by James Ransome |
| Gouache is an opaque watercolor paint. | *Kitten's First Full Moon* by Kevin Henkes<br>*Spider and the Fly* by Mary Howitt, illustrated by Tony DiTerlizzi<br>*So Happy!* by Kevin Henkes, illustrated by Anita Lobel |

*(continued)*

**TABLE 4.2**
*(continued)*

# Media Used in Illustrations

| Painterly Media | Example |
|---|---|
| Tempera uses opaque water-based or eggyolk-based paints. | *The Miracle of Saint Nicholas* by Gloria Whelan, illustrated by Judith Brown<br>*The Very Hungry Caterpillar* by Eric Carle |
| Watercolor creates a translucent image. | *Tuesday* by David Wiesner<br>*Orange Pear Apple Bear* by Emily Gravett<br>*Beach* by Elisha Cooper |
| Crayon uses crayons, craypas, pastels, or water crayons. | *How Many Days to America? A Thanksgiving Story* by Eve Bunting, illustrated by Beth Peck<br>*The Baby Sitter* by Tomie dePaola |
| Pencil drawing is used to create strong lines, shaded areas, smudged shadows, and fine details. | *Song and Dance Man* by Karen Ackerman, illustrated by Steven Gammell<br>*Jumanji* by Chris Van Allsburg |
| Charcoal is a smoky black smudge technique that produces images that appear to be like shadows. | *The Keeping Quilt* by Patricia Polacco<br>*Olivia Counts* by Ian Falconer<br>*Wolves* by Emily Gravett |
| Pen and ink are used to create shapes, shadows, and textures. | *Casey at the Bat* by Ernest Lawrence Thayer, illustrated by Christopher Bing<br>*Wizzle* by William Steig, illustrated by Quentin Blake |
| Graphic Media | Example |
| Scratchboard is when a black ink layer is scratched away to show white beneath the surface. Once completed, color may be added. | *The Faithful Friend* by San Souci<br>*The Lamp, the Ice, and the Boat Called Fish* by Jacqueline Briggs Martin, illustrated by Beth Krommes |
| Woodcuts are images carved into a block of wood; ink and paint are applied to the wood and transferred to paper. | *Snowflake Bentley* by Jacqueline Briggs Martin, illustrated by Mary Azarian<br>*Bull Run* by Paul Fleischman |
| Linoleum cuts are like woodcuts but produce a cleaner line. | *Hilda Hen's Scary Night* by Martha Wormell<br>*Spring: An Alphabet Acrostic* by Steven Schnur, illustrated by Leslie Evans |
| Collage uses an arrangement of more than one type of material such as torn pieces of fabric, paper, or other materials on the page. Montage is the arrangement of only one type of material on a page. | *Golem* by David Wisniewski<br>*Living Color* by Steve Jenkins<br>*Rosa* by Nikki Giovanni, illustrated by Bryan Collier |

*(continued)*

**TABLE 4.2**

*(continued)*

# Media Used in Illustrations

| Painterly Media | Example |
|---|---|
| Stone lithography is engraving on stone and then putting it on paper. | *Abraham Lincoln* by Ingri and Edgar d'Aulaire<br>*The Princess and the Pea* by Rachel Isadora (ceramic tile) |
| Photography uses real-world photographs as illustrations in the story. | *Nic Bishop Spiders* by Nic Bishop<br>*Stranger in the Woods* by Carl Sams and Jean Stoick<br>*Wolves* by Seymour Simon |
| Mixed media use graphic and painterly techniques together to create a unique image on the page. | *Waiting for Gregory* by Kimberly Holt, illustrated by G. Swiatkowskas<br>*Comets, Stars, the Moon, and Mars: Space Poems and Paintings* by Douglas Florian<br>*17 Things I'm Not Allowed to Do Anymore* by Jenny Offill, illustrated by Nancy Carpenter |
| Computer-generated graphics uses a computer program to create art. | *Cook-a-Doodle-Doo!* by Janet Stevens<br>*ABC Pop!* by Rachel Isadora<br>*Bow-Wow Bugs A Bug* by Mark Newgarden and Megan Cash |

As previously mentioned, Chris Van Allsburg's use of conté pencil was effective in creating a magical realism in *Jumanji,* and Jacqueline Briggs Martin's use of scratchboard illustrations for *The Lamp, the Ice, and the Boat Called Fish* captures the strength and grace of Iñupiaq culture. Jerry Pinkney's use of watercolors in Julius Lester's *John Henry* conveys both the superior strength and the warm sense of humanity of this tall-tale figure.

## ELEMENTS OF ILLUSTRATIONS IN CONTEXT

As we have seen, many meaningful choices go into the design and illustration of a picturebook. This section considers additional choices illustrators must make specific to the context of a particular picturebook.

**Framing.** You may have noticed that most of the illustrations in *The Man Who Walked Between the Towers* are framed (a box around the illustration). Nodelman (1988) notes that a frame around a picture not only makes it appear neater, but it also gives the reader a less energetic, unemotional, objective view of the story. The story begins like this:

"Once there were two towers side by side" as Gerstein tells the story of Philippe Petit as if we are looking back in time, through newspaper clippings. Gerstein manipulates the use of frames to achieve different effects throughout the story. When Petit is remembering his walk between the steeples of Notre Dame Cathedral, the outline of the frames becomes distorted and the tone of the colors becomes darker to reflect the difference in time. When Petit's accomplices are assisting him in getting equipment and cable to the top of the towers, we see a montage of frames. On the pages in which the officers rush to the roof, Gerstein explains, "I distorted the picture frames. I tried to twist that space, pull one edge toward the reader and the other edge away. I tried to stretch and open up the space" (Silvey, 2004, p. 56). Then, we see a small framed close-up of Petit's foot on the wire that yields to two gate-folds of the walk.

The gate-folds are not framed; rather, the illustrations go to the edge of all four sides of the pages. This is called "full-bleed." Moebius (1986) states, "Framed, the illustration provides a limited glimpse 'into' a world. Unframed, the illustration constitutes a total experience, the view from 'within'" (p. 150). The gate-folds give the following impression:

We are within Petit's world, on the high wire with him. No longer spectators, we are full participants in the experience of Petit's walk. The different perspectives of the two gate-folds allow us to have two different experiences, one with Petit on the high wire and one as a spectator below.

In *Where the Wild Things Are,* Sendak also uses frames that lead up to three full-bleed layouts that depict the wild rumpus. Interestingly, the frames start out small, and as Max becomes angrier for being sent to his room with no supper, the frames become larger, taking up increasingly more space until they fill both sides of the double-page spreads. As Max's anger subsides and he begins to think of home, the illustrations become smaller again. David Wiesner's unconventional *The Three Pigs* begins with a framed illustration of a wolf looking down on the first pig building his house of straw, much like the illustrations of other traditional versions of the story. But as we turn the page, we realize that this story is going to be anything but traditional as we see the first pig literally blown out of the frame by the wolf. When we turn the page again, we find that the two other pigs have also left the frame of the picture to find safety from the huffing and puffing wolf. Breaking the frame breaks the boundary between the world created in the story and the real world. The three pigs leave the story in which they have been traditionally bound to enter into other stories. Each time they enter into another story, the page is framed. Finally, the pigs decide to go home to their own story, which is again framed. (See illustration 6 in the Part 2 color insert Visual Discussion 2.)

Frames vary in shape and size according to the meaning of the story. In *Grandfather's Journey*, Allen Say consistently places framed illustrations on each page. Each frame is bordered by a thin black line, giving this story of the immigrant experience of the author's grandfather the appearance and emotional feel of looking at his personal photo album. Many of Jan Brett's illustrations in *Annie and the Wild Animals* are framed with borders that add additional information to the story. The frames depict other animals living in the woods and give clues to what will happen next in the story. Books with no frames focus more centrally on action and emotion (Nodelman, 1988). The illustrations in Jane Yolen's

*Owl Moon* are all full-bleed, giving us a feeling of going along for the journey with a father and his daughter as they go owling.

**Arrangement.** Page arrangement refers to the ways illustrators choose to manipulate words and pictures within the space on the page. Typically, words are on the left side of the page and the pictures are on the right, or the pictures are at the top of the page and the words are at the bottom.

> On the pages of *The Man Who Walked Between the Towers,* in which there is only one framed illustration, the words are placed below the frame. In moments of intense action there are two or more frames on each page, the words are above, between, or below the frames. We tend to look at the pictures first when viewing a picturebook, so when the words in *The Man Who Walked Between the Towers* precede the picture, we are unsure of what to do first, which creates another level of tension to these already tense scenes.

The use of multiple frames, or montage, on a page is another way to create action, motion, or the passing of time that Gerstein uses very effectively throughout the story. Gerstein uses more than one frame on several pages, with the following exception:

> The scene in which Petit's friends carry cable and equipment to the top of the towers is a series of six frames, all conveying a sense of action and passage of time.

On the last double-page spread of the book, the left side contains only the words "Now the towers are gone," and the right side is a full-bleed illustration of the New York cityscape looking very empty and ominous without the Twin Towers. This is the only time in the book that words or illustration appears in isolation. The asymmetrical imbalance between a page full of color and another with nothing but a few words adds a dramatic tension to the story.

This technique is also used throughout *Where the Wild Things Are*. Nodelman (1988) observes, "The only pages with both words and pictures on them that seem relatively balanced are the ones directly before and after the wild rumpus, which have equal blocks of words under the picture on both sides of the spread. In this way as well as in every other, this book builds toward and then away from that central sequence" (p. 54). Chris Van Allsburg uses this approach for a different purpose in *Jumanji, The Garden of Abdul Gasazi, The Wreck of the Zephyr,* and *The Z Was Zapped.* The words on the left-hand page are in large type, which provides an overall balance to the images on each right-hand page.

**Narrative Sequence.** Gerstein said, "I think of a picturebook as a hand-held theatre, entered by opening it and operated by turning its pages (no batteries, you don't have to plug it in)" (p. 408). Gerstein's comparison of a picturebook to a handheld theater underscores the importance of visual narrative in both art forms. Both use action, setting, perspective, and distance to create a meaningful, engaging experience for the viewer.

Yet, the director of a play has more time to tell the story, whereas the illustrator only has a few pages. Therefore, rather than a succession of visual images, as in a play, a picturebook has gaps between images that the viewer must fill in. On the other hand, one cannot stop a scene in a play to think about its implications or make predictions about what will occur next. One of the best things about a picturebook is that we can pore over the pictures as long as we like, turn back to previous pages in the book, or read the book again and again. An illustrator can capitalize on this opportunity by creating recurring motifs, patterns, or rhythms in the illustrative sequence.

Another important aspect of a visual narrative is the beginning and ending. Sipe (2001) elaborates, "One way of critically examining the narrative structure of a picturebook is to look at the first and last illustrations and to try to understand how they are connected" (p. 37). In *Testing the Ice*, Sharon Robinson's childhood memoir of her father, the story opens in 1955 with Jackie Robinson sliding into home plate scoring the run that would win the Brooklyn Dodgers the World Series against the New York Yankees. By the end of the story, Jackie has retired to his home in Connecticut and faces his fear of water by going out on the frozen lake to be sure it was safe for his children and their friends to skate on. Just as Jackie Robinson "tested the ice" by being the first African American player in Major League Baseball, he once again faced his challenge and conquered it, but this time, for the safety of his family.

*Watch*

*Watch an interview with Sharon Robinson and Kadir Nelson.*

**Page Turns.** In one illustration of *The Man Who Walked Between the Towers*, Gerstein shows us the following:

> A small framed close-up of Philippe Petit's foot stepping on the wire. We cannot help but feel the suspense, to ask ourselves, "Is he really going to do it?"

We ask ourselves this even though we know he is going to do it from the picture on the front cover. We cannot help but to fall victim to the suspense. Everything has built to this climactic point. We hold our breath as we turn the page. This is what Barbara Bader (1976) calls "the drama of the turning of the page" (p. 1). Because of the limited space to tell the story, illustrators must make careful choices about what pictures to include. The illustrations that are included are only snapshots, leaving gaps in time and space. Unlike novels, each turn of the page in a picturebook presents the illustrator with an opportunity to change perspective, redirect feelings or attention, create suspense and drama, and confirm or foil predications (Sipe, 2001).

> Early in *The Man Who Walked Between the Towers*, we see Petit sitting on the back of a park bench in what appears to be spring or summer, the twin towers in the background, with a rope in his hands and a contemplative look on his face.

The text reads as follows:

> "And so Philippe—that was the young man's name—began to plan to do it secretly. The buildings are not quite finished, he thought. Maybe if I dressed as a construction worker. . . ."

The ellipses suggest that Petit just might try to come up with a plan, as impossible as that might seem. The page turn allows us to engage in this speculation. How will he go about planning such a feat? When we turn the page, we see the following:

> It is August and we see a montage of frames, all depicting Petit's friends maneuvering cable and equipment to the top of the towers.

Clearly much has happened between the two pages. Petit had to contact his friends, convince them to help him in performing an illegal act, gather the necessary supplies, and plan how to get the equipment to the top of the tower. The turning of the page allows us to see Petit as determined, persistent, and diligent. Carefully planned page turns are "far from being meaningless necessities, they have increased our engagement and pleasure, contributing positively to our total experience of the book" (Sipe, 2001, p. 39).

## Writing Style in Picturebooks

In picturebooks, the author does not have to say absolutely everything because the illustrator shows what the author leaves out. The text is shaped by the fact that there are illustrations, and the picture is shaped by the fact that there is text that results in great efficiency in communicating meaning. Although the language in picturebooks can be characterized by extreme economy, this is not to say that it is exempt from the usual canons of style. Good writing is good writing at any level.

Because picturebooks are categorized by their unique format and not by genre, picturebooks employ both narrative and expository writing. In this section, we will discuss narrative writing as it appears in both fiction and nonfiction.

Gerstein masterfully uses artistic technique and design to capture Petit's unbelievable determination, extreme talent, and sheer delight in accomplishing his death-defying act. But the text that accompanies the illustrations is just as important.  Philippe Petit documented his walk between the towers in his memoir *To Reach the Clouds* (2002), which is 241 pages long. *The Man Who Walked Between the Towers* is 37 pages long. Condensing the story emphasizes the significance of the instances we see: "They clearly become the most significant moments out of all the possible ones we might have seen, the ones most worthy of our attention" (Nodelman, 1988, p. 244). The text that accompanies the 37 "moments" we see in *The Man Who Walked Between the Towers* must convey the whole story, be interrelated, and make us ask "What's next?" until those moments reach a climax and a satisfying ending. Authors must use effective writing techniques to craft text in such a way as to achieve so much in such a brief time. These techniques certainly are not unique to picturebooks but make the most of limited writing space.

### CRAFTING POETIC WRITING

*Watch*

*Watch an interview with Philippe Petit.*

*Watch*

*Watch an interview with Mordicai Gerstein and hear him read from* The Man Who Walked Between the Towers.

In an interview about writing *The Man Who Walked Between the Towers*, Gerstein states, "I always create the story first, before I begin any art. I work as a writer; then I put the manuscript away and come back to the project as the illustrator. I read the text aloud as I am working on it, writing for voice" (Lukehart, 2003, p. 125). Gerstein, as with many authors, knows that the eye does not pick up what only the ear can hear. He reads the text aloud to listen for rhythm, pacing, and tone, the combination of which becomes the author's voice—music to our ears. Voice comes from the craft of writing. Craft in text is a particular way of using words that seems deliberate or by design—that goes beyond simply choosing words that will get the meaning across—to where words sing. We can see much craft at work in Gerstein's writing:

> In one of the first scenes, Petit has his back to the viewer looking at the towers; sizing them up. Listen: "He looked not at the towers but at the space between them and thought, what a wonderful place to stretch a rope; a wire on which to walk."

This language is poetic—the words just roll off the tongue. It has a natural rhythm and the alliteration of the consonant "t" in the first part and the "w" in the second part ties them together. Also notice the interesting sentence structure: Rather than just come right out with the idea of Petit walking between the towers, Gerstein builds up to it, saving the surprise for the end. In the second sentence on the same page, the text continues:

> "Once the idea came to him he knew he had to do it! If he saw three balls, he had to juggle. If he saw two towers, he had to walk! That's how he was."

Notice how almost every word is a single syllable, how the repetition of "If he saw" provides rhythm along with the repetition of the word "he." We have more insight into the character of Petit through this sparse description than if Gerstein had simply told us he was an aerialist.

Sonia Landes (1985) writes:

> I once asked Maurice Sendak whether the first line of *Wild Things* came naturally, or if he had to hammer it out. He said, "I'm sure it didn't. Nothing comes naturally. It had to be shaped and shaped. I think if there is any model I used, it's a kind of rough model of how children sound. I've listened to children playing, and that breathless pacing is what is so wonderful and I'm trying to catch it." (p. 54)

Sendak achieves this sense of breathless pacing by spreading one sentence across the first three double-page spreads of the book, breaking it in strategic places for page turns. One sentence spread across nine pages creates the feeling of experiencing a conscious flow of thought for the reader.

*Listen*

*Listen to an interview with Maurice Sendak.*

In the next sentence, Sendak uses *assonance*, or the repetition of the vowel sounds in words:

> That very night in Max's room a forest grew.

*Max* and *that* and *room* and *grew* are the two vowel sounds that repeat and connect the rhythmic phrases together.

Sendak's stories for children have certainly endured the test of time. Written in 1963, *Where the Wild Things Are* is still one of the most popular books for young children today. The language is so memorable that even though my son is in high school now, we still say, "I'll eat you up—I love you so!" These are the books we want to share with our children—books that echo in our memory.

### CRAFTING PROSAIC WRITING

*Read*

*Read* The Polar Express.

Writing does not have to be poetic to be beautiful. In *The Polar Express*, about a boy who rides a train to the North Pole to receive the first gift of Christmas from Santa Claus himself, Van Allsburg uses *prosaic writing*—a more straightforward style of writing. In the scene where the children see the North Pole for the first time, he describes it as follows:

> The mountains turned into hills, the hills to snow-covered plains. We crossed a barren desert of ice—the Great Polar Ice Cap. Lights appeared in the distance. They looked like the lights of a strange ocean liner sailing on a frozen sea. "There," said the conductor, "is the North Pole."
>
> © 1985 Chris Van Allsburg. By permission.

Neumeyer (1990) writes, "This prosaic writing is worth noting because, like the bass accompaniment to a melody, it keeps being the 'ground,' the linguistic background against which the miraculous picture story is set" (p. 6).

In the nonfiction book *A Drop of Water,* author Walter Wick combines science and art when he uses stop-action photography and magnification to bring new perspective to the origins, characteristics, and uses of water. Here, Wick describes a magnified photograph of water droplets on the head of a pin: "A drop of water falls through the air. Down it splashes, breaking apart into tiny droplets. What would you see if you could break water into even smaller bits?" (© Walter Wick. By permission, p. 7). This style of writing allows us to speculate on what we know (and what to learn) about the properties of water while fully absorbing the marvel of the photographs.

Table 4.3 presents many other examples of the writer's craft used in picturebooks.

## TABLE 4.3 — Other Crafting Techniques

**Watch** ✺
Watch an interview with Kathleen Krull.

| Technique | Definition | Example |
|---|---|---|
| Leads | The opening line or lines of a book intended to grab the reader's attention and make him or her want to read more. | *Wilma Unlimited,* the biography of Wilma Rudolph, written by Kathleen Krull, begins, "No one expected such a tiny girl to have a first birthday. In Clarksville, Tennessee, in 1940, life for a baby who weighed just over four pounds at birth was sure to be limited." |
| Figurative language | Figurative language provides new ways of looking at the world by comparing things that are different in enough ways so that their similarities, when pointed out, are interesting, unique, or surprising. | In Stephen Kramer's nonfiction book *Hidden Worlds: Looking Through a Scientist's Microscope,* the opening sentence reads, "Imagine what it would be like to look into the eyes of a carpet beetle, / examine grains of pollen on a sunflower petal, / or take a peek at red blood cells the size of jelly doughnuts!" (See illustration 3 in the Part 2 color insert.) |

*(continued)*

**TABLE 4.3**

(*continued*)

# Other Crafting Techniques

| Technique | Definition | Example |
|---|---|---|
| Making a long story short | Many times authors and illustrators must tell a long story in a short period of time. Writers must use effective crafting techniques to move the story along. | Cynthia Rylant uses this technique in *The Relatives Came*, which is about a family who leaves their home in Virginia and drives to visit relatives. Rylant writes, "So they drank up all their pop and ate up all their crackers and traveled up all those miles until finally they pulled into our yard." |
| Repetition of a sentence or phrase | Just as the repetition of images in illustrations can emphasize the importance of themes or make connections, so can the repetition of sentences or phrases within a story. | In Cynthia Rylant's memoir of her childhood with her grandparents, *When I Was Young in the Mountains*, the title is the recurring first line throughout the story. The first page reads, "When I was young in the mountains, Grandfather came home in the evening covered with the black dust of a coal mine. Only his lips were clean, and he used them to kiss the top of my head." |
| Understatement | Understatement gives power to writing because of what is *not* said and shows that an author trusts readers to make important, personal connections with the story. | In the last double spread of *The Man Who Walked Between the Towers*, the left page contains text only and the right page is a full-bleed illustration. The text on the left page reads, "Now the towers are gone." |

# Guidelines for Selecting Picturebooks

Picturebook illustrations will only provide meaningful learning and comprehension if they come from high-quality picturebooks. When sharing books with children, teachers and other adults must choose picturebooks with illustrations that extend or expand the text, as discussed earlier in this chapter. It is essential that the content and illustrations of all picturebooks, fiction or nonfiction, be authentic, current, and accurate. The content or information should be current; the author should have good credentials and provide source notes; the illustrations should depict the people of a culture as individuals and artifacts must be accurate; and the language, whether narrative or expository, should be engaging and should never be condescending.

Table 4.4 supplies criteria to assist with the selection of exemplary picturebooks.

## CONSIDERATIONS

The content of picturebooks crosses all genres, so the considerations and controversial issues specific to each genre (discussed in each genre chapter) also apply to picturebooks. However, some of the issues that often prompt the initiation of challenges are due to the illustrations in picturebooks.

Books for which objections have been made include: Maurice Sendak's *In the Night Kitchen* because of the nudity of the main character, a young boy, promoting allegations that this nudity might encourage child molestation (some librarians drew shorts or diapers on the nude boy); William Steig's *The Amazing Bone* on the basis that one of the animal characters uses tobacco and *Sylvester and the Magic Pebble* due to the portrayal of policemen as pigs; Maurice Sendak's *Where the Wild Things Are* and *Halloween ABC* for involving witchcraft; and Garth Williams' *The Rabbits' Wedding* for showing an "interracial" rabbit couple.

*And Tango Makes Three*, written by Justin Richardson and Peter Parnell and illustrated by Henry Cole, is based on the true story of Roy and Silo, two male Chinstrap Penguins at New York City's Central Park Zoo, who formed a couple and were given an abandoned egg to hatch and raise. This picturebook received critical acclaim from reviewers and educational organizations; however, it is the fourth most challenged book of 2000-2009 (ALA) for promoting a homosexual lifestyle. Those who challenge books on the basis of sexual content and other issues such as witchcraft believe that children must be protected from early exposure to these topics because it may lead to experimentation.

Teachers and librarians must remain aware of controversial and sensitive issues in children's picturebooks, follow the guidelines for evaluating picturebooks for literary and illustrative quality, bias and stereotypes, and involve the school faculty and community in discussions about children's picturebooks (for more information, see the Censorship Section in Chapter 7).

*And Tango Makes Three* by Justin Richardson and Peter Parnell, illustrated by Henry Cole is about two male penguins in the NY Central Park Zoo who hatched and raised an adopted chick. The book has been challenged for promoting a homosexual lifestyle.

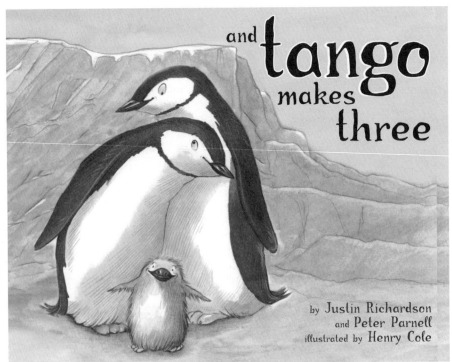

Simon and Schuster, Inc.

**TABLE 4.4**

# Criteria for Selecting Picturebooks

- Physical elements such as the size, shape, cover, endpapers, frontmatter, paper, and binding must add to the overall theme of the book.

- Visual elements such as color, line, shape, texture, style, media, point of view, and distance must develop, reflect, and enhance the story and theme.

- Compositional elements such as framing, arrangement on the page, narrative sequence, and page turns must develop, reflect, and enhance the story and theme.

- Illustrations must allow the reader to go beyond the surface level into a deeper level of understanding.

- Accuracy, currency, and authenticity must be present.

- Writing style should be engaging and follow guidelines for literary quality.

- The following questions can assist in applying the preceding criteria. Ask yourself the following questions as a starting point for locating books that meet the selection criteria:

- Do the illustrations make us see something we've not seen before, or see something familiar in a new way?

- Does the art intrigue us because of where it is placed, how it is presented, or what visual elements are used?

- How do the illustrations extend, expand, or add to the text?

- Do the illustrations present people of a culture as individuals and the artifacts of a culture accurately?

- In nonfiction books, is the copyright current to include recent information or knowledge about a subject or topic?

- Will children find the book engaging and interesting?

## The Role of Picturebooks in Reading Development

Picturebooks can play an important role in children's language and literacy development by enriching their learning experiences through storytelling, elaborating on concepts, or conveying information. They also provide opportunities to develop children's comprehension and visual literacy. In this section, we take a close look at visual literacy and meaning making with picturebooks.

### VISUAL LITERACY THROUGH PICTUREBOOKS

A picturebook for children, as outlined for the Caldecott Award, is "one that essentially provides the child with a visual experience" (Definitions section, online document). For this visual experience to be meaningful, given the relationship between the illustrations and text in picturebooks, children must learn how to analyze the ways images make meanings. Visual literacy is the ability to interpret meaning through graphic stimuli such as paintings, TV, movies, photographs, illustrations in texts, and the Internet. With today's ever-changing technology, children are bombarded with visual images every day. Visual literacy provides an alternative way of interpreting, building, and comprehending knowledge from various media using higher-order thinking (Richards & Anderson, 2003). Goldstone (1989) explains as follows:

> Children come to school with the ability to interpret on a literal level and perceive the image as a whole. However, the higher-order thinking skills of analyzing, synthesizing, and interpreting the visual images does not come naturally. To be able to interpret visual images from pictorial or media sources, the viewer must use abstract thinking skills. This is ultimately what the educational system is trying to promote (p. 592).

Picturebooks provide a unique opportunity to assist children in learning how to sort, recognize, and understand the many forms of visual information because they are able to return to the visual images to explore, reflect, and critique those images.

## MAKING MEANING FROM PICTUREBOOKS

To understand how to read picturebooks, children must recognize the structural features that promote comprehension. Children read and respond more successfully and with greater confidence to a text if they know how it is constructed and how it conveys meaning. Children need specific information on how to integrate visual and verbal information to enhance appreciation and comprehension of the picturebook.

Unsworth and Wheeler (2002) identify three kinds of meanings that are made simultaneously from visual/verbal meaning-making systems:

- *Referential meanings* involve the visual representations of events, objects, people, and the circumstances in which they occur.
- *Interpersonal or interactive meanings* involve the kind of relationship that is constructed between the viewer and what is viewed. These relationships are influenced by the use of a close-up or distant view of the character, whether characters look directly at the viewer or not, and whether the viewer looks down on or up to the characters.
- *Compositional meanings* involve the layout of the illustrations in the picturebook, including the location of elements to the left or right of the page, their size, and any type of borders used to influence attention given to illustrations.

All three of these meaning-making systems are important as children consider the details from illustration to illustration. For example, Philippe Petit's relationship with the people of New York City adds to the referential meaning of the story *The Man Who Walked Between the Towers*:

> When we are first introduced to Petit, he is riding a unicycle, juggling, and walking a tightrope between two trees. It is in the details that we see that he is encircled by people who are all wearing smiles or expressions of awe. In each picture in which Petit is performing, he always has a crowd of people looking on, fascinated by his talent.

The text works with the illustrations as Petit is actively described with verbs such as *rode, juggled, walked,* and *danced.* The fact that people find his talent entertaining and thrilling adds to the complexity of the story when we find out that his daredevil feats are against the law. Like the onlookers in the story, we are attracted by Petit's performance, but our excitement is tempered by the illegality of it. When the police rush to the top of the Twin Towers to arrest Petit, we find ourselves rooting for him, and when he is arrested and sentenced, we feel his punishment (to perform in the park) is completely justified.

The use of color, perspective, and distance in Gerstein's illustrations helps to create interpersonal meaning with the reader. As previously mentioned, the color palate of shades of blue and green of low intensity and light tone creates a mood that is happy, light, and fun. In the double gate-fold pages, Gerstein masterfully uses perspective and distance to create a feeling of vertigo and fear but also of freedom and sheer delight. Even though Petit's death-defying feat was perilous and illegal, through the use of color, perspective, and distance, our relationship to the story remains enjoyable and hopeful.

The use of frames, full-bleed layouts, and left-right positioning are compositional elements that add to the meaning of the story. Gerstein uses frames to convey a sense of objectivity, as if we were looking back in time until we witness Petit's walk between the towers, which are full-bleed and bring us into the action.

> When Petit begins his walk, we see him move from the left side of the page, a position of security, to the right side of the page, a position of risk and adventure.
>
> This is also mirrored in the text. For example, the police are first shown on a double-page spread with two frames stretched across both pages. In the first frame, Petit is walking to the left and the police are on the right.
>
> The text above the first frame is on the left side where Petit is walking and reads, "Officers rushed to the roofs of the towers. 'You're under arrest!' they shouted through bullhorns. Philippe turned and walked the other way."
>
> Underneath the first frame on the right side where the police are gathered, the text reads, "Who would come and get him?"

This placement of illustrations and text or composition creates meaning in the story.

## HOW TO READ PICTUREBOOKS

To use these meaning-making systems effectively, children need to know how to integrate visual and verbal information into a meaningful whole. Using your knowledge of illustrations and narrative writing in picturebooks from reading the first part of this chapter, you can assist children in learning how to read illustrations and text to increase their appreciation, comprehension, visual literacy, language, and concept knowledge. Unsworth and Wheeler (2002) point out, "Far from lessening children's enjoyment of literature, analysing the means by which images make meanings helps them feel they are getting closer to the texts and what it is they enjoy about them" (p. 69). The following structure is one way adults can scaffold children's understanding of how to make meaning from integrating pictures and text in picturebooks by reading aloud and modeling.

A critical first step is to select a picturebook in which the pictures are an integral part of the story and that meets the developmental needs and cultural context of the children with whom you will share the book (see "Categories of Picturebooks" on pages 82–84). Then be sure the children are within easy viewing range of the book (more information on reading aloud to children is in Chapter 13). If children cannot see the book, they will probably disengage from the experience.

**Orientation.** When presenting the book to children, access their prior knowledge and experiences that will affect how they engage with and comprehend the book. First, present the children with the front cover of the book:

> The front cover of *The Man Who Walked Between the Towers* shows a foot on a wire high above a cityscape. Opening the cover so that the back is also shown, the other foot comes into view along with an extension of the city and seaport below. An orientation to this book might begin with telling children that this book is about Philippe Petit, a tightrope walker who walked between the World Trade Towers in New York City.

To access prior knowledge and bring in previous experiences, ask the children if they have been to a circus and seen a tightrope walker or if they have been to New York City (unless, of course, you live there). Some children may remember the destruction of the towers or have family members who were affected by their destruction. Children who may not have had these experiences will benefit from this conversation while the adult fills in gaps where needed.

Ask the children for other observations. What else do they see? From looking at the front cover, children might comment on how high up the tightrope walker is, creating a sense of excitement and trepidation. This is a good time to point out how the illustrator created this feeling through the perspective he presents, the size of the objects, and the distance of the objects from the viewer. Invite students to speculate as to why Philippe Petit would want to walk between the towers and why the illustrator only shows Petit's feet on the wire. Continue the orientation to the book by explicitly drawing children's attention to other physical features of the book: endpapers, title page, dedication, and acknowledgments. This information will add to the children's understanding of when the story takes place and why the author chose to write Philippe Petit's story, which is very interesting. Also, they learn the parts of a book.

**Looking at the Whole Picture.** When we read picturebooks, the first thing we do is look at the picture. As you bring children to the beginning of the story, relate prior knowledge and predictions to the first illustration.

> The first page of *The Man Who Walked Between the Towers* depicts New York City from a distance, the World Trade Centers towering above the other buildings against the background of a blue sky.

Give children the opportunity to express their thoughts about the illustration on this page by asking what they notice. Many will notice how tall the towers are compared to the other buildings in the city. Some children might notice that it is a beautiful day, and others might comment on how the illustration looks like a picture or a postcard. Bring to the children's attention the role color plays in creating the feeling of a pleasant day or how the relative sizes of the objects create the feeling of height between the towers and other buildings.

**Reading the Text.** After looking at the picture, read the accompanying text. Under the picture of the first page of *The Man Who Walked Between the Towers*, the text reads as follows:

> "Once there were two towers side by side. They were each a quarter of a mile high; one thousand three hundred and forty feet. The tallest buildings in New York City."

Children might notice that the story starts like many fairy tales with which they are familiar. This provides a great opportunity to point out the writing technique the author uses to convey the setting.

**Looking Back at the Picture.** After reading the text, refer back to the illustration and focus on how the text and illustration are interrelated by asking the following questions:

- What does the picture show you about the words in the story? (directly interprets the words)
- What does the picture show you that adds more to the words in the story? (extends or expands the meaning of the words)
- What does the picture show you that adds meaning the author did not mention in the words?

Then return to the picture and ask, "What does the picture show you about the words in the story?" Point out or elicit from the children that most of the text is concerned with the height of the towers, which is emphasized effectively through the illustrations.

Next ask, "What does the picture show you that adds more to the words in the story?" The text tells us that the story takes place back in time: "Once there were two towers side by side." Again, point out or elicit from the children that the illustration extends our understanding of the setting through the use of the frame, which gives us a feeling of distance, of looking at a photograph.

Finally ask, "What does the picture show you that adds meaning the author did not mention in the words?" Children may not have noticed Philippe Petit looking at the towers from a distance in the far left-hand corner of the picture with his top hat in his hand. He is not mentioned in the text. Because we already know that he will walk between the towers, we can imagine that Philippe is thinking about the towers quite differently from the way they are architecturally described in the text. Also, the position of Philippe to the towers is to the extreme far left, placing him safely on the ground and at the same time emphasizing their relative size to each other. As we know, this position will change to the complete opposite. This provides an opportunity for the children to bring insight to the text and to build anticipation.

Through this process children are actively engaged in asking questions that lead to new questions, predictions, inferences, and determining the importance of the visual and verbal information presented in the picturebook. In other words, children are engaged in analyzing, interpreting, and synthesizing—the highest level of comprehension or higher-order thinking. This process moves children beyond literal understanding that may come from surface level reading and viewing to a deeper, more thoughtful and insightful understanding.

**Bringing New Knowledge to the Next Illustration.** Once the page is turned, the process starts over: First, look at the whole illustration; next, read the text; then, go back to the illustration and question the ways in which it interprets, extends, or adds to the ideas from the text while explicitly discussing the illustrative elements and techniques illustrators use. Children will bring new knowledge, predictions, and ideas to each page that builds on the process of reading illustrations, making connections to the text, and comprehending the story.

**After You Read the Book.** After the story has been read, consider how the illustrations and text worked together to create an overall theme to the story. In *The Man Who Walked Between the Towers*, the use of color, perspective, distance, and framing creates a context for imagination, perspective taking, and remembrance. Together, the words and pictures reinforce, counterpoint, anticipate, and expand on one another. By considering the work as a whole, children must synthesize multiple sources of information, and through this process they can begin to understand how an author's narrative style and artist's illustrative style is developed and used together to create meaning in picturebooks.

**Classroom Strategy for Reading Picturebooks.** After several times of modeling the process with different picturebooks, children will begin to look for visual elements and textual connections and will gradually take over the process themselves. As a temporary scaffold, and as a way to monitor and assess individual children's processing, the PTP-Q³ (Picture-Text-Picture, 3 Questions) strategy chart can be used (see Figure 4.2). After

**FIGURE 4.2**

A second grade teacher uses the PTP-Q³ strategy with *The Raft* by Jim LaMarche

modeling how to read picturebooks using the strategy outlined here several times, allow children to think through the process on their own intermittently throughout the book. Children can share their thoughts with each other as you move through the book. The chart provides a means of assessing each child's strategic processing as they approach particular pages throughout the book.

The goal is for children to use this structure for reading picturebooks on their own. Teachers and other adults serve as powerful models when sharing books with children and demonstrating their own approach to reading a book, but they must also be given time and opportunity to read picturebooks on their own and with peers in guided and independent situations.

## Opportunities for Reader Response

Children respond to the illustrations in *The Man Who Walked Between the Towers* with wonder and amazement. I presented this book to a group of third graders, and as the pages were turned and new illustrations were revealed, the children gasped. Their responses to the dizzying heights, views, and movement depicted as Petit walked between the towers are captured in the written responses in "The Child's Voice" below.

### T H E • C H I L D ' S • V O I C E

Third Graders Respond to *The Man Who Walked Between The Towers*

"The illustrations made me feel like I was really in the story. When Philippe was walking on the rope in between the two towers, I could feel the breeze against my face." **Grace**

"I felt like he was actually moving in the pictures. I felt like he was actually going and dancing." **Michael**

"The pictures had lots of detail and it showed things to tell that it was in New York City. The author tried to make it interesting for the reader." **Robert**

"I think the flip-out made it look like he was moving on the rope through the picture." **Adrianna**

"It [the illustrations] makes me feel the movement because, for example, when he walked from one Twin Tower to the other, you can see him so far one time and in the next he is farther." **Ally**

—*What elements of illustration were used to create the visual "feel" that these children experienced?*

As these responses indicate, the illustrations had a powerful effect on the children's aesthetic and emotional reaction to and understanding of *The Man Who Walked Between the Towers.* Such an experience gives children the opportunity to do more than just comprehend. Picturebooks have the potential for producing "a state of mind where new and personal meaning can take shape" (Marantz, 1992, p. 51), in which children may make connections to themselves, to the author, to the illustrator, to other texts, and to their world. Allowing students to engage in discussion about illustrations helps them to connect their prior knowledge to illustrations within a picturebook. Story elements like characters, setting, events, and themes are represented in the illustrations of a picturebook in ways that enhance or elaborate on their literary descriptions. When viewing story elements, each child will bring his or her own meaning to those represented in the illustrations. By drawing on knowledge of picturebooks, an understanding of what constitutes artistic and literary merit in picturebooks, and on the craft of authors and artists who create picturebooks, teachers can do many things to scaffold children's transactions with picturebooks.

## MODELING AND DISCUSSION

Eeds and Peterson (1995) have the following to say about discussing a book with children:

> [The teacher can] move talk beyond mere sharing of impressions and reactions toward that deeper level of noticing and insight that we call dialogue. It is in these moments of dialogue with others that our understanding and appreciation of literature are deepened. (p. 10)

Stopping during read alouds to model your own thinking and response to what you are reading can demonstrate for children how good readers engage with text when they read.

## LITERATURE RESPONSE JOURNAL

Provide children with the time to respond to their reading in a response journal. Some children who are hesitant to discuss a book orally might respond in writing. Also, writing allows children time to reflect and organize their thoughts. The format should be open, providing children the opportunity to write freely rather than to be directed by a set of predetermined questions. Teachers can model this process for children on chart paper or an overhead projector, demonstrating open and honest reflection and how to organize thinking when responding in writing.

## MAKING BOOKS

After children have been introduced to the book design elements and writing techniques discussed in this chapter, they can use their knowledge to publish their own stories (see the photo on page 77). Books can be constructed, or commercially prepared blank books can be purchased for their compositions. Include a title page, author/illustrator information, and a dedication page, as well as source notes (in the back) that include research information. These books can be placed in the classroom library for other children to read.

*These children are making their own books, which reinforces their knowledge of book design elements and sense of authorship.*

© Ellen B. Senisi/The Image Works.

## DRAMA: READER'S THEATER

Reader's theater is an activity in which students read directly from scripts (no memorizing lines) mainly without props, costumes, or sets, although sometimes these are used. A part or all of a picturebook can be used for the script, and it may be modified to include more roles. Teachers can introduce children to this fun activity and then gradually turn over the responsibility to the students for writing the script, assigning parts, obtaining props if desired, and performing for each other. Children are encouraged to read with expression and use gestures appropriate for their character. This encourages a deeper insight into the character and an understanding of the story.

## RESEARCH: AUTHOR/ILLUSTRATOR STUDY

Allowing children to learn about an author or illustrator by reading several of his or her works brings them closer to the author/illustrator's life and works. Carol Jenkins, author of *The Allure of Authors* (1999), believes that "children attach themselves to authors without direction from us. They return time and again to these authors for many of the same reasons we return: emotional sustenance, wisdom, appreciation of the author's craft, and intrigue with author as person and as writer" (p. 14). Jenkins believes that author studies invite children to respond aesthetically, critically, and biographically to an author's body of work, significantly expanding their literary and literacy understanding. Information for author studies can be obtained in the biographies, memoirs, and websites of many authors and illustrators.

# Special Topic: Graphic Novels

In 2007, the Michael L. Printz Award for excellence in young adult literature was awarded to *American Born Chinese* by Gene Luen Yang. Reviewers hailed *American Born Chinese* as "a well-crafted work that aptly explores issues of self-image, cultural identity,

*American Born Chinese* is an affecting story about growing up different and learning to accept who you are.

transformation, and self-acceptance" (Crawford, 2006, p. 240) and compared it to such literary greats as Toni Morrison's *Bluest Eye* and Laurence Yep's *Dragonwings*. Yet, the selection of *American Born Chinese* for the Printz Award was unprecedented because it is a graphic novel—the first ever to be selected in the history of the award.

### WHAT ARE GRAPHIC NOVELS?

Graphic novels are simply book-length comics. Comics usually range from short strips in the newspaper to comic books that can be up to 20 pages long, whereas graphic novels range from 50 to 600 pages in length. Like picturebooks, graphic novels are defined by their format. One popular and very recognizable style of graphic novel is *Manga*. These are Japanese print comics that have a particular artistic style such as exaggerated eyes and simplified features of characters.

There is an increasing diversity of genre in graphic novels that can range from memoir and nonfiction to realistic fiction and fantasy. The perception that graphic novels are not "real" books could only be held by those who are not familiar with them. As with picturebooks, graphic novels can be challenging, imaginative, intelligent, and gripping, and can convey a story as well as any book.

Though relatively new, graphic novels have quickly inherited many common misconceptions traditionally associated with comics. Those unfamiliar with graphic novels may erroneously assume they contain violence and sex; are only about superheroes; or aren't "real" books. Some graphic novels are R-rated, but they are not intended for children and do not represent the majority of the graphic novels available.

## ELEMENTS OF GRAPHIC NOVELS

Graphic novels employ the same trademark format as comics, called *sequential art*: the combination of text, art, and images (Brenner, 2006). Visual and textual information are presented in a series of sequenced panels. There may be many smaller panels on a page that suggest action or a larger panel that conveys more visual and/or textual information and takes longer to read. The space between the panels is called the gutter. As with page turns in a picturebook, much can happen between panels, and readers must be able to follow the action and draw conclusions. The placement and succession of the panels is important to the development of the plot and appropriate pacing of the story.

Thought bubbles, speech bubbles, font size, and lines to express action or emotion are used to show what the characters are thinking, speaking, or doing. As with picturebooks, readers must read both text and pictures to fully understand the story. Graphic artists must be good visual storytellers who are able to convey as much information as possible through the artwork and text in a limited amount of space. The best writers and artists work together to create text and images that work seamlessly and that lead the reader through the page. For example, look at this series of panels from *Amelia Rules!*

As with other children's books, the best graphic novels can be evaluated according to their literary merit and artistic quality. Reviews of graphic novels are widely published both in professional journals and on the Internet (see Print and Online Resources at the end of the chapter). Public libraries have long been advocates of graphic novels and are a good place to become familiar with many of the most popular titles (see Creating Your Classroom Library at the end of the chapter).

*Notice how the frame spreads across the page, giving the reader a sense of time and space; how the text bubbles show who is speaking; and how line is used to show action and emotion.*

## BENEFITS OF GRAPHIC NOVELS IN THE CLASSROOM

If you've ever observed children reading graphic novels, you know they are very popular. Beyond popularity however, research supports many benefits for children who read graphic novels. Graphic novels

- promote critical and visual literacy (Lavin, 1998; Thompson, 2008; Weiner, 2004)
- present alternative perspectives of culture, history, and life in an accessible way (Schwarz, 2002)
- consistently engage male readers (Smith & Wilhelm, 2002)
- motivate and engage reluctant readers (Gorman, 2003)
- benefit English Language Learners (Cary, 2004; Krashen, 1996; Liu, 2004)

*Watch*

*Watch a webcast of Gene Yang discussing graphic novels.*

Gene Yang, author of *American Born Chinese*, was a high school computer-science teacher and algebra teacher. When he had to be absent from class, he drew out his lessons in comics for the substitute teacher to use, and the students had an overwhelmingly positive response. "Comics are visual, like a film or a television program, but you have the ability to reread things if you need to, which really aids the learning process" (Engberg, 2007, p. 75).

The combination of images and text in graphic novels provides an excellent opportunity for higher-order thinking skills and critical analysis. Literary classics such as *The Wind in the Willows* and *Canterbury Tales* have been retold in graphic novels. Students can make comparisons between the traditional version and the graphic novel. *Howtoons: The Possibilities Are Endless!* uses cartoons that teach young readers "how to" find imaginative new uses for common household items to build, create, and explore things. *Storm in the Barn*, the 2010 Scott O'Dell award winner, has his share of ordinary challenges, but he also has to deal with the effects of the Dust Bowl, including rising tensions in his small town and the spread of a shadowy illness the Dust Bowl. Graphic novels cross all genres and make excellent additions to all areas of the curriculum.

## Making the Connection Across the Curriculum

Fiction and nonfiction picturebooks can provide background knowledge as well as deepen and extend knowledge about a diverse range of people, places, events, concepts, and experiences within any content area across the grades. In addition to picture story books, subjects across the curriculum can be found in the form of poetry, alphabet books, and pop-up books.

### MATH

*Watch*

*Watch an interview with Lane Smith who illustrated* Math Curse *and Science Verse.*

*G Is for Google* by David Schwartz presents complex math concepts such as network theory and probability through fun cartoons in an alphabet book format. In *A Remainder of One* by Elinor J. Pinczes, a squadron of 25 ants has difficulty finding a symmetrical formation until they learn to divide. *Math Curse* by Jon Scieszka deals with numbers in everyday life. When the teacher tells her class, "You know, you can think of almost everything as a math problem" one student acquires a math anxiety that becomes a real curse. This wacky whimsical take on math anxiety clearly express the child's feelings of befuddlement and frustration, as well eventual joy when she overcomes the math curse.

## SCIENCE

Science is the topic of many picturebooks. *Starry Messenger* by Peter Sis is a beautifully illustrated book about the brilliant astronomer Galileo's life from childhood to his final days as a prisoner of the Church. *Science Verse* by Jon Scieszka follows the inception of *Math Curse*, when a boy hears his teacher say, "If you listen closely enough, you can hear the poetry of science in everything," he is stricken with a "curse of science verse." What follows is a series of poems about topics in science that are parodies of famous poems and songs. *Ubiquitous: Celebrating Nature's Survivors* by Joyce Sidman blends poetry, science, and art in a collection that celebrates the Earth's most resilient and long-lived species that have avoided extinction to become nature's survivors.

## ART

*M is for Music* by Kathryn Krull is an alphabetical compendium of the people and things that make us sing. *Lives of the Artists: Masterpieces, Messes (and What the Neighbors Thought)* by Kathryn Krull is a collection of short biographies about 15 famous artists of European heritage that focus on the subjects' personal lives and eccentricities. Many picturebooks have been written about the lives of famous painters, but these pop-up books make the lives and times of these artists come to life: *Leonardo's Studio: A Pop-Up Experience* and *Van Gogh's House: A Pop-Up Experience* by Bob Hersey, and *A Walk in Monet's Garden: A Pop-Up Book* by Francesca Crespi.

## HISTORY

Picturebooks can bridge the past and the present in the history or social studies curriculum. For example, a series of picturebooks that tells about the Underground Railroad can provide children with a personal connection and perspective on the people and the period of time. *Barefoot: Escape on the Underground Railroad* by Pamela Edwards follows the overgrown path that an escaping slave stealthily follows one evening whose flight is aided by the wild animals of forest and swamp. *A Good Night for Freedom* by Barbara Morrow is the first-person narrative of a young girl who discovers two runaway slave girls hiding in the home of Quaker abolitionist Levi Coffin and must decide whether to protect the girls or tell the slave catchers. *Liberty Street* by Candice Ransom is told in the voice of Kezia, a young slave girl in Fredericksburg, Virginia. Missus Grace, a widow who owns Kezia and her family, sells Kezia's father to pay her husband's debts. Kezia's mother sends her to the home of a free black woman who teaches slave children to read and write and makes plans for her daughter to escape through the Underground Railroad to Canada. Ann Petry's biography *Harriet Tubman: Conductor of the Underground Railroad* presents the story of the courageous woman who guided over 300 slaves to freedom, and Raymond Bial's *The Underground Railroad* combines firsthand accounts and black-and-white period reproductions and full-color photographs to explain how the Underground Railroad worked, why it was necessary, and the hardships involved in the journey north. *Remember the Bridge: Poems of a People* pairs Carole Weatherford's poetry with photographs and engravings of the time that traces 400 years of African-American history. Together, these stories and poems provide background and insight into a time that is only briefly mentioned in most textbooks.

# Top 10 Read Alouds

## PICTUREBOOKS

1. **The Chicken Chasing Queen of Lamar County** by Janice Harrington, illustrated by Shelley Jackson (2007, Farrar, Straus and Giroux). A young farm girl tries to catch her favorite chicken, until she learns something about the hen that makes her change her ways.

2. **My Garden** by Kevin Henkes (2010, HarperCollins). After helping her mother weed, water, and chase the rabbits from their garden, a young girl imagines her dream garden complete with jellybean bushes, chocolate rabbits, and tomatoes the size of beach balls.

3. **Click, Clack, Moo: Cows That Type** by Doreen Cronin, illustrated by Betsy Lewin (2000, Simon & Schuster). When Farmer Brown's cows find a typewriter in the barn, they start making demands, and they go on strike when the farmer refuses to give them what they want.

4. **Jazz** by Walter Dean Myers, illustrated by Christopher Myers (2006, Holiday House). Illustrations and rhyming text celebrate the roots of jazz music.

5. **Knuffle Bunny: A Cautionary Tale** by Mo Willems (2004, Hyperion). A trip to the laundromat leads to a momentous occasion when Trixie, too young to speak, realizes that something important is missing and struggles to explain the problem to her father.

6. **Officer Buckle and Gloria** by Peggy Rathmann (1995, Putnam). The children at Napville Elementary School always ignore Officer Buckle's safety tips, until a police dog named Gloria accompanies him when he gives his safety speeches.

7. **Owl Moon** written by Jane Yolen, illustrated by John Schoenherr (1987, Philomel). On a winter's night under a full moon, a father and daughter trek into the woods to see the great horned owl.

8. **Velma Gratch and the Way Cool Butterfly** by Alan Madison, illustrated by Kevin Hawkes (2007, Schwartz & Wade). Velma starts first grade in the shadow of her memorable older sisters, and while her newfound interest in butterflies helps her to stand out, it also leads to an interesting complication.

9. **What Do You Do with a Tail Like This?** by Steve Jenkins (2003, Houghton Mifflin). Explores the many amazing things animals can do with their ears, eyes, mouths, noses, feet, and tails.

10. **Where in the Wild?: Camouflaged Creatures Concealed . . . and Revealed** by David Schwartz and Yael Schy, photographs by Dwight Kuhn (2007, Tricycle Press). Ten creatures camouflaged in creative photographs and accompanied by poems that offer clues about each animal's identity along with a full page of facts.

# Activities for Professional Development

## Think Critically About Children's Literature

1. Use the framework for picturebook criticism to evaluate a picturebook. Compare your analysis to the reviews of your picturebook by critics in children's literature journals such as *Horn Book Magazine* or *School Library Journal*. Do you agree with the evaluation in the journal? Why or why not?

## Bring Children's Literature into the Classroom

2. Read aloud a picturebook to a group of children, modeling the PTP-Q$^3$ strategy. Then engage children in using the strategy through guided and independent practice. As the children begin to understand how picturebooks work, observe their development of visual literacy and comprehension of the visual and verbal information in picturebooks.

## Learn About Authors and Illustrators

3. Visit the Virtual Children's Book Exhibit at the Cotsen Children's Library, Princeton University (http://library.princeton.edu/libraries/cotsen/exhibitions/index.html). The virtual exhibit showcases illustrations from children's books within the themes of swimming, magic lanterns, insects, and the art of Beatrix Potter. Each thematic exhibit features approximately 15 illustrations from a variety of artists, cultures, and time periods. The illustrations are beautifully displayed along with information about the books and the authors/illustrators from which the illustrations were taken. As you look through the illustrations within each theme, think about how the illustrations differ across artists, cultures, and time periods.

4. Collect several books by a single author/illustrator such as Chris Van Allsburg, Maurice Sendak, Barbara Cooney, or Leo Lionni. Then collect several books by one author such as Cynthia Rylant, Eve Bunting, or Mem Fox that are illustrated by different artists. Compare how the author/illustrator's vision is conveyed to that of the artists' vision for a book written by a different author.

5. Visit the website for Project ECLIPSE: Exemplary Children's Literature Interface Project for Scholarly Education (http://www.eclipse.rutgers.edu). The site traces both verbal and visual variants of Mother Goose rhymes over time and across cultures. It also allows the reader the unique opportunity to follow the development of a picturebook, *Kisses from Rosa* by Petra Mathers, from its conception through the various revisions of both text and illustration to the published book.

   - Click on *Kisses from Rosa*. Then click on the links to follow the creation of *Kisses from Rosa* from the interview with the author through the many versions of the book.
   - Then click on "Notes on Creating a Visual Interpretive Analysis." Read this page to understand the purpose of a visual interpretive analysis: a tool to look closely and deeply at the way an illustration from a picturebook creates meaning that enhances and extends the story.
   - Finally, click on "Visual Interpretive Analysis of *Kisses from Rosa*." Then click on "The Beginning and Going Home" to see how Mathers uses line, balance, and color/contrast in the beginning and end of the story.
   - Go back to the main menu and click on each of the next four links: "Rosa Playing on the Floor," "Rosa's Mother Receiving Kisses," "Rosa and Aunt Mookie Unpack," and "Rosa Wakes Up in a Crib." After viewing the illustrations and reading the text within each link, respond to the questions on interrelationships established among illustrations and text.

6. How does this activity expand your understanding of how the visual and verbal work together to create meaning in a picturebook?

# Print and Online Resources

## Print Resources

Arizpe, E., & Styles, M. (2003). *Children reading pictures: Interpreting visual texts.* New York: RoutledgeFalmer.

Carter, J. (2007). *Building literacy connections with graphic novels: Page by page, panel by panel.* Urbana, IL: National Council of Teachers of English.

Cary, S. (2004). *Going graphic: Comics at work in the multilingual classroom.* Portsmouth, NH: Heinemann.

Eric Carle Museum of Art. (2007). *Artist to artist: 23 major illustrators talk to children about their art.* New York: Philomel.

Gravett, P. (2005). *Graphic novels: Everything you need to know.* New York: HarperCollins.

Lewis, D. (2001). *Reading contemporary picturebooks: Picturing text.* New York: Routledge Falmer.

Nodelman, P. (1988). *Words about pictures: The narrative art of children's picture books.* Athens: The University of Georgia Press.

Pawuk, M. (2007). *Graphic novels: A genre guide to comic books, manga, and more.* Westport, CT: Libraries Unlimited.

Richey, V., & Puckett, K. (1992). *Wordless/almost wordless picture books: A guide.* Englewood, CO: Libraries Unlimited.

Rudiger, H. (2006). Reading lessons: Graphic novels 101. *Horn Book Magazine, 82*(2), 126–134.

Spitz. E. (1999). *Inside picture books.* New Haven, CT: Yale University Press.

Thompson, T. (2008). *Adventures in Graphica: Using Comics and Graphic Novels to Teach Comprehension, 2-6.* Portland, ME: Stenhouse

## Online Resources

*American Library Association's Caldecott Medal*
**http://www.ala.org/ala/mgrps/divs/alsc/ awardsgrants/bookmedia/caldecottmedal/ caldecottmedal.cfm**

The American Library Association annually bestows the prestigious Caldecott Medal to the picturebook with the most outstanding illustrations. Information on past winners and honor books, plus other resources are available on the ALA site.

*American Library Association's Great Graphic Novels for Teens*
**http://www.ala.org/ala/mgrps/divs/yalsa/ booklistsawards/greatgraphicnovelsforteens/ gn.cfm**

This website houses ALA's annual list of Great Graphic Novels for Teens.

*Children's Picturebook Database*
**http://www.lib.muohio.edu/pictbks**
The Children's Picture Book Database at Miami University contains searchable abstracts of over 5,000 picturebooks for children, preschool to grade 3.

*Cooperative Children's Book Center (CCBC) Charlotte Zolotow Award*
**http://www.education.wisc.edu/ccbc/books/ zolotow.asp**
In 1998, the CCBC established the Charlotte Zolotow Lecture and Award for outstanding writing in a picturebook. The CCBC site houses webcasts of the winners' lectures, including Angela Johnson, Linda Sue Park, Kevin Henkes, and Katherine Paterson.

*Cooperative Children's Book Center: Graphic Novels*
**http://www.education.wisc.edu/ccbc/books/ graphicnovels.asp**
Includes review sources, articles, book lists, and additional resources on graphic novels.

*The Graphic Classroom*
**http://graphicclassroom.blogspot.com**
The Graphic Classroom is a resource for teachers and librarians to help them stock high quality, educational-worthy, graphic novels and comics in their classroom or school library. The blog includes reviews and ratings of graphic novels and comics.

*Picturing Books*
**http://www.picturingbooks.com**
A website that provides information and resources on every aspect of the picturebook.

*Themed Reviews of Wordless Picturebooks*
**http://www.childrenslit.com/childrenslit/ th_wordless.html**
An annotated list of 50 wordless picturebooks sponsored by the Children's Literature website.

Visit the companion website at **www.cengage.com/education/johnson** to find links related to the Read/Watch/Listen icons noted throughout the chapter, as well as additional resources.

# Creating Your Classroom Library

*Abuela* by Arthur Dorros. While riding on a bus with her grandmother, a little girl imagines that they are carried up into the sky and fly over the sights of New York City.

*A Chair for My Mother* by Vera B. Williams. A child, her waitress mother, and her grandmother save dimes to buy a comfortable armchair after all their furniture is lost in a fire.

*Alexander and the Terrible, Horrible, No Good, Very Bad Day* by Judith Viorst, illustrated by Ray Cruz. Recounts the events of a day when everything goes wrong for Alexander.

*Caps for Sale: A Tale of a Peddler, Some Monkeys and Their Monkey Business* by Esphyr Slobodkina. A band of mischievous monkeys steals every one of a peddler's caps while he takes a nap under a tree

*The Carrot Seed* by Ruth Krauss; illustrated by Crockett Johnson. A young boy plants a carrot seed and, although the adults tell him that nothing will happen, he just knows it will come up.

*Chicka Chicka Boom Boom* by Bill Martin, Jr. and John Archambault; illustrated by Lois Ehlert. An alphabet rhyme/chant that relates what happens when the whole alphabet tries to climb a coconut tree.

*Corduroy* by Don Freeman. A teddy bear in a department store wants a number of things, but, when a little girl finally buys him, he finds what he has always wanted most of all.

*Crow Call* by Lois Lowry, illustrated by Bagram Ibatoulline. Nine-year-old Liz accompanies the stranger who is her father, just returned from the war, when he goes hunting for crows in Pennsylvania farmland.

*Curious George* by H. A. Rey. The adventures of a curious monkey.

*Don't Let the Pigeon Drive the Bus!* by Mo Willems. When the bus driver leaves the bus for a while, the pigeon wants to drive the bus so badly that he starts to dream himself behind the steering wheel vroom-vroom-vroom.

*Fire Truck* by Peter Sis. Matt, who loves fire trucks, wakes up one morning to find that he has become a fire truck, with one driver, two ladders, three hoses, and ten boots.

*The Firekeeper's Son* by Linda Sue Park; illustrated by Julie Downing. In eighteenth-century Korea, after Sang-hee's father injures his ankle, Sang-hee attempts to take over the task of lighting the evening fire that signals to the palace that all is well. Includes historical notes.

*First the Egg* by Laura Seeger. This brief but vibrantly illustrated book describes familiar transformations or cycles in nature such as egg to chicken, tadpole to frog, seed to flower, and caterpillar to butterfly.

*Freight Train* by Donald Crews. Brief text and illustrations trace the journey of a colorful train as it goes through tunnels, by cities, and over trestles.

*George and Martha* by James Marshall. Relates several episodes in the friendship of two hippoppotamuses.

*Goin' Someplace Special* by Patricia McKissack; illustrated by Jerry Pinkney. In segregated 1950s' Nashville, a young African American girl braves a series of indignities and obstacles to get to one of the few integrated places in town: the public library.

*Good Night, Gorilla* by Peggy Rathmann. An unobservant zookeeper is followed home by all the animals he thinks he has left behind in the zoo

*Gone Wild: An Endangered Animal Alphabet* by David McLimans. This black-and-white iconic alphabet book is sophisticated enough to intrigue and captivate readers of any age. A contemporary interpretation of an illuminated alphabet melds animals and letters into 26 unique and elegant graphic images.

*Growing Vegetable Soup* by Denise Fleming. A father and child grow vegetables and then make them into a soup.

*Harold and the Purple Crayon* by Crockett Johnson. Harold goes for a walk in the moonlight with his purple crayon and creates many fantastic adventures.

*Harry the Dirty Dog* by Gene Zion; illustrated by Margaret Graham. A little dog who hates baths hides his scrubbing brush then becomes so dirty that his family does not recognize him.

*Horton Hatches the Egg* by Dr. Seuss. When a lazy bird hatching an egg wants a vacation, she asks Horton, the elephant, to sit on her egg—which he does through all sorts of hazards and waits until he is rewarded for doing what he said he would.

*The House in the Night* by Susan Marie Swanson; illustrated by Beth Krommes. Illustrations and easy-to-read text explore the light that makes a house in the night a home filled with light.

*If You Give a Mouse a Cookie* by Laura J. Numeroff. Relating the cycle of requests a mouse is likely to make after you give him a cookie takes the reader through a young child's day.

*January's Sparrow* by Patricia Polacco. After a fellow slave is beaten to death, Sadie and her family flee the plantation for freedom through the Underground Railroad.

*The Keeping Quilt* by Patricia Polacco. A homemade quilt ties together the lives of four generations of an immigrant Jewish family, remaining a symbol of their enduring love and faith.

*Lilly's Purple Plastic Purse* by Kevin Henkes. Lilly loves everything about school, especially her teacher, but when he asks her to wait a while before showing her new purse, she does something for which she is very sorry later.

*Lyle, Lyle, Crocodile* by Bernard Waber. The helpful, happy crocodile living on East 88th St. causes a neighborhood feud.

*Machines at Work* by Byron Barton. During a busy day at the construction site, the workers use a variety of machines to knock down a building and begin constructing a new one.

*Madeline* by Ludwig Bemelmans. The story of a school girl in Paris.

*Make Way for Ducklings* by Robert McCloskey. Mr. and Mrs. Mallard found a quiet place to raise their babies then took them to the pond in the Boston Public Garden where there were peanuts to eat.

*Mike Mulligan and his Steam Shovel* by Virginia L. Burton. The story of an Irish steam-shovel artist and his old-fashioned steam-shovel, Mary Anne.

*Millions of Cats* by Wanda Gág. The story of a peasant who goes off in search of one kitten and returns with trillions of cats.

*Miss Nelson is Missing!* by Harry Allard; illustrated by James Marshall. The kids in Room 207 take advantage of their teacher's good nature until she disappears and they are faced with a vile substitute.

*My Friend Rabbit* by Eric Rohmann. Something always seems to go wrong when Rabbit is around, but Mouse lets him play with his toy plane anyway because he is his good friend

*My Great Aunt Arizona* by Gloria Houston; illustrated by Susan Lamb. An Appalachian girl, Arizona Houston Hughes, grows up to become a teacher who influences generations of schoolchildren.

*The Napping House* by Audrey Wood; illustrated by Don Wood. In this cumulative tale, a wakeful flea atop a number of sleeping creatures causes a commotion, with just one bite.

*No, David!* by David Shannon. A young boy is depicted doing a variety of naughty things for which he is repeatedly admonished, but finally he gets a hug.

*Olivia* by Ian Falconer. Whether at home getting ready for the day, enjoying the beach, or at bedtime, Olivia is a feisty pig who has too much energy for her own good.

*Papa, Please Get the Moon for Me* by Eric Carle. Monica's father fulfills her request for the moon by taking it down after it is small enough to carry, but it continues to change in size.

*The Salamander Room* by Anne Mazer; illustrated by Steve Johnson. A young boy finds a salamander and thinks of the many things he can do to make a perfect home for it.

*Scarecrow* by Cynthia Rylant; illustrated by Lauren Stringer. Although made of straw and borrowed clothes, a scarecrow appreciates his peaceful, gentle life and the privilege of watching nature at work.

*Scaredy Squirrel* by Mélanie Watt. Meet Scaredy Squirrel, a squirrel who never leaves his nut tree because he's afraid of the unknown "out there." But then, something unexpected happens that may just change his outlook.

*The Spider and the Fly* based on the poem by Mary Howitt; illustrated by Tony DiTerlizzi. An illustrated version of the well-known poem about a wily spider who preys on the vanity and innocence of a little fly.

*The Snowy Day* by Ezra Jack Keats. A story of a young boy explores the magic world of snow—snowball fight, snowman making, sliding down the snow way, etc. He loves the snow fall.

*Strega Nona* by Tomie De Paola. A retelling of an old Italian tale about what happens when Strega Nona leaves her apprentice alone with her magic pasta pot, and he is determined to show the townspeople how it works.

*Swimmy* by Leo Lionni. Swimmy, the only black fish of the entire school, devises for himself and his adopted brothers and sisters a safer way to live in the sea.

*Tar Beach* by Faith Ringgold. A young girl dreams of flying above her Harlem home, claiming all she sees for herself and her family. Based on the author's quilt painting of the same name.

*Tell Me A Story, Mama* by Angela Johnson, illustrated by David Soma. A young girl and her mother remember together all the girl's favorite stories about her mother's childhood

*Ten, Nine, Eight* by Molly Bang. Numbers from ten to one are part of this lullaby that observes the room of a little girl going to bed.

*There Was An Old Lady Who Swallowed A Fly* by Simms Taback. Presents the traditional version of a famous American folk poem first heard in the U.S. in the 1940s with illustrations on die-cut pages that reveal all that the old lady swallows.

*Tuesday* by David Wiesner. Frogs rise on their lily pads, float through the air, and explore the nearby houses while their inhabitants sleep.

*Uptown* by Collier Bryan. A tour of the sights of Harlem, including the Metro-North Train, brownstones, shopping on 125th Street, a barber shop, summer basketball, the Boy's Choir, and sunset over the Harlem River.

*The Very Hungry Caterpillar* by Eric Carle. Follows the progress of a little caterpillar as he eats his way through a varied quantity of food until, full at last, he forms a cocoon around himself and goes to sleep.

*We Are the Ship: The Story of Negro League Baseball* by Kadir Nelson. Using an "Everyman" player as his narrator, Kadir Nelson tells the story of Negro League baseball from its beginnings in the 1920s through the decline after Jackie Robinson crossed over to the majors in 1947.

*The Wheels on the Bus* adapted and illustrated by Paul O. Zelinsky. Through the use of movable illustrations, the wheels on the bus go round, the wipers swish, the doors open and close, and the people go in and out in this adaptation of the traditional song.

*When I Was Young in the Mountains* by Cynthia Rylant; illustrated by Diane Goode.

Reminiscences of the pleasures of life in the mountains as a child.

*Whistle for Willie* by Ezra Jack Keats. A little Black boy tries very hard to learn how to whistle for his dog.

*Wolves* by Emily Gravett. When Rabbit goes to the library and checks out a book about wolves, he learns things he would rather not know.

*Yoko* by Rosemary Wells. When Yoko brings sushi to school for lunch, her classmates make fun of what she eats—until one of them tries it for himself.

## GRAPHIC NOVELS: PRIMARY (GRADES K-2)

*Akiko Pocket Size* series by Mark Crilley (Sirius Entertainment)

*Amelia Rules!* series by Jim Gownley (Renaissance Press)

*Baby Mouse* series by Jennifer and Matthew Holm (Random House)

*Benny and Penny* series by Geoffrey Hayes (Raw Junior)

*Billions of Bats: A Buzz Beaker Brainstorm* by Scott Nickel (Stone Arch)

*Comic Adventures of Boots* series by Satoshi Kitamura (Farrar, Straus and Giroux)

*Greek Myths for Young Children* by Marcia Williams (Candlewick)

*Jack and the Box* by Art Spiegelman (TOON Books)

*Little Lit: Folklore & Fairy Tale Funnies* series by Art Speigelman and Françoise Mouley (Joanna Cotler)

*Little Vampire Goes to School* by Joann Sfar (Simon & Schuster)

*Magic Pickle* by Scott Morse (Oni Press)

*Master Man: A Tall Tale of Nigeria* by Aaron Shepard (HarperCollins)

*Mo and Jo: Fighting Together Forever* by Jay Lynch and Dean Haspiel (Raw Junior)

*Midsummer Knight* by Gregory Rogers (Roaring Brook)

*Otto's Orange Day* by Jay Lynch and Frank Cammuso (TOON Books)

*Rapunzel's Revenge* by Sharon, Dean and Nathan Hale (Bloomsbury)

*Sardine in Outer Space* by Emmanuel Guibert and Joann Sfar (First Second Books)

*Scary Godmother* series by Jill Thompson (Sirius Entertainment)

*Silly Lilly* series by Agnes Rosenstiehl (TOON Books)

*Stinky* by Eleanor Davis (Raw Junior)

*Tiny Tyrant* by Lewis Trondheim (Roaring Brook)

**GRAPHIC NOVELS: INTERMEDIATE
(GRADES 3 AND UP)**

*Alison Dare* series by J. Torres and J. Bone (Oni Press)

*Amulet, Book One: The Stonekeeper* by Kazu Kibuishi (Graphix)

*Amy Unbounded* by Rachel Hartman (Pug House Press)

*Bone* series by Jeff Smith (Graphix)

*City of Light, City of Dark* by Avi (Orchard Books)

*Creepy Crawly Crime* (Joey Fly, Private Eye) by Aaron Reynolds and Neil Numberman (Henry Holt)

*Graphic Myths and Legends* by various authors (Graphic Universe)

*Hikaru No Go* series by Yumi Hotta (VIZ Media LLC)

*The Hobbit* by J. R. R. Tolkein, adapted by Sean Deming and Chuck Dixon (Ballantine Books)

*Insect Ninja* by Aaron Reynolds and Erik Lervold (Stone Arch Books)

*Into the Volcano* by Don Wood (Blue Sky Press)

*The Last Knight* by Will Eisner and Miguel de Cervantes Saavedra (Nantier Beall Minoustchine Publishing)

*Lunch Lady* series by Jarrett Krosoczka (Knopf)

*Seadogs: An Epic Ocean Operetta* by Lisa Wheeler (Atheneum)

*Superman for All Seasons* by Jeph Loeb (DC Comics)

*To Dance: A Ballerina's Graphic Novel* by Siena Cherson Siegel (Atheneum)

*The TOON Treasury of Classic Children's Comics* by Art Spiegelman and Françoise Mouly (Abraham ComicArts)

*Treasure Island* retold by Wim Coleman and Pat Perrin (Stone Arch)

*Ultimate Spider-Man* series by Brian Bendis (Marvel Comics)

*Warriors* series by Erin Hunter (TokyoPop)

*The Wind in the Willows* series by Kenneth Graeme, adapted by Michel Plessix (Nantier Beall Minoustchine Publishing)

*X-Men Evolution* series by Devin Grayson (Marvel Comics)

# References

American Library Association. *Terms and criteria: Randolph Caldecott Medal.* http://www.ala.org/ala/alsc/awardsscholarships/literaryawds/caldecottmedal/caldecottterms/caldecottterms.htm.

Bader, B. (1976). *American picturebooks from Noah's ark to the beast within.* New York: Macmillan.

Bang, M. (1991). *Picture this: Perception and composition.* Boston: Little, Brown.

Brenner, R. (2006). Graphic novels 101: FAQ. *Horn Book Magazine, 82*(2), 123–125.

Carroll, L. (1865). *Alice's adventures in wonderland.* London: Macmillan.

Cary, S. (2004). *Going graphic: Comics at work in the multilingual classroom.* Portsmouth, NH: Heinemann.

Crawford, P. (2006). American born Chinese. *School Library Journal, 52*(9), 240.

Eeds, M., & Peterson, R. (1995). What teachers need to know about the literary craft. In N. L. Roser & M. G. Martinez (Eds.), *Book talk and beyond: Children and teachers respond to literature* (pp. 10–23). Newark, DE: International Reading Association.

Elster, C. (1998). Influences of texts and pictures on shared and emergent readings. *Research in the Teaching of English, 32,* 43–78.

Engberg, G. (2007). The Booklist interview: Gene Luen Yang. *Booklist, 103*(13), 75.

Gerstein, M. (2003). *The man who walked between the towers.* Brookfield, CT: Roaring Brook Press.

Gerstein, M. (2004). Caldecott Medal acceptance. *The Horn Book Magazine, 80*(4), 405–409.

Golden, J., & Gerber, A. (1990). A semiotic perspective of text: The picture story book event. *Journal of Reading Behavior, 22,* 203–219.

Goldstone, B. (1989). Visual interpretation of children's books. *The Reading Teacher, 42,* 592–595.

Goldstone, B. (1989). Visual interpretation of children's books. *The Reading Teacher, 42,* 592–595.

Goldstone, B. (2002). Whaz up with our books? Changing picture book codes and teaching implications. *The Reading Teacher, 55*(4), 362–370.

Gorman, M. (2003). *Getting graphic: Using graphic novels to promote literacy with preteens and teens.* Columbus, OH: Linworth Publishing.

Gownley, J. (2006). *Amelia rules! Volume 1: The whole world's crazy.* Ashuelot, NH: Renaissance Press.

Hearne, B., & Sutton, R. (1992). *Evaluating children's books: A critical look.* Urbana-Champaign: The University of Illinois Press.

Jenkins, C. (1999). *The allure of authors: Author studies in the elementary classroom.* Portsmouth, NH: Heinemann.

*Kirkus Reviews.* (2003). *The man who walked between the towers* (book review), 7(5), 1017.

Krashen, S. (1996). *Every person a reader: An alternative to the California task force report on reading.* Culver City, CA: Language Education Associates.

Landes, S. (1985). Picture books as literature. *Children's Literature Association Quarterly, 10*(2), 51–54.

Lanes, S. (1980). *The art of Maurice Sendak.* New York: Delacorte Press.

Lavin, M. (1998). Comic books and graphic novels for libraries: What to buy. *Serials Review, 24*(2), 31–46.

Lewis, D. (2001). *Reading contemporary picturebooks: Picturing text.* New York: RoutledgeFalmer.

Liu, J. (2004). Effects of comic strips on L2 learners' reading comprehension. *TESOL Quarterly, 38,* 225–245.

Lukehart, W. (2003). The man who walked between the towers. *School Library Journal, 49*(11), 125.

Marantz, K. (1977). The picture book as art object: A call for balanced reviewing. *Wilson Library Bulletin,* 148–151.

Marantz, S. (1992). *Picture books for looking and learning: Awakening visual perceptions through the art of children's books.* Phoenix, AZ: Oryx Press.

Moebius, W. (1986). Introduction to picturebook codes. *Work and Image, 2*(2), 141–158.

Neumeyer, P. (1990). How picture books mean: The case of Chris Van Allsburg. *The Children's Literature Association Quarterly, 15*(1), 2–8.

Nodelman, P. (1988). *Words about pictures: The narrative art of children's picture books.* Athens: The University of Georgia Press.

Petit, P. (2002). *To reach the clouds.* New York: North Point Press.

Polese, C. (1993). Little eagle lots of owls. *School Library Journal, 39*(6), 73.

Richards, J., & Anderson, N. (2003). What do I *See*? What do I *Think*? What do I *Wonder*? (STW): A visual literacy strategy to help emergent readers focus on storybook illustrations. *The Reading Teacher, 56*(5), 442–444.

Robinson, L. (2003). [Review of Mordicai Gerstein's *The Man Who Walked Between the Towers*]. *The Horn Book Magazine, 79*(6), 763–764.

Rochman, H. (2003). The man who walked between the towers. *Booklist, 100*(5), 498.

Schwarcz, J. (1982). *Ways of the illustrator: Visual communication in children's literature.* Chicago: American Library Association.

Schwarz, G. (2002). Graphic novels for multiple literacies. *Journal of Adolescent & Adult Literacy, 46,* 262–265.

Silvey, A. (2004). Sitting on top of the world. *School Library Journal, 50*(5), 54–57.

Sipe, L. (2001). Picturebooks as aesthetic objects. *Literacy Teaching and Learning, 6*(1), 23–42.

Smith, M., & Wilhelm, J. (2002). *Reading don't fix no Chevys.* Portsmouth, NH: Heinemann.

Thompson, T. (2008) *Adventures in graphica: Using Comics and Graphic Novels to Teach Comprehension, 2–6.* Portland, ME: Stenhouse

Unsworth, L., & Wheeler, J. (2002). Revaluing the role of images in reviewing picture books. *Reading, Literacy, and Language, 36,* 68–74.

Weiner, S. (2004). Show, don't tell: Graphic novels in the classroom. *English Journal, 94*(2). 114–117.

# 5 Traditional Literature

> One of the most striking things about children's books is how widely they are known by adults. Probably almost everyone in America and Britain today is familiar with "Cinderella" and Alice's Adventures in Wonderland; not one in ten will have read James Joyce.
> —Alison Lurie, 1990, p. 189

Do you know the four most powerful words in the English language? They are "once upon a time." I recently heard this public service announcement on television, which was intended to encourage parents to read to their children. You might ask why, out of all the words in the English language, these four are the *most* powerful? The answer is because these four words evoke strong feelings and images for most adults. When most grown-ups hear or read the words "once upon a time," they instantly enter a world where wishes come true and good always triumphs over evil. Jacobs and Tunnell (2004) state, "Traditional fantasy is a wonderful metaphor for human existence, and because of its rich imagery and dreamlike quality, it speaks to us deeply" (p. 75).

## Defining Traditional Literature

*Traditional literature, also known as folk literature* or oral literature, is the canon of tales, stories, and poems of a people that have been passed down by word of mouth through many generations. These stories have become the cultural heritage of groups of people all around the world, recrafted and reshaped through multiple retellings to fit the needs of the audiences of a particular place or time. Folklore includes a variety of oral lore, including legends, folktales, fables, myths, and tall tales that emerged from the people of a particular culture. Myths and legends were often told by religious leaders or professional poets whose function was to recite the great deeds of the leaders or the history of the people. Folktales and fables were told in a range of settings, from formal community functions, such as funerals, to family gatherings and recreational occasions. Tall tales of larger-than-life heroes were told around the campfire by many settlers as they braved the vast frontier.

Rudyard Kipling's *Just-So Stories* and Hans Christian Andersen's well-known tales, such as *The Little Mermaid, The Princess and the Pea,* and *The Emperor's New Clothes,* did not originate from oral tradition but were written by these authors and followed the model for folktales.

Likewise, many contemporary authors have rewritten traditional tales to include modern settings and gender roles, reversed point of view, and twisted plot lines to add humor. Some of these "fractured" folktales include Jon Scieszka's *The True Story of the Three Little Pigs,* in which we see the story from the wolf's point of view, whereas the original story was from the pigs' point of view. Helen Ketteman's *Bubba the Cowboy Prince* reverses the gender roles in the traditional Cinderella story, and in Diane Stanley's *Rumpelstiltskin's Daughter,* the miller's daughter marries Rumpelstiltskin. Unlike traditional tales, which are cataloged in the nonfiction section of the library (Dewey decimal 398 for folktales, 290 for mythology), literary and fractured folktales are cataloged as fiction (FIC).

## FROM ORAL TELLINGS TO WRITTEN LITERATURE

Because traditional stories were handed down orally, no one knows who told the tales first. Folklore became folk literature when it was recorded in written form. Stories from folklore come from all countries and cultures. The stories are sometimes associated with the name of the person who first collected the oral version and wrote it down. For example, the French courtier Charles Perrault and the German scholars the Grimm Brothers collected many of the European tales such as *Cinderella, Sleeping Beauty,* and *Little Red Riding Hood.* The British scholars Joseph Jacobs and Andrew Lang collected stories such as *The Three Little Pigs* and *The Little Red Hen,* and Scandinavian stories such as *The Three Billy Goats Gruff* were collected by Peter Asbjørnsen and Jorgen Moe.

Russell (2005) maintains that folk literature proliferated around the world because it met a variety of human needs:

- The need to explain the natural world in the absence of scientific information
- The need to articulate our fears and dreams, thus making them accessible and manageable
- The need to impose some order on the apparent random, even chaotic, nature of life, thus helping us to understand our place in the universe
- The need to entertain each other, as well as ourselves (p. 149)

Sometimes folktales are infamous for their characters, such as Baba Yaga from Russian folktales; the Arabian Nights from the Middle East; *Yeh-Shen,* the oldest written variant of Cinderella, from China; tricksters Anansi the spider and Zomo the rabbit from Africa; and Iktomi and Coyote from the American Indians.

## TRADITIONAL TALES: THE PROVINCE OF CHILDREN

Why are so many stories from all over the world alike? Usually it is because themes such as those in the Cinderella stories—perseverance, punishment of evil, reward of kindness, and justice—are fundamental values and motivations that are universal. Traditional literature transmits values to children. Many cultures have their own versions of Cinderella or other traditional tales. For example, there are almost 700 versions of the Cinderella story (Opie & Opie, 1974).

*Listen*

Listen to an interview with experts on the stories of Hans Christian Andersen and read the stories.

*Watch*

Watch an interview with Jon Scieszka.

*Read*

*Read* Grimm's Fairy Tales.

*Craft's retelling of Cinderella abounds with lavish detail inspired by the opulent styles of seventeenth- and eighteenth-century France.*

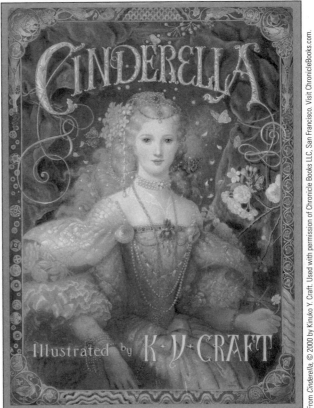

Although traditional literature was never meant to be for children only, once the tales were written down, they slowly become the province of children. Horning (1997) reports that this happened for four main reasons:

1. The common characteristics traditional stories share make them very appealing and accessible to children: concentrated action, stock characters, patterned language, elements of fantasy, and simple themes such as good versus evil and weak overcoming the strong and powerful.
2. The emphasis on oral storytelling by librarians who draw heavily from traditional oral sources, which creates a demand for publishing in this area.
3. The increasing demand for multicultural literature from non-European sources over the past ten years. Traditional tales have ready-made characters and plots that can be extracted from sources in the public domain that require no royalty payments.
4. The power of the stories themselves. The tales have survived for their sheer power as stories that deal with universal truths (pp. 47–48).

It is important for children to become familiar with the rich heritage of folk literature that has come down to us from cultures around the world.

# Benefits and Considerations of Traditional Literature

## BENEFITS

Traditional literature can play important roles in children's understanding of the rich oral heritage handed down from cultures around the world:

- It helps children understand the personal dimension and standards of behavior of a culture and at the same time reduce stereotypes. According to Young and Ferguson (1995), "Folklore contain[s] references to a society's values: what the people value; what they laugh at; what they scorn, fear, or desire; and how they see themselves" (pp. 490–491). Stories help us understand and appreciate other people and hold many valuable lessons, as well as help us understand the universality of common beliefs and values.

- It provides children with a framework for the literature, drama, and art they will later encounter. Referred to as "the mother of all literature," literally all character types, basic plots, and themes have been explored in traditional tales. Indeed, many fantasy stories echo literary patterns found in all fiction and nonfiction, and when we read, we forge links between what we are reading and texts we already know. "The Child's Voice" feature on this page presents a journal entry by a third grader who made an inter-textual connection between *Stone Fox* by John Gardiner and the tall tale of *John Henry* by Julius Lester. (See illustration 1 in the Part 2 Visual Discussion.)

- It provides entertainment and pleasure: children enjoy reading and hearing folktales.

- It provides strong rhythm, rhyme, and repetition of patterns. Traditional stories are tailored to children's developing memory and imagination and to their unique way of viewing the world.

The benefits of sharing traditional literature with children are why traditional tales are shared in homes and classrooms around the world. Yet, there are many adults who object to sharing some traditional literature with children because they are too violent, are antifeminist, or perpetuate stereotypes.

## THE • CHILD'S • VOICE

**A Third Grader's Journal Entry: Understanding How Literature Works**

I think this book is very good. And I thought that when Stone Fox let Willy win that it was very nice. I think Stone Fox did that because he saw how Willy really needed that money more than he did. When the book said that search light's heart burst and she suddenly died, it reminded me when John Henry died he had broke in two. They both died because they worked them selves too hard. And they were trying to win a race.

*—How does a child's understanding of traditional tales provide a foundation for understanding other archetypes in literature?*

## CONSIDERATIONS

**Violence in Traditional Tales.** Of course, the stories we are familiar with today differ greatly from the original versions, which were not written for children and reflect the time in which they were told. Nodelman and Reimer (2003) say the following:

> The first written records of the tales make it clear they weren't originally written for children at all—at least, not children with the tastes and interests that North American adults usually assume modern children have. In a version of "Sleeping Beauty" recorded in Giambattista Basile's Pentameron in 1634, for example, the prince so likes the looks of the sleeping princess that he climbs into bed with her and enjoys "the first fruits of love" (374). Then he deserts her, leaving her pregnant but still sleeping. She doesn't wake up until one of the twins she has given birth to in her sleep gets hungry enough to suck from her finger the enchanted piece of flax that kept her sleeping. (pp. 304–305)

*Read* Histoires ou Contes du Temps Passé.

*Read different versions of* Little Red Riding Hood.

When the story of *Sleeping Beauty* appeared in Charles Perrault's *Histoires ou Contes du Temps Passé* (*Stories of Past Times*, 1697), the pregnancy occurs after she awakens, and the prince and Sleeping Beauty marry immediately after the prince awakens her (Nodelman & Reimer, 2003). Even though there were different ideas about the nature of children during Perrault's time, he believed they should not be that knowledgeable.

In Perrault's version of *Little Red Riding Hood*, the story ends with the child being eaten by the wolf—basically, that she got what she deserved because she didn't listen to her mother. In the Grimm version, written almost a century and a half later, Little Red Riding Hood is rescued by a woodcutter. The Grimm Brothers combined the best features of the authentic versions of the tale and "in the process of adding to and deleting from the tales they heard, the Grimms gave preference to events and characterizations that suited their own middle-class, Christian values" (Nodelman & Reimer, 2003, p. 307).

Many adults feel that the violence in many of the traditional tales is inappropriate for or frightening to young children. Even though these stories are representative of only a small number of tales on the whole, they are some of the most popular and best known in North America. In response to adult criticism, retellings of these tales have taken a much softer approach. Lurie (1990) states the following:

> Sentimental editors bowdlerize and rewrite, often without admitting it. . . . Nobody gets eaten, nobody gets rescued, nobody gets punished. This is supposed to make children feel safer—even though the wolf is still wandering around outside somewhere, waiting for the next little girl (p. 23).

Many critics of such "bowdlerization" of traditional tales blame the attitudes of adults toward goodness and justice—especially in North America—on popular media, Disney in particular. The knowledge many children and adults have about traditional tales come from watching Disney movies. According to Nodelman (1988), "Many adults do believe that figures like Walt Disney's cardboard heroines are more suitable. Years of familiarity have persuaded them to identify such colorful and relatively simple images with the tastes and interests of children." (p. 38)

**Responding to Sexism in Traditional Tales.** Zipes (2002) asserts, "If we examine in depth the folktales gathered by the Grimm Brothers, we learn that . . . [s]uch tales as 'Cinderella,' 'Little Red Riding Hood,' 'King Thrushbeard,' and 'Rapunzel' are decidedly biased against females who must either be put in their places or have their identity defined by males" (p. 154).

*A variation on the classic story of Cinderella with the dazzle and fashion of the roaring twenties.*

*Listen* ✺

*Listen to an interview with Jack Zipes, a leading authority on fairy tales.*

Feminist fairy tales have become popular in recent years in response to female bias in popular fairy tales and movies. *Ella's Big Chance: A Jazz-Age Cinderella* by Shirley Hughes, *Princess Furball* by Charlotte Huck, *Cinder Edna* by Ellen Jackson, and *Prince Cinders* by Babette Cole are just a few of the titles that present strong female characters who do not wait for Prince Charming to determine their fate. These stories provide strong female role models. Many of my female students find these stories not only enjoyable but satisfying because they grew up in a time when women's rights were a major issue (see "The Teacher's Voice" below). Yet, without the "outmoded, sexist schema" (Nodelman & Reimer, 2003, p. 320) depicted in some traditional tales, feminist fairy tales lose most of their humor and purpose. Adults have a firm understanding of gender roles in society, but children may not, so such themes may be confusing or not make any sense at all.

*Watch* ✺

*Watch a webcast with Gail Carson Levine.*

**Stereotypes in Traditional Tales from Around the World.** Most educators and children's literature experts believe it is enriching and informative to read folktales from around the world to children. A conscious effort is needed on the part of adults to introduce children to people of different cultures in other genres. Otherwise, stereotypes are perpetuated. However, if the only multicultural literature children are exposed to is that of traditional literature, children may end up believing that these people are either extinct or are part of a world that is unlike the contemporary world. According to Rudman (1997), "Being able to see people of different races doing everyday, mundane

# THE · TEACHER'S · VOICE

This modern version of <u>Cinderella</u> is refreshing and engaging. It takes the story of Cinderella and provides context and depth to the story. It answers a question I always had as a child: Why didn't Cinderella just tell everyone to bugger off and do as she pleased? Cinderella, and many other such stories, really made little sense to those of us who were young in the early to mid-seventies. We were being raised with the idea of equality for women and "woman power," so I think we were confused about Cinderella when she was presented as a "brave" protagonist.

In any event, this "cognitive dissonance" that has plagued me for over 30 years is at least partially resolved and explained by <u>Ella Enchanted</u>. Ella is a complex and an interesting character who does act bravely against her curse of obedience. She is presented as noble and thoughtful, caring and self-sacrificing in the name of love. Happily, she is also an intelligent girl, breaking old stereotypes of the fairy tale princess-to-be.

I also appreciated that the author made the relationship between Prince Char (I just got it—Prince Charming) and Ella one that developed. She had reason to be in love with Char beyond the fact he was a prince. He loved her for her intelligence and personality. This is such an important message for kids who would read this book.

Although set in a fantasy land with the elements typical of fantasy, the emotions, conflicts, and relationships are realistic and complex. The author underscores this realism with the language in which she writes. At first, I was turned off by her common tone and telling. Only later did I realize that she was using the language to merge the fantasy world with the realism of the characters and their emotions.

I also appreciate that she defines what "happily ever after" looks like. Ella is an equal to the prince even though she doesn't assume the title of Princess. She travels, speaks languages, and enjoys her power to say yes and no. Again, the author is giving us a modern interpretation that includes an empowered heroine who accepts and gives love and happiness on her own terms.

*—How does this teacher's knowledge of the traditional version
of Cinderella affect her interpretation of Ella Enchanted?*

tasks—and not only in exotic or esoteric circumstances—is critical for children if they are to get a balanced view. Currently, it is difficult to find indigenous peoples from any continent in contemporary and realistic stories" (p. 369). Teachers must integrate contemporary fiction and nonfiction multicultural literature across the curriculum to provide children with a balanced view.

## Categories of Traditional Literature

Traditional tales have no identifying author because they have been handed down through the centuries by word of mouth until they were eventually written down. Folklorists who have collected these stories over time disagree as to how they should be categorized. See the "Categories of Traditional Literature" chart and Table 5.1 (on page 126), which both summarize the most commonly agreed upon categories and organizational patterns.

## Categories of Traditional Literature

| Subgenre | Definition | Characters | Setting | Themes | Teller's Beliefs | Examples |
|---|---|---|---|---|---|---|
| **Fable** | A brief story in which the moral is explicitly stated | Animals talk as human beings/one dimensional | Anyplace, anytime | Universal lessons to be learned that reflect the values of the culture | Not told as fact | *The Town Mouse and the Country Mouse* *The Boy Who Cried Wolf* *The Dog in the Manger* |
| **Myth** | Explains aspects of culture or how something came to be in the natural world | People who have super-powers | "In the beginning . . ."Before and during creation | Supernatural creators; origins of the world, natural phenomena, animals and people | Told as fact | *When the Beginning Began: Stories About God, the Creatures and Us* *The First Strawberries* *Favorite Norse Myths* |
| **Legend** | Traditional narrative based on historical truth | Historical figures such as saints, kings, heroes | "When father was king . . . ." Recent past | Founding of a nation; courage/ perseverance of heroes; unusual occurrences | Told as fact | *King Arthur Tales* *The Girl Who Dreamed Only Geese and Other Tales of the Far North* *Fa Mulan* |

*(continued)*

# Categories of Traditional Literature *(continued)*

| Subgenre | Definition | Characters | Setting | Themes | Teller's Beliefs | Examples |
|---|---|---|---|---|---|---|
| **Religious Stories** | Stories of important events and people of different religions | Prominent religious figures | Biblical time period | Peace, hope, faith, forgiveness, salvation | Told as fact | *Wonders and Miracles: A Passover Companion* *Noah's Ark* *A Time to Love: Stories from the Old Testament* |
| **Tall Tale** | Exaggerated humorous stories of characters that perform impossible acts | Historical figures given superhuman strengths, "larger than life" | "In the early days of our country…" Mostly North America | Frontier settlement Hard work | Not told as fact | *John Henry* *Paul Bunyan* *Lies and Other Tall Tales* |
| **Folktale** | A fairy, human, or animal tale passed down by word of mouth | Human or animal characters/ symbolic and flat | "Long ago and far away" Far distant past | Universal truths that reflect the values of the times/ societies | Not told as fact | See Table 5.1 |

**TABLE 5.1**

# Subgenres of Folktales

| Subgenre | Definition | Examples |
|---|---|---|
| Pourquoi (Why) Tales | Explain how certain animal traits, characteristics, or human customs came to be | *How Animals Got Their Tails* *Her Seven Brothers* *Story of the Milky Way* |
| Beast Tales | Stories in which animals talk and behave as people | *The Three Little Pigs* *Three Billy Goats Gruff* *The Little Red Hen* *Puss in Boots* |

*(continued)*

**TABLE 5.1**
(*continued*)

# Subgenres of Folktales

| Subgenre | Definition | Example |
|---|---|---|
| Cumulative Tales | Increasing repetition of details that build to a quick climax | *The Old Woman and Her Pig*<br>*The Gingerbread Boy*<br>*Chicken Little* |
| Fairy Tales | Simple narratives dealing with magic and the supernatural; glorious fulfillment of human desires | *Lon Po Po: A Red Riding Hood Story from China*<br>*Jack and the Beanstalk*<br>*Cendrillion: A Caribbean Cinderella* |
| Realistic Tales | Tale could possibly be true or the tales began as true, but through retellings it takes place in the folklore of its culture | *Dick Wittington and His Cat*<br>*Johnny Appleseed*<br>*Zlateh the Goat* |
| Noodlehead/Jack Tales | Humorous stories of characters who are good at heart but lack good judgment | *Noodlehead Stories: World Tales Kids Can Read and Tell*<br>*The Six Fools* |
| Trickster Tales | The main character plays tricks to outsmart those in power | *Anansi the Spider: A Tale from the Ashanti*<br>*Raven: A Trickster Tale from the Pacific Northwest*<br>*Tales of Uncle Remus* |

## Evaluating and Selecting Traditional Literature

Because of the nature of traditional literature, it must be evaluated according to a different set of criteria. Literary elements of character, setting, and plot are not fully developed. Characters in these stories are stereotypes symbolic of certain fundamental human qualities such as good, evil, jealousy, or foolishness. There may be one or two lines of text establishing the setting, usually the distant past, but then the story jumps directly into the action. Plots are simple, predictable, and direct, reflecting the oral tradition in which they were born. They had to be easy to remember, because the stories were recited and not written down. The action quickly rises to a climax and then concludes with a satisfactory ending such as "they lived happily ever after." Some plots are cumulative or add-on, as in *The Gingerbread Boy,* or cyclical, as in destruction and rebirth in creation myths like Hamilton's *In the Beginning: Creation Stories from Around the World.* The themes in traditional tales reflect what was important to the cultures from which they originated. Many themes are represented across cultures—for example, good versus evil, perseverance and diligence, kindness, greed, and fear.

# Evaluation Criteria

| Cultural Consideration | | |
|---|---|---|
| | **Narrative** | **Illustrations** |
| **Accuracy** | Does the story accurately: <br> • present historical information and cultural details with richness of written details? <br> • mirror the culture through dialogue and relationships? <br> • give central treatment of important cultural issues? | Do the illustrative translations accurately: <br> • depict cultural artifacts and details? <br> • depict the cultural setting? |
| **Authenticity** | Does the story authentically: <br> • reflect the culture of origin? <br> • ensure value implications in the story are compatible with both universal human rights and the beliefs and values for the recipient culture? | Do the illustrative translations: <br> • use an authentic art form that is in sync with the cultural reality? <br> • remain faithful to and corroborate the values found in the story? |
| **Authority** | • Is the author an insider writing about his or her own culture? If so, does the author have good credentials and local community endorsement? <br> • Is the author an outsider to the culture he or she is writing about? If so, did the author include source citations, notes, and critical reviews? | • Is the artist an insider illustrating his or her own culture? If so, does the artist have good credentials and local community endorsement? <br> • Is the artist an outsider to the culture he or she is illustrating? If so, did the author include source citations, notes, and critical reviews? |

**Criteria for Evaluating and Selecting Traditional Literature**

**Criteria for Evaluating and Selecting Traditional Literature (cont.)**

| | Literary Consideration | |
|---|---|---|
| | **Narrative** | **Illustrations** |
| Literary/ Illustrative Style | • Does the retelling offer something unique in the way it is told or the culture from which the retelling is derived?<br>• Does the retelling extend the available folklore from the culture?<br>• Does the author's style reflect that of the culture portrayed?<br>• Does the story stand on its own compared to other translations or authoritative versions?<br>• Is the story engaging and does it come to life when read aloud through robust, vivid language, rhythm, and repetition? | • Does the artist's style bring freshness or novelty to the story yet remain in keeping with the culture?<br>• Are the illustrations appropriately balanced with the text?<br>• Are the illustrations visually pleasing? |
| Plot | • Is the plot well structured or simple enough for children to follow? | • Do the illustrations enhance the text and add dimension to the plot? |
| Theme | • Is the theme(s) appropriate and relevant to contemporary children? | • Do the elements of illustrations (discussed in depth in Chapter 4) come together in a satisfying whole to support the overall theme of the story? |

Based on the work of Hearn (1993), Mellon (1987), Norton (2001), Mo and Shen (2003), and Yokota (1993).

The cultural roots and interrelated themes across many tales from different cultures are at the heart of evaluating traditional literature. Yet, folktales—especially in picturebooks—represent an extremely high percentage of multicultural books used in classrooms. Therefore, it is essential that traditional literature accurately and authentically portray the culture of origin.

## AUTHENTICITY AND ACCURACY OF TRADITIONAL LITERATURE

How do we know if a story is truly representative of the culture from which the story originated centuries ago? Because very few authors have access to original oral sources of folk literature, they must rely on printed versions collected or retold by others from a different time and with different purposes and audiences than the original. But how can we be sure that authors and illustrators have remained true to the values, beliefs, and cultural backgrounds of the people portrayed in traditional literature? Folklore critic and scholar Betsy Hearne (1993) stresses the importance of establishing cultural authority, citing the sources for folklore, and training adults who select and interact with the literature. Hearne also assessed the methods authors use for citing sources in picturebook folktales. She found that authors' source acknowledgment practices fall between nonexistent source notes and model source notes that cite the sources the author used, any changes the author made in his or her retelling, and the cultural context in which the story was told.

*Listen*

Listen to an interview with Judy Sierra.

At the end of her book, *Nursery Tales from Around the World,* Judy Sierra provided extensive notes that include the written source for each tale in the collection along with an indication of whether she retold a particular text to update some of the vocabulary.

Authors and illustrators need to establish cultural credibility by engaging in active research on all aspects of the culture they are trying to depict instead of being satisfied with expressing only the exotic and superficial aspects of a culture. Caldecott Medal winner Paul Goble does extensive research before writing a traditional American Indian myth or legend:

> When I retell and illustrate an Indian legend or a moment of history, I want to visit the people and see the places I write about. . . . I try to get details right in my stories and illustrations, because mistakes would be rude to Indian people, and to my readers. . . . When I am working on retelling a traditional myth or legend, I often ask Indian people to tell me the story. I want to hear them tell it in their own words. Sometimes they cannot because the memory of it died with their grandparents. I always have a lot of questions in my mind. Sometimes I find the answers in museum archives, sometimes in state historical societies; at other times the answers come by thinking hard. (pp. 18–26)

Mo and Shen (1997) maintain that in addition to carefully selecting and adapting stories that are authentic to the culture of origin, authors and illustrators must ensure that the values they imply are compatible with both universal human rights and the values of the recipient's culture. The following chart provides criteria for analyzing and critiquing both cultural and literary aspects of traditional literature. An example of how to evaluate a book is then provided, using the picturebook *Yeh-Shen: A Cinderella Story from China.* (See illustration 2 in the Part 2 Visual Discussion.)

# *A Closer Look*

## Yeh-Shen: A Cinderella Story from China

"In the dim past, even before the Ch'in and the Han dynasties, there lived a cave chief of southern China by the name of Wu. As was the custom in those days, Chief Wu had taken two wives. Each wife presented Wu with a baby daughter. But one of the wives sickened and died, and not too many days after that Chief Wu took to his bed and died too. Yeh-Shen, the little orphan, grew to girlhood in her stepmother's home." (first opening)

**Synopsis.** So begins Yeh-Shen, retold by Ai-Ling Louie and illustrated by Ed Young (1982, Philomel Books). The story is about a young girl who overcomes the wickedness of her stepsister and stepmother to become the bride of a prince. Yeh-Shen predates the earliest European version of Cinderella by 1,000 years.

**Authority.** The inside front and back flaps of the dust jacket of the book and information on the copyright page tell us that the author, Ai-Ling Louie, heard the story of Yeh-Shen from her grandmother when she immigrated from southern China. The tale had been told in her family for three generations. Research led Louie to an ancient Chinese manuscript that appeared in The Miscellaneous Record of Yu Yang, authored by Tuan Ch'eng-Shih, that confirmed that the story had been told in China since the days of the T'ang dynasty (A.D. 618–907). Tuan's book became part of an encyclopedic work that went through many editions. The Hsueh Chin T'ao Yun edition from the Ch'ing dynasty (1644–1912) is reproduced and included in the frontmatter of the book.

Ed Young, the illustrator, was born in Tientsin, China, grew up in Shanghai, and came to the United States in his late teens, where he attended college and art school. He is a renowned illustrator of other children's books of Chinese folklore, including the Caldecott Medal winner *Lon Po Po: A Red Riding Hood Story from China* and Caldecott Honor winners *The Emperor and the Kite* and *Seven Blind Mice*. The artwork for *Yeh-Shen* took over two years to complete, with Ed Young making two trips to China to research the traditional costumes and customs of the people in the area in which the tale is set.

**Author Accuracy.** The original translated text begins:

"During the time of the Ch'in and Han dynasties, a cave chief named Wu married two wives, and each gave birth to baby girls. Before long, Chief Wu and one wife died, leaving one baby, Yeh-Shen, to be reared by her stepmother."

Louie's retelling remains true to the translation, but it adds details of historical location and cultural custom that enhance the reader's knowledge. Louie also elaborates and enriches the language of the story. Together, the story is richer in detail and more pleasing to the ear.

Louie also adds dialogue to the original text that enhances our understanding of the relationships in the story. After the stepmother kills Yeh-Shen's beautiful fish, she is overcome with grief, and her tears fall into the water from which a spirit in the form of a wise old man arises. The translated text describes his interaction with Yeh-Shen as follows:

> "Yeh-Shen was distraught when she learned of the fish's death. As she sat crying she heard a voice and looked up to see a wise old man wearing the coarsest of clothes and with hair hanging down over his shoulders. He told her that the bones of the fish were filled with a powerful spirit and that when she was in serious need, she was to kneel before the bones and tell them of her heart's desires. She was warned not to waste their gifts."

With Louie's addition of dialogue, the scene is described as follows:

> "'Ah, poor child!' a voice said. Yeh-Shen sat up to find a very old man looking down at her. He wore the coarsest of clothes, and his hair flowed down over his shoulders. 'Kind uncle, who may you be?' Yeh-Shen asked. 'That is not important, my child. All you must know is that I have been sent to tell you of the wondrous powers of your fish.' 'My fish, but sir. . . .' The girl's eyes filled with tears, and she could not go on. The old man sighed and said, 'Yes, my child, your fish is no longer alive, and I must tell you that your stepmother is once more the cause of your sorrow.' Yeh-Shen gasped in horror, but the old man went on. 'Let us not dwell on things that are past,' he said, 'for I have come bringing you a gift. Now you must listen carefully to this: The bones of your fish are filled with a powerful spirit. Whenever you are in serious need, you must kneel before them and let them know your heart's desire. But do not waste their gifts.'" (third opening)

The addition of dialogue adds depth to the story by giving the reader a stronger sense of the honored place that spirits hold in the Chinese culture and the effect the spirit had on Yeh-Shen. Louie adds detail and dialogue throughout the story.

Louie also decided to keep the ending of the story, which some consider too violent. After the prince marries Yeh-Shen, they return to his castle but do not bring the stepmother and stepsister because they were so unkind to Yeh-Shen. "They remained in their cave home, where one day, it is said, they were crushed to death in a shower of flying stones." Louie, an elementary school teacher, obviously made the decision to keep the original ending to the story because she felt that American children could handle the stepmother's and stepsister's "just desert" in the end.

**Illustrative Accuracy.** Young's depictions of traditional Chinese dress and hairstyles are accurate for the time period. Although often the characters are not facing the reader or are too far away to distinguish, the closer pictures show a clear difference between the facial features of the older stepmother and the younger Yeh-Shen. The composition of the illustrations provides a limited, if not nonexistent, view of the setting.

**Author Authenticity.** Yeh-Shen reflects the essence of ninth-century Chinese culture. The cultural symbol of the fish as good luck and prosperity is a critical aspect of the story. The beauty of Yeh-Shen's "tiny" feet is emphasized in the story, paralleling the practice of foot binding during the Ch'ing dynasty.

**Illustrative Authenticity.** Young uses either three or four panel frames on each double spread throughout the book, which are representative, to some degree, of large wall paintings that were often divided into panels in China. Although this is an innovative approach to composition in picturebooks, it is effective in suggesting the cultural setting. Even though pastels and watercolors are not traditional Chinese media, the shimmering effect of the merged watercolors and limited lighting are typical of Chinese paintings. Young uses simple page design and blank space, which are also traditional.

**Literary Style.** Until the publication of Yeh-Shen, a picturebook version of this story did not exist, so the addition of this telling extended the folklore from China as well as our knowledge of the original version of Cinderella. The author's poetic simplicity is very much in keeping with the original translated text and with Chinese literary tradition. The following excerpt highlights some of the author's use of robust and vivid language that evokes emotion:

> "At once she found herself dressed in a gown of azure blue with a cloak of kingfisher feathers draped around her shoulders. Best of all, on her tiny feet were the most beautiful slippers she had ever seen. They were woven of golden threads, in a pattern like the scales of a fish, and the glistening soles were made of solid gold." (fifth opening)

*Watch*

*Watch a webcast of illustrator Ed Young.*

**Illustrative Style.** Young's combination of innovative style and authentic Chinese art creates an imaginative interpretation of the story while maintaining the aesthetic feel of the Chinese culture. His use of simple page design consisting of panels and white space with misty, jewel illustrations uniquely balances the sparse text while allowing the reader to bring his or her own interpretations and imagined details to the story.

**Plot.** The simple story structure of the fairy tale is preserved in this version. The story begins with a statement of setting and moves immediately to the problem: Yeh-Shen's mother and father die, leaving her to be raised by her wicked stepmother. The story then moves immediately into the action: The stepmother kills Yeh-Shen's beloved pet, but its bones become the magical power that allows her to attend the festival and ultimately marry the prince in the end. Sparse detail and archetypical characters lead to the story's swift movement into the action. Young's use of panels, white space, and directional movement created by his use of line and object placement complement the rapid action in the story.

**Themes.** The typical themes in Cinderella tales are also present in Yeh-Shen: kindness, generosity, patience, endurance, and gratitude. Young's use of color and shading captures the essence of these themes. His development of the motif of the fish throughout the book is a subtle and effective reminder of the magic power at work and the cultural connection of fish as a symbol of good luck and prosperity.

How do we know that *Yeh-Shen* is an excellent example of a well-researched, well-written, and well-illustrated retelling of the Chinese folktale? The book meets critical criteria for sharing traditional literature with children. It provides information on the backgrounds of the author and illustrator, includes research into the origin of the folktale, provides a comparison of the text to the original, and offers cultural accuracy and authenticity in the text and illustrations. Knowing about traditional literature helps teachers and other adults to select and use folktales appropriately to build children's language and literacy development.

## The Role of Traditional Literature in Literacy Development

Many adults read nursery rhymes to children at a very young age. The brief, simple structure, rhyme, rhythm, and repetition of traditional stories are just right for developing literary language and understanding basic story structure in early childhood.

To demonstrate effective reading of traditional literature for children, model your own thinking and strategy use, while explicitly discussing the origin and culture of the tales. When sharing traditional tales in picturebook format, the guidelines for reading picturebooks in Chapter 4 remain appropriate and effective. This section describes some ways that traditional literature can be used to assist in children's reading and language development.

### DEVELOPMENT OF LITERARY LANGUAGE

Children quickly develop oral language at a very early age to communicate with the people in their lives. Oral language is not the same as literary language, or the language used in books. For instance, when Yeh-Shen first sees the vision of the old man, she exclaims, "Kind Uncle, who may you be?" Because we do not talk like that, it is important for children to understand that the language in books can be different from the way we speak. As a matter of fact, if children do not acquire an understanding of literary language, they may have difficulty comprehending text at higher levels. Reading aloud to children deposits literary language in the mind. Literary language also uses a more extensive vocabulary than we use in everyday conversations, so children are exposed to words they might not hear or learn otherwise. The brevity, structure, and style of traditional tales hold children's attention even at a young age, while introducing them to literary language and rich vocabulary.

### DEVELOPMENT OF ABSTRACT AND INFERENTIAL THINKING

Literary language is full of complex patterns and literary devices, including metaphorical language that requires readers to think abstractly and make inferences. Traditional tales are very brief; much is left out that we must fill in on our own. For instance, what do we know about the character of Yeh-Shen? We know she wept over the death of her fish and she did many chores for her stepmother, but not much more. How did she feel about the prince not allowing her stepmother and stepsister to live in the palace? How did she feel about their deaths at the end of the story? Traditional tales such as fables are known for their witty maxims such as *sour grapes, a wolf in sheep's clothing, crying wolf, actions speak louder than words, slow and steady wins the race,* and *honesty is the best policy.* Maxims are used to suggest meaning that isn't conveyed through more lengthy writing so that the reader must infer how the maxim is developed by the story.

**FIGURE 5.1**

First-Grade Students' List of Common Elements in Fairy Tales

# What We Noticed About Fairy Tales

- Once upon a time … & Long ago …
- End happily ever after
- Magic
- Have characters such as kings & queens
- Take place in faraway places
- Have a good character & a bad character
- Sometimes characters are turned into animals
- Animals can talk
- Teach a lesson

## HOW STORIES WORK: UNDERSTANDING STORY STRUCTURE

The literary elements come together to form the structure or organization of fiction stories. Traditional tales present a stripped-down version of the story elements or story "grammar" in a simple story. Since there are no complex details, it is easy to identify the characters, setting, problem, events, and resolution. It is important for children to understand how these elements come together in a story. Teachers can use visual structures to support children's understanding of how traditional tales work. In Figure 5.1, a first-grade teacher created an anchor chart with her children as they discussed what they noticed about the elements of fairy tales. The anchor chart provided a concrete representation of their thinking. This chart can be used for reference as more tales are read and compared (Figure 5.2). It can also be used to scaffold children's retelling of a tale.

Providing children with the opportunity to retell a story requires them to use prior knowledge, an understanding of how text works, and an understanding of literary language. Teachers must model retelling a story many times and then guide children through the process before engaging children in retelling. The brevity of traditional tales is a great place to begin.

*Read*

*Read more about retelling activities.*

# Opportunities for Reader Response

When reading a traditional tale aloud to children or when children have had time to read tales on their own, there should be plenty of time for discussion. Discussion requires the orchestration of what the listener remembers and what he or she interprets while in the process of listening. This orchestration results in the listener holding longer episodes of the story in her memory and building memory capacity.

## DISCUSSION

Discussion allows children to continually make connections and voice their predictions and inferences throughout the story and share their thinking with each other. The average

**FIGURE 5.2**

First-Grade Students' Comparisons of Folktales

# Cinderella

| Title | Characters | Problem | Resolution |
|---|---|---|---|
| Cinderella | Cinderella, Stepmother, 2 Stepsisters, prince fairy godmother. | Her family was mean to her. She was not allowed to go to the ball. | Her Fairy Godmother helped her get to the ball. The glass slipper fit. She lived happily-ever-after. |
| Bubba the Cowboy Prince | Bubba, Dwayne, Milton, Stepdaddy, Miz Lurleen, Fairy Godcow. | His family made him do all the work. They wouldn't let him go to the ball. | His Fairy Godcow helped him go to the ball. Miz Lurleen liked him best. They lived happily-ever-after. |
| Princess Furball | Furball, King, Father, Cook, Ogre, Nurse | Her father wanted her to marry the Ogre. She ran away. She was so poor & had to be a servant. | She was clever. She used her gifts to get the king's attention. He fell in love w/her. |

classroom has children from cultures that have a rich oral tradition and/or are depicted in traditional tales. Teachers and children must not respond in ways that would be considered disrespectful of or trivializing to their culture.

Teachers should openly discuss issues of violence, antifeminism, and stereotyping with children as they pertain to the traditional tales they are reading. Research has shown that by comparing and contrasting variations of traditional tales, these issues become apparent and should be discussed openly. According to Mello (2001), "When students are presented with a variety of gender roles from disparate cultural texts, they begin to examine their own understanding of how to assign value to gender roles and gendered relationships" (p. 554).

## ORAL STORYTELLING

Many children come to school already having experienced rich cultural traditions of storytelling (Long & Sibberson, 2006). Storytelling in the early childhood classroom is an excellent technique for bridging home and school communities and for fostering growth in literary language, story structure, and comprehension. Children acquire language through active participation, and literature provides rich language models. To encourage children in your classroom to retell stories, model storytelling for them (Table 5.2).

*Read* ✴

*Read more about oral storytelling activities.*

Prior to modeling storytelling for children, be sure to let them know that eventually they will be telling the story themselves. Teachers must model the act of storytelling many times before asking children to tell a story. Children can take turns telling stories to each other during share time or scheduled center time, or they can tell their story into a tape recorder or camcorder to be listened to or viewed by other children, their parents, or the teacher at another time.

## STUDENTS WRITE THEIR OWN VERSIONS

Once children have read many versions of traditional tales and thoroughly understand their structure, they can write their own. Sierra (1996) says, "Suppose that instead of a Gingerbread Boy there were a runaway pizza, or tortilla, or bagel. What would its journey be like? What hungry people and animals might it encounter? Who would be the one to eat it?" (p. xii). An anchor chart can be used to scaffold children's writing. "The Child's Voice" feature on the next page provides an example of a third grader's tall tale.

## SUPPORTING ENGLISH LANGUAGE LEARNERS

The genre of books read with children has a basic effect on the interactions around those books. Research on culture and reader response indicates that readers are most interested in texts directly related to their own experiences. Paul Boyd-Batstone (1997), a third-grade bilingual teacher in Long Beach, California, found that his Spanish-English students could not define the problem in the story *The Rabbit and the Turnip*, a cumulative Chinese folktale in which a hungry rabbit finds a turnip in the snow at Christmas, only to give it away to a hungry donkey, who in turn gives it away to another hungry animal, and so on until it ends up back in the paws of the generous rabbit. Paul's students were perplexed by what seemed to be a simple, straightforward story problem. Paul asked his students what they found wrong with the story. The students immediately indicated that the story was not believable because the color of the turnip in the book

**TABLE 5.2**

# How to Model Storytelling for Children

1. Select stories with good plot structures.

2. Be sure you know the story thoroughly so you can retell it in your own words. Include any rhythmical or repetitive phrases.

3. Be expressive, changing your voice to reflect dialogue, intonation, and inflection.

4. Tell the story slowly and with animation of body, hand gestures, and facial expressions.

5. Use props and other creative storytelling techniques such as puppets, stuffed animals, cutout characters and settings, a felt-board, and dolls.

# THE · CHILD'S · VOICE

> A Third Grader
> Writes a Tall Tale

In old Texas lived a woman named Annie Mae. She was the best reading and storytelling woman in Texas. She started reading and writing before she could even see! Everyone from miles around knew Annie Mae the girl who could read and write before she could see! They even loved to tell and retell her amazing storys about what she has written and how she has helped people. Now one day Annie Mae went to visit her friend Trinket. Trinket had been having big problems with reading. He couldn't read a lick. He couldn't read because he wasn't paying attention in school. All he did was sit there and stare at the pretty girls! Finally Trinket told Annie Mae his problem and she said, "Reading was as easy as licking your teeth." So Trinket was about to ask how was she going to help him to read. But before he could even ask her, she had already gone home. But of course she came back with some books. She had so many books that it filled the sky all the way to heaven. Then she opened Trinket's head and stuck all the books in his head. Finally she gave him a book to read. And he just started reading faster than a Jaguar can outrun a horse. He read so fast that he read a 700 page book in one minute! Now one day a person that knew everything and knew every word in the world asked Trinket would he be in a reading contest. And he said, "Yes!" Well see that person didn't know what was coming! When the man said "on your mark get set read!" Trinket read that book in 2 minutes. The other guy read it in 10 days and that's 240 hours! After that context Texas has past the word on about Trinket and soon Texas had a new tale to tell about how Annie Mae helped another person.

—*What do you notice about this child's use of literary language and the use of the literary device of exaggeration, which defines a tall tale?*

was not correct and turnips do not grow in the snow. As it turned out, one student's grandfather grew turnips in Mexico. Capitalizing on their knowledge of turnips, Paul wrote the students' comments on a chart, encouraged the children to bring in photographs of turnips, and then wrote stories about life on a turnip ranch. Boyd-Batstone (1997) said the following:

What I began to realize was that transmitting notions of story structure was not the best approach for literature instruction. Transactional instruction, which looks for authentic responses to literature from students, was a much more effective and enjoyable way to teach. Transaction instruction invited Javier to bring to light the lived-through cultural experiences that he brought to school. This is vitally important in light of the need for the bilingual educator to provide culturally responsive instruction. (p. 189)

*Read*

*Read about digital storytelling with ELL students.*

By asking open-ended questions, students of all cultures have the opportunity to share their thoughts and experiences relating to the genre of traditional literature in a meaningful way.

## Making the Connection Across the Curriculum

Once upon a time the famous physicist Albert Einstein was confronted by an overly concerned woman who sought advice on how to raise her small son to become a successful scientist. In particular she wanted to know what kinds of books she should read to her son.
"Fairy tales," Einstein responded without hesitation.
"Fine, but what else should I read to him after that?" the mother asked.
"More fairy tales," Einstein stated.
"And after that?"
"Even more fairy tales," replied the great scientist, and he waved his pipe like a wizard pronouncing a happy end to a long adventure.

JACK ZIPES, 2002, P. 1

### SOCIAL STUDIES

Traditional tales can be used to introduce and expand upon many topics. When studying history or social studies, children can learn a great deal about a particular country and its people by analyzing traditional tales from that country. For example, Kathryn Pierce (2002), a third-grade teacher, used African folktales to teach a social studies unit on the cultures of the grasslands, specifically Kenya and the Masai people. She read *Why Mosquitoes Buzz in People's Ears* and *Who's in Rabbit's House?: A Masai Tale* by Verna Aardema to begin the unit. For several days, Kathryn continued to read African folktales aloud, and students read independently. Students then began to write their own folktales. Their learning became evident when the children inserted information learned in the study into the writing of their folktales, "especially by creating new animal characters such as gazelles or African buffalo" (p. 4).

Similarities and differences among cultures can also be explored. The tale of *Yeh-Shen* conveys much information about Chinese culture during the ninth century: hair styles, dress, and the beauty of small feet—all of which are stereotypes that continue to be perpetrated in our society today. As a starting point, have students create a chart of culturally specific details of what life is like in China today. Students can prepare the chart in small groups or individual research projects.

## LANGUAGE ARTS

Myths and legends are typically studied in English classes, but they can be used in social studies to discuss how early humanity explained the natural world in the absence of scientific information. Children can also find allusions to myths or mythical characters referred to frequently in everyday vocabulary, art, advertising, scientific and medical terms, and literature, such as Venus pencils, Achilles tendon, arachnid, the Olympics, the names of the planets, and the days of the week.

*Read* 

*Read an interview with Donna Jo Napoli.*

Many folktales and fairy tales have been developed into longer books. Donna Jo Napoli has written several stories based on folktales: *The Prince of the Pond*, *Jimmy, The Pickpocket of the Palace,* and *Gracie, the Pixie of the Puddle* (The Frog Prince), *Bound* (Chinese Cinderella Yeh-Shen), *The Magic Circle* (Hansel and Gretel), *Crazy Jack* (Jack and the Beanstalk), *Beast* (Beauty and the Beast), *Spinners* (Rumpelstiltskin), and *Zel* (Rapunzel). Older children can see how Napoli recreates these folktales with fuller characters, more developed settings, and more intricate plot structures.

Many times, tall tales are based on real people who were given a larger-than-life twist, such as Daniel Boone. Children can research the actual historical character to determine the point at which a character turns into a tall tale. By identifying the literary devices of understatement and exaggeration, children can choose any figure in history and create their own tall tales.

## MATH AND SCIENCE

Even mathematical principles can be illustrated by using folk literature, such as exponential growth in Demi's *One Grain of Rice: A Mathematical Folktale* and Hong's *Two of Everything: A Chinese Folktale.* Pourquoi or "why" tales, such as Hausman's *How Chipmunk Got Tiny Feet: Native American Animal Origin Stories,* can be used to discuss animal camouflage and adaptation in science class.

# Top 10 Read Alouds

## TRADITIONAL TALES

1. **Glass Slipper, Gold Sandal: A Worldwide Cinderella** by Paul Fleischman, illustrated by Julie Paschkis (2007, Henry Holt). The author draws from a variety of folk traditions to put together this version of Cinderella, including elements from Mexico, Iran, Korea, Russia, Appalachia, and more.

2. **How the Stars Fell into the Sky: A Navajo Legend** by Jerrie Oughton, illustrated by Lisa Desimini (1996, Houghton Mifflin). A retelling of the Navajo legend that explains the patterns of the stars in the sky.

3. **The Hunter** by Mary Casanova, illustrated by Ed Young (2000, Atheneum). After learning to understand the language of animals, Hai Li Bu the hunter sacrifices himself to save his village.

4. **Lion and the Mouse** by Jerry Pinkney (2009, Little, Brown). In this wordless retelling of an Aesop fable set in the African Serengeti, an adventuresome mouse proves that even small creatures are capable of great deeds when she rescues the King of the Jungle.

5. **Where the Mountain Meets the Moon** by Grace Lin (2009, Little, Brown). Minli, an adventurous girl from a poor village, buys a magical goldfish and then joins a dragon who cannot fly on a quest to find the Old Man of the Moon in hopes of bringing life to Fruitless Mountain and freshness to Jade River.

6. **Peggony-Po: A Whale of a Tale** by Andrea Pinkney, illustrated by Brian Pinkney (2006, Hyperion). Peggony-Po, carved out of wood by his father, a one-legged whaler, determines to catch the huge whale that ate his father's leg.

7. **Rapunzel** by Paul Zelinsky (1997, Dutton). A retelling of a folktale in which a beautiful girl with long, golden hair is kept imprisoned in a lonely tower by a sorceress.

8. **Silly & Sillier: Read Aloud Tales from Around the World** by Judy Sierra, illustrated by Valeri Gorbachev (2002, Knopf). A compilation of folktales from 20 different cultures, each of which contains elements suited to storytelling for young children.

9. **The Three Princes: A Tale from the Middle East** by Eric Kimmel, illustrated by Leonard Fisher (1994, Holiday House). A princess promises to marry the prince who finds the most precious treasure.

10. **Why Mosquitoes Buzz in People's Ears** by Verna Aardema, illustrated by Leo and Diane Dillon (1975, Dial). A retelling of a traditional West African tale that reveals how the mosquito developed its annoying habit.

# Activities for Professional Development

## Think Critically About Children's Literature

1. Snow White is a common fairy tale that has many versions from around the world. Comparing and contrasting the different versions of characters, settings, actions, and themes can reveal cultural differences and universal themes. To experience this, go to Kay Vandergrift's site: http://comminfo. rutgers.edu/professional-development/ childlit/snowwhite.html. From here, click "Snow White" Text. Here, Vandergrift, a children's literature expert, has reprinted the original 1898 version of the Grimm's fairy tale. Throughout the text, certain phrases are hyperlinked. When clicked, the reader can compare the hyperlinked text to thirty-six other versions. What are the differences among the textual interpretations of the story? Are the different versions intended for different audiences? Go back to the main menu and click "Snow White" Illustrations. Here, Vandergrift provides illustrations from different versions of Snow White over time. As you look at the pictures, think about the questions Vandergrift poses after each set of illustrations.

2. Find the original version of your favorite fairy tale, possibly by Charles Perrault or the Grimm Brothers, and compare it to subsequent retellings. How do different retellings reflect the time period of when it was published and the audience for which it was intended? Rewrite the traditional tale to reflect the current time period.

3. Visit the virtual Osborne Collection's sixtieth anniversary exhibit, *When Cinderella Went to the Ball: Five Hundred Years of Fairy Tales.* (http://ve.torontopubliclibrary. ca/cinderella/index.html). The exhibit "progresses from a fifteenth-century Venetian wonder tale (*Historia di Lionbruno,* 1476), through "classic" stories and collections by Charles Perrault, the Brothers Grimm and others, to today's spin-offs, spoofs and "post-modern" interpretations." How have the illustrations for fairy tales changed over the years. What were the influences for these changes?

4. During a professional development session with 12 classroom teachers, Dr. Mileidis Gort presents research-based principles that support English language learners' literacy and language development. To view this professional development session, go to the Annenberg Media video series, *Teaching Reading K–2 Workshop,* at http://www.learner.org/ resources/series175.html.

   • Read the description of the *Teaching Reading K–2 Workshop* and then click on "enter the series website." Then click on "supporting the English Language Learner." Click on "video summary" to read about the video you will be viewing.

   • The teachers watch a classroom excerpt showing a teacher using the folktale *The Runaway Rice Cake* by Ying Chang Compestine with a classroom of English language learners. After the teachers watch the classroom excerpt, they discuss how various versions of folktales extend the students' understanding of reading and writing.

   • Later in the video, the teachers create a lesson plan around children's books, including The Legend of the Bluebonnet by Tomie dePaola. Return to the video and watch the following segments: lecture, classroom excerpts, and discussion. After watching each video segment, respond to the questions provided. This video series shows how teachers create effective literacy lessons for English language learners.

# Print and Online Resources

## Print Resources

Bettelheim, B. (1976). *The uses of enchantment: The meaning and importance of fairy tales.* New York: Random House.

Bomhold, C., & Elder, T. (2008). *Twice upon a time: A guide to fractured, altered, and retold folk and fairy tales.* Santa Barbara, CA: Libraries Unlimited.

Charles, V. (2010). *Fairy tales in the classroom: Teaching students to write stories with meaning through traditional tales.* Markham, Ontario: Fitzhenry & Whiteside.

Kimbell-Lopez, K. (1999). *Connecting with traditional literature: Using folktales, fables, and legends to strengthen students' reading and writing.* Needham Heights, MA: Allyn & Bacon.

Lurie, A. (1990). *Don't tell the grown-ups: The subversive power of children's literature.* New York: Little, Brown.

Zipes, J. (2002). *Breaking the magic spell: Radical theories of folk & fairy tales.* Lexington: University Press of Kentucky.

 **ONLINE RESOURCES**

### The Cinderella Project
**http://www.usm.edu/english/fairytales/ cinderella/cinderella.html**
Hosted by the University of Southern Mississippi, the Cinderella Project houses text and image archives containing a dozen English versions of the fairy tale. From this site, the *Little Red Riding Hood Project* and the *Jack and the Beanstalk and Jack the Giant-Killer Project* may also be accessed, each housing multiple versions of the respective fairy tale.

### Kay Vandergrift's Scholarly Snow White
**http://comminfo.rutgers.edu/professional-development/childlit/snowwhite.html**
This site, developed by Dr. Kay Vandergrift of Rutgers University, brings together a number of resources on the tale of *Snow White* so that groups or individuals can focus on the traditional tale and study it in different versions and variants published over an extended time frame.

### The Rosetta Project
**http://www.childrensbooksonline.org**
The Rosetta Project is an online collection of antique books, many of which are traditional tales. The books are divided into prereader, early reader, intermediate reader, and advanced reader.

### Scholastic's Myths, Folktales, and Fairy Tales
**http://teacher.scholastic.com/writewit/mff/ index.htm**
On this website, students learn from authors Jane Yolen, Alma Flor Ada and Rafe Martin, Nina Jaffe, and John Sciezka to develop their skills in writing myths, fairy tales, and folktales. Each "workshop" provides step-by-step guidance through the writing process.

### SurLaLune Fairy Tales
**http://www.surlalunefairytales.com**
SurLaLune Fairy Tales features 49 annotated fairy tales, including their histories, similar tales across cultures, modern interpretations, and over 1,500 illustrations. Also discover over 1,600 folktales & fairy tales from around the world in more than 40 full-text eBooks. A discussion forum is also available. A link to Introduction to Fairy Tale Studies, an assortment of questions, essays, guides, links, is provided.

### Telling Stories: Using Drama and Multimedia with ESL Students
**http://www.prel.org/eslstrategies/multimedia.html**
Technology-based projects allow ESL students to draw on their cultural strengths and background experiences, which may otherwise go unnoticed. This site, sponsored by Pacific Resources for Education and Learning (PREL), has lesson plans and examples of creative projects that incorporate visual and aural media to address different learning styles and modalities such as creating digital books, digital storytelling, and digital show and tell. By constructing knowledge, students become active learners, researchers, and producers and can take pride in their accomplishments.

Visit the companion website at **www.cengage.com/education/johnson** to find links related to the Read/Watch/Listen icons noted throughout the chapter, as well as additional resources.

# Creating Your Classroom Library

## COLLECTIONS

*Aesop's Fables* by Jerry Pinkney (2000, SeaStar Books). A collection of nearly 60 fables from Aesop, including such familiar ones as "The Grasshopper and the Ants," "The North Wind and the Sun," "Androcles and the Lion," "The Troublesome Dog," and "The Fox and the Stork."

*Aesop's Fables* by Lisbeth Zweger (1991, Simon & Schuster). Twelve illustrated fables including familiar and not-so-familiar tales.

*The Annotated Classic Fairy Tales* edited by Maria Tarter (2002, Norton). This collection includes 26 fairy tales, biographies of the authors/collectors, and biographies of the illustrators.

*The Complete Fairy Tales of Charles Perrault* translated by Neil Philip and Nicoletta Simborowski, illustrated by Sally Holmes (1993, Houghton Mifflin). This collection includes all 11 tales attributed to Perrault.

*Favorite Folktales from Around the World* edited by Jane Yolen (1986, Pantheon). The 160 tales from the oral tradition are grouped thematically.

*Favorite Greek Myths* by Mary Osborne, illustrated by Troy Howell (1989, Scholastic). Twelve illustrated Greek myths, with an index of Greek names and words in the English language from Greek myths.

*The Great Fairy Tale Tradition: From Straparola and Basile to the Brothers Grimm* edited and translated by Jack Zipes (2001, Norton). This collection includes 116 fairy tales grouped thematically and accompanied by detailed introductions and annotations. Seven "criticism" selections provide insight into different aspects of the fairy tale tradition.

*The People Could Fly: American Black Folktales* told by Virginia Hamilton (1985, Random House). Retold Afro-American folktales of animals, fantasy, the supernatural, and desire for freedom, born of the sorrow of the slaves, but passed on in hope.

*Porch Lies: Tales of Slicksters, Tricksters, and Other Wily Characters* by Patricia McKissack (2006, Random House). Side-splittingly funny, spine-chillingly spooky, this anthology is filled with bad characters who know exactly how to charm.

## PICTUREBOOKS

*Anansi and the Moss-Covered Rock* by Eric A. Kimmel, illustrated by Janet Stevens (1988, Holiday House). Anansi the Spider uses a strange moss-covered rock in the forest to trick all the other animals, until Little Bush Deer decides he needs to learn a lesson.

*Beautiful Blackbird* by Ashley Bryan (2003, Atheneum). In a story of the Ila people, the colorful birds of Africa ask Blackbird, who they think is the most beautiful of all the birds, to decorate them with some of his "blackening brew."

*The Bossy Gallito: A Traditional Cuban Folk Tale* retold by Lucia M. Gonzalez, illustrated by Lulu Delacre (1994, Scholastic). In this cumulative Cuban folktale, a bossy rooster dirties his beak when he eats a kernel of corn and must find a way to clean it before his parrot uncle's wedding.

*The Girl Who Loved Wild Horses* by Paul Goble (1985, Bradbury). Although she is fond of her people, a girl prefers to live among the wild horses, where she is truly happy and free.

*Golem* by David Wisniewski (1996, Houghton Mifflin). A saintly rabbi miraculously brings to life a clay giant, who helps him watch over the Jews of sixteenth-century Prague.

*It Could Always be Worse: A Yiddish Folk Tale* retold by Margot Zemach (1976, Farrar, Straus and Giroux). Unable to stand his overcrowded and noisy home any longer, a poor man goes to the Rabbi for advice.

*John Henry* by Julius Lester; illustrated by Jerry Pinkney (1994, Dial). Retells the life of the legendary African American hero who raced against a steam drill to cut through a mountain.

*The Little Red Hen: An Old Story* by Margot Zemach (1983, Farrar, Straus and Giroux). A retelling of the traditional tale about the little red hen whose lazy friends are unwilling to help her plant, harvest, or grind the wheat into flour, but all are willing to help her eat the bread that she makes from it.

*Little Red Riding Hood* by Grimm Brothers, illustrated by T. Hyman (1982, Holiday House). On her way to deliver a basket of food to her sick grandmother, Elisabeth encounters a sly wolf.

*Mabela the Clever* by Margaret MacDonald (2000, Albert Whitman). An African folktale about a mouse who pays close attention to her surroundings and avoids being tricked by the cat.

*Mufaro's Beautiful Daughters: An African Tale* by John Steptoe (1987, Amistad). Mufaro's two beautiful daughters, one bad-tempered, one kind and sweet, go before the king, who is looking for a wife. An African variant of *Cinderella*.

*The Rough-Face Girl* by Rafe Martin, illustrated by David Shannon (1992, Putnam). In this Algonquin Indian version of the Cinderella story, the Rough-Face Girl and her two beautiful but heartless sisters compete for the affections of the Invisible Being.

*Rumpelstiltskin* by Paul Zelinsky (1986, Dutton). A strange little man helps the miller's daughter spin straw into gold for the king on the condition that she will give him her first-born child. Retold and illustrated by Paul O. Zelinsky.

*Sir Gawain and the Loathly Lady* retold by Selina Hastings, illustrated by Juan Wijngarrd (1981, Lothrop Lee & Shepard). After a horrible hag saves King Arthur's life by answering a riddle, Sir Gawain agrees to marry her and thus releases her from an evil enchantment.

*Snow White and the Seven Dwarfs* by Grimm Brothers, translated by Randall Jarrell, illustrated by Nancy Burkert (1972, Farrar, Straus and Giroux). A stunning version of the Grimms' classic story.

*Swamp Angel* by Anne Isaacs, illustrated by Paul Zelinsky (1994, Dutton). Along with other amazing feats, Angelica Longrider, also known as Swamp Angel, wrestles a huge bear, known as Thundering Tarnation, to save the winter supplies of the settlers in Tennessee.

*The Three Bears* by Paul Galdone (1985, Perfection Learning). Three bears return from a walk and find a little girl asleep in baby bear's bed.

*Tops & Bottoms* by Janet Stevens (1995, Harcourt). Hare turns his bad luck around by striking a clever deal with the rich and lazy bear down the road. Caldecott Honor book.

*Trisba & Sula: A Miskitu Folktale from Nicaragua* adapted by Joan MacCracken (2005, Triffin). A young Miskitu man loses his father and must provide for his mother. Initially, he hunts too many deer. With a magical twist, his love for a beautiful young woman helps him realize his unwise practice.

*Yummy: Eight Favorite Fairy Tales* by Lucy Cousins (2009, Candlewick). Eight classic stories are retold and illustrated by the author.

*Zomo the Rabbit: A Trickster Tale from West Africa* retold and illustrated by Gerald McDermott (1992, Harcourt Brace Jovanovich). Zomo the Rabbit, an African trickster, sets out to gain wisdom.

## OTHER CHAPTER BOOKS AND COLLECTIONS

*American Tall Tales* by Mary Osborne, illustrated by Michael McCurdy (1991, Knopf.). A collection of tall tales about such American folk heroes as Sally Ann Thunder Ann Whirlwind, Pecos Bill, John Henry, and Paul Bunyan.

*Best-Loved Folktales of the World* by Joanna Cole (1983, Anchor). A collection of more than 200 folktales and fairy tales from all over the world.

*Complete Brothers Grimm Fairy Tales* edited by Lilly Owens (1993, Gramercy). The collection presents all 215 illustrated stories recorded by the Brothers Grimm.

*Complete Hans Christian Andersen Fairy Tales* edited by Lilly Owens (1993, Gramercy). The collection consists of 159 illustrated tales.

*Her Stories: African American Folktales, Fairy Tales and True Tales* told by Virginia Hamilton, illustrated by Leo and Diane Dillon (1995, Blue Sky). A collection of 17 tales, each featuring an African-American woman or girl as the main character.

# References

Boyd-Batstone, P. (1997). Learning to walk together in a third-grade bilingual classroom: From transmission to transaction instruction in literature. In N. Karolides (Ed.), *Reader response in elementary classrooms: Quest and discovery* (pp. 187–212). Mahwah, NJ: Erlbaum.

Goble, P. (1994). *Hau kola: Hello friend.* Katonah, NY: Richard Owen.

Hearne, B. (1993). Cite the source: Reducing cultural chaos in picture books, part one. *School Library Journal, 39*(7), 22–27.

Horning, K. (1997). *From cover to cover: Evaluating and reviewing children's books.* New York: HarperCollins.

Jacobs, J., & Tunnell, M. (2004). *Children's literature, briefly* (3rd ed.). Upper Saddle River, NJ: Merrill.

Long, S., & Sibberson, F. (2006). Broadening visions of what counts: Honoring home and community literacies. *School Talk, 11*(4).

Louie, A. (1982). *Yeh-Shen: A Cinderella story from China.* New York: Philomel.

Lurie, A. (1990). *Don't tell the grown-ups: The subversive power of children's literature.* Boston: Little, Brown.

Mello, R. (2001). Cinderella meets Ulysses. *Language Arts, 78*(6), 548–555.

Mellon, C. (1987). Folk tales as picture books: Visual literacy or oral tradition? *School Library Journal, 33,* 46–48.

Mo, W., & Shen, W. (1997). Reexamining the issue of authenticity in picture books. *Children's Literature in Education, 28*(2), 85–93.

Mo, W., & Shen W. (2003). Accuracy is not enough: The role of cultural values in the authenticity of picture books. In D. Fox & K. Short (Eds.), *Stories matter: The complexity of cultural authenticity in children's literature* (pp. 198–212). Urbana, IL: National Council of Teachers of English.

Nodelman, P. (1988). *Words about pictures.* Athens: University of Georgia Press.

Nodelman, P., & Reimer, M. (2003). *The pleasures of children's literature* (3rd ed.). Boston: Allyn & Bacon.

Norton, D. (2001). *Multicultural children's literature: Through the eyes of many children.* Upper Saddle River, NJ: Merrill.

Opie, I., & Opie, P. (1974). *The classic fairy tales.* London: Oxford University Press.

Pierce, K. (2002). Studying African folktales in the primary grades. In J. Hansen & V. Vasquez (Eds.), *School talk: Genre studies* (pp. 3–4). Urbana, IL: National Council of Teachers of English.

Rudman, M. (1997). Folktales, fairy tales and legends: Fantasy and the imagination. In D. Muse (Ed.), *The New Press guide to multicultural resources for young readers* (p. 369). New York: New Press.

Russell, D. (2005) *Literature for children* (5th ed.). Boston: Allyn & Bacon.

Sierra, J. (1996). *Nursery tales around the world.* New York: Houghton Mifflin.

Yokota, J. (1993). Issues in selecting multicultural children's literature. *Language Arts, 70*(3), 156–176.

Young, T., & Ferguson, P. (1995). From Anansi to Zomo: Trickster tales in the classroom. *The Reading Teacher, 48*(6), 490–503.

Zipes, J. (2002). *Breaking the magic spell: Radical theories of folk and fairy tales.* Lexington: University Press of Kentucky.

# Modern Fantasy

> What is most important about fantasy, what separates and frees it from the boundaries of other genres, is that it is an undistilled version of human imagination—momentary worlds and magic that may be at odds with the rational truth, yet continue to reflect our culture and times.
>
> —*Melissa Thomas, 2003, p. 63*

On July 20, 2007, my son, Derek, and I joined the line in front of a local bookstore awaiting the release of the seventh and final book in the Harry Potter series: *Harry Potter and the Deathly Hallows.* Yes, there was a *very* long line to get in the store. Yes, the books could not be purchased until midnight and we didn't get ours until after 1:00 a.m. Yes, people came dressed in Harry Potter paraphernalia and speculated on how the author, J. K. Rowling, would end the series. Call us naive for buying into the hype of mass marketing by Scholastic, the U.S. publisher of the Harry Potter books, and a little crazy for staying up until 2:30 a.m. reading our prize—but we were in fantasy heaven!

## Defining Modern Fantasy

*Watch*

*Watch J. K. Rowling reading an excerpt from* Harry Potter and the Deathly Hallows *and an interview about her thoughts on ending the series.*

*My son, like many children,* is an avid reader of fantasy. With its roots in folktales, legends, and myths, fantasy takes us beyond the world as we know it, defying the natural laws of physics, to a world where animals can talk, people can perform magic, and other worlds exist. Even though there are parallels between folklore and modern fantasy, such as heroes taking on great danger and rising to impossible challenges, folklore is grounded in cultural belief and shaped by the storyteller, whereas modern fantasy is shaped by the author's artistic vision.

A testament to the power of fantasy is that almost half of the books identified in *One Hundred Books That Shaped the Century* (Breen, Fader, Odean, & Sutherland, 2000) are fantasy, and half of the books listed in *100 Best Books for Children* (Silvey, 2004) are fantasy. Why does fantasy hold such a lofty position? One reason may be that fantasy unites the child's view of the world with her inherent fascination for magic. The meanings fantasy generates come out of the author's ability to refer to the "real world" recognized by the reader and, at the same time, to create an "other world" that the reader can accept in its context. At the intersection where fantasy blends with reality, fantasy writers are able to speak to our deepest emotions, our darkest fears, and our highest hopes.

## CATEGORIES AND MOTIFS IN MODERN FANTASY

Modern fantasy stories are classified into two categories: low fantasy and high fantasy. Stories considered to be low fantasy take place in the real world but magical elements of fantasy make them impossible. E. B. White's *Charlotte's Web* and Beatrix Potter's *The Tale of Peter Rabbit* are both examples of low fantasy that are classified as animal fantasy because the animals in the story live in a realistic place, but they are able to speak. Margery Williams's *The Velveteen Rabbit* and Michael Bond's *A Bear Called Paddington* are low fantasy and are classified as toy fantasy because the toys, which also live in the real world, are "alive." Stories about animals and toys that talk are among the best-loved fantasy and are excellent stories for introducing young children to this genre. The fact that the animals and toys can talk and are given human characteristics is the only magical element or motif in these stories; everything else is consistent with the real world. Other categories of fantasy are listed in Table 6.1. Stories considered to be low fantasy are usually lighthearted and center on concerns of younger children, such as home, family, or self-identity.

| TABLE 6.1 | | |
|---|---|---|
| **Categories in Modern Fantasy** | | |
| **Category** | **Description** | **Selected Examples** |
| Animals | Attributes human thoughts, feelings, and language through animals that have human characteristics | *Wind in the Willows* by Kenneth Grahame *Whittington* by Alan Armstrong *Emmy and the Incredible Shrinking Rats* by Lynne Jonell |
| Toys and Objects | Demonstrates belief in human characteristics children give their playthings | *Winnie the Pooh* by A. A. Milne *The Mouse and His Child* by Russell Hoban *Toys Go Out* by Emily Jenkins |
| Miniature Worlds | Highlights human emotions by displaying them in action on a miniscule level | *The Borrowers* by Mary Norton *The Littles* by John Peterson *The Doll People* by Ann Martin |

*(continued)*

**TABLE 6.1**

*(continued)*

# Categories in Modern Fantasy

| Category | Description | Selected Examples |
|---|---|---|
| Time Warps | Focus on central character going through difficult adjustment periods, such as loneliness, alienation, and sensitivity associated with time travel | *Inkspell* by Cornelia Funke *When You Reach Me* by Rebecca Stead *11 Birthdays* by Wendy Mass |
| Unreal Worlds | Setting of the story is in a fantasy land, although the great amount of detail makes the fantasy world believable to the reader | *Coraline* by Neil Gaiman *The Phantom Tollbooth* by Norton Juster *The BFG* by Roald Dahl |
| Ghost Stories | Stories about ghosts and spirits who haunt the real or imaginary world | *The Blue Ghost* by Marion Bauer *Golden & Grey* by Louise Arnold *The Seer of Shadows* by Avi |
| Magic Powers | Characters possess magical objects, know a magical saying, or have magical powers themselves | *Magic by the Book* by Nina Bernstein *Half Magic* by Edward Eager *My Father's Dragon* by Ruth Stiles Gannett |
| Preposterous Characters/ Situations | Characters developed through vivid and descriptive images of dress, features, and actions | *James and the Giant Peach* by Roald Dahl *Whales on Stilts* by M. T. Anderson *The Magic School Bus* by Joanna Cole |
| Quest Tales | Borrow magical settings and characters from traditional tales of heroism; a common theme is the victory of good over evil; often becomes a search for an inner enemy rather than an outer enemy | *The Book of Three* by Lloyd Alexander *The Golden Compass* by Philip Pullman *The Lightning Thief* by Rick Riordan |

High fantasy takes the information and experiences from the real world and projects them into an "other world." According to Winters and Schmidt (2001), "High fantasy involves difficult and arduous journeys, supernatural characters who are both benign and malignant, a gathered set of companions who will contribute to the fulfilling of the quest, a quest object that is often magical, a cause that is just and right, and tasks that test the

*Read*

*Read* The Wonderful Wizard of Oz *and the* Oz Collection.

worth of the protagonist" (p. 199). High fantasy employs most if not all of the six fantasy motifs (Figure 6.1) within the same story. Stories of high fantasy typically have a serious tone and are read by older children. Examples of high fantasy that have endured over the years are L. Frank Baum's *The Wonderful Wizard of Oz*, J. R. R. Tolkien's *The Lord of the Rings* trilogy, and C. S. Lewis's *The Lion, the Witch and the Wardrobe.*

The Land of Oz, Middle Earth, and Narnia are magical "other worlds" created by the authors in which unlikely heroes such as Dorothy, Frodo, Lucy, Peter, Edmund, and Susan embark upon an arduous quest involving fantastic objects such as a pair of ruby slippers, a golden ring, and a wardrobe that ultimately takes them through many battles with special characters such as winged monkeys, Orcs, fauns, and centaurs in the fight against evil. At the end of the quest, the children have grown toward maturity and independence rather than the security of home and family. Literary folktales and science fiction are unique categories of fantasy and are discussed in the next section.

**Literary Folktales.** As discussed in Chapter 5, contemporary writers intentionally use folklore elements in stories or expand upon well-known traditional tales to create

---

**FIGURE 6.1**

# Motifs in Modern Fantasy

Low fantasy ........

High fantasy ........

| Motifs | Definition | Examples |
|---|---|---|
| Magic | A basic element in fantasy | Talking animals in *Charlotte's Web* |
| Other Worlds | A special place or world in which magic is used freely. The story may start in the realistic world and move to a magical world or take place entirely in the magical world. | The wizard world in the *Harry Potter* series Middle Earth in *The Lord of the Rings* |
| Good vs. Evil | A basic theme in modern fantasy that gives rise to the conflict in the story | Dorothy and the wicked witch in *The Wizard of Oz* |
| Heroism | The hero's quest takes him or her on a circular journey that ends where it began | The children in *The Lion, the Witch and the Wardrobe* |
| Special Character Types | Characters from the legendary past (fairies, giants, ogres) or the author's imagination | The ogre in *Shrek!* The hobbits in *The Lord of the Rings* |
| Fantastic Objects | Magical objects that assist in accomplishing a heroic or evil deed | Magic wands, brooms, slippers, rings |

full-length novels. These stories are called literary folktales. Sometimes these stories are confused with traditional tales because they are so similar. In *The Book Without Words*, Avi creates a fable with a clear message about humanity and the evils of materialism. In *Bound*, Donna Napoli maintains the central story of *Yen-Shen*, the Chinese version of Cinderella, while fleshing out and enriching the story with well-rounded characters and information about a specific time and place in Chinese history. In *Bella at Midnight*, Diane Stanley gives the female role in the tale of Cinderella a few twists and deviations from the original. Instead of a modest heroine patiently awaiting a prince to rescue her, Bella is a spirited and courageous girl with the ambition to take matters into her own hands. In *The Looking Glass Wars*, author Frank Beddor puts quite a spin on *Alice in Wonderland*. In this version, young Alyss Heart is cast out of Wonderland by her evil Aunt Redd and finds herself living in Victorian Oxford as Alice Liddell as she struggles to keep memories of her kingdom until she can return and claim her rightful throne.

*Listen*

Listen to an excerpt of The Looking Glass Wars.

Fractured folktales deliberately imitate traditional tales but add modern settings and gender roles as well as reversed points of view and twisted plot lines to add humor, such as in Jon Scieszka's *Squids Will Be Squids*.

**Science Fiction.** Science fiction is a type of fantasy in which the author hypothesizes about the future or the nature of the universe based on real scientific concepts. Whereas fantasy stories are based on unexplainable magic that could never happen, science fiction stories have the possibility of happening given enough time, new knowledge, and advancements in technology. Armed with a plausible premise, science fiction writers make readers believe the unbelievable because they convince them it is possible. Therefore, the setting, characters, and plot must be consistent, logical, and believable. This requires detailed descriptions of the scientific concepts or principles and the characters' understanding and acceptance of them.

Themes in science fiction typically resemble that of heroic fantasy, with magic replaced by technology. The story might start out in the real world and move to another world through some scientific process, as in *A Wrinkle in Time* by Madeleine L'Engle, or take place wholly in another world or in the future, as in *The Giver* by Lois Lowry, *The City of Ember* by Jeanne DuPrau, and *The House of the Scorpion* by Nancy Farmer. The hero in the story usually struggles to fight some form of evil such as aliens, robots, mind control, or environmental catastrophes. Yet, at the heart of science fiction are serious questions about our own world that can be explored from a safe distance with clearer vision. Many times students have strong reactions to science fiction. In "The Teacher's Voice" on page 152, a teacher in a children's literature course responds to *The House of the Scorpion*. (See illustration 4 in the Part 2 Visual Discussion.)

*Watch*

Watch a video of Nancy Farmer.

In *A Wrinkle in Time,* L'Engle creates a realistic foundation with the main characters of Meg Murry and Charles Wallace, the children of eminent scientists. They are very intelligent and do not fit in with other children in their town. When their father, secretly engaged in work for the government, disappears in his effort to fight the "dark thing," the children use theoretical physics to induce time and space travel to the fifth dimension to find their father and fight the evil power of "It." Meg's deep love for her father and Charles is what saves them. Unthinking conformity, scientific irresponsibility, and the power of love are all thought-provoking themes explored in this story.

Good science fiction allows children to consider possibilities that go well beyond their everyday reality, thus educating the imagination. By entering the world of possibility and speculation, science fiction nurtures children's capacity for invention and intuition.

# T H E · T E A C H E R ' S · V O I C E

A *Journal Response to* The House of the Scorpion

The House of the Scorpion by Nancy Farmer is science fiction and reminiscent, in many ways, of The Giver. Matteo Alacrán, the protagonist, is a clone of El Patron, the drug lord and leader of Opium. Opium is one of many countries bordering the U.S. and what was once Mexico.

The young Matteo is raised in seclusion and secrecy by Celia, a servant of El Patron, until he is five. Out of curiosity, he breaks a window and is discovered. He is thrown into a stable/dungeon until El Patron becomes aware of his plight.

As the story continues, Matteo is at once given special treatment and ostracized as an animal. Like Jonas from The Giver, his destiny has been selected for him. Unlike Jonas, however, Matteo does not fully understand his fate. Where Jonas explored the dangers of his environment and society philosophically, Matteo experiences his dangers firsthand. He discovers ejits, or people whose brains have been stunted to provide nonresistant labor.

Matteo is forced to flee Opium to save his own life, but he returns to save the others who live in Opium. Jonas left his society to save it and return its memories. Both are presented as heroic but reluctant.

I found The House of the Scorpion to be frightening. Biologically, everything seemed possible. Description of life for the immediate servants and family of El Patron did not seem far-fetched. The ecological disaster and political systems presented seem possible in the next few hundred years. The level of evil of those in power did not seem unrealistic. All of the characters were presented as complicated people with conflicting motivations and emotions. This added to the realism and to the themes of good and evil coexisting and struggling against one another among and within each other.

In Kate DiCamillo's Newbery acceptance speech, she addresses, much more eloquently than I, the theme of good and evil existing in every person. She quotes Einstein's perspective on living life as though everything were a miracle or as though nothing was. I'd like to think that Matteo came to the first conclusion. Though he was genetically engineered and ultimately manipulated by intentions larger than his own, his own life is a miracle as is his survival of it.

I don't generally like science fiction, but I found this book compelling and engrossing. On some level, it was like an ancient Greek epic. There was a clear sense of journey—at times literal and at times metaphorical.

*—How does this teacher's comparison of* The House of the Scorpion *to* The Giver *and other sources inform her response?*

# Benefits and Considerations of Modern Fantasy

Fantasy writers can explore complex ideas on a symbolic level that would otherwise be difficult to convey to young readers. Well-written fantasy is simply a metaphor that illustrates the truth about life in a way that realistic fiction or informational writing cannot. Jacobs and Tunnell (2008) explain as follows:

> Children can read directly about friendship, sacrifice, selfishness, the fear of death, and death itself, but the insight is somehow more meaningful when shown metaphorically through the lives of Wilbur the pig, Templeton the rat, and Charlotte the spider in *Charlotte's Web*. (p. 122)

*Watch*

*Watch an interview with Anita Silvey.*

Of course, the only way to know this is true is to ask adults how fantasy literature shaped them as children. In the book *Everything I Need to Know I Learned from a Children's Book* (2009), children's literature expert Anita Silvey does just that. Of the 110 essays of accomplished Americans—businessmen, politicians, artists, athletes, authors, and actors—over half reveal that fantasy literature provided them with inspiration, understanding, and motivation and instilled principles and the desire for storytelling. For example, expert photographer and author Maureen Taylor writes,

> At the end of fifth grade my favorite childhood book was Madeline L'Engle's *A Wrinkle in Time*. I read it through several times in one summer. I still own a copy. Meg was my hero. I immediately identified with her—we had poor handwriting, were clumsy, and wore glasses. I felt I understood her angst because we were both at an awkward age. I found it refreshing that a female protagonist could be intelligent and engage in scientific inquiry. It was a very powerful book for me . . . *From A Wrinkle in Time* I learned to believe in myself and—from Meg I learned that it was important to question everything. (p. 97)

Fantasy is perfectly suited to thoughtful exploration of philosophical issues at a level that can be understood and appreciated by children.

### BENEFITS

I recently attended a presentation by Newbery author Lois Lowry, during which she shared a story that illustrates how fantasy literature like *Charlotte's Web* can bring insight to reality for children. Her son Ben, then eight years old, took his bunny rabbit, Barney, outside to play on the lawn when suddenly the neighbor's German shepherd came bounding out of his own yard and grabbed Barney by the neck. Ben rescued Barney, who was mortally wounded, and placed him in his bed. Lowry (2005) continues the story:

> Some time later Ben came to me and told me that Barney had died. Together we planned a funeral. And Ben explained what he had been thinking about as he lay there beside Barney. He was remembering, he told me, the saddest sentence he had ever read. Page 171 of *Charlotte's Web*. "No one was with her when she died," was the sentence. There is something profoundly moving about a man, a gifted writer, E. B. White, who was able to put down on a page eight words "No one was with her when she died" . . . . that went to the heart of a little boy and taught him something about loneliness and loss. (p. 9)

*In this beloved classic, Wilbur the pig is devastated when he learns he is destined to be the farmer's Christmas dinner until Charlotte, his spider friend, uses her "terrific" webs to help him.*

A gifted writer herself, Lois Lowry knows a thing or two about writing fantasy stories that speak to the hearts and minds of children. Her Newbery award–winning book, *The Giver*, is set in a futuristic utopian world with no poverty, no crime, no sickness, no unemployment, and no memories of the past. When 12-year-old Jonas is chosen to be the community's Receiver of Memories under the guidance of one of the Elders, an old man known as the Giver, he discovers the disturbing truth about his utopian world and struggles against the weight of its hypocrisy. The fact that this story takes place in a futuristic society that does not exist provides enough distance from reality for us to question our own deeply held values and beliefs.

*Watch*

*Watch a video of Lois Lowry.*

### CONSIDERATIONS

*The Giver* ranked twenty-second out of the one hundred most frequently challenged books from 2000 to 2009 (American Library Association). When a book is challenged by an individual or group, it is an attempt to ban or restrict materials in a public library or school, based on the objections of a person or group. A successful challenge results in materials being banned or restricted (see Chapter 7 for more information on censorship). One of the reasons given for a recent challenge to *The Giver* by a parent group was a statement about the book on the inside jacket cover: "In the telling it questions every value we have taken for granted and reexamines our most deeply held beliefs." One parent commented, "Everything presented to the kids should be positive or historical, not nega-tive" (*Kansas City Star*, 2005). Lowry (2005) responded by explaining how important it was for people to question their own beliefs and values every day and to teach their children to do the same.

The *Harry Potter* series ranked first on the list of most frequently challenged books from 2000 to 2009. Some adults believe that reading about magic spells and witches will lead children to practices of witchcraft, Satanism, or the occult. J. K. Rowling has said that she believes children can tell the difference between reality and fantasy and that she has never heard of a child wanting to be a witch after reading her books (Schafer, 2000). Furthermore, Strimel (2004) argues that the scenarios presented in the series teach chil-dren strategies for coping with both physical and psychological victimization and allows children to "analyze terror-related questions such as why some people are considered evil, why difference is often believed to be bad, and why good people do bad things" (p. 35). Strimel provides evidence for her assertion through children's letters about Harry Potter written for an essay contest titled "How Harry Potter Books Changed My Life," conducted by Scholastic, the U.S. publisher of the *Harry Potter* series. The children's essays explained how Harry, Ron, Hermione, or one of the books' other characters had helped them to cope with illness, abuse, bullying, or lack of self-esteem. Lehr (2008) writes "Children need to think of themselves as independent agents and to consider how they can choose to live heroically. Children cannot survive without heroes. Perhaps that is why Harry Potter [and friends] continues to disarm us with their courageous chutzpah" (p. 307).

*Set in a tightly controlled futuristic society, 12-year-old Jonas is given his lifetime assignment as the receiver of memories, shared by only one other, the Giver, and discovers the awful truth about the society in which he lives.*

Children must find a strong sense of self with which to deal with their struggles, whether they are external or internal. Through fantasy, that struggle for self-knowledge becomes clear. In her Newbery acceptance speech for *The Tale of Despereaux,* Kate DiCamillo (2004) said the following:

> There are people who believe that stories for children should not have darkness in them. There are people who believe that children know nothing of darkness. Children's hearts, like our hearts, are complicated. And children need, just as we do, stories that reflect the truth of their own experience of being human. The truth is this: we all do battle with the darkness that is inside of us and outside of us. Stories that embody this truth offer great comfort because they tell us we do not do battle alone. (p. 397)

Through fantasy, hope is kept alive. Children who immerse themselves in fantasy experience the many forms of darkness vicariously and emerge with a sense of hope and empowerment that will carry them through uncertainty and the unknown.

## Evaluating and Selecting Modern Fantasy

> Someone once called unicorns "animals that never were and always are." And that's what fantasy is, too.
>
> JANE YOLEN, 1997, P. 3

Like all good books, quality modern fantasy employs the basic literary elements to create an engaging and a believable story. But as Barron (2001) explains, "If any of [those elements] seem false, the whole story will fail. And if any of them seem true, both individually and together the story can achieve a convincing narrative structure, a believable hero, and even a lasting spiritual depth" (p. 53). Originality and believability are both key to the effectiveness of fantasy.

We expect good fantasy to be imaginative, unusual, and bold. Characters such as Alice and the Cheshire Cat, Peter Pan and Tinker Bell, Matilda, and Winnie and Jessie, and settings such as Hogwarts, Narnia, and the Hundred Acre Wood live on in our memory because the stories are so original.

Believability is achieved when the reader suspends disbelief and enters the fantasy world of the story. To suspend disbelief, however, the reader must have a sense that the story is true. Barron (2001) elaborates, "For as paradoxical as it sounds, the best fantasy is true. It must be—to win our honest belief in a brand-new world with brand-new rules" (p. 53). To achieve believability, the writer must adhere to the criteria listed in Table 6.2.

**TABLE 6.2**

## How a Writer Makes Fantasy Seem Believable

- Provides vivid descriptions of characters, setting, and action by giving us sensual details: the colors, sounds, textures, tastes, and smells of the fantasy worlds.

- Engages the hearts of the reader by grounding the story in reality and the human condition: humor, joy, grief, pride, shame, hope, and despair.

- Maintains consistency by abiding by the rules established in the fantasy world. Veering from the rules causes the reader to stop and speculate about the viability of the story, preventing suspension of disbelief.

Fantasy writers often incorporate extensive prefaces or prologues (*Fly By Night* by Frances Hardinge), construct detailed maps (*The Changeling* by Delia Sherman), invent new languages, and include pronunciation guides (*Eragon* by Christopher Paolini) as additional ways to create believability in the secondary world created in the story. Criteria for evaluating modern fantasy can be found below.

# Evaluation Criteria

**Criteria for Evaluating Modern Fantasy**

| Element | Criteria | Description |
|---|---|---|
| Setting | Does the context of the story describe a fantasy world that is detailed and believable? | Made believable through the use of rich detail consistently throughout the story so that the reader can see, hear, and feel the story. |
| Plot | Are the events in the story imaginative while also being logical to the world where the story takes place? | Suspend disbelief and bring the reader to accept the possibility that it could happen. Imaginative events are logically consistent throughout the story world. |
| Characters | Do the characters behave logically and consistently throughout the story? | Internally coherent characters that can be human, nonhuman, or supernatural that exhibit human traits and have strong emotions. Although characters may grow or change throughout the story, their behavior remains consistent. |
| Style | Is the structure of the story understandable, allowing the reader to create solid and vivid images? | Establish the setting using rich images and vivid figurative language. Authentic dialogue and a clear structure build characterization and help the reader to follow the action. |
| Theme | Can the themes of the story be connected to the life and experiences of the reader? | Modern fantasy demonstrates universal struggles, values, and emotions to help the reader keep an open mind and explore unlimited possibilities. |

# The Role of Modern Fantasy in Literacy Development

Although fantasy is very popular with children, many parents and educators question the value of "make-believe" and consider it to be little more than fluff. In the article *Stepping into the Wardrobe: A Fantasy Genre Study*, fourth-grade teachers Maria Cruz and Kate Pollock (2004) admit to this same thinking: "At first we thought of fantasy as a fun, albeit somewhat shallow, genre. We thought it lacked the seriousness of more respected genres such as memoir and historical fiction" (p. 185). When given an opportunity to create their own genre study, they chose fantasy not only because they thought it was fun but also because their students held so much passion for it. Once these teachers immersed themselves in reading many fantasy books, they gained a newfound appreciation for the genre:

> Fantasy is a rich genre with strong roots in history, religion, science, and the classic literary canon. This feature of the genre supports opportunities to extend and enrich our students' reading. As a matter of fact, the genre is so rich we believe that a class could easily study it for an entire year and still not completely exhaust its depth. (p. 193)

Many children will enter classrooms with a love for fantasy stories. Teachers and librarians can capitalize on this familiarity and interest to develop children's imagination and literary knowledge.

## READING ALOUD

Once again, read alouds are an excellent way to immerse children in fantasy while modeling and demonstrating how fantasy works. Picturebooks are a wonderful way to begin because they can be read quickly and easily discussed in their entirety. Create an anchor chart with what the children notice about fantasy stories. From this chart, children can begin to form a definition of fantasy as a genre.

## CLARIFYING DIFFERENCES AMONG GENRES

Compare the fantasy chart to what the children know about folktales and realistic fiction. In Figure 6.2, a second-grade teacher conducted an author study on Patricia Polacco. After each book, the children applied their knowledge of fantasy, folklore, and memoir to categorize the books.

## DISCUSSING MOTIFS

As the children's knowledge of what makes a book a fantasy continues to develop, create a chart of the six characteristics of fantasy, and after each read aloud, fill in the motifs used in the book. For example, Cruz and Pollock, the fourth-grade teachers who conducted a fantasy genre study with their students, read aloud *The New Kid at School,* a book in the *Dragon Slayer's Academy* series by Kate McMullan. The students noticed that the hero, Wiglaf, is different from his brothers and not liked by his family. They also noticed that Wiglaf's love of all creatures made his goal of becoming a dragon slayer more difficult. Cruz and Pollock (2004) write, "We named their observations so that they had a common vocabulary that was shared by other readers of fantasy. Students recognized Wiglaf as a character with a 'heroic flaw' who is 'alienated' (p. 190). By scaffolding the students' understanding of how these elements work in fantasy, Cruz and Pollock

**FIGURE 6.2**

Second-Grade Students' Chart on Genres

*Watch*

*Watch a video interview with Patricia Polacco.*

## Patricia Polacco

| Contemporary Fantasy | Memoir Family History | Ukrainian Folktale |
|---|---|---|
| • Aunt Chip & the Triple Creek Dam Affair | • The Butterfly | • Rechenka's Eggs |
| • Christmas Tapestry | • Mr. Lincoln's Way | • Luba & the Wren |
| • Just Plain Fancy | • Betty Doll | • Babushka's Doll |
| • Welcome Comfort | • The Keeping Quilt | • Babushka Baba Yaga |
| • Appelemando's Dreams | • Thank You Mr. Falker | |
| | • My Rotten Red-headed Older Brother | |
| | • My Ol' Man | |
| | • When Lightning Comes in a Jar | |
| | • Meteor | |
| | • Some Birthday | |
| | • The Trees of the Dancing Goats | |
| | • Thunder Cake | |
| | • The Bee Tree | |

have given their students the language they need to apply their understanding of these elements in their future reading. Table 6.3 shows an example of a motif chart that can be used to support children's understanding of fantasy motifs as they are read and discussed as a class and as they are read independently.

## SCAFFOLDING: CHARACTERIZATION, SETTING, AND PLOT

Characterization, setting, and plot in fantasy stories can sometimes be complex and difficult to understand. Charts can serve as excellent scaffolds as children learn how these elements work in fantasy. There can be many characters in fantasy stories, and some children may have trouble keeping track of all of them and identifying their significance in the story. A character map or T-chart can help them keep track by charting the characters' relationships to other characters through dialogue and actions. Setting can be equally challenging. Some fantasy books start out in the real world and move to a secondary world, whereas others start out in the secondary world. A chart that requires students to attend to the feelings, sounds, smells, tastes, and looks of the setting can help them

**TABLE 6.3**

# Recognizing Motifs in Fantasy Books

| Book Title | Magic | Other Worlds | Good vs. Evil | Heroism | Special Characters | Fantastic Objects |
|---|---|---|---|---|---|---|
| *The Paper Bag Princess* | X | X | X | X | X | X |
| *Tuck Everlasting* | X | | X | X | | X |

differentiate between the real world and that of a secondary world. Finally, the plot of a fantasy story can sometimes be difficult to follow. A chart or graph can help children recognize plot structures particular to fantasy, such as the circular journey of the hero's quest.

### DISCUSSING THE TRUTH IN FANTASY

*Watch*

*Watch an interview with Kevin Henkes.*

It is important for children of all ages to understand that at the heart of all fantasy lies the truth about ourselves and the world around us. In Figure 6.3, a first-grade teacher read aloud and recorded several books by author/illustrator Kevin Henkes.

After each read aloud, the teacher wrote what the children learned from the book. In this way, children can begin to understand that even though a fantasy story cannot happen in the real world, it still shows the basic struggles we all face in our lives.

### IDENTIFYING LITERARY DEVICES

The literary devices of personification (toys and other inanimate objects have human characteristics, such as talking) and anthropomorphism (animals have human characteristics, such as wearing clothes) are unique to the genre of fantasy. In the classroom, draw children's attention to these devices when reading aloud and sharing books so they can use specific language to identify these literary devices when reading independently.

### USING VISUALIZATION

Several years ago, I asked my son if he wanted to go see the first Harry Potter movie. He didn't. When I asked him why not, he replied, "I don't want to ruin the pictures in my mind."

Rosenblatt (1978, 1983) stressed the difference between "text" as simply words on a page and the reader's "lived-through" experience of the text as it is imagined, visualized, and experienced in the mind's eye. When we visualize, we create pictures or a movie in our mind that are all our own because the images are evoked through a combination of the author's words and our own background knowledge (Harvey & Goudvis, 2007). Consequently, visualizing strengthens our inferential thinking. Research supports the fact that less proficient readers do not employ mental imagery and visualization in reading as an important element of active reading, comprehension, comprehension monitoring, and response (Purcell-Gates, 1991; Wilhelm, 2007).

**FIGURE 6.3**

First-Grade Students' Chart on the Fantasy Books of Kevin Henkes

# Kevin Henkes

| Title | What we learned from the book |
|---|---|
| Lilly's Purple Plastic Purse | • Be patient.<br>• Say you are sorry if you hurt someone's feelings. |
| Chrysanthemum | • Don't tease someone about their name.<br>• Treat others the way you want to be treated. |
| Wemberly Worried | • Sometimes you should not worry and take a chance.<br>• Everyone makes mistakes. |
| Julius the Baby of the World | • Don't be jealous.<br>• Don't be a bully.<br>• Your parents will always love you. |
| Chester's Way | • We can be friends with people who are different from us. |
| Owen | • Sometimes it is hard to grow up! |
| Sheila Rae, the Brave | • It is easier to be brave when someone is with you.<br>• Little brothers or sisters can help us. |

Visualizing is critical to understanding the elements of fantasy if the reader is to become immersed in the imaginative characters, setting, and events the author has created. We can assist children with using the strategy of visualization:

1. Begin by modeling the strategy through reading aloud.
2. Choose a picturebook that evokes strong mental images. Although picurebooks have illustrations that help us to interpret the text, as discussed in Chapter 4, much can happen from one page turn to the next. For example, in *Abuela,* by Arthur Dorros, Rosalba, a Hispanic-American child, imagines she's rising into the air over the park in New York and flying away with her abuela, or grandmother. The third page opening shows Rosalba in the park feeding the birds with her abuela. The text reads, "'Tantos pájaros,' Abuela says / as a flock of birds surrounds us. / So many birds. / They're picking up the bread we brought." The next page shows Rosalba high over the park, looking down. The text reads, "What if they picked me up, / and carried me / high above the park? / What if I could fly?"
3. Ask students to visualize what they think happened between the pages and draw a picture.

Visualization with excerpts from chapter books is also very effective. Select a chapter in which the author creates imagery through the use of details to "show" the reader how the characters, setting, or action looks, smells, sounds, or feels. Ask the students to draw a picture of what they visualized and share them with each other. In this way, children can begin to understand that not everyone visualized the same thing, but they still can all be accurate. These student drawings are also an effective way to monitor students' comprehension.

## Opportunities for Reader Response

Abundant opportunities to learn how fantasy works is important to students' comprehension. However, just as important are opportunities for students to become engaged in discussing and writing fantasy to extend and deepen their understanding and interpretation of the genre.

### CULTURALLY RESPONSIVE DISCUSSION

In his autobiography *The Lost Garden*, Laurence Yep (1991) writes about his experience of being born in China and moving to America at the age of 10 and how the discovery of fantasy helped him cope with his situation more so than realistic fiction:

> In the Oz books, you usually have some child taken out of his or her everyday world and taken to a new land where he or she must learn new customs and adjust to new people. There was no time for being stunned or for complaining. The children took in the situation and adapted. Unlike the Homer Price books, the Oz books talked about survival. They dealt with the real mysteries of life—like finding yourself and your place in the world. And that was something I tried to do every day I got on and off the bus. (p. 77)

*Read* Skeleton Man *and view a presentation by Joseph Bruchac.*

Although there are few multicultural fantasy books available, several exceptional modern fantasy stories that have multicultural main characters and reflect the experiences of children from diverse backgrounds exist, such as *Skeleton Man* by Joseph Bruchac (American Indian), *A Million Fish . . . More or Less* by Patricia McKissack (African American), and *The Tiger's Apprentice* by Laurence Yep (Asian). Classrooms must contain fantasy books that reflect the interests and experiences of a diverse group of children to engage all children in the classroom (see list of fantasy books with multicultural characters at the end of this chapter).

### RESPONDING THROUGH PERSONAL WRITING

Students can create fantasy stories from personal experiences. In their book, *Learning About Genres: Reading and Writing with Young Children,* authors and literacy teachers Debbie Rickards and Shirley Hawes (2005) describe a process in which they have students write a five-page fantasy (with room for illustrations) based on real-life events. The teachers use literature as a way to give students ideas and make connections to their own lives. For example, after reading *Lilly's Purple Plastic Purse,* the story of a little mouse who brought her new plastic purse to school to show her friends, written by Kevin Henkes, Rickards asked the children if they had ever brought something special to school to show their friends. Rickards went on to point out how Kevin Henkes had written about something that happened to a mouse that could actually happen to any one of them. Together they brainstormed a list of things that could really happen to people, and then the children imagined these same things happening to animals. Rickards then modeled how she would write her own story.

Children must be immersed in reading fantasy with many opportunities to analyze and discuss the structure and craft elements before they will be ready to write their own fantasy stories. Writing fantasy stories helps children understand the characteristics of fantasy and the author's craft at a deeper level.

## Making the Connection Across the Curriculum

Fantasy is a unique way to bring insight and provocative thinking to the content areas. This section examines ideas for using fantasy books when children are studying history, science, and language arts.

### HISTORY

Many time-warp fantasies take the reader back in time to experience events in history. These books offer children insight into a time in history they might be learning about in social studies or history class. The value of the time-warp fantasy is that children become enthusiastic about the material, which often has characters with which they can identify. This engagement aids in the child's understanding and retention of the historical material they are studying. In Jane Yolen's *Devil's Arithmetic*, 12-year-old Hannah resents the embarrassing traditions of her Jewish heritage. During Passover Seder, Hannah is chosen to open the door to welcome the prophet Elijah. When she reluctantly opens the door, time travel places her in the middle of a small Jewish village in Nazi-occupied Poland. She is captured by the Nazis and taken to a death camp, where she is befriended by a young girl named Rivka, who teaches her how to fight the dehumanizing processes in the camp and hold onto her identity. When at last their luck runs out and Rivka is chosen, Hannah goes in her stead. As the door to the gas chamber closes behind her, she is returned to the door of her grandparents' apartment, waiting for Elijah. With her memories of the present and the past, Hannah fully understands the importance of her Jewish family traditions and the importance of remembering. Several books in the *Magic Tree House* series by Mary Pope Osborne, such as *Civil War on Sunday*, the *Time Warp Trio* books by Jon Scieszka, such as *Tut, Tut* and *Viking It and Liking It*, and *The Kane Chronicles* by Rick Riordan, such as the *Red Pyramid*, also transport the main characters back in time to experience historical events.

### SCIENCE

Science fiction engages children in thinking about scientific principles and extrapolating how they could be used in the future. For example, the technology of cloning is explored in *Anna to the Infinite Power* by Mildred Ames and *The House of the Scorpion* by Nancy Farmer. Philip Pullman's *His Dark Materials* trilogy (*The Golden Compass*, *The Subtle Knife*, and *The Amber Spyglass*) is about parallel worlds where demons and winged creatures live side by side with humans and a mysterious entity called Dust could have the power to unite the universes.

Mary and John Gribbin, award-winning science writers for both adults and children, wrote *The Science of Philip Pullman's His Dark Materials* in which they draw on string theory and space time, quantum physics, and chaos theory to explain real science behind the fantasy trilogy. The effects of nuclear disaster are contemplated in Louise Lawrence's *Children of the Dust* and Karen Hesse's *Phoenix Rising*. *The Ear, the Eye and the Arm* by Nancy Farmer and *The Last Book in the Universe* by Rodman Philbrick present futuristic societies that appear to be utopias due to the influence of technology to create highly efficient, ideal worlds only to discover the negative implications of such social planning. Most of the *Magic School Bus* books also explore science topics. Fantasy books can stimulate curiosity and the capacity for invention.

## LANGUAGE ARTS

*Watch a presentation by Jane Yolen.*

Much of modern fantasy is derived from the literary canon—myths, legends, epics, and ballads of literature. Many fantasy authors borrow directly from the characters and motifs of folklore. English and language arts teachers can assist children in making these important connections. Some literary experts believe that children cannot fully appreciate the literature of fantasy until they become familiar with the stories of folklore upon which they lean. Jane Yolen (1981) asserts, "A child who has never met Merlin—how can he or she really recognize the wizards in Earthsea? The child who has never heard of Arthur—how can he or she totally appreciate Susan Cooper's *The Grey King*?" (p. 15). English and language arts teachers can assist children in making these important connections.

# Top 10 Read Alouds

### FANTASY

1. **Gossamer** by Lois Lowry (2006, Thorndike). While learning to bestow dreams, a young dream giver tries to save an eight-year-old boy from the effects of both his abusive past and the nightmares inflicted on him by the frightening Sinisteeds.

2. **The Graveyard Book** by Neil Gaiman, illustrated by Dave McKean (2008, HarperCollins). After the grisly murder of his entire family, a toddler wanders into a graveyard where the ghosts and other supernatural residents agree to raise him as one of their own.

3. **I, Coriander** by Sally Gardner (2005, Dial). In seventeenth-century London, Coriander, a girl who has inherited magic from her mother, must find a way to use this magic in order to save both herself and an inhabitant of the fairy world where her mother was born.

4. **The Invention of Hugo Cabret** by Brian Selznick (2007, Scholastic). When 12-year-old Hugo, an orphan living and repairing clocks within the walls of a Paris train station in 1931, meets a mysterious toy seller and his goddaughter, his undercover life and his biggest secret are jeopardized.

5. **Savvy** by Ingrid Law (2008, Dial). Recounts the adventures of Mibs Beaumont, whose thirteenth birthday has revealed her "savvy"–a magical power unique to each member of her family–just as her father is injured in a terrible accident.

6. **The Tale of Despereaux: Being the Story of a Mouse, a Princess, Some Soup and a Spool of Thread** by Kate DiCamillo, illustrated by Timothy Ering (2003, Candlewick). This book tells of the adventures of Despereaux Tilling, a small mouse of unusual talents, the princess that he loves, the servant girl who longs to be a princess, and a devious rat determined to bring ruin to them all.

7. **Toys Go Out** by Emily Jenkins, illustrated by Paul Zelinsky (2006, Schwartz & Wade). Six stories relate the adventures of three best friends, who happen to be toys.

8. **Tuck Everlasting** by Natalie Babbitt (1975, Farrar). The Tuck family is confronted with an agonizing situation when they discover that a ten-year-old girl and a malicious stranger now share their secret about a spring whose water prevents one from ever growing older.

9. **Wait Till Helen Comes** by Mary Downing Hahn (1986, Houghton Mifflin). Molly and Michael dislike their spooky new stepsister Heather but realize that they must try to save her when she seems ready to follow a ghost child to her doom.

10. **Where the Mountain Meets the Moon** by Grace Lin, (2009, Little, Brown). Minli, an adventurous girl from a poor village, buys a magical goldfish, and then joins a dragon who cannot fly on a quest to find the Old Man of the Moon in hopes of bringing life to Fruitless Mountain and freshness to Jade River.

*Watch*

*Watch a presentation by Natalie Babbitt.*

# Activities for Professional Development

## Think Critically About Children's Literature

**1.** Many fantasy books for children have been turned into movies, such as *The Golden Compass, The Tale of Despereaux, Harry Potter, The Chronicles of Narnia, Charlie and the Chocolate Factory, The Lord of the Rings,* and *Tuck Everlasting.* Select one of these books to read and then watch the movie. Did the movie use special effects successfully to create the magical elements in the book? Why or why not?

**2.** Listen to National Public Radio show *Children's Fantasy Literature in the Modern World,* featuring three prominent authors of children's fantasy: Neil Gaiman (*The Graveyard Book, Caroline*), Christopher Paolini (*Eragon* series), and Tamora Pierce (*Circle of Magic Quartet, Trickster's Queen*) as they discuss how children's literature appeals to both old and young alike. The authors also discuss controversial topics such as violence in fantasy, using fantasy to teach morals, and feminine roles in fantasy. Reflect on the authors' discussion. Do you agree with their positions on these topics? Explain.

## Bring Children's Literature into the Classroom

**3.** Although fantasy is not the most censored genre, several books, such as the *Harry Potter* series, are among those most often challenged. For many teachers and librarians, it is difficult to understand why not everyone shares their excitement about the phenomenal impact Harry Potter has had on children's reading. Some religious groups, however, believe that witchcraft and wizardry actually exist, and they are concerned that their children might find it acceptable. How would you respond to this concern brought to you by the parent of a child in your class or library?

## Learn About Authors and Illustrators

**4.** Listen to one or both of the following online interviews with authors of children's fantasy:

- Kate DiCamillo has written several critically acclaimed books for children, including the fantasy novels *The Magician's Elephant, The Tale of Despereaux, The Journey of Edward Tulane,* and the *Mercy Watson* series. Go to the *School Library Journal* website (http://www.schoollibraryjournal.com/flashVideo/element_id/2140018711/taxid/33733.html?starting=13). After watching the interview (approximately 19 minutes), reflect on how Kate DiCamillo's real-life experiences have influenced her writing. How does the theme of darkness and light in DiCamillo's stories reflect her own life? How does the theme of darkness and light in her stories, as in many other fantasy stories, convey a sense of hope to children?

- Susan Cooper is an award-winning children's author of *The Dark is Rising* series and *The Boggart* series. Go to The Forum Network website (http://forum-network.org/lecture/susan-cooper-role-fantasy-childrens-lives). In this interview, Cooper explores the ways that literary fantasy helps children understand the world of adulthood. How do children understand fantasy? What does it add to their lives? Why do adults find fantasy in children's literature objectionable, even threatening?

# Print and Online Resources

## Print Resources

Johansen, K. (2005). *Quests and kingdoms: A grown-up's guide to children's fantasy.* Sackville, New Brunswick: Sybertooth.

Levine, G. (2006). *Writing magic: Creating stories that fly.* New York: HarperCollins.

Marcus, L. (Ed.). (2006). *The wand in the word: Conversations with writers of fantasy.* Cambridge, MA: Candlewick.

Mikkelsen, N. (2005). *Powerful magic: Learning from children's responses to fantasy literature.* New York: Teachers College Press.

Silvey, A. (2009). *Everything I need to know I learned from a children's book*. New York: Roaring Brook Press.

## Online Resources

*American Library Association's page on Intellectual Freedom*
**http://www.ala.org**
The American Library Association's website on Intellectual Freedom has a wealth of information for teachers and librarians on how to handle challenged books, the top 100 banned books by year and decade, information for Banned Books Week, and much more.

*The Golden Duck Awards for Excellence in Science Fiction*
**http://www.goldenduck.org**
The Golden Duck Awards are given in the categories of picturebooks, middle grades, and young adults. This site lists the criteria for the award, along with online resources for teachers to promote the use of science fiction in the classroom.

*The Science Fiction and Fantasy Bibliography*
**http://www.sfbooklist.co.uk**
A database of more than 4500 science fiction and fantasy authors, with links to websites and book information.

*Readkiddoread*
**http://www.readkiddoread.com**
*Readkiddoread* is sponsored by the author James Patterson and is dedicated to helping parents and educators connect their children with the books that will turn them into lifelong readers. Type "fantasy" (or any genre/theme/topic) in the search box at the top of the webpage for an excellent annotated list of books.

*The Library of Congress Center for the Book*
**http://www.read.gov/books**
*The Library of Congress Center for the Book* has a digitized collection of classic children's books that include many in the fantasy genre such as *The Arabian Nights, The Secret Garden,* and *The Wonderful Wizard of Oz.*

Visit the companion website at **www.cengage.com/education/johnson** to find links related to the Read/Watch/Listen icons noted throughout the chapter, as well as additional resources.

# Creating Your Classroom Library

### FANTASY SERIES FOR YOUNGER READERS

*Adventures of Captain Underpants* series by Dave Pilkey

*Amelia Bedelia* series by Peggy Parish

*Arthur* series by Marc Brown

*A Series of Unfortunate Events* by Lemony Snicket

*Berenstain Bears* books by Jan and Stan Berenstain

*Bunnicula* series by James and Deborah Howe

*Clifford, the Big Red Dog* series by Norman Bridwell

*Commander Toad* series by Jane Yolen

*Dragon Slayer's Academy* series by Kate McMullan

*Eddie Dickens Trilogy* by Philip Ardagh

*Frances* books by Russell Hoban and Lillian Hoban

*Frog and Toad* series by Arnold Lobel

*Froggy* books by Jonathan London

*George and Martha* books by James Marshall

*Harvey Angell Trilogy* by Diana Hendry

*Little Bear* books by Holmelund Minarik

*Magic School Bus* series by Joanna Cole

*Magic Tree House* series by Mary Pope Osborne

*Mercy Watson* series by Kate DiCamillo

*Olivia* books by Ian Falconer

*Paddington Bear Adventures* by Michael Bond

*Pippi Longstocking* series by Astrid Lindgren

*Poppleton* series by Cynthia Rylant

*Secrets of Droon* series by Tony Abbot

*Spiderwick Chronicles* by Holly Black

*Sideways Stories from Wayside School* series by Louis Sachar

*Tales from Dimwood Forest* series by Avi

*Time Warp Trio* by Jon Scieszka

*Young Merlin Trilogy* by Jane Yolen

## FANTASY SERIES FOR OLDER READERS

*39 Clues* series by various authors

*Among the Hidden* series by Margaret Haddix

*Artemis Fowl* series by Eoin Colfer

*Bartimaeus Trilogy* by Jonathan Stroud

*The Borrowers* series by Mary Norton

*Chronicles of Chrestomanci* series by Diana Wynne Jones

*Dark Is Rising* series by Susan Cooper

*Dragon* series by Laurence Yep

*Dragon Chronicles* by Susan Fletcher

*Earthsea* series by Ursula Le Guin

*The Edge Chronicles* by Paul Stewart

*The Enchanted Forest Chronicles* by Patricia Wrede

*Fire Us Trilogy* by Jennifer Armstrong and Nancy Butcher

*Harry Potter* series by J. K. Rowling

*Hermux Tantamoq Adventure* series by Michael Hoeye

*His Dark Materials Trilogy* by Philip Pullman

*Inheritance Trilogy* by Christopher Paolini

*Isis Trilogy* by Monica Hughes

*Lewis Barnavelt* series by Brad Strickland

*The Littles* by John Peterson

*Lord of the Rings Trilogy* by J. R. R. Tolkien

*Lost Years of Merlin* series by T. A. Barron

*Pit Dragon Trilogy* by Jane Yolen

*Prydian Chronicles* by Lloyd Alexander

*Redwall* series by Brian Jacques

*Seventh Tower* series by Garth Nix

*Time Quartet* by Madeleine L'Engle

*Tripod Trilogy* by John Christopher

*Unicorn Chronicles* by Bruce Coville

*Warriors* series by Erin Hunter

## FANTASY BOOKS WITH MULTICULTURAL CHARACTERS

*The Abhorsen Trilogy* by Garth Nix

*Abuela* by Arthur Dorros

*Aunt Harriet's Underground Railroad in the Sky* by Faith Ringgold

*The Big Fish* by Marcia Wakland

*The Boggart* by Susan Cooper

*Bonjour, Mr. Satie* by Tomie dePaola

*The Clone Codes* by Patricia, Fred and John McKissack

*The Conch Bearer* series by Chitra Divakaruni

*The Dream Stair* by Betsy James

*The Ear, the Eye and the Arm* by Nancy Farmer

*The Feverbird's Claw* by Jane Kurtz

*Galax-Arena* by Gillian Rubenstein

*The Ghost of Grania O'Malley* by Jane Stemp

*The Golden Hour* by Maiya Williams

*Haroun and the Sea of Stories* by Salman Rushdie

*Johnny Maxwell Trilogy* by Terry Pratchett

*Justice Trilogy* by Virginia Hamilton

*Maya Running* by Anjali Banerjee

*The Mer-Child* by Robin Morgan

*North Country Christmas* by Shelly Gill

*Noughts and Crosses Trilogy* by Malorie Blackman

*Pay the Piper* by Jane Yolen

*Pig-Heart Boy* by Malorie Blackman

*Sweetwater* by Laurence Yep

*Tar Beach* by Faith Ringgold

*This Is the Key to the Kingdom* by Diane Allison

*Three Wishes* by Lucille Clifton

*Walking the Boundaries* by Jackie French

*The Wizard of Washington Square* by Jane Yolen

# References

American Library Association. http://www.ala.org/ala/oif/bannedbooksweek/bbwlinks/100mostfrequently.htm.

Barron, T. A. (2001). Truth and dragons. *School Library Journal, 47*(6), 52–54.

Breen, K., Fader, E., Odean, K., & Sutherland, Z. (2000). One hundred books that shaped the century. *School Library Journal, 46*(1), 50–59.

Cruz, M., & Pollock, K. (2004). Stepping into the wardrobe: A fantasy genre study. *Language Arts, 81*(3), 184–195.

DiCamillo, K. (2004). Newbery Medal acceptance. *Horn Book Magazine, 80*(4), 395–400.

Dorros, A. (1991). *Abuela.* New York: Dutton.

Harvey, S., & Goudvis, A. (2007). *Strategies that work* (2nd ed.). York, ME: Stenhouse.

Jacobs, J., & Tunnell, M. (2008). *Children's literature, briefly* (4th ed.). Upper Saddle River, NJ: Merrill/Prentice Hall.

*Kansas City Star* (2005, January 6). "Officials consider challenge to book."

Lehr, S. (2008). *Shattering the looking glass: Challenge, risk and controversy in children's literature.* Norwood, MA: Christopher-Gordon.

Lowry, L. (2005, March). *How everything turns away.* Speech given at the University of Richmond, VA. http://www.loislowry.com/speeches.html.

Purcell-Gates, V. (1991). On the outside looking in: A study of remedial-readers' meaning-making while reading literature. *Journal of Reading Behavior, 23*(2), 235–254.

Rickards, D., & Hawes, S. (2005). *Learning about literary genres: Reading and writing with young children.* Norwood, MA: Christopher-Gordon.

Rosenblatt, L. (1978). *The reader, the text, the poem: The transactional theory of the literary work.* Carbondale: Southern Illinois University Press.

Rosenblatt, L. (1983). *Literature as exploration.* New York: The Modern Language Association of America.

Schafer, E. (2000). *Exploring Harry Potter.* Osprey, FL: Beacham Publishing.

Silvey, A. (2009). *Everything I need to know I learned from a children's book.* NY: Roaring Brook Press.

Silvey, A. (2004). *100 best books for children.* Boston: Houghton Mifflin.

Strimel, C. (2004). The politics of terror: Rereading Harry Potter. *Children's Literature in Education, 35*(1), 35–52.

Thomas, M. (2003). Teaching fantasy: Overcoming the stigma of fluff. *English Journal, 92*(5), 60–64.

Wilhelm, J. (2007). *You've gotta BE the book* (2nd ed.). New York: Teachers College Press.

Winters, C., & Schmidt, G. (2001). *Edging the boundaries of children's literature.* Boston: Allyn & Bacon.

Yep, L. (1991). *The lost garden.* New York: Simon & Schuster.

Yolen, J. (1981). *Touch magic: Fantasy, faerie and folklore in the literature of childhood.* New York: Philomel.

Yolen, J. (1997). *Twelve impossible things before breakfast.* New York: Harcourt.

# 7 Realistic Fiction

This response from sixth grader Britney Titensor (The Center for the Book in the Library of Congress, 2006) shows how convincingly true to life the stories of realistic fiction can be. Realistic fiction helps children see their own lives, empathize with other people, and understand the complexity of human interaction.

Imagine two girls, both in the sixth grade but really quite different. The first girl lives in the arid desert of Afghanistan; the second, in the snowy mountains of Wyoming. The first girl educates herself by reading the banned books her father illegally hid, while the second attends school openly every day (even when she would rather be shopping). The first girl can only leave her house in secrecy for fear of being shot or beaten by soldiers. The second girl spends her time hanging out with friends or building snow forts in her yard. You know the first girl well. She is your courageous character, Parvana. The second girl is me. The remarkable thing is the friendship we developed through the pages of The Breadwinner, a friendship that has changed my view of the world forever.
—*Excerpt from Britney Titensor's Response to* The Breadwinner

## Defining Realistic Fiction

*Realistic fiction is realistic* in the sense that the setting, characters, and events are plausible—they reflect contemporary places, people, and situations. Yet, these stories are fiction because the characters and events did not really happen even though many authors write stories based on their own childhood experiences. Newbery award–winning author Cynthia Kadohata (2005) affirms, "Out of our homes, I believe, grow our stories" (p. 412). Her book *Kira, Kira* is a story of learning to appreciate the "kira-kira," or glittering in everyday life.

Categories within realistic fiction range from lighthearted, humorous stories to the conflicting feelings and difficult choices presented in stories about growing up (see "Categories in Realistic Fiction" on page 171). Of course, these categories can overlap. For example, *Yolanda's Genius* by Carol Fenner is told from the perspective of Yolanda, a fifth grader who is big and

*Listen*

Listen to an interview with Cynthia Kadohata.

# Categories of Realistic Fiction

| Category | Description | Example |
|---|---|---|
| **Survival / Adventure** | Exciting fast-paced plot with the conflict often between person and nature. Characters control much of the action and change as a result of the action. | *Hatchet* by Gary Paulsen<br>*The Wanderer* by Sharon Creech<br>*The Thief Lord* by Cornelia Funke |
| **Mystery** | Marked by suspense with fast-paced action and a logical solution that is foreshadowed through the presentation of clues. Action centers on finding an answer to the focus question: Who did it? What happened? Where is it? | *The Egypt Game* by Zilpha Keatley Snyder<br>*The Westing Game* by Ellen Raskin<br>*Chasing Vermeer* by Blue Balliett |
| **Humor** | Characters are involved in funny situations and the actions that follow heighten the humor. | *The Trolls* by Polly Horvath<br>*Ramona* by Beverly Cleary<br>*Millicent Min, Girl Genius* by Lisa Yee |
| **Animals** | Characters grow and change as a result of a realistic relationship with an animal. | *Because of Winn-Dixie* by Kate DiCamillo<br>*The Trouble with Tuck* by Theodore Taylor<br>*Shiloh* by Phyllis R. Naylor |
| **Sports** | Action revolves around the tensions and thrills that accompany a particular sport. | *Free Baseball* by Sue Corbett<br>*Wrestling Sturbridge* by Rich Wallace<br>*Taking Sides* by Gary Soto |
| **Family** | A strong need for family, both traditional and nontraditional, is depicted as characters show responsibility, loyalty, or unity to overcome conflicts. | *Yolanda's Genius* by Carol Fenner<br>*Anastasia Krupnik* by Lois Lowry<br>*Ida B.* by Katherine Hannigan |
| **Growing Up** | Characters cope with increasing independence from adults and confront the accompanying conflicting feelings and difficult choices and challenges. | *Criss Cross* by Lynne Perkins<br>*Baseball in April and Other Stories* by Gary Soto<br>*Wringer* by Jerry Spinelli |

strong for her age. The book is about Yolanda's fierce protection and advocacy of her brother, who is still unable to read after completing first grade. It is also about Yolanda growing up as she experiences the awkwardness of being the new kid in school and the desire to be noticed by boys. In almost all realistic fiction, the characters emerge at the end of the story with a fuller understanding of themselves. Maybe this is why realistic fiction is a popular genre with children. Everyone, including children, wants to understand and be understood.

## Benefits and Considerations of Realistic Fiction

### BENEFITS

Children benefit from reading realistic fiction in several ways. Good realistic fiction has the following characteristics:

- It honestly portrays the realities of life so children can gain a more in-depth understanding of human problems and relationships.
- It helps expand children's frames of reference and ability to see the world from another perspective.
- It helps children understand and take comfort in knowing that their problems are not unique and they are not alone in the world.
- It allows children to experience vicariously interactions with the characters in books.
- It provides a literary framework for the development of a sense of personal and civic competency and the ability to make improvements in our own lives and the lives of others.

Good realistic fiction portrays the real world in all its contexts. Life is full of ups and downs; it can be funny, painful, tumultuous, joyful, and distressing. We share the ups and downs of life with each other through stories, which connect us and help us see that we are not alone in our thoughts, experiences, and emotions. Children and adults in all societies and cultures want books that reflect and confirm their lives. Since our society is diverse and human nature is complex, realistic fiction reflects all of the sensitive topics common in our world: divorce, death, abuse, sexuality, and poverty. Good literature does not resolve these complex issues with easy answers; it considers these problems with the seriousness they require.

### CONSIDERATIONS

**Moralizing.** After interviewing Newbery author Kate DiCamillo, Irene Cooper (2006) wrote the following:

> [DiCamillo] gets prickly when people ask her what message she wants to convey in her stories, especially since she doesn't think adult authors are asked that kind of question. DiCamillo acknowledges that, when she's finished with her books, she can see that they contain things that are "valuable and good," but she is also aware that she would "fail miserably" if she sat down to write a story designed to teach someone something. (p. 112)

Some adults hold the perception that books for young people should convey a lesson or learning experience. James McCosh, the eleventh president of Princeton University, once said that one should not read a book that "thinks for you" but one that "makes you think." This is true of any book and any genre. Authors must trust their readers to be able to think for themselves and avoid any tone of condescension in their writing. Most authors of realistic fiction acknowledge that they do not write with a moral or lesson in mind. Here are the comments of some of them.

**Louis Sachar:** "It's not something I think about while I'm writing a book. I'm too caught up in just trying to write the story to worry about its significance. . . . I'm just trying to please one reader: myself. I try to write a story I like." (1999)

**Judy Blume** (in an interview about *Are You There, God? It's Me, Margaret*): "I was really writing about the kind of kid I was in sixth grade, the late developer." (Kloberdanz & Blume, 2002)

**Katherine Paterson:** "When our son, David, was eight years old, his best friend was struck and killed by lightning. Out of the grief and devastation of this event, I began to write a story. I am deeply grateful that *Bridge to Terabithia*, which I wrote for myself and my family, has proved to be such a comfort to many people young and old." (Censored, 1995)

**Cynthia Rylant:** "It is as if we, as children, just *felt* the life, then after we grew up we wanted to *see* it. So we create stories and paintings and music, not so much for the world as for ourselves." (1989)

**Julius Lester:** "I write because there is something I want to know, and the only way I can know it is to write." (2006)

*Listen*

*Listen to interviews with Louis Sachar, Judy Blume, and Katherine Paterson, and listen to an excerpt from* Missing May *by Cynthia Rylant.*

Realistic fiction can offer children the opportunity to closely observe the decision–making process when it comes to moral issues. The characters in many Newbery medal–winning realistic fiction books are involved in making decisions based on thinking about their experiences. Reflective decision making, according to Friedman and Cataldo (2002), "demonstrates that good decisions evolve from a process of inquiry where the decision maker recognizes and questions personal biases; casts preconceived notions about race, ethnicity, and gender aside; and resolves dilemmas in ways that model social justice" (p. 102).

Britney Titensor's earlier response to *The Breadwinner* indicated that her view of the world has changed from reading the story. She continues, "These lessons and my friendship with this young Afghan girl have changed me and my reaction to people I meet. You have given me a friend. You have given me Parvana, and Parvana will always be a part of who I have become." It is apparent that Britney connected with the main character, Pavana, and, this story made an impact on her life.

**Bias and Stereotyping.** For realistic fiction to portray the real world in all its contexts, it must accurately and authentically reflect the lives of all who live in it. Contemporary realistic fiction must be examined for racism, cultural inaccuracies, sexism, ageism, and treatment of people with physical, mental or behavioral impairments. Criteria for cultural considerations described in Chapters 5 and 11 apply to realistic fiction.

*Realistic fiction challenges the reader to understand the complexity of human interaction—an essential life skill that is addressed only rarely in one's life.*

## Evaluating and Selecting Realistic Fiction

> *I hope some of the sad books I write make children think. I hope some of the "not sad" ones make them laugh. I hope I always write books that children want to read.*
>
> EVE BUNTING, 1995, P. 26

The crux of good realistic fiction lies in its credibility: How believable are the characters and the setting? Is the plot believable? The theme must be meaningful, and the writing style must be engaging and effective. These elements are the criteria for well-written realistic fiction (see "Evaluation Criteria for Realistic Fiction" on page 175). To add to credibility, authors may include a preface, author's note, epilogue, or afterword to help readers understand their purposes for telling the story.

Credibility is also achieved when the author avoids "teaching and preaching" to the reader by conveying the story honestly and trusting the reader to understand the insights offered in the book. Equally important to a book's credibility is the avoidance of bias or stereotypes of all people depicted in the story. Additionally, it is critical that sensitive issues in children's literature, such as abuse, sexual relationships, or homelessness, be presented with feeling and depth of emotion and not sensationalized.

**Criteria for Evaluating Realistic Fiction**

# Evaluation Criteria

| Element | Criteria | Description |
|---|---|---|
| Characterization | Do the characters consistently act like real people within their age group and cultural background? Do they grow, change, and develop over the course of the story? | Characters act like real people: credible, authentic, not stereotypic, and fully developed as multidimensional human beings that show change and development throughout the story. |
| Setting | Does the setting seem real and appropriate to the story? | Setting depicts the contemporary world as we know it and supports the events of the story. |
| Plot | Is the action consistent with everyday contemporary problems that are developmentally appropriate for the intended age group? Does the author avoid manipulative devices of sentimentality and sensationalism? | Action deals with familiar everyday problems of today's world that are understood and believed by the target audience and solved in authentic ways. |
| Theme | Is the theme relevant and does it engage the child's interest? Does the story allow the reader to make his or her own moral judgments based on the insights in the book? | Reflects important issues of contemporary society that are applicable to children's lives and tied intrinsically to the plot, characterization, and setting. |
| Style | Is the writing style engaging and imaginative? Does the author's use of figurative language and dialogue help the reader understand the complex nature of human relationships? | Engages the reader with vivid descriptions; believable dialogue; and language that reflects today's dialect, slang, and figures of speech. |

## Controversial and Sensitive Issues

Ursula Nordstrom, the director of Harper's Department of Books for Boys and Girls from 1940 to 1973, edited a major portion of children's classics of our time, including *Stuart Little*, *Charlotte's Web*, and *Where the Wild Things Are*. In *Dear Genius: The Letters of Ursula Nordstrom*, editor Leonard Marcus writes, "Nordstrom brought devotion and verve to the quest for originality and honesty in books for young people, a readership she believed had long been ill served by the sentimental illustrations and false pieties of their elders" (p. xl). Nordstrom's authors were among the first to address topics such as racial tension, homosexuality, and divorce in such books as *I'll Get There, It Better Be Worth the*

*Trip* by John Donovan, *Harriet the Spy* by Louise Fitzhugh, and *It's Like This, Cat* by Emily Neville, which won the 1964 Newbery Award.

Though prior to the 1960's some children's literature dealt with sensitive issues such as E. Nesbit's *The Railway Children* (1906, father's imprisonment), L. M. Montgomery's *Emily of New Moon* (1923, adultery), and Elizabeth Enright's *The Saturdays* (1941, kidnapping), more often children's realistic fiction depicted a romantic, sentimental, and idealistic view of childhood. The 1960s brought stories with more candid emotions, blunt language, and serious ideas. Some believe this movement began with the book *The Outsiders* by S. E. Hinton, which is about teenage gangs and alienated youth in Tulsa, Oklahoma, during the 1960s. *The Outsiders* has sold 14 million copies (Smith, 2005). In a recent interview, Hinton was asked why she thought *The Outsiders* has endured the test of time. She replied, "Today black and minority kids identify with the Greasers as outsiders. There is universality in being an adolescent outsider." *The Outsiders* presented issues that until that time had been missing from children's literature: gang violence, death, children living without parents, and abuse. Since then, many children's books have been published that deal with issues considered taboo in earlier years. Issues of sexuality, violence, drug use, physical and mental challenges, divorce, and child abuse are common in children's literature today (see Table 7.1). However, it should be noted that there are still many books published every year that present a sentimental and idealistic view of children.

**TABLE 7.1**

## Realistic Fiction About Controversial Issues

| Topic | Examples |
|---|---|
| Death | *I Remember Miss Perry* by Pat Brisson<br>*Olive's Ocean* by Kevin Henkes<br>*Getting Near to Baby* by Audrey Couloumbis |
| Divorce | *Dear Mr. Henshaw* by Beverly Cleary<br>*How Tia Lola Came to Stay* by Julia Alvarez<br>*Buttermilk Hill* by Ruth White |
| Moral Choices | *Maniac Magee* by Jerry Spinelli<br>*Shiloh* by Phyllis R. Naylor<br>*The Hundred Dresses* by Eleanor Estes |
| Mental, Physical, and Behavioral Challenges | *A Corner of the Universe* by Ann Martin<br>*So B. It* by Sarah Weeks<br>*Joey Pigza Swallowed the Key* by Jack Gantos |
| Abuse | *Jumping the Scratch* by Sarah Weeks<br>*Cracker Jackson* by Betsy Byars<br>*Silent to the Bone* by E. L. Konigsburg |
| Homelessness and Poverty | *The Road to Paris* by Nikki Grimes<br>*Pictures of Hollis Woods* by Patricia Reilly Giff<br>*How to Steal a Dog* by Barbara O'Connor |
| Sexism and Sexuality | *Oliver Button Is a Sissy* by Tomie dePaola<br>*Are You There God? It's Me, Margaret* by Judy Blume<br>*Totally Joe* by James Howe |

## CENSORSHIP

In *Dear Clueless: The Rejection Letters of Edna Albertson*, Peter Sieruta (1998, p. 704) created a fictional children's editor, Edna Albertson, as a satire of Ursula Nordstrom. One of the fictional editor's rejection letters follows:

---

May 20, 1966

Dear Mrs. Konigsburg:

Thank you for showing us your two manuscripts. Unfortunately, we must say "no" to both. I feel the story of the runaway children will only encourage others to emulate their behavior. Dear, we can't have the Metropolitan Museum filled wall to wall with run-aways, can we? As for the story about the new girl at school and the young witch, I note in the illustrations that Jennifer is a Negro. We are not publishing books about Negroes at this time, as we feel the trend may blow over. Also, have you considered shortening your titles? How about simply *The Mixed-up Files* and *Me, Elizabeth* (or perhaps just *Me, Liz*)? Think about it.

---

Unfortunately, the fictional letter does reflect how the content of children's books was and still is censored by editors and other adults, but especially in the early and mid part of the twentieth century. Realistic fiction is the genre most often challenged or banned in children's literature (see special section: *Perspectives on Censorship*).

As you may know, the two realistic fiction titles to which the fictional Albertson refers, *The Mixed-up Files of Mrs. Basil E. Frankweiler* and *Jennifer, Hecate, Macbeth, William McKinley, and Me, Elizabeth* received the 1968 Newbery Medal and Newbery Honor awards, respectively, in the same year. In her Newbery acceptance speech, Konigsburg (1997) spoke of her love of words and language: "Language demands being treated with dignity. It makes demands, but it also delivers rewards, for precise language helps shape precise thinking" (p. 405). Good realistic fiction demands that readers think hard and articulately about what they are doing and what they want to accomplish. It is the "shaping of precise thinking" for which some adults have a problem.

*Watch*

*Watch a presentation by E. L. Konigsburg.*

Some adults argue that children should not be exposed to what they consider the inappropriate issues or offensive language that appears in some works of realistic fiction for children. For example, when *The Higher Power of Lucky* by Susan Patron won the 2007 Newbery Medal, many librarians across the country refused to purchase the book for school libraries because the word *scrotum* appears on the first page of the text. In *The Higher Power of Lucky,* ten-year-old aspiring scientist Lucky Trimble seeks the Higher Power that will bring stability to her life. (See illustration 5 in the Part 2 Visual Discussion.) Her mother is dead, and her father has left Lucky in the care of his ex-wife, who is her legal guardian. In the opening scene, Lucky is eavesdropping on a 12-step Alcoholics Anonymous meeting in which Short Sammy is telling a story about how he found his Higher Power:

Sammy told of the day when he had drunk half a gallon of rum listening to Johnny Cash all morning in his parked '62 Cadillac, then fallen out of the car when he saw a rattlesnake on the passenger seat biting his dog, Roy, on the scrotum. (p. 1)

A few pages later, Lucky reflects on the word:

> Scrotum sounded to Lucky like something green that comes up when you have the flu and cough too much. It sounded medical and secret, but also important, and Lucky was glad she was a girl and would never have such an aspect as a scrotum to her own body. Deep inside she thought she would be interested in seeing an actual scrotum. But at the same time—and this is where Lucky's brain was very complicated—she definitely did not want to see one. (p. 7)

Taken in context of the entire book, Lucky's reflection on the word *scrotum* is symbolic of her trying to make sense of the world and to find her place in it. Yet, on February 18, 2007, the *New York Times* reported that many librarians were concerned about parents' objections and their own discomfort about having to explain the word to children (Bosman, 2007).

Realism demands realistic portrayals, and writers must be able to depict scenes and characters realistically if they want them to be presented fully and honestly. Winters and Schmidt (2001) state the following:

> In showing the reader the bent world, the mirror of realism can sometimes show ugliness. If that mirror is angled merely to revel in that ugliness, or merely to nuzzle in the unseemly, the grotesque, the bawdy, the obscene, then realism has lost its purpose. If the mirror is meant to show a full character, a full story, then that mirror willy-nilly must show the bent world for what it is, a mixture of joy and sorrow, gladness and despair, beauty and ugliness, responsibility and manipulation. What realism can show most vividly, in fact, is the suggestion that great joy, great beauty, great responsibility may come out of a reaction to their opposites. (p. 237)

## RECOMMENDING REALISTIC FICTION FOR CHILDREN

*Ms. Washington would read good books, too, not silly ones where kids just learned how to behave right. The kids in her books did fun things, brave things, magical things. She'd walk by my desk and set a book on it. "I thought you might want to read this," she'd whisper. And I'd just leave it there, like I wasn't one bit interested. Then I'd slip it into my backpack at the end of the day. I'd take it out in my room at home with the door locked, and she was right—I did like it. A lot. But I wouldn't tell her.*

KATHERINE HANNIGAN, 2004, P. 130

This excerpt is from the book *Ida B . . . and Her Plans to Maximize Fun, Avoid Disaster, and (Possibly) Save the World* by Katherine Hannigan. Ida B., an only child, loves to spend time outside on the family's orchard indulging in creative endeavors. When her mother develops cancer, her parents sell part of the orchard and send Ida B. to public school instead of homeschooling her as they had before. The changes leave her feeling fiercely angry and betrayed. With the help of a wise and caring fourth-grade teacher and the enduring love of her mother and father, Ida B. slowly begins to heal.

Ms. Washington did not "slip" Ida books about a girl whose mother has cancer or require her to read the books. One of the books Ms. Washington recommended, *Alexandra Potemkin and the Space Shuttle to Planet Z*, transported Ida into another world, and that may have been the best thing for her. It's not that recommending a book about

*The mother of the protagonist in this book, Ida, has cancer. Some children might enjoy reading a book that is reflective of their own situation, whereas others may not.*

a child whose parent has cancer would have been wrong, but it certainly should be the child's decision to read it. Rudman (1995) writes, "When a book is assigned as medicine, the chances of it being accepted are slim. Rather, if informal strategies are used, such as amassing many books on a given theme, then the likelihood of success is enhanced" (p. 3). Teachers who are very knowledgeable about their students' developmental levels and children's literature in general might want to recommend such books to help children who are struggling with personal problems to draw personal insights and be willing to discuss their feelings.

## The Role of Realistic Fiction in Literacy Development

Because many children are drawn to realistic fiction, it provides the perfect opportunity for teachers to build on children's interests to expand their knowledge of literary language and devices and to deepen comprehension. The following are some suggestions for developing literacy with realistic fiction.

## READING ALOUD

Lucy Calkins (2001) writes, "Helping children think about texts is as essential to the teaching of reading as it is to the whole of our lives, and the most powerful way to teach this kind of thinking is through book talks based on read-aloud books" (p. 226). Reading aloud realistic fiction picturebooks allows students to experience short, common texts that take them deeper into "living" the book while the teacher models and demonstrates how realistic fiction works.

**Immersing Children in Realistic Fiction.** After reading aloud several realistic fiction picturebooks, create an anchor chart that documents what children notice about the stories. Compare and contrast this chart to other genre charts (fantasy, traditional literature) to assist children in defining the genre of realistic fiction.

**Depositing Literary Language in the Mind.** Books use language to convey meaning in powerful ways. Skilled writers understand how language works and will use this knowledge to craft language in creative ways. When reading aloud, pause to comment on words or phrases the authors use to grab the readers' attention, precisely convey meaning, or paint a vivid picture in the readers' mind. Provide opportunities for children to share the "powerful phrases" they hear during read alouds or find in their own books during independent reading. Figure 7.1 shows a chart that a third-grade teacher kept of the powerful phrases Eve Bunting wrote in her realistic fiction picturebooks. Often, the most powerful phrases evoke strong feelings and provide a way to talk about the book. Many times, as with Eve Bunting's books in Figure 7.1, it is the use of figurative language, such as metaphors, similes, and personification that creates powerful phrases. Thinking together about the craft a writer uses to create strong images or set the mood or tone can assist children with understanding how language works and how to use it in their own writing.

*Watch*

*Watch an interview with Eve Bunting.*

## SCAFFOLDING COMPREHENSION

Many children who have experience with books come to school with a basic understanding of story structure. As literary knowledge increases, children read longer texts with more complex story elements and literary devices. If children are to become engaged, gain new insights and perspectives from reading, and become empowered to imagine new realities, teachers must develop their basic understanding of literary elements and devices and comprehension strategies.

*Read*

*Read* Brave Irene.

**Understanding Literary Elements and Devices.** Picturebooks can serve as a bridge from children's basic understanding of story elements to more subtle features, such as characters' reactions and motives. For example, survival and adventure stories in realistic fiction revolve around a character-against-nature conflict. Picturebooks such as *Brave Irene*, written and illustrated by William Steig, illustrate the tension that occurs when characters are forced to battle nature.

In the book, when her mother, a dressmaker, falls ill, Irene must fight a raging snowstorm to deliver a dress in time for the duchess's ball. Irene's tenacity and resolve come through when she is forced to confront the ferocity of nature. Discussing Irene's battle with nature and how she survived can prepare children for longer books in which

**FIGURE 7.1**

Anchor Chart
Documenting
Memorable Language
While Reading
Aloud Picturebooks
by Eve Bunting

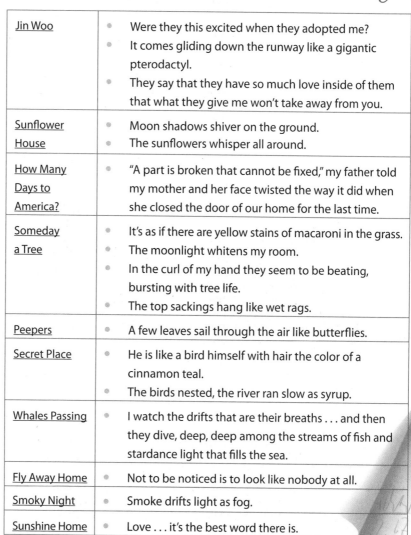

## Powerful Phrases from Eve Bunting

| Jin Woo | • Were they this excited when they adopted me?<br>• It comes gliding down the runway like a gigantic pterodactyl.<br>• They say that they have so much love inside of them that what they give me won't take away from you. |
|---|---|
| Sunflower House | • Moon shadows shiver on the ground.<br>• The sunflowers whisper all around. |
| How Many Days to America? | • "A part is broken that cannot be fixed," my father told my mother and her face twisted the way it did when she closed the door of our home for the last time. |
| Someday a Tree | • It's as if there are yellow stains of macaroni in the grass.<br>• The moonlight whitens my room.<br>• In the curl of my hand they seem to be beating, bursting with tree life.<br>• The top sackings hang like wet rags. |
| Peepers | • A few leaves sail through the air like butterflies. |
| Secret Place | • He is like a bird himself with hair the color of a cinnamon teal.<br>• The birds nested, the river ran slow as syrup. |
| Whales Passing | • I watch the drifts that are their breaths . . . and then they dive, deep, deep among the streams of fish and stardance light that fills the sea. |
| Fly Away Home | • Not to be noticed is to look like nobody at all. |
| Smoky Night | • Smoke drifts light as fog. |
| Sunshine Home | • Love . . . it's the best word there is. |

*Watch*

*Watch an interview with Gary Paulsen and Jean Craighead George.*

a character's persistence and determination to survive will be tested, such as *Hatchet* by Gary Paulsen and *Julie of the Wolves* by Jean Craighead George.

Character-against-self conflict is common in realistic fiction in which the main character(s) often struggle with internal conflict as they confront moral issues or difficult situations and usually come to a deeper understanding of themselves. In the picturebook *Sam, Bangs, and Moonshine*, written and illustrated by Evaline Ness, Samantha, a fisherman's daughter, dreams rich and lovely dreams—moonshine, her father calls them. But when her tall stories bring disaster to her friend Thomas and her cat Bangs, Samantha learns to distinguish between moonshine and reality. Discussing Samantha's struggle to deal with the loss of her mother and how that ultimately affected the people she cared about can prepare children for understanding characters' perspectives and inner struggles in longer books such as *A Fine White Dust* and *Missing May* by Cynthia Rylant.

In addition to conflict patterns, authors also use literary devices such as flashbacks, foreshadowing and story-within-a-story to compel inferential thinking and to build layers of meaning. For example, the picturebook *Miss Rumphius*, written and illustrated by Barbara Cooney, uses the technique of flashback as an aging *Miss Rumphius* remembers many experiences throughout her life. Barbara Cooney uses this technique as a way for the reader to look into Miss Rumphius's past to understand why she now feels the urgent need to give something back to the world. This can lead to a discussion of transition techniques used by an author to signal that a flashback will follow. Some longer books that include these techniques include *Belle Prater's Boy* by Ruth White, *Yolanda's Genius* by Carol Fenner, and *Wringer* by Jerry Spinelli. Flashbacks, flashforwards, and epilogues provide the reader with a broader sense of time.

Complex plot structures and characterization can make a story less accessible to readers. Therefore, it is essential that teachers build upon children's current understandings and make connections to more sophisticated structures. Analyzing literary elements and devices helps readers experience so much more in a text. Students learn to peel away layers of meaning and to think more deeply about issues and relationships.

*Read and Listen*

*Read the first draft of* Because of Winn-Dixie *and listen to Kate DiCamillo reflect on her writing process.*

**Questioning, Predicting, and Inferring.** Picturebooks can also be used as a way to scaffold children's comprehension strategies as they move into longer texts. Teachers can model questioning, predicting, and inferring, which require the reader to draw on his or her knowledge of how literary elements are developed and literary devices are employed in the story. Figure 7.2 shows how a third-grade teacher used an anchor chart to document strategy use during a study of Eve Bunting's picturebooks. She then extended this process to the chapter book *Because of Winn-Dixie* by Kate DiCamillo (see Figure 7.3). Children can learn how to use these strategies when they read longer books and how to build on previous knowledge from chapter to chapter.

**Releasing Responsibility to Children.** Scaffolding is a temporary support that is provided by teachers as children learn to engage in critical analysis of literature. Slowly, this scaffolding must fall away as children internalize these strategies and use them during independent reading. Share sheets (see Figure 7.4) are one way children can make visible their thinking while reading. A share sheet is a blank piece of paper (or Post-it note) on which students respond as they are reading. The student writes his or her name, date, and reading assignment in the center and then divides the page into sections. The student writes one type of response to the reading in each section. Share sheets encourage multiple responses to a text and provide a way for students to reflect on their reading and to share their reflections in literature circles. Children of all ages can use share sheets to monitor their comprehension and during book discussions. Teachers can use them to assess students' understanding of strategies. The strategies on the share sheet can be assigned and changed as necessary.

**FIGURE 7.2**

Anchor Chart for
Prompting Questioning,
Predicting, and
Inferencing While
Reading Aloud
Picturebooks by
Eve Bunting

# Eve Bunting

| Title | Questions | Predictions/Inferences |
|---|---|---|
| Fly Away Home | • Why don't they have a home?<br>• Where is the mom?<br>• What happens if you get noticed?<br>• Will they ever get a home? | • Maybe they don't have much money—or their house burned down.<br>• She left them like in Because of Winn-Dixie.<br>• They make you leave the airport.<br>• Yes—We hope so! |
| Sunshine Home | • What is the Sunshine Home?<br>• How did Gram fall?<br>• Why was Timmie scared to go inside and see Gram?<br>• Why is Mom using that sparkly voice?<br>• Where is Timmie's Grandpa?<br>• Is Gram really happy? | • A nursing home.<br>• Sometimes old people fall and their bones are easily broken.<br>• He thought Gram would be different.<br>• She is trying to let Timmie know that it's OK.<br>• Maybe he died.<br>• No—she misses home/family. |
| The Memory String | • What happened to Laura's mom?<br>• Why does Laura pull out the memory string so much?<br>• How did her mom die?<br>• Will Laura's feelings change toward Jane? | • Died/Divorced.<br>• She doesn't like her stepmom. She misses her mom & wants her stepmom to know it.<br>• She got sick/accident.<br>• Yes—Jane is kind and loving. |
| The Wall | • What is the wall for?<br>• Which war?<br>• Why do people leave things?<br>• Why did we have the war?<br>• Why did so many people die?<br>• What does it mean . . . "The wall is for all of us." | • A memorial for people who died in a war. So many names!<br>• Vietnam war.<br>• Gifts for people who died.<br>• Trying to help others/freedom.<br>• War is terrible—people die.<br>• It represents the people who died, but the living go there to remember them. |

**FIGURE 7.3**

Anchor Chart Supporting Literary Elements and Comprehension Strategies During a Chapter Book Read Aloud of *Because of Winn-Dixie*, Written by Kate DiCamillo

# Because of Winn-Dixie

| Characters | Setting | Questions | Predictions/Inference |
|---|---|---|---|
| • India Opal Buloni<br>• Winn-Dixie<br>• The store manager | • Last summer<br>• Winn-Dixie grocery store | • Where did Winn-Dixie come from?<br>• Who owns him?<br><br>• Will Opal get to keep him? | **Chapter 1**<br>• He's a stray (ribs showing, matted fur)<br>• He ran away or he is lost (no one claims him)<br>• Yes (the book's title gives us a clue |
| • Preacher/ Dad<br>• Opal<br>• Winn-Dixie | • Naomi, Florida<br>• Friendly Cornas Trailer Park | • Where is her mom?<br><br>• Does she have brothers/ sisters? | **Chapter 2**<br>• Maybe she died or her parents are divorced<br>• No (the trailer park) rules — she is an exception |
| • Preacher/ Dad<br>• Opal<br>• Winn-Dixie | • Opal's house (trailer park) | • Why is Opal thinking about her mother more since they moved?<br>• Why is Opal afraid her dad will get mad if she asks about her mom? | **Chapter 3**<br>• She is getting older — better able understand<br><br><br>• He is still hurt about her leaving |
| • Opal (has red hair & freckles like her mom)<br>• Preacher<br>• Winn-Dixie | | • Where is Opal's mom?<br>• Will she ever come back? | **Chapter 4**<br>• Someplace for people who drink |

**FIGURE 7.4**

Example of a
Share Sheet

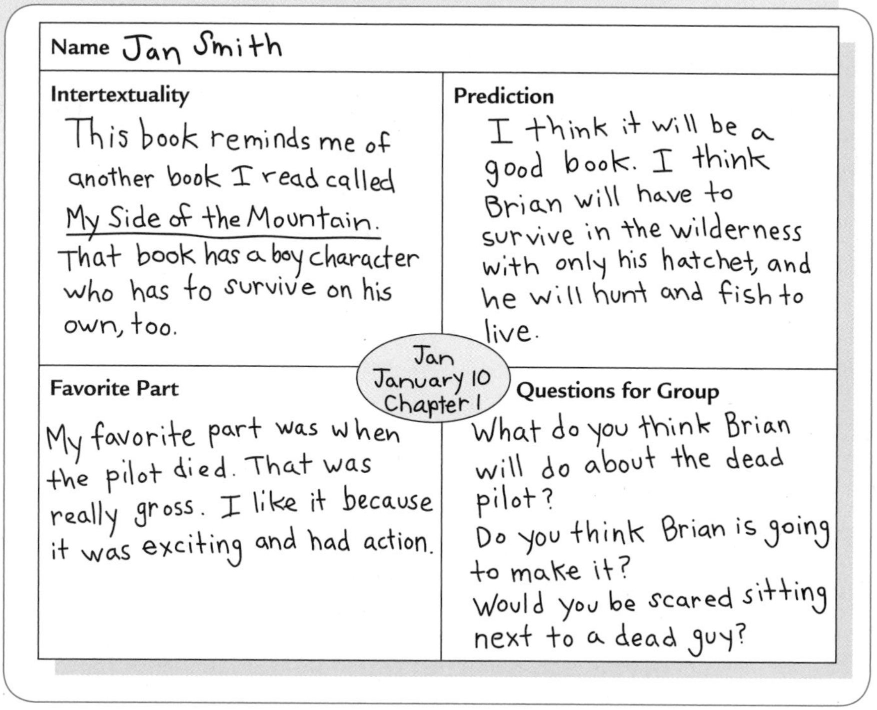

T. Raphael, L. Pardo, & K. Highfield (2002). *Book club: A literature-based curriculum*, p. 106. Reprinted by permission of Small Planet Communications, Inc.

Name Jan Smith

**Intertextuality**

This book reminds me of another book I read called My Side of the Mountain. That book has a boy character who has to survive on his own, too.

**Prediction**

I think it will be a good book. I think Brian will have to survive in the wilderness with only his hatchet, and he will hunt and fish to live.

Jan
January 10
Chapter 1

**Favorite Part**

My favorite part was when the pilot died. That was really gross. I like it because it was exciting and had action.

**Questions for Group**

What do you think Brian will do about the dead pilot?
Do you think Brian is going to make it?
Would you be scared sitting next to a dead guy?

## Opportunities for Reader Response

Realistic fiction is particularly compatible with reader response activities such as open-ended discussion and reader response journals. These are important to this genre because realistic fiction addresses issues and topics that are close to the hearts and lives of children and allows them to gain new perspectives on culture and sensitive issues. Group discussion and personal written responses not only provide children with advance reading strategies and intellectual development, but with the chance to identify with characters and their peers.

### OPEN-ENDED DISCUSSION

According to Calkins (2001), "We teach children to think with and between and against texts by helping them say aloud, in conversations with us and with others, the thoughts they will eventually be able to develop without the interaction of conversation" and that talk, like reading and writing, "is *the* major motor" of intellectual development (p. 226). Researchers such as Richard Allington (2002) have noted that classroom talk is critical to reading instruction.

Themes within realistic fiction often involve controversial and sensitive issues that some teachers may not feel comfortable discussing or are not explicitly taught in the academic curriculum. For example, in *Maniac Magee* by Jerry Spinelli, after his parents die, Jeffrey "Maniac" Magee's life becomes legendary—he can outrun dogs, hit a home run off the best pitcher in the neighborhood, and untie a knot no one can undo. Moreover,

*Listen*

*Listen to an excerpt of* Maniac Magee.

he confronts racism on the tough side of a small town where there is racial tension between rival factions. Teachers may not feel comfortable discussing such complex concepts as home and race relations which are not typically taught in the elementary academic curriculum.

As a result, teachers may ignore, transpose, or marginalize students' spontaneous and honest comments about many aspects of human interaction in children's realistic fiction (Brooks & Thompson, 2005).

Brooks and Thompson (2005) point out that although suppressing open and honest conversations constricts the learning of all students, it can be most harmful to students from low socioeconomic backgrounds who depend on teachers to bridge the gap between their own cultural capital and the mainstream cultural and social perspectives:

*Watch*

*Watch a presentation by Sharon Creech.*

For these vulnerable and often disenfranchised students, the larger the incongruence between the predominant cultural capital of their schools and themselves, the less effectively the teaching of the explicit curriculum can stimulate their learning or develop social justice understandings. (p. 49)

## THE • TEACHER'S • VOICE

**Journal Response to *Walk Two Moons* by Sharon Creech**

Salamanca, the protagonist of <u>Walk Two Moons</u>, is the narrator of this story in a story in a story. At one level, this is the story of Sal and her grandparents as they drive from Ohio to Idaho to "visit" Sal's mother. Sal is anxious to arrive in Lewiston, Idaho, on or before her mother's birthday. As the reader, all we know is that Sal's mother left their home in Bybanks, Kentucky, leaving Sal and her father behind. We also know that she is not coming back. I felt frustration and anger at a woman who would just leave this little girl behind.

To make the trip pass, Sal tells her grandparents the story of her friend Phoebe. Phoebe's family represents an ideal that Sal at once longs for and seems not to believe. Over the journey, we learn that Phoebe's world falls apart when her perfect mother leaves the family with a son she put up for adoption when she was very young. Phoebe's family survives and seems strengthened by the crisis.

Meanwhile, the reader is not at all sure that Sal's journey will end as well. Sal herself says, "I did not really expect to survive the trip." I had to read all the way to the end to figure out Sal's mother had died in a bus crash and was not coming back because she was buried in Idaho. This made me want to reread the book because I realized how carefully the author had used clues and foreshadowing throughout the text. Nevertheless, I can't imagine not being surprised by realizing the actual fate of Sal's mother.

It is as though the author took us through the stages of grief although we start in the middle among anger and bargaining. At the end of the book, we experience the shock that Sal must have felt. We realize, too, that the journey was necessary for Sal's acceptance and understanding of the tragedy. We learn that her anger toward her mother could only be dissipated when she made the journey ("walked two moons") that her mother had.

This leads to the other story within the story: that of the grandparents' gift to Sal. By taking Sal on the same journey her mother took, they are giving her the opportunity to see the last things her mother saw and to heal some of the hurt surrounding the circumstances of her mother's death. It seemed appropriate that Sal was forced to make the last most dangerous part of the journey alone. She needed to face the reality of her mother's passing in a way no one could do for her.

Sadly, the trip costs her grandmother's life. Yet, through the gift of the trip despite its toll, Creech creates hope and compassion. Sal is given a gift of unselfish love that offsets the mother's act of walking out on the family.

This book is one of the best I've ever read, adult or otherwise. I will have my own copy and reread it again. Perhaps I am overly fond of the book because I lost my mother when I was young and so could identify with the protagonist. I think the themes of love, forgiveness, understanding, and compassion are universal. I also think the story is brilliantly crafted and told in a style that cannot help but draw in the reader.

—*What personal, intertextual, or thematic connections did this teacher make with* Walk Two Moons *that lead her to believe "this book is one of the best I've ever read . . . "?*

Some parents are opposed to teachers sharing books about cultural backgrounds that are different from the teacher's. This attitude, however, can result in missed opportunities to understand the complexity of social relationships and failure to acknowledge students' perspectives. In addition to communicating with parents and garnering support from professionals inside and outside the school setting, teachers must work to establish classroom environments that foster interdependent exploration, emotional safety, flexibility, and complexity (Brooks & Thompson, 2005). We must model, demonstrate, facilitate, and provide feedback to students as they learn to value personal response, listen carefully, and consider others' responses, and support responses with evidence.

### READING RESPONSE JOURNALS

Reading response journals are an opportunity to reflect on reading in personally satisfying ways. Students may make personal, intertextual, or thematic connections (see the examples in "The Teacher's Voice" and "The Child's Voice"). Since children make strong connections with characters and themes in realistic fiction, journal response can also

## THE · CHILD'S · VOICE

Second Grader's
Journal Response to *The
Summer My Father Was
Ten* by Pat Brisson

When the dad in this story was ten, he helped tear up the garden that belonged to an old man. This book is a sad book because I feel bad for the old man. On the page where the dad wants to say sorry I would definitily say it then and help clean up the mess. I think it was really mean what they did because I mean what would you think if you had a garden you worked hard on but then it got ruined? I mean that would be really mean and I would be really sad. This book made me stop and think!

Questions – Did this story really happen? How did the old man feel when they destroyed his garden? What happened to the old man, did he die?

—*What personal, intertextual, or thematic connections did this student make with the text that prompted her to ask questions about the story?*

be a tool for extending thinking. As children reflect on their reading, they may explore new perspectives, examine personal issues, or question the boundaries that their family, school, or society has placed on them. Some teachers may question this type of response because it doesn't seem to be connected to what "counts" as learning to read. Reader response is inextricably connected to students' experiences in and out of school and thus to our social conditions. It makes sense that when we ask children to make connections, comprehend deeply, and think critically, they respond in ways that take them to new mental places.

## Making the Connection Across the Curriculum

Many times there is a disconnection between the topics taught in the content areas and what children perceive as applicable to life in the real world. Realistic fiction can provide a bridge for children to connect with characters who use their knowledge of science, social studies, and math to make informed decisions in their lives.

### SCIENCE

In *Hatchet,* written by Gary Paulsen, 13-year-old Brian spends 54 days in the Canadian wilderness after a plane crash, learning to survive with only the aid of a hatchet given to him by his mother. He is also learning to survive his parents' divorce. Ten-year-old Leigh Botts is also trying to cope with his parents' divorce and being the new boy in school in

*Dear Mr. Henshaw,* written by Beverly Cleary and illustrated by Paul Zelinsky. In letters to his favorite author, Leigh carefully describes the steps he takes to set an alarm in his lunch box when he finds someone is stealing his food. In *Phineas L. MacGuire . . . Erupts!,* by Frances Dowell, fourth-grade science whiz Phineas MacGuire (Mac) is forced to team up with the quirky new boy in class on a science fair project. Although there are a few mishaps along the way, the science project, a volcano, has a successful eruption and Mac just might have a new best friend. Three science experiments are included: an erupting volcano, a microwave marshmallow roast, and an exploding film canister. Teachers can pair these books with class experiments and discuss how science knowledge is important in everyday life.

## MATH

Math comes into everyday life in *Math Curse,* written by Jon Scieszka and illustrated by Lane Smith, when the teacher tells her class that they can think of almost everything as a math problem. One student acquires a math anxiety, which becomes a real curse. In *Counting on Frank,* written and illustrated by Rod Clement, a boy and his dog present amusing counting, size comparison, and mathematical facts. In *Alexander, Who Used to Be Rich Last Sunday,* written by Judith Viorst and illustrated by Ray Cruz, Alexander's grandparents give him a dollar, and he is suddenly rich! Although his money quickly disappears, he comes to realize all the things that can be done with a dollar. In *Mr. Chickee's Funny Money,* written by Christopher Paul Curtis, Mr. Chickee, a blind man in the neighborhood, gives nine-year-old Steven a quadrillion-dollar bill. As president of the Flint Future Detectives Club, Steven, with the help of his best friends, Russell and Zoopy the giant dog, must outsmart Agent Fondoo of the U.S. Treasury Department and his team of Secret Government Agents who want the money back.

## SOCIAL STUDIES

Current events and issues of contemporary times also become more meaningful when children can connect the events to characters they come to know and care about in realistic fiction. The Middle East and the war in Iraq may seem far removed from the daily lives of many children, whereas others have parents or relatives who are serving in the war. Books can provide bridges to conversations that help children understand Middle Eastern customs and cultures. In the picturebook *One Green Apple,* by Eve Bunting, the story is told through the eyes of Farah, a Muslim girl who is attending a new school in a new country and feels isolated and lonely because she does not speak English. When she joins her class on a field trip to an apple orchard, Farah discovers there are lots of things that look and sound the same as they did at home. When she joins the class in making apple cider, Farah connects with the other students and begins to feel she belongs. *Under the Persimmon Tree,* written by Suzanne Staples, takes place in northern Afghanistan after 9/11 during the Afghan war. When Najmah's father and brother are taken by the Taliban and her mother and baby brother are killed in a bombing raid, Najmah begins a dangerous journey across the border to Peshawar, Pakistan, where she meets an American woman who is conducting a school for refugee children.

## LANGUAGE ARTS

Censorship is the topic of several books for children that shed light on this issue. For younger children, *Arthur and the Scare-Your-Pants-Off Club,* by Marc Brown, presents the story of a parent group that bans a series of scary books from the local public library, so Arthur and his friends create a plan to get their favorite books returned. In *The Last Safe Place on Earth*, author Richard Peck paints a perfect picture of life in Walden Woods for 15-year-old Todd, until his dream girl comes to baby-sit for his sister and reveals the forces of fundamentalism and censorship at work in the town. Teachers can use these books to help children understand the motives behind censorship and how it affects the lives of everyone when books are removed from library circulation.

## Special Topic: Perspectives on Censorship

*Restriction of free thought and free speech is the most dangerous of all subversions. It is the one un-American act that could most easily defeat us.*

U.S. Supreme Court Justice William O. Douglas

The First Amendment guarantees every citizen, regardless of age, the right to free speech, which extends to books and other mediums of expression that communicate a message, and includes the right to disseminate and receive the messages contained therein. Censorship is the suppression of these messages that certain individuals, groups or government officials find objectionable or dangerous. Educators must balance the principles of the First Amendment and the demands of Censorship against concerns such as maintaining the integrity of the educational curriculum, meeting state education requirements, respecting the judgments of professional staff, and addressing deeply held beliefs in students and members of the community.

### WHAT ARE CHALLENGED AND BANNED BOOKS?

A challenge is an attempt by an individual or group to remove or restrict materials from the curriculum or library based upon objectionable ideas and information. The form and intent of challenges can range from an expression of concern to an oral complaint to a formal written complaint submitted to a school board or library board of trustees. The board may determine to deny the challenge and return the material to the classroom or library collection or it may censor or ban the material by restricting, relocating or removing it from the classroom or collection, preventing open access to any other student or patron. School officials, however, may not censor a book simply because they do not like the ideas or information conveyed. They may only censor books based on educational suitability as long as the motivation is for other reasons such as preventing students from obscene or vulgar content (Board of Education, Island Trees Union Free School District vs. Pico, 1982).

### WHO CHALLENGES BOOKS AND WHY?

According to the American Library Association's Office for Intellectual Freedom (2010), of the 4,006 book challenges initiated from 2000-2009, almost 60% were made by parents and almost 80% of those were to school and classroom libraries. Sexual content (22%), offensive language (21%), suitability for the intended age group (15%), violence (9%), and homosexuality (5%) were the most frequently cited reasons for seeking removal of books from libraries (see Table 7.2 for all reasons cited by challengers). However, many challengers admit to not examining a work in its entirety; thus, the majority of objections raised are about isolated passages or features of the materials such as explicit illustrations, descriptions of sexual activity or profanity rather than the ideas or themes of the work as a whole (Reichman, 2001).

**TABLE 7.2**

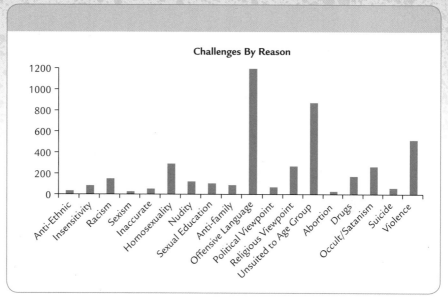

## 2000-2009 Challenges by Reason

The top 15 challenged books from 2000–2009 are listed in Table 7.3. This total number of challenges in this decade is down by over 1700 challenges from the previous decade (also listed in Table 7.3) due in large part to the commitment of librarians, teachers, parents, students and other concerned citizens.

Of the top 15 challenged books from 2000–2009, only three books appear on the list for the first time as compared to the previous decade; all others remained on the list, with a slight shift in order. Clearly, the same books are censored year after year. Ironically, according to a 2010 National Education Association poll, Harry Potter is children's favorite book series.

Censorship rarely achieves its goal. Often, censored books become best sellers right after a highly publicized challenge and students find ways around censored material. Susan Patron (2007), a public school librarian and author of the Newbery award winning book *The Higher Power of Lucky,* said the following:

*Watch*

*Watch an interview with Susan Patron.*

> If I were a parent of a middle-grade child, I would want to make decisions about my child's reading myself—I'd be appalled that my school librarian had decided to take on the role of censor and deny my child access to a major award-winning book. And if I were a ten-year-old and learned that adults were worried that the current Newbery book was not appropriate for me, I'd figure out a way to get my mitts on it anyway, its allure intensified by the exciting forbiddenness—by the unexpressed but obvious fear on the part of these adults.

In fact, Patron's assertion that children will seek out reading material to which adults object has been substantiated by research. Jenkins's review of research found, "Forbidding reading materials will not diminish reader interest in or desire for the material. Indeed, research indicates that censorship heightens readers' interest in the material" (2008, p. 233). Adults who expect children's books to serve as role models for children's conduct or language argue that inappropriate language and events do not belong in children's literature.

**TABLE 7.3**

# Top 15 Banned/Challenged Books

| | 2000–2009 | 1990–1999 |
|---|---|---|
| 1. | *Harry Potter* (series) by J.K. Rowling | *Scary Stories* (series) by Alvin Schwartz |
| 2. | *Alice series* by Phyllis Reynolds Naylor | *Daddy's Roommate* by Michael Willhoite |
| 3 | *The Chocolate War* by Robert Cromier | *I Know Why the Caged Bird Sings* by Maya Angelou |
| 4. | *And Tango Makes Three* by Justin Richardson/Peter Parnell | *The Chocolate War* by Robert Cormier |
| 5. | *Of Mice and Men* by John Steinbeck | *The Adventures of Huckleberry Finn* by Mark Twain |
| 6. | *I Know Why the Caged Bird Sings* by Maya Angelou | *Of Mice and Men* by John Steinbeck |
| 7. | *Scary Stories* (series) by Alvin Schwartz | *Forever* by Judy Blume |
| 8. | *His Dark Materials* (series) by Philip Pullman | *Bridge to Terabithia* by Katherine Paterson |
| 9. | *The Perks of Being a Wallflower* by Stephen Chbosky | *Heather Has Two Mommies* by Leslea Newman |
| 10. | *Fallen Angels* by Walter Dean Meyers | *The Catcher in the Rye* by J.D. Salinger |
| 11. | *It's Perfectly Normal* by Robie Harris | *The Giver* by Lois Lowry |
| 12. | *Captain Underpants* (series) by Dav Pilkey | *My Brother Sam is Dead* by James Lincoln Collier and Christopher Collier |
| 13. | *The Adventures of Huckleberry Finn* by Mark Twain | *It's Perfectly Normal* by Robie Harris |
| 14. | *The Bluest Eye* by Toni Morrison | *Alice* (series) by Phyllis Reynolds Naylor |
| 15. | *Forever* by Judy Blume | *Goosebumps* (series) by R.L. Stine |

When I discuss the controversy surrounding *The Higher Power of Lucky* (discussed earlier in this chapter) with the teachers in my children's literature class, many agree with the librarians in the *New York Times* article. They are not comfortable with reading and possibly discussing the word "scrotum" with their students. When I ask why, the ensuing discussion requires the teachers to reflect on and question their own belief systems to understand their reaction.

In many ways, parents, teachers, librarians, and other adults are the "hidden censors" and serve as the gatekeepers of literature for children. A very important first step in understanding censorship is to understand our own beliefs, values, and biases. It is not until we understand, question, analyze and evaluate our own beliefs and biases that we are able to come to a personal judgment that empowers us to take ownership of ideas and control of our own intellectual and moral lives. The struggle to recognize our own beliefs and biases combined with an understanding of child development and standards for literary merit will ensure that we are providing a balanced curriculum that will enable our students to become not only readers but also lovers of literature.

## THE BALANCING ACT

The American Library Association maintains that "parents—and only parents—have the right and the responsibility to restrict the access of their children—and only their children—to library resources" (APA, 2010). Parents often hold very deep and diverse political, moral, and religious perspectives and values they wish to pass on to their children and they have the right to guard against books they consider inappropriate regardless of professional judgment or literary merit.

On the other hand, the National Council of Teachers of English contends,

> English teachers must be free to employ books, classic or contemporary, which do not lie to the young about the perilous but wondrous times we live in, books which talk of the fears, hopes, joys, and frustrations people experience, books about people not only as they are but as they can be. English teachers forced through the pressures of censorship to use only safe or antiseptic works are placed in the morally or intellectually untenable position of lying to their students about the nature and condition of mankind. (NCTE, 1981)

Parents and teachers may seem to have contradictory rights and obligations; however, the compromise lies in the balance. Yes, parents have the right to make decisions about the reading materials of their own children, but they do not have the right to make that decision for other peoples' children. A vast majority of parents trust the professional judgment of their children's teachers and librarians, and it is the responsibility of these educators' to ensure that students have access to books that will challenge them to consider new ideas and broaden their perspectives.

**Critical Literacy.** Rather than prohibiting children from reading controversial books, teachers can use them to promote critical literacy. Several discussion strategies such as problem posing, alternative perspectives, and Questioning the Author are discussed in this book and can be used to promote critical literacy with controversial issues. For example, a group of fourth grade girls were reading *Shiloh* by Phyllis Reynolds Naylor in their book club. The teacher knew that her students were socially and emotionally at a developmental level in which their concept of right and wrong was becoming more flexible. *Shiloh*, a 1992 Newbery award winner, is the story of Marty, a boy who finds a lost beagle in the hills behind his West Virginia home and tries to hide it from his family and the dog's real owner, a mean-spirited man known to shoot deer out of season and to mistreat his dogs. The teacher believed that the book depicted the real world of young people and would challenge the girls to consider new ideas and perspectives. As they read independently, they took notes and then met several times to engage in conversation before they finished reading the book.

The teacher, who observed the group's discussions, noted that the girls often commented on the profanity used in the book by Shiloh's owner, Judd. The girls really enjoyed the book but the profanity continued to raise questions. The teacher used a Questioning the Author approach to engage the girls in thinking about why the author would include this language in the text and how it shaped their thinking about the character, Judd. After talking with each other and getting the opinions of their classmates and parents, the girls decided that the author could have used different words that depicted Judd as a mean character yet did not expose children to bad words. After summarizing their thoughts in writing, the girls decided to express their opinion in a letter to Phyllis Reynolds Naylor. The letter the girls composed is in Table 7.4 followed by Phyllis Reynolds Naylor's response.

**TABLE 7.4**

## Letter from Fourth Graders to Phyllis Reynolds Naylor

Dear Mrs. Naylor,

We are in fourth grade at Woodrow Wilson School. We are reading your book, Shiloh. We like the book and we like the dog, Shiloh. When we were reading this, we had problems with one thing. This book had bad words in it like the d-word and the h-word, and it said, "Shut up." We were wondering why did you put these words in this book? We were hoping you could loosen up the bad words. Can't you make your characters seem mean without the bad words because little kids shouldn't be reading them?

We love your books and when you write a new book, please don't use words that children should not hear. If you do, then it will encourage kids to say those words. We want the kids to enjoy your books without hearing those words.

We really love your books very much because we think Shiloh and Marty seem real and you had a lot of inspiration on Marty and Shiloh. We can't wait to read the next one, Shiloh Season.

Sincerely, your friends,
Niesha, Calley, and Torey

## Response from Phyllis Reynolds Naylor to Fourth Graders

Dear Niesha, Calley, and Torey,

Thank you for your polite and thoughtful letter. I hope my answer will get to you as I've written it, as I want to be polite and thoughtful too. I'm so glad you enjoyed my book Shiloh. I had never planned to write it until I met the real-life, abused dog in West Virginia, who became my inspiration for the book.

**TABLE 7.4**

(*continued*)

# Letter from Fourth Graders to Phyllis Reynolds Naylor

I need to disagree with you, however, about the words I used. I think a long time about each word that goes into my books. A story is only as meaningful to the reader as it is able to affect him emotionally. My job as an author is not only to tell you about a character, but to make you feel what Marty is feeling. Marty not only loathes Judd Travers, but he fears him; he is disgusted by him. And yet, this eleven year-old boy has to somehow figure out a way to win the respect of this cruel, crude man.

In the story, when Marty asks Judd if he has names for his dogs, Judd could have replied, "Git, Scram and Out, *that's* my dogs' names." And the reader might have chuckled a little, because even a grouchy grandfather might have said the same thing. But when I have Judd answer, "Git, Scram, Out and Dammit, *that's* my dog's names," doesn't that sort of give you a chill? Doesn't that turn your mind against this man? Doesn't it make you wonder what kind of person would give a dog a cuss word for a name?

And you know what? I don't agree with you that the two words you object to in this book are going to encourage kids to say those words, because I think you're smarter than that. What about the things Judd does? He also kicks and starves his dogs. Does that mean I'm encouraging children to go home and kick the family pet? Judd cheats shop owners, he kills deer out of season, what about those? Should a writer say, "Judd wasn't kind to his dogs," and let it go. Would that be much of a story?

It's okay to disagree with an author. It's wonderful that you discuss things like this in your classroom, and I trust that my letter will start another discussion. But I hope you'll remember that I carefully choose the words in my books, that it is my job to make my story as real and as powerful as I can. And I trust you boys and girls to copy the things you read about that are examples of your real values and that you, like Marty, can choose to do the right thing.

Best wishes,
Phyllis Reynolds Naylor

*This letter was reprinted with the permission of Phyllis Reynolds Naylor.*

When the girls received Phyllis Reynolds Naylor's letter, they were very excited. After carefully reading and discussing the contents with the girls, the teacher brought the issue to the whole class in a grand conversation. The girls and the class were particularly moved by Naylor's example of why a "cuss word" was more effective in characterizing Judd Travers than other word choices. They were also affected by the author's assertion that "the two words you object to in this book are going to encourage kids to say those words, because I think you're smarter than that." They reflected on their own thinking and began to see the book as a whole rather than a sum of its parts. After the class discussed the specific use of profanity in *Shiloh*, the teacher broadened the discussion to include profanity in books for children in general.

The teacher could have told the students the same information contained in the letter from Naylor, but it would not have been nearly as effective. The process of discussion and questioning, gathering information, and initiating an action for finding an answer to their question engaged the students in the important work of critical analysis. To be truly literate in the twenty-first century, children must be able to do more than read and respond superficially to text; they also need to understand how language works, how to find and question the story being told, and how to act on their new awareness. Using controversial books promotes stimulating class discussions that lead to the development of critical literacy and assists children with reading many other books more critically.

**How to Respond to a Book Challenge.** Despite the care taken to select worthwhile books for student reading and the qualifications of teachers selecting and recommending books, occasional objections to a work will undoubtedly arise. Table 7.5 provides actions, questions, and resources for addressing challenges to children's books.

Teachers and librarians can help to reduce censorship by remaining aware of controversial and sensitive issues in children's literature, following the guidelines for evaluating books for literary quality, bias and stereotypes, and involving the school faculty and community in discussions about children's literature. Prevalent controversial issues have been discussed in each genre chapter of this book along with strategies for supporting children in thinking critically about these issues. Online and print resources and professional development activities related to censorship are at the end of this chapter.

**TABLE 7.5**

# What Teachers Can Do to Handle Challenges to Children's Books

| Action | Questions | Resources |
|---|---|---|
| Keep current in the field. | • What elements in literature are offensive to censors?<br>• What happens when personal and community standards conflict?<br>• To what extent are school materials censored by the selection of administrators, librarians, and teachers?<br>• Which books are you personally willing to fight for? Why?<br>• What biases do you have? How do they influence you? | Maintain a file of material on censorship, including newspaper clippings, reference sources, and policy statements from various organizations, both partisan and nonpartisan. Reference book reviews by relevant sources, such as these:<br>*Horn Book Magazine*<br>*School Library Journal*<br>*The Bulletin of the Center for Children's Literature*<br>*Booklist*<br>*Children's Literature Review*<br>*Kaleidoscope: Multicultural Booklist for Grades K–8*<br>*Adventuring with Books*<br>*Jewish Children's Books: How to Choose Them, How to Use Them* |

**TABLE 7.5**

(*continued*)

# What Teachers Can Do to Handle Challenges to Children's Books

| Action | Questions | Resources |
|---|---|---|
| Obtain selection criteria from national professional organizations. | • What professional organizations offer support in the form of policies, online information, or advocacy? Is your school aware of these policies?<br>• How can these policies assist you in selecting books for the classroom? | Assemble support from professional organizations, such as these:<br>• American Library Association<br>• The Council on Interracial Books for Children<br>• The National Council of Teachers of English<br>• The International Reading Association |
| Communicate with parents. | • Have you held open conversations about children's literature with parents?<br>• Have you provided parents with the information they need to make informed choices about their children's reading material such as offering copies of class novels to parents who want to read them?<br>• Have you discussed with parents the value and appeal of books that may be considered controversial?<br>• Have you requested that parents submit written family standards that would be honored in recommending books for independent reading? | Provide an opportunity to have an open discussion with parents about children's literature during a special event, open house, or through written communication. Invite parents to read the books that might be in question. Discuss changes in children's books over the years and the value and appeal of these books for children. Share written responses from children about these books, or have children join in the discussion. |
| Evaluate books with children. | • Are the children in your class able to critically evaluate books? If not, how can you engage them in judging books for quality?<br>• How can you assist children in understanding the concept of censorship and how it affects them? | Engage children in comparing/contrasting various versions of folktales/fairy tales as a way to think about quality in books. In this way, you will provide children with tools of the mind to begin thinking critically about books. For older readers, have honest conversations about books that have controversial language/issues connecting back to the criteria for quality literature. |

(*continued*)

**TABLE 7.5**

*(continued)*

# What Teachers Can Do to Handle Challenges to Children's Books

| Action | Questions | Resources |
|---|---|---|
| Prepare a school policy statement. | • Does your school have a policy in place for selecting books for school and class-room libraries? | With the participation of the school's faculty, librarian, and administration and community members, construct a selection policy that establishes reasons for including a book in the school or classroom library. Keep everyone in the school and community informed of new acquisitions. Draft a policy for dealing with book challenges. |
| Adopt a formal complaint procedure. | • What support will you have from the school administration for book challenges?<br>• Does your school have a policy in place for handling book challenges? | The National Council of Teachers of English provides guidelines for coping with censorship. These guidelines suggest that the individual objecting to a book fill out "The Citizen's Request for Reconsideration of a Work" form. This form assumes that the individual has read the work in its entirety, which alone may discourage minor objections. Completed forms should be reviewed by a committee that will report its findings and recommendations. Sample policies are also available on the American Library Association's website. |

Adapted from M. Jalongo & A. Creany (1991).

# Top 10 Read Alouds

**REALISTIC FICTION**

1. **Alvin Ho: Allergic to Girls, School, and Other Scary Things** by Lenore Look, illustrated by LeUyen Pham (2008, Schwartz & Wade). A young boy in Concord, Massachusetts, who loves superheroes and comes from a long line of brave Chinese farmer-warriors, wants to make friends, but first he must overcome his fear of everything.

2. **Each Little Bird That Sings** by Deborah Wiles (2005, Gulliver). Comfort Snow berger is well acquainted with death because her family runs the funeral parlor in their small southern town, but even so, the ten-year-old is unprepared for the series of heart-wrenching events that begins on the first day of Easter vacation with the sudden death of her beloved Great-Uncle Edisto.

3. **Feathers** by Jacqueline Woodson (2007, Putnam). When a new, white student nicknamed "The Jesus Boy" joins her sixth grade class in the winter of 1971, Frannie's growing friendship with him makes her start to see some things in a new light.

4. **The Penderwicks: A Summer Tale of Four Sisters, Two Rabbits, and a Very Interesting Boy** by Jeanne Birdsall (2005, Knopf). While vacationing with their widowed father in the Berkshire Mountains, four lovable sisters, ages 4 through 12, share adventures with a local boy, much to the dismay of his snobbish mother.

5. **Pictures of Hollis Woods** by Patricia Reilly Giff (2002, Wendy Lamb Books). A troublesome 12-year-old orphan, staying with an elderly artist who relies on her, remembers the only other time she was happy in a foster home with a family who truly seemed to care about her.

6. **Ruby Holler** by Sharon Creech (2002, HarperCollins). Thirteen-year-old fraternal twins Dallas and Florida have grown up in a terrible orphanage, but their lives change forever when an eccentric but sweet older couple invite them to go on an adventure that begins in an almost magical place called Ruby Holler.

7. **Ruby Lu, Brave and True** by Lenore Look (2004, Simon & Schuster). "Almost-eight-year-old" Ruby Lu spends time with her baby brother, goes to Chinese school, performs magic tricks, learns to drive, and has adventures with both old and new friends.

8. **Rules** by Cynthia Lord (2006, Scholastic Press). Frustrated at life with an autistic brother, twelve-year-old Catherine longs for a normal existence, but her world is further complicated by a friendship with a young paraplegic.

9. **The Talented Clementine** by Sara Pennypacker (2007, Hyperion). Eight-year-old Clementine, convinced that she has no talents, tries to find a way to avoid participating in the class talent show.

10. **The Year of the Dog** by Grace Lin (2006, Little, Brown). Frustrated at her seeming lack of talent for anything, a young Taiwanese-American girl sets out to apply the lessons of the Chinese Year of the Dog—making best friends and finding oneself—to her own life.

# Activities for Professional Development

## Think Critically About Children's Literature

1. Select a topic, such as death or divorce, in children's realistic fiction, and then find several realistic fiction picturebooks and novels from different time periods and cultures that deal with this topic. How has the treatment of this topic changed over time?

2. Visit the American Library Association's (ALA) Banned Books Week webpage. Banned Books Week celebrates the freedom to choose, to express an opinion, and to have available unorthodox or unpopular viewpoints to anyone who wishes to read them. Explore the resources available to teachers and librarians. Did anything surprise you? Do you disagree with any of the materials provided? What opinions might be expressed in children's books that you feel uncomfortable having available for children to read? Why? Discuss these issues with your classmates.

3. The Kerlan Collection at the University of Minnesota is one of the world's great children's literature research collections. The Collection includes books, original manuscripts and illustrations, and many related materials including a censorship portfolio that includes The Anatomy of a Book Challenge: Lois Lowry's *The Giver*. Go to: http://special.lib.umn.edu/clrc/kerlan/censorship/challenge.php. You will see that the portfolio is divided into four parts which follow the process of a book challenge: the book, the challenge, the response from the school district and the response from Lois Lowry. Many of the documents in each section are available online. As you read the documents in each section, record your thoughts on the issues, opinions, and perspectives presented from all sides. Then, write a reflective summary of the case as a whole and share with your classmate.

## Children's Literature in the Classroom

4. Interview peers in your class and/or colleagues at your school or library about ways they select realistic fiction for their classrooms. Ask if they have had specific books that caused controversy. If so, how did they handle the situation? Interview a school librarian and ask what policies the school or district has in place for handling book challenges.

# Print and Online Resources

## Print Resources

Reichman, H. (2001). *Censorship and selection: Issues and answers for schools* (3rd ed.) Chicago: ALA.

Roser, N., & Martinez, M. (Eds.) (2005). *What a character! Character study as a guide to literary meaning making in grades K–8.* Newark, DE: International Reading Association.

Silvey, A. (2004). *100 best books for children.* Boston: Houghton Mifflin.

 **Online Resources**

*Censorship, the Internet, Intellectual Freedom, and Youth*
**http://www.scils.rutgers.edu/~kvander/censorship.html**
Written and compiled by Professor Emerita Kay Vandergrift of Rutgers University, this webpage offers a brief discussion of censorship, the Internet, intellectual freedom, and youth along with a compilation of online resources.

*CCBC Intellectual Freedom Services*
**http://www.education.wisc.edu/ccbc/freedom/default.asp**
This site is part of the Cooperative Children's Book Center which specializes in intellectual freedom issues as they relate to children's and teens' access to materials in libraries and classrooms. A rich depository of resources, the site includes suggested steps to take when materials are challenged, a list of education and advocacy groups and a "what if" library of questions and answers about book challenges.

*eThemes*
**http://www.emints.org/ethemes/index.shtml**
eThemes is an extensive database of content-rich, age-appropriate resources organized around specific themes. These resources are created for educators to use in their classrooms. The themes

include specific books and themes within the realistic fiction genre.

*Juvenile Series and Sequels*
**http://www.mcpl.lib.mo.us/readers/series/juv**
Many realistic fiction books are part of a series. This searchable database hosted by the Mid-Continent Public Library has over 23,000 series or sequels titles classified into three categories: young adult, juvenile, and juvenile easy.

*KidSPEAK!*
**http://www.kidspeakonline.org**
Missing from the debate over protecting kids from harmful material have been the kids themselves.

KidSPEAK will provide a means for kids to enter this discussion, which so vitally affects their rights. The site provides a forum for students to talk about books, learn more about censorship and find ways to support their right to freedom of speech.

*National Council of Teachers of English Anti-Censorship Center*
**http://www.ncte.org/action/anti-censorship**
This webpage of NCTE offers advice, helpful documents, and other support to teachers faced with challenges to literary works, films and videos, drama productions, or teaching methods.

Visit the companion website at **www.cengage.com/education/johnson** to find

links related to the Read/Watch/Listen icons noted throughout the chapter, as well as additional resources.

## Creating Your Classroom library

### PICTUREBOOKS

*All the World* by Liz Garton Scanlon, illustrated by Marla Frazee (2009, Simon & Schuster). Following a circle of family and friends through the course of a day from morning till night, this book affirms the importance of all things great and small in our world, from the tiniest shell on the beach, to warm family connections, to the widest sunset sky.

*Flower Garden* by Eve Bunting (1994, Harcourt). Helped by her father, a young girl prepares a flower garden as a birthday surprise for her mother.

*Fred Stays with Me!* written by Nancy Coffelt, illustrated by Tricia Tusa (2007, Little, Brown). A child describes how he lives sometimes with his mother and sometimes with his father, but his dog is his constant companion.

*Nana Upstairs & Nana Downstairs* by Tomie dePaola (1973, Putnam). Four-year-old Tommy enjoys his relationship with both his grandmother and great-grandmother, but he eventually learns to face their inevitable deaths.

*The Old Woman Who Named Things* by Cynthia Rylant (1996, Harcourt). An old woman who has outlived all her friends is reluctant to become too attached to the stray dog that visits her each day.

*Pictures from Our Vacation* by Lynne Perkins (2007, Greenwillow). Given a camera that takes and prints tiny pictures just before leaving for the family farm in Canada, a young girl records a vacation that gets off to a slow start, but winds up being a family reunion filled with good memories.

*The Relatives Came* by Cynthia Rylant (1985, Atheneum). The relatives come to visit from Virginia, and everyone has a wonderful time.

*Shortcut* by Donald Crews (1992, Greenwillow). Children taking a shortcut by walking along a railroad track find excitement and danger when a train approaches.

*Weslandia* by Paul Fleischman (1999, Candlewick). Wesley's garden produces a crop of huge, strange plants that provide him with clothing, shelter, food, and drink, thus helping him create his own civilization and changing his life.

*Wilfrid Gordon McDonald Partridge* by Mem Fox (1985, Kane/Miller). A small boy tries to discover the meaning of "memory" so he can restore that of an elderly friend.

### OLDER READERS

*A View from Saturday* by E. L. Konigsburg (1996, Atheneum). Four students, with their own individual stories, develop a special bond and attract the attention of their teacher, a paraplegic, who chooses them to represent their sixth-grade class in the Academic Bowl competition.

*The Aurora County All-Stars* by Deborah Wiles (2007, Harcourt). For most boys in a small Mississippi town, the biggest concern one hot summer is whether their annual July 4th baseball game will be cancelled due to their county's anniversary pageant, but after the death of the old man to whom twelve-year-old star pitcher House Jackson has been secretly reading for a year, House uncovers secrets about the man and the history of baseball in Aurora County that could fix everything.

*Chasing Vermeer* by Blue Balliett (2004, Scholastic). When strange and seemingly unrelated events start to happen and a precious Vermeer painting disappears, eleven-year-olds Petra and Calder combine their talents to solve an international art scandal.

*Frindle* by Andrew Clements (1996, Simon & Schuster). When he decides to turn his fifth-grade teacher's love of the dictionary around on her, clever Nick Allen invents a new word and begins a chain of events that quickly moves beyond his control.

*The Great Gilly Hopkins* by Katherine Paterson (1978, HarperCollins). An 11-year-old foster child tries to cope with her longings and fears as she schemes against everyone who tries to be friendly.

*Holes* by Louis Sachar (1998, Farrar, Straus and Giroux). As further evidence of his family's bad fortune, which they attribute to a curse on a distant relative, Stanley Yelnats is sent to a hellish correctional camp in the Texas desert where he finds his first real friend, a treasure, and a new sense of himself.

*Julie of the Wolves* by Jean Craighead George (1994, HarperCollins). When Julie returns to her father's Eskimo village, she struggles to find a way to save her beloved wolves in a changing Arctic world, and she falls in love with a young Siberian man.

*Moxy Maxwell Does Not Love Stuart Little* by Peggy Gifford (2007, Schwartz & Wade). With summer coming to an end, about-to-be-fourth-grader Moxy Maxwell does a hundred different things to avoid reading her assigned summer reading book.

*Tales of a Fourth Grade Nothing* by Judy Blume (1972, Dutton). Peter finds his demanding two-year-old brother an ever-increasing problem.

*The Small Adventure of Popeye and Elvis* (2009, Farrar, Straus and Giroux). In Fayette, South Carolina, the highlight of Popeye's summer is learning vocabulary words with his grandmother until a motor home gets stuck nearby and Elvis, the oldest boy living inside, joins Popeye in finding the source of strange boats floating down the creek.

*The Trouble with Tuck* by Theodore Taylor (1981, Delacorte). A young girl trains her blind dog to follow and trust a seeing-eye companion dog.

*The Westing Game* by Ellen Raskin (1978, Dutton). The mysterious death of an eccentric millionaire brings together an unlikely assortment of heirs, who must uncover the circumstances of his death before they can claim their inheritance.

*Where the Red Fern Grows* by Wilson Rawls (1961, Curtis). A young boy living in the Ozarks achieves his heart's desire when he becomes the owner of two redbone hounds and teaches them to be champion hunters.

*Wringer* by Jerry Spinelli (1997, HarperCollins). As Palmer comes of age, he must either accept the violence of being a wringer at his town's annual Pigeon Day or find the courage to oppose it.

## REALISTIC FICTION SERIES BOOKS FOR YOUNGER READERS

*A to Z Mysteries* by Ron Roy

*Akimbo and the Crocodile Man* by Alexander McCall Smith

*Aldo Applesauce* by Joanna Hurwitz

*Amber Brown* by Paula Danziger

*Baby-Sitters Club* by Ann Martin

*Bailey School Kids* by Debbie Dadey and Marsha Thornton Jones

*The Boxcar Children* by Gertrude Warner

*Cam Jansen* by David Adler

*Diary of A Wimpy Kid* by Jeff Kinney

*Einstein Anderson, Science Detective* by Seymour Simon

*Henry and Mudge* by Cynthia Rylant

*Horrible Harry* by Suzy Kline

*Ivy and Bean* by Annie Barrows

*Jackson Jones* by Mary Quattlebaum

*Judy Moody* by Megan McDonald

*Julian Stories* by Ann Cameron

*Junebug* by Alice Mead

*Junie B. Jones* by Barbara Park

*Magnolia Street* by Angela Johnson

*Marvin Redpost* by Louis Sachar

*Nate the Great* by Marjorie Sharmat

*Owen Foote* by Stephanie Greene

*Pee Wee Scouts* by Judy Delton

*Polk Street School* by Patricia Reilly Giff

*Ramona Quimby* by Beverly Cleary

*Saddle Club* by Bonnie Bryant

*Sam* books by Lois Lowry

*Willimena Rules!* by Valerie Wilson Wesley

*Zach Files* by Dan Greenburg

## REALISTIC FICTION SERIES BOOKS FOR OLDER READERS

*Alex Rider Adventures* by Anthony Horowitz

*Alice* by Phyllis Reynolds Naylor

*Anastasia* by Lois Lowry

*Bingo Brown* by Betsy Cromer

*Black Beauty* series by Walter Farley

*Encyclopedia Brown* by Donald J. Sobol

*Ernestine & Amanda* series by Sandra Belton

*Famous Five* by Enid Blyton

*Flint Future Detective* series by Christopher Paul Curtis

*Fudge* books by Judy Blume

*The Great Brain* series by John Fitzgerald

*Hardy Boys* by Franklin W. Dixon

*Henry Reed* books by Keith Robertson

*Joey Pigza* by Jack Gantos

*Katie Kazoo, Switcheroo* by Nancy E. Krulik

*Mad Scientists' Club* by Bertrand R. Brinley

*Matthew Martin* by Paula Danziger

*Nancy Drew* by Carolyn Keene

*On the Run* series by Gordon Korman

*Sammy Keyes* by Wendelin Van Draanen

*Sebastian Barth Mysteries* by James Howe

*Soup* by Robert Newton Peck

*Yang* series by Lensey Namioka

*Young Bond* by Charlie Higson

## REALISTIC FICTION BOOKS WITH MULTICULTURAL CHARACTERS
### Picturebooks

*Allison* by Allen Say

*Angel Child, Dragon Child* by Michele Surat

*Annie and the Old One* by Miska Miles

*Bigmama's* by Donald Crews

*Billy the Great* by Rosa Guy

*Chin Chiang and the Dragon's Dance* by Ian Wallace

*The Day Gogo Went to Vote: South Africa, April 1994* by Elinor Sisulu

*The Flower Garden* by Eve Bunting

*The Hundred Penny Box* by Sharon Mathis

*Jonathan and His Mommy* by Irene Smalls-Hector

*The Keeping Quilt* by Patricia Polacco

*Little Cliff and the Porch People* by Clifton Taulbert

*The Lotus Seed* by Sherry Garland

*Mama, Do You Love Me?* by Barbara Joosse

*Maria Molina and the Days of the Dead* by Kathleen Krull

*My Aunt Otilia's Spirits* by Richard Garcia

*The Patchwork Quilt* by Valerie Flaurnoy

*Song of the Swallows* by Leo Politi

*Too Many Tamales* by Gary Soto

**Chapter Books**

*A Girl Named Disaster* by Nancy Farmer

*And Now Miguel* by Joseph Krumgold

*Beware of Kissing Lizard Lips* by Phyllis Shalant

*Black Star, Bright Dawn* by Scott O'Dell

*Bobby vs. Girls (Accidentally)* by Lisa Yee

*Child of the Owl* by Lawrence Yep

*Cousins* by Virginia Hamilton

*Felita* by Nicholasa Mohr

*Going Home* by Eve Bunting

*Habibi* by Naomi Shihab Nye

*Heaven* by Angela Johnson

*Living Up the Street* by Gary Soto

*Love That Dog* by Sharon Creech

*M. C. Higgins, the Great* by Virginia Hamilton

*Make Way for Dyamonde Daniel* by Nikki Grimes

*Miracle's Boys* by Jacqueline Woodson

*The Most Beautiful Place in the World* by Ann Cameron

*The Mouse Rap* by Walter Dean Myers

*Nikki and Deja* by Karen English

*Only One Year* by Andrea Cheng

*Pageant* by Kathryn Lasky

*Philip Hall Likes Me, I Reckon* by Bette Greene

*The Planet of Junior Brown* by Virginia Hamilton

*The Road to Paris* by Nikki Grimes

*Ruby and the Booker Boys* series by Derrick Barnes

*Scorpions* by Walter Dean Myers

*Shadow of a Bull* by Maia Wojciechowska

*Sister* by Eloise Greenfield

*Songs of Faith* by Angela Johnson

*The Storyteller's Beads* by Jane Kurtz

*Sunny Holiday* by Coleen Paratore

*Taking Sides* by Gary Soto

*The Talking Earth* by Jean Craighead George

*Time Pieces* by Virginia Hamilton

*Yang the Third and Her Impossible Family* by Lensey Namioka

*Year of the Boar and Jackie Robinson* by Betty Lord

*Yolanda's Genius* by Carol Fenner

*Zeely* by Virginia Hamilton

# References

Allington, R. (2002). What I've learned about effective reading instruction. *Phi Delta Kappan*, 740–747.

American Library Association (ALA, 2010). Frequently challenged books by decade. Available: http://www.ala.org/ala/issuesadvocacy/index.cfm.

American Library Association (ALA). *ALA free access to libraries for minors: An interpretation of the Library Bill of Right.* Available: http://www.ala.org/Template.cfm?Section=interpretations&Template=/ContentManagement/ContentDisplay.cfm&ContentID=8639.

Bosman, J. (2007). With one word, children's book sets off uproar. *New York Times*. Available: http://www.nytimes.com/2007/02/18/books/18newb.html?n=top%2freference%2ftimes.

Brooks, J., & Thompson, E. (2005). Social justice in the classroom. *Educational Leadership, 63*(1), 48–52.

Board of Education, Island Trees Union Free School District No. 26 v. Pico, 457 U.S. 853, 102 S.Ct. 2799, 73 L.Ed.2d 435 (1982).

Bunting, E. (1995). *Once upon a time*. Katonah, NY: Richard Owens.

Calkins, L. (2001). *The art of teaching reading*. New York: Addison-Wesley.

Censored. (1995, February). *Parenting, 9,* 104–109.

Cooper, I. (2006). There's something about Edward. *Booklist, 102*(9–10), 112.

Douglas, W. (1953). The one un-American act. *Nieman Reports*, 7(1), p. 20.

Friedman, A., & Cataldo, C. (2002). Characters at crossroads: Reflective decision makers in contemporary Newbery books. *The Reading Teacher, 56*(2), 102–112.

Hannigan, K. (2004). *Ida B: . . . and her plans to maximize fun, avoid disaster, and (possibly) save the world.* New York: Greenwillow.

Jalongo, M., & Creany, A. (1991). Censorship in children's literature: What every educator should know. *Childhood Education, 67*(3), 143–148.

Jenkins, C. (2008). Book challenges, challenging books, and young readers: The research picture. *Language Arts, 85*(3), 228–236.

Kadohata, C. (2005). Newbery Medal acceptance. *The Horn Book Magazine, 81*(4), 409–417.

Kloberdanz, K., & Blume, J. (2002, Sept.–Oct.). Back in Blume: Everything's coming up roses for the writer who has helped three generations through adolescence. *Book, 36*(2), 22.

Konigsburg, E. L. (1997). Newbery Medal acceptance. *The Horn Book Magazine, 73*(4), 404–414.

Lester, J. (2006, August 11). Writing from experience. Message posted to child lit electronic mailing list, archived at https://email.rutgers.edu/pipermail/child_lit.

Marcus, L. (1998). *Dear genius: The letters of Ursula Nordstrom.* New York: HarperCollins.

National Education Association (NEA). *What is America's favorite children's book series?: Harry Potter' series tops list of NEA's Read Across America favorite book series poll.* Available: http://www.nea.org/home/38249.htm.

National Council of Teachers of English (NCTE) (1981). The right to read and the English teacher. Available: http://www.ncte.org/positions/statements/righttoreadguideline.

Patron, S. (2006). *The higher power of Lucky.* New York: Atheneum.

Patron, S. (2007). Susan Patron's response. *Publishers Weekly* [online]. Available: http://www.publishersweekly.com/index.asp?layout=articleprint&articleid=CA6416836.

Raphael, T., Pardo, L., & Highfield, K. (2002). *Book club: A literature-based curriculum.* Lawrence, MA: Small Planet Communications.

Reichman, H. (2001). *Censorship and selection: Issues and answers for schools* (3rd ed.). Chicago: American Library Association.

Rudman, M. (1995). *Children's literature: An issues approach* (3rd ed.). White Plains, NY: Longman.

Rylant, C. (1989). *But, I'll be back again: An album.* New York: Orchard Books.

Sachar, L. (1999). Newbery Medal acceptance. *The Horn Book Magazine, 75*(4), 410–417.

Sieruta, P. (1998). Dear Clueless: The rejection letters of Edna Albertson. *The Horn Book Magazine, 74*(6), 703–707.

Smith, D. (2005, September 7). S. E. Hinton, out of the shadows. Available http://www.detnews.com/2005/books/0509/16/0ent-306965.htm. Accessed Sept. 22, 2005.

The Center for the Book in the Library of Congress (2006). *Letters about literature.* Retrieved August 4, 2007, from http://www.loc.gov/loc/cfbook/LAL2006-levelone.two.html.

Weekly Reader's *Read* Magazine (1995). *Dear author: Students write about the books that changed their lives.* Berkeley, CA: Conari Press.

Winters, C., & Schmidt, G. (2001). *Edging the boundaries of children's literature.* Needham Heights, MA: Allyn & Bacon.

# 8  Historical Fiction

This excerpt from Karen Cushman's (1996) Newbery acceptance speech for *Midwife's Apprentice* provides a fitting metaphor for the role of historical fiction for children. Children's knowledge of history is based primarily on what is conveyed through print, usually in the form of textbooks, which present historical facts about specific events and time periods. These facts from textbooks do not speak to us in a way that helps us understand our humanity, that helps us grow. Good historical fiction provides us with an opportunity to connect with people and events in the past, and in doing so, it helps us consider both the present and the future.

> Among a native Australian people, it is said, when the rice crop shows sign of failure, the women go into the rice field, bend down, and relate to it the history of its origins; the rice, now understanding why it is there, begins again to grow. Aha, I thought, as I read this passage, such is the importance of stories. That is why I write. When the book is finished and I hold it in my hands, I can see myself bending down to whisper it into the ear of a child.
> —*Karen Cushman, 1996, p. 413*

## Defining Historical Fiction

*Historical fiction brings together* historical fact and imagination. We can never experience the lives of the people and events of the past, but we can come as close as possible through historical fiction. Authors craft historical fiction by weaving together pieces of factual information and filling in the gaps of available information with imagination. The success of a work of historical fiction depends on the author's ability to combine the facts of the event, their vision of the meaning of the event, and the fictional tale surrounding the event. The successful union of these three elements brings to life the spirit of the time period (Winters & Schmidt, 2001).

## AUTHENTIC HISTORICAL TIME AND EVENTS

Stories that fall within the genre of historical fiction are neither fantasy nor nonfiction, but they are realistic in the sense that they are possible—the setting is authentic, the characters could have or did exist, and the plot is at least believable, if not true to life. Yet, these stories are not considered realistic fiction because they are set in the past. Experts disagree about what constitutes "the past." Some say a book must be set 25 years in the past to be considered historical fiction; others say 50, and still others say a book is *historical* if it takes place any time prior to the present. The exact number of years doesn't matter. Time is relative—what was a long time ago for a child might seem "just like yesterday" to an adult. For example, *The Watsons Go to Birmingham—1963,* written by Christopher Paul Curtis, is considered historical fiction because it takes place during the early days of the civil rights movement. This time period may seem like a long time ago to children, but for many adults who lived through this time, it may seem like "only yesterday."

*Listen*

Listen to excerpts from A Single Shard *and* Crispin: The Cross of Lead.

Many stories of historical fiction take place during time periods before the life of the author. *A Single Shard,* written by Linda Sue Park, takes place in twelfth-century Korea; *Crispin: The Cross of Lead,* written by Avi, is set in fourteenth-century England; and *Beyond the Burning Time,* by Kathryn Lasky, is set in seventeenth-century America. Since the authors have no personal experiences during the time periods written about, they must rely entirely on primary and secondary sources. Most authors of this type of historical fiction spend hundreds of hours researching historical documents, visiting historical locations and museums, and conducting interviews.

Another type of historical fiction is when the author writes about his or her own experiences, usually as a child, in fictional format. *Homesick* by Jean Fritz is a memoir of the author's early childhood growing up in turbulent China in the mid-1920s. *Caddie Woodlawn* by Carol Ryrie Brink is the story of the author's grandmother growing up in the woods of Wisconsin in 1864. In *The Upstairs Room,* author Johanna Reiss chronicles her survival as a Jewish child in Holland during the Holocaust. Authors of this type of historical fiction must have a keen power of observation and an excellent memory. Other books that were originally written as contemporary realistic fiction are now considered historical fiction—for example, *Little Women* by Louisa May Alcott, *Journey to Jo'berg* by Beverly Naidoo, and *Snow Treasure* by Marie McSwigan. All of these books were considered contemporary realistic fiction when they were published, but they have since become historical fiction.

*Read*

Read Little Women.

Children can and do understand historical time and are capable of reconstructing patterns and sequences of historical events as they are represented in story form. Children's ability to understand cause-and-effect relationships, a fundamental aspect of historical reasoning, is developmental and takes place over time. By the end of fifth grade, students have acquired a good grasp of historical time periods in U.S. history (Hodge, 1991; VanSledright, 2002). Research suggests that historical narrative is more interesting and comprehensible to students than the expository writing of social studies textbooks and that students' interest and ability to learn and retain historical information increase (Levstik & Barton, 2010). Historical fiction is categorized around major time periods or events in history (see "Categories of Historical Fiction").

## CREATING A SENSE OF REALISM

Although historical information can be gained, a book of historical fiction is first and foremost a story. For children to engage in historical fiction, authors must create a sense of realism in their work that brings the time period alive regardless of how much the time

*The Watsons Go to Birmingham—1963 blends the fictional account of an African-American family with the factual events of the violent summer of 1963 as seen through the innocent eyes of ten-year-old Kenny.*

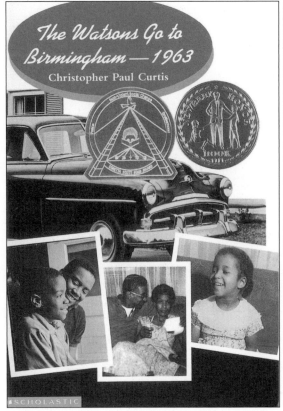

period, setting, or culture separates the story from the reader. Authors achieve a sense of realism in a variety of ways:

- The use of a distinctive narrative format, such as a journal or diary entries
- An authentic setting and dialogue of the time period
- The characters' responses to historical events

*Watch*

*Watch an interview with Christopher Paul Curtis and listen to an excerpt of* The Watsons Go to Birmingham—1963.

For example, in *The Watsons Go to Birmingham—1963,* Christopher Paul Curtis blends the fictional account of an African-American family with the factual events of the violent summer of 1963 and brings the story to life through the innocent and genuine protagonist of ten-year-old Kenny. When Kenny's family decides to visit his grandmother in Birmingham, Alabama, the reader experiences through Kenny's eyes the burning of the Sixteenth Avenue Baptist Church with four little girls trapped inside. It is Kenny's response to this horrific event that affects the reader. Good historical fiction presents a story about human characters who have the same essential nature as the reader, a nature that does not change over time and shows the commonalities of humanity. Avi (2003), who has written many historical fiction novels for children, imparts, "That's all we who write hope to do: create stories that will enable our young readers to find the stirrings of their souls" (p. 414).

Within the genre of historical fiction, there are categories: different time periods and events in history that are often represented in historical fiction (see "Categories of Historical Fiction"). All historical fiction should represent authentic times and events and invoke a sense of realism.

# Benefits and Considerations of Historical Fiction

Historical fiction has not been favored by children in the past, but it is beginning to see a new resurgence. One bookseller called historical fiction the "new fantasy," stating, "Interest in magical peoples and places, in other worlds and times, has paved the way for greater appetite for learning about different historical periods" (Owens, 2003, p. 22).

## BENEFITS

Historical fiction, like the genre of fantasy, creates another world, a deliberately evoked world that is very different from but has strong connections to our own world. Winters and Schmidt (2001) state, "The writer of historical fiction creates another world, but it is a world firmly rooted in the real world and, in creating it, to allow the reader to see his or her own world more fully, from more perspective, from deeper inside" (p. 264). Historical fiction creates a sense of life as it was lived at the time. Historical fiction

- conveys a sense of life as it was lived.
- happens to ordinary people.
- broadens perspectives.
- helps children understand that the present and future are linked to actions of the past.

Textbooks present history in a stripped-down, depersonalized way that can make students feel detached and insignificant. Reading personalized accounts of history as told through the eyes of realistic characters connects children to life as people experienced it then—whether in their own parents' generation or many generations in the past.

At one time, children's historical fiction consisted mainly of stories about well-known figures and events of the past. Today's historical fiction still includes these figures, but usually they are secondary to the lives of the common people of the time. Children are naturally curious about the people and events of the past; they want to know the truth about what really happened. Avi (2003) writes the following:

> Truth is always the harshest reality, even as it is the more liberating one. For the paradox of writing is this: the greater the writing, the more it reveals. . . the *ordinary*. That is to say, great writing reveals what we know—but never noticed before. Great writing identifies that most elusive of all things—that which we have seen but had not noticed, that did not seem to exist until it was named. (p. 412)

Historical fiction helps children realize they are not just outsiders looking in on great historical events; it helps them appreciate that everyone plays a role in shaping history. Through historical fiction, children can determine their role in history and position their own lives in the succession of generations. They can find common bonds with people who are distant in time and space, recognizing in them a part of our common humanity while understanding the differences that separate us.

Historical fiction provides a means to a balanced view of historical events and experiences from the multiple perspectives of the individuals or groups who participated. Tunnell and Ammon (1993) provide an example of how historical fiction can provide a multicultural perspective on the westward expansion in the United States in the nineteenth century, typically presented in a positive light in textbooks:

> Today, although most historians recognize the benefits of westward expansion for Anglo-American and Mexican families migrating from the East, they also acknowledge that migration and hunger for land wrought destruction upon Native American and

# Categories of Historical Fiction

| Time/Event | Description | Examples |
|---|---|---|
| Ancient Times | Stories about ancient civilizations including Ancient Greece, Rome, and Egypt. Often focuses on a character considered an outsider and an independent thinker. Themes include survival, courage, honor, and development of compassion. | *Mara, Daughter of the Nile* by Eloise McGraw<br>*The Thieves of Ostia* by Caroline Lawrence<br>*The Bronze Bow* by Elizabeth George Speare |
| Medieval Times | Stories that take place during the Middle Ages, which begins after the fall of the Roman Empire. In this period, battles with the barbarian tribes take place in Europe. Stories often mix fact and fiction. Stories about knights are common. Themes include loyalty and overcoming handicaps. | *Matilda Bone* by Karen Cushman<br>*A Door in the Wall* by Marguerite De Angeli<br>*The King's Shadow* by Elizabeth Alder |
| Colonial Times | Stories about the settlements at Jamestown, Plymouth, and Boston. Includes stories about the continued move westward, American Indians, and the Salem witch trials. Themes include courage, survival, and persecution. | *The Witch of Blackbird Pond* by Elizabeth G. Speare<br>*The Courage of Sarah Noble* by Alice Dalgliesh<br>*Constance: A Story of Early Plymouth* by Patricia Clapp |
| Revolutionary Era | Stories about the events surrounding the Revolutionary War. Often focuses on a character that stays and defends the home during the war or one who becomes involved in the war. Themes include divided loyalties between family, freedom, commitment to a cause, and injustice. | *Early Thunder* by Jean Fritz<br>*Woods Runner* by Gary Paulsen<br>*Katie's Truck* by Ann Turner |
| Early Frontier Era | Stories about the move westward before the Civil War. Includes the different perspectives of the settlers and American Indians. Themes include friendship, faith, longing for ownership of land, hardship, and family bonds. | *Lyddie* by Katherine Paterson<br>*Sarah, Plain and Tall* by Patricia MacLachlan<br>*Adaline Falling Star* by Mary Pope Osborne |
| Civil War | Books that describe the antebellum period, slavery, and the War between the States. Battles are not glorified. Themes include divided loyalty, the tragedy of war, and freedom. They also portray prejudice and hate as destructive. | *Shades of Grey* by Carolyn Reeder<br>*Charlie Skedaddle* by Patricia Beatty<br>*Nettie's Trip South* by Ann Turner |
| Post–Civil War | Stories about the move westward, the Industrial Revolution, and immigrants. The poor working conditions in the factories are often depicted. Themes include looking for a better life, desire to own land, family bonds, seeking fortune, and hardship. | *Little House on the Prairie* by Laura Ingalls Wilder<br>*Immigrant Girl* by Brett Harvey<br>*Worth* by A. LaFaye |

*(continued)*

# Categories of Historical Fiction *(continued)*

| Time/Event | Description | Examples |
|---|---|---|
| World War I | Stories surrounding the events of World War I and its aftermath. Focuses on characters in different countries. Themes include destructive nature of war, survival, prejudice, and discrimination. | *Summer Soldiers* by Susan Lindquist *No Hero for the Kaiser* by Rudolf Frank *Letters from Rifka* by Karen Hesse |
| Great Depression | Stories surrounding the economic depression in the 1930s. Books often portray the hardships faced by main characters. Themes include survival, money does not create happiness, effects of poverty, and homelessness. | *Out of the Dust* by Karen Hesse *Bud, Not Buddy* by Christopher Paul Curtis *The Song of the Trees* by Mildred D. Taylor |
| World War II | Stories surrounding World War II, Hitler's rise and fall, and Japanese military activity. Often focuses on characters who struggle with the effects of war. Many stories focus on the Holocaust. Themes include hatred, prejudice, religious and personal freedom, survival, and suffering caused by war. | *Number the Stars* by Lois Lowry *Year of Impossible Goodbyes* by Sook Nyul Choi *Lily's Crossing* by Patricia Reilly Giff |
| Post–World War II | Stories about the continued conflict in Korea, Vietnam, and Cambodia. The early 1960s saw the assassination of President John F. Kennedy. Themes include the consequences of war, social change, and humanity. | *The Wall* by Eve Bunting *When JFK Was My Father* by Amy Gordon *Grandfather's Dream* by Holly Keller |
| Civil Rights Movement | Stories about the fight for civil rights that took place from the late 1800s through the mid-1960s. Focuses on the discrimination in the South and the struggle for equal rights. Themes include human suffering, injustice, tolerance, and understanding. | *Francie* by Karen English *Roll of Thunder, Hear My Cry* by Mildred Taylor *Elijah of Buxton* by Christopher Paul Curtis |

Mexican peoples and cultures. As children mature, they can learn to see past events such as the "westward migration" from the multiple perspectives of the people involved. In short, the young can learn to respect and appreciate how people from different races, ethnicities, classes, regions, and genders interpret and evaluate historical experiences. (p. 2)

Many picturebooks and novels available today (including the following) bring to the forefront the perspectives of people from different races, ethnicities, classes, regions, and genders about this time period that have typically been depicted from a limited viewpoint in textbooks.

- *I Have Heard of a Land,* by Joyce Carol Thomas and illustrated by Floyd Cooper, centers on the migration of African-American pioneers to Oklahoma (Floyd Cooper received a 1999 Coretta Scott King Honor Award for illustration).

- In *Zebra-Riding Cowboy,* based on a western folk song, author Angela Medearis and illustrator Maria Brusca tell the story of an educated fellow mistaken for a greenhorn who proves his cowboy ability by riding a wild horse. The book also examines the roles of African-American and Hispanic cowboys in the nineteenth century.
- *Cheyenne Again,* written by Eve Bunting and illustrated by Irving Toddy, is the story of Young Bull, a Cheyenne boy in the late 1880s who struggles to hold onto his heritage when he is taken to a boarding school to learn the white man's ways.
- The novel *Forty Acres and Maybe a Mule,* written by Harriette Robinet, tells the story of 12-year-old Pascal, born with a withered leg and hand, who joins other former slaves in a search of 40 acres of farmland promised by the Freedmen's Bureau during Reconstruction, only to be evicted after a short time.
- *The Birchbark House* and the sequel *The Game of Silence,* by Louise Erdrich, captures both the everyday life and devastating effect of the Westward Expansion in the mid 1800s from the point of view of Omakayas, a young American Indian girl. (See illustration 8 in the Part 2 color insert.) The sole survivor of a smallpox epidemic, Omakayas is adopted by a family in the Ojibwa tribe who lives on an island in Lake Superior, when a white man brings smallpox to the community and is later threatened with eviction.

*Listen*

*Listen to an interview with Louise Erdrich.*

Historical fiction transports readers to places, times, and cultures not otherwise possible. It provides an insider's perspective to the human characteristics of the people involved in an event. According to Tunnell (1993), "Children need to know not so much the events and dates of history as the people—the big names and the little ones—who *are* our history" (p. 84). The typical survey approach provided by most textbooks just can't accomplish this.

Brozo and Tomlinson (1986) believe that by asking the following three questions about a historical event, children can unveil salient concepts that define the human condition:

- What are the driving forces behind the events?
- What phenomena affected ordinary people?
- What universal patterns of behavior should be explained? (p. 289)

Tunnell (1993) continues, "Prejudice, man's inhumanity to man, and man's driving need for freedom are but a few examples of salient history concepts that are only hinted at or ignored in history textbooks" (p. 85). Knowledge of these concepts in history helps children understand the human condition and thus establish relevance: the students' realization that democratic ideals are difficult to reach but worthy of persistent pursuit.

Writers of historical fiction work in both the past and the present. Authors work in the past to clarify the present, and they work in the present as a vantage point to comment on the past. Ellen Klages, winner of the 2007 Scott O'Dell Award for historical fiction for *The Green Glass Sea,* compares historical fiction to a time machine that can transport the reader from the outside looking in to the center of the events of history:

History isn't just dates and facts and places. It's people and their lives and their stories. Sometimes it's extraordinary people in ordinary times, changing the world. And sometimes it's ordinary people in extraordinary times, as the world changes around them. By seeing the past through their eyes—how they live, what they do, how they think—we get a new perspective on the present. (Bird, 2007)

Louise Erdrich's *Birchbark House* is an example of how an author used the past to inform the present by advancing to the forefront the neglected voice of the American Indian. Erdrich also uses the perspective of the present to comment on the horrific treatment of American Indians by the white majority. In an interview (Rochman, 1999), Erdrich explained her feelings:

Smallpox wiped out 9 of 10 people. It's such an inconceivable horror. And it's so undocumented by native people because everything comes down orally…. A few accounts that have come down show that a lot of the native people also migrated because they wanted to avoid the diseases…. The romantic portrayals of the past leave out this reality….. The terrible stories are there, but one of the reasons why I love writing about this culture is that it's so rich, and it's so funny, and there's so much warmth (p. 1427).

Writers of historical fiction have the opportunity to show how the past of all cultures impacts and gives meaning to the present of all cultures, ultimately teaching us about ourselves. (See "The Teacher's Voice" below for an example of how one teacher responded to historical fiction.)

## THE • TEACHER'S • VOICE

**Response to *The Truth About Sparrows* by Marian Hale**

Marian Hale creates characters and a setting so realistic that I've never read a better account of life during the Great Depression. Hale shows the reader the suffering of the time in a way that reminds me of John Steinbeck's <u>East of Eden</u> or <u>Grapes of Wrath.</u>

Against that backdrop, the author develops complex and interesting characters. Told from the first person point of view in the voice of Sadie, a 13-year-old, Hale explores the conflicts of Sadie's own heart. Sadie is so realistic because she struggles with herself and her own attitudes in the way many people do. She is plagued with self-doubt and a desire to be better. Yet, through her actions we see her as a better person than she perceives herself.

Marian Hale explores the questions What is home? Where is home? Who is family? What is suffering? What is hope? What is faith? Sadie also has to learn about forgiveness of herself and others. She must learn acceptance of others and her situation.

I like that the story ends with Christmas with its symbolism for new life and new hope. I think Marian Hale expertly crafted the book as she took Sadie through a painful period of growth and realization. Although there is some dialect in the dialogue, the story is told with dignity and wisdom.

I like this book better than <u>Out of the Dust</u>. Though that story captures the emotion of the times, Hale's story is much more realistic and universal in its themes. Sadie and her family are as real as people I know. I also enjoyed this book because it gave me a better awareness of what my grandparents and father lived through.

I don't think the setting becomes its own character as in <u>Teacher's Funeral</u>, but I do think the author moves beyond setting to create a condition against which all else happens. This story, then, becomes very powerful as an example of historical fiction.

*—How does this teacher use her knowledge of other books of historical fiction as a way to analyze the quality of* The Truth About Sparrows?

## CONSIDERATIONS

For an author to create a realistic depiction of the time in historical fiction, the characters' language, emotions, thoughts, concerns, and experiences must match those of a culture. Yet, this can be difficult when the attitudes and values of another time are repugnant to today's society. Nikolajeva (2005) said the following:

> This [importance of historical and social context] is extremely important in children's literature because young readers may not be aware of the change in values over time; for instance, child abandonment and abuse were once acceptable acts in children's literature, but not today. Readers cannot judge a parent beating his children in a Victorian novel by the same measure used to judge a contemporary parent. The societal norms encoded in such adjectives as nice, virtuous, well-mannered, and even pretty differ considerably over time and from culture to culture. However, readers do not always have the knowledge of exactly what these qualities denoted in their time. Young readers, lacking such knowledge, can fall victim to racist, sexist, and other types of prejudice through characters. (p. 194)

*Listen*

*Listen to an excerpt of* Roll of Thunder, Hear My Cry.

**Historical and Social Context.** Most children's literature experts agree that *Roll of Thunder, Hear My Cry,* written by Mildred Taylor, is an outstanding book of historical fiction. It is on the list of *One Hundred Books That Shaped the Century* (Breen, Fade, Odean, & Sutherland, 2000) and *100 Best Books for Children* (Silvey, 2004). Yet, it was also one of the top ten most challenged books in 2002—cited for insensitivity, racism, and offensive language. The criteria for judging such content should be born out of the context. Is the material authentic and is it used in an accurate social context? The following excerpt from *Roll of Thunder* is a conversation that conveys the tension of the time:

> "It's sho' a shame, all right," said T.J.'s father, a frail, sickly man with a hacking cough. "These folks gettin' so bad in here. Heard tell they lynched a boy a few days ago at Crosston."
>
> "And ain't a thing gonna be done 'bout it," said Mr. Lanier. "That's what's so terrible! When Henrietta went to the sheriff and told him what she'd seed, he called her a liar and sent her on home. Now I hear tells that some of them men that done it been 'round braggin' 'bout it. Sayin' they'd do it again if some other uppity nigger get out of line."
>
> Mrs. Avery tisked, "Lord have mercy!" (p. 29)

In the author's note, Mildred Taylor writes, "By the fireside in our northern home or in the South where I was born, I learned a history not then written in books but one passed from generation to generation on the steps of moonlit porches and beside dying fires in one-room houses" (p. vii). As a cultural insider, Taylor is able to articulate assumptions with which she has always been a part and to enable readers to experience a sense of the time period in which the story is set. In other words, the social context that Taylor conveys is true to her experience.

**The Harsh Truth of History.** Not so long ago, it was the prevailing opinion that the author of children's books had an obligation to moderate information about the unpleasant aspects of our history—to soften such human injustices as the internment of Japanese Americans during World War II or the suffering of African slaves. Ching (2005) writes as follows:

Researchers, librarians, and book critics have long debated and deliberated over the aspect of "safety" related to violent content. However, they have not fully challenged the structures of American imagination that associate critiques of American nationalism with violence inappropriate for young readers. I believe that safe narratives "protect" young readers from fully comprehending the violence that modern nation states necessitate in their formation and sustained unity. (p. 134)

Authors of historical fiction must take into consideration the maturity of the child reader. If the events of history are presented in such a way that a child cannot understand or cope with the meaning, then the story has failed. Yet, the past cannot be "tidied up" in such a way as to mask the truth, accuracy, and importance of historical events. One way for the writer of historical fiction to mitigate the harshness of the past is to provide a mediating voice and consciousness that has suffered through the events and now comes to tell their meaning. In *The Watsons Go to Birmingham—1963*, the burning of the Sixteenth Avenue Baptist Church with four little girls inside is conveyed through Kenny as he thinks about his own sister Joey's narrow escape:

"Why would they hurt some little kids like that?... It's just not fair. What about those other kids, you know they had brothers and sisters and mommas and daddies who loved them just as much as we love Joey, how come no one came and got them out of that church? How's it fair? How come their relatives couldn't come and warn them?" (p. 202)

The reader empathizes with Kenny as he struggles to understand what caused the church burning, but he is confronted with the fact that there is no easy answer. His older brother, Byron, replies, "Kenny, things ain't ever going to be fair... But you just gotta understand that that's the way it is and keep on steppin'" (p. 203). When considering whether a book of historical fiction is appropriate for children, think about the developmental level of the children and the quality of the literature, and consult with other teachers, librarians, specialists, parents, and members of the community.

## Evaluating and Selecting Historical Fiction

Like all good fiction, books of historical fiction must first tell an interesting and engaging story. Thus, historical fiction is evaluated according to the same criteria as fantasy and realistic fiction (see "Evaluation Criteria" on page 217).

- Strong character development
- A credible and engaging plot
- An effective writing style
- A detailed and believable setting
- A relevant theme

Yet, a special requirement of historical fiction is that it must balance the fictional story with the known facts of the time period. The historical facts and details of the time must not overwhelm the telling of the story but must serve as a scaffold that guides the depiction of details of the people, places, events, values, and norms of the culture portrayed. Although authors of historical fiction have the leeway to invent characters and plot, they must not veer from the historical record or breach the spirit and value of the times.

**Criteria for Selecting Historical Fiction**

# Evaluation Criteria for Historical Fiction

| Element | Criteria | Description |
|---|---|---|
| Setting | Are authentic details provided to bring the setting to life? | Details bring place and time of story to life. Place and time are described in detail so the reader can create mental images and make connections to the setting of the story. |
| Plot | Are the conflicts in the story appropriate for the time period in which the story is set? | The conflict and resolution of conflict must be authentic to the time period of the story. The conflict most often occurs when the character leaves his or her own environment and enters another. |
| Characters | Are the characters believable for the time period in which they lived? | Characters are developed through their language, thought, and actions. They must accurately depict the beliefs and values of the time period. Historical figures are often secondary characters in the story. |
| Style | Do historically authentic language patterns keep with the mood and characterization of the story? | Language is accessible to children and influences the mood of the story. Figurative language is used to clarify the plot and other elements of the story. |
| Theme | Are the themes representational of larger historical concerns? | Themes must be relevant to the reader in today's society. Common themes include independence, loyalty, and honor. |
| Historical Accuracy and Cultural Authenticity | Does the story accurately present historical information and cultural details? Does the story authentically reflect the culture depicted? | Source notes are provided for citing sources in novels and picturebooks. |
| Authority | Is the author an insider who is writing about his or her own culture or an outsider? | If the author is an insider, she or he must have good credentials and local community endorsement; if the author is an outsider, she or he must include source citations, notes and critical reviews. |

The author's ability to take on the perspective of other people living in the past or in other cultures is crucial to authenticity. To do so effectively requires the author to conduct extensive research. Winters and Schmidt (2001) note, "Historical fiction…allows the reader to enter into the time period and to experience the action from the inside; when this experience allows the reader to understand another culture's perspective it is especially valuable" (p. 265).

To misrepresent the events of a time or present inaccurate information is to violate an important bond of trust between author and child. Ann Rinaldi's *My Heart Is on the Ground: The Diary of Nannie Little Rose, A Sioux Girl* is one of many books in the popular *Dear America* historical fiction series written by various authors and published by Scholastic. In diary format, Nannie Little Rose describes her first year of schooling at Carlisle Indian Industrial School in Carlisle, Pennsylvania, from December 1879 to October 1880. The book includes many historical and cultural inaccuracies that reinforce stereotypical perspectives of American Indians. Rinaldi, a cultural outsider, did consult Indian boarding school sources, but critical reviewers (Molin, 2005) note that she altered text into stereotypical Indian speak, replicated source text verbatim, changed identities or other characteristics in ways that distorted reality, and decontextualized historical speeches. No one from the American Indian community was consulted on the book. Unfortunately, early reviews by professional journals such as *School Library Journal, Booklist,* and *Kirkus Reviews* highly recommended *My Heart Is on the Ground.* Noll (2003) explains, "For readers unfamiliar with the culture portrayed in a particular piece of literature, determining accuracy and merit is not always easy… especially when the distortions are consistent with their own cultural and literary experiences" (pp. 184–185). There are resources available to teachers, librarians, and parents who evaluate and select multicultural literature, among them: *Through Indian Eyes: The Native Experience in Books for Children* by Slapin and Seale and *A Broken Flute: The Native Experience in Books for Children* by Seale and Slapin.

## The Role of Historical Fiction in Literacy Development

Many children in the primary and intermediate grades have little, if any, prior knowledge of history. The ability to comprehend depends on prior knowledge. Therefore, one key aspect of understanding historical fiction is the ability to access and build upon prior knowledge.

### READING ALOUD

Children's understanding of history is greatly enhanced when the context in which a historical event takes place is presented and discussed within a framework of other interrelated events. Picturebooks present pertinent historical information and illustrations in a brief yet complex and stimulating way that can be used to incrementally develop children's background knowledge of a particular historical event.

There are many picturebooks available on the same historical event but from different contexts or perspectives. For example, African Americans' flight for freedom through the Underground Railroad has been documented in several picturebooks:

*Watch*

*Watch an interview with Pamela Duncan Edwards.*

- *Barefoot: Escape on the Underground Railroad,* by Pamela Duncan Edwards and illustrated by Henry Cole, is the story of an escaping slave whose flight is aided by the wild animals of forest and swamp.
- *Follow the Drinking Gourd,* written and illustrated by Jeanette Winter, explains how the directions in a song, "The Drinking Gourd," help runaway slaves journey north along the Underground Railroad to freedom in Canada.

- *Sweet Clara and the Freedom Quilt*, written and illustrated by Deborah Hopkinson, tells the story of a young slave who stitches a quilt with a map pattern that guides her to freedom in the North.
- *Liberty Street*, by Candice F. Ransom and illustrated by Eric Velasquez, depicts how a mother sends her daughter to the home of a free black woman, who teaches slave children to read and write, and makes plans for her daughter to join a group preparing to take the Underground Railroad to Canada.
- *Show Way*, by Jacqueline Woodson and illustrated by Hudson Talbott, shows how the quilt-making tradition is passed down through successive generations of women in the author's family to sew messages and directions into quilt patterns—a *show way*—to find the road to freedom. (See illustration 7 in the Part 2 color insert.)

*Watch*

*Watch an interview with Jacqueline Woodson.*

After reading each book, create an anchor chart with children, documenting what they noticed about historical fiction. The chart serves to support students' developing understanding of what constitutes historical fiction and also what they have taken away from the books about the Underground Railroad. In this way, students develop prior knowledge of the time period and the genre that will be helpful when they go on to read longer works of historical fiction.

*This picturebook is one of many about the Underground Railroad. Historical fiction picturebooks have many benefits, including helping children to develop prior knowledge of historical events.*

## QUESTIONING THE AUTHOR

Young readers can develop the ability to understand the author's perspective and to determine if a book is historically accurate and culturally authentic. This is no small task, even for adults. However, children can learn to be perceptive readers of historical fiction if given the time and strategies. Questioning the Author (QtA; Beck & McKeown, 2006) is a technique in which the teacher supports students' interaction with the text by intervening at selected points and asking guiding queries. The following are four queries found to be useful in addressing narrative text:

*Characters and their motivations:*

- How do things look for this character now?
- Given what the author has already told us about this character, what do you think he's up to?

*Author's craft and plot:*

- How has the author let you know that something has changed?
- How has the author settled this for us?

For example, after reading the excerpt cited earlier from *The Watsons Go to Birmingham— 1963,* in which Kenny questions why anyone would want to hurt little kids, the teacher could ask students to think about how things look for this character now. Kenny is very upset by the church burning and his sister's narrow escape. He has started sleeping behind the couch in the hopes that the magical powers that heal wounded animals that hide behind the couch will also heal his pain. Students must draw on their knowledge of Kenny's character and family to predict how they think he will deal with his distress.

Students respond to these prompts by contributing ideas that other students or the teacher may build upon, refine, or challenge. Finally, students and the teacher work together to think through ideas and build understanding.

When planning a QtA lesson, teachers should keep in mind these three goals:

1. Identify the major understandings students should construct, and anticipate potential problems in the text.
2. Segment the text to focus on information needed to build understandings.
3. Develop queries that promote the building of those understandings (p. 74).

The Questioning the Author approach provides students with a set of useful thinking strategies for all genres, especially historical fiction, since the queries and discussion help children sort out the real from the imaginary. QtA also provides a scaffold for children's independent book discussions, which are covered in the next section.

# Opportunities for Reader Response

Historical fiction provides an array of opportunities for reader response. Here are some ideas for book discussion that encourage readers to voice their opinions and rethink their ideas and ways to use drama to connect to history.

## BOOK DISCUSSIONS

Literature conversations provide an avenue for deep comprehension of text. Conversation provides students with the practice necessary to orchestrate the use of cognitive strategies that become the basis for critical thinking. Although reading and thinking about historical fiction require teacher modeling, scaffolding, and direct instruction, students must be given time to reflect on their learning. Discussion groups and buddy reading can provide an excellent opportunity for children to use their own strategies.

I once observed two third-grade girls discussing *The Last Princess: The Story of Princess Ka'iulani of Hawaii*, written by Fay Stanley and illustrated by Diane Stanley, the story of Hawaii's last heir to the throne, who was denied her right to rule when the monarchy was abolished.

One of the girls asked the other, "Do you think the story is true? America doesn't have kings and queens or princesses, and Hawaii is part of America. Maybe the story is a fairy tale because this same author wrote one of my favorite books, *Rumpelstiltskin's Daughter*."

The other girl replied, "I think the story is true because Hawaii was the last state to become part of America, so it could have had kings and queens before then. Also, at the back of the book is a list of all of the books the author used to help write the story."

The first girl reflected on this comment. "I feel very sad for Princess Ka'iulani. It's unfair that she was not able to become the princess." The other girl agreed, and they talked about how hard the princess had worked to help her country.

Finally, they discussed how Princess Ka'iulani died. Opening the book to a specific page, one of the girls read, "Her real disease was despair" (p. 34). "Do you think someone can really die of despair?" she asked.

The other girl pointed out, "My aunt is very sad most of the time, and my mother is worried about her committing suicide." The girls knew that Princess Ka'iulani didn't commit suicide but that her sadness may have played a role in her inability to recover from her illness.

This brief conversation provided an opportunity for these two children to hear each other's point of view, and the conflicting ideas that emerged encouraged them to rethink their opinions. Through conversations with peers, children become involved in understanding and negotiating ideas and perspectives that promote reflection and insight.

## DRAMA

Drama can be a wonderful way to enhance students' understanding and connection to the events of the past. Play is an integral part of most children's lives, imagining themselves as other people, in other places, times, and situations. Play acting is a way of learning about the world, with the child in the center of the process. Acting in the classroom can make learning about distant people, places, and times more personal and help them to understand the viewpoints of the people involved.

When children are given responsibility for writing, producing, and performing the play, the experience becomes even more meaningful and engaging as they take ownership in their learning. Historical fiction picturebooks and chapter books can be a great source for plays. Kornfeld and Leyden (2005) implemented a five-month integrated unit centered on historical plays with first graders. The plays were based on picturebooks about African-American experiences and perspectives. The children were given the responsibility, with teacher and parent support, for all aspects of the production. Kornfeld and Leyden (2005) write, "In this unit, students were listening, speaking, reading, and writing, not because they were being told to do so—and not merely in pursuit of particular standards—but because they were seeking to fulfill what they considered a pressing need to reach their goals for the plays" (p. 235).

When acting out *I Am Rosa Parks*, one child, who was playing the role of a waitress who rudely asks black customers to leave the restaurant, broke down in tears stating, "I just can't do it...I don't want to talk so mean to him. It's not right!" Role playing provided

**TABLE 8.1**

# Using Drama in the Classroom

| |
|---|
| **1.** Start small, one play at a time. |
| **2.** Find someone to work with you to provide encouragement and to share the workload. |
| **3.** Bring in parent volunteers to assist with costumes, rehearsals, backdrops, and props. |
| **4.** Don't start planning with standards first, since it is the authenticity of the experience that develops many literacy skills. |
| **5.** Make sure the topics explored in the literature are meaningful and important to the students. |
| **6.** Allow the students to take charge of their learning (Kornfeld & Leyden, 2005, p. 237). |

this child with a sense of living as a member of that time, and her values clashed with the accepted values of the time. "She may have previously been aware of the existence of racism past and present, but it had had no meaning to her until she participated in the play" (p. 236). See Table 8.1 for guidelines for using drama in the classroom and Table 8.2 for picturebooks that can be turned into plays.

## Making the Connection Across the Curriculum

Over the years, researchers have repeatedly found that students have negative attitudes toward social studies. A study by Zhao and Hoge (2005) found that students in grades K–5 did not like social studies, did not know much about social studies, and did not think social studies was relevant to their lives. The study also found that students received limited or no social studies instruction in the primary grades, and teachers in the upper grades used a textbook-centered approach driven by state and local curriculum guides. History textbooks have long been criticized for being inconsiderate to the reader due to the use of an omniscient, unquestionable narrator, mundane expository style, and disconnected and decontextualized events. VanSledright (2002) believes there must be a shift in the view of history promoted in the classroom, which would require "dropping the idea that history can be understood as an objective, fact-based account that mirrors the 'real' past and instead viewing history as a set of representations of the past authored by persons who are telling stories employing different frameworks, making different assumptions, and relaying varying subtexts" (p. 131).

### HISTORY

The use of historical fiction and other genres, such as nonfiction and poetry, along with the history textbook and primary and secondary sources can provide a more balanced and robust approach to representations of the past and enhance children's interest,

**TABLE 8.2**

# Picturebooks to Use for Plays

*Bobbin Girl* by Emily Arnold McCully (1996, Dial). A ten-year-old bobbin girl working in a textile mill in Lowell, Massachusetts, in the 1830s must make a difficult decision: Will she participate in the first workers' strike in Lowell?

*Charlotte* by Janet Lunn (1998, Tundra Books). After the end of the Revolutionary War in New York, ten-year-old Charlotte witnesses the deportation of Loyalists, including her cousin's family.

*Coming on Home Soon* by Jacqueline Woodson (2004, Putnam). After Mama takes a job in Chicago during World War II, Ada Ruth stays with Grandma but misses her mother who loves her more than rain and snow.

*The Memory Coat* by Elvira Woodruff (1999, Scholastic). In the early 1900s, two cousins leave their Russian shtetl with the rest of their family to come to America, hopeful that they will all pass the dreaded inspection at Ellis Island.

*Sunsets of the West* by Tony Johnston (2002, Putnam). Pa and his family pack up their belongings and undertake the difficult journey to a new life in the West.

*Uncle Jed's Barbershop* by Margaret Mitchell (1993, Simon & Schuster). Despite serious obstacles and setbacks, Sarah Jean's Uncle Jed, the only black barber in the county, pursues his dream of saving enough money to open his own barbershop.

understanding, and critical thinking about history. Yet, essential to the effectiveness of a multiple text approach is students' ability to assess the validity and reliability of text sources. Rather than accepting all books at face value, children must learn to assess the author's perspective and how that perspective may affect an author's selection of source information to judge the quality of information in the text.

One way to involve children in this process is to compare and analyze two or more books about the same historical event or time period. For example, Esther Forbe's *Johnny Tremain,* published in 1943, presents an ideal view of the American Revolution in which the patriots are seen as a united people fighting a just war for freedom and equality. In contrast, James and Christopher Collier's *My Brother Sam Is Dead*, written in 1974, presents the colonists as a divided people as many remained loyal to the king of England. The book's protagonist questions the values of the revolution and ultimately chooses not to become a part of it. Finally, in Avi's *The Fighting Ground*, published in 1984, 13-year-old Jonathan can't wait to fight in the war. When he does fight, he is taken prisoner by three Hessian soldiers. The horror and brutality he encounters changes his understanding of war and life forever as he decides that all war is appalling. Interestingly, *Johnny Tremain* was written during World War II, *My Brother Sam Is Dead* was written during the Vietnam War, and *The Fighting Ground* was written toward the end of the Cold War.

Another important consideration of author perspective is the sociopolitical viewpoint. Eve Bunting's *So Far from the Sea* is a picturebook, illustrated by Chris Soentpiet, that recounts nine-year-old Laura Iwasaki and her Japanese-American family's 1972 visit to the site of the former Manzanar War Relocation Camp in eastern California. Thirty years earlier, her father and his parents were interned there, along with 10,000 other Japanese Americans during World War II. Her grandfather is buried there. At the story's end, Laura whispers, "It was wrong." Her father answers, "Sometimes in the end there is no right or wrong.... It is just a thing that happened long years ago. A thing that cannot be changed" (p. 30).

*Listen to an interview with Allen Say about* Home of the Brave.

Allen Say's picturebook *Home of the Brave* also remembers the internment of Japanese Americans, although he uses a very different approach. In dreamlike sequences, a man symbolically confronts the trauma of his family's internment as he meets a group of children all with strange name tags pinned on their coats. The man feels the helplessness of the children, but he releases the name tags into the air so they can find their way home with the hope for a time when Americans will be seen as one people—not judged, mistrusted, or segregated because of their individual heritage.

Both books present powerful, rich texts and illustrations that bring dignity to the Japanese-American community. Yet, Ching and Pataray-Ching (2003) point out that in *So Far from the Sea*, Laura's father's response to her accusation that "It was wrong" excuses and justifies the government actions and "adopts the rhetoric of forgetting and erasure" (p. 125), whereas *Home of the Brave* does not excuse the racial injustice. Up to the end of the book, the man and the children wish to go home but remain lost together: "Each individual seems to dream of a home in America that the nation has yet to realize" (p. 125). Ching and Pataray-Ching (2003) write, "Bunting's text predominately merges with nationalist discourse; Say's text merges with and pushes the boundaries of this discourse. Bunting's text importantly remembers and honors the sacrifice of interned Japanese Americans. Say's text does the same and additionally moves the reader to an uncomfortable position" (p. 127). Although *So Far from the Sea* may be a more "comfortable" reading, teachers can use this text as a way to question the national discourse surrounding this and other events in the history of the United States and other countries around the world in which the cultural majority have subjugated the cultural minority.

## SCIENCE AND MATH

Historical fiction can also promote a deeper understanding of the time period, events, and circumstances that surrounded the discovery of science and math concepts. These books are great for using in conjunction with science or math lessons to enable deeper understanding and a personal connection to the material. *Ben Franklin and His First Kite,* by Stephen Krensky and illustrated by Bert Dodson, is about Franklin's first experiment with a kite and conveys a number of known facts about the man. Throughout the easy-to-read story, Franklin has conversations with his friends and parents, and his observations are described in detail.

*Read an interview with Ellen Klages about* The Green Glass Sea *and the sequel* White Sands, Red Menace.

Ellen Klages's *The Green Glass Sea* is set in 1943. Ten-year-old Dewey Kerrigan travels west on a train to live with her mathematician father—but no one will tell her exactly where he is. It turns out that Dewey's father is part of the Manhattan Project in Los Alamos, New Mexico, but Dewey is only told that he is working on a top secret government program. The secretive scientific community and what Dewey knows only as "the gadget" adds mystery and tension but "Screwy Dewey," as her classmates call her, finds lots of people to talk with about building radios (including Robert Oppenheimer or "Oppie") and science stuff. However, after the atomic bomb test succeeds, ethical concerns of both youngsters and adults intensify as the characters learn how it is ultimately used.

Jacqueline Davies's *The Boy Who Drew Birds: A Story of John James Audubon* introduces the reader to the young 18-year-old French naturalist John James Audubon as he tries to determine whether individual birds return to the same nests in the spring by using a silver thread to band some fledgling peewee flycatchers. *Maria's Comet,* by Deborah Hopkinson and illustrated by Deborah Lanino, is a fictionalized first-person account of astronomer Maria Mitchell's Nantucket childhood. The girl is much influenced by her astronomer father, who goes up to the roof of their house each night to "sweep the sky" with his telescope. Here, her dream of following his avocation is sparked the night her older brother,

Andrew, runs away to sea. The concluding author's note highlights Maria Mitchell's later accomplishments and explains several astronomical terms used in the narrative.

## LANGUAGE ARTS

The lives of famous authors are also brought to life in several historical fiction books. *Richard Wright and the Library Card,* by William Miller and illustrated by Gregory Christie, chronicles the early life of the African-American author of *Black Boy* and *Native Son.* Seventeen-year-old Richard Wright's hunger to read inspires him to borrow the library card of a white coworker in Memphis in the 1920s, when public library borrowing privileges did not extend to blacks. He goes to the library with a forged note requesting permission to check out books for the man. An author's note acknowledges that this story is based on a scene from Wright's auto-biography *Black Boy.*

    *More Than Anything Else,* by Marie Bradby and illustrated by Chris Soentpiet, is based on the childhood of Booker T. Washington. He tells of leaving his cabin before dark to work all day shoveling salt with his father and older brother: What Booker really wants to do is read and teach others to read. Finally, he finds a newspaper man who teaches him the alphabet, and Booker knows that literacy will bring freedom.

## ART

Art history can be brought to life through historical fiction about famous artists. Laurence Anholt has written and illustrated an imaginative and accessible picturebook series introducing history's great artists: *Leonardo and the Flying Boy, Picasso and the Girl with a Ponytail, Camille and the Sunflowers: A Story About Vincent Van Gogh, Degas and the Little Dancer,* and *The Magical Garden of Claude Monet.* In Jon Scieska's time warp trio book *Da Wild, Da Crazy, Da Vinci,* illustrated by Adam McCauley, three young Brooklyn friends are sent to sixteenth-century Italy, where they meet Leonardo da Vinci, outwit Machiavelli, and learn about famous inventors and their discoveries. For older readers, *The Second Mrs. Gioconda,* by E. L. Konigsburg relates how Leonardo da Vinci came to paint the *Mona Lisa* from the point of view of his servant, Salai.

# Top 10 Read Alouds

## HISTORICAL FICTION

1. **Blood on the River: Jamestown 1607** by Elisa Carbone (2006, Viking). Traveling to the New World in 1606 as the page to Captain John Smith, 12-year-old orphan Samuel Collier settles in the new colony of Jamestown, where he must quickly learn to distinguish between friend and foe.

2. **Catherine, Called Birdy** by Karen Cushman (1994, Houghton Mifflin). The 13-year-old daughter of an English country knight keeps a journal in which she records the events of her life, particularly her longing for adventures beyond the usual role of women and her efforts to avoid an arranged marriage.

3. **Fever, 1793** by Laurie Halse Anderson (2000, Simon & Schuster). In 1793 Philadelphia, sixteen-year-old Matilda Cook, separated from her sick mother, learns about perseverance and self-reliance when she is forced to cope with the horrors of a yellow fever epidemic.

4. **Esperanza Rising** by Pam Munoz Ryan (2000, Scholastic). Esperanza and her mother are forced to leave their life of wealth and privilege in Mexico to go work in the labor camps of southern California, where they must adapt to the harsh circumstances facing Mexican farm workers on the eve of the Great Depression.

5. **I Am the Mummy Heb-Nefert** by Eve Bunting, illustrated by David Christiana (1997, Harcourt). A mummy recalls her past life in ancient Egypt as the beautiful wife of the Pharaoh's brother.

6. **The Legend of Bass Reeves: Being the True and Fictional Account of the Most Valiant Marshal in the West** by Gary Paulsen (2006, Random House). An account of the life of Bass Reeves who was born into slavery, and became the most successful U.S. Marshal of the Wild West.

7. **The Mostly True Adventures of Homer P. Figg** by Rodman Philbrick (2009, Scholastic). Twelve-year-old Homer, a poor but clever orphan, has extraordinary adventures after running away from his evil uncle to rescue his brother, who has been sold into service in the Civil War.

8. **One Crazy Summer** by Rita Garcia Williams (2010, HarperCollins). In the summer of 1968, after travelling from Brooklyn to Oakland, California, to spend a month with the mother they barely know, eleven-year-old Delphine and her two younger sisters arrive to a cold welcome as they discover that their mother, a dedicated poet and printer, is resentful of the intrusion of their visit and wants them to attend a nearby Black Panther summer camp.

9. **Whittington** by Alan Armstrong (2005, Random House). Whittington, a feline descendant of Dick Whittington's famous cat of English folklore, appears at a rundown barnyard plagued by rats and restores harmony while telling his ancestor's story.

10. **Yellow Star** by Jennifer Roy (2006, Cavendish). From 1939, when Sylvia is four-and-a-half years old, to 1945, when she has just turned 10, a Jewish girl and her family struggle to survive in Poland's Lodz ghetto during the Nazi occupation.

# Activities for Professional Development

### Think Critically About Children's Literature

1. Several books of historical fiction have won Newbery awards, the latest being *Kira, Kira* (2005, Kadohata), *Crispin: The Cross of Lead* (2003, Avi), *A Single Shard* (2002, Park), *A Year Down Yonder* (2001, Peck), and *Bud, Not Buddy* (2000, Curtis). Read the Newbery acceptance speech of one or more of these authors (published in *Horn Book Magazine*). What compelled the author(s) to write historical fiction? How did the author(s) ensure the work was accurate and authentic?

### Bring Children's Literature into the Classroom

2. Picturebooks have become a popular format for historical fiction. Given the brevity of picturebooks and the potentially disturbing subject matter of many aspects of history, it is important that teachers not only make sure a picturebook is appropriate but think through how the picturebook will be shared with students to ensure understanding. Select a historical fiction picturebook, and prepare a Questioning the Author lesson following the planning steps described earlier in the chapter.

### Learn About Authors and Illustrators

3. The National Book Festival is held annually in Washington, D.C. Visit the website of the National Book Festival online. Webcasts are available of all authors for the past five years. Click on "authors" and then, "Richard Peck" under "Children & Teens." Then click on "webcast" to view the video (approximately 32 minutes) of Richard Peck's 2006 presentation. After watching the video, respond to the following questions:

   - Peck states that his stories come from other people's memories. He remembers the impetus for *Fair Weather* was from the conversations of the old men who hung out at his father's gas station. They often spoke of riding the Ferris wheel at the Columbian Exposition of 1893. Peck states that he wrote about the Ferris wheel, "not because I had ridden the Ferris wheel, but because I had not." Explain what you believe Peck is trying to say about writing historical fiction.
   - Peck states, "Fiction isn't what was, fiction is what ought to have been, and a novelist is one who believes history can always be improved upon." What do you believe Peck means by this statement?

4. Many times, authors of historical fiction write from their own family history. The Kerlen Collection of children's literature at the University of Minnesota has two digital portfolios that provide a unique and transparent look at the process of writing historical fiction. Go to: http://special.lib.umn.edu/clrc/kerlan/resources.php. You will see two digital portfolios. The first is for Carol Ryrie Brink's *Caddie Woodlawn* which includes an on-line presentation in PowerPoint format that provides samples of the correspondence between Brink and her grandmother. Also included are historical photographs, original drafts of the story, background information on the setting and times of the story, a bibliography of related American Indian resources, and teaching activities.

   The second portfolio is for Karen Hesse's *Letters from Rifka* which explores the research process of Hesse in preparing for her book including letters to her aunt, notes on her family and her family tree, notes on her historical research about the book, characters, and setting. This portfolio pulls together family and immigration history with authorship for grade school students. Choose one of these portfolios, read and analyze the documents and write a review that reflects your understanding of the author, the author's writing process, and historical fiction.

# Print and Online Resources

### Print Resources

I., McKeown, M. (2006). *Improving Comprehension with Questioning the Author: A Fresh and Expanded View of a Powerful Approach.* New York: Scholastic.

Gillespie, J. (2008). *Historical Fiction for Young Readers (Grades 4–8): An Introduction.* Westport, CT: Libraries Unlimited.

Loewen, J. (2008). *Lies my teacher told me: Everything your American history textbook got wrong.* New York: New Press.

Roser, N. & Martinez, M. (Eds.). (2005). *What a character! Character study as a guide to literacy meaning making in grades K–8.* Newark, DE: International Reading Association.

Seale, D., & Slapin, B. (2005). *A broken flute: The native experience in books for children.* Walnut Creek, CA: AltaMira Press.

 **Online Resources**

*Carol Hurst's Children's Literature Site*
**http://www.carolhurst.com/index.html**
This site houses a collection of reviews of great books for kids; ideas of ways to use them in the classroom; and collections of books and activities about particular subjects, curriculum areas, themes, and professional topics. Many historical themes and topics are included with recommended children's books, activities, and approaches.

*Historical Fiction Book Lists*
**bookgirl3.tripod.com/historicalfiction.html**
Books are categorized by continent and subdivided by countries or historical eras. Each country/era book list is divided by grade level. A cover picture of the book, a synopsis, and number of pages are provided for each entry.

*National Council for the Social Studies (NCSS) Notable Books*
**http://www.socialstudies.org/resources/notable**
The books that appear in the annotated book lists on the NCSS website were evaluated and selected by a Book Review Committee appointed by the National Council for the Social Studies (NCSS) and assembled in cooperation with the Children's Book Council (CBC). The books are written primarily for children in grades K–8 and emphasize human relations, represent a diversity of groups, and are sensitive to a broad range of cultural experiences.

*Scott O'Dell Award for Historical Fiction*
**http://www.scottodell.com/odellaward.html**
An annual award bestowed to a meritorious book published in the previous year for children or young adults. Scott O'Dell established this award in 1982 to encourage other writers—particularly new authors—to focus on historical fiction.

Visit the companion website at **www.cengage.com/education/johnson** to find links related to the Read/Watch/Listen icons noted throughout the chapter, as well as additional resources.

# Creating Your Classroom Library

## PICTUREBOOKS

*A Sweet Smell of Roses* by Angela Johnson, illustrated by Eric Velasquez (2005, Simon & Schuster). A stirring yet jubilant glimpse of the youth involvement that played an invaluable role in the civil rights movement.

*The Bracelet* by Yoshiko Uchida, illustrated by Joanna Yardley (1993, Philomel). Emi, a Japanese American in the second grade, is sent with her family to an internment camp during World War II, but the loss of the bracelet her best friend has given her proves that she does not need a physical reminder of that friendship.

*Crossing Bok Chitto* by Tim Tingle, illustrated by Jeanne Bridges (2006, Cinco Puntos Press). In the 1800s, a Choctaw girl becomes friends with a slave boy from a plantation across the great river, and when she learns that his family is in trouble, she helps them cross to freedom.

*Dandelions* by Eve Bunting, illustrated by Greg Shed (1995, Harcourt). Zoe and her family find strength in each other as they make a new home in the Nebraska territory.

*The Gardener* by Sarah Stewart, illustrated by David Small (1997, Farrar, Straus and Giroux). A series of letters relates what happens when, after her father loses his job, Lydia Grace goes to live with her Uncle Jim in the city but takes her love for gardening with her.

*Grandfather's Journey* by Allen Say (1993, Houghton Mifflin). A Japanese-American man recounts his grandfather's journey to America, which he later also undertakes, and the feelings of being torn by a love for two different countries.

*The Lotus Seed* by Sherry Garland, illustrated by Tatsuro Kiuchi (1993, Harcourt). A young Vietnamese girl saves a lotus seed and carries it with her everywhere to remember a brave emperor and the homeland that she must flee.

*Malian's Song* by Marge Bruchac, illustrated by William Maughan (2006, The Vermont Folklife Center). Young Malian lives with her family in an Abenaki village near Montreal in the mid-eighteenth century. One night, Malian's life changes abruptly when her father orders her to run to their tribe's winter camp and she never sees him again.

*Peppe the Lamplighter* by Elisa Bartone, illustrated by Ted Lewin (1993, HarperCollins). Peppe's father is upset when he learns that Peppe has taken a job lighting the gas streetlamps in his New York City neighborhood.

*Star of Fear, Star of Hope* by Jo Hoestlandt, illustrated by Johanna Kang (1996, Walker). Nine-year-old Helen is confused by the disappearance of her Jewish friend during the German occupation of Paris.

## CHAPTER BOOKS

*A Single Shard* by Linda Sue Park (2003, Houghton Mifflin). Tree-year, a 13-year-old orphan in medieval Korea, lives under a bridge in a potters' village, and longs to learn how to throw the delicate celadon ceramics himself.

*A Long Way from Chicago* by Richard Peck (1998, Dial). A boy recounts his annual summer trips to rural Illinois with his sister during the Great Depression to visit their larger-than-life grandmother.

*Al Capone Does My Shirts* by Gennifer Choldenko (2004, Putnam). A 12-year-old boy named Moose moves to Alcatraz Island in 1935 when guards' families were housed there, and has to contend with his extraordinary new environment in addition to life with his autistic sister.

*Boston Jane: An Adventure* by Jennifer Holm (2001, HarperCollins). Schooled in the lessons of etiquette for young ladies of 1854, Miss Jane Peck of Philadelphia finds little use for manners during her long sea voyage to the Pacific Northwest and while living among the American traders and Chinook Indians of Washington Territory.

*Bread and Roses, Too* by Katherine Paterson (2006, Houghton Mifflin). Jake and Rosa, two children, form an unlikely friendship as they try to survive and understand the 1912 Bread and Roses strike of mill workers in Lawrence, Massachusetts.

*Bud, Not Buddy* by Christopher Paul Curtis (1999, Delacorte). Ten-year-old Bud, a motherless boy living in Flint, Michigan, during the Great Depression, escapes a cruel foster home and sets out in search of the man he believes to be his father—the renowned bandleader, H. E. Calloway of Grand Rapids.

*Bull Run* by Paul Fleischman (1993, Harper). Northerners, Southerners, generals, couriers, dreaming boys, and worried sisters describe the glory, the horror, the thrill, and the disillusionment of the first battle of the Civil War.

*Counting on Grace* by Elizabeth Winthrop (2006, Wendy Lamb). It's 1910 in Pownal, Vermont. At age 12, Grace and her best friend, Arthur, must go to work in the mill, helping their mothers work the looms. Together Grace and Arthur write a secret letter to the Child Labor Board about underage children working in the mill. A few weeks later, Lewis Hine, a famous reformer, arrives undercover to gather evidence. Grace meets him and appears in some of his photographs, changing her life forever.

*Crispin: The Cross of Lead* by Avi (2002, Hyperion). Falsely accused of theft and murder, an orphaned peasant boy in fourteenth-century England flees his village and meets a larger-than-life juggler who has a dangerous secret.

*The Evolution of Calpurnia Tate* by Jacqueline Kelly (2009, Henry Holt). In central Texas in 1899, eleven-year-old Callie Vee Tate learns about love from the older three of her six brothers and studies the natural world with her grandfather which leads to an important discovery.

*Give Me Liberty* by Laura Elliott (2006, HarperCollins). Follows the life of thirteen-year-old Nathaniel Dunn, from May 1774 to December 1775, as he serves his indentureship with a music teacher in Williamsburg, Virginia, and witnesses the growing rift between patriots and loyalists, culminating in the American Revolution.

*Lizzie Bright and the Buckminster Boy* by Gary Schmidt (2004, Houghton Mifflin). In 1911, Turner Buckminster hates his new home of Phippsburg, Maine, but things improve when he meets Lizzie Bright Griffin, a girl from a poor, nearby island community founded by former slaves that the town fathers—and Turner's—want to change into a tourist spot.

*The Loud Silence of Francine Green* by Karen Cushman (2006, Houghton Mifflin). In 1949, 13-year-old Francine goes to Catholic school in Los Angeles, where she becomes best friends with a girl who questions authority and is frequently punished by the nuns, causing Francine to question her own values.

*Midwife's Apprentice* by Karen Hesse (1995, Houghton Mifflin). In medieval England, a nameless, homeless girl is taken in by a sharp-tempered midwife, and in spite of obstacles and hardship, eventually gains the three things she most wants: a full belly, a contented heart, and a place in this world.

*Nightjohn* by Gary Paulsen (1993, Delacorte). Twelve-year-old Sarny's brutal life as a slave becomes even more dangerous when a newly arrived slave offers to teach her how to read.

*Rodzina* by Karen Cushman (2003, Houghton Mifflin). A 12-year-old Polish-American girl is boarded onto an orphan train in Chicago with fears about traveling to the West and a life of unpaid slavery.

*Rosa* by Nikki Giovanni, illustrated by Bryan Collier (2005, Holt). The story of Rosa Park's refusal to give up her seat on a Montgomery, Alabama, bus is recounted along with the important changes in civil rights that followed.

*Season of Gifts* by Richard Peck (2009, Dial). Relates the surprising gifts bestowed on twelve-year-old Bob Barnhart and his family, who have recently moved to a small Illinois town in 1958, by their larger-than-life neighbor, Mrs. Dowdel.

*Sing Down the Moon* by Scott O'Dell (1970, Houghton Mifflin). A young Navajo girl recounts the events of 1864 when her tribe was forced to march to Fort Sumner as prisoners of the white soldiers.

*The True Confessions of Charlotte Doyle* by Avi (1990, Scholastic). As the only passenger, and the only female, on a transatlantic voyage in 1832, 13-year-old Charlotte finds herself caught between a murderous captain and a mutinous crew.

*Under the Blood Red Sun* by Graham Salisbury (1994, Delacorte). Tomikazu Nakaji's biggest concerns are baseball, homework, and a local bully, until life with his Japanese family in Hawaii changes drastically after the bombing of Pearl Harbor in December 1941.

*Uprising* by Margaret Peterson Haddix (2007, Simon & Schuster). In 1927, at the urging of twenty-one-year-old Harriet, Mrs. Livingston reluctantly recalls her experiences at the Triangle Shirtwaist factory, including miserable working conditions that led to a strike, then the fire that took the lives of her two best friends, when Harriet, the boss's daughter, was only five years old.

*Victory* by Susan Cooper (2006, Margaret K. McElderry). Alternating chapters follow the mysterious connection between a homesick English girl living in present-day America and an 11-year-old boy serving in the British Royal Navy in 1803 aboard the H.M.S., commanded by Admiral Horatio Nelson.

*Weedflower* by Cynthia Kadohata (2006, Atheneum). After 12-year-old Sumiko and her Japanese-American family are relocated from their flower farm in southern California to an internment camp on a Mojave Indian reservation in Arizona, she helps her family and neighbors, befriends a local American Indian boy, and tries to hold onto her dream of owning a flower shop.

## HISTORICAL FICTION SERIES BOOKS

*American Diaries* series by various authors

*American Girl* series by various authors

*Boston Jane* series by Jennifer Holm

*Children of America* series by various authors

*Chronicles of Ancient Darkness* by Michelle Paver

*Dear America* series by various authors

*Ellis Island* series by Joan Nixion

*First Person Fiction* series by various authors

*Gladiators from Capua* series by Caroline Lawrence

*Golden Mountain Chronicles* by Laurence Yep

*Great Episodes* series by various authors

*The Holocaust Remembrance* series by Kathy Kacer

*Joe Joe in the City* series by Jean Alicia Elster

*Journey Through Time* series by Roberta Angeletti

*The Lady Grace Mysteries* by Grace Cavendish

*Life and Times* series by various authors

*Little House* series by Laura Ingalls Wilder

*Little Maid* series by Alice Curtis

*Magic Tree House* series by Mary Pope Osborne

*My America* series by various authors

*My Name Is America* series by various authors

*On Time's Wing* series by various authors

*Once Upon America* series by various authors

*Orphan Train* series by Joan Nixion

*Pirate Hunter* series by Brad Stickland and Thomas Fuller

*The Roman Mysteries* series by Caroline Lawrence

*Royal Diaries* series by various authors

*Time Warp Trio* by Jon Scieska

*Vesper Holly Adventures* by Lloyd Alexander

*Unsolved Mysteries from History* series by Jane Yolen and Heide Stemple

# References

Avi (2003). Newbery Medal acceptance. *Hornbook, 79*(4), 407–414.

Beck, I., & McKeown, M. (2006). *Improving comprehension with questioning the author: A fresh and expanded view of a powerful approach.* New York: Scholastic.

Bird, E. (2007, April 13). O'Dell speech 2007: Full and unabridged text. Message posted to http://fusenumber8.blogspot.com.

Breen, K., Fade, E., Odean, K., & Sutherland, Z. (2000). One hundred books that shaped the century. *School Library Journal, 46*(1), 50–59.

Brozo, W., & Tomlinson, C. (1986). Literature: The key to lively content courses. *The Reading Teacher, 40*(3), 288–293.

Ching, S. (2005). Multicultural children's literature as an instrument of power. *Language Arts, 83*(2), 128–136.

Ching, S., & Pataray-Ching, J. (2003). Toward a socio-political framework for Asian American children's literature. *The New Advocate, 16*(2), 123–128.

Curtis, C. (1995). *The Watsons go to Birmingham—1963.* New York: Delacorte.

Cushman, K. (1996). Newbery Medal acceptance. *Hornbook, 72*(4), 413–419.

Hodge, J. (1991). A survey investigation of students' historical time knowledge. *Journal of Social Studies Research, 15,* 16–29.

Kornfeld, J., & Leyden, G. (2005). Acting out: Literature, drama, and connecting with history. *The Reading Teacher, 59*(3), 230–238.

Levstik, L., & Barton, K. (2010). *Doing history: Investigating with children in the elementary and middle schools.* Mahwah, NJ: Erlbaum.

Molin, P. (2005). Historical fiction: The controversy over *My Heart Is on the Ground.* In P. Molin (Ed.), *American Indian themes in young adult literature.* Lanham, MD: Scarecrow Press.

Nikolajeva, M. (2005). Toward a theory of character in children's fiction (pp. 182–204). In N. Roser & M. Martinez (Eds.), *What a character! Character study as a guide to literacy meaning making in grades K–8.* Newark, DE: International Reading Association.

Noll, E. (2003). Accuracy and authenticity in American Indian children's literature: The social responsibility of authors and illustrators. In D. Fox & K. Short (Eds.), *Stories matter: The complexity of cultural authenticity in children's literature.* (pp. 182–197). Urbana, IL: National Council of Teachers of English.

Owens, J. (2003, March 28). History, the new fantasy. *The Bookseller,* 22–24.

Rochman, H. (1999). Little house on the lake. *Booklist, 95*(15), 1427.

Silvey, A. (2004). *100 best books for children.* Boston: Houghton Mifflin.

Taylor, M. (1976). *Roll of thunder, hear my cry.* New York: Dial.

Tunnell, M. (1993). Unmasking the fiction of history: Children's historical literature begins to come of age. In M. Tunnell & R. Ammon (Eds.), *The story of ourselves: Teaching history through children's literature.* (pp. 79–90). Portsmouth, NH: Heinemann.

Tunnell, M., & Ammon, R. (1993). *The story of ourselves: Teaching history through children's literature.* Portsmouth, NH: Heinemann.

VanSledright, B. (2002). Fifth graders investigating history in the classroom: Results from a researcher-practitioner design experiment. *The Elementary School Journal, 103*(2), 131–160.

Winters, C., & Schmidt, G. (2001). *Edging the boundaries of children's literature.* Boston: Allyn & Bacon.

Zhao, Y., & Hoge, J. (2005). What elementary students and teachers say about social studies. *The Social Studies, 96*(5), 216–222.

# Poetry

*9*

They read books, Sophie talking and turning the pages and pointing. Byrd's voice was smooth, like the velvet of her hat.

> "so much depends
> upon
> a red wheel
> barrow
> glazed with rain
> water
> beside the white
> chickens."

"That's William Carlos Williams," Byrd said to Sophie.

> "She doesn't understand," I said. "She doesn't need to understand, dear," said Byrd. "She likes the way the words sound."

*Patricia MacLachlan, 1993, pp. 80–81*

*Baby*, by Patricia MacLachlan, is the story of a family who cares for a baby who was left behind by vacationers. In caring for the baby, Sophie, they teach her games and new words. Ultimately, Sophie helps the family come to terms with the death of their own infant son. *Baby* is a story of memory, love, loss, risk, and the power of language. As Byrd so eloquently states, "Sometimes poetry—words—give us a small, lovely look at ourselves" (p. 69).

## Watch

*Watch an interview with Patricia MacLachlan.*

*Poetry is the first genre* that children hear through lullabies, nursery rhymes, and Mother Goose. As they grow older, children recite riddles, raps, and jump rope rhymes. When they enter school, teachers use nursery rhymes to teach children to read and write, and as they move through the grades, poetry introduces children to new vocabulary and the power of word choice and word order to deepen and broaden knowledge, understanding, and perspective. As with William Carlos Williams's poem *The Red Wheelbarrow* (© 1938 New Directions Publishing Corp. By permission.), a short and simple poem can raise difficult and complex questions.

# Defining Poetry

*Poetry, at its most basic, is a short, lyrical response to the world. It is emotion under extreme pressure or recollection in a small space. It is the coal of experience so compressed it becomes a diamond.*

JANE YOLEN, 2003, P. 66

This description from Jane Yolen's (2003) book *Take Joy* captures the essence of poetry—the distillation of experience through the concentrated use of language and form that creates rhythm, sound, image, and meaning in a way that helps us see the new in the ordinary. As with sculpture, photography, painting, and music, poetry speaks to adults and children in ways that cause us to pause and reflect. This power of poetry lies in the work of the poet who renders that hard lump of words into jewels of emotion. Authors of fine poetry construct meaning through the careful use of poetic techniques, such as metaphor, to create vivid imagery and rhyme for a resonating sound. The way a poem looks on the page also conveys meaning. When a poet chooses a one-word line or a break in a thought, he is helping the reader shape the poem in her mind and voice. The shape of the poem is chosen to build up an emotional rhythm or effect. Together, sound, image, and shape produce language in its most beautiful form and create an emotional effect on the reader that is unparalleled by other genres.

# Benefits and Considerations of Poetry

Poetry for children should convey the experiences and perceptions of the child in a way that is meaningful and not condescending, didactic, or simplified. Consider the following poem from the book *A Maze Me: Poems for Girls* by Naomi Shihab Nye:

### In the School Cafeteria

Your face makes me feel like a lighthouse
    beaming across waves.
We don't even know one another,
    yet each day I am looking for your face.
Walking slowly among tables, I balance my tray,
    glancing to the side.
You're not here today.
Are you sick?
Why are you absent?
And why, among all these faces,
is there only one I want to see?
Whatever the reason
your absence is not excused
by me.

From *A Maze Me: Poems for Girls* by Naomi Shihab Nye, p. 37.
© 2005 Naomi Shihab Nye. By permission.

*Watch*

*Watch a presentation with Naomi Shihab Nye.*

Naomi Nye's poem creates an easy kinship with the reader. Her poetry speaks directly to the child, to her senses, imaginations, emotions, feelings, and childhood experiences. She captures a short, brief, glimpse into a moment in time that has been silent until poetry rises to speak.

### BENEFITS

In *Sahara Special* by Esmé Codell, Sahara is struggling with school and her feelings since her father left. She gets a fresh start with a new and unique teacher, Miss Poitier—or Miss Pointy, as the children call her—who supports Sahara's writing talents and the individuality of her classmates. Sahara knows that Miss Pointy loves poetry: "She gives us copies of poems by famous poets, one every couple of days, but she doesn't quiz us about them, so most of the kids throw them in the garbage can" (p. 110). Her favorite poem, *Autobiographia Literaria* by Frank O'Hara (1971), causes Sahara to pause and reflect on her own life:

### Autobiographia Literaria by Frank O'Hara

When I was a child
I played by myself in a
corner of the schoolyard
all alone.

I hated dolls and I
hated games, animals were
not friendly and birds
flew away.

If anyone was looking
for me I hid behind a
tree and cried out"I am
an orphan."

And here I am, the
center of all beauty!
writing these poems!
Imagine!

From *The Collected Poems of Frank O'Hara* by Maureen Granville-Smith, p. 11.
© 1971 Maureen Granville-Smith. By permission.

When I'm alone opening a can of corn in the kitchen with dirty dishes piled high, I imagine coming out from behind a tree and being the center of all beauty, which doesn't seem likely, but Frank O'Hara said it happened. All he had to do was come out from behind a tree, and he was Somewhere Else. I say his words over and over again, like a spell, if I say it maybe a thousand times it will come true for me, too. Maybe the poems are a test, like Cinderella's slipper. Maybe if you can make them fit, you can be queen. That would be useful (p. 112).

*Listen*

*Listen to an excerpt of Sahara Special.*

Sahara finds herself in Frank O'Hara's poem. She struggles with her own feelings of abandonment by her father and the isolation and loneliness of not having friends. She finds hope in the poem, hope that one day she will come out from behind her feelings and become "the center of all beauty," just like Frank O'Hara. When teachers and children explore together the features of poetry—words, sound, images—and especially the relationship between these features and the aesthetic and meaning-making responses that poems inspire, wonderful things happen. Fine poetry should do the following:

- Nurture a love and appreciation for the sound and power of language
- Engage children in a new or heightened understanding of the world, themselves, and others
- Broaden experiences with and connections to new concepts in all content areas
- Validate our human experience
- Provide opportunities for children of all linguistic and cultural backgrounds to develop important oral language skills through reading and performing poetry

The poem *The Seed,* which appears in Aileen Fisher's book *Always Wondering,* also illustrates how poetry achieves these benefits:

### The Seed

How does it know,
this little seed,
if it is to grow to a flower or weed,
if it is to be a vine or shoot,
or grow to a tree with a long deep root?
A seed is so small,
where do you suppose it stores up all
of the things it knows?

From *Always Wondering* by Aileen Fisher, p. 68.
© 1991 Aileen Fisher. By permission.

This poem has a delightful rhythm and sound brought about through structure and rhyme. It presents an accessible and uncomplicated image, one we have all thought about at one time or another. Many of us remember from school observing a seed sprouting from a pot of dirt. We may have wondered, "How does the seed know how to grow?" Fisher presents the seed as something that "knows" and as a result creates a new relationship between the reader and the seed. Now we look at the seed in a new light—as we would any living thing that has knowledge. This relationship brings forth a new way of thinking about the germination process and allows us to ponder the question: Where do you suppose it stores up all the things it knows? Compare the way of thinking inspired by the poem to this introduction to the life processes of plants in a science book: "Throughout their lives, plants and animals undergo a series of orderly and identifiable changes." Which words make you want to learn more? Robert Frost said a poem begins in delight and ends in wisdom. The wisdom of this poem is achieved by its ability to reveal a way of seeing.

## CONSIDERATIONS

For the benefits of poetry to be realized, children must be exposed at an early age to a range of the best poetry and engage in a variety of forms of response to poetry. Children who are given many opportunities to read and write poetry on their own possess a remarkable understanding of the genre (McClure, 1994), whereas children who have not had this exposure typically don't understand what poetry is or how it differs from prose (Fisher, 1994). The key to early, positive experiences with poetry is the influence of parents, librarians, and teachers.

## Teachers as Readers of Poetry

### Look

The moon thumbs through the night's book.
Finds a lake where nothing is printed.
Draws a straight line. That's all
it can. That's enough.
Thick line. Straight toward you.
—Look.

From *Night Open* by Rolf Jacobsen Rosenberg, 2000, p. 44.
© Rolf Jacobsen. By permission.

Jacobsen's poem is undeniably delightful, but many teachers do not like poetry and thus avoid reading and writing poetry in the classroom. Block and Mangieri (2002) conducted a study of teachers' recreational reading in 1981 and a follow-up study in 2001. When the results were compared, the percentage of teachers who were knowledgeable of recent titles in poetry improved from 3 percent in 1981 to 27 percent in 2001. Although this is a significant improvement over the 20-year period between studies, it is disappointing when you consider that less than one-third of the teachers surveyed were familiar with a recent published title of children's poetry. Even more disappointing is that only 7 of the 549 teachers surveyed reported providing reading activities specific to poetry. Teachers are not alone in their dislike of poetry. *Reading at Risk: A Survey of Literary Reading in America* (2004), a report by the National Endowment for the Arts, reported the 2002 results of a comprehensive survey of the reading trends of the adult population conducted every decade since 1982. The percentage of people reading or listening to poetry decreased substantially from approximately 20 percent of adults in 1982 to 14 percent in 2002. Tarr and Flynn (2002) assert the following:

> Here in the United States, we seem to take poetry for granted. Unquestionably, we live in anti-poetic times. Poetry has become dispensable in an age that values information over art, and consequently fewer and fewer of our teachers seem equipped to teach poetry to our children. (p. 2)

Why do so many people dislike poetry? Often, it is for many of the same reasons children today turn up their noses at poetry. Ralph Fletcher's (2002) experience reflects that of many children:

> I often run into kids who don't like to write poems. "Poems are boring," one girl muttered when I visited her classroom. She complained that her teacher had spent hour after hour dissecting poems and pulling out similes, metaphors, and symbolism. "If I had one wish," she told me, "it would be that I'd never have to analyze another poem for the rest of my life. (p. 8)

Children's experiences with poetry in the classroom must be "to motivate—not murder—interest and delight in poetry" (Sloan, 2003, p. 25). How can teachers create for themselves and their students a sense of joy in reading poetry? Booth and Moore (1988) make suggestions to enlighten our thinking about poetry (Table 9.1).

**TABLE 9.1**

# Bringing Poetry into the Classroom

For the students:

- Read poems aloud to children with energy, passion, and delight. Read poems to children that you personally enjoy, and not for other apparent teaching purposes.

- Schedule times for poetry reading by groups of children and by individuals who are ready to share. Then, join in with children, clapping along, tasting the words. Sing and chant poems and songs aloud and alongside the children, letting the joys of language reach them through the ear and the eye.

- Encourage children to write in a poetic fashion, using all of the tools that poets use—from models, shapes, and patterns to ideas and concepts.

- Use poems all the time, in a quiet moment, as a lesson, as part of another subject's content, such as *The Seed* for a science unit on plants.

- Give poetry a prominent place in your classroom library. Provide resources and dozens of poetry anthologies (by single poets, collections, picturebook versions) to share, and for children to peruse on their own.

- Explore poets as well as poems, letting the children come to know the writer of words, through reading many poems by one poet, and perhaps by sharing information about the poet's life and work.

- At the classroom listening center, provide recordings of poems on CD or from websites.

- Use poems in big-book formats, on overhead transparencies, on chart paper, on mobiles, incorporating them into visual arts, writing them large and small, with felt pens and chalk, and careful calligraphy.

- Collect poetic language to share with children from ads, stories, novels, songs, or magazines—letting the children learn from living language about the power of words.

- Ask children to bring poetry to school to build their private anthologies, and write and share their own poems with the class.

For the teacher:

- Ask consultants, librarians, authors, and book store clerks to keep you posted on new releases so your own repertoire of children's poems constantly grows and changes.

- Share with other teachers poems that work, poems that draw children again and again.

- Do not insist that students give a "correct" response to a poem but rather observe and listen to responses of the children and build on them.

- Do not be afraid to teach about poems, thus giving children knowledge and information to strengthen their poem power, but never teach the technique without context, without the child wanting or needing to know (pp. 24–26).

It is essential that teachers reacquaint themselves with the power and pleasure of poetry. Poetry brings light "straight toward you," as Rolf Jacobsen's poem makes apparent, and it is important that we "Look!"

### Children as Readers of Poetry

**Cuckoo!**

The cuckoo in our cuckoo clock
was wedded to an octopus,
she laid a single wooden egg,
and hatched a cuckoocloctopus.

From *The New Kid on the Block* by Jack Prelutsky, p. 19.
© 1984 Jack Pelutsky. By permission.

*Watch*

*Watch an interview with and listen to poems by Jack Prelutsky.*

Even the most reluctant readers of poetry love Jack Prelutsky. That's one of the reasons he was named the first children's poet laureate by the Poetry Foundation. Prelutsky knows what kids like—funny, scary, but also imaginative and perceptive.

Children should be exposed to a variety of poems to gain a broad appreciation for all that poetry has to offer.

Kutiper and Wilson (1993) summarized the results of several studies of children's poetry preferences and found the following:

### Children's poetry preferences:

- The narrative form of poetry was popular with readers of all ages, whereas free verse and haiku were the most disliked.
- Students preferred poems that contained rhyme, rhythm, and sound.
- Children most enjoyed poetry that contained humor, familiar experiences, and animals.
- Younger students (elementary and middle school/junior high age) preferred contemporary poems.
- Students disliked poems that contained visual imagery or figurative language (p. 29).

*Listen*

*Listen to some of Shel Silverstein's poems and a tribute to his work.*

Kutiper and Wilson (1993) also found that the humorous contemporary poetry of Shel Silverstein and Jack Prelutsky dominated the circulation volume of school libraries.

The popularity of this light, humorous poetry crosses the grade levels with its ability to delight children and young adults and should certainly be a part of any school or classroom library. Yet, if children are only exposed to this type of poetry, then they will never develop a genuine interest in it. Kutiper and Wilson (1993) assert as follows:

One would not suppose that a steady diet of popular music would prepare youngsters to appreciate Beethoven or Chopin. By the same token, a steady diet of Silverstein and Prelutsky will probably not prepare young readers for Frost, Dickinson, or the poetry of countless other word artists. (p. 34)

Former fifth-grade teacher Janine Certo (2004) agrees with Kutiper and Wilson, stating, "Children, too, deserve a diet of poetry that blends laughter with elements of insight, human experience, and wonder so that they can make meaning of the world and their unique perspective" (p. 271). Certo wanted her students to experience the fun of Silverstein, but she also wanted them to mature as readers and writers of poetry. Recognizing that the poetry teachers select for use in the classroom greatly affects the long-term impression poetry will leave with children, she scanned classic children's and adult poetry collections and anthologies for suitable poems. Certo selected poems that were not too complex or abstract but would enhance students' perceptions and enrich their lives. She states, "It is the teacher's responsibility to assure and to reassure children that their imagination and their experiences of the world are major factors in understanding the poem" (p. 269). Certo shared information about the poems' authors and read the poems aloud to her students. She gave students the opportunity to read the poems themselves and to respond to the poems on their own terms without pressure. Through this sequence, Certo found her students to be empowered by poetry.

## Types of Poetry

Poetry can be categorized by the kind of poem it is, such as a nursery rhyme or a folk poem, or by its form, such as *The Tower*, a concrete or shape poem in which the arrangement on the page indicates the poem's subject. Some forms of poetry have specific rules, such as haiku, which usually include 17 syllables arranged in lines of 5, 7, and 5 syllables. Other forms of poetry, such as free verse, do not have rules. (See "Categories of Poetry" on page 240.)

Because children prefer funny, narrative poems that rhyme, it is important to include such poems in class. But if teachers want to broaden children's interests in and appreciation for poetry, they must expand the depth and breadth of the poetry. This does not mean a tedious analysis of structure or form but a discussion of rhyme, pattern, and category. Poems can be presented in a collection by a single author, a collection by multiple authors, or an illustrated book of a single poem. Each brings its own pleasures to the reader.

### SINGLE ILLUSTRATED POETRY

*Read* Harlem *by Walter Dean Myers.*

A single illustrated poem consists of only one poem presented in an illustrated picturebook format. For a single poem to comprise an entire picturebook, a single line or stanza may constitute an entire page. Thus, the illustrations play a major role in the development of the poem's meaning. The Caldecott Honor winning *Harlem*, written by Walter Dean Myers, celebrates the people, sights, and sounds of Harlem. Christopher Myers's illustrations, a combination of bold collage, ink, and gouache, create a subtext of textures and colors of the city and people and seem to personify the words themselves.

In *Long Night Moon*, Cynthia Rylant sets the stage by explaining, "Long ago Native Americans gave names to the full moons they watched throughout the year. Each month had a moon. And each moon had a name." Twelve poems are presented, one for each month of the year. Illustrator Mark Siegel explains in a note that he spent many hours walking around at night to capture the "astonishing and complex face" that nature reveals at night.

In *Hush! A Thai Lullaby,* also a Caldecott Honor book, author Minfong Ho uses rhymed, repetitive, onomatopoetic text in a question-and-answer format, as a mother, having just put her toddler to sleep, says "Hush!" to a succession of noises around her and finds out which animal is making each sound. Illustrator Holly Meade uses cut-paper-and-ink illustrations in earth tones with the varied textures of the paper to depict traditional Thai textiles, basketry, and building styles.

*The Tower is a concrete poem from a collection of concrete poems by John Grandits in* Technically, It's Not My Fault. *Playing on a familiar tale, Grandits uses creative technical design and wacky humor to create a delightful and accessible poem.*

THE TOWER

hair hair hair hair hair hair
hair hair hair hair hair
hair hair hair hair hair

Rapunzel, Rapunzel, let down your hair, I said. And she did. I started climbing. Watch out for my hair, she said, I don't want split ends. Take your boots off, I just washed it, she said. Watch out for my barrette, it's my favorite! she said. Why are you slowing down? Aren't you strong enough to rescue me? Why did you stop? What kind of prince are you, anyway? I climbed back down. I've heard about this other princess who's asleep—a real beauty.

## POETRY COLLECTIONS

Possibly the most common type of poetry for children is a collection of poems by a single poet. Sometimes the collection of poetry is unified by a common theme. Children's poet Ralph Fletcher says the following:

> Concocting a poetry collection is akin to putting together the menu for a dinner party. You can't limit your focus to the chicken satay appetizer or the fresh dinner rolls. You have to make sure that each dish works harmoniously with the other dishes and courses being served. With a poetry collection, I know each poem will "rub against" all the other poems. As I write each poem I ask myself, will it fit in the collection? If I put it in the section, will it help that poem shine? (Kurkjian, Livingston, Young, & Fletcher, 2006, p. 601)

*Watch*

*Watch a presentation by Janet Wong and listen to her read a poem from* Night Dreams.

The poems in Janet Wong's *Night Dreams* are about some of the many dreams she or her friends have had. *Hailstones and Halibut Bones*, written by Mary O'Neill and illustrated by John Wallner, consists of 12 poems that reflect the author's feelings about various colors: "Like acrobats on a high trapeze / The colors pose and bend their knees/Twist and turn and leap and blend / Into shapes and feelings without end." Diane Ackerman's *Animal Sense* shows how animals use their senses of sight, touch, taste, smell, and hearing

# Categories of Poetry

| Category | Description | Examples |
|---|---|---|
| **Mother Goose and Nursery Rhymes** | Passed down from the oral tradition, these poems or verses often contain nonsensical lyrics and strong rhyme. | *Mamá Goose: A Latino Nursery Treasury*, selected by Alma Ada and Isabel Campoy<br>*Sing a Song of Six Pence* by Jane Chapman<br>*My Very First Mother Goose*, edited by Iona Opie |
| **Jump Rope Poems** | Poems passed from children to children. Contain rhythm and rhyme. | *Skipping Around the World* by Francelia Butler<br>*Miss Mary Mack and Other Children's Street Rhymes* by Joanna Cole and Stephanie Calmenson |
| **Folk Poems** | Folk songs that contain rhymes. They can be hundreds of years old. Also very popular with children. | "There Was an Old Lady Who Swallowed a Fly" in John Langstaff's *Oh, A-Hunting We Will Go*<br>*Granny Will Your Dog Bite? And Other Mountain Rhymes*, collected by Gerald Milnes |
| **Lyrical** | A brief poem emphasizing sound and picture imagery rather than narrative or dramatic movement. | "The Swing" by Robert Louis Stevenson in *A Child's Garden of Verses*<br>"The Lone Dog" by Irene McLeod in Helen Tibbet's *Favorite Poems Old and New* |
| **Narrative** | Tells a story often with rapid action and a chronological order. Relates to a particular event or tale. | *Brown Honey and Broomwheat Tea* by Joyce Carol Thomas<br>*The Night Before Christmas* by Clement Moore<br>*The Midnight Ride of Paul Revere* by Henry Wadsworth Longfellow |
| **Free Verse** | A poem with no specific form, rhyme, or pattern, but evokes strong feeling. | *Worlds Apart: Traveling with Fernie and Me* by Gary Soto<br>*Speak to Me (and I Will Listen Between the Lines)* by Karen English<br>*Confetti: Poems for Children* by Pat Mora |
| **Nonsense Verse** | Poetry that is entertaining for children but doesn't make much sense. | "They Went to Sea in a Sieve" by Edward Lear<br>"Chester" by Shel Silverstein |
| **Sonnets** | A 14-line rhyming poem in iambic pentameter. | *A Wreath for Emmet Till* by Marilyn Nelson<br>"Emily Dickinson's House" by Jane Yolen in *Take Joy* |
| **Ballads** | A narrative folk song developed in Europe during the middle ages that is often accompanied by instruments. The focus is typically heroic or tragic. | "On Top of Old Smoky" in X. J. Kennedy's *Knock at a Star*<br>"Get Up and Bar the Door" in *The Oxford Book of Poetry for Children*, edited by Edward Blishen |

*(continued)*

# Categories of Poetry (continued)

| Category | Description | Examples |
|---|---|---|
| **Limericks** | A short five-line poem in which the first, second, and fifth lines rhyme and have three pronounced beats, while the third and fourth lines rhyme and have two pronounced beats each. | *The Hopeful Trout and Other Limericks* by John Ciardi<br>*The Book of Pigericks* by Arnold Lobel<br>*Timothy Tunny Swallowed a Bunny* by Bill Grossman |
| **Concrete Poems** | The poet emphasizes meaning by shaping the poem into a picture. | *Technically, It's Not My Fault* by John Grandits<br>*Doodle Dandies* by J. Patrick Lewis<br>*A Poke in the I* by Paul Janeczko |
| **Haiku** | A type of Japanese poetry that consists of three lines. The first line has five syllables, the second line has seven syllables, and the final line has five syllables. | *If Not for the Cat* by Jack Prelutsky<br>*Stone Bench in an Empty Park* by Paul Janeczko<br>*A Pocketful of Poems* by Nikki Grimes |
| **Poetry Novels** | An entire novel written in poetic form. | *Love That Dog* by Sharon Creech<br>*Spinning Through the Universe* by Helen Frost<br>*Locomotion* by Jacqueline Woodson |
| **Other Forms/ Elements of Poetry** | There are many other forms/ elements of poetry not listed here. See the resources to the right for more detailed information about other forms and elements of poetry. | *A Kick in the Head: An Everyday Guide to Poetic Forms* by Paul Janeczko<br>*Poetry Matters: Writing a Poem from the Inside Out* by Ralph Fletcher<br>*R Is for Rhyme: A Poetry Alphabet* by Judy Young |

to guide them in ways that are similar to and different from our own. Peter Sis's sketches add whimsy without distracting from the words.

## POETRY ANTHOLOGIES

An anthology is a collection of poems by various poets. The poems can be about a variety of topics within an overarching theme, such as *Light-Gathering Poems*, in which editor Liz Rosenberg collected poems from the 1700s to the present that she believes inspire and bring forth light. Anthologies can also be a collection of poems by poets on a single topic, such as *Science Spectacular* and *Marvelous Math*, selected by Lee Bennett Hopkins. When creating an anthology, Lee Bennett Hopkins (1993) says:

> First, I come up with an idea for a topic. Then I search for all the poems I can find on that subject. I look through the hundreds of books I have in my library and I search for new books in bookstores. I read and reread hundreds of poets' works, whittling away until I've found just the right poems for my anthology. (pp. 26–27)

A carefully crafted anthology is an invaluable resource for the classroom, providing teachers and children with poems from a range of forms, topics, and poets (see the list of anthologies at the end of this chapter).

## Elements of Poetry

The elements of poetry are the devices poets use to craft sound, image, and form that come together to create imagination and depth of emotion that is the hallmark of quality poetry. Table 9.2 provides a description and examples of the major elements of poetry. Teachers can introduce children to the elements of poetry through reading aloud a variety of poems and discussing the technique used by the poet to create the rhythm, sound, or shape. Children can try to use these elements in their own poetry writing.

**TABLE 9.2**

# Elements of Poetry

| Element | Description | Examples |
|---|---|---|
| Rhythm | The beat or movement of words in a poem. The meter or stress, number of syllables, and pattern of syllables, affect the rhythm of the poem. | "The Pickety Fence" by David McCord in *One at a Time* "From a Railway Carriage" by Robert Lewis Stevenson in *A Child's Garden of Verses* |
| Rhyme/ Sound Pattern | Affects the musical quality of poetry. The sounds of words convey the intended meaning of the poem. The repletion of initial consonants (alliteration), vowels (assonance), the use of words that make a sound (onomatopoeia) or the repletion of particular words, lines, phrases or verses in a poem all contribute to the creation of rhyme in poetry. | "Beautiful Soup" by Lewis Carroll in *Alice's Adventures in Wonderland* *A Foot in the Mouth: Poems to Speak, Sing and Shout* compiled by Paul B. Janeczko |
| Imagery | Involves one or more of the five senses—to see, feel, hear, taste, smell, and/or touch the environment created by the poem. Figurative language such as simile, metaphor, and personification is often used to clarify and enhance the reader's experience with the poem. | *Dirty Laundry Pile: Poems in Different Voices* by Paul Janeczko "April Rain Song" by Langston Hughes in *The Dream Keeper and Other Poems* "Summer Grass" by Carl Sandburg from *Grassroots*, illustrated by Wendell Minor |
| Shape | Words may be organized in a way to add meaning and/ or create a visual image of the poem. The concrete poem is an example. | *Falling Down the Page: A Book of List Poems* edited by Georgia Heard *Doodle Dandies: Poems That Take Shape* by J. Patrick Lewis |

# Evaluating and Selecting Poetry

**Great, Good, Bad**

A great book is a homing device
For navigating paradise.

A good book somehow makes you care
About the comfort of a chair.

A bad book owes to many trees
A forest of apologies.

From *Please Bury Me in the Library* by J. Patrick Lewis, p. 10.
© 2005 J. Patrick Lewis. By permission.

The boundaries of what constitutes poetry for children are lenient. Winters and Schmidt (2001) write the following:

> While there are certainly those poems specifically written for the child audience, there are also poems that have been brought into the arena. The commonality here is that all of these poems are able to be enjoyed and understood, at least on the literal level, by a child audience. (p. 77)

Evaluating and selecting poetry for children must necessarily take into consideration readability, subject matter, language, and form, as described in "Evaluation Criteria."

As with other genres, poetry should avoid nostalgia, sentimentality, sarcasm, and didacticism. The emotional appeal of poetry for children should honestly reflect the real emotions of childhood. Poets of quality children's poetry often draw on their own experiences as a child. Nikki Grimes (2000) writes:

> When I was growing up, I rarely found beautiful images of myself in the pages of a book, and that's precisely why I chose to write books for young people like me. I wanted them to meet girls like Zuri and Danitra in *Meet Danitra Brown*, like LaTasha in *Come Sunday*, boys like Damon, and men like Blue in *My Man Blue*. These were people from my neighborhood, from my world. People who walked and talked the way I did, who danced the way I danced, and who worshipped the way I worshipped. These were people whose stories I knew and wanted to tell, people who looked and felt like me. (pp. 2–3)

*Watch*

*Watch an interview with Nikki Grimes.*

Teachers and parents can help children find voices in poetry that reflect the child's own experiences and emotions as well as those of others. Therefore, any poetry collection should include poetry from diverse cultures. Janet Wong (2005) reflects, "Many people come up to me and say how much my books affected their Asian-American students. What I really prefer, though, is to think of how many non-Asian students I've reached, kids who were surprised to find themselves identifying with something in one of my books. . . . Too often kids are directed to read only those books that deal with their own ethnicity" (p. 232). Similarly, Ashley Bryan (Pavonetti, 2002) affirms, "Very often, somebody will say, 'Oh, that's a black poet and there are only white children in my class'" but "to reach out and include the loveliest of work of the many different peoples of our country is what opens that sense of wonder in a child" (pp. 66–67).

*Watch*

*Watch Ashley Bryan give a presentation.*

# Evaluation Criteria

**Criteria for Evaluating Poetry**

| Element | Criteria | Description |
|---|---|---|
| Readability | Can children understand the poem when reading alone or with the help of an adult? | While one should not assume that a child will not understand a certain poem and write it down to a particular level, children need to read poems that they can generally understand. If they do not, it is unlikely that the poem will be appealing to them. |
| Subject Matter | Does the poem contain a subject or an experience with which the child is familiar? Does the subject evoke a feeling or response from the child? | If the poem contains a subject or an experience with which the child is familiar, it is more likely to be understood. The subject matter should appeal to the child and evoke emotion, such as inspiration, encouragement, or laughter. |
| Language | Does the author use language to create images in the poem? Does the author manipulate language by playing with the sounds through repetition or rhyme? | Images of sight, smell, taste, and touch should be used in different ways. It should encourage the child to imagine or think in other ways. Repetition and rhyme should allow children to play with sounds which appeal to them. |
| Form | Could the child replicate or borrow the form when writing poetry? | The form should be something the child can adapt and use in his or her writing. |

**Criteria for Evaluating Poetry**

As with other genres, excellent multicultural poetry honestly and accurately portrays a particular culture while also including common themes, emotions, and experiences familiar to all children (see Chapter 11 for more guidance on providing multicultural literature).

## CHALLENGING PERSPECTIVES ON POETRY

The language that poets use to create strong emotions in poetry is often political and steeped in the history of oppression. For example, in *Pass It On: African American Poetry for Children*, editor Wade Hudson included the poem "Incident" by Countee Cullen. In this poem, Cullen relates the experience of an eight-year-old child who is the object of a racial slur on a Baltimore bus, an adaptation of a personal experience. The poem addresses the issues of racial discrimination and inequality in American society and the use of a racial slur creates the desired effect of outrage and disbelief. However, many teachers would not feel comfortable sharing "Incident" with children. I am not suggesting that the use of oppressive or other strong language is appropriate for school. Yet, language is one of the most intimate expressions of identity and poetry often strongly connects to issues of identity and validation. Poetry can be used to affirm a child's home language and culture and can help a teacher learn more about their students' lives. For an example of how two teachers used poetry to teach about race and racism that connected with their students' identity, see the Opportunities for Reader Response section of this chapter.

## The Role of Poetry in Literacy Development

Besides bringing joy and insight, poetry contributes to children's literacy development. In the primary grades, nursery rhymes can be used to develop phonemic awareness, alphabet knowledge, one-to-one correspondence, word parts, and rhyme. Older students benefit from the precise language in poetry such as rich vocabulary and figurative language. Many children come to school knowing only poetry from nursery rhymes, riddles, raps, and jump rope. Other children do not even have that much experience with poetry. So it is essential that teachers provide opportunities for children to experience poetry throughout the school day.

### SHARING POETRY

> There was an Old Lady whose folly
> Induced her to sit in a holly;
> Whereupon, by a thorn
> Her dress being torn,
> She quickly became melancholy.

From *A Kick in the Head: An Everyday Guide to Poetic Forms* by Paul Janeczko, p. 20

Addressing the deficiency in the poetry that is usually read aloud to children, Laminack and Wadsworth (2006) state, "We encourage you to pause a moment every day to put the rhythms and cadences of poetry into the air and into the ear. Day after day, as you layer poem upon poem, those sounds begin to gather in the silent spaces and hover there like bees gathering one by one, gathering into a swarm" (p. 113). One, two, or even a few bees cannot make a hive, make honey, or make people run for cover. Yet, a swarm of bees is a powerful force. Such is true for reading poetry—one, two, or even a few poems sprinkled throughout the year will not make a difference in children's interest in poetry, but one, two, or even a few poems every day throughout the curriculum over the course of a school year *will* make a difference.

Reading aloud affords the teacher an opportunity to model the sound, rhythm, and pattern of poetry along with the delight, reflection, and wisdom poetry brings. Laminack and Wadsworth (2006) offer a weekly format for including poetry in daily read alouds in Figure 9.1.

**FIGURE 9.1**

Suggested Weekly Format for Sharing Poetry Daily

**Older Students—Poems on overhead 2 or 3 times a week**

| NOVEMBER 2008 | | | | |
|---|---|---|---|---|
| **Monday** | **Tuesday** | **Wednesday** | **Thursday** | **Friday** |
| 3 Read the poem once. Stop to think aloud and let your students know how you make decisions about the sound of poetry when you read. Then, let students read through the poem silently, followed by choral reading. Distribute a copy to students. | 4 Read the poem aloud to students to refresh the sound in their ears. Then, ask the students to read the poem in pairs or small groups, inviting them to try alternative ways of reading that match the meaning of the poem. | 5 Start over with a new poem following Monday's format. | 6 Follow Tuesday's format. | 7 Pause after every five poems, and encourage students to find favorites to share through poetry performance or poetry cafe. |
| 10 | 11 | 12 | 13 | 14 |

**Younger Students—Poems on chart, 1 poem a week**

| NOVEMBER 2008 | | | | |
|---|---|---|---|---|
| **Monday** | **Tuesday** | **Wednesday** | **Thursday** | **Friday** |
| 3 Read the poem once so students can hear the pacing, cadence, and meaning of the language. Invite them to read the poem with you a second time. | 4 Read the poem together on the first reading; then divide students into two groups to read alternate lines or stanzas. | 5 Read the poem together as a group during the first reading, and then give students a copy of the poems to read in pairs or small groups. | 6 Devote the time to performances or reading of the poem by individuals, pairs, or small groups. | 7 Same as Thursday. |
|  |  |  |  |  |
| 10 | 11 | 12 | 13 | 14 |

Adapted from L. Laminack & R. Wadsworth, *Learning under the influence of language and literature: Making the most of read-alouds across the day* (pp. 114–115). Portsmouth, NH: Heinemann, 2006.

## LISTENING TO POETRY

Hearing poetry read aloud by the authors can also be an excellent experience for children. Younger readers will enjoy the antics of the happy, carefree, and mischievous swarm of bees in *Happy Bees*, written by Arthur Yorinks and illustrated by Carey Armstrong-Ellis. The poem is the first tune on the accompanying CD along with nine other songs. For readers of all ages, *Once Upon a Poem: Favorite Poems That Tell Stories,* edited by Kevin Crossley-Holland offers a CD with dramatized selected works from 15 exciting and enjoyable stories. The illustrated poems each begin with a quotation from one of today's favorite authors including J. K. Rowling, Avi, Philip Pullman, and Cornelia Funke. Jon Scieszka and illustrator Lane Smith read aloud poems from the hilarious *Science Verse* in which a student is cursed after his teacher tells his class they can hear the poetry of science in everything:

### Mary Had a...

Mary had a little worm.
She thought it was a chigger.
But everything that Mary ate,
Only made it bigger.
It came with her to school one day,
And gave the kids a fright,
Especially when the teacher said,
"Now that's a parasite."

From *Science Verse* by Jon Scieszka. © 2004 Jon Scieszka. By permission.

For older readers, *Poetry Speaks to Children,* edited by Elise Paschen, includes great poets past and living from Robert Frost to Sylvia Plath and Langston Hughes reading their works. Additional poems in print form along with biographies of the poets allow the reader to further explore the poets' works.

## ELEMENTS OF POETRY

> I don't think it's wrong to tell students about simile, metaphor, and personification, but the explanations should have an organic origin. . . . Taught out of context, without an understanding of how poets use them, the labels become another way to turn students off to poetry—to make them yawn at the mention of the word.
>
> GEORGIA HEARD, 1989, P. 69

Teachers can record what children notice about poetry on an anchor chart (Figure 9.2). This ongoing documentation will help children realize that there are many forms and elements of poetry. Recording students' observations about poetry as it develops over time keeps learning in context and organic, as Georgia Heard (1989) suggests. When teachers carefully select poetry, read it aloud every day, and model their own thinking as they read, children will naturally learn to recognize the elements and forms of poetry. This is powerful learning! Teachers can then ask children to look for examples of the elements and forms of poetry in their independent reading.

*Watch*

*Watch an interview with Jacqueline Woodson in which she reads an excerpt from* Locomotion.

## IMAGERY

Imagery is at the heart of poetry, so visualization is integral to reading poetry. When we visualize, we create pictures in our minds. Poetry, more than any other genre, relies on imagery to convey meaning. In *Locomotion*, author Jacqueline Woodson conveys the story of 11-year-old Lonnie through a series of 60 free verse poems.

**FIGURE 9.2**

Anchor Chart for Poetry

## What We Noticed About Poetry

| | |
|---|---|
| Tell about experiences | Some lines can be a pattern |
| Sound like a song | Some lines ask questions then the next lines answer |
| Some words rhyme | Can look like a list |
| Some words don't rhyme | Punctuation can be different |
| Emotions  feelings | Some have shapes |
| Titles | |
| Some words can repeat | |

In these poems, Lonnie writes about his life after the death of his parents in a fire when he was seven years old. He also writes about the separation from his younger sister, Lili, living in a foster home, and finding his poetic voice at school. Lonnie explains that he is telling his story in a book of poems "because poetry's short," and "every time I try to / tell the whole story my mind goes *Bequiet*" (p. 1). Only, it is not his mind's voice that is telling him to be quiet, it is the voice of his foster mother, Miss Edna. Woodson uses figurative language to bring to life how it might feel when Miss Edna's constant *"Be quiet!"* keeps Lonnie from thinking:

> But when Miss Edna's voice comes on, the ideas in my
> head go out like a candle and all you see left is this little
> string of smoke that disappears real quick
> before I even have a chance to find out
> what it's trying to say. (p. 1)

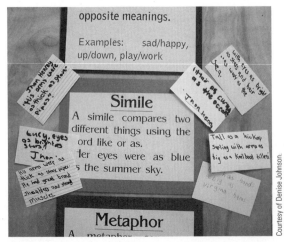

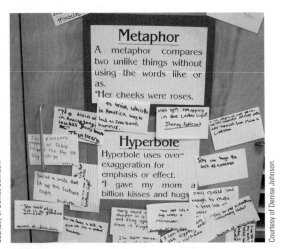

*A third-grade teacher posted the meanings of some elements of figurative language and asked students to record examples on index cards when they came across them in their independent reading.*

Visualizing is inferring with mental images rather than words. Imagery assists the reader in making meaning out of poetry, which goes beyond the literal and implies and suggests other meanings, feelings, and ideas. Figurative language is language that is not literal. The smoke looks like a piece of string because it is long and narrow. This language requires the reader to think beyond the text. It stimulates the senses and automatically engages the brain in creating visual images in the mind of the reader. Learning to think beyond the literal meaning and being able to imagine what is suggested by words are invaluable tools. However, the reader needs sufficient background knowledge for stimulating the mental image. Most of us have watched a candle being blown out, and that experience evokes a mental image that allows us to compare the disappearance of an idea to the extinguishing of a candle flame and thus creates a deeper understanding of what Lonnie must feel. Dorn and Soffos (2005) write the following:

> The reader's ability to construct pictorial images from the writer's words is essential for deepening the reader's comprehension. In fact, deep comprehension is greatly impaired—if not impossible—if the reader is unable to construct mental bridges between the author's message and the reader's experiences. (p. 9)

Teachers can assist children with understanding when and how to use the strategy of visualization by modeling during the think aloud process.

For example, a teacher might read the following poem by Douglas Florian:

### The Daddy Longlegs

O Daddy
Daddy O
How'd you get
Those legs to grow
So very long
And lean in size?
From spiderobic
Exercise?
Did you drink milk?
Or chew on cheese?
And by the way,
Where are your knees?
O Daddy
Daddy O
How'd you get
Those legs to grow?

From *Insectlopedia* by Douglas Florian, p. 10.
© 1998 Douglas Florian. By permission.

After reading the poem, the teacher might pause to think aloud about how the word *spiderobics* paints a picture in her mind of a spider doing aerobics with really long legs. After discussing how this word helped with visualizing, the teacher adds *spiderobics* to a chart on which she recorded words from poetry that created emotion, imagery, or music (Figure 9.3). Children can then use this chart to assist them with writing their own poetry.

**FIGURE 9.3**

A Chart Recording
Words Found
in Poetry That
Create Emotion,
Imagery, or Music

## Three Pillars of Poetry

| Emotion | *Imagery* | *Music* |
|---|---|---|
| terrorize | lean | Oh Daddy |
| fuss | spiderobic | Daddy Oh |
| faithful | swarm | left-right, |
| exhausted | roam | left-right |
| sorrow | glide | whirl-twirl |
| frantic | seize | red, red rose |
| awkward | swoop | barn owl, |
| joy | precarious | barn owl |
| love | shattered | red headed |
| happiness | soothe | tap, tap, |
| lonely | gaze | tapping |
| | exotic | |
| | smidgen | |

## INFERRING

There's a power in leaving things out. It's the power of negative space in art. What you don't say may ring louder in the air than what you do. It's often more powerful to imply something than to state it.

Paul Fleischman, 2003, p. 87

Throughout *Locomotion*, Lonnie reflects on the memories he holds of his parents:

You know honeysuckle talc powder?
Mama used to smell like that. She told me
honeysuckle's really a flower but all I know
is the powder that smells like Mama.
Sometimes when the missing gets real bad
I go to the drugstore and before the guard starts
following me around like I'm gonna steal something
I go to the cosmetics lady and ask her if she has it.
When she says yeah, I say
*Can I smell it to see if it's the right one?*
Even though the cosmetics ladies roll their eyes at me
they let me smell it.
And for those few seconds, Mama's alive
again.

From *Locomotion* by Jacqueline Woodson, p. 7.
© 2003 Jacqueline Woodson. By permission.

As with visual imagery, the text acts as a stimulus, activating the mind of the reader to ask questions and infer actions. We can visualize Lonnie at the drugstore counter and we can relate to the experience of a smell recalling a memory. We can make concrete connections to Lonnie, but what does he mean by "for those few seconds, Mama's alive again"? Did his mother come back to life? Here, the reader must infer the meaning of this event from multiple sources of information—the story is realistic, not fantasy; a smell can evoke a strong memory; memories can feel real sometimes. By drawing on background knowledge and orchestrating multiple sources of information, the reader can "read between the lines" to infer that Lonnie's mother was not really alive, but his memory of her was so vivid at that moment, that she seemed alive. Loss of a parent is something most children fear, and the connections between Lonnie's trip to the drugstore, the smell of his mother's talc, and the almost real memory of his mother come together to reveal his powerful yearning for her. Poetry, like all stories, is full of complex relationships, and the reader's comprehension depends on the mind's ability to see these relationships.

Readers also infer from line breaks and white space. For instance, reread the first part of *Locomotion*.

> You know honeysuckle talc powder?
> Mama used to smell like that. She told me
> honeysuckle's really a flower but all I know
> is the powder that smells like Mama.

Now, read the third sentence without the line breaks: "She told me honeysuckle's really a flower but all I know is the powder that smells like Mama." The poem reads differently than the sentence. The line breaks are used to shape the meaning and effect of the poem. This creates drama and allows the reader to experience the sadness and loss of Lonnie's mother. The line breaks are not secondary to the language and the images but emphasize and harmonize them, shaping the reading and understanding of a poem.

White space is used by poets to suggest a pause, a change in direction, or a passing of time. As you read this poem by Kristine O'Connell George, think about the purpose of the space:

### Skating in the Wind

> I crouched.
> My brother Bill shoved hard.
> I held up my jacket;
> the wind caught it, shaped it taut like a sail.
>
> The wind slammed into my back.
>
> My skates clattered.
> Skidding,
> Skimming,
> like butter in a hot skillet.
>
> Mouth dry,
> The wind roared in my ears.
>
> Bill said I was almost flying.
>
> Until the fence.

From *Poetry Speaks to Children* by Kristine O'Connell George, p. 79.
© Kristine O'Connell George. By permission.

The first stanza depicts a seemingly innocent shove that sends the ice skater across the ice. Then, there is a pause before the single line "The wind slammed into my back," which takes the reader in an unexpected direction. The wind puts a twist on what was thought to be a fun skate across the ice. The second pause allows the reader to infer what might happen next given this new information. The second stanza confirms the reader's prediction that the wind sent the ice skater uncontrollably across the ice. The third and forth pauses allow the reader to engage fully in the panic of the skater. Then, the second to last sentence, "Bill said I was almost flying" gives the reader the impression that the skater made it to safety with just a hint of glee at the prospect of "flying" across the ice. The pause before the last sentence allows the reader to take a breath at the prospect of the ice skater's victory. Then the author delivers the final punch in the last line as the reader learns of the impending fence. White space played an important role in the reading of this poem by setting up opportunities for the reader to infer the action in the poem.

Again, teachers can model the strategy of inferring through think alouds, making visible a complex process. Children should be encouraged to think aloud on their own when reading independently or in groups with the teacher as a "guide on the side" to scaffold and support as necessary. Like visualization, inferring is critical to our ability to think deeply about poetry.

### ORAL FLUENCY: PERFORMING POETRY

Poetry is meant to be read aloud the same way music is meant to be played. When poems are read aloud, the rhythm or cadence reinforces the meaning. When reading poetry aloud, children learn that meaning can be influenced through manipulation of intonation, pitch, or stress of certain words or phrases. In other words, how a poem is read matters. Children of all ages can learn much about interpreting poetry by practicing different ways in which it can be read aloud. One way to achieve this is through choral reading or performance poetry.

*Listen*

*Listen to Kristine O'Connell George read several poems.*

**ALL MY FAULT?**

The guinea pig has fleas,
there are grass stains on my knees,
          AND IT'S ALL MY FAULT?
There's mustard on the floor,
and flies came in the door,
          AND IT'S ALL MY FAULT?
The milk is warm and sour,
all the bread has been devoured.
          THAT TOO IS ALL MY FAULT?
Why, when I walk into the room,
do you always start to fume
          LIKE IT'S ALL MY FAULT?
Did I cause the national debt?
the creeping ozone threat?
          IS *THAT* ALL MY FAULT?
How 'bout overpopulation?
Did I pollute the habitation?
          IS *THAT* ALL MY FAULT?
Was I born to take the blame?
A guilty face to fit your frame?
          LIKE, THIS IS ALL MY FAULT?
I didn't make the traffic slow,
but that delinquent video
          is mine.
          That one is all my fault.

From *Wham! It's a Poetry Jam* by Sara Holbrook, p. 264.
© 2002 Sara Holbrook. By permission.

The preceding poem, "All My Fault" is from Sara Holbrook's (2002) book *Wham! It's a Poetry Jam.* It is written in a call and response form of choral reading. Choral reading involves dividing a poem so that individuals or groups of students read designated parts of a poem. One or more students take turns reading the lines in black type, while the whole class comes in on the lines in blue type. Some poetry books are specifically written for two or more voices. Poetry for two voices is another type of choral reading. The Newbery-winning *Joyful Noise: Poems for Two Voices,* written by Paul Fleischman, consists of 14 poems about insects. Here is the first stanza of "Grasshoppers."

### Grasshoppers

Sap's rising

|  |  |
|---|---|
|  | Ground's warming |
| Grasshoppers are | Grasshoppers are |
| hatching out | hatching out |
| Autumn-laid eggs | |
| | splitting |
| Young stepping | |
| | into spring |

From *Joyful Noise* by Paul Fleischman, p. 3.
© 1988 Paul Fleischman. By permission.

*Listen*

*Listen to a choral reading of several poems from* Joyful Noise *and* I Am Phoenix.

The class can be divided into two groups, each taking a side of the poem and reading alternately until they have corresponding lines in which they read simultaneously. I Am Phoenix: Poems for Two Voices and Big Talk: Poems for Four Voices are also written by Paul Fleischman. Math Talk: Mathematical Ideas in Poems for Two Voices by Theoni Pappas and Farmer's Garden: Rhymes for Two Voices by David L. Harrison are also excellent resources.

Choral reading can also be conducted in a cumulative style in which one student reads the first line and another student joins in reading the second line in a cumulative manner picking up additional voices until the end of a stanza or the end of the poem. The reverse can also take place in which the whole class starts reading the poem together and then voices drop off until only one or a few remain at the end.

Poetry does not have to be written specifically for choral reading—many poems can be used for this purpose. After children feel comfortable with choral reading, let them select their own poems to perform. You may be amazed at how they choose to interpret a poem through performance if given the opportunity. Encourage students to combine their performance with music, add artwork or create props, or include sound effects, gestures, or body movement.

Choral reading allows children to experience the power of language, actively interpret poetry, and delight in reading poetry aloud. In addition, choral reading also increases all students' oral fluency and may be especially beneficial for ESL students. Hadaway, Vardell, and Young (2001) write, "For English L2 learners, teacher-guided choral reading of poetry meets many of the conditions that are critical in fostering oral language proficiency. Moreover, the focus on poetry is ideal when one considers the unique qualities of the genre: its brevity, strong rhythm, focused content, strong emotional connection, and powerful imagery" (p. 804).

## Opportunities for Reader Response

A powerful aspect of poetry is its potential to engage readers' minds, elicit intense emotional and sensory reactions, and arouse intrinsic passions. Reader response can be an excellent way for students to reflect on poetry and their reaction to it.

### REFLECTING ON POETRY

My son's sixth-grade teacher asked her students to read and respond to the poem "I'm Nobody!" by Emily Dickinson.

### I'm Nobody!

I'm Nobody! Who are you?
Are you nobody, too?
Then there's a pair of us—don't tell!
They'd banish us, you know.

How dreary to be Somebody!
How public, like a frog
To tell your name the livelong day
To an admiring bog!

From Emily Dickinson, *The Complete Poems of Emily Dickinson*, p. 288.
© 1951, 1955, 1979, 1983 Emily Dickinson. By permission.

"I'm Nobody!" is commonly included in middle school English anthologies. The teacher asked the students to respond to the question "Are you somebody or nobody?" Derek's response is in "The Child's Voice." Middle school can be a stressful, uncertain time for some students who suddenly find themselves segmented into a social group that did not exist in elementary school. Derek's response, prompted by Emily Dickinson's poem, is much more reflective of his emotions than it would have been if the teacher had simply asked, "How do you feel about middle school?"

James Damico and Ruthie Riddle (2004) used poetry in a fifth-grade classroom that included children of a wide range of economic and racial diversities. Their goal

## THE • CHILD'S • VOICE

Sixth Grader's Response to "I'm Nobody!" by Emily Dickinson

"This is not an easy question and it took a lot of thought, but in the end, I'm Somebody, but really only by a little. I have few but wonderful and supportive friends, five to be exact. I really think that's the only thing that makes me Somebody because I can't go to the mall without my parents, I don't have a cell phone, I stay inside a lot, I'm good at only about two sports, and I'm not really with the crowd. But really, I don't think any of those things matter in the end. Most kids don't really know me and some don't really want to. But, I have good friends and I do well in school and my parents are proud of me most of the time. So, I may not be in with the crowd, but I'm in with mine. And that's what matters."

*—In what ways could the teacher get the students in this sixth grade class to use their responses to "I'm Nobody" to reflect on the elements of poetry that create depth of emotion?*

was to evoke feelings and provoke thoughts and ideas about complex social issues. They exposed the fifth graders to poetry that dealt with race and racism that connected to a social studies unit on slavery and freedom: Sherman Alexie's *Powwow at the End of the World* and several poems by Janet Wong, including *Bombs Bursting in Air, Speak Up, Noise,* and *Math.* The poetry was used as a catalyst for critical conversations that broadened the content focus on African Americans to include issues that affected American Indians and Asian Americans. The poetry offered the students an opportunity to think about the question "What does it mean to be American?" After reading each poem aloud, Riddle asked the students to respond to an open-ended writing prompt: "What does the poem make you think or feel?" "Speak Up," a dialogue between a European American and a Korean American, is one of the poems to which students responded:

**Speak Up**

You're Korean, aren't you?

                    Yes.

Why don't you speak
Korean?

                    Just don't, I guess.

Say something Korean.

                    I don't speak it.
                    I can't.

C'mon. Say something.

                    *Halmoni.* Grandmother.
                    *Haraboji.* Grandfather.
                    *Imo.* Aunt.

Say some other stuff.
Sounds funny.
Sounds strange.

                    Hey, let's listen to you
                    for a change.

Listen to me?

                    Say some foreign words.

But I'm American,
Can't you see?

                    Your family came from
                    somewhere else.
                    Sometime.

But I was born here.

                    So was I.

From *Good Luck Gold and Other Poems* by Janet Wong, p. 5.
© 1994 Janet S. Wong. By permission.

Damico and Riddle (2004) describe the students' responses to "Speak Up":

Many of the students described how the ending of the poem was "powerful," indicating that it helped them "think about something I never really thought of." One student wrote in his journal, "No one is really official American because everybody's family came from somewhere else." Similarly, Crissy pointed out that discerning American identity is complicated because all Americans, just like the character in "Speak Up," came from somewhere else at some time. Crissy wrote, "Because everyone that is born in America is American. But in another way everyone who is American is also something else." (p. 143)

Damico concludes, "these poems encouraged [the students] to "think about stuff I've never thought of before." In other words, the students' responses, their feelings of "being moved," were part of developing more informed understandings about the world, enabling them to critique and question, for example, why prejudice and discrimination persist and who or what counts as American" (p. 144). Providing children with an opportunity for public and private response to poetry through a variety of avenues—whole/ small group, peer discussion, and journal writing—allows for critical reflection and the "transformative potential of poetry" (p. 145).

## WRITING POETRY

*It has been said that writing a poem for someone else is like giving blood because it comes from the heart of the writer and goes to the heart of the receiver. Poems are filled with words from the heart.*

RALPH FLETCHER, 2002, P. 7

Language, thinking, and feeling come together as students become intimately involved in the process of writing poetry. The poem in Figure 9.4 was written by a first grader after experiencing the loss of his best friend. He dealt with his loss the best way he knew how—through his words. Poetry allowed Dylan to express a very big emotion— sadness and loss of one's best friend—in a small space. As Calkins (1994) affirms, "Writing allows us to turn chaos into something beautiful, to frame selected moments, to uncover and celebrate the organizing patterns of our existing" (p. 253).

Unfortunately, many children have misconceptions about what poetry is and how to write it based on their limited knowledge of the types of poetry. Reading poetry aloud to children, pausing to notice the elements and forms of poetry and children reading poetry independently and chorally every day will broaden their knowledge of what constitutes good poetry. At this point, children are ready to write poetry.

It might seem like a good idea to require students to write poems within a specific form, such as haiku, or to write using certain elements, such as simile or metaphor. Yet, as Regie Routman (2005) notes, this can actually make writing harder and less pleasurable:

When I began teaching children to write free verse, I made writing harder for them by first teaching individual parts. I would say, *Today, we'll learn how to do line breaks [or use white space or craft ending]*. Not only did that slow down the process, it took away the enjoyment. To my surprise, I found kids, even kindergartners, grasped the whole of poetry easily in one fell swoop—the title, the line breaks, the white space, the rhythm—when I started by reading and writing poems and noticing what poets do. After kids wrote their own heartfelt poems, we celebrated these poems and then dealt with specifics as we focused on what each writer was trying to do. (p. 142)

In Lucy Calkins's (1994) classic book *The Art of Teaching Writing,* she reflects on her experience watching poet Georgia Heard teach several groups of children to write poetry. Georgia Heard always encouraged the children to write from the heart, to take an image from their own lives and picture it, to write about what they see and feel in that mental picture.

**FIGURE 9.4**

First Grader's
Published Poem

**Split Up**

My friend
My only friend
He moved
It felt like a bullet went through my heart.
But I will always remember
His smile
I bet he will remember my smile, too.

By Dylan Spradlin

Courtesy of Denise Johnson.

Routman (2005) suggests a lesson framework that gradually releases responsibility to students after showing them how to write poetry through demonstration, shared demonstration, guided practice, and, finally, independent practice (Table 9.3).

After students have published their poetry, create a class anthology. Children like to read one another's poetry, so place the anthology in the class library. Over time, there will be many collections that will reflect students' experiences from joy to wisdom.

## Making the Connection Across the Curriculum

Poetry helps broaden children's experiences with new concepts and provides fresh outlooks on the ordinary things that surround them, making poetry a perfect complement to content area subjects.

# Guidelines for Teachers: Steps for Writing Poetry with Children

1. Select a real audience and purpose for writing.

2. Read, examine, and discuss examples and characteristics of poetry (immersion, demonstration).

3. What do you notice? (shared demonstration).

4. Talk before writing (shared and guided practice).

5. Provide sustained writing time with feedback (guided and independent practice).

6. Conference with students (guided and independent practice).

7. Share, celebrate, and reflect.

8. Revisit drafts (guided and independent practice).

9. Conference with students.

10. Proofread and edit.

11. Publish

Source: R. Routman, *Writing essentials* (Portsmouth, NH: Heinemann, 2005), p. 306.

## MATH

Greg Tang has written several math poetry books, including *Math for All Seasons* (2002) and *The Grapes of Math* (2001), that use rhymed couplets to show how to group together objects and look for patterns to speed up the calculation process. *Math Talk: Mathematical Ideas in Poems for Two Voices* by Theoni Pappas (1991) includes poems intended to be read chorally about topics from triangles to fractals, googles, and tessellations. The poems in *Marvelous Math* (1997), selected by Lee Bennett Hopkins, include a variety of poems about math from various poets, including *Pythagoras* by Madeleine Comora and *Math Makes Me Feel Safe* by Betsy Franco.

## GEOGRAPHY AND SOCIAL STUDIES

Children can experience a year in the lives of the Amish and Mennonite communities of Pennsylvania Dutch Country through poetry in Linda Oatman High's *A Humble Life: Plain Poems* (2001). The journey continues in *My America: A Poetry Atlas of the United States* (2000), selected by Lee Bennett Hopkins. The selections explore seven regions of the United States, including geography, climate, and urban or rural features. Classic and contemporary poets such as Langston Hughes, Carl Sandburg, Nikki Giovanni, David McCord, X. J. Kennedy, Myra Cohn Livingston, and Lee Bennett Hopkins are represented.

The journey expands to include monuments of the world in J. Patrick Lewis's *Monumental Verses* (2005). Lewis pairs poetry of varying forms with the artistry of well-known architectural marvels throughout the world photographed by National Geographic. The 13 monuments include Stonehenge, Machu Picchu, the Statue of Liberty, and the Great Wall of China.

## SCIENCE

Add a spark to science with *Night Wonders* (2005) by Jane Ann Peddicord: "Beside a dark and quiet sea / beneath a starlit canopy, / I shone my light upon a star / and wondered, *What is out that far?*" (p. 2). So begins this book of poetry that takes us past stars into intergalactic space and back to Earth again. Each poem is captioned with factual information and paired with a spectacular photo or picture of space on the facing page.

Back on the ground we find *Lizards, Frogs, and Polliwogs* (2001) by Douglas Florian, which includes a collection of humorous poems about such reptiles and amphibians as the glass frog, the gecko, and the rattlesnake. A gila monster retorts, "They call me monster just because / I have short legs and clumsy claws, / and poison in my jaws, / And look / Like someone's composition book" (p. 21). Each poem is accompanied by a whimsical full-page illustration. Along the same line, Florian has written poems about assorted insects in *insectlopedia* (1998) and various animals in *mammalabilia* (2000). *Song of the Water Boatman and Other Pond Poems* by Joyce Sidman and illustrated by Beckie Prange is a collection of vivid poems that provides an insightful look at some of the animals, insects, and plants that are found in ponds, with accompanying information about each. A glossary of science terms is included in the back of this unique and striking collection. (See illustration 9 in the Part 2 color insert.)

# Top 10 Read Alouds

## POETRY

1. **19 Varieties of Gazelle: Poems of the Middle East** by Naomi Shihab Nye (2002, Greenwillow). A collection of poems about the Middle East and about being Arab American.

2. **A Pocketful of Poems** by Nikki Grimes, illustrated by John Steptoe (2001, Houghton Mifflin). Poems and haiku verses provide glimpses of life in the city.

3. **Blues Journey** by Walter Dean Myers, illustrated by Christopher Myers (2003, Holiday House). The African experience in America is celebrated with a soulful, affecting blues poem.

4. **Days to Celebrate: A Full Year of Poetry, People, Holidays, History, Fascinating Facts, and More** by Lee Bennett Hopkins, illustrated by Stephen Alcorn (2005, Greenwillow). Provides a listing of events, births of famous people, and holidays, with information and poetry about the 12 months of the year.

5. **Hummingbird Nest: A Journal of Poems** by Kristine O'Connell George, illustrated by Barry Moser (2004, Harcourt). When a mother hummingbird builds a nest on a family's porch, they watch and record her actions and the birth and development of her fledglings.

6. **Mirror, Mirror: A Book of Reversible Verse** by Marilyn Singer, illustrated by Josée Massee (2010, Dutton). A collection of short poems which, when reversed, provide new perspectives on the fairy tale characters they feature.

7. **Moon, Have You Met My Mother? The Collected Poems of Karla Kuskin,** illustrated by Sergio Ruzzier (2003, HarperCollins). This collection contains Kuskin's most celebrated poems, as well as new works never before published.

8. **¡Muu, Moo! Rimas de animals/Animal Nursery Rhymes** selected by Alma Flor Ada and F. Isabel Campoy, illustrated by Vivi Escrivá (2010, HarperCollins). A collection of animal-themed nursery rhymes in Spanish, from Spain and Latin America, with English translations.

9. **Red Sings from Treetops: A Year in Colors** by Joyce Sidman, illustrated by Pamela Zagarenski (2009, Houghton Mifflin). The names of colors are woven into unrhymed poems that celebrate the seasons.

10. **Sweethearts of Rhythm: The Story of the Greatest All-Girl Swing Band in the World** by Marilyn Nelson, illustrated by Jerry Pinkney (2009, Penguin). A chronology of the 1940s, all-female, interracial jazz band that made its way from Mississippi to the most famous ballrooms in the country during the hard years of the war.

# Activities For Professional Development

## Think Critically About Children's Literature

1. As discussed in this chapter, many teachers do not like poetry. How do you feel about poetry? Discuss your own experiences with poetry in school and how they shaped your like, dislike, or indifference to poetry. Make a point of reading poetry by different poets as often as possible and note the types of poems and poets you enjoy most.

## Bring Children's Literature into the Classroom

2. If possible, share a few poems you enjoy with children. How did they react? Do they have a favorite? Consider submitting the children's favorite poem or your favorite poem to the Favorite Poem Project at http://www.favoritepoem.org.

3. Go to the Annenberg Media video series *Engaging with Literature 3–5.* Read the description of the *Engaging* with *Literature 3–5* video series. Click on "enter the series website" and then "starting out." Read about the video you are about to view. In this video session, Jonathan Holden begins exploring poetry with his fourth-grade class. He carefully guides them as they create and explore individual and rich envisionments of the text through discussion and writing. The class explores poems from *Baseball, Snakes, and Summer Squash* by Donald H. Graves and *Hey You! C'Mere: A Poetry Slam* by Elizabeth Swados. View the "classroom snapshot" and "classroom lesson plan" from the menu on the left. Then view the video. After watching each video segment, respond to the questions under the "professional reflection" link.

## Learn About Authors and Illustrators

4. In September 2008, Mary Ann Hoberman was named the second poet laureate by the Poetry Foundation to raise awareness of the genre and to encourage more poets to write for children. Hoberman is a prolific writer of children's poetry with over 40 books, including *A House is a House for Me* (1978); *The Llama Who Had No Pajama: 100 Favorite Poems* (2006); and *All Kinds of Families!* (2009). Read several of Hoberman's poems. Why do you think she was named the children's poet laureate? Whom would you nominate for the next children's poet laureate? Visit the Poetry Foundation at http://www.poetryfoundation.org for more information on Mary Ann Hoberman, Jack Prelutsky and for more resources on children's poetry.

5. In poetry, image is everything—from gathering ideas to the choice of words and spacing and layout. In creating imagery, much of the author's and publisher's work is never evident in the final process unless you know what went on "behind the scenes." Poet Barbara Esbensen worked to have the best word choices and used spacing to help convey mood and meaning. Many original drafts for several of her poems, in the sequence of how they were developed, are available online through the Kerlan Collection at the University of Minnesota. Go to: http://special.lib.umn.edu/clrc/kerlan/esbensen/downloads.php and click on Writing Poetry Part 1 and Part 2 to access the original drafts as well as lesson plans for using the drafts with students in the classroom.

# Print and Online Resources

## Print Resources

Fandel, J. (2006). *Understanding poetry: Rhyme, meter, and other word music.* Huntington Beach, CA: Creative Press.

Flynn, N., & McPhillips, S. (2000). *A note slipped under the door: Teaching from poems we love.* Portland, ME: Stenhouse.

Heard, G. (1999). *Awakening the heart: Exploring poetry in elementary and middle school.* Portsmouth, NH: Heinemann.

Holbrook, S. (2005). *Practical poetry: A Nonstandard Approach to Meeting Content-Area Standards.* Portsmouth, NH: Heinemann.

Holbrook, S. (2002). *Wham! It's a poetry jam: Discovering performance poetry.* Honesdale, PA: Boyds Mills Press.

Kohl, H. (1999). *A grain of poetry.* New York: HarperCollins.

Prelutsky, J. (2008). *Pizza, pigs, and poetry: How to write a poem.* New York: Greeenwillow.

Sloan, G. (2003). *Give them poetry! A guide for sharing poetry with children K–8.* New York: Teachers College Press.

Styles, M. (1997). *From the Garden to the Street: Three Hundred Years of Poetry for Children.* New York: Cassell.

## Online Resources

### Academy of American Poets
**http://www.poets.org**
The website of the Academy of American Poets features over 1,250 poems, along with biographies, photos, and other information on more than 450 poets. The "Serious Play" page within the site also provides links for ideas on teaching poetry to children, links to interesting sites, information on appropriate poets, and dozens of great poems for younger children, some with audio.

### Favorite Poem Project
**http://www.favoritepoem.org**
Founded by Robert Pinsky, the 39th Poet Laureate of the United States, the Favorite Poem Project houses a collection of 50 short video documentaries showcasing individual Americans reading and speaking personally about poems they love.

### Lee Bennett Hopkins Poetry Award
**http://www.pabook.libraries.psu.edu/activities/hopkins/index.html**
The Lee Bennett Hopkins Award is presented annually to an American poet or anthologist for the most outstanding new book of children's poetry published in the previous calendar year. Selected by a panel of nationally recognized teachers, librarians, and scholars, the Lee Bennett Hopkins Award for Children's Poetry is the first award of its kind in the United States.

### Shel Silverstein YouTube Channel
**http://www.youtube.com/shelsilversteinbooks**
The ShelSilversteinBooks Channel on YouTube has several animated excerpts from most famous works including *Lafcadio, The Lion Who Shot Back,* "Backward Bill" from *A Light in the Attic,* and excerpt from *The Giving Tree,* "The Toy Eater" from *Falling Up,* "Runny on Round Mushmore" from *Runny Babbit,* and "Ickle Me, Pickle Me, Tickle Me Too" from *Where the Sidewalk Ends.*

### Poetry 18
**http://www.loc.gov/poetry/180**
Selected by former Poet Laureate Billy Collins, Poetry 180 is designed to make it easy for students to hear or read a poem on each of the 180 days of the school year.

### Poetry Writing with Jack Prelutsky
**http://teacher.scholastic.com/writewit/poetry/jack_home.htm**
Hosted by Scholastic, the Writing with Writers site allows students to proceed through a series of activities such as reading about the poet, reading one of his poems, brainstorming ideas for poems, and writing a poem (which can be published online) with poem starters for those who choose to use them, complete with a certificate of achievement signed by Jack Prelutsky himself!

Visit the companion website at **www.cengage.com/education/johnson** to find links related to the Read/Watch/Listen icons noted throughout the chapter, as well as additional resources.

# Creating Your Classroom Library

## SINGLE ILLUSTRATED POEMS

Janeczko, P., & Lewis, J. P. (2006). *Wing nuts: Screwy haiku.* New York: Little, Brown.

Crist-Evans, C. (1999). *Moon over Tennessee: A boy's Civil War journal.* Boston: Houghton Mifflin.

Cyrus, K. (2005). *Hotel deep: Light verse from dark water.* New York: Harcourt.

Kuskin, K. (2006). *So, what's it like to be a cat?* Illustrated by B. Lewin. New York: Atheneum.

Myers, W. (2009). *Looking like me.* Illustrated by Christopher Myers. New York: Egmont.

## COLLECTIONS AND ANTHOLOGIES OF POETRY AND NURSERY RHYMES

Crossley-Holland, K. (2004). *Once upon a poem.* New York: Scholastic.

dePaola, T. (1988). *Tomie dePaola's book of poems.* New York: Putnam.

de Regniers, B., Moore, E., White, M., & Carr, J. (compilers) (1988). *Sing a song of popcorn.* New York: Scholastic.

George, K. (2001). *Toasting marshmallows: Camping poems.* Boston: Houghton Mifflin.

Fletcher, R. (2005). *A writing kind of day: Poems for young poets.* New York: Boyds Mills.

Hall, D. (Ed.) (1999). *The Oxford illustrated book of American children's poems.* New York: Oxford University Press

Heard, G. (2002). *This place I know: Poems of comfort.* New York: Candlewick.

Hopkins, L. (2004). *Wonderful words: Poems about reading, writing, speaking, and listening.* New York: Simon & Schuster.

Hopkins, L. (2010). *Sharing the seasons: A book of poems.* New York: Simon & Schuster.

Kennedy, X. J., & Kennedy, D. M. (1999). *A knock at a star: A child's introduction to poetry.* Illustrated by K. L. Baker. New York: Little, Brown.

Lewis, J. P. (2005). *Vherses: A celebration of outstanding women.* Mankato, MN: Creative Editions.

Nye, N. (2005). *You & yours.* Rochester, NY: BOA Editions.

Prelutsky, J. (2006). *Behold the Bold Umbrellaphant: And Other Poems.* New York: Greenwillow.

Sidman, J. (2006). *Meow Ruff: A Story in Concrete Poetry*. New York: Houghton Mifflin.

Sierra, J. (1996). *Nursery tales around the world.* Boston: Houghton Mifflin.

Singer, M. (2005). *Central heating*: Poems about fire and warmth. New York: Knopf.

Wong, J. (2000). *Night garden.* Illustrated by J. Paschkis. New York: Simon & Schuster.

## MULTICULTURAL POETRY

Bryan, A. (1997). *Ashley Bryan's ABC of African American poetry.* New York: Atheneum.

English, K. (2004). *Speak to me and I will listen between the lines.* New York: Farrar, Straus and Giroux.

Giovanni, N. (2008). *Hip Hop Speaks to Children: A Celebration of Poetry with a Beat.* Naperville, IL: Sourcebooks Jabberwocky.

Myers, W. (1993). *Brown angels: An album of pictures and free verse.* New York: HarperCollins.

Myers, W. (2004). *Here in Harlem: Poems in many voices.* New York: Holiday House.

Nelson, M. (2003). *Fortune's bones: The Manumission requiem.* Honesdale, PA: Front Street.

Nelson, M. (2005). *A wreath for Emmett Till.* Boston: Houghton Mifflin.

Sneve, V. (1989). *Dancing teepees. Poems of American Indian youth.* New York: Holiday House.

Swann, B. (1998). *Touching the distance: Native American riddle-poems.* New York: Harcourt.

Thomas, J. (2002). *Growing glory.* New York: HarperCollins.

Weatherford, C. (2002). *Remember the bridge: Poems of a people.* New York: Philomel.

Wong, J. (1994). *Good luck gold and other poems.* New York: Macmillian.

# References

Block, C. C., & Mangieri, J. N. (2002). Recreational reading: 20 years later. *The Reading Teacher, 55*(6), 572–580.

Booth, D., & Moore, D. (1988). *Poems please: Sharing poetry with children.* Ontario, Canada: Pembroke.

Calkins, L. (1994). *The art of teaching writing* (2nd ed.). Portsmouth, NH: Heinemann.

Certo, J. (2004). Cold plums and the old men in the water: Let children read and write "great" poetry. *The Reading Teacher, 58*(3), 266–271.

Codell, E. (2003). *Sahara special.* New York: Hyperion.

Damico, J. S., & Riddle, R. (2004). From answers to questions: A beginning teacher learns to teach for social justice. *Language Arts, 82(1),* 36–46.

Dickinson, E. (1960)."I'm nobody!" (p. 288). In T. H. Johnson (Ed.), *The complete poems of Emily Dickinson.* Boston: Little, Brown.

Dorn, L., & Soffos, C. (2005). *Teaching for deep comprehension.* Portland, ME: Stenhouse.

Fisher, A. (1991). *Always wondering.* New York: HarperCollins.

Fisher, C. (1994). Sharing poetry in the classroom: Building a concept of poem. In J. Hickman, B. Cullinan, & S. Hepler (Eds.), *Children's literature in the classroom: Extending Charlotte's Web.* (pp. 53–66). Norwood, MA: Christopher-Gordon.

Fleischman, P. (1988). *Joyful noise: Poems for two voices.* New York: Harper & Row.

Fletcher, R. (2002). *Poetry matters: Writing a poem from the inside out.* New York: HarperCollins.

Florian, D. (1998). *insectlopedia.* New York: Harcourt.

Grimes, N. (2000). The power of poetry. *Booklinks, 9*(4), 32–37.

Hadaway, N., Vardell, S., & Young, T. (2001). Scaffolding oral language development through poetry for students learning English. *The Reading Teacher, 54(8),* 796–806.

Heard, G. (1989). *For the good of the Earth and the sun: Teaching poetry.* Portsmouth, NH: Heinemann.

Holbrook, S. (2002). *Wham! It's a poetry jam: Discovering performance poetry.* Honesdale, PA: Boyds Mills.

Hopkins, L. B. (1993). *The writing bug.* Katonah, NY: Richard Owens.

Janeczko, P. (2005). *A kick in the head: An everyday guide to poetic forms.* New York: Candlewick.

Kurkjian, C., Livingston, N., Young, T., & Fletcher, R. (2006). A pickle of poems. *The Reading Teacher, 59*(6), 598–608.

Kutiper, K., & Wilson, P. (1993). Updating poetry preferences: A look at the poetry children really like. *The Reading Teacher, 47*(1), 28–35.

Laminack, L., & Wadsworth, R. (2006). *Learning under the influence of language and literature: Making the most of read-alouds across the day.* Portsmouth, NH: Heinemann.

Lewis, J. P. (2005). *Please bury me in the library.* New York: Harcourt.

MacLachlan, P. (1993). *Baby.* New York: Delacorte.

McClure, A. (1994). Wordspinning: Children writing poetry. In J. Hickman, B. Cullinan, & S. Hepler (Eds.), *Children's literature in the classroom: Extending* Charlotte's Web (pp. 67–82). Norwood, MA: Christopher-Gordon.

National Endowment for the Arts (2004). *Reading at risk: A survey of literary reading in America.* Washington, DC: NEA.

Nye, N. (2005). *A maze me.* New York: Greenwillow.

O'Hara, F. (1971). "Autobiographia literaria" (p. 11), from *The collected poems of Frank O'Hara.* New York: Knopf.

Paschen, E. (2005). *Poetry speaks to children.* Naperville, IL: Sourcebooks.

Pavonetti, L. (2002). Ashley Bryan: Beautiful language, wondrous words. *Journal of Children's Literature, 28*(2), 62–71.

Pavonetti, L. (2003). Paul Fleischman: A partner in celebrating language and reading. *Journal of Children's Literature, 29*(2), 85–93.

Prelutsky, J. (1984). *The new kid on the block.* New York: Scholastic.

Rosenberg, L. (2000). *Light-gathering poems.* New York: Henry Holt.

Routman, R. (2005). *Writing essentials.* Portsmouth, NH: Heinemann.

Sloan, G. (2003*). Give them poetry!* New York: Teachers College Press.

Tarr, A., & Flynn, R. (2002)."The trouble isn't making poems, the trouble's finding somebody that will listen to them": Negotiating a place for poetry in children's literature studies. *Children's Literature Association Quarterly, 27*(1), 2–3.

Winters, C., & Schmidt, G. (2001). *Edging the boundaries of children's literature.* Boston: Allyn & Bacon.

Wong, J. (1994). *Good luck gold and other poems.* New York: Macmillian.

Woodson, J. (2003). *Locomotion.* New York: Putnam.

Yolen, J. (2003). *Take joy.* Waukesha, WI: Kalmbach Publishing.

Young, T., & Vardell, S. (2005)."Speaking up"with Janet Wong. *Language Arts, 82*(3), 230–234.

# 10 Nonfiction: Biographies and Informational Books

On Easter Sunday, April 9, 1939, Marian Anderson performed an open-air concert on the steps of the Lincoln Memorial in front of 75,000 people. This would become a historic event in the struggle for civil rights. In *The Voice That Challenged a Nation: Marian Anderson and the Struggle for Equal Rights*, Russell Freedman (2004) captures both the anticipation and the hope of the people and the grace and strength of Marian Anderson through his plain yet eloquent prose. Throughout, Freedman weaves archival photographs and quotations to establish historical and cultural context that masterfully conveys Anderson's triumphant story.

> The massive figure of Abraham Lincoln gazed down at her as she looked out at the expectant throng. Silencing the ovation with a slight wave of her hand, she paused. A profound hush settled over the crowd. For that moment, Marian Anderson seemed vulnerable and alone. Then she closed her eyes, lifted her head, clasped her hands before her, and began to sing.
>
> *Russell Freedman, 2004, p. 3*

*Approximately four years before* Marian Anderson stood on the steps of the Lincoln Memorial, Admiral Richard Byrd stepped onto the frozen tundra of Antarctica. In March of 1934, Byrd began his six-month seclusion in the bitterly cold, dark, yet beautiful, continent of Antarctica. In his book *Black Whiteness: Admiral Byrd Alone in the Antarctic*, Robert Burleigh's (1998) spare, poetic prose movingly renders the severe surroundings in which Byrd performed daily meteorological studies in temperatures of –60° with only a flashlight, a lantern, and a small gas lamp:

*Watch*

*Watch a presentation by Russell Freedman.*

### Blizzard

Like an incoming tide, the snow rises:
over his ankles,
above his knees,
> against his chest,
> exploding into his eyes
> "like millions of tiny pellets."

No night has ever seemed so dark.
The flashlight's beam blackens.
The trapdoor, weighted by the sudden snow,
is stuck tight.

> From *Black Whiteness: Admiral Byrd Alone in the Antarctic* by
> Robert Burleigh, p. 16. © 1998 Robert Burleigh. By permission.

Burleigh effectively integrates passages taken from Byrd's daily journal into the text, which adds authenticity and conviction to the already mesmerizing account. Combined with Walter Krudop's illustrations that reflect the faint play of light on the stark blue of the Antarctic climate and the golden glow of the poorly heated shelter, Burleigh captures the desolation, loneliness, determination, and courage of Admiral Byrd's remarkable voyage.

## Defining Nonfiction

*The Voice That Challenged a Nation* and *Black Whiteness* are works of nonfiction. Nonfiction is the *literature* of fact consisting of biographies and informational books that revolve around the social and scientific world. The foundation of all nonfiction is truth. Nonfiction has come a long way from the dry recitation of facts, badly reproduced photographs, and practical prose that many adults remember; however, this reputation continues to haunt the genre. The hallmark of today's quality nonfiction is a piece of literature that is "absolutely enchanting" (Gill, 2010). The vision of the author guides the organization, creativity, presentation, and originality of the work. Together, these elements define the author's style. Freedman (1992) writes the following:

> Certainly, the basic purpose of nonfiction is to inform, to instruct, hopefully to enlighten. But, that's not enough. An effective nonfiction book must animate its subject, infuse it with life, it must create a vivid and believable world that the reader will enter willingly and leave only with reluctance. A good nonfiction book should be a pleasure to read. (p. 3)

The Caldecott has been awarded three times to books of nonfiction: *The Man Who Walked Between the Towers* (2004), *So You Want to Be President?* (2001), and *Snowflake Bentley* (1999). The Newbery has been awarded to a nonfiction title only once—to *Lincoln: A Photobiography* (1988). To recognize excellence in nonfiction, the American Library Association established the Robert F. Sibert Informational Book Award, which *Almost Astronauts: 13 Women Who Dared to Dream*, written by Tanya Lee Stone, won in 2010. The Children's Book Guild honors an author or author/illustrator whose total work has contributed significantly to the quality of nonfiction for children. Sy Montgomery was presented the award in 2010 for her significant contribution to nonfiction children's books including *Kakapo Rescue: Saving the World's Strangest Parrot, The Ghost of the Mountain: An Expedition Among Snow Leopards in Mongolia* and *The Snake Scientist*. The National Council of Teachers of English established the Orbis Pictus Award for Outstanding Nonfiction for Children, awarded annually since 1989. The 2010 Orbis Pictus Award was given to

*The Secret World of Walter Anderson* by Hester Bass, illustrated by E.B. Lewis. Information about these awards is provided through the associations' websites and publications (also provided at the end of this chapter).

## Benefits and Considerations of Nonfiction

How did you react upon reading the title of this chapter? Did visions of facts, figures, encyclopedias, and book reports parade through your mind? If so, you're not alone. Many adults remember nonfiction as a source of information for completing school assignments. Yet, nonfiction has come a long way. Unfortunately, teachers' preconceived ideas about nonfiction can lead to little exposure and instruction with informational text for children. The following are benefits and considerations for including nonfiction in the literacy curriculum.

### BENEFITS

Children of all ages prefer reading nonfiction when given the opportunity (see Dreher 2000; Davila & Patrick, 2010; Duke, Bennett-Armistead, & Roberts, 2002; and Duke, 2003a for reviews). Yet, for many reasons teachers have limited children's exposure to nonfiction trade books (Donovan & Smolkin, 2001). The predominance of narrative text in basal readers (Caswell & Duke, 1998), a reliance on the limited selection of nonfiction books in classroom or school libraries (Duke, 2000), and teachers' lack of knowledge about how to help children understand expository reading material (Walker, Kragler, Martin, & Arnett, 2003) have all contributed to the dearth of such books in the classroom. Teachers must recognize the positive effects of nonfiction on students. Duke (2003b) offers six reasons why nonfiction should be included in classroom reading instruction:

1. It offers a key to success in later schooling.
2. It is ubiquitous in the larger society.
3. It is the preferred reading material for some children.
4. It addresses children's interests and questions.
5. It builds knowledge of the natural and social world.
6. It includes many important text features (pp. 3–5).

Nonfiction trade books engage and motivate children's reading and interest in subject matter knowledge in a way that textbooks cannot. Equally, if not more importantly, nonfiction trade books expose children to nonfiction text features that dominate the majority of reading and writing that they will encounter later in school and in the workplace. Several research studies analyzed by Palincsar and Duke (2004) reveal that integrating information books with reading instruction promotes both general literacy knowledge and subject matter knowledge.

As you become more familiar with the quality of nonfiction books, check out the non-fiction section of your school or public library. Look for a variety of current biographies and information books for independent reading that will pique students' interests and would be excellent for reading aloud. As teachers discover new and exciting nonfiction books, they must become advocates for increasing the nonfiction collection in the school library.

### CONSIDERATIONS

When making decisions about nonfiction in the classroom, it is important to consider the role of children's preferences, text accuracy, and multicultural understanding in the selection and use of children's literature.

**Preference for Nonfiction.** As I sat in my office surrounded by biographies and informational books in preparation for writing this chapter, my son exclaimed, "You've finally gotten to the best chapter!" Like many children, he has always loved nonfiction. Mohr (2006) observed that first-grade girls and boys prefer nonfiction books, although girls chose a wider variety of texts, whereas boys' choices relied solely on topic and content of interest to them. Research has found that boys in particular are drawn to nonfiction (Brozo, 2002; Coles & Hall, 2001; Davila & Patrick, 2010; Murphy & Elwood, 1998; Smith & Wilhelm, 2004; Taylor, 2005; see Table 10.1). Boys prefer texts that connect directly to their lives—desires, concerns, experiences—and that are appropriately challenging and in which they can become totally immersed (Smith & Wilhelm, 2004). Such texts include information books, magazines, and Internet sites that schools often don't recognize or embrace (Coles & Hall, 2001). In fact, a review of research by Davila and Patrick (2010) indicate that children currently prefer to read magazines, comics, and websites.

Children deserve the opportunity to read books they choose every day. Classroom libraries must reflect the interests of all children, and high-quality, visually, intellectually, and emotionally appealing nonfiction should constitute a significant part of the collection. In this way, boys are given the chance to read books they find interesting, motivating, and engaging. Yet, boys must be exposed to a variety of genres to participate in school literacy practices. Educators must make efforts to provide structured opportunities for boys and girls to become emotionally engaged with text and to talk about and write about texts they are reading. Smith and Wilhelm (2004) suggest (1) "sequencing instruction so that success with one text or interpretive activity lays the groundwork for success in the next" and (2) "use think-aloud strategies and drama and visual art activities as supports to build on students' strengths in other semiotic systems so that they may be applied to more traditional forms of text" (p. 460). Here are some other strategies for engaging boys in reading:

**TABLE 10.1**

# Myths and Facts About Nonfiction Biography and Information Books

| Myth | Fact |
|------|------|
| 1. Nonfiction is only a dry recitation of facts, badly reproduced photographs, and practical prose. | Today's quality nonfiction is a piece of literature that is a work of art. |
| 2. The information in textbooks is more effective than trade books for learning about a content area. | Problems with textbooks have been a major force driving the trend toward using trade books. Trade books generally are more up to date, contain less overwhelming vocabulary, and provide a more focused, in-depth look at particular subjects. |
| 3. Both boys and girls would rather read fiction than nonfiction. | Children of all ages prefer reading nonfiction when given the opportunity. First-grade girls and boys prefer nonfiction books; however, generally, boys are more drawn to nonfiction than girls. |

*Listen*

*Listen to an interview
with Jon Scieszka about
boys and reading.*

- Form a"boys-only"book club.
- Assemble a"guys' rack"section of the classroom library.
- Incorporate inquiry-based research projects and Internet projects.
- Invite men into the classroom to give book talks.

## Accuracy and Cultural Authenticity

*Award-winning prose floats on mastery of subject matter, mastery that comes from re-
search both wide and deep. While it may be possible to ruin good information with bad
writing, even good writing cannot overcome bad information.*

JULIE JENSEN, 2001, P. 3

Because nonfiction is the literature of fact, the accuracy of the factual material in both
biography and informational books is crucial. Authors of nonfiction spend a great deal of
time researching their topic prior to writing. The craft is in wrapping this information into
a story. Diane Stanley compares this process to a collage:

> You have all of these different materials. Your position is not to put words in your
> subjects' mouths or invent things, but to choose from all of these elements, and put
> them together in such a way that you paint a picture of the person and entertain
> your reader and give a sense of the person and their world. Each writer would prob-
> ably come up with different choices, tell the same basic facts but bring a different
> quality in their approach to it. That's how you put your stamp on it, in making
> choices. (Devereaux, 1996, p. 216).
>
> From *Black Whiteness: Admiral Byrd Alone in the Antarctic* by Robert Burleigh, p. 16

Prior to the 1980s it was common for authors to fictionalize dialogue in children's biography or to change or dramatize tedious abstract historical accounts or informational details.
Today, authors of nonfiction are expected to provide extensive source notes, glossaries, tables
of important dates or information, and other supplemental information. Fictionalized text
and inaccuracies are unacceptable. For example, Susan Jeffers's rendition of Chief Seattle's
speech in *Brother Eagle, Sister Sky* (1991) has received criticism for inaccurately portraying
the culture of Chief Seattle and changing the text and intent of his original speech (see
reviews by Doris Seal in *A Broken Flute* and Patricia Dooley in *School Library Journal*, 1991).
An excellent example of accuracy and authenticity in a picturebook is James Giblin's *The
Amazing Life of Benjamin Franklin*. Through a focused narrative, Giblin presents a great deal
of information about the famous American, including his difficulties as well as his accomplishments. The appendices include a list of important dates from Franklin's life, a selected
list of his inventions, selected sayings from *Poor Richard's Almanack,* a descriptive listing of
historic sites associated with Franklin, and a bibliography with source notes. An artist's note
by illustrator Michael Dooling indicates that research was necessary not only to accurately
depict Benjamin Franklin but also to set him against an authentic colonial context.

An excellent example of an informational text is *The Tarantula Scientist* (2004),
which describes the research Samuel Marshall and his students are doing on tarantulas,
written by Sy Montgomery, with photographs by Nic Bishop. (See illustration 11 in the
Part 2 Visual Discussion.) The backmatter provides a list of spider statistics, a glossary
of specialized vocabulary of arachnologists, a section on how the book was researched,
a selected bibliography, a list of websites, and information on buying a tarantula. Such
extensive documentation not only allows for verification of accuracy, but it whets the
reader's appetite for more information. During the reading of a nonfiction text, teachers
can model reading the narrative and referring to the sources and source notes to show
how readers decide if the information is accurate. For instance, a teacher might model
asking questions such as, How does the author know that? and What do we learn from

*The writing style and illustrations in The Amazing Life of Benjamin Franklin inform and engage the reader without romanticizing or sentimentalizing Franklin's brilliance or contributions and includes appendices that enrich and expand on the text.*

the source notes? These are questions students must learn to ask themselves as they read nonfiction texts.

Teachers must not assume the information in trade books is accurate and not take the time to check for accuracy before sharing them with children. For example, many primary grade teachers use favorite fiction books to teach science concepts. *The Very Hungry Caterpillar* (1969), written and illustrated by Eric Carle, describes the metamorphosis of a caterpillar, but Carle has the caterpillar transform in a cocoon (moth) rather than a chrysalis. In *The Mixed Up Chameleon* (1975), written and illustrated by Eric Carle; *A Color of His Own*, written and illustrated by Leo Lionni (1975); and *The Yucky Reptile Alphabet Book* (1989), written and illustrated by Jerry Pallotta, green chameleons change to bright red, yellow, and white, colors a chameleon cannot assume (Rice, 2002). In all of these books, the illustrations play a major role in conveying misinformation about the subject. Children cannot always discriminate between accurate and inaccurate information. A review of research by Rice (2002) indicates that science misconceptions developed in the early years are very likely to be retained into adulthood.

Rather than dispensing with these books, teachers can bring inaccuracies to the attention of children, presenting the correct information and discussing why the author might have chosen to write the book with inaccuracies. For example, is it possible that Eric Carle chose a cocoon rather than a chrysalis because it is more commonly known and easier to read and pronounce by young children?

One way to differentiate fiction and nonfiction books is to look at how they are categorized in the library. *The Very Hungry Caterpillar, The Mixed Up Chameleon, A Color of His Own*, and *The Yucky Reptile Alphabet Book* are cataloged in the Juvenile Easy (JE) section of the library, which means that it is a fiction picturebook. Books that are nonfiction are given

*Watch*

*Watch a video of Eric Carle discussing the creation of* The Very Hungry Caterpillar.

a Dewey Decimal number between 000 and 999 and are separated from the JE books. Of course, many books classified as JE contain accurate information and some books in the nonfiction section do not contain accurate information. Therefore, it is always best to carefully evaluate the information in a book before sharing it with children.

When an author realizes inaccurate information has been published, he or she may request that the publisher revise the information in subsequent printings. For example, after the publication of *The Man Who Walked Between the Towers*, Mordicai Gerstein discovered that the width of the rope on which Philippe Petit walked was incorrect, and he revised the illustration and the text to depict the correct width of seven-eighths of an inch. A reviewer noticed that *Coming to America: A Muslim Family's Story* written by Bernard Wolf included inaccurate information about why Muslims face Mecca when they pray. The publisher, acknowledging the inaccuracy, corrected the information in question in subsequent printings.

**Promoting Multicultural Understanding.** In *Number the Stars*, Lois Lowry fictionalizes a true account of how the Danish resistance in Copenhagen during the Nazi occupation in 1940 made it possible for almost 8,000 Jews to be smuggled to safety in Sweden. The story is told through the eyes of ten-year-old Annemarie Johansen, whose family harbors her best friend, Ellen Rosen, and helps smuggle Ellen's family out of the country. *Number the Stars* brings insight to children who might otherwise not understand the extent to which personal and collective sacrifices were made by both the Jewish and non-Jewish people in their attempts to survive. In *Darkness Over Denmark: The Danish Resistance and the Rescue of the Jews*, Ellen Levine recounts the true-life dramas of 21 Danes she interviewed, ranging in age from 2 to 28, who escaped, assisted with escapes, or joined the resistance during the Nazi takeover of Denmark. Levine alternates their stories with the history of the war as it affected Denmark and the rest of Europe; these stories come together to make these ever more distant events come alive. Levine (2000) writes, "I wanted to tell the story of the Danish resistance and rescue in part through the people who experienced it. In the end, the truth is richer than any made-up story." (p. viii). The well-chosen black-and-white period photographs add a feeling of immediacy and significance to the text. Levine provides perspective to the successes of Denmark by including its own Nazi membership, traitors, and failed rescue attempts:

> Novels and histories about Denmark during the war focus on the extraordinary rescue of the Danish Jews. But not all of Denmark's Jews escaped. Nearly 500 were captured and sent to Theresienstadt concentration camp. A number of them had gotten no warning, others ignored it. Some were betrayed by stickers (informers). Still others were too weak or exhausted to flee. A small number of Jews died while trying to escape. Others, unwilling to risk falling into the hands of the Nazis, took their own lives. Their stories are also part of Denmark's history. (p. 92)

*Darkness Over Denmark* brings an accurate, relevant, and in-depth look at the lives of Danish people who participated in this historic event. In addition to source notes, a bibliography, and an excellent chronology, a "who's who" list provides a brief biography and photo of the major figures discussed in the book.

Nonfiction can further multicultural understanding by contributing to diverse students' self-esteem and awareness, helping children of diverse cultures appreciate the contributions of their ancestors, contributing to the development of respect across cultures, enhancing students' identification with members of diverse cultures, illustrating the history of various diverse cultures in this country and abroad, and providing up-to-the-minute portrayals of the everyday lives of youngsters from diverse cultures living today. Table 10.2 offers ways nonfiction can be used for multicultural understanding, along with relevant titles.

**TABLE 10.2**

# Goals of Multicultural Understanding with Nonfiction

| Goal | Examples |
|---|---|
| **Contribute to students' self-esteem and self-awareness.** | *Su Dongpo: Chinese Genius* by Demi<br>*The Tequila Worm* by Viola Canales<br>*Calavera Abecedario: A Day of the Dead Alphabet Book* by Jeanette Winter |
| **Help children of diverse cultures appreciate the contribution of their ancestors.** | *How Smart Are We* by W. Nikola-Lisa<br>*José: Born to Dance* by Susanna Reich<br>*Quiet Hero: The Ira Hayes Story* by S. D. Nelson |
| **Contribute to the development of respect across cultures.** | *Celebrate Connections Among Cultures* by Jan Reynolds<br>*Paths to Peace* by Jane Zalben<br>*How People Live* by Dena Freeman |
| **Enhance students' identifcation with members of diverse cultures.** | *Coming to America: A Muslim Family's Story* by Bernard Wolf<br>*One Year in Beijing* by Xiaohong Wang<br>*Linda Brown, You Are Not Alone: The Brown v. Board of Education Decision* by Joyce Carol Thomas |
| **Illustrate the history of various diverse cultures in this country and abroad.** | *Freedom Walkers: The Story of the Montgomery Bus Boycott* by Russell Freedman<br>*Rattlesnake Mesa: Stories from a Native American Childhood* by Ednah New Rider Weber<br>*Mexico and Central America: A Fiesta of Cultures, Crafts, and Activities* by Mary Turck |
| **Provide up-to-the-minute portrayals of everyday lives of youngsters from diverse cultures living today.** | *Children of Native America Today* by Yvonne Dennis<br>*You and Me Together: Moms, Dads, and Kids Around the World* by Barbara Kerley<br>*Families* by Susan Kuklin |

Adapted from B. Moss, *Exploring the literature of fact: Children's nonfiction trade books in the elementary classroom* (New York: Guilford, 2003), p. 20.

# Evaluating and Selecting Biographies

This is how Betty Carter (2003), a reviewer of biography for *Horn Book Magazine,* remembers biographies from her childhood:

> A larger-than-life, near-perfect individual to be honored and emulated; a lack of historical context within which to place the subject; an endless tally of accomplishments that show little relationship to either character or reader; and an organizing structure that revolves around birth and death dates rather than an implied theme concerning the subject's life.  (p. 165)

Does this sound familiar? If so, hopefully you have given biographies another chance. Biographies have changed significantly in the past decade. Biographers today conduct extensive research, including visiting original sites and studying original materials and then selecting those details that balance fact, meaning, and significance. Biographies must "show rather than tell . . . illuminate an aspect or point of view about the subject's life, thereby giving it either pattern or meaning" (p. 170). The evaluation and selection of biographies involves determining the accuracy and authenticity of the information about the subject, the authority of the author, and how skillfully the author crafts the information into an interesting, well-told story.

## BIOGRAPHICAL SUBJECTS

James Giblin, the author of more than 20 biographies for children, including the *Good Brother, Bad Brother: The Story of Edwin Booth and John Wilkes Booth* (2005), considers finding the pattern of a subject's life this way:

> When I was young I did some acting, and I remember one teacher talking about the "through line" of the character—what it is that the character is seeking, what behavioral pattern would he or she develop to achieve this goal? I find that's a useful exercise to apply to biography. (Frederick, 2002, p. 84)

Children read biographies for the same reasons as adults: to see how other people from all walks of life lived and dealt with their problems. Today's biographies for children highlight not only the lives of historical icons but also the lives of everyday heroes (see Table 10.3 for biographical subjects and examples).

## CATEGORIES OF BIOGRAPHY

Biographies typically fall into one of three categories: authentic, fictionalized, and autobiographies and memoirs (see Categories of Biography).

Milton Meltzer (1993) has written nearly 100 books dealing with history, biography, and social issues. When discussing his preparation for writing, Meltzer reflects as follows:

> In preparing to write such a history I read as widely as possible in the available sources, both primary and secondary, making notes on what I think I may want to use. At the same time I hunt everywhere for the documentary material that will let people speak their own words. I don't mean only the kings and generals—the Lords of Creation—I mean the anonymous ones upon whom society rests and without whom the superstructure would collapse. Their words are found in letters, journals, diaries, autobiographies, in songs and poems, in speeches, in court testimony and legislative hearings, in newspaper reports, in eyewitness accounts, and, more recently, in oral history interviews. I want the reader to discover how it felt to be alive at that time, I want the reader to share directly in that experience, to know the doubts, the hopes, the fears, the anger and the joy of the men, women, and children who were the blood and bone of that history. (p. 28)

**TABLE 10.3**

# Biographical Subjects

| Subject | Description | Examples |
|---|---|---|
| **Discovery and Exploration** | Books about the exploration of earth and space and the discovery of scientific theories and inventions that have moved civilization forward. | *Team Moon: How 400,000 People Landed the Apollo 11 on the Moon* by Catherine Thimmesh<br><br>*American Slave, American Hero: York of the Lewis and Clark Expedition* by Laurence Pringle<br><br>*Marvelous Mattie: How Margaret E. Knight Became an Inventor* by Emily Arnold McCully |
| **Political Leaders and Social Activists** | Includes presidents, senators, kings, and queens, as well as people who are actively trying to instigate social change. Often these figures are controversial. | *Madam President: The Extraordinary, True (and Evolving) Story of Women in Politics* by Catherine Thimmesh<br><br>*The Bus Ride That Changed History: The Story of Rosa Parks* by Pamela Edwards<br><br>*George Did It* by Suzanne Jurmain |
| **Artists and Authors** | Stories about famous artists and authors. Focuses less on pop culture than biographies about people in the arts. Many authors of children's books have written autobiographies and memoirs. | *26 Fairmount Avenue* by Tomie dePaola<br><br>*The Illustrator's Notebook* by Mohieddine Ellabbad<br><br>*José! Born to Dance* by Susanna Reich |
| **People Who Have Persevered** | Stories about people who have overcome insurmountable odds or persecution and discrimination due to political or religious beliefs, physical or mental challenges, homelessness, poverty, abuse, nontraditional families, or sexual orientation. | *Selvakumar Knew Better* by Virginia Kroll<br><br>*Shadow Life: A Portrait of Anne Frank and Her Family* by Barry Denenberg<br><br>*Dare To Dream! 25 Extraordinary Lives* by Sandra Humphrey<br><br>*Perfect Timing: How Isaac Murphy Became One of the World's Greatest Jockeys* by Patsi B. Trollinger<br><br>*Dizzy* by Jonah Winter |

It is clear from Meltzer's description that he has a passion for his subject matter and a clear vision for how to convey that passion in a way that encourages children's curiosity and wonder. The type of biography Meltzer writes is authentic, in that everything he writes about his subjects is verifiable and not fictionalized in any way.

A *complete biography*, such as Meltzer's *Walt Whitman* (2002), reconstructs Whitman's entire life span, integrating many black-and-white photographs, reproductions, and facsimiles of Whitman's work with the background on the turbulent political and social times in which he lived. A *partial biography* covers only part of a person's life, usually a dramatic or historically significant event. Many authors write partial biographies because of their own interest in a certain event or aspect of the subject's life and because covering the subject's entire life would make the book too long and difficult for young readers. For example, Kathleen Krull's partial biography *Wilma Unlimited*, illustrated by David Diaz, is about the childhood of the Olympic champion Wilma Rudolph. Krull states, "The story of how she overcame those obstacles [disabilities, poverty, all kinds of disadvantages] and ended up at the Olympics as a runner winning three Gold Medals at the Olympics—first woman to do that—was probably the most amazing life story that I've ever heard." Krull is also the author of many *collective biographies*, which contain a number of short biographical sketches of people with common attributes, such as those in her *Lives of* series (i.e., *Lives of the Musicians, Lives of Extraordinary Women, Lives of Pirates*). Jennifer Armstrong's *The American Story: 100 True Tales from American History* (2006) is, a collection of one hundred brief stories about real people and occurrences in American history, arranged in chronological order by year from 1565 to 2000.

Authors of authentic biographies attempt to capture the factual information of the lives of the people they are documenting, providing an objective and balanced view. However, what the biographer captures in objectivity, he loses in distance since he will never be able to fully capture what was in subject's heart and mind. On the other hand, autobiographies and memoirs are written about the author's own life, thus they are subjective but also provide a unique perspective that only this type of biography can capture. In the autobiographical picturebook *The Wall: Growing Up Behind the Iron Curtain* (2007), author and illustrator Peter Sis documents his life growing up in Czechoslovakia under Soviet rule. Through annotated illustrations, journals, maps, and dreamscapes, he shows what life was like for a child who lived on the "Red side—the Communist side—of the Iron Curtain," eventually escaping to America. In the Afterward, Sis writes, "I have always drawn everything, I have tried to draw my life—before America—for [my children]." Children are often very interested in learning about the lives of the authors and illustrations whose books they enjoy and admire.

Russell Freedman notes, "A children's biography doesn't have to be comprehensive, and it doesn't have to be definitive. It does have to be accurate, to the extent that's possible. And most of all, it has to be a piece of literature, a compelling read" (Sutton, 2002, p. 703). Sometimes, to achieve a stronger sense of story, biographers change the sequence of events or fictionalize the context of an event. In the foreword to her childhood memoir, *Homesick: My Own Story*, Jean Fritz (1982) writes the following:

> When I started to write about my childhood in China, I found that my memory came out in lumps. Although I could for the most part arrange them in the proper sequence, I discovered that my preoccupation with the time and literal accuracy was squeezing the life out of what I had to say. So I decided to forget about sequence and just get on with it. Since my childhood feels like a story, I decided to tell it that way, letting the events fall as they would into the shape of a story, lacing them together with fictional bits, adding a piece here and there when memory didn't give me all I needed. . . . The people are real; the places are dear to me. But most important, the form I have used has given me the freedom to recreate the emotions that I remember so vividly. Strictly speaking, I have to call this book fiction, but it does not feel like fiction to me. It is my story, told as truly as I can tell it. (p. 7)

Fritz's perspective on her childhood as seen from adulthood provides an insight that is achieved through an adept blend of truth and storytelling (see "The Teacher's Voice" below). Just because a biography is fictionalized doesn't mean it is not based on truth, but it is up to the reader to decide if the author has gone beyond the reasonable boundary of biography. Look for source notes and other documentation and ask questions such as, Has the spirit of the truth been maintained? Are the foundational facts accurate?

# THE • TEACHER'S • VOICE

> A Response to *Homesick: My Own Story*

The day has been redeemed! I finished *Homesick* just this moment. Jean Fritz is an eloquent writer and storyteller. From the beginning, I was able to relate to Jean and her sense that she belonged somewhere other than where she found herself. The voice of the author came through so strongly that I felt immediately as though she were my grandmother telling me about her childhood.

Jean Fritz captures the right moments, thoughts, and feelings of a young girl. For example, she describes her frustrations at being told to "be good." I know <u>exactly</u> what she means and how a seemingly innocuous comment by an adult, in the midst of family chaos, can become a curse. She captures that.

Fritz also relates honestly feelings of pessimism, hope, disappointment, and anger. Her family becomes very real for the reader. Despite the specific time and locations of the story, it has a universal quality and that sense of timelessness that good literature captures.

Like Richard Peck, Jean Fritz makes the setting and the land so vital to the story that they become characters. When Jean says she loves the Yangtze River, I know exactly what she means. I feel as strongly about the Missouri and the York. When she describes her grandparents' farm in Pennsylvania, I can see the same in Missouri and Oklahoma. And when she writes about her grandmother, I can almost see and hear my own Grandma Lea.

Like <u>The Watsons Go to Birmingham</u>, the story of Jean and her family is set against world changing events in history. Fritz includes a postscript to help the reader understand the complicated events in China at that time. During the story, however, the events are relayed and interpreted through their impact on specific characters. This is far more effective than trying to incorporate history lessons in the middle of the story.

—How does this teacher convey the effectiveness of Fritz's blend of truth and storytelling in *Homesick: My Own Story*?

*Watch*

*Watch interviews with many of these authors.*

## Categories of Biography

| Category | Description | Examples |
|---|---|---|
| **Authentic Biography** | True nonfiction. Uses only primary data such as letters, diaries, and interviews. No fictionalized details created. Authentic biography can range from covering the entire life of a subject to only one event or period in a subject's life. | *Shipwrecked! The True Adventures of a Japanese Boy* by Rhoda Blumburg<br><br>*The Adventures of Marco Polo* by Russell Freedman<br><br>*Who's Saying What in Jamestown, Thomas Savage?* by Jean Fritz<br><br>*Harvesting Hope: The Story of Cesar Chavez* by Kathleen Krull |
| **Fictionalized Biography/ Biographical Fiction** | Invented dialogue is present in fictionalized biographies. Invented dialogue, secondary characters, and actions are present in biographical fiction. Achievements are accurately described in both. | *Snowshoe Thompson* by Nancy Levinson<br><br>*Maria's Comet* by Deborah Hopkinson<br><br>*The Dreamer* by Pam Munoz Ryan<br><br>*Here Comes the Garbage Barge!* by Jonah Winter |
| **Autobiographies and Memoirs** | Autobiography is when the author writes about his or her own life. A memoir is a story about a certain period in the author's life, interpreted by the author in the present. | *Guts* by Gary Paulsen<br><br>*Buzz Aldrin: Reaching for the Moon* by Buzz Aldrin and Wendy Minor<br><br>*Marshfield Dreams: When I Was a Kid* by Ralph Fletcher |

### EVALUATING BIOGRAPHY

Biography is written in a narrative format. Each biographer's unique style must come through in how he or she selects, organizes, and designs the information in an unbiased manner. In this way, evaluating biography is very similar to evaluating fiction (see "Evaluation Criteria" on page 279). Vardell (1991) writes the following:

> The evaluation of fiction and nonfiction may be surprisingly similar. For an information book must be interesting and well-written, use rich and vivid language, reflect the author's unique voice and passion, and involve and stimulate the reader, just as a good work of fiction should. (p. 478)

## Evaluating and Selecting Informational Books

Informational books are available on a wide array of topics from joke books to insects to the Harlem Renaissance. It is the variety of topics, visual appeal, and compelling details that draw children to informational books. In *Fast Food! Gulp! Gulp!* (2001)

# Evaluation Criteria

**Criteria for Evaluating Biographies**

| Element | Criteria | Description |
|---|---|---|
| Setting | Does the author's description accurately portray where the subject lived, worked, and played? | The author should provide details reflective of the time period and place in which the character lived. These details should support the development of the character. |
| Plot | Are the events in the story based on fact? Do they help the reader understand what occurred in the subject's life? | While the events can be presented in many ways and from different perspectives, they should have a factual basis to them. They should help highlight the contributions of the subject. |
| Characters | Does the author present a balanced depiction of the character? Is the subject worthy of a biography? | The author should not present an overly critical or glorified depiction of the character. The characters should be dynamic and act in realistic ways. This is one of the most important elements of a biography. |
| Style | Are crafting techniques used to make the character and the story interesting to the reader? | Authors can use a variety of crafting techniques to create a vivid picture of the subject's life and achievements. These techniques, such as anecdotes, dialogue, and flashbacks supported by pictures and quotes, help the story come alive for the reader. |
| Theme | Does the author tie the setting, plot, and characters together in a way that makes the contributions of the character evident? | The author must interpret the events and details of a subject's life to identify a central theme based on the subject's accomplishments without judgment or bias. |
| Accuracy, Authority, and Cultural Authenticity | Is the information current and accurate? Is the author an expert on the subject? Do the story or illustrations authentically reflect the beliefs and values of the culture discussed? | The information needs to be up to date and verifiable through a variety of documentation. Facts should support generalizations. The author should be qualified to write about the topic. Biases and stereotypes should be avoided. |

# Categories of Informational Books

| Category | Description | Examples |
|---|---|---|
| **Nature** | Books about the natural world. Includes books about animals, plants, geology, geography, and the human body. | *I'm A Pill Bug* by Yukihisa Tokuda<br><br>*An Island Grows* by Lola Schaefer<br><br>*The Great Brain Book: An Inside Look at the Inside of Your Head* by H. P. Newquist<br><br>*A Place for Butterflies* by Melissa Stewart<br><br>*Our Seasons* by Grace Lin<br><br>*Almost Gone: The World's Rarest Animals* by Steve Jenkins |
| **People and Cultures** | Books about people and cultures in the United States and other parts of the world. Introduces children to similarities and differences among peoples of the world. | *Celebrate Connections Among Cultures* by Jan Reynolds<br><br>*How to Survive in Antarctica* by Lucy Bledsoe<br><br>*Drumbeat in Our Feet* by Patricia Keeler |
| **History** | Books that provide an in-depth look into people, places, and events in history. | *The American Story: 100 True Tales from American History* by Jennifer Armstrong<br>*Freeze Frame: A Photographic History of the Winter Olympics* by Sue Macy<br>*Nobody Gonna Turn Me 'Round: Stories and Songs about the Civil Rights Movement* by Doreen Rappaport |
| **Discoveries and How Things Work** | Books about past discoveries. Includes books on astronomy, space, and technology. Books about how things work, including books about appliances and machines. Diagrams are important. | *Destination: Space* by Seymour Simon<br><br>*New How Things Work: From Lawn Mowers to Surgical Robots and Everything in Between* by John Langone<br><br>*So You Want to Be an Inventor?* by Judith St. George |
| **Hobbies, Crafts, Creative Arts, How-to Books, Sports, and Recreation** | Children like looking into their interests. Books contain directions and background information. Drawings are important in creative art books. | *What Athletes Are Made of* by Hanoch Piven<br><br>*The Green Eggs and Ham Cookbook* by Georgeanne Brennan<br><br>*Spilling Ink: A Young Writer's Handbook* by Ellen Potter and Anne Mazer<br><br>*Faces, Places, and Inner Spaces: A Guide to Looking at Art* by Jean Sousa |

author Bernard Waber takes the reader on a tour of the frenzied world of fast food, "Pick! Pick! / Lick! Lick! / Slurp! Slurp! / Burp! Burp!" Children of all ages love the *The Guinness Book of World Records,* filled with hundreds of photographs of the world's largest, tallest, heaviest, and most extreme. *Phineas Gage: A Gruesome But True Story About Brain Science* (2002), by John Fleischman, chronicles the scientific details behind the story of a man who was shot through the head with a 13-pound iron rod and lived. *The Frog Scientist* (2009) describes the research Tyrone Hayes and his students are doing to discover the effects pesticides have on frogs and, in turn, on people and the environment, written by Pamela Turner, with photographs by Andy Comins. The backmatter provides a list of featured frogs and toads, a glossary, a selected bibliography, a list of websites, and multimedia.

The evaluation and selection of informational books involves deciding on how well the author distilled and organized his or her extensive research into an appealing, interesting, and accessible format that involves and stimulates the reader through well-written prose.

*Listen*

*Listen to an interview with Tyrone Hayes about the effects of pesticides on frogs.*

## CATEGORIES OF INFORMATIONAL BOOKS

Informational books consist of primarily expository text structure—meaning to inform, explain, describe, or persuade. The organization of the structure of expository text is dependent on the form, among them concept books, picturebooks, photographic essays, Internet websites, journals and diaries, how-to books, field guides, newspaper articles, brochures, pamphlets, maps, and reference books.

Ninety-five percent of school and public libraries organize informational books by the Dewey Decimal System, with the following main classes:

000 Computers, information, and general reference
100 Philosophy and psychology
200 Religion
300 Social sciences (includes folk literature)
400 Language
500 Science
600 Technology
700 Arts and recreation
800 Literature (includes poetry)
900 History and geography

Since these ten classes are broad in scope—each includes nine subcategories and each subcategory includes nine more subcategories—they can become unwieldy as far as determining quickly what information is included in informational books. Therefore, the categories of informational books outlined in "Categories of Informational Books" are more specific and useful for teachers. Children's literature classifies folk literature (included in 300) and poetry (included in 800) as separate genres from nonfiction.

## EVALUATING INFORMATIONAL BOOKS

Sophie Webb (2000) is a biologist and an artist who went to Antarctica for two months to study the Adélie penguin. She wrote about her experiences in *My Season with*

*Penguins: An Antarctic Journal.* The journal format allows Webb to chronicle her experiences so the reader understands the scientific method used to document her observations as well as learning about the habitat and behavior of the penguins. The journal format also allows Webb to include amusing facts and anecdotes that bring a personal feel to the book:

> 18 December
> The Adélie nest is a shallow scrape (a depression dug in the ground by a penguin). The rim is formed by small rocks that the birds have collected. These rocks are much prized. A very large nest of rocks is often an indicator of a bird's stature—signifying, for example, a bird's level of fitness or its success as a parent. I see a bird sneak up behind another that is sleeping, stretch out its neck, and gently steal a stone from the edge of the nest. The almost sly expression on its face turns to guilt as its theft is discovered. It hurries back to its nest with its prize. (p. 21)

Most children can relate to doing something they are not supposed to do and feeling guilty about it. In this journal entry, Webb has brought the actions of one penguin into a child's realm of experience by giving him human characteristics such as

*Written in a journal format, My Season with Penguins draws the reader into the world of the Antarctic.*

being sneaky, sly, and guilty. Webb also makes the text accessible by defining *scrape*, a word with which most children are not familiar. The journal entries are accompanied by Webb's notebook-like sketches, complete with captions describing the pictures, which are very useful in interpreting the text. The end of the book contains a one-page glossary that defines the technical terms used throughout the book.

*My Season with Penguins* is an excellent example of an informational book. The author is an authority on the subject, and, based on references and acknowledgments, the information is accurate and organized in a way that makes the content easily accessible and reader friendly. The overall design and use of illustrations adds to the

# Evaluation Criteria

**Criteria for Evaluating Informational Books**

| Element | Criteria | Description |
|---|---|---|
| Organization | Is the book clearly organized in a way that shows the relationship between concepts? Does it organize the information in a way that aids in the understanding of the concepts? | There should be a clear pattern and sequence. Headings and subheadings can help organize the information. The organization needs to be logical and relate to the intended audience. |
| Style | Is the writing interesting? Does it show the author's enthusiasm for the topic? Does it draw the reader in by the use of language? | The information should be presented in a way that encourages the reader's involvement. The author's enthusiasm and relationship to the topic should be made evident by the tone of the work. A good work is precise with descriptive language. |
| Design and Illustrations | Is the design visually appealing? Does it support and add to the content? Do the illustrations help solidify the reader's understanding of the topic? | The illustrations should relate to the topic on the given page and enhance the reader's understanding of the subject matter. Illustrations should be explained through captions or in the text. The format should be clear and appealing. |
| Accuracy, Authority, and Cultural Authenticity | Is the information current and accurate? Is the author an expert on the topic? Do the information and illustrations authentically reflect the beliefs and values of the culture discussed? | The information needs to be up to date and verified by individuals in the field. The author should be qualified to write about the topic. Facts should support generalizations. Biases and stereotypes should be avoided. |

understanding of the text, and the writing style conveys the author's enthusiasm for her subject and engages the reader.

Applying the criteria in "Evaluation Criteria" will ensure that children have access to only the best of the genre. Award-winning nonfiction, such as the Siebert, Orbis Pictus, and Children's Book Guild awards, as well as notable trade books selected by professional organizations such as the National Association of Science Teacher's *Outstanding Science Trade Books for Students K–12* and the National Council of Teachers of Social Studies' *Notable Trade Books for Young People* are also excellent resources (information on these sources can be found in the resources section at the end of this chapter).

# The Role of Nonfiction in Literacy Development

Duke's (2000) study of 20 first-grade classrooms (10 in low-SES districts and 10 in high SES) revealed that very little time during the school day was devoted to informational text—a mean of 3.6 percent minutes per day. Additionally, classrooms in low-SES districts had less informational text and spent less time in activities—just 1.4 minutes per day. Duke argued that the lack of exposure to informational texts in first-grade classrooms in general, and low-SES classrooms in particular, may help explain why many children have difficulty with informational reading and writing later in school—for example, during what has been termed the "fourth-grade slump" (Chall, Jacobs, & Baldwin, 1990).

Although Duke's research was with primary grades, the lack of exposure to nonfiction at an early age has lasting effects into intermediate, middle, and high school, since children who are not provided with instruction on how to read nonfiction texts early in school will not have the necessary strategies for content area reading that predominates later in school. Duke (2004) recommends four strategies for improving comprehension of informational text:

- Increase students' access to informational text.
- Increase the time students spend working with informational text in instructional activities.
- Explicitly teach comprehension strategies.
- Create opportunities for students to use informational text for authentic purposes (p. 40).

Each of these recommendations is discussed in the following sections.

## INCREASING ACCESS AND TIME TO READ INFORMATIONAL TEXTS

The availability of quality nonfiction books has increased significantly in the past decade. Educators must ensure that a considerable portion of school and classroom libraries is devoted to nonfiction texts. This necessarily includes access to magazines and the Internet. Not only does this provide for the interests, motivation, and engagement of students who prefer nonfiction, but it sends a strong message that reading outside of school, which is predominately nonfiction, is also important inside of school.

Access to a critical mass of nonfiction books in the classroom is an important first step, but it must be extended into opportunities for instruction. Characteristics and conventions of expository text are significantly different from narrative text. With narrative text, we read for aesthetic reasons, using our knowledge of how stories work, and reading from cover to cover to find out what the story is about. With expository text, we read to learn more about a subject in which we are interested. Expository text doesn't follow a

**TABLE 10.4**

# Comparison of Narrative and Expository Texts

| Narrative | Expository |
|---|---|
| Follows a familiar story structure—characters, plot, theme, and setting—in the order of events | Organized by description, sequence, comparison/contrast, cause-effect, and problem-solution |
| Reader reads for aesthetic purposes: enjoyment, intrigue, etc. | Reader reads to find out information |
| Illustrations extend text meaning | Illustrations (usually with captions) are used to clarify or explain |
| Written in past tense | Written in present tense |
| Uses dialogue and familiar vocabulary | Does not use dialogue; uses technical vocabulary |
| Concepts are usually related to the experiences of the reader | Subject may be about abstract concepts unfamiliar to the reader |
| Reader gets meaning from events and characters | Reader gets meaning from information |
| Reader suspends disbelief | Reader assumes information is accurate |
| Plot holds reader's attention | Reader attends to organization of information |
| Reader may read material quickly | Reader uses flexible, slower reading rate |
| Uses prose paragraph style | Uses headings, subheadings, titles, table of contents, indexes, and glossaries |

typical story structure but rather an organization that makes sense for the content, such as cause and effect, sequence or chronological order, description, problem-solution, or comparison-contrast. We might not read the whole book but use the table of contents or index to find a particular part of the book we are interested in reading (see Table 10.4 for comparisons of narrative and expository texts).

Reading aloud to children while modeling effective strategies for reading nonfiction text can familiarize children with the unique characteristics and conventions of expository text. When thinking about books to read aloud, nonfiction might not be your first choice, but we must make a conscientious choice to include nonfiction in our read alouds just as we would fiction. The following are some guidelines for selecting and reading aloud nonfiction.

- **Select only quality nonfiction.** Choose only those texts that meet the evaluation criteria of quality biographies and information books. This ensures that books will be accurate and information will be presented in an accessible, appealing, and interesting way and that the writing style is engaging.

- **Select information from a variety of media.** Include nonfiction to read aloud from newspapers, magazines, pamphlets, articles from the Internet, and brochures. Many times information from these sources connects with topics in the content area curriculum and makes an authentic real-world connection to reading nonfiction for information.
- **Choose books that reflect children's interests.** Read aloud nonfiction books that reflect children's interests and books they recommend, including those that blend fact and fiction, such as the *Magic School Bus* series by Joanna Cole. Provide opportunities for children to compare and contrast the differences between fiction and nonfiction, documenting their thinking on a chart, as in Figure 10.1.
- **Consider reading only a portion of the book.** A nonfiction book does not necessarily have to be read from cover to cover. Read aloud a particular section of a book that you find interesting and model how to find it by using the table of contents or the index.
- **Read aloud nonfiction with expression just as you would fiction.** Make sure all children can see and hear you, and give them time to discuss the read aloud along the way.
- **Discuss unfamiliar words.** Use unfamiliar or technical vocabulary as an opportunity to stop and think aloud about how to figure out unknown words. Encourage children to listen for "powerful words or phrases" in nonfiction.
- **Stop to discuss the organization and features.** Pause at appropriate times to discuss the organization of the text and identify special features and their purpose. Keep a chart of what the children notice that can be revisited and added to over time, as in Figure 10.2.
- **Reread favorite nonfiction titles,** and make the books that are read aloud available for children to read independently.

**FIGURE 10.1**

Comparing and Contrasting Elements in Fiction and Nonfiction

| Fiction | Same | Nonfiction |
|---|---|---|
| Setting | Pictures or illustrations | Table of contents |
| Characters | Title | True - real |
| Events | | Index |
| Resolution | Authors | Information that helps |
| Stories | Illustrators or | you learn |
| Beginning, middle, end | photographers | Labels |
| Connections with our life | Fun to read | Close-up pictures |
| | | Captions |
| Not true | | Diagrams |
| Speech bubbles | | Maps |
| Dialogue | | Bold words |
| | | Special science words |

# Biographies

What information about a person's life can we find out in biographies?

- Their childhood
- When they were born and died (and how they died)
- What makes them special—how they overcame problems
- About their family
- The events in their life—whom they met
- If they were poor or rich
- What they looked like
- Accomplishments
- Nicknames
- Contributions: how they helped others, inventions
- Quotations

## TEACHING COMPREHENSION STRATEGIES

In addition to reading aloud and modeling effective reading strategies, explicit teaching of comprehension strategies can foster comprehension development (Duke & Pearson, 2002). The same comprehension strategies that appear to improve comprehension of fiction apply to nonfiction:

- Monitoring students' understanding and making adjustments as needed
- Activating and applying relevant prior knowledge
- Generating questions
- Thinking aloud
- Attending to and uncovering text structure
- Drawing inferences
- Constructing visual representations
- Summarizing

Teachers must help children understand the differences in when, how, and why the strategies are used with nonfiction.

**Literal Comprehension.** The ability to recall basic information is necessary for many literal comprehension skills such as retelling, synthesizing, visualizing, summarizing, recognizing the main idea and locating details, understanding text structure, and figuring out new vocabulary. Literal understanding is the foundation for higher-level comprehension such as interpreting and evaluating information.

Tony Stead (2006) has worked extensively with K–5 students on reading and writing nonfiction. He discovered that limited and inaccurate prior knowledge interfered with students' comprehension. In an effort to access students' background knowledge in a way that facilitated making accurate predictions and asking relevant questions, Stead developed the *reading and analyzing nonfiction (RAN) strategy* (Table 10.5), extending the KWL (Know, Want to know, Learned) strategy (Ogle, 1986).

*Watch*

*Watch a video of Tony Stead helping children select nonfiction books.*

**TABLE 10.5**

# The RAN Strategy: Reading and Analyzing Nonfiction Strategies

| What I Think I Know | Confirmed | Misconceptions | New Information | Wonderings |
|---|---|---|---|---|
| Children state information they think is correct about the topic. | Children research to confirm prior knowledge. | Children research to discard prior knowledge. | Children research to find additional information not stated in prior knowledge. | Children raise questions based on the new information gathered. |

T. Stead, *Reality checks: Teaching reading comprehension with nonfiction, K–5* (Portland, ME: Stenhouse, 2006), p. 18. Copyright © 2004, reproduced with permission of Stenhouse Publishers.

The first step in the RAN strategy is a prereading activity in which the children brainstorm what they think they know about the topic under study and post their ideas on the chart with sticky notes. During reading, as the teacher and children read and research the topic, they either confirm their prior knowledge by moving sticky notes into column two or realize it is a misconception by moving the notes into column three. In this way, children are comparing and contrasting information explicitly stated in the text or shown through illustrations. Children should be given the opportunity to discuss their thinking with partners, keeping each child focused and giving him time to talk. Section four encourages children to think about information that that was not part of their prior knowledge but is new learning, which constitutes much of the literal understandings of the text. Many times, this new information leads children to ask questions that are then recorded in the fifth column: "Wonderings." Stead (2006) writes, "By encouraging children to make connections with prior knowledge I was also developing interpretive understandings. Evaluative understandings are also strengthened as children begin to question the validity of the information we are reading when it differs from other sources we have read in the past" (p. 19).

**Postreading Retellings.** Retellings are a postreading activity in which children recall what they remember after reading or listening to a particular text. Through retellings, children develop reading flexibility as they learn about text forms and conventions. They also discover how stories are structured. Retellings provide teachers with an understanding of "*how* as well as *how much*" information children retain after reading or listening to nonfiction text (Moss, 2003, p. 712). Moss suggests the following two-part sequence to facilitate students' development of expository retelling skills.

**Step 1: Teacher modeling of retellings.** First, brainstorm children's prior knowledge. Column one of the RAN strategy would be an excellent way to start. Then, read the text aloud, pointing out specific text features that facilitate retelling, such as signal words, the table of contents, headings, bolded words, maps, charts, or diagrams. After reading, retell the text as completely as possible, allowing students to add missing information and to go back into the text to reread for parts that might have been missed. Finally, model more elaborate retellings by including analogies, personal anecdotes, and imagery, making the text your own.

**Step 2: Students practice retellings.** Ask children to brainstorm their prior knowledge, as in the first step of phase one. Then, read the text aloud or have children read it silently, encouraging them to predict what the text might be about and to think about what the organizing pattern might be by previewing the text, table of contents, and headings. Then, ask students what they remember about the text, and record their responses on chart paper. Scaffold students' recall with pictures from the text or by asking questions that prompt sequencing of events: What did you learn first . . . next . . . after that? Then, reread the text aloud or ask children to reread silently to look for information missed during the retelling. Add this information to the chart paper. Finally, encourage students to make personal connections between their lives and the text or the world and the text.

Once children have experience with large group retellings, they can move to small group and paired retellings. Moss (2003) believes that English language learners may particularly benefit from retellings because the concrete nature of informational text can help them build bridges between their first and second languages.

**Inferential Comprehension.** Inferring is a strategy that has been discussed in several of the fiction genre chapters in this book, but it is also an essential strategy for nonfiction. Inferring requires the reader to use stated facts in the text and personal knowledge and experiences to make meaning beyond the text. For example, consider the journal entry discussed earlier by Sophie Webb from *My Season with Penguins* in which one of the penguins stole a coveted rock from the nest of an incubating penguin. The facts stated in the text are that some penguins have higher stature than others, as indicated by their large nest of rocks, and some penguins (presumably of lesser stature) will steal those rocks if given the chance. What inferences can we make from this information? One might infer that the social structure of penguins is like that of humans. Many people desire the material possessions of others, and some even resort to stealing to get what they want. This text-to-world connection requires the reader to understand the literal facts and then connect those facts to personal experience. Stead (2006) states, "Even though it is important for readers to be able to recall facts and locate new information, it is when they connect with the information they read that even deeper meaning occurs" (p. 90).

Teachers can model inferring and making connections before and during read alouds and by allowing children to talk about the connections they make to the content. Every child has her own set of experiences and will make different connections. Discussing these differences helps children to understand a variety of perspectives and to gain new insight. During independent reading, children can record their connections on sticky notes to discuss with the teacher during conferences and during small group discussions with peers.

**Evaluative Comprehension and Critical Thinking.** Evaluative comprehension requires the reader to use explicit information in the text, implicit understandings, and personal knowledge and experiences to make judgments about the content of material being read. Evaluative understandings come from critically thinking about such aspects of text as fact versus opinion; reality versus fantasy; validity, adequacy, and relevance of the text; and author's bias, intent, and point of view (Stead, 2006, p. 115). If we want children to become good consumers of information, they must be able to critically analyze print and media sources.

One way to engage children in the process of evaluative comprehension is by pairing nonfiction and fiction books on the same topic. Giles and Pierce (2001) write, "Juxtaposing fiction and nonfiction builds on the natural curiosity of students. The fictional accounts draw readers into the story world, while the nonfiction texts add facts and depth to students' understanding" (p. 578). For example, the fiction book *The Great Kapok Tree*, written and illustrated by Lynn Cherry, is about how the different animals who live in a great kapok tree in the Brazilian rainforest try to convince a man with an axe of the importance of not cutting down their home. The book's environmental message is clear: Save the rainforest! The book does not explain why the rainforest is being destroyed and what can be done to save it. Students can be encouraged to think about their own knowledge of disappearing resources such as the flattening of a playground to make room for more parking spaces or the demolition of historic buildings to build more modern, space-efficient buildings. What have people done in the past to protect or preserve property they believe is an asset to society? Drawing on students' implicit understandings, *The Great Kapok Tree* can be paired with a nonfiction text such as *Nature's Green Umbrella: Tropical Rain Forests*, written and illustrated by Gail Gibbons, to provide accurate information about rainforests, including why rainforests are being destroyed and ways people are currently trying to save them:

*Watch*

*Watch a video of Gail Gibbons discussing ways to make nonfiction visually exciting.*

> Many people are working hard to save the tropical rain forests from destruction. . . .
> One way is to create protected places called *reserves*. In some reserves only *selective cutting* is done. This means that loggers and farmers can cut down certain trees, but others must be left to grow. Some people think *extractive reserves* will also help. In these reserves, people are allowed to take only limited amounts of fruit, plants, nuts, and latex for the production of rubber, and other natural products.

Students can be prompted to use the explicit information in the texts and implicit understandings from their background knowledge and experiences to make judgments about whether these efforts will result in the survival of rainforests. Students can conduct research to discover if reserves, selective cutting, or extractive reserves have assisted in the preservation of the rainforest.

### USING INFORMATIONAL TEXTS FOR AUTHENTIC PURPOSES

Most of us read a variety of nonfiction texts every day—newspapers, Internet articles, magazines, cookbooks, vacation brochures—because they present information of interest to us. "In contrast," Duke (2004) asserts, "students in school usually read informational text to answer questions at the back of the chapter to complete a test prep worksheet, or simply because the teacher said so" (p. 42). Children must be given opportunities to read and write nonfiction texts for authentic reasons.

Most children are truly interested in many of the topics studied in school and, if given the chance, will engage in further reading and writing about these texts independently. For instance, I worked with a third-grade teacher who set up dry and aquatic habitats in small terrariums placed on the students' desks to study over a period of time. The students kept a journal in which they documented the changes in the habitats. They researched the environments and life cycles of the worms and fish in the habitats by reading books, Internet articles, and magazine articles. The students created their own books based on their observations and what they learned and then placed their books in the classroom library for everyone to read.

It was a pleasure to observe these students at work researching the habitats— they were excited about their work and enthusiastically shared their findings with each other and the teacher. These children were reading and writing to learn more about something they were interested in rather than to complete an assignment for the teacher. Engagement in reading for authentic purposes results in increased motivation, comprehension, and strategic reading.

## Opportunities for Reader Response

Most people read nonfiction with an efferent stance or with the expectation that they are going to learn something. Yet, it is the aesthetic or emotional response to what we read that makes the information meaningful. Typically, a strong emotional response is associated with fiction with its well-developed characters and plot lines. However, we do react emotionally to nonfiction. For example, if I read a newspaper article about a robbery that took place in a part of the city that is far away from where I live, I might not have the same response as if the robbery took place in a neighborhood close to my house. I am more likely to discuss the article with my family and neighbors and look for articles that follow up on the story in the next few days or weeks. I have connected the information in the article to my own situation, feelings, and thinking. The ability to make these connections is important for all levels of comprehension.

Modeling, scaffolding, discussing, and recording students' connections to prior knowledge and experiences are an important part of all of the strategies presented in the previous section. Students should be encouraged to write their thoughts and feelings about nonfiction books in their reading response journal just like they would for a fiction book. In *"The Child's Voice"* below, a third grader wrote a response to *The Mary Celeste: An Unsolved Mystery from History* (1999). This book is one in a series of unsolved

## THE • CHILD'S • VOICE

Third Grader's Response to *The Mary Celeste: Unsolved Mystery from History*

> The Mary Cesletse
> I'm thinking that maybe the people on the Mary Cesletse saw the people on the ea graft and thought they were pirates. So the people on the Mary Cesletse jumped on the life boat and sailed to the Island 6 miles away. And they tied up the ship at night. But they left their stuff on. But in the morning somehow it got lose. That's I think happend. Also I think you should read this book Because it is extrodanary!

—How was the idea of a real unsolved mystery motivating and engaging for this third grader?

mystery books written by Jane Yolen and Heidi Stemple. All the books are based on real, unsolved mysteries.

In this mystery, the ship *Mary Celeste* sailed out of New York in 1872 and never returned. When found by the crew of the *Dei Gratia,* the brig was in seaworthy condition and almost completely in order, but everyone on it had vanished. At the end of each mystery, several of the most plausible theories are presented that might explain what really happened.

## Making the Connection Across the Curriculum

Content area textbooks cannot match the flexibility, depth, or quality provided by trade books. Problems with textbooks have been a major force driving the trend toward using trade books. Trade books generally do the following:

- Are more up-to-date
- Contain less overwhelming vocabulary
- Provide a more focused, in-depth look at particular subjects
- Accommodate differences in learning styles
- Have more interesting and less confusing storylines that help children remember concepts
- Contain colorful pictures and graphics
- Provide context for understanding difficult concepts
- Have a more positive view of women and minorities

When any one textbook becomes the total curriculum, we shortchange students (Routman, 2008). Collectively, the drawbacks inherent in textbooks are why many children have difficulty reading and connecting with textbooks and why nonfiction trade books are the perfect supplement to textbooks. Following are a few nonfiction titles that are great for science, math, and social studies.

### SCIENCE

Plants and animals are common in the school science curriculum, but many books bring out more uncommon aspects of these topics. *Gregor Mendel: The Friar Who Grew Peas,* written by Cheryl Bardoe and illustrated by Joseph Smith, depicts how the father of genetics conducted carefully controlled experiments in cross-breeding plants. An extensive author's note presents further information. *Hungry Plants,* written by Mary Batten and illustrated by Paul Mirocha, provides basic facts about the structure and behavior of one of children's favorite plants, the Venus flytrap, along with a few of the other 600 kinds of carnivorous plants that exist. *Extreme Animals: The Toughest Creatures on Earth,* written by Nicola Davies and illustrated by Neal Layton, is about animals that have adapted to survive in conditions that would kill a human. *Little Lost Bat,* written by Sandra Markle and illustrated by Alan Marks, tells the story of one newborn Mexican free-tailed bat that loses its mother, while providing incredible facts about the more than 20 million bats that live in a cave close to Austin, Texas.

### MATH

Uncommon ways of thinking about math can be highlighted through nonfiction books. *Math-terpieces: The Art of Problem-Solving,* written by Greg Tang, uses the artwork of 12 famous painters as an aid in developing problem-solving skills through grouping.

Featuring panda cubs born in the San Diego Zoo, *Panda Math: Learning About Subtraction from Hua Mei and Mei Sheng,* by Ann Whitehead Nagda, serves double duty as it presents addition and subtraction exercises along with interesting facts about panda bears. Additional titles that use the same structure include *Polar Bear Math: Learning About Fractions from Klondike and Snow; Tiger Math: Learning to Graph from a Baby Tiger;* and *Chimp Math: Learning About Time from a Baby Chimpanzee. Great Estimations,* by Bruce Goldstone, uses amazing photographs of toys, pipe cleaners, marbles, peanuts, and other small items to learn to estimate the size of groups of approximately 10, 100, and even 1,000 things on sight.

*Read*

Shipwreck at the Bottom of the World *won the Orbis Pictus Award. Read Jennifer Armstrong's acceptance speech.*

## SOCIAL STUDIES

Historical events not commonly discussed in social studies textbooks are the topic of many nonfiction books. *Shipwreck at the Bottom of the World: The Extraordinary True Story of Shackleton and the Endurance,* by Jennifer Armstrong, describes the events of Sir Ernest Shackleton's 1914 Antarctic expedition when, after being trapped in a frozen sea for nine months, he was forced to make a very long and perilous journey across ice and stormy seas to reach an inhabited land.

In the *Children of the Great Depression,* Russell Freedman presents a photo-essay of those who endured the Depression, including schooling, work life, home life, leisure activities, and the lives of children who rode the rails. *Let Me Play: The Story of Title IX: The Law That Changed the Future of Girls in America,* by Karen Blumenthal, describes the evolution of the groundbreaking law that bans sex discrimination in U.S. education. Alternating between profiles of groundbreaking female athletes and legislators and highlights of the women's movement, the text moves from the early twentieth century through today.

# Top 10 Read Alouds

## NONFICTION

1. **A Platypus, Probably** by Sneed Collard III, illustrated by Andrew Plant (2005, Charlesbridge). Follow a female platypus as she hunts for food, finds a mate, builds a shelter, and cares for her pups.

2. **An Egg Is Quiet** by Dianna Aston, illustrated by Sylvia Long (2006, Chronicle). Introduces readers to more than 60 types of eggs and an array of egg facts.

3. **Claudette Colvin: Twice Toward Justice** by Phillip Hoose, (2009, Farrar, Straus and Giroux). The long-overlooked story of a teenager who refused to give her seat to a white woman nine months before Rosa Parks refused to give up her seat on a Montgomery bus. This meticulously researched book fuses history with Colvin's recollections of her experiences as a linchpin in the case that ended the historic boycott.

4. **How We Are Smart** by W. Nikola-Lisa, illustrated by Sean Qualls (2006, Lee & Low). Through direct quotations, verse, and prose, the achievements of a diverse group of people who illustrate Dr. Howard Gardner's theory of multiple intelligences is presented. Includes information about the eight basic ways people can be "smart" with suggested activities.

5. **Down, Down, Down: A Journey to the Bottom of the Sea** by Steve Jenkins (2009, Houghton Mifflin). Provides a top-to-bottom look at the ocean, from birds and waves to thermal vents and ooze.

6. **Photo by Brady: A Picture of the Civil War** by Jennifer Armstrong (2005, Atheneum). In *Photo by Brady,* Jennifer Armstrong tells the story of the Civil War as seen through the lenses of its recorders.

7. **Pick Me Up: Stuff You Need to Know** by Jeremy Leslie and David Roberts (2006, Dorling Kindersley). With full-color spreads and vivid design, this "unencyclopedia" for the Internet generation gives fresh and fascinating contexts for classic information—making looking up information easier than ever.

8. **Moonshot: The Flight of Apollo 11** by Brian Floca (2009, Atheneum). Here is the story of the Apollo 11 mission to the Moon—a story of leaving and returning during the summer of 1969, and a story of home, seen whole, from far away by steady astronauts in their great machines.

9. **The Way We Work: Getting to Know the Amazing Human Body** by David Macaulay (2008, Houghton Mifflin). Explore everything from bones to bronchioles, noses to neurons in this clear, comprehensive and utterly engaging guide to the human body.

10. **Who Was First? Discovering the Americas** by Russell Freedman (2007, Houghton Mifflin). Before Columbus, Admiral of the ocean sea, did China discover America? Leif the Lucky? Who really discovered America?

# Activities for Professional Development

## Think Critically About Children's Literature

1.  Select a topic taught in the elementary or middle school content area curriculum, such as science or social studies. Compare the extent and range of content and illustrations on the topic in a textbook to that of a nonfiction trade book. Which is more effective in conveying the information? Why? Would the two sources of information complement each other?

2.  Select a historical or realistic fiction book on a topic of interest to you. Find a nonfiction book on the same topic. Compare how the different genres inform your knowledge of the topic. How could you use the two books to promote critical thinking with students?

3.  A recent study by Broemmel and Rearden (2006) found that science books selected by participating teachers for the annual Teacher's Choices list were of high literary quality and had accurate and appropriate science content. The Teacher's Choices lists are published annually in the November issue of *The Reading Teacher* and are also available online. Access the most recent Teacher's Choices list and locate several information books. Critique three books according to the criteria in this chapter. Do you agree that the books belong on the list? Why or why not?

## Learn About Authors and Illustrators

4.  Interviews with two prominent children's nonfiction authors, Gail Gibbons and Seymour Simon, are available at the Reading Rockets website. View the videos for both authors. How do these authors make nonfiction interesting and accessible to young children? What insight did you gain about reading, writing, and publishing information texts from viewing these videos?

# Print and Online Resources

## Print Resources

Dorfman, L. & Cappelli, R. (2009). *Nonfiction Mentor Texts: Teaching Informational Writing Through Children's Literature, K-8*. Portland, ME: Stenhouse.

Duke, N., & Bennett-Armistead, S. (2003). *Reading & writing informational text in the primary grades: Researched-based practices*. New York: Scholastic.

Hoyt, L., Mooney, M., & Parkes, B. (2003). *Exploring informational texts: From theory to practice*. Portsmouth, NH: Heinemann.

Moss, B. (2004). Teaching expository text structures through information trade book retellings. *The Reading Teacher, 57*(8), 710–718.

Stead, T. (2006). *Reality checks: Teaching reading comprehension with nonfiction K–5*. Portland, ME: Stenhouse.

Zarnowski, M. (2003). *History makers: A questioning approach to reading & writing biographies*. Portsmouth, NH: Heinemann.

Zarnowski, M. (2006). *Making Sense of History: Using High-Quality Literature and Hands-On Experiences to Build Content Knowledge*. New York: Scholastic.

 **Online Resources**

*100 Best Nonfiction Books, PreK-8*
**http://www.rif.org/educators/books/100_nonfiction .mspx**
Hosted on the Reading Is Fundamental website, this list of 100 Best Nonfiction Books were selected and annotated by Judy Freeman. Judy chose the nonfiction books that have had the most impact on her teaching, have broken new ground, have taught her something extraordinary, and have wowed readers.

*Boston Globe Horn Book Award for Nonfiction*
**http://www.hbook.com/bghb/default.asp**
First presented in 1967 and customarily announced in June, the *Boston Globe*–Horn Book Awards are among the most prestigious honors in the field of children's and young adult literature. Winners are selected in three categories: Picture Book, Fiction and Poetry, and Nonfiction. Two Honor Books may be named in each category. On occasion, a book will receive a special citation for its high quality and overall creative excellence. The winning titles must be published in the United States, but they may be written or illustrated by citizens of any country.

The awards are chosen by an independent panel of three judges who are annually appointed by the editor of the Horn Book.

### INK Think Tank
**http://www.inkthinktank.com**
The INK (Interesting Nonfiction for Kids) Think Tank is composed of a group of talented authors who research and write about nonfiction topics. The INK Think Tank Database is a versatile search engine designed to produce lists of award-winning nonfiction books that give your students all the information required by National Education Standards and the curriculum practices of your school district.

### National Association of Science Teachers: Outstanding Science Trade Books for Students K–12
**http://www.nsta.org/publications/ostb**
Since 1973, the a review panel of the National Science Teachers Association (NSTA) in cooperation with the Children's Book Council (CBC) has selected the Outstanding Science Trade Books for Children. The panel uses rigorous selection guidelines relating to the presentation of material.

### National Council of Teachers of Social Studies Notable Trade Books for Young People
**http://www.socialstudies.org/resources/notable**
The books that appear in these annotated book lists were evaluated and selected by a Book Review Committee appointed by National Council for the Social Studies (NCSS) and assembled in cooperation with the Children's Book Council (CBC). NCSS and CBC have cooperated on this annual bibliography since 1972. Books selected for this bibliography are written primarily for children in grades K–8. The selection committee looks for books that emphasize human relations, represent a diversity of groups and are sensitive to a broad range of cultural experiences, present an original theme or a fresh slant on a traditional topic, are easily readable and of high literary quality, and have a pleasing format and, when appropriate, illustrations that enrich the text.

### Orbis Pictus Nonfiction Award
**http://www.ncte.org/awards/orbispictus**
NCTE, through the Committee on the Orbis Pictus Award for Outstanding Nonfiction for Children, has established an annual award for promoting and recognizing excellence in the writing of nonfiction for children. The name *Orbis Pictus* commemorates the work of Johannes Amos Comenius, *Orbis Pictus—The World in Pictures* (1657), considered to be the first book actually planned for children.

### Robert F. Sibert Informational Book Medal
**http://www.ala.org/ala/mgrps/divs/alsc/ awardsgrants/bookmedia/sibertmedal/index.cfm**
The Robert F. Sibert Informational Book Award, established by the Association for Library Service to Children in 2001, is awarded annually to the author (including coauthors or author/illustrators) of the most distinguished informational book published in English during the preceding year.

Visit the companion website at **www.cengage.com/education/johnson** to find links related to the Read/Watch/Listen icons noted throughout the chapter, as well as additional resources.

## Creating Your Classroom Library

### CHILDREN'S NONFICTION MAGAZINES

*Cobblestone*

*Highlights Magazine*

*Muse*

*National Geographic News for Kids*

*Ranger Rick*

*Sports Illustrated for Kids*

*Time for Kids*

*Zillions*

### CHILDREN'S INFORMATION WEBSITES

*National Geographic Explorer for Kids*
**http://kids.nationalgeographic.com**
*National Geographic Kids*, geared toward readers ages 6 to 14, is an interactive, multitopic magazine covering animals, entertainment, science, technology, current events, and cultures from around the world.

*New York Times Learning Network*
**http://www.nytimes.com/learning**
With news, activities, and lesson plans for grades 3 through high school, the New York Times Learning Network really does have something for everyone. Includes news summaries, a daily news quiz, an interactive crossword puzzle with educational Web links, Word of the Day, and On This Day.

*Scholastic News for Kids*
**http://teacher.scholastic.com/scholasticnews**
Junior Scholastic Online combines original reporting with an interactive news quiz (ten multiple-choice questions about the week's current events), a NewsZone RealAudio Radio broadcast, and an opinion poll. Some of the content is only for Junior Scholastic print subscribers.

*Sports Illustrated for Kids*
**http://www.sikids.com**
SIKids.com is the online counterpart to *Sports Illustrated for Kids* magazine with the purpose of creating a fun, safe environment for kids, filled with news, games, and interactive features on the Internet.

*Time for Kids*
**http://www.timeforkids.com**
Timeforkids.com, the online version of *Time for Kids* magazine, is the news, homework helper, and exploration destination for kids on the Internet. The site keeps kids on top of the news and lets them create, learn, get involved, explore, play games, and access tools to help with homework.

## INFORMATIONAL BOOKS

*Children of the Great Depression* by Russell Freedman (2005, Houghton Mifflin). Life was hard for children during the Great Depression: kids had to do without new clothes, shoes, or toys, and many couldn't attend school because they had to work. Even so, life still had its bright spots. Take a closer look at the lives of young Americans during this era.

*ER Vets: Life in an Animal Emergency Room* by Donna Jackson (2005, Houghton Mifflin). Witness the excitement and drama of life in an animal emergency room as the ER vets work to heal the creatures we consider part of our families.

*George vs. George: The American Revolution as Seen from Both Sides* by Rosalyn Schanzer (2004, National Geographic). Explores how the characters and lives of King George III of England and George Washington affected the progress and outcome of the American Revolution.

*How Many Baby Pandas?* by Sandra Markle (2009, Walker). Looks at the eight panda pairs that were born at China's Wolong Giant Panda Breeding and Research Center in 2005, examining how they live, grow, and play and the steps that are being taken to prepare them for their release into the wild.

*I Face the Wind* by Vicki Cobb, illustrated by Julia Gorton (2003, HarperCollins). Introduces the characteristics and actions of the wind through simple hands-on activities.

*I See a Kookaburra!* by Steve Jenkins and Robin Page (2005, Houghton Mifflin). Learn how many animals grow and thrive in very different environments.

*Mapping the World* by Sylvia Johnson (1999, Atheneum). A history of mapmaking showing how maps both reflect and change people's view of the world.

*The Mysterious Universe: Supernovae, Dark Energy, and Black Holes* by Ellen Jackson, photographs by Nic Bishop (2008, Houghton Mifflin). Follows scientist Alex Filippenko and the High-Z Supernova Search Team in their work to search for supernovae and dark energy.

*The Prairie Builders: Reconstructing America's Lost Grasslands* by Sneed Collard III (2005, Houghton Mifflin). Join the scientists working in the Neal Smith National Wildlife Refuge as they work to rebuild the tallgrass prairie that once covered much of the Midwest and restore the native plants and animals to the region.

*Ready Set Grow!* (2010, DK). Step-by-step photographs show young gardeners how to grow plants from seed, how to propagate plants, when to harvest seeds, how long different plants take to grow, what to do about pests, and much more.

*Secrets of the Sphinx* by James Giblin, illustrations by Bargram Ibatoulline (2004, Scholastic). Discusses some of Egypt's most famous artifacts and monuments, including the pyramids, the Rosetta Stone, and, especially, the Great Sphinx, presenting research and speculation about their origins and their future.

*Starry Messenger: Galileo Galilei* by Peter Sis (1996, Farrar, Straus and Giroux). Describes the life and work of the courageous man who changed the way people saw the galaxy by offering objective evidence that the earth was not the fixed center of the universe.

*Surprising Sharks* by Nicola Davies, illustrated by James Croft (2003, Candlewick). Introduces many different species of sharks, pointing out such characteristics as the small size of the dwarf lantern shark and the physical characteristics and behavior that makes sharks killing machines.

*Wild and Swampy* by Jim Arnosky (2000, HarperCollins). Describes and portrays the birds, snakes, and other animals that can be seen in a swamp.

## SERIES INFORMATIONAL BOOKS

### Younger Readers

*A Child's Day* by various authors, published by Benchmark

*All About . . .* by various authors, published by Scholastic

*Eyewitness Juniors* by various authors, published by Knopf

*First Step* by various authors, published by Lerner

*Let's-Read-and-Find-Out Science* by various authors, published by Scholastic

*Nic Bishop* by Nic Bishop, published by Scholastic

*Postcards from . . .* by various authors, published by Steck-Vaughn

*Read and Wonder* by various authors, published by Candlewick

*Rookie Read-About* by various authors, published by Children's Press

*See More Readers* by Seymour Simon, published by Scholastic

*Watch Me Grow* by various authors, published by DK

### Older Readers

*Animal Predators* by Sandra Markle, published by Carolrhoda

*Careers in Search and Rescue Operations* by various authors, published by Rosen

*Coming to America* by various authors, published by Barron's

*Crossroads America* by various authors, published by National Geographic

*Earthworks* by Roy A. Gallant, published by Benchmark

*Environmental Disasters* by various authors, published by World Almanac

*From Sea to Shining Sea* by various authors, published by Children's Press

*Holocaust in History* by various authors, published by Enslow

*The Human Body* by various authors, published by Child's World

*Journey to Freedom: The African American Library* by various authors, published by Child's World

*Life Balance* by various authors, published by Franklin Watts

*Mighty Math* by various authors, published by Child's World

*People of the Ancient World* by various authors, published by Franklin Watts

*Science on the Edge* by various authors, published by Gale/Blackbirch

*Scientist in the Field* by various authors, published by Houghton Mifflin

*True Books* by various authors, published by Children's Press

*Voyages through Time* by Peter Ackroyd, published by DK

## BIOGRAPHY

*Bad News for Outlaws: The Remarkable Life of Bass Reeves, Deputy U. S. Marshal* by Vaunda Nelson; illustrations by R. Gregory Christie (2009, Lerner). This biography profiles the life of Bass Reeves, a former slave who was recruited as a deputy United States Marshal in the area that was to become Oklahoma.

*Blockhead: The Life of Fibonacci* by Joseph D'Agnese, illustrated by John O'Brien (2010, Holt). The entertaining biography of medieval mathematician Leonardo Fibonacci.

*The Boy Who Invented TV: The Story of Philo Farnsworth* by Kathleen Krull, illustrated by Greg Couch (2009,

Knopf). This picture-book biography explains how Farnsworth held on to his dream to develop television and the scientific concepts behind it.

*The Dinosaurs of Waterhouse Hawkins: An Illuminating History of Mr. Waterhouse Hawkins, Artist and Lecturer* by Barbara Kerley (2001, Scholastic). The true story of Victorian artist Benjamin Waterhouse Hawkins, who built life-sized models of dinosaurs in the hope of educating the world about these awe-inspiring ancient animals and what they were like.

*Good Brother, Bad Brother: The Story of Edwin Booth and John Wilkes Booth* by James Giblin (2005, Houghton Mifflin). Most people know the name John Wilkes Booth, but few likely have heard of his elder brother Edwin. Find out about the brothers through firsthand accounts. Learn how alike and how different they were, and how each made a lasting impression on American history.

*The Life and Death of Crazy Horse* by Russell Freedman, illustrated by Amos Bad Heart Bull (1996, Holiday House). A biography of the Oglala leader who relentlessly resisted the white man's attempt to take over Indian lands.

*Lincoln Tells a Joke: How Laughter Saved the President (and the Country)* by Kathleen Krull and Paul Brewer, illustrated by Stacy Innerst (2010, Harcourt). This unusual biography of Lincoln highlights his life and presidency while focusing on what made Lincoln's sense of humor so distinctive—and so necessary to surviving his tough life and time.

*Sir Walter Ralegh and the Quest for El Dorado* by Marc Aronson (2000, Houghton Mifflin). Recounts the adventurous life of the English explorer and courtier who spelled his name "Ralegh" and led many expeditions to the New World.

*Wangari's Trees of Peace: A True Story from Africa* by Jeanette Winter (2008, Harcourt). This true story of Wangari Maathai, environmentalist and winner of the Nobel Peace Prize, is a shining example of how one woman's passion, vision, and determination inspired great change.

*We Are the Ship: The Story of Negro League Baseball* by Kadir Nelson (2008, Hyperion). Using an "Everyman" player as his narrator, Kadir Nelson tells the story of Negro League baseball from its beginnings in the 1920s through the decline after Jackie Robinson crossed over to the majors in 1947.

## COLLECTIVE BIOGRAPHIES

*50 American Heroes Every Kid Should Meet* by Dennis Denenberg, illustrated by Lorraine Roscoe (2001, Millbrook Press). A compilation of short biographies of men and women from different eras, professions, and ethnic backgrounds. The alphabetically arranged, double-page entries include expected names, such as Mary McLeod Bethune, Thomas Jefferson, and Harriet Tubman, as well as the unexpected, such as Martha Graham, Yo-Yo Ma, and Cal Ripken Jr., with justification by the authors.

*Guide to Collective Biographies for Children and Young Adults* by Sue Barancik (2004, Scarecrow Press). This text indexes 721 titles for children and young adults to provide access to 5,760 notable individuals from early to modern times. All of the referenced titles were published between 1988 and 2002.

*Victory or Death: Stories of the American Revolution* by Doreen Rappaport and Joan Verniero (2003, HarperCollins). Inspiring stories about lives of people—famous and unknown—who took part in the fight for independence.

## SERIES BIOGRAPHIES

### Younger Readers

*First Biographies* by various authors, published by Pebble Press

*Life and Work of . . .* by various authors, published by Heinemann

*On My Own Biographies* by various authors, published by Carolrhoda

*Picture Book Biographies* by David Adler, published by Holiday House

*Rookie Biographies* by various authors, published by Children's Press

*Scholastic Biographies* by various authors, published by Scholastic

## OLDER READERS

*Childhood of Famous Americans* by various authors, published by Aladdin

*Civil War Library* by various authors, published by Enslow

*Dell Yearling Biography* by various authors, published by Yearling

*DK Biography* by various authors, published by DK

*Giants of Science* by various authors, published by Viking

*Historical American Biographies* by various authors, published by Enslow

*Matt Christopher Sports Biographies* by Matt Christopher, published by Little, Brown

*Milton Meltzer Biographies* by Milton Meltzer, published by Franklin Watts

*National Geographic World History Biographies* by various authors, published by National Geographic

*Sports Achievers Biographies* by various authors, published by Lerner

*Time for Kids Historical Biographies* by various authors, published by Harper Trophy

*Who Was . . . ? Historical Biographies* by various authors, published by Grossett and Dunlap

# References

Broemmel, A., & Rearden, K. (2006). Should teachers use the Teachers' Choices books in science classes? *The Reading Teacher, 60*(3), 254–265.

Brozo, W. (2002). *To be a boy, to be a reader.* Newark, DE: International Reading Association.

Burleigh, R. (1998). *Black whiteness: Admiral Byrd alone in the Antarctic.* New York: Atheneum.

Carter, B. (2000). A universe of information: The future of nonfiction. *The Horn Book Magazine, 76*(6), 697–707.

Carter, B. (2003). Reviewing biography. *The Horn Book Magazine, 79*(2), 165–175.

Caswell, L., & Duke, N. (1998). Non-narrative as catalyst for literacy development. *Language Arts, 75*(2), 108–117.

Chall, J., Jacobs, V., & Baldwin, L. (1990). *The reading crisis: Why poor children fall behind.* Cambridge, MA: Harvard University Press.

Coles, M., & Hall, C. (2001). Boys, books and breaking boundaries: Developing literacy in and out of school. In W. Martino & B. Meyenn (Eds.), *What about the boys? Issues of masculinity in schools* (pp. 211–221). Buckingham, UK: Open University Press.

Davila, D., & Patrick, L. (2010). Asking the experts: What children have to say about their reading preferences. *Langague Arts, 87*(3), 199-210.

Devereaux, E. (1996). Diane Stanley: Illustrating a life. *Publishers Weekly, 243*(30), 216–217.

Donovan, C., & Smolkin, L. (2001). Genre and other factors influencing teachers' book selections for science instruction. *Reading Research Quarterly, 36,* 412–440.

Dooley, P. (1991). Brother Eagle, Sister Sky. *School Library Journal, 37*(9), 228.

Dreher, M. (2000). Fostering reading for learning. In L. Baker, M. Hreher, & J. Guthrie (Eds.), *Engaging young readers: Promoting achievement and motivation* (pp. 94–118). New York: Guilford.

Duke, N. (2000). 3.6 minutes per day: The scarcity of informational texts in first grade. *Reading Research Quarterly, 35*(2), 202–224.

Duke, N. (2003a). Reading to learn from the very beginning: Informational literacy in early childhood. *Young Children, 58*(2), 14–20.

Duke, N. (2003b). Bringing informational texts into focus. In L. Hoyt, M. Mooney, & B. Parkes (Eds.), *Exploring informational texts: From theory to practice* (pp. 1–7). Portsmouth, NH: Heinemann.

Duke, N. (2004). The case for informational text. *Educational Leadership, 61*(6), 40–44.

Duke, N., Bennett-Armistead, V., & Roberts, E. (2002). Incorporating information text in the primary grades. In C. Roller (Ed.), *Comprehensive reading instruction across the grade levels.* Newark, DE: International Reading Association.

Duke, N., & Pearson, P. D. (2002). Effective practices for developing reading comprehension. In A. Farstrup & S. J. Samuels (Eds.), *What research has to say about reading instruction* (3rd ed.). Newark, DE: International Reading Association.

Fredrick, H. (2002). PW talks with James Cross Giblin. *Publishers Weekly, 249*(13), 84.

Freedman, R. (1992). Fact or fiction? In E. Freeman & D. Person (Eds.), *Using nonfiction trade books in the elementary classroom: From ants to zeppelins.* Urbana, IL: National Council of Teachers of English.

Freedman, R. (2004). *The voice that challenged a nation: Marian Anderson and the struggle for equal rights.* Boston: Houghton Mifflin.

Fritz, J. (1982). *Homesick: My own story.* New York: Putnam.

Gibbons, G. (1994). *Nature's green umbrella: Tropical rain forests.* New York: Morrow.

Giles, C., & Pierce, K. (2001). Pairing fact and fiction for deep understanding. *Language Arts, 78*(6), 579–588.

Gill, S. (2010). What teachers need to know about the "new" nonfiction. *The Reading Teacher, 63*(4), 260–267.

Jensen, J. (2001). The quality of prose in Orbis Pictus Award books. In M. Zarnowski, R. Kerper, & J. Jensen (Eds.), *The best in children's nonfiction: Reading, writing, & teaching Orbis Pictus Award books* (pp. 3–12). Urbana, IL: National Council of Teachers of English.

Levine, E. (2000). *Darkness over Denmark: The Danish resistance and the rescue of the Jews.* New York: Holiday House.

Meltzer, M. (1993). Voices from the past. In M. Tunnell & R. Ammon (Eds.), *The story of ourselves: Teaching history through children's literature.* Portsmouth, NH: Heinemann.

Mohr, K. (2006). Children's choices for recreational reading: A three-part investigation of selection preferences, rationales, and processes. *Journal of Literacy Research, 38*(1), 81–104.

Moss, B. (2003). *Exploring the literature of fact: Children's nonfiction trade books in the elementary classroom.* New York: Guilford.

Murphy, P., & Elwood, J. (1998). Failing boys. In D. Epstein, J. Ellwood, V. Hey, & J. Maw (Eds.), *Failing boys: Issues in gender and achievement.* Buckingham, UK: Open University Press.

Ogle, D. (1986). KWL: A teaching model that develops active reading of expository text. *The Reading Teacher, 39,* 563–570.

Palincsar, A., & Duke, N. (2004). The role of text and text-reader interactions in young children's reading development and achievement. *The Elementary School Journal, 105*(2), 183–197.

Rice, D. (2002). Using trade books in teaching elementary science: Facts and fallacies. *The Reading Teacher, 55*(6), 552–565.

Routman, R. (2008). *Teaching essentials.* Portsmouth, NH: Heinemann.

Smith, M., & Wilhelm, J. (2004). "I just like being good at it": The importance of competence in the literate lives of young men. *Journal of Adolescent & Adult Literacy, 47*(6), 454–461.

Stead, T. (2006). *Reality checks: Teaching reading comprehension with n-onfiction K–5.* Portland, ME: Stenhouse.

Sutton, R. (2002). An interview with Russell Freedman. *The Horn Book Magazine, 78*(6), 695–704.

Taylor, D. (2005). "Not just boring stories": Reconsidering the gender gap for boys. *Journal of Adolescent & Adult Literacy, 48*(6), 290–298.

Vardell, S. (1991). A new 'picture of the world': The NCTE Orbis Pictus Award for outstanding nonfiction for children. *Language Arts, 68*(6), 474–479.

Walker, C., Kragler, S., Martin, L., & Arnett, A. (2003). Facilitating the use of informational texts in a 1st-grade classroom. *Childhood Education, 79*(3), 152–159.

Webb, S. (2000). *My season with penguins: An Antarctic journal.* Boston: Houghton Mifflin.

# 11 Diverse Perspectives in Children's Literature

> I write because our lives are stories. If enough of those stories are told, then perhaps we will begin to see that our lives are the same. The differences are merely in the details.
>
> *Julius Lester, 2005*

In Chapter 2, multicultural literature is defined as "a group of works used to break the monopoly of the mainstream culture and make the curriculum pluralistic" (Cai, 2002, p. 4). Nieto (2000) defines culture as "the values, traditions, social and political relationships, and worldview created, shared, and transformed by a group of people bound together by a common history, geographic location, language, social class, and/or religion, and how these are transformed by those who share them" (p. 138). Inherent in this definition of *culture* is a range of perspectives that have traditionally been marginalized due to race, gender, ethnicity, language, exceptionality, age, social class, religion, or sexual orientation. The definition does not include international literature, which deals with world cultures outside of the United States and will be discussed later in this chapter.

*Today, there is more high-quality* multicultural children's literature available than ever before, but we still have a long way to go. It is essential for educators to understand the importance of including multicultural literature in the curriculum and to be able to select and recommend high-quality multicultural literature for children. This chapter is not intended to isolate the literature of diverse cultures from other literature discussed in this book. Indeed, many multicultural books have been discussed in the previous chapters but were evaluated primarily on the basis of genre criteria. The purpose of a separate chapter on multicultural literature is to examine more closely the quality of cultural content.

*Julius Lester tells his own story in a light and engaging tone, allowing the reader to think about differences. Lester points out, "Beneath everyone's skin are the same hard bones."*

*Watch*

*Watch a video of Julius Lester discuss literary point of view as a sacred trust between the writer and reader.*

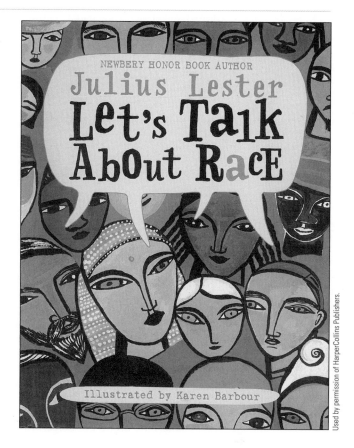

Used by permission of HarperCollins Publishers.

# The Books: Multicultural Children's Literature

*In truth, everything in my life in 1951 that was personal and had value was white. All the authors I studied, all the historical figures, with the exception of George Washington Carver, and all those figures I looked upon as having importance were white men. I didn't mind that they were men, or even white men. What I did mind was that being white seemed to play so important a part in the assigning of values. I knew that the vague thought I had had earlier, that goodness and intelligence could somehow lift a person above the idea of race, was wrong. I wondered where and how I would fit into a society that basically didn't like me.*

WALTER DEAN MYERS, 2001, P. 113

This poignant excerpt from *Bad Boy: A Memoir* by Walter Dean Myers gives the reader insight into a 15-year-old Myers's growing awareness of racism and his own identity as a black man. In the 1940s and 1950s diverse literature for children and young adults—literature that was not exclusively about white culture—was almost nonexistent.

Yet, Myers's passion for reading eventually led him to read more, and he found a few books that offered perspectives on different types of people. Myers writes the following:

> *The Gay Genius* by Lin Yutang told the story of Su Tung Po, the Chinese poet, artist, philosopher, and civil servant. What attracted me especially to the book was that the poet rose through the ranks of civil servant by taking tests and was appreciated as a poet at the same time that he was a civil servant. Race was taken out of the equation. It seemed a civilized way of conducting one's life. (p. 125)

*Watch*

*Watch a video of Walter Dean Myers discussing his journey to becoming an author.*

Walter Dean Myers went on to become a proliferate award-winning author and has written many books in which children and young adults see a more diverse portrait. They see people like themselves facing challenges and solving problems.

## THE NEED FOR MORE MULTICULTURAL LITERATURE

In an interview (Day, 2006), Francisco Jiménez, author of *The Circuit: Stories from the Life of a Migrant Child* (1997) and *Breaking Through* (2001), stated that he "believes it is extremely valuable to document the Mexican-American experience, knowing that when we read about the various experiences of ethnic groups in our multicultural society, we better understand who the United States is as a nation" (p. 269). Yet, in a recent synthesis of research on Hispanic portrayal in children's literature from 1966 to 2003, Nilsson (2005) found that although improvements have been made in a greater number of books with Hispanic characters and themes, "compared to the proportion of Hispanics who presently make up the United States population, there is indication that the relative proportion of Hispanic representation in children's literature has lost major ground" (p. 545). In fact, since 2002 a steady decline in the number of books published in the United States for children each year by and about people of color has been documented by the Cooperative Children's Book Center (Horning, Lindgren, Rudiger, & Schiliesman, 2006). Efforts have been made in recent years to increase the publication and recognition that multicultural children's literature deserves.

## PUBLISHERS AND AWARDS IN MULTICULTURAL LITERATURE

Many large publishing houses have established imprints devoted exclusively to publishing multicultural titles, such as *Jump at the Sun,* an imprint of Hyperion, which was launched by notable African-American children's author Andrea Davis Pinkney. Independent publishers such as Lee & Low that focus specifically on multicultural literature have also increased. Founded in 1991 by Tom Low and Philip Lee, both Chinese Americans, Lee & Low is one of the few minority-owned publishing companies in the country. "When we started the company, there was a lot of interest in multicultural books," says Tom Low, "but most of the titles were folktales about exotic people from distant lands. We felt strongly that it was important to have books with a contemporary setting that reflects how we live today" (http://www.leeandlow.com).

Several awards for multicultural children's literature have been established to highlight outstanding books and their creators:

- The American Library Association bestows several awards, including the Coretta Scott King Award "given to an African-American author and an African-American illustrator for an outstandingly inspirational and educational contribution. The books promote understanding and appreciation of the culture of all peoples and their contribution to the realization of the American dream."

- The Pura Belpré Medal is presented to a "Latino/Latina writer and illustrator whose work best portrays, affirms, and celebrates the Latino cultural experience in an outstanding work of literature for children and youth."
- The Schneider Family Book Awards honor an author or illustrator for a book that "embodies an artistic expression of the disability experience for child and adolescent audiences." Three annual awards are given in these categories: birth through grade school (ages birth–10), middle school (ages 11–13) and teens (ages 13–18).
- The Tomás Rivera Mexican American Children's Book Award, bestowed by Texas State University at San Marcos, is given annually to an author/illustrator that aesthetically reflects the lives of Mexican-American children and young adults in the southwestern United States.
- The Américas Book Award for Children's and Young Adult Literature, sponsored by the National Consortium of Latin American Studies Programs housed at the University of Wisconsin, is given annually to books published in English or Spanish that portray Latin America, the Caribbean, or Latinos in the United States authentically and engagingly.
- The Asian Pacific American Literary Award is given by the National Conference on Asian Pacific American Librarians every three years to Asian Pacific American writers in three categories, one of which is literature for children and young adults.
- Lambda Literary Award in the category of children's and young adult literature seeks to recognize excellence in the field of lesbian, gay, bisexual, and transgender literature.
- Ezra Jack Keats Awards recognize excellence in children's literature by new authors and illustrators, who, like the late author/illustrator Ezra Jack Keats, offer fresh and positive views of the multicultural world inhabited by children today.

Descriptions and links to the websites for these awards are provided in the Online Resources at the end of this chapter.

Although the numbers of multicultural books recently published has declined slightly, the overall number of books published in the last decade far exceeds that of any previous decade. Still, we must become advocates for high-quality multicultural literature by challenging publishing houses to increase the number of titles published each year.

The awards listed here are one way to find quality multicultural literature for children. Many teachers and librarians consult professional journals and magazines, such as *Horn Book Magazine, Publishers Weekly,* and *School Library Journal,* that publish reviews of books to select multicultural books for classroom use. We must encourage these sources not only to include more reviews of multicultural literature but to ensure that reviewers hold authors to high standards of accuracy and authenticity. Teachers and librarians must have excellent multicultural books from which to choose along with an ongoing obligation to share these books with children.

## The Child: What Does Diversity Mean?

The ability to see other cultures and life experiences is important in developing children's perspective, insight, and possibilities as they progress to becoming citizens of the world. And children need to see their own cultures and values reflected in the books they read. The following characteristics of the current population provide some insight into the diversity of the United States today.

## DIVERSITY IN CULTURE, LANGUAGE, AND RELIGION

According to the U.S. Census Bureau (2001), the population of the United States grew by 32.7 million people between 1990 and 2000, the largest census-to-census increase in history. The greatest percentage of growth in the population was in cultural groups other than European American:

- People of color (a collective term for people of African-American, Latino, Asian-American and American Indian backgrounds) currently constitute 25 percent of the population, but as we move further into the twenty-first century, they will comprise one-third of the population.
- Forty percent of children under the age of 18 are members of cultural groups other than European American.
- Twenty-seven percent of the population has a religious affiliation other than Christianity.
- Eighteen percent of children under the age of 18 live in homes where English is not spoken (U.S. Census Bureau, 2004).

## DIVERSITY IN SOCIAL CLASS, AGE, EXCEPTIONALITY, AND FAMILY STRUCTURE

Classrooms across the country represent small microcosms of the population. Although some states and regions, such as Texas, New Mexico, Florida, California, and Arizona, have higher proportions of certain cultural groups, all classrooms reflect the diversity in the population to some degree. One of our country's strengths is its diversity, and it should be celebrated. Yet, an increase in the diversity of other characteristics of the population shows some of the problems our culture must resolve:

- Twenty-six percent of the population is under the age of 18, the second largest age group in the United States. Twelve percent of the population is over the age of 65, the smallest age group in the United States. The discrepancy between the sizes of these two populations increases the likelihood that children and young adults do not understand the social and economic issues facing the elderly.
- Seventeen percent of children under the age of 18 live in poverty.
- Thirty-two percent live with a single or adoptive parent or unrelated caregiver.
- Forty-seven percent moved one or more times in the last five years.
- Six percent have a physical or mental disability (U.S. Census Bureau, 2004).

## EDUCATING ALL CHILDREN

Unfortunately, these characteristics can predict high percentages of academic failure. A recent longitudinal study by the National Center for Educational Statistics (NCES, 2006) followed 22,782 children from 944 schools across the United States from kindergarten through fifth grade from 1998 to 2004. The study collected descriptive statistics and test score data in the areas of reading, math, and science, and came up with the following findings:

- Children who live in poverty scored lower than students at or above the poverty level.
- Students living in single-parent families were less likely to score in the top third than those in two-parent families.
- Students whose primary home language is English outperformed those whose home language was not English.

- African-American students scored lower than students in other cultural groups.
- Boys scored higher than girls in the areas of math and science.
- Students who changed schools three or more times over the course of the study were less likely to score in the top third than students who moved two or fewer times.

Without successful intervention, these children are at risk of failure. This is a staggering reality that no school or educator can ignore: *We are failing to educate students from diverse backgrounds in our school systems.*

The implication of such failure is what Barr and Parrett (2001) call an "apartheid of ignorance"—"a tragic separation in our society between those who are educated and those who are not" (p. 9). They go on to emphasize, "Those who have a formal education can obtain the economic opportunities that surround them and can access the continuing education that is needed to keep pace with the ever changing technological world. Without education the door is slammed shut" (p. 9). Au (2006) posits five major explanations supported by research for the lack of school success experienced by many students of diverse backgrounds:

*Watch*

*Watch a video of Kathy Au on closing the literary achievement gap.*

1. **Discrimination:** The instruction students of diverse backgrounds receive is qualitatively different from that of other students. Students of diverse backgrounds are disproportionately placed in special education programs; are more likely to be in low reading groups or pulled from class for remedial reading; and are more likely to be retained, suspended, or expelled.
2. **Inferior education:** Urban schools with a high proportion of students of diverse backgrounds and low-income students have deteriorating buildings, outdated textbooks, inexperienced teachers, surroundings that expose students to violence, less time to spend on reading instruction, and testing practices that limit students' opportunities to learn.
3. **Linguistic differences:** Many schools give low status to the home language by excluding or limiting the use of instruction in the home language in many school programs.
4. **Cultural differences:** Students have difficulty learning in school because instruction does not follow their community's values and standards for behavior.
5. **Higher-level thinking:** Without realizing it, teachers may subconsciously absorb long-standing stereotypes that lead them to expect a lower level of academic performance from students of diverse backgrounds (pp. 19–31).

Public schools in the United States have demonstrated, at best, only isolated, marginal success with children of diverse cultural and social backgrounds at risk of failure. Barr and Parrett (2001) assert, "The tragedy of the apartheid of ignorance is that education research has documented and demonstrated that everyone can learn effectively, especially if the efforts start early and if schools and communities have the *will* to make it happen" (p. 9).

## ACKNOWLEDGING AND ACCEPTING MULTICULTURAL DIVERSITY

Programs and practices that discriminate against at-risk children must be eliminated, and ineffective traditional teaching and learning approaches must be redesigned and restructured. Au (1998) proposes that schools assume a diverse constructivist orientation that "attempts to look at how schools devalue and could revalue the cultural capital of students of diverse backgrounds" (p. 306). Au also suggests that educators look at the power relations between teachers and students that privilege mainstream knowledge over that of students of diverse backgrounds. Nieto (1996) maintains that in our pluralistic society, "students of all backgrounds, languages, and experiences need to be acknowledged, valued, and used as important sources of their education" (p. 8). Educators must inquire into the ways knowledge is related to cultural identity and shaped by ethnicity, primary language, and social class. Eighty-three percent of teachers are European Americans from middle-class backgrounds, and 75 percent are female (see Figure 11.1). The experiences students bring to literacy events may be significantly different from educators' experiences and expectations. Au (1998) asserts, "The revaluing process includes teachers' acceptance of students as cultural beings. It also encompasses the manner in which teachers receive and extend students' literacy efforts and encourage students to interact with peers and with texts" (p. 306).

**FIGURE 11.1**

The Case for Multicultural Education and Diverse Perspectives in Literature

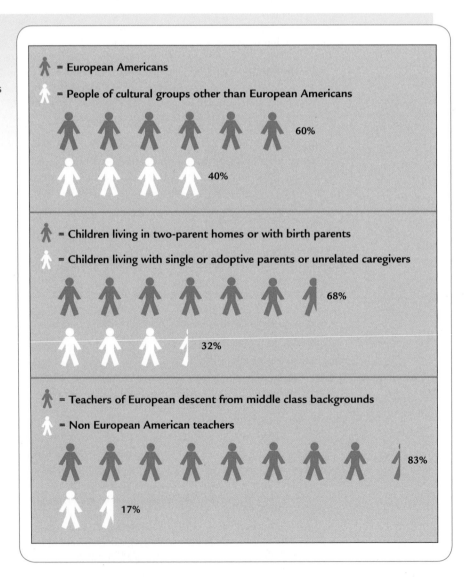

# Benefits and Considerations of Multicultural Literature

Research has shown that the use of multicultural literature that accurately depicts the experiences of diverse groups may improve the literacy achievement of students of diverse backgrounds by increasing their motivation to read, their appreciation and understanding of their own language and cultural heritage, their respect for their own life experience as a topic for writing, and cross-cultural understanding (Amour, 2003; Au, 1998; DeNicolo & Franquiz, 2006; Jordan, 1988; Lee, 1991; Louie, 2006; Spears-Bunton, 1990).

## BENEFITS

Rudine Sims Bishop (2007), noted African-American professor of children's literature, uses the metaphor of multicultural literature serving as a mirror and a window for the reader. As a mirror, it shows children reflections of themselves; as a window, it shows them what other people are like. Multicultural literature helps children to see themselves reflected in stories, and it shows them how people unlike them feel, think, and live. There are many benefits to using multicultural literature in the classroom:

- It provides enjoyment of quality literature that meets the criteria of literary and artistic merit.
- It presents information and knowledge about the historical and continuing contributions of the people of diverse cultures who live in the United States.
- It connects children to the world by exposing them to diverse viewpoints other than the mainstream.
- It fosters awareness, appreciation, and understanding of people who are different from and similar to themselves.
- It promotes critical inquiry into issues of equal representation of how people of diverse cultures are depicted in all books.

Quality multicultural literature can play an important role in providing vicarious experiences in relating to and understanding others—whether they are like ourselves or very different.

# Special Topic: Sharing "Risky" Books

Every book written for children represents a set of beliefs and values, most being that of the European-American mainstream. It makes sense that since most teachers are European Americans, they would naturally select books that represent their mainstream beliefs. Research supports the fact that many teachers are hesitant, if not completely unwilling, to share multicultural books with children, especially those considered controversial (Bonilla, 1998; Stallworth, Gibbons, & Fauber, 2006; Williams, 2002). A study of teachers' perspectives on using multicultural literature by Stallworth, Gibbons, and Fauber (2006) found that fear of censorship, lack of resources, lack of expertise, and time constraints due to mandates, standards, and high-stakes testing were the reasons teachers cited most as to why they do not include multicultural literature in the English language arts curriculum. Additionally, Bonilla (1998) found that some of her preservice teachers rejected multicultural books that portray racism or sexism because the books failed to represent dominant social values or myths. They believed racism and sexism were identified as a social problem, or they feared such books might frighten or corrupt children. Yet,

Escamilla and Nathenson-Mejía (2003) and Colby and Lyon (2004) found that by asking preservice teachers to examine their own beliefs, heightened awareness and effective practices regarding the use of multicultural children's literature can be achieved.

On the other side of the issue, some parents object to teachers sharing books that are different from the teacher's culture. Parents may feel that because of the teacher's "outsider" status, he or she might not be capable of discussing the cultural experience represented in the books without hurting the children in the class. In her article *Outside Teachers: Children's Literature and Cultural Tension,* Vivian Yenika-Agbaw (2003) states, "Like outsiders who write about cultural experiences they are not necessarily part of, readers sharing stories with children that deal with cultural experiences they are unfamiliar with must be wary of the possibility of misunderstandings, perhaps due to what I'll reluctantly term 'cultural illiteracy'" (p. 7).

The alternative is for teachers and parents to share only those books that fall within their own culture. As Yenika-Agbaw notes, "That would exclude too many voices and experiences, hence depriving our children of the opportunity to understand facets of our humanity" (p. 8). Why should teachers and parents move out of their comfort zone and risk sharing books with children that challenge the status quo or encourage "risky" conversations? Based on my own observations in numerous classrooms, along with those of other researchers (Lewison, Leland, Flint, & Möller, 2002), the reasons for sharing "risky" books are presented in Table 11.1.

Multicultural books with controversial social issues provide opportunities for teachers and children to engage in conversations that explore diversity and difference, to look at perspectives different from our own, and to question our political and democratic suppositions. These conversations are too important to leave outside the classroom door. Gallo (1994) asserts, "If we do not provide our students with a variety of literature—however controversial—and teach them to read it and discuss it critically, we cannot hope that they will ever develop into sensitive, thoughtful, and reasonable adults" (p. 118).

**TABLE 11.1**

# Reasons for Sharing "Risky" Books

1. *It promotes critical thinking:* When children are given the opportunity to read and discuss books about meaningful topics that connect their lives, there is a remarkable level of intellectual engagement that occurs.

2. *Few truly "safe" children's books are available:* Even seemingly innocuous books, such as *Click, Clack, Moo* (Cronin), *The Grouchy Ladybug* (Carle), and *Pinduli* (Cannon), all have underlying themes of power, prejudice, or violence.

3. *It promotes the value of diversity and difference:* Reading books about diverse social issues topics makes it possible for silenced voices to be heard and for multiple perspectives to be explored.

4. *It encourages cross-curricular connections:* Including books about diverse social issues in the social studies curriculum makes it possible for children to acquire a more complex, multifaceted view of the United States.

The reasons that teachers and parents are wary of multicultural books that deal with potentially controversial social issues are complex and deeply ingrained in personal and institutional bias. Teachers and parents should work collaboratively with other people in and out of the school setting to explore culturally sensitive books that are outside their cultural experiences or could stir controversy within particular cultural communities, including the school psychologist, reading specialist, special educator, administrators, parents, other community members, and outside consultants. The importance of communicating with parents cannot be overemphasized. When educators and parents work together, barriers that sometimes create cultural misunderstandings can be broken down. In addition, evaluating books for literary quality and for sexism and racism (see "Evaluating and Selecting Multicultural Literature," page 319) allows teachers and parents to engage in critical conversations that promote cross-cultural understanding. Furthermore, such ongoing dialogue can counter simplistic reform initiatives that do not address the deeply embedded inequalities and complexities of our education systems.

The decision to share "risky" books with children can seem difficult, yet a more complete understanding of the types of quality books available can assist teachers in expanding their repertoire of multicultural children's literature. In the next section, we take a look at the categories of multicultural literature.

## Categories of Multicultural Literature

Although multicultural children's literature crosses all genres (as evidenced by the genre chapters of this book), the purpose of this chapter is to look more closely at the content of multicultural literature. Therefore, multicultural books have been divided into three major categories according to the diverse perspectives they represent: cultural diversity, religious diversity, and other diverse perspectives.

### CULTURAL DIVERSITY

*Little one, whoever you are, wherever you are, there are little ones just like you all over the world. Their lives may be different from yours, and their words may be very different from yours. But inside, their hearts are just like yours.*

MEM FOX, 1997

Table 11.2 presents the literature of the four most predominant cultural groups— African American, Asian American, Latino/Latina American, and American Indian—and examples of notable titles. Obviously, not all books fall neatly into any one category. Arnold Adoff's *Black Is Brown Is Tan,* illustrated by Emily McCully, and Bob Graham's *Oscar's Half Birthday* are two examples of books that depict biracial children.

Of course, it is not enough to count the diverse faces in a book. The significance is in how the members of various cultures are portrayed. The degree of cultural specificity in books varies from merely visual inclusion of diverse faces to books based entirely on specific cultural aspects. Cultural specificity ranges from culturally neutral books to culturally specific:

- **Culturally neutral:** Books that include culturally diverse characters, but the topics of the books are about something else. Example titles include *Brown Bear, Brown Bear What Do You See?* by Bill Martin Jr. and *Can You Top That?* by W. Nikola-Lisa.

**TABLE 11.2**

# Predominant Cultural Groups in the United States and Their Representation in Multicultural Children's Literature

*Watch interviews with many of these authors.*

| Category | Description | Notable Authors |
|---|---|---|
| **African Americans** | African-American children's literature covers a diverse span of time and culture, including slavery and the civil rights movement to the current time period. Includes experiences of the inner city and the middle class. Books are found in all genres. | Eloise Greenfield<br>Virginia Hamilton<br>Walter Dean Myers<br>Jacqueline Woodson<br>Mildred Taylor<br>Patricia and Fred McKissack<br>Julius Lester<br>Leo and Diane Dillon<br>Nikki Grimes<br>Andrea and Jerry Pinkney |
| **Latino/Latina Americans** | Compared to the population, the amount of Latino/Latina literature is quite low, although more books of quality are being published. The body of literature includes a good variety of subcultures. Often contains Spanish vocabulary interspersed throughout the book. Books cross all genres. | Gary Soto<br>Alma Flor Ada<br>Francisco X. Alarcon<br>Rodolfo Anaya<br>Lulu Delacre<br>David Diaz<br>Juan Felipe Herrera<br>Nicholasa Mohr<br>Pat Mora<br>Luis Rodriguez |
| **Asian Americans** | Compared to the population, the number of books is small but increasing. Contains characters from countries including Korea, Taiwan, China, Philippines, Japan, Vietnam, and Hawaii. Books cross all genres. | Allen Say<br>Laurence Yep<br>Janet Wong<br>Linda Sue Park<br>Yoshiko Uchida<br>Ed Young<br>Ken Mochizuki<br>Lensey Namioka<br>Chris Soentpiet<br>Paul Yee |
| **American Indians** | Until the 1970s, portrayals were often inaccurate. Themes include respect for wisdom, patience, harmony with nature, and respect for animals. Books cross all genres. | Joseph Bruchac<br>Michael Dorris<br>Louise Erdrich<br>Michael Arvaarluk Kusagak<br>Michael Lacapa<br>George Little Child<br>Cynthia Leitich Smith<br>Virginia Driving Hawk Sneve<br>Clifford Trafzer (Richard Red Hawk) |

- **Culturally generic:** Books that focus on culturally diverse characters but include few details that differentiate a culture from the larger American culture. Example titles include *Hot Day on Abbott Avenue* by Karen English, *My Best Friend* by Mary Ann Rodman, and *Emma's Rug* by Allen Say.
- **Culturally specific:** Books that incorporate specific, culturally authentic details that define characters, plots, and themes. Example titles include *I Love Saturdays y domingos* by Alma Flor Ada, *Dragonwings* by Laurence Yep, and *Eagle Song* by Joseph Bruchac.

A full range of books that depict diversity is necessary. Books differ in the degree and the specificity of their emphasis and, accordingly, in the cultural understandings that they offer to the reader.

## RELIGIOUS DIVERSITY

*Knowledge about religions is not only characteristic of an educated person, but also is absolutely necessary for understanding and living in a world of diversity.*

NCSS, 1998

The United States is the most religiously diverse country in the world. Classrooms reflect not only children's cultural diversity but also their religious diversity. Green and Oldendorf (2005) write, "If we want children to feel safe and cared for at school and if we want to respect their families' hopes and beliefs, it is important that we know about their deepest convictions and values" (p. 210). Classrooms where religious diversity is honored help children develop and preserve their cultural identity and their understanding of history, literature, art, and music.

Although many teachers believe they should respect their students' diverse religious traditions, they may not think they can teach about religions, or they may feel uncomfortable teaching about religions different from their own. Green and Oldendorf (2005) state, "Most teachers in the United States accept the principle of separation of church and state and, therefore, find it confusing when they try to determine the content for a curriculum on religious diversity. As a result, some teachers choose not to bring up religion at all" (p. 210). But when teachers omit such literature, it deprives children of the opportunity to learn about religion's impact on society.

In their article *Teaching Religious Diversity Through Children's Literature* (2005), Green and Oldendorf recommend four guidelines for including content about religion:

1. Introduce children to content about religion, rather than about the practice of a particular religion.
2. Include a wide variety of religions in their study.
3. Refrain from promoting or denigrating any religion.
4. Facilitate children's awareness of religious differences, without advocating acceptance of one over another (p. 216).

Table 11.3 describes six of the most predominant religions in the United States beyond Christianity and provides examples of children's literature for each.

*Families around the world celebrate faith in many different ways through praying, singing, learning, helping, caring, and more. "Faith highlights the common threads that bring people together in reverence and joy." With simple text and stunning photographs from many cultures and religious traditions,* Faith *celebrates the ways in which people worship around the globe. Thematically organized back matter gives additional information on common expressions of faith, and a glossary describes particular religions and elements of faith depicted in the book.*

Charlesbridge Publishing.

**TABLE 11.3**

## Predominant Religions in the United States Represented in Multicultural Children's Literature

| Religion | Description | Examples |
|---|---|---|
| **American Indian Spirituality** | American Indian spirituality is not considered a religion in the same sense as other world religions. American Indian beliefs and practices are a fundamental part of who American Indians are. Traditionally, American Indians believe in a deity, either a supreme being or a dual divinity—that is, a Creator and a mythical individual, such as a hero or a trickster. Additionally, there are spirits that control the natural world and may be perceived as one force with the Creator. Most American Indians practice a blend of traditional beliefs and Christianity. | *Native North American Wisdom and Gifts* by Niki Walker and Bobbie Kalman<br><br>*The First Americans: The Story of Where They Came From and Who They Became* by Anthony Aveni<br><br>*Moccasin Thunder: American Indian Stories for Today* by Lori Carlson |

*(continued)*

**TABLE 11.3**
(*continued*)

# Predominant Religions in the United States Represented in Multicultural Children's Literature

| Religion | Description | Examples |
| --- | --- | --- |
| **Hinduism** | Hinduism is one of the world's oldest and most-practiced religions: Hindus believe in many gods and goddesses, of which three predominate: Brahma, the creator; Vishnu, the preserver; and Shiva, who destroys and then regenerates. Three important concepts within Hinduism are dharma, practicing a life of virtue, truthfulness, nonviolence, and patience; karma, the belief that thoughts, words, and actions in this life should be completed without the expectation of a worldly reward; and reincarnation, the belief that following death, the soul is reborn into a new body. Hindus worship at shrines at home and in temples. | *How Ganesh Got His Elephant Head* by Harish Johari and Vatsala Sperling<br><br>*This Is My Faith: Hinduism* by Anita Ganeri<br><br>*The Illustrated Encyclopedia of Hinduism* by James Lochtefeld |
| **Buddhism** | Buddha, meaning Awakened One, does not include belief in a god. Followers believe the teachings of Siddhartha, a Hindu prince who became the Buddha and whose teachings provide guidance for their lives. Through meditation and compassion for others, Buddhists strive to realize that their individual selves are not the focus of attention. Buddhism is based on four noble truths: (1) life inevitably involves suffering, is imperfect, and is unsatisfactory; (2) suffering originates in desire; (3) when desire ends, suffering ends; and (4) humans can end desire and suffering by following the eightfold path, which offers guidance for daily livingdhists worship at shrines at home and in temples. | *The Dalai Lama: A Life of Compassion* by Sheila Rivera<br><br>*Buddha Boy* by Kathe Koja<br><br>*Far Beyond the Garden Gate* by Don Brown<br><br>*The Prince Who Ran Away* by Anne Rockwell |

(*continued*)

Adapted from C. Green & S. Oldendorf (2005). Teaching religious diversity through children's literature. *Childhood Education, 81*(4), 209–218.

**TABLE 11.3**

*(continued)*

# Predominant Religions in the United States Represented in Multicultural Children's Literature

| Religion | Description | Examples |
|---|---|---|
| **Judaism** | Jews believe that God made a covenant with Abraham through which the Jews became "God's chosen people" and agreed to keep the Ten Commandments, which form the core of Jewish values. Prayers are an important part of Jewish life. There are specific prayers for different times of the day, for the Sabbath, and for holy days, as well as individual prayers communicated directly to God. Jews worship in synagogues, and rabbis are the teachers within the Jewish community. | *Hanukkah, Shmanukkah!* by Esmé Codell<br><br>*Wonders and Miracles* by Eric Kimmel<br><br>*Celebrating Passover* by Diane Hoyt-Goldsmith<br><br>*Festival of Lights: The Story of Hanukkah* by Maida Silverman |
| **Islam** | Islam, meaning "full submission," was founded by the prophet Muhammad 1,400 years ago. Muhammad received messages from God that were eventually written down and became the Koran, the sacred Islamic guide to moral and social behavior. Those who practice Islam are known as Muslims, meaning "obedient ones." Two major sects of Islam are the Sunni, who make up about 90 percent of all Muslims, and Shi'ah. Muslims believe in Allah, the all-powerful, and only God, and his prophet Muhammad and pray in mosques. | *Muhammad* by Lisa Bakhtiar<br><br>*Muslim Child: Understanding Islam Through Stories and Poems* by Rukhsana Khan<br><br>*Celebrating Ramadan* by Diane Hoyt-Goldsmith<br><br>*What Will You See Inside a Mosque?* by Rukhsana Khan |

## OTHER DIVERSE PERSPECTIVES

*I'd like to think my books, what they're about, is opening the mind and the heart of the reader, to make the reader more open and compassionate, toward him- or herself and toward other people.*

James Howe (Owens, 2006)

*Listen to an excerpt from books in the* Bunnicula *series.*

James Howe's books—the popular *Bunnicula* series, *The Misfits,* and, most recently, *Totally Joe*—are about learning to accept those who are different from you. Howe states, "I really want kids to think about the assumptions they make. I mean really thinking through issues and asking hard questions" (Owens, 2006).

Literature can play an important role in providing vicarious experience in interacting with others who are like us or very different and provides opportunities for critical conversations in which children think through their own biases, fears, and preconceived or unexamined ideas about diverse issues in our society. Table 11.4 describes some of the diverse perspectives represented in multicultural children's literature. For more in-depth information and book lists for many of the diverse perspectives listed below, see the print resources section at the end of this chapter.

**TABLE 11.4**

## Other Diverse Perspectives Represented in Multicultural Children's Literature

| Perspective | Description | Examples |
|---|---|---|
| **Aging** | Books depicting the elderly in a variety of stages and states of life. Elders should not be portrayed as only senile and close to death but also as intellectually competent, capable, independent, active, vibrant, and engaged individuals who are treated with the dignity and respect they deserve and who also have faws like everyone else. | *Jazzy Miz Mozetta* by Brenda Roberts<br><br>*The Hello, Goodbye Window* by Norton Juster<br><br>*The Old Woman Who Named Things* by Cynthia Rylant<br><br>*Are You Going to Be Good?* by Cari Best<br><br>*Grandfathers: Reminiscences, Poems, Recipes, and Photos of the Keepers of Our Traditions* by Nikki Giovanni |
| **Gender Equity** | Books devoid of stereotypes that have traditionally constrained gender roles in society. Characters should depict males and females as individuals; personalities, achievements, and occupations should be gender free. The language used to designate genders should be equitable. | *Oliver Button Is a Sissy* by Tomie dePaola<br><br>*Let Me Play: The Story of Title IX: The Law That Changed the Future of Girls in America* by Karen Blumenthal<br><br>*100 Things Guys Need to Know* by Bill Zimmerman<br><br>*Boy v. Girl: How Gender Shapes Who We Are, What We Want, and How We Get Along* by George Abrahams and Sheila Ahlbrand |

*(continued)*

**TABLE 11.4**

(*continued*)

# Other Diverse Perspectives Represented in Multicultural Children's Literature

| Perspective | Description | Examples |
|---|---|---|
| **Exceptionalities** | Books portraying characters with physical, mental, or behavioral challenges and giftedness must avoid stereotypes and focus on what they can do. Characters with exceptionalities should be shown in major and minor roles as respected individuals capable of coping with their situation and helping others. | *Out of My Mind* by Sharon Draper *Granny Torrelli Makes Soup* by Sharon Creech<br><br>*Do You Remember the Color Blue? And Other Questions Kids Ask About Blindness* by Sally Alexander *Chang and the Bamboo Flute* by Elizabeth Hill<br><br>*Anything But Typical* by Nora Baskin |
| **Language** | Books written in English and another language or books about people who speak one or more languages other than English. Books must avoid stereotypes in the characters' speech, and the dialogue should sound natural, not forced. Non-English words must be spelled and used correctly. | *Code Talker: A Novel About the Navajo Marines of World War Two* by Joseph Bruchac<br><br>*I Hate English!* by Ellen Levine *Poems to Dream Together/Poemas Para Soñar Juntos* by Francisco X. Alarcón<br><br>*Yum! Yuck! A Foldout Book of People Sounds* by Linda Sue Park |
| **Social Diversity** | Books portraying poverty, low social class, homelessness, illiteracy, or migrant life. It is important for characters and settings to be believable, authentic, and not stereotyped. | *A Chair for My Mother* by Vera B. Williams<br><br>*The Wednesday Surprise* by Eve Bunting<br><br>*The Teddy Bear* by David McPhail *First Day in Grapes* by L. Perez |
| **Family Structures** | Books about a variety of family social structures including adoption (international and intercultural adoption), divorced families, single-parent families, blended families and multiple siblings, foster families, extended families, same-sex parents, and biracial parents. | *Black Is Brown Is Tan* by Arnold Adoff<br><br>*The White Swan Express: A Story About Adoption* by Jean Okimoto and Elaine Aoki<br><br>*Celebrating Families* by Rosemarie Hausherr<br><br>*And Tango Makes Three* by Justin Richardson and Peter Parnell<br><br>*Our Gracie Aunt* by Jacqueline Woodson |

# Evaluating and Selecting Multicultural Literature

Evaluating multicultural children's literature that is outside one's own culture or religion can be a seemingly daunting task. Lack of exposure to information about diverse cultures, religions, and perspectives in elementary and secondary schools and in the teacher preparation programs as well as lack of personal experience may mean that teachers must construct a complex set of new knowledge. Mendoza and Reese (2001) explain, "In the process, they may also need to deconstruct misinformation and biases they have absorbed, which adds an emotional challenge to the problem of finding time to locate and use available resources for helping children learn about other cultures." An individual's level of cultural awareness and understanding will affect how he or she interprets and uses children's literature.

The Council on Interracial Books for Children has published criteria for analyzing children's books for racism and sexism. See Table 11.5 for questions that, according to McLaughlin and DeVoogd (2004), should help teachers and other adults "challenge the text—to see past the literal meaning of the text to examine issues such as what the author wants readers to believe and which gender, ethnic group, or philosophy is focused on in the text and which is missing, discounted, or marginalized" (p. 62). Evaluating literature according to genre criteria without considering cultural and historical accuracy and authenticity can lead to missing important misconceptions or misrepresentations about a cultural or religious group. "Critical multicultural analysis of children's literature equips the reader with strategies to unmask dominant ideologies, integrate what they know about themselves with what they learn about others, and translate their reading and thinking in to social action" (Botelho & Rudman, 2009, p. 9). Challenging the text or reading against the grain can open our eyes to how every text emphasizes certain perspectives while discounting and silencing others. Mendoza and Reese (2001) state the following:

> The point of reading against the grain is not to find "perfect" multicultural books. No such thing exists, nor is it likely that there are any books that are free of ideology. The purpose is to help illuminate the places that bias, stereotypes, and misinformation might be hidden—hidden, perhaps, even from the authors and illustrators who produce the images.

Learning how to recognize quality multicultural literature is an ongoing process that takes time and commitment. According to McLaughlin and DeVoogd (2004), "It is a process that involves learning, understanding, and changing over time. This includes developing theoretical, research, and pedagogical repertoires, changing with time and circumstance, engaging in self critical practices, and remaining open to possibilities" (p. 33). Engaging children in learning to critically analyze books is extremely important and will be discussed later in this chapter.

## CONSIDERATIONS IN SELECTING MULTICULTURAL CHILDREN'S LITERATURE

Multicultural literature that has high literary quality and accurately and authentically reflects cultural, religious, or social groups is at the core of evaluating and selecting books to share with children. Realizing their own deficiencies in cultural awareness, some

Adapted from I. Fountas & G. Pinnell (2001). *Guiding readers and writers*. Portsmouth, NH: Heinemann, p. 407. Fountas and Pinnell adapted the chart from *10 Quick Ways to Analyze Children's Books for Racism and Sexism*, Council on Interracial Books for Children.

**TABLE 11.5**

# Analyzing Children's Books for Racism and Sexism

| What to Do | What to Ask | Probing Questions |
|---|---|---|
| **1. Look at the illustrations.** | • Are there stereotypes or is there tokenism?<br>• How are minority roles depicted? | • Although not always obvious, look for variations that in any way demean or ridicule characters because of their race or sex.<br>• If there are racial minority characters in the illustrations, do they look just like whites except for being tinted or colored in? Do all minority faces look stereotypically alike or are they depicted as genuine individuals with distinctive features?<br>• Do the illustrations depict minorities in subservient and passive roles or in leadership and action roles? Are males the active "doers" and females the inactive observers? |
| **2. Examine the story line.** | • Are white roles and ideas of success the only standards for success?<br>• How are problems of minorities presented and viewed?<br>• Are the causes of poverty and oppression explained?<br>• Is passive acceptance or active resistance encouraged?<br>• Are the achievements of female characters based on initiative or superficial, stereotypic traits? | • Does it take "white" behavior standards for a minority person to "get ahead"?<br>• Is "making it" in the dominant white society projected as the only ideal?<br>• To gain acceptance and approval, do persons of color have to exhibit extraordinary qualities—excel in sports, get all A's, and so on?<br>• In friendships between white and nonwhite children, is the child of color the one who does most of the understanding and forgiving?<br>• Are minority people considered to be "the problem"?<br>• Are the oppressions faced by minorities and women represented as related to social injustice?<br>• Are the reasons for poverty and oppression explained, or are they accepted as inevitable?<br>• Does the story line encourage passive acceptance or active resistance?<br>• Is a particular problem that is faced by a racial minority person or female resolved through the benevolent intervention of a white person or male?<br>• Are the achievements of girls and women based on their own initiative and intelligence, or are they due to their good looks or to their relationships with boys?<br>• Are sex roles incidental or critical to characterization and plot?<br>• Could the same story be told if the sex roles were reversed? |

*(continued)*

**TABLE 11.5**

*(continued)*

# Analyzing Children's Books for Racism and Sexism

| What to Do | What to Ask | Probing Questions |
|---|---|---|
| **3. Look at the characters' lives.** | • Do the lives of people of color represent stereotypes or contrast unfavorably with white norms?<br>• Are the lives of minorities represented in a simplistic way, or do they offer genuine insights? | • Are minority persons and their setting depicted in such a way that they contrast unfavorably with the unstated norm of white middle-class suburbia?<br>• If the minority group in question is depicted as "different," are negative value judgments implied?<br>• Are minorities depicted exclusively in ghettos, barrios, or migrant camps? If the illustrations and text attempt to depict another culture, do they go beyond over-simplifications and offer genuine insight into another lifestyle?<br>• Look for inaccuracy and inappropriateness in the depiction of other cultures.<br>• Watch for instances of the "quaint-natives-in-costume" syndrome (most noticeable in areas like clothing and custom but extending to behavior and personality traits as well). |
| **4. Analyze the relationships between people.** | • Do whites have power and leadership, relegating people of color and females to subordinate roles?<br>• Are the family relationships presented in a stereotypic way?<br>• Is it recognized that societal conditions are among the reasons for family problems and separations? | • Do the whites in the story possess the power, take the leadership, and make the important decisions?<br>• Do racial minorities and females of all races function in essentially supporting roles?<br>• How are family relationships depicted? In black families, is the mother always dominant? In Hispanic families, are there always lots of children?<br>• If the family is separated, are societal conditions—for example, unemployment, poverty—cited among the reasons for the separation? |
| **5. Discover the role of models and heroes.** | • Are people of color depicted as "safe" heroes who avoid conflict with the establishment?<br>• Do minority heroes resemble white heroes?<br>• In whose interests does the hero work?<br>• Are there persons with whom children of color can readily identify with positive results? | • For many years, books showed only "safe" minority heroes—those who avoided serious conflict with the white establishment of their time. Minority groups today are insisting on the right to define their own heroes (of both sexes) based on their own concepts and struggles for justice.<br>• When minority heroes do appear, are they admired for the same qualities that have made white heroes famous or because what they have done has benefited white people?<br>• Are norms established that limit any child's aspirations and self-concept?<br>• What effect can it have on images of the color white as the ultimate in beauty, cleanliness, and virtue and black as evil, dirty, and menacing? |

*(continued)*

**TABLE 11.5**

*(continued)*

# Analyzing Children's Books for Racism and Sexism

| What to Do | What to Ask | Probing Questions |
|---|---|---|
| | • Does the story portray norms that are within the aspirations of children of color?<br>• Does the story portray norms that are within the reach of females who do not conform to stereotyped standards of beauty? | • Does the book counteract or reinforce this positive association with the color white and negative association with black?<br>• What happens to a girl's self-image when she reads that boys perform all of the brave and important deeds? What about a girl's self-esteem if she is not "fair" of skin or slim of body?<br>• In a particular story, is there any character with whom a minority child can readily identify to a positive and constructive end? |
| **6. Consider the author's or illustrator's background and perspective.** | • Is the author or illustrator a member of the group being written about?<br>• If not, what qualifies the author or illustrator to present the subject?<br>• Does the author's perspective substantially weaken or strengthen the value of the work?<br>• Do omissions and distortions directly influence the overall message of the book? | • Analyze the biographical material on the jacket flap or the back of the book. If a story deals with a minority theme, what qualifies the author or illustrator to deal with the subject?<br>• If the author and illustrator are not members of the minority being written about, is their anything in their background that would specifically recommend them as the creators of this book?<br>• No author can be wholly objective. All authors write out of a cultural, as well as a personal context. Children's books in the past have traditionally come from authors who were white and who were members of the middle class, with one result being that a single ethnocentric perspective has dominated children's literature in the United States.<br>• Is the perspective patriarchal or feminist? Is it solely Eurocentric, or do minority cultural perspectives also appear? |
| **7. Look at the language.** | • Are there "loaded" words that have insulting overtones?<br>• Is there sexist language that excludes or diminishes women?<br>• How is the male pronoun used? | • Examples of loaded adjectives (usually racist) are *savage, primitive, lazy, superstitious, treacherous, wily, crafty, inscrutable, docile,* and *backward.*<br>• Look for use of the male pronoun to refer to both males and females. Although the generic use of the word *man* was accepted in the past, its use today is outmoded. The following examples show how sexist language can be avoided: *ancestors* instead of *forefathers; chairperson* instead of *chairman; community* instead of *brotherhood; firefighters* instead of *firemen; manufactured* instead of *manmade; the human family* instead of *the family of man.* |

*(continued)*

**TABLE 11.5**

*(continued)*

# Analyzing Children's Books for Racism and Sexism

| What to Do | What to Ask | Probing Questions |
|---|---|---|
| 8. **Use copyright dates as a warning to examine the book closely.** | • Given the time of writing, indicated by publication, how likely is the book to be overtly racist or sexist? | • Not until the early 1970s has the children's book world begun to even remotely reflect the realities of a multiracial society. The new direction resulted from the emergence of minority authors writing about their own experiences.<br>• Nonsexist books, with rare exceptions, were not published before 1973.<br>• The copyright dates can be a clue as to how likely the book is to be overtly racist or sexist, although a recent copyright date, of course, is no guarantee of a book's relevance or sensitivity.<br>• The copyright date only means the year the book was published. It usually takes about two years from the time a manuscript is submitted to the publisher to the time it is actually printed and put on the market. This time lag meant very little in the past, but in a time of rapid change and changing consciousness, when children's book publishing is attempting to become "relevant," it is becoming increasingly significant. |

teachers may rely on the work of well-known authors and illustrators and reviews of books in journals such as *Horn Book Magazine* and *School Library Journal*. However, there are pitfalls to each of these approaches, as highlighted by Mendoza and Reese (2001) through their comparison of two books about Mexican-American families (Table 11.6). *A Day's Work*, written by the very popular Eve Bunting and illustrated by well-known illustrator Ronald Himler, is compared to *A Gift from Papa Diego*, written by first-time children's author Benjamin Saenz and illustrated by little-known illustrator Geronimo Garcia. As you can see in Table 11.6, very different messages are conveyed in each book. *A Day's Work* is the story of a boy and his grandfather that presents a moral lesson, whereas *A Gift from Papa Diego*, also about a boy and his grandfather, concentrates on the affection and closeness of a particular family.

Both books were given very high reviews by the review journals, and *A Day's Work* was a 1994 Américas Commended Title and a notable children's trade book in the field of social studies. *A Day's Work*, which was published by a large press, has received more recognition than *A Gift from Papa Diego*, which was published by a small press, so public and school libraries and bookstores are more likely to have copies of *A Day's Work* than *A Gift from Papa Diego*.

By comparing *A Day's Work* and *A Gift from Papa Diego* it becomes apparent why no single book can adequately represent any cultural group. All cultural groups consist of a rich tapestry of complex, multifaceted peoples, histories, traditions, and religions. In order to present an accurate, authentic depiction of any culture, teachers must seek out many titles that present an accurate and authentic window and mirror.

**TABLE 11.6**

# Comparison of Two Books About Mexican-American Families

| | A Day's Work | A Gift from Papa Diego |
|---|---|---|
| **Content** | Children who look at the pages in this book see Mexican Americans who do the following:<br>• Wait for work<br>• Scramble for work<br>• Lie to get work<br>• Push others out of the way to get work<br>• Work close to an area of high-priced homes<br>• Work hard and make a serious mistake<br>• Rest after working, not knowing they have made the mistake<br>• Are scolded by an employer<br>• Feel ashamed, dismayed, at fault<br>• Seek to correct the mistake<br>• Face the consequences of their actions, thereby winning the employer's respect<br>• Are at a disadvantage if they do not speak English<br>• In childhood, mediate between adults who speak English and those who speak Spanish<br>• Walk home together<br>• Are males in a male work world | Children who look at the pages in this book see Mexican Americans who do the following:<br>• Think about things and explore the world<br>• Have father-son talks about family issues<br>• Hug each other<br>• Wear a tie to work<br>• Read<br>• Imagine and daydream<br>• Long to cross a border that separates them from loved ones<br>• Have family conversations while preparing food<br>• Experience sibling rivalry<br>• Play the guitar and sing to a loved one<br>• Greet each other with affection<br>• Act on a mistaken idea, with no harm done<br>• Do kind things for others<br>• As adults, are sources of love and guidance<br>• As children, play, go the school, and interact with family members<br>• Eat together as a family<br>• Are in all stages of life: infant/child/parent/grandparent<br>• Are female, are male<br>• Write books or illustrate them |
| **Illustrations** | Watercolor and gouache illustrations are expressive and evocative with a kind of gravity that sometimes hints at threats or overwhelming situations. | Photos of three-dimensional painted terra cotta creations create a light, cheerful mood but with a solid, substantial feeling. |

Adapted from J. Mendoza & D. Reese (2001). Examining multicultural picture books for the early childhood classroom: Possibilities and pitfalls. *Early Childhood Research and Practice*, 3(2).

*(continued)*

**TABLE 11.6**

*(continued)*

# Comparison of Two Books About Mexican-American Families

| | *A Day's Work* | *A Gift from Papa Diego* |
|---|---|---|
| **Cultural Markers** | • Integrates a few Spanish words<br>• Refers to two specific foods<br>• No mention of a specific area of Mexico or relationship to specific customs | • Spanish text and Spanish phrases are embedded in the English text<br>• The mention of four specific foods<br>• Family discussions of Chihuahua and the U.S.-Mexican border<br>• The special birthday song Little Diego's family sings |
| **Ancillary Information** | No ancillary information included in the book. | At the back of the book is a page of notes about the places in the book, a glossary of Spanish terms, and an author-illustrator biography page. |
| **Author** | Eve Bunting is a well-known, award-winning author of books about people of color who live in poverty but an outsider to the Mexican-American culture. | Benjamin Saenz is a little-known author. *A Gift from Papa Diego* is his first children's book. He is a cultural insider. |
| **Illustrator** | Ronald Himler is a well-known award-winning illustrator who is a cultural outsider. | Geronimo Garcia is a little-known illustrator who is a cultural insider. |
| **Publisher** | Clarion is a subsidiary of Houghton Mifflin Company, a large publishing house. | Cinco Puntos Press is a small press with strong connections to Latino/Latina communities. |

# International Literature

*I would hope that writing for young people might serve as an invitation to get to know some of those other slightly different folks out there in the world—without fear, without ever thinking of "otherness" as a threat. . . Those people unlike us: how to have empathy with them, for them? Those lives seemingly unlike our own: how are we connected, ultimately? We all sleep, eat, have dreams and loves and hopes and sorrows. I want writing to be connected to all of this.*

NAOMI SHIHAB NYE

*Listen*

*Listen to Naomi Shihab Nye read her poetry.*

As Naomi Shihab Nye (Castro, 2002, p. 227) reminds us, children's literature from other cultures and languages helps connect us to other people around the world. Inspired by the events of September 11, 2001, Nye wrote *19 Varieties of Gazelle: Poems of the Middle East*, a collection of poems about the Middle East and about being an Arab American living in the United States. She felt a "huge shadow had been cast across the lives of so many innocent people and an ancient culture's pride." Her natural response was to write, to grasp "onto details to stay afloat."

Isaacs (2006) writes the following:

> Our society's values are not universal, and what we see as acts of good will aren't always taken that way. We may feel connected to the rest of the world by television, telecommunications, and the Internet, but these links are ephemeral. Our attention shifts from one story to the next, and the fleeting moments of sympathy and understanding are quickly lost. Furthermore, our preconceptions about other cultures can easily cloud our vision. How can we get beyond our own experiences? How can we help our children see the world more clearly and pave the way for genuine empathy? One way, of course, is through reading. (p. 40)

International literature can give us insight into the inner thoughts and external lives of our global neighbors. Compelling stories, poems, and nonfiction can provide cultural knowledge that goes beyond the narrow coverage in textbooks and reflects the culture and language diversity found in our own classrooms—helping children see themselves as citizens of the world.

International literature has one or more of the following features:

1. It was originally written in a language other than English and subsequently translated.
2. It was originally written in English, but in a country other than the United States.
3. It was written for children of another culture by a long-term member of that culture.

International books must adhere to standards of literary quality and accuracy and authenticity just as any other children's book.

## TRANSLATED CHILDREN'S LITERATURE

The Mildred L. Batchelder Award is a citation awarded by the American Library Association to an American publisher for a children's book considered to be the most outstanding translated book of the year. Books eligible for the award are those originally published in a foreign language in a foreign country and subsequently published in the United States. The purpose of the award is to encourage international exchange of high-quality children's books by recognizing U.S. publishers of such books in translation. This award honors Mildred L. Batchelder, a former executive director of the Association for Library Services to Children. According to Batchelder (1972, pp. 307–315), children in all countries should have good books in translation from many parts of the world (see Table 11.7).

The 2010 winner of the Mildred L. Batchelder Award is *A Faraway Island*, written by Annika Thor and translated from Swedish by Linda Schenck. The book tells the story of two Jewish sisters from Vienna, Austria, twelve-year-old Stephie and her younger sister Nellie, who are sent by their parents to Sweden to escape the Nazis. Nellie adapts easily, but Stephie faces painful challenges. *Rose Blanche,* by Christophe Gallaz and Roberto

Innocenti; *Hiroshima No Pika,* by Toshi Maruki (both past Batchelder Award winners); and *Faithful Elephants,* by Yukio Tsuchiya, are popular translated titles that depict the lives of innocent victims of World War II. Both *Rose Blanche* and *Faithful Elephants* have been criticized for inaccurate translations that convey false historical information (Kawabata and Vandergrift, 1998; Stan, 2004). Faithfulness to the original text is essential in the translation of text. Stan (2004) states, "Cultural, aesthetic, national, ideological, pedagogical, and economic issues are all at work in shaping these translations" (p. 31). As with all texts, teachers must read translated texts with a critical stance and not depend solely on journal reviews and award committees.

## BOOKS WRITTEN IN ENGLISH FROM OTHER COUNTRIES

*Harry Potter, The Chronicles of Narnia, His Dark Materials* trilogy, *Koala Lou, The Dark Is Rising* series, *Little Bear* stories, *James and the Giant Peach* . . . do these titles sound familiar? They are much-loved books by authors from the English language countries of Canada, Australia, United Kingdom, Ireland, and New Zealand. These books make up the majority of international books in the United States because they need no translation and can be readily acquired. It is common for some words or phrases in books from other English language countries to be adapted, since some expressions and forms of speech are regional and may be confusing for children in the United States. For example, the first book in the Harry Potter series when released in the United Kingdom was titled *Harry Potter and the Philosopher's Stone* but changed to *Harry Potter and the Sorcerer's Stone* when released in the United States. Changes were made to reduce unfamiliar language or colloquialisms of the United Kingdom, yet they were largely met with criticism by many readers, who felt that such changes were unnecessary and even condescending.

The United States Board on Books for Young People (USBBY) annually compiles the International Children's Books List. USBBY serves as the U.S. national section

**TABLE 11.7**

# Benefits of Reading Translated Books

| | |
|---|---|
| **1.** | Children of one country who come to know the books and stories of many countries have made a beginning toward international understanding. |
| **2.** | Knowing the classic stories of a country creates an attitude for understanding toward the people for whom that literature is a heritage. |
| **3.** | Children who know they are reading in translation the same stories that children in other countries are reading, develop a sense of nearness with those in other lands. |
| **4.** | Interchange of children's books between countries through translation enhances communication between the peoples of those countries, and, if the books chosen for traveling from language to language are worthy books, the resulting communication is deeper, richer, more sympathetic, and more enduring. |

of the International Board on Books for Young People (IBBY), which was founded to promote international understanding and good will through books for children and teenagers. The books chosen for the list represent the best of the books from other countries published in the United States and range from kindergarten through grade 12.

Every other year, IBBY presents the Hans Christian Andersen Medals to an author and an illustrator, living at the time of the nomination, whose complete works have made a lasting contribution to children's literature. The Hans Christian Andersen Medal is the highest international recognition given to an author and an illustrator of children's books. David Almond from the United Kingdom is the winner of the 2010 Hans Christian Andersen Author Award, and Jutta Bauer from Germany is the winner for illustration. Past recipients from the United States include authors Katherine Paterson, Paula Fox, Virginia Hamilton, Scott O'Dell, and Meindert DeJong and illustrator Maurice Sendak.

*Read*

*Connect to the USSBY's website for the annual lists of international books and for more information about the Hans Christian Andersen Medal.*

## The Role of Multicultural and International Literature in Literacy Development

> *Teachers are very powerful in determining the kind of society we will have in the future, because they are educating our future leaders, people who are going to be doing what needs to be done in our society to continue a democracy and autonomy that sustains everyone.*
>
> Francisco Jiménez (Day, 2006, p. 269)

According to Jiménez (Day, 2006, p. 269), educators are in an excellent position to make children aware of this literature. Storybook reading of books from other cultures positively affects student attitudes toward a wide range of diverse perspectives, such as single-parent families, the elderly, the unemployed, families from different cultural and ethnic groups, and children with physical and mental challenges (Wham, Barnhart, & Cook, 1996). Reading and deep discussion of culturally specific multicultural literature increases students' ability to examine the values, beliefs, and events in their personal and collective lives and the ability to view literacy as an empowering force in the classroom (DeNicolo & Franquiz, 2006).

### CRITICAL LITERACY

In Chapter 2, reader response was described as how each reader brings his or her own background knowledge and previous experience to a text that determines how the text is interpreted and what meaning is derived from it. It makes sense that children bring their cultural worlds to this interaction. "[B]y consciously incorporating a critical perspective into their responses, students will be able to elevate their aesthetic and efferent responses to multicultural literature to a higher level of critical reading" (Cai, 2008, p. 219). Critical literacy invites readers to move beyond the author's message to question, examine, or dispute the power relations that exist between readers and authors. McLaughlin and DeVoogd (2004, pp. 14–16) point out four Principles of Critical Literacy (Table 11.8).

**TABLE 11.8**

# Principles of Critical Literacy

1. Critical literacy focuses on issues of power and promotes reflection, transformation, and action. Readers use their power to question the perspective presented by the author to engage in reflection about whose voice might be missing, discounted, or silent in the text. Drawing on their background knowledge, readers might transform the author's perspective by choosing the alternative view that might result in taking action, such as researching the topic, writing a letter, and so forth.

2. Critical literacy focuses on the problem and its complexity. Readers raise questions and seek alternative explanations as a way of more fully acknowledging and understanding the complexity of the situation.

3. Critical literacy strategies are dynamic and adapt to the contexts in which they are used. No one set of methods for critical literacy work the same in all contexts all the time. Depending on the instructional goals and on what is happening in the classroom, teachers will adapt methods that promote critical literacy to their context.

4. Critical literacy disrupts the commonplace by examining it from multiple perspectives. Examining the point-of-view from which a text is written and brainstorming other perspectives that may or may not be represented challenges students to expand their thinking and discover diverse beliefs, positions, and understandings.

## STRATEGIES FOR TEACHING CRITICAL LITERACY

Two strategies can help readers think about texts from a critical perspective: problem posing and alternative perspectives (McLaughlin & DeVoogd, 2004). *Problem posing* is a strategy that requires the reader to use questions to engage in critical analysis:

- Who is in the text/picture/situation? Who is missing?
- Whose voices are represented? Whose voices are marginalized or discounted?
- What are the intentions of the author? What does the author want the reader to think?
- What would an alternative text/picture/situation say?
- How can the reader use this information to promote equity? (p. 41)

*Alternative perspectives* is exploring viewpoints of different characters in a story or different people in real-life situations. These characters or people may be present in the story or situation, or they may be created or imagined by the reader. Formats students can use to share perspectives include focus groups, dramatization, poetry, and song lyrics (McLaughlin & DeVoogd, 2004, p. 49).

The guided comprehension direct instruction framework (McLaughlin & DeVoogd, 2004, p. 38) in Table 11.9 can be used to teach the critical literacy strategies of problem posing and alternative perspectives. The next section offers an example of critical literacy in the classroom, using the children's book *The Lady in the Box,* which is about a homeless woman.

**TABLE 11.9**

# Guided Comprehension: Modeling

1. Explain what the critical literacy strategy is and how it works.

2. Demonstrate the strategy, using a think aloud, a read aloud, and an overhead projector or a chalkboard.

3. Guide the students to work in small groups or with partners to create responses.

4. Practice by having students work with partners or independently to apply the critical literacy strategy.

5. Reflect on how the strategy helps students read from a critical stance.

## Opportunities for Reader Response

*Conversation is a basis for critical thinking. It is the thread that ties together cognitive strategies and provides students with the practice that becomes the foundation for reading, writing, and thinking.*

A. KETCH, 2005, P. 8

The critical literacy strategies outlined in the previous section provide excellent opportunities for students to respond critically to reading. For example, recently I observed a fourth-grade teacher read aloud to her students Ann McGovern's *The Lady in the Box*, a picturebook about two children who bring food and warm clothing to a homeless lady living in their neighborhood during the Christmas season. Their desire to help the lady goes against their mother's admonition to never talk to strangers. When a store owner orders the homeless lady to leave her usual spot in front of his deli, the children tell their mother, who then decides to help the lady, too.

Before reading the book, the teacher accessed the students' prior knowledge of homeless people. The majority of students had encountered the homeless on different occasions, mostly outside their suburban residential locations. During the reading, the teacher paused to allow students to discuss events in the story and to convey their own thoughts about the characters' actions. Most of the students were sympathetic to the homeless lady's plight, sharing stories of giving money, food, or other items to homeless people, although a few mentioned their parents' warning that giving handouts to the homeless didn't help them because it discouraged them from trying to become self-sufficient.

After the reading, the teacher modeled thinking aloud about whose voices were represented in the story and whose voices were marginalized or discounted. Since the book was about a homeless lady and how the efforts of a mother and two children made a difference in her life, the teacher thought the voice of the homeless was represented in the book. Then the teacher modeled reflecting on the comments of those few students who mentioned how helping the homeless made them more dependent. She prompted the students to think about whose voices were marginalized or discounted in the story. She asked the children to work in triads to share their perspectives and ideas.

When it was time for the students to share, several indicated that the voice of the store owner was marginalized and the voices of those who did not help the homeless were not represented. The teacher asked the students to think about what the store owner would say if he were allowed to include his perspective or what some of the other citizens who chose to walk past the homeless lady without helping her would say if they were allowed to include their perspectives. Again, the students formed triads and engaged in critical conversations with each other, which required most of them to think about the homeless from a different perspective—the perspective of the people who did not choose to help the lady in the box. Finally, the teacher asked the students to reflect on how the story would be different if these perspectives were included in the story. One student commented that if he were the store owner, he would help the lady in the box even if it would make her more dependent because he would not want her to be hungry. Considering his comment, another student turned to him and said that if the store owner continued to give the lady food and risked losing business, he would eventually have to close down and wouldn't be able to help the lady anyway. This exchange demonstrates how the guided comprehension direct instruction framework can support students in their thinking about a common social situation by examining it from multiple perspectives. By prompting the students to examine the point of view from which the text was written and then thinking through other perspectives that were not represented, the students were challenged to expand their thinking and discover different beliefs, positions, and understandings.

## Making the Connection Across the Curriculum

Many children's books are available in which the main character(s) engage in critical thinking. These books can be used across the content areas as examples of how critical thinking in a diverse society leads to deeper understanding and knowledge of cultures, religions, or perspectives and, in turn, leads to reflective decision making.

### READING AND LANGUAGE ARTS

*The Hard-Times Jar*, written by Ethel Smothers and illustrated by John Holyfield, is an autobiographical account of the author's childhood. Emma, the daughter of poor migrant workers living in Florida, longs to own a real book. When Emma turns eight and her family moves to Pennsylvania for apple picking, she must attend school for the first time. Emma discovers she is the only "chocolate-brown" child in her new third-grade classroom, but she soon discovers the treasure of the school library.

*Watch*

*Watch a video of Pat Mora as she discusses the special librarian who opened the world of reading for her.*

The love of books and reading is also the theme of *Tomas and the Library Lady*, written by Pat Mora and illustrated by Raul Colon. This is a fictionalized story of a brief period in the life of Tomas Rivera, who became the chancellor of the University of California at Riverside and grew up in a migrant family. One summer during his childhood, Tomas visits a local library while his family works the harvest. The librarian introduces him to stories about dinosaurs, horses, and American Indians and encourages him to take home some books, where he shares them with his family. When Tomas's family must return to Texas, the librarian gives him a book of his own to keep. Both *The Hard-Times Jar* and *Tomas and the Library Lady* are beautifully illustrated and written, conveying the love of family, the compassion of a librarian, and the joy of reading.

## SOCIAL STUDIES

*Coming to America: A Muslim Family's Story* written and illustrated by Bernard Wolf, describes the daily life of the Mahmoud family from their immigration to New York City from Egypt to how they spend their time at school, work, and home. (See illustration 12 in the Part 2 color insert.) Rather than focus solely on the Mahmouds' religious beliefs, Wolf portrays them as individuals through interactions with non-Muslim friends and food and through their engagement in typical American activities, such as watching television and playing basketball. The Mahmouds' Friday attendance at a mosque is depicted as one facet of a hard-working, loving family.

David Macaulay, well known for his books on architecture, continues his familiar design in *Mosque*, which takes place in sixteenth-century Istanbul, where a wealthy patron has hired an architect to create a mosque and supporting buildings. Based on a composite of actual historical people and mosques, the story provides detailed activities of the architect and workers as the reader follows the building of the complex from its planning to completion.

*Watch*

*Watch an interview with David Macaulay as he discusses the making of* Mosque.

## SCIENCE

In *Project Mulberry*, written by Linda Sue Park, Julia Song and her family are the only Koreans living in her new neighborhood in Plainfield, Illinois. When Julia and her good

*Macaulay's use of a combination of labeled architectural drawings, sketches, and detailed descriptions effectively conveys beliefs, practices, culture, and the social context of the Muslim religion and Islamic society.*

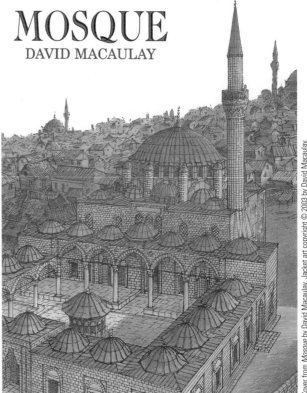

MOSQUE
DAVID MACAULAY

friend and neighbor Patrick decide to raise silkworms for their science fair project, Julia is not excited because silkworms are too Korean, and she wants a real American project. Julia's attitude slowly changes as she realizes that to get the silk, the worms must die. Linda Sue Park brings to life the amazement of silkworms and how silk is made. Julia also must deal with her mother's attitude toward African Americans. A truly distinctive aspect of the book is the discussions that take place between Linda Sue Park and Julia at the end of each chapter. The author and main character discuss the "story inside the story," such as where the author's ideas came from and how the characters take on a life of their own. These conversations provide the reader with a unique and an insightful look into the writing process.

*Read*

*Read the journal Linda Sue Park kept while raising the silkworms for this book.*

Students will be enthralled with *Guinea Pig Scientists: Bold Self-Experimenters in Science and Medicine,* written by Mel Boring and Leslie Dendy and illustrated by C. B. Mordan, a unique and interesting look at the scientists from the past several centuries who became their own guinea pigs or test subjects. The authors chose ten mesmerizing case studies from hundreds of examples gathered over a decade of research. The significance of each experiment in advancing our understanding of science and medicine are discussed. Topics include guinea pig scientists who inoculated themselves with deadly tropical diseases, tested internal body temperatures in extreme heat and cold conditions, inhaled various gasses to discover one suitable for anesthetic use, and swallowed various unusual things. The book is gross enough to captivate young scientists but still convincingly discourages readers from trying the experiments. Each captivating biography is provocative, lively, and compelling, with black-and-white sketches and photographs, a timeline, and well-documented resource lists and endnotes.

## MATH

*One Leaf Rides the Wind: Counting in a Japanese Garden,* written by Celeste Mannis and illustrated by Susan Hartung, introduces readers to haiku and aspects of Japanese culture. A Japanese girl dressed in a kimono explores a traditional temple garden and counts its fixtures one to ten, along with three lines of haiku for each number and a brief explanation. For example, the fifth object the child finds is a pagoda. The poem reads "Smiling pagoda. / Five roofs stretch to the heavens. / We shelter beneath." The accompanying explanation states, "The gently upturned roofs of the pagoda stand for earth, water, fire, wind, and sky. With its soaring silhouette, the pagoda is a prominent feature in the garden, and a favorite place to pray or meditate." The last spread shows the entire garden, providing readers the opportunity to find the ten objects on their own. The book simply and elegantly brings together math, poetry, and Japanese culture.

In *The History of Counting*, author Denise Schmandt-Besserat uses her background as an archaeologist to assist children in understanding how and why the early counting techniques of the ancient Middle East evolved into our contemporary method. For example, the ancient Sumerians did not have zero in their counting system, and the ancient Greeks used the 27 letters of their alphabet as numbers. With these counting techniques, it is easy for children to see why our current system of counting evolved.

# Top 10 Read Alouds

## Multicultural Literature

1.  **El Barrio by Debbi Chocolate, illustrated** by David Diaz (2009, Holt). A young boy explores his vibrant Latino neighborhood, with its vegetable gardens instead of lawns, Nativity parades, quinceañera parties, and tejana and salsa music.

2.  **Faith** by Maya Ajmera, Magda Nakassis, Cynthia Pon (2009, Charlesbridge). Explores the many ways in which the world celebrates and practices religious belief, highlighting the common threads.

3.  **I Lost My Tooth in Africa** by Penda Diakité, illustrated by Baba Diakité (2006, Scholastic). While visiting her father's family in Mali, a young girl loses a tooth, places it under a calabash, and receives a hen and a rooster from the African Tooth Fairy.

4.  **Jazzy Miz Mozetta** by Brenda Roberts, illustrated by Frank Morrison (2004, Farrar, Straus and Giroux). On a beautiful evening, Miz Mozetta puts on her red dress and blue shoes and dances the jitterbug just like she did many years before.

5.  **Only One Year** by Andrea Cheng, illustrated by Nicole Wong (2010, Lee & Low). Nine-year-old Sharon has conflicted feelings towards her copycat little sister and rambunctious toddler brother, who is sent to China for a year to live with relatives.

6.  **Poems to Dream Together/Poemas Par Soñar Juntos** by Francisco X. Alacron, illustrated by Paula Barragan (2005, Lee & Low). A bilingual collection of poetry celebrating family, community, nature, and the positive power of dreams to shape the future.

7.  **Rickshaw Girl** by Mitali Perkins, illustrated by Jamie Hogan (2007, Charlesbridge). In her Bangladesh village, 10-year-old Naimi excels at painting designs called alpanas, but to help her impoverished family financially, she would have to be a boy—or disguise herself as one.

8.  **Saltypie: A Choctaw Journey from Darkness into Light** by Tim Tingle, illustrated by Karen Clarkson (2010, Cinco Puntos Press). Choctaw author Tim Tingle tells the story of his family's move and the problems encountered by his Choctaw grandmother—from her orphan days at an Indian boarding school to hardships encountered in her new home on the Texas Gulf Coast.

9.  **Uncle Peter's Amazing Chinese Wedding** by Lenore Look, illustrated by Yumi Heo (2006, Atheneum). A Chinese-American girl describes the festivities surrounding her uncle's wedding and the customs behind each one.

10. **We** by Alice Schertle, illustrated by Kenneth Addison (2007, Lee & Low). Provides readers with a sweeping glimpse into the rich diversity of people and the spread of culture, technology, and societies.

# Activities for Professional Development

## THINK CRITICALLY ABOUT CHILDREN'S LITERATURE

1. *En cada cabeza, el mundo* is a dichos, or proverb, meaning *in every mind, the world.* In an online article titled *Family Dichos: Bringing the Language of Home into the Classroom,* author Ruth Shagoury explains that in her family, when someone acted differently or in a way that the family didn't understand, her mother would recite this proverb as a reminder to respect people's differences. Read Shagoury's article at http://www.choiceliteracy.com/public/150.cfm. Think about how family dichos can be used in your own classroom to bridge home and family cultures and traditions.

2. A report by the Northwest Evaluation Association titled *Achievement Gaps: An Examination of Differences in Student Achievement and Growth* (2006) (http://www.nwea.org/research/achievementgap.asp) confirmed previous reports of an achievement gap for poor and minority students. Yet, this report found that schools and teachers are giving equal attention to and are equally effective with these groups, although the rate of growth is not sufficient to close the achievement gap. The researchers concluded, "What we see as a gap in student performance in different groups is made up of thousands of individual students engaging in academic content in thousands of unique ways." How does the use of multicultural literature assist educators with meeting diverse students' unique needs with engagement in academic content?

3. The Annenberg Media video series *Teaching Multicultural Literature* features eight one-hour videos featuring teachers from across the country as they model approaches that make multicultural literature meaningful for students in grades five to eight. As units unfold over time, students engage in critical discussions of race, class, and social justice that inspire action for change. The featured teachers, along with leading educators, provide reflection and commentary throughout the programs. Authors share information about their writings through interviews and classroom visits. Go to the series at http://www.learner.org/resources/series203.html. Click on "enter the series website." Then choose one of the videos from the menu on the right side of the page.

   - Read the overview and the author and literary works information.
   - Read the video summary, which includes PDF files of reading guides, poetry, graphic organizers, rubrics, or other material used in the video.
   - Watch the video. Teaching strategies, student work, teacher commentary, and resources are available to view from the menu.
   - Reflect on the multicultural literature and teaching strategies the teachers used in the videos. How did the literature and strategies promote student engagement and critical thinking about issues related to diversity?

## BRING CHILDREN'S LITERATURE INTO THE CLASSROOM

4. The ReadWriteThink website, established in 2002, is a partnership between the International Reading Association (IRA), the National Council of Teachers of English (NCTE), and the Verizon Foundation. NCTE and IRA are working together to provide educators and students with access to the highest-quality practices and resources in reading and language arts instruction through free, Internet-based content. Lessons are available on learning language, learning about language, and learning through language. Go to the website at http://www.readwritethink.org. Under "Search Resources" on the left, select a grade level, and under "Resource Type" select "lesson plan". Under "Learning Objective", select "critical thinking." Browse through the lessons. Select one lesson to try in an elementary classroom. Share the lesson you selected with your classmates, and discuss how to make the lesson most effective.

# Print and Online Resources

## PRINT RESOURCES

Ada, A. (2003). *A magical encounter: Latino children's literature in the classroom* (2nd ed.). New York: Allyn & Bacon.

Bishop, R. (2007). *Free within ourselves: The development of African American children's literature.* Portsmouth, NH: Heinemann.

Botelho, M., & Rudman, M. (2009). *Critical multicultural analysis of children's literature: Mirrors, windows, and doors.* New York: Routledge.

Cowhey, M. (2006). *Black ants and Buddhists: Thinking critically and teaching differently in the primary grades.* Portland, ME: Stenhouse.

Day, F. (2000). *Lesbian and gay voices: An annotated bibliography and guide to literature for children and young adults.* Westport, CT: Greenwood Press.

Dozier, C., Johnston, P., & Rogers, R. (2006). *Critical literacy, critical teaching: Tools for preparing responsive teachers.* New York: Teachers College Press.

Dyches, T. (2008). *Teaching about disabilities through children's literature.* Westport, CT: Libraries Unlimited.

East, K., & Thomas, R. (2007). *Across cultures: A guide to multicultural literature for children.* Santa Barbara, CA: Libraries Unlimited.

Fox, D., & Short, K. (Eds.) (2003). *Stories matter: The complexity of cultural authenticity in children's literature.* Urbana, IL: National Council of Teachers of English.

Freeman, E., & Lehman, B. (2001*). Global perspectives in children's literature.* Boston: Allyn & Bacon.

Gebel, D. (2006). *Crossing boundaries with children's books.* Lanham, MD: Scarecrow Press.

Hallford, D., & Zaghini, E. (2005).*Outside in: Children's books in translation.* London: Milet.

Hansen-Krening, N. (2003). *Kaleidoscope: A multicultural booklist for grades K–8* (4th ed.). Urbana, IL: National Council of Teachers of English.

Henderson, D., & May, J. (2005). *Exploring culturally diverse literature for children and adults: Learning to listen in new ways.* Boston: Pearson.

*Multicultural review* (published quarterly by The Goldman Group, Inc.). A journal dedicated to a better understanding of ethnic, racial, and religious diversity.

NCTE Position statement: Supporting linguistically and culturally diverse learners in English education. http://www.ncte.org/groups/cee/positions/122892.htm.

Reid, S. (2002). *Book bridges for ESL students: Using young adult and children's literature to teach ESL.* Lanham, MD: Scarecrow Press.

Seale, D., & Slapin, B. (Eds.) (2005). *A broken flute: The Native experience in books for children.* Lanham, MD: AltaMira Press.

## Online Resources

*Barahona Center for the Study of Books in Spanish for Children and Adolescents*
**http://www.csusm.edu/csb/english**
Sponsored by California State University San Marcos, the Barahona Center is a database of Spanish books for children and adolescents. The database allows the user to search by age, subject, grade, setting, publisher or publication date, and reviewer. Recommended lists and special lists of award-winning books that have been translated into Spanish are available.

*Cooperative Children's Book Center: 50 Multicultural Books Every Child Should Know*
**http://www.education.wisc.edu/ccbc/books/detailListBooks.asp?idBookLists=42**
Compiled by Ginny Moore Kruse and Kathleen T. Horning, the list of multicultural books about people of color ranges from preschool through age 12. A list of 30 books is also available for older readers. Many other list are also available including: Spanish/English bilingual books, gay and lesbian themes and topics, and book featuring interracial families.

*Database of Award-Winning Children's Literature*
**http://www.dawcl.com/introduction.html**
One way to find quality multicultural children's literature is by choosing books that have won awards. Yet, knowing about and finding all of the awards can be an arduous task. Not anymore! The *Database of Award-Winning Children's Literature* (DAWCL) is a data-base of almost 7,000 books from 73 awards across six English-speaking countries. The database allows the user to create a tailored reading list of quality children's literature or to find out if a book has won one of the indexed awards.

*Growing Up Around the World: Books as Passports to Global Understanding for Children in the United States*
**http://www.ala.org/ala/mgrps/divs/alsc/ compubs/booklists/growingupwrld/ GrowingUpAroundWorld.cfm**
*Growing Up Around the World* is a project of the International Relations Committee of the Association for Library Service to Children. The purpose of the project is to make books that accurately depict contemporary life in other countries more widely available to American children. The project includes bibliographies representing five regions: Africa, the Americas, Asia and the Middle East, Australia and New Zealand, and Europe.

*Kay Vandergrift's Children's Literature Page*
**http://www.scils.rutgers.edu/~kvander/ ChildrenLit/index.html**
Kay Vandergrift, Professor Emerita in the School of Communication, Information and Library Studies at Rutgers University, has composed a comprehensive website that includes resources and children's literature bibliographies on American Indians, Asian Americans, African Americans, Hispanic Americans, Islamic traditions and Muslim cultures, sensitive issues, and female stories.

*Multicultural Children's Literature*
**http://www.multiculturalchildrenslit.com**
This website contains links to annotated bibliographies of children's multicultural books appropriate for the elementary grades (K–6). Cultural groups currently listed include African Americans, Chinese Americans, Latino/Hispanic Americans, Japanese Americans, Jewish Americans, American Indians, and Korean Americans.

*World of Words*
**http://wowlit.org**
Housed at the University of Arizona, *WOW* is committed to promoting intercultural understanding and global perspectives. The website has a searchable database with over 25,000 volumes of children's and adolescent literature focusing on world cultures and indigenous peoples. There is also a link to the *WOW Review: Reading Across Cultures*, an electronic journal of critical reviews on children's and adolescent literature that highlight intercultural understanding and global perspectives; WOW Currents, a blog focusing on personal response and extensions to culture; and WOW Stories, focusing on reading critically through global inquiry.

*Oyate*
**http://www.oyate.org**
Oyate is a Native organization that works to ensure that the lives and histories of Native peoples are portrayed honestly. Oyate's work includes evaluation of texts, resource materials, and fiction by and about Native peoples.

**Awards and Honors**
*Américas Award*
**http://www4.uwm.edu/clacs/aa/index.cfm**
This award recognizes U.S. published works of fiction, poetry, folklore, or selected nonfiction for children and young adults that authentically and engagingly relate to Latin America, the Caribbean, or Latinos in the United States.

*Asian Pacific American Award for Literature*
**http://www.apalaweb.org/awards/awards.htm**
The Asian/Pacific American Librarians Association bestows the Asian/Pacific American Award for Literature for books by or about Asian Pacific Americans.

*Coretta Scott King Award*
**http://www.ala.org/ala/awardsgrants/index.cfm**
The Coretta Scott King Book Award is presented annually by the Coretta Scott King Committee of the American Library Association's Ethnic Multicultural Information Exchange Round Table (EMIERT). The award (or awards) is given to an African American author and an African American illustrator for an outstandingly inspirational and educational contribution. The books promote understanding and appreciation of the culture of all peoples and their contribution to the realization of the American dream.

*The Ezra Jack Keats New Writer and New Illustrator Awards*
**http://kids.nypl.org/reading/keatsawards.cfm**
The Ezra Jack Keats Awards are given annually to an outstanding new writer and illustrator of picture books for children that portray the goals and values of Ezra Jack Keats as expressed in his multicultural books including: the universal qualities of childhood, a strong belief in family and community, and creativity and love of learning.

*Hans Christian Andersen Award*
**http://www.ibby.org**
Every other year, the International Board on Books for Young People presents the Hans Christian

Andersen Awards to a living author and illustrator whose complete works have made a lasting contribution to children's literature.

### The Lambda Literary Awards
**http://www.lambdaliterary.org**
Since 1989 the Lambda Literary Awards have been given to the finest lesbian, gay, bisexual and transgendered literature available in the United States. The "Lammy" is the most prestigious, competitive, and comprehensive literary award offered specifically to LGBT authors.

### Mildred L. Batchelder Award
**http://www.ala.org/ala/awardsgrants/index.cfm**
The Mildred L. Batchelder award is a citation awarded to an American publisher for a children's book considered to be the most outstanding of those books originally published in a foreign language in a foreign country and subsequently translated into English and published in the United States.

### Native Writers Circle of the Americas Award
**http://www.wordcraftcircle.org**
These are the only literature awards bestowed on Native American Indian writers by Native American Indian people. The awards are given in three categories: Lifetime Achievement Awards, First Book Awards for Poetry, and First Book Awards for Prose.

### Notable Books for A Global Society
**http://mysite.verizon.net/vzeeioxu/id13.html**
The Committee of the Children's Literature and Reading Special Interest Group of the International Reading Association selects 25 outstanding trade books annually for enhancing student understanding of people and cultures throughout the world. The committee reviews books representing all genres intended for students K-12.

### The Pura Belpré Award
**http://www.ala.org/ala/awardsgrants/index.cfm**
The Pura Belpré Award, established in 1996, is presented to a Latino/Latina writer and illustrator whose work best portrays, affirms, and celebrates the Latino cultural experience in an outstanding work of literature for children and youth.

### Reading the World Award
**http://soe.usfca.edu/institutes/reading_world/rtw_award.html**
The Reading the World Award, presented at the annual Reading the World Conference on -multicultural children's literature, is given to an individual in recognition of outstanding contributions in making quality literature accessible to children and young adults and to recognize those who have enriched the lives of children through multicultural literature.

### The Schneider Family Book Awards
**http://www.ala.org/ala/awardsgrants/index.cfm**
The Schneider Family Book Awards honor an author or illustrator for a book that embodies an artistic expression of the disability experience for child and adolescent audiences. Three awards are given annually in each of the following categories: birth through grade school (ages birth–10), middle school (ages 11–13) and teens (ages 13–18). The book must emphasize the artistic expression of the disability experience for children and/or adolescent audiences. The book must portray some aspect of living with a disability or that of a friend or family member, whether the disability is physical, mental, or emotional.

### Tomas Rivera Mexican American Children's Book Award
**http://www.education.txstate.edu/departments/Tomas-Rivera-Book-Award-Project-Link.html**
This award is given annually to the author/illustrator of the most distinguished book for children and young adults that authentically reflect the lives and experiences of Mexican Americans in the United States.

### The USBBY Outstanding International Books List
**http://www.usbby.org**
USBBY selects an annual list of Outstanding International Books for children and young adults. Books are selected from international books that are published during the calendar year deemed most outstanding.

Visit the companion website at **www.cengage.com/education/johnson** to find links related to the Read/Watch/Listen icons noted throughout the chapter, as well as additional resources.

# References

Amour, M. (2003). Connecting children's stories to children's literature: Meeting diversity needs. *Early Childhood Education Journal, 31*(1), 47–51.

Au, K. (1998). Social constructivism and the school literacy learning of students of diverse backgrounds. *Journal of Literacy Research, 30*(2), 297–319.

Au, K. (2006). *Multicultural issues and literacy achievement.* Mahwah, NJ: Erlbaum.

Barr, R., & Parrett, W. (2001). *Hope fulfilled for at-risk and violent youth: K–12 programs that work* (2nd ed.). Boston: Allyn & Bacon.

Batchelder, M. (1972). *Translations of children's books.* Minneapolis: Minnesota Libraries.

Bishop, R. (2007). *Free within ourselves: The development of African American children's literature.* Portsmouth, NH: Heinemann.

Botelho, M., & Rudman, M. (2009). *Critical multicultural analysis of children's literature: Mirrors, windows, and doors.* New York: Routledge.

Bonilla, J. (1998). Outrageous viewpoints: Teachers' criteria for rejecting works of children's literature. *Language Arts, 75*(4), 287–295.

Cai, M. (2002). *Multicultural literature for children and young adults: Critical issues.* Westport, CT: Greenwood Press.

Cai, M. (2008). Transactional theory and the study of multicultural literature. *Language Arts, 85*(3), 212–220.

Castro, J. (2002). Nomad, switchboard, poet: Naomi Shihab Nye's multicultural literature for young readers: An interview. *MELUS, 27*(2), 225–236.

Colby, S., & Lyon, A. (2004). Heightening awareness about the importance of using multicultural literature. *Multicultural Education, 11*(3), 24–28.

Day, D. (2006). Persevering with hope: Francisco Jiménez. *Language Arts, 83*(3), 266–270.

DeNicolo, C., & Franquiz, M. (2006). "Do I have to say it?" Critical encounters with multicultural children's literature. *Language Arts, 84*(2), 157–170.

Escamilla, K., & Nathenson-Mejía, S. (2003). Preparing culturally responsive teachers: Using Latino children's literature in teacher education. *Equity & Excellence in Education, 36,* 238–248.

Fountas, I., & Pinnell, G. (2001). *Guiding readers and writers.* Portsmouth, NH: Heineman.

Fox, M. (1997). *Whoever you are.* New York: Harcourt.

Gallo, D. (1994). Censorship of young adult literature. In J. Simmons (Ed.), *Censorship, a threat to reading, learning and thinking* (pp. 115–122). Newark, DE: International Reading Association.

Green, C., & Oldendorf, S. (2005). Teaching religious diversity through children's literature. *Childhood Education, 81*(4), 209–218.

Horning, K., Lingren, M., Rudiger, H., & Schiliesman, M. (2006). *Publishing in 2005.* Accessed March 30, 2006, from http://www.education.wisc.edu/ccbc/books/choiceintro06.asp.

Isaacs, K. (2006). It's a big world after all. *School Library Journal, 52*(2), 40–45.

Jordan, J. (1988). Nobody mean more to me than you and the future life of Willie Jordan. *Harvard Educational Review, 58,* 363–374.

Kawabata, A., & Vandergrift, K. (1998). History into myth: The anatomy of a picture book. *Bookbird, 36*(2), 6–12.

Ketch, A. (2005). Conversation: The comprehension connection. *The Reading Teacher, 59*(1), 8–13.

Lee, C. (1991). Big picture talkers/words walking without masters: The instructional implications of ethnic voices for an expanded literacy. *Journal of Negro Education, 60,* 291–304.

Lester, J. (2005). *Let's talk about race.* New York: Amistad.

Lewison, M., Leland, C., Flint, A., & Möller, K. (2002). Dangerous discourses: Using controversial books to support engagement, diversity, and democracy. *The New Advocate, 15*(3), 215–226.

Louie, B. (2006). Guiding principles for teaching multicultural literature. *The Reading Teacher, 59*(5), 438–448.

McLaughlin, M., & DeVoogd, G. (2004). *Critical literacy: Enhancing students' comprehension of text.* New York: Scholastic.

Mendoza, J., & Reese, D. (2001). Examining multicultural picture books for the early childhood classroom: Possibilities and pitfalls. *Early Childhood Research and Practice, 3*(2). Available at myess http://ecrp.uiuc.edu/v3n2/mendoza.html.

Myers, W. (2001). *Bad boy: A memoir.* New York: HarperCollins.

NCES (2006). Characteristics of schools, districts, teachers, principals, and school libraries in the United States: 2003-04 Schools and staffing survey. Accessed March 25, 2006, from http://nces.ed.gov/pubs2006/2006313.pdf.

NCSS (1998). *Study about religions in the social studies curriculum.* National Council for the Social Studies, in its Curriculum Standards for Social Studies. Available at http://www.socialstudies.org/positions/religion.

Nieto, S. (2000). *Affirming diversity: The sociopolitical context of multicultural education* (3rd ed.). New York: Longman.

Nieto, S. (1996). *Affirming diversity* (2nd ed.). New York: Longman.

Nieto, S. (2000). *Affirming diversity: A sociopolitical context of multicultural education* (3rd ed.). New York: Longman.

Nilsson, N. (2005). How does Hispanic portrayal in children's books measure up after 40 years? The answer is "It depends." *The Reading Teacher, 58*(6), 534–548.

Owens, T. (2006). Totally James. *Teaching Tolerance Magazine, 29.* Online document available: http://www.tolerance.org/teach/magazine/features.jsp?p=0&is=38.

Spears-Bunton, L. (1990). Welcome to my house: African American and European American students' responses to Virginia Hamilton's *House of Dies Drear. Journal of Negro Education, 59,* 566–576.

Stallworth, J., Gibbons, L., & Fauber, L. (2006). It's not on the list: An exploration of teachers' perspectives on using multicultural literature. *Journal of Adolescent & Adult Literacy, 49*(6), 478–489.

Stan, S. (2004). *Rose Blanche* in translation. *Children's Literature in Education, 35*(1): 21–32.

U.S. Census Bureau (2001, April). Population change and distribution 1990–2000. Accessed March 25, 2006, from http://www.census.gov/prod/2001pubs/c2kbr01-2.pdf.

U.S. Census Bureau (2004, March). Children and the households they live in: 2000. Accessed March 25, 2006, from http://www.census.gov/prod/2004pubs/censr-14.pdf.

Wham, M., Barnhart, J., & Cook, G. (1996). Enhancing multicultural awareness through the storybook reading experience. *Journal of Research and Development in Education, 30,* 1–9.

Williams, S. (2002). Reading *Daddy's Roommate:* Preservice teachers respond to a controversial text. *The New Advocate, 15*(3), 231–236.

Yenika-Agbaw, V. (2003). Outside teachers: Children's literature and cultural tension. *English Leadership Quarterly, 26*(2), 7–11.

# The New Literacies: The World of Online Children's Literature

*12*

I'm too excited to end this letter here. I have diarrhea of the pen. I really wish you had a computer so we could send each other e-mail too. Then we could practically talk to each other with the computers instead of having to wait three or four days for our letters to be delivered via snail mail. With e-mail we could write to each other several times a day. We could tell each other everything that happens, practically as it happens. For instance, right now I could tell you what I made for supper. With e-mail that would be interesting because you could read about it this very evening. With snail mail you won't read about it until three days after the meal, so who cares?

*Paula Danziger, 2000, pp. 4-5*

Danziger says in her book *Snail Mail No More*, the Internet has narrowed the gap between people all over the world. Unlike the "olden days," when a letter could take several days or even weeks to arrive at its destination, Internet communication is almost instantaneous. Electronic mail (e-mail), listservs, instant messaging (IM), chat rooms, discussion boards, wikis, and weblogs (blogs) allow people to share ideas, opinions, and information. Renowned literacy expert Frank Smith (2006) writes, "Technology extends our abilities to see, reach, feel, examine, and communicate" (p. 108).

*Smith (2006) believes that technology* is part of who we are:

It exists as a significant part of the external landscape. We can neither dislodge nor ignore it. It is a fully functioning part of our environment when we are born, as natural and inevitable in our minds as the earth and the sky. It becomes part of our baseline for constructing a world—a substantial and influential part in most peoples' minds. (p. 109)

Children today are digital natives. Ninety-three percent of children ages 8–18 spend an average of 90 minutes a day using the computer at home (Kaiser Foundation, 2010). Almost 75% of this time is spent on social networking, instant messaging, watching videos and playing computer games. Even very young children come to school having either firsthand experience or experience with their parents' or siblings' use of e-mail, cell phones, iPods, and digital cameras (see Table 12.1 for definitions of these and other terms related to communication technology). However, only a small percentage of children use the Internet to explore interests or to find information beyond what they have access to at school or in their community (Ito, et al., 2008; Kaiser Foundation, 2010). This lack of engagement with online networks as a learning resource suggests new ways of thinking about the role of classroom teachers.

Although children come to school already familiar with digital media, they do not necessarily know how to fully access and engage with them. Digital texts and Information Communication Technologies (ICT) are quickly becoming the predominant way people read and communicate at work and home (Horrigan, 2007). What would it mean to really exploit the potential of the learning opportunities available through online resources and networks? Teachers can use these tools to extend children's understanding, motivation, and engagement with children's literature in authentic ways that also extend opportunities to acquire the skills and strategies needed to live and work in the rapidly changing technological world.

**TABLE 12.1**

# Selected Technology Terms

| Term | Definition |
|------|------------|
| Bookmark | In a web browser, bookmarks allow you to keep a list of pages you want to revisit. |
| Chat Room | An online venue where people who share a common interest can communicate in real time—typing out conversations on their keyboards. |
| Discussion Board | Online bulletin boards where people can "post" and respond to messages. |
| Hyperlink | An image or word on a web page that, when clicked, takes you to a different part of that web page or a different website altogether. |
| Information Communication Technologies (ICT) | ICT is an umbrella term that includes any communication device or application such as radio, television, cellular phones, personal digital assistants (PDAs), MP3 players, and computer and network hardware and software. |
| Interactive Whiteboard | An interactive whiteboard is a large interactive screen connected to a computer and projector. The screen is touch sensitive, which means that you can control it by using your finger or pen as a mouse. |
| Instant Messenger | Allows two people to have a short conversation instantly. |

**TABLE 12.1**

(*continued*)

# Selected Technology Terms

| Term | Definition |
|------|-----------|
| Listserv or Mailing List | A list of e-mail addresses. You can send an e-mail to all the people on a mailing list at the same time. |
| MP3 | The standard for audio compression, especially music. |
| Personal Digital Assistant (PDA) | A digital device that can include the functionality of a computer, a mobile phone, a music player, and a camera. |
| Podcast | An audio file, usually in MP3 format, that is available online. The files can be downloaded and listened to at the user's convenience. |
| Webcam | Video camera whose content is fed to a website. |
| Weblog, or Blog | Interactive online journals. The person writing the weblog is known as a "blogger," and the process of keeping an online diary is known as "blogging." |
| Wikis | Server program that allows anyone to edit or add content. |

## Defining Digital Texts

Traditional text presents content in a fixed linear format. Digital text separates the content from the way it is displayed, making the text flexible in several key ways. Imagine a book where you could change the color or size of the type or have the option to listen to the book instead of reading it. Digital texts offer varied visual display such as font color, size, shape, and background color, and other displays such as audio and video can be offered. Digital text can also be linked for access to other pages on the same website or externally. Internal and external links can provide important structural labels and semantic information that can be identified and displayed in different ways.

Links can be used to embed a variety of learning supports, like prompts to stop and predict, summarize, question, or visualize; internal links to definitions of key words; and links to external websites with additional information. Research-based learning strategies can become part of a text, helping students gain meaning. These unique features of digital text differentiate it from other genres.

Currently, there are several "hybrid books" on the market that combine a traditional book with high-quality video and the power of the Internet into a single, complete story. The result is often an enriching experience that expands our traditional view of storytelling. Though these hybrid books are not common, several have become popular with students. The *Amanda Project* features three teens who investigate the disappearance of a mutual friend. On a companion website, readers can upload their own "clues" to Amanda's presence. *Skeleton Creek* alternates between the written diary of Ryan, a housebound teen trying to investigate strange occurrences in his home town, and the video missives of his best friend, Sarah, which are accessed by logging onto a website. The *39 Clues* books follow Amy Cahill and her brother Dan as they travel the world to hunt for the clues that unlock the family's power. Each book comes with six game cards and an online component that reveals important information about the Cahills and unlocks clues. Educators must be prepared to teach students the skills and strategies they need to successfully read and comprehend across multiple media.

## DIGITAL TEXT AS A UNIQUE GENRE

Why should digital texts be considered a *genre*? Digital texts are similar to other genres—in fact, all genres can be found online. Digital texts are distinguished from other genres by the interactive structure. Digital texts are not linear. Hyperlinks embedded in websites allow the reader to go to completely different web pages or to a digital picture, video, or audio. The path of hyperlinks selected by the reader influences the direction and content of the text. In this way the reader's purpose and choices determine the reading sequence rather than the author. Due to the unique nature of digital text, we use different comprehension strategies than with traditional print texts. Thus, knowing when and why to click a particular hyperlink is a strategic process that influences comprehension. For example, have you ever been reading a website, clicked on a hyperlink for more information, started reading the new information, and continued to click on interesting links, only to realize that you have no idea how you got to that point or how to get back to the original website? This can be frustrating for adults and children. Negative experiences can develop into poor attitudes toward reading online just as with reading traditional print.

For a child to engage in reading online, a transaction must take place between the reader and the text. For this transaction to be successful, the reader, the text, the reading activity, and the context must all be taken into consideration. Figure 12.1 represents the reading transaction and focuses on the features or issues important to consider for optimal engagement and comprehension. Since the *text* format is interactive, students have control over the direction of the text. They must sort through and manipulate different media formats to create meaning. For this reason, it is important that the teacher create a purpose for the *reading activity*. Teachers also must show students how to determine if information on the Internet is accurate and unbiased. Since the nature of the Internet is interactive, the *reader* can become more engaged in the reading activity. Like conventional print, the reader's previous experience with the Internet can affect how successfully they manipulate the Web to create meaning. In addition, teachers can use the different features of the Web to motivate students.

The *social context* influences the text, the reading activity, and the reader to affect comprehension. The Internet provides opportunities for students locally, nationally, and internationally to work together. To prepare children to successfully interact with Information Communication Technologies (ICTs), teachers can scaffold students' acquisition of the new literacies required to comprehend and compose online.

## THE NEW LITERACIES

The term *new literacies* has been defined as the "skills, strategies, and dispositions necessary to successfully use and adapt to the rapidly changing information and communication

**FIGURE 12.1**

The Reading Transaction as It Relates to Digital Texts and ICT

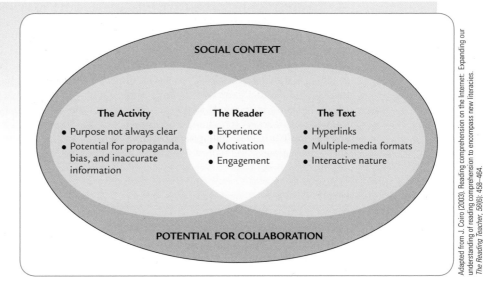

Adapted from J. Coiro (2003). Reading comprehension on the Internet: Expanding our understanding of reading comprehension to encompass new literacies. *The Reading Teacher, 56*(6): 458–464.

technologies and contexts that continuously emerge in our world and influence all areas of our personal and professional lives" (Leu, Kinzer, Coiro, & Cammack, 2004, p. 1572). The acquisition of these skills, strategies, and dispositions allows us to identify, locate, crucially evaluate, synthesize, and communicate to others information from the Internet and other ICTs. It is critical for students to acquire the skills and strategies of the new literacies to read, write, view, navigate, and communicate.

## Benefits and Considerations of the New Literacies

*It is now possible for more people than ever to collaborate and compete in real time with more other people on more different kinds of work from more different corners of the planet and on more equal footing than at any previous time in the history of the world—using computers, e-mail, fiber-optic networks, teleconferencing, and dynamic new software. . . The global competitive playing field [is] being leveled. The world [is] being flattened.*

THOMAS FRIEDMAN, 2006, P. 8

*Listen*

*Listen to a presentation by Thomas Friedman*

This excerpt from *The World Is Flat* by Thomas Friedman is an account of how globalization has shifted into high speed due to rapid advances in technology and communications. Although specialized and localized jobs such as brain surgeons, lawyers, musicians, plumbers, and sales clerks will continue to be needed, as the world gets "flatter," more and more middle-class jobs, such as accountants and factory workers, will be digitized, automated, or outsourced to other countries that can do the work cheaper. Since the middle class is the foundation of our economic and political stability, what does this mean for America? Will the backbone of America be broken? According to Friedman, "There is nothing about the flat world—nothing—that Americans cannot handle, as long as we roll up our sleeves [and] educate our young people the right way for these times" (p. 322).

There are a broad range of skills and strategies children of today will need to successfully live and work in the 21st century. These skills include the use of technology but also creativity and innovation, critical thinking and problem solving, communication, collaboration, flexibility and adaptability, initiation and self-direction, social and cross-cultural skills, and productivity and accountability. Educators must view literacy as a matter of engaging in the ever-developing process of using reading and writing as tools for thinking and learning in order to expand students' understanding of themselves and the world.

In response to the need for further evolution of the national standards for English language arts learners (presented in chapter three), NCTE presented the Framework for 21st Century Curriculum and Assessment (see Figure 12.2). The framework presents what 21st century readers and writers need to know and be able to do.

**FIGURE 12.2**

NCTE Framework
for 21st Century
Curriculum and
Assessment

### Develop proficiency with the tools of technology

Students in the 21st century should have experience with and develop skills around technological tools used in the classroom and the world around them. Through this they will learn about technology and learn through technology. In addition, they must be able to select the most appropriate tools to address particular needs.

- Do students use technology as a tool for communication, research, and creation of new works?
- Do students evaluate and use digital tools and resources that match the work they are doing?
- Do students find relevant and reliable sources that meet their needs?
- Do students take risks and try new things with tools available to them?
- Do students, independently and collaboratively, solve problems as they arise in their work?
- Do students use a variety of tools correctly and efficiently?

### Build relationships with others to pose and solve problems collaboratively and cross-culturally

Students in the 21st century need interpersonal skills in order to work collaboratively in both face-to-face and virtual environments to use and develop problem-solving skills. When learning experiences are grounded in well informed teaching practices, the use of technology allows a wider range of voices to be heard, exposing students to opinions and norms outside of their own.

- Do students work in a group in ways that allow them to create new knowledge or to solve problems that can't be created or solved individually?
- Do students work in groups to create new sources that can't be created or solved by individuals?
- Do students work in groups whose members have diverse perspectives and areas of expertise?
- Do students build on one another's thinking to gain new understanding?
- Do students learn to share disagreements and new ways of thinking in ways that positively impact the work?
- Do students gain new understandings by being part of a group or team?

National Council of Teachers of English (2008). *NCTE framework for 21st century curriculum and assessment.* Available from http://www.ncte.org/library/NCTEFiles/Resources/Positions/Framework_21stCent_Curr_Assessment.pdf.

**FIGURE 12.2**

(*continued*)

### Design and share information for global communities that have a variety of purposes

Students in the 21st century must be aware of the global nature of our world and be able to select, organize, and design information to be shared, understood, and distributed beyond their classrooms.

- Do students use inquiry to ask questions and solve problems?
- Do students critically analyze a variety of information from a variety of sources?
- Do students take responsibility for communicating their ideas in a variety of ways?
- Do students choose tools to share information that match their need and audience?
- Do students share and publish their work in a variety of ways?
- Do students solve real problems and share results with real audiences?
- Do students publish in ways that meet the needs of a particular, authentic audience?

### Manage, analyze, and synthesize multiple streams of simultaneously presented information

Students in the 21st century must be able to take information from multiple places and in a variety of different formats, determine its reliability, and create new knowledge from that information.

- Do students create new ideas using knowledge gained?
- Do students locate information from a variety of sources?
- Do students analyze the credibility of information and its appropriateness in meeting their needs?
- Do students synthesize information from a variety of sources?
- Do students manage new information to help them solve problems?
- Do students use information to make decisions as informed citizens?

### Create, critique, analyze, and evaluate multimedia texts

Students in the 21st century must be critical consumers and creators of multimedia texts.

- Do students use tools to create new thinking or to communicate original perspectives?
- Do students communicate information and ideas in a variety of forms?
- Do students communicate information and ideas to different audiences?
- Do students articulate thoughts and ideas so that others can understand and act on them?
- Do students analyze and evaluate the multimedia sources that they use?
- Do students evaluate multimedia sources for the effects of visuals, sounds, hyperlinks, and other features on the text's meaning or emotional impact?
- Do students evaluate their own multimedia works?

(*continued*)

**FIGURE 12.2**
(*continued*)

**Attend to the ethical responsibilities required by complex environments**

Students in the 21st century must understand and adhere to legal and ethical practices as they use resources and create information.

- Do students share information in ways that consider all sources?
- Do students practice the safe and legal use of technology?
- Do students create products that are both informative and ethical?
- Do students understand the concepts of collaborative production, group and individual contribution, and group and individual ownership?

It is important to understand that computer technology will not replace foundational literacies required by traditional books and print but rather build on and extend them. The ability to analyze pictures and text, respond to literature, comprehend, infer and evaluate, use critical literacy, see other perspectives, and build on prior knowledge and use vocabulary knowledge remain fundamental to the use of ICTs. As new technologies and complex information networks become more proliferate, reading, writing, and communication will take new forms, thus requiring new literacies for their effective use. The ability to use new literacies is necessary to fully engage with digital texts and ICTs. Teachers are perfectly positioned to build and extend these skills and strategies within the literacy curriculum.

## BENEFITS

There are many benefits to including digital texts and ICTs in the literacy curriculum. And because digital texts and ICTs are relatively new literacies, there are some important aspects to consider when bringing these into the classroom. The next section examines the benefits of digital texts and story worlds, how digital texts can increase critical thinking, and how this genre promotes understanding diversity.

## CLASSROOM READING MATERIALS AND STORY WORLDS

The Internet allows teachers and librarians to literally bring a whole world of books or e-literature into the classroom. Some e-literature is simply traditional forms of books that have been put on the Internet, whereas others are interactive in that children can have the book read to them, have the words pronounced or defined for them, or engage in related activities. The Internet also opens up opportunities to find out more information about a book's setting, events, and author that make for a richer and more meaningful reading experience.

**Online Read Alouds.** Children enjoy hearing books read aloud by their parents, teachers, and librarians, who serve as models for reading. The Screen Actors Guild Foundation has capitalized on this influence by hosting BookPALS Storyline Online, which allows children to watch streaming videos of celebrities such as Elijah Wood, Amanda Bynes, and Jason Alexander reading and discussing children's picturebooks. Currently there are 22 picturebooks that would appeal to all children. One exceptional example is the reading of *No Mirrors in My Nana's House,* written by Ysaye Barnwell and illustrated by Synthia St. James, which is read by Tia and Tamera Mowry. Included in the video is

*Listen*

*Listen to* No Mirrors
in My Nana's House
*by Ysaye Barnwell.*

the song from which the book originated performed by a capella quintet Sweet Honey and the Rock, of which the book's author, Ysaye Barnwell, is a member. Information about each book, author, and celebrity reader is provided along with related activities.

The structure or organization of online read alouds follows that of traditional print; stories are read from start to finish with little or no other functionality. For video recordings of books such as Storybook Online, students need to know how to start and stop the recording and to turn on or off the captions. For online books that show the print and pictures accompanied by audio, students will need to learn how to navigate page turns on the computer. However simple this may seem, it is important for students to be very familiar with how to use the navigation controls. Teachers must model and guide students through the process many times to ensure that students are actively engaged in a successful read aloud experience and do not become frustrated.

**Online Books.** Thousands of free books are available on the Internet that are digitized versions of the traditional print books. A unique and invaluable collection is the International Children's Digital Library (ICDL); see Figure 12.3. This global collection currently includes approximately 4,000 books in 54 languages for children ages 3-13. The browser interface is in 15 languages. The computer interface technologies that support searching, browsing, reading, and sharing books have been developed by interdisciplinary researchers and a team of 7- to 11-year-old children. As a result, the ICDL's interface allows children to search for new books and retrieve previously read books through categories they can easily understand, such as true or make believe, book color, length, how a book makes them feel, or spinning a globe. An advanced search interface is also available for older children and adults.

The collection is focused on books that help children understand the world around them and the global society in which they live. The books represent exemplary artistic, historic, and literary qualities. For example, *The Complete Collection of Pictures and Songs,* written by Randolph Caldecott (1887), is a part of this collection. Books are presented in the way they are read in their country (i.e., written from left to right) or in dual languages.

**FIGURE 12.3**

The Main Page of
the International
Children's Digital
Library

This collection is especially beneficial for English language learners for books in their home language that are difficult to find in print in America. For example, there are 422 books from Persia written in Farsi and 25 books from the Philippines written in Tagalog.

The structure of online books is very similar to traditional texts. Usually, the only functionality is the navigation controls. Additionally, the book may be broken into parts and accessed from an entry point, often a hyperlinked table of contents, so when finished with one chapter, the student will need to be able to navigate back to the table of contents to access the next chapter. The most challenging part of online books may be using the search interface that allows the reader to find, select, and read books. However, the exciting aspect of such online collections of online books such as the IDCL is that students can actually select books of their choice. Therefore, teachers must model and guide students in learning how to use the search interface and, as with any independent reading context, students must know how to determine if a book is "just right" or too hard.

**Interactive Storybooks.** Interactive storybooks can also be found online. They transform traditional print stories by adding graphics, sound, animation, and video to create interactive texts, much like a storybook on a CD-ROM. Glasgow (1996) examined CD-ROM storybooks at different stages in children's reading development and found that in the emergent stage they can be helpful in reducing dependence on text by integrating print, images, sound, motion, and color. In addition, students can track text from left to right and top to bottom because the text is highlighted as it is read. Older students can benefit from work with unknown vocabulary, since some interactive storybooks have accompanying graphics that show the meaning of the word that takes into account individual student differences. Further, the interactive nature of online storybooks helps students become more personally involved as they engage with the storybook.

Teachers may be concerned that students will become distracted by the interactive features and games rather than reading the text. A way to scaffold students' effective engagement with interactive storybooks is to read aloud and model the use of the storybook online with children. By modeling and thinking aloud about how to use the interactive features on the online storybook appropriately, students can observe how to interact and problem solve. Children can then be given the opportunity to engage with the online storybook independently during centers or during independent reading time.

One outstanding site for interactive storybooks is the TumbleBook Library, a collection of animated talking picturebooks offered through participating public libraries (Figure 12.4). The TumbleBook Library consists of 146 highly popular picturebooks for K–5 students. The audio and graphics can be turned off, and children can read the books themselves. Some books include a word helper.

**Virtual Meet the Author.** In the past few years, several children's book authors have visited my hometown so students could meet them in person and hear them read from their books. These authors included Christopher Paul Curtis, Lois Lowry, and Russell Freedman. There is something magical about meeting an author—hearing the stories of their inspiration and listening to them read their works. Although there is no substitute for the thrill of meeting an author in person, author visits can be very expensive and time consuming for schools to host. However, virtual author visits allow readers and authors to "meet." Virtual meetings are more affordable and provide access to authors who are geographically distant or prefer not to travel. A quick Internet search will produce authors' websites, e-mail addresses, and their publishers' contact information. Some websites list authors who are willing to conduct virtual visits or provide transcripts of past author chats.

Virtual author visits can be conducted via e-mail, bulletin board connection, virtual chat, or live broadcast via webcam. The type of communication technology,

**FIGURE 12.4**

A Page from the E-book *The Diary of a Worm* by Dorin Cronin
As the text is read by a narrator, the text is highlighted so children are able to visually rack the text.

the cost, and date/time frame will be determined by the author/publisher and the teacher/librarian. It can take some time to work out the details, so take this into consideration in the overall time frame of the event. Table 12.2 gives a few suggestions for preparing for the virtual visit to ensure it goes smoothly and is meaningful for all involved.

**TABLE 12.2**

# Preparing for a Virtual Author Visit

- Make sure you have access to multiple copies of most of the author's works.

- Read and discuss the author's works well in advance of the virtual visit. Depending on the number and type of books the author has written, this can take at least three to four weeks.

- Collect questions for the author ahead of time.

- Discuss netiquette and discussion procedures with the students.

- Check and double check that all equipment and necessary software is working, and design a backup plan if there is a technology problem or network failure.

- Use a projector to broadcast the computer screen or webcam so all students can see the communication.

- If connecting via e-mail, bulletin board, or virtual chat, be sure students read all posts before asking follow-up questions.

- Monitor the time and allow students to ask impromptu questions if there is enough time.

**Webcasts of Authors and Illustrators.** Another way to bring an author into the classroom is through online author videos (also called webcasts or podcasts). Reading Rockets (http://www.readingrockets.org) is an educational initiative of the public broadcasting station WETA. This website provides information and resources on how young kids learn to read and hosts over 40 online videos of renowned children's authors and illustrators. In addition to each author/illustrator interview is a transcript of the interview, a biography of the author's/illustrator's life, and a bibliography of the author's/illustrator's works.

The National Book Festival (http://www.loc.gov/bookfest), sponsored by the Library of Congress and held annually since 2001, brings more than 70 award-winning authors, illustrators, and poets to the nation's capital each year. Each author's presentation is videotaped and published on the Web. Over 150 distinguished children's and young adult authors and illustrators are featured. Table 12.3 presents some additional sites for online read alouds, interactive books, and virtual author visits.

---

**TABLE 12.3**

# Online Resources for Read Alouds, Interactive Books, and Virtual Author Visits

## Online Read Alouds

- **BookHive.com's Zinger Tales** http://www.bookhive.org. This site includes videos of storytellers telling stories rather than reading a book aloud; it is an excellent source for students to see and hear how to tell stories.

- **Storybook Online** http://www.storybookonline.net includes 17 books or poems read aloud, one of which is Roald Dahl's reading of "Little Red Riding Hood and the Wolf" from his book *Revolting Rhymes*. The pictures in the books are not shown, so children will need a copy of the book to see the pictures and read the text as it is read aloud.

- **Librivox** http://librivox.org. LibriVox provides free audiobooks from the public domain. The children's catalog offers almost 60 titles, including *The Wind in the Willows*, *The Secret Garden*, and *The Wizard of Oz*.

## Online Books and Magazines

- **Children's Books Online.** The Rosetta Project http://www.childrensbooksonline.org. This children's online library is a volunteer-driven project that features scanned historical children's books. Many are translated into several languages.

- **Literature.org** http://www.literature.org provides over 200 free e-texts for K–adult of the world's most famous novels, plays, short stories, poems, and historical documents, organized alphabetically and by categories.

- **Project Gutenburg** http://promo.net/pg/index.html. Over 6,200 classic books such as Shakespeare, Poe, Dante, and favorites like the Sherlock Holmes stories by Sir Arthur Conan Doyle, the Tarzan and Mars books of Edgar Rice Burroughs, *Alice's Adventures in Wonderland* as told by Lewis Carroll, and thousands of others.

**TABLE 12.3**

(*continued*)

# Online Resources for Read Alouds, Interactive Books, and Virtual Author Visits

- **Aesop's Fables** http://www.aesopfables.com. Includes a collection of over 650 fables with many morals listed. Some of the fables have an option that allows the reader to listen to it being read. Also, lesson suggestions of purposes are provided for teachers.

- **Academy of American Poets** http://www.poets.org. Sponsored by the Academy of American Poets, this searchable site contains biographies of poets. A message board allows users to discuss, share, and criticize poems, books, and current events in the field of poetry.

## Online Interactive Storybooks

- **Mythic Journeys** http://mythicjourneys.org/bigmyth/index.htm. Includes several creation stories from different cultures around the world.

- **Clifford Books online** http://pbskids.org. Read and listen to several of the popular Clifford stories online.

- **Storybook Web** http://www.ltscotland.org.uk/storybook. Based on popular stories by Scottish children's authors Scoular Anderson, Debi Gliori, Mairi Hedderwick, and Frank Rodgers. Children can watch and listen to the authors reading excerpts from their stories and answering questions about how they get their ideas for writing.

- **Kids' Corner** http://wiredforbooks.org/kids.htm. Hosted by Ohio University's Telecommunications Center, this site provides several illustrated stories by Beatrix Potter, some of which have an audio slide show in English, French, German, and Japanese.

- **Between the Lions** http://pbskids.org/lions. The popular Public Broadcasting System show hosts a different e-book each week on its website. A pop-up "word helper" pronounces and defines pre-identified words on several of the pages.

## Authors Who Conduct Virtual Visits

- **Kate's Book Blog** http://kmessner.livejournal.com/106020.html. Author Kate Messner has composed a list of authors by age level who offer free 20-minute Skype chats with book clubs that have read one of their books.

- **Scholastic's Visiting Author Series** http://www2.scholastic.com. Scholastic Books hosts several authors throughout the year. Children and teachers post questions via a discussion board over a two-week period, and then, on a set date, the author joins the discussion. Transcripts of past author discussions are available.

- **Skype an Author Network** http://skypeanauthor.wetpaint.com. The Skype-an-Author Network allows teachers and librarians to connect with children's and young adult authors registered on the network for virtual school visits via Skype. Two types of visits are available, free for 10 to 15 minutes and in-depth (30-60 minutes) with the charge to be determined by the author.

- **Toni Buzzeo's website** http://www.tonibuzzeo.com/visitvirtual.html. Author Toni Buzzeo's website lists the e-mail addresses of authors who will conduct virtual visits.

## Special Topic: Digital Literacy in the Classroom

Teachers and librarians can use authors' websites to assist children in getting to know the author, which will make the author's works more meaningful. One first-grade class conducted an author study on Mem Fox. After reading aloud to the children a few of her books, the teacher shared Mem Fox's website with them. The teacher gathered the children around the computer monitor in a shared reading fashion (she did not have a projector to broadcast the computer screen) and read aloud to the children parts of the information about Mem Fox. As she did so, she thought aloud about how she made decisions to click on certain hyperlinks or which buttons she needed to use to go back and forth within the website. In this way, she modeled the decision-making process one must use to find the needed information.

After reading about Mem Fox, the teacher created a chart with the children, on which they recorded information learned from the website along with the books they had read in which the children could see a connection to Mem Fox's life. In parentheses, children identified books by Mem Fox that included some of the biographical details from her life. (See Figure 12.5.)

From the author information gained through the website, the children were able to make important connections to how the stories relate to Mem Fox's life and where she got ideas for writing many of her books.

Almost every author has a website or is port of the publisher's website. Author websites often offer a showcase of their works, appearances, interviews, speeches, and other

**FIGURE 12.5**

Making Connections: An Author's Website and Her Books

### What We Learned About Mem Fox's Life @ memfox.net

- She was born in Australia (Possum Magic).
- She moved to Africa when she was a little girl.
- Her parents were missionaries who lived on a farm (Hattie and the Fox).
- Wilfrid Gordon McDonald Partridge was her father's name (Wilfrid Gordon McDonald Partridge).
- She went to college in London. She liked the Beatles, wore miniskirts, and dyed her hair.
- Mem didn't get to know her grandfather until he was 90 years old and living in a nursing home (Sophie).
- When Mem lived on the farm in Africa, her mom worried about the dangers of the African wildlife (Possum Magic).
- She has a younger sister (Koala Lou, Harriet You'll Drive Me Wild!).
- She has written 53 children's books.
- Her first book was Possum Magic.

news about the author. In addition, some authors include an online journal or blog that updates the audience on their daily lives, what they are currently writing, or their opinions on a variety of topics (Johnson, 2010). Some have activity resources, such as worksheets, that go along with their books. Table 12.4 contains a few selected authors' websites.

**TABLE 12.4**

# Selected Author Websites

| Title | Description | Books/Web Address |
|---|---|---|
| Jan Brett | Jan Brett's site has almost 3,600 pages of resources that go along with her picture-books; 20 videos of Brett demonstrating how to draw different animals or characters in her books and interviews with the author about her books | *The Mitten: A Ukrainian Folktale*<br>*Town Mouse, Country Mouse*<br>*The Hat*<br>http://ww.janbrett.com |
| Eric Carle | Carle's website has a Q/A section, a bulletin board that allows parents and teachers to offer suggestions of how to use the books, and a photo and video section on how Carle creates his illustrations and pictures of his family. | *Brown Bear, Brown Bear, What Do You See?*<br>*The Very Hungry Caterpillar*<br>*The Very Lonely Firefly*<br>http://www.eric-carle.com |
| Cynthia Leitich Smith | Includes author's blogs, substantial resources for the author's books, appearances, information about her writing life, and a wealth of information and resources on children's and young adult literature. | *Tantalize*<br>*Jingle Dancer*<br>*Indian Shoes*<br>*Santa Knows*<br>http://www.cynthialeitichsmith.com |
| J. Patrick Lewis | Includes personal photos from the poet's life and school visits, transcripts of interviews, poems, and upcoming appearances | *Please Bury Me in the Library*<br>*Doodle Dandies: Poems That Take Shape*<br>*Once Upon a Tomb: A Collection of Gravely Humorous Verses*<br>http://www.jpatricklewis.com |

*(continued)*

**TABLE 12.4**

(*continued*)

# Selected Author Websites

| Title | Description | Books/Web Address |
|-------|-------------|-------------------|
| Lois Lowry | Includes the author's blog, a video of an interview with the author in her home, schedule of appearances, and transcripts of the author's speeches. | *Anastasia* series<br>*Number the Stars*<br>*The Giver*<br>*Gossamer*<br>http://www.loislowry.com |
| J. K. Rowling | An interactive website that includes the latest news, an online journal by Rowling, quashed rumors, extra information on characters and stories that did not make it into the books. | *The Harry Potter series*<br>http://www.jkrowling.com |
| Nikki Giovanni | Includes a Truth Is On Its Way webcast, video clips of Giovanni reading her poetry, and interview transcripts. | *Ego-tripping & Other Poems for Young People*<br>*The Girls in the Circle*<br>*Rosa*<br>http://nikki-giovanni.com |
| Jane Yolen | Includes an online journal, interview transcripts, thoughts on writing, and frequently asked questions. | *Owl Moon*<br>*How Do Dinosaurs Say Goodnight?*<br>*The Devil's Arithmetic*<br>http://www.janeyolen.com |

## ENHANCED CRITICAL THINKING SKILLS

The Internet is a portal to a vast amount of information on just about any topic. This can be very motivating for students, since it provides an avenue to conduct research on issues and interests posed by them. Yet, anyone can publish anything on the Internet, so students must learn how to gather and critically evaluate information found on the Web. Learning how to effectively conduct a search, compare and contrast information found on different websites, and validate the information develops critical literacy skills.

**Searching for Information Online.** For children to find websites on the Internet that support their research and interests, they must learn how to effectively use a web browser to conduct a search. This is essential because a haphazard approach to finding information can lead to only frustration. The skills and strategies for conducting a productive search are unique to the Internet. The SEARCH strategy can be an effective way to teach children how to search for information on the Internet (Henry, 2006, p. 618) (see Figure 12.6).

**FIGURE 12.6**

The Search Strategy for Finding Information on the Internet

**S**et a purpose for searching.
**E**mploy effective search strategies.
**A**nalyze search engine results.
**R**ead critically and synthesize information.
**C**ite your sources.
**H**ow successful was your search?

**Set a purpose for searching.** The first and most crucial step is for students to have a goal in mind to focus their search task. Teachers can help children with this step by asking students to think about what information they are trying to locate. For example, if a child wanted to learn more about spiders as pets, she might want to know what types of spiders make the best pets, the environment she would need to house a spider, and the type of food it eats.

**Employ effective search strategies.** Next, help children to use prior knowledge about the topic of the search and use keywords as effective search strategies. Henry (2006) relates, "Providing students with a basic knowledge foundation of the topic to be explored causes searches to become more focused as the selection of appropriate keywords becomes easier" (p. 618). A child who would like to know more about having spiders as pets should be encouraged to brainstorm all she already knows about spiders before she starts her search.

**Analyze search engine results.** Once the search results have been displayed, children must then be able to determine which results will provide the most relevant information to the search goal. When a web page has been selected, children should skim the page for the URL, make inferences, and look for highlighted terms to determine if the information is relevant. Based on prior knowledge and the questions about pet spiders

Google Search Results on Spiders

Ten **Spider** Pets - **Pet Spiders | Pet Spider** Care
Raising pet spiders can be a fascinating experience. There are both advantages and disadvantages to raising a pet spider such as a tarantula or wolf spider.
www.tenspider.net/Pets/T3_Pet_Exotic_Invert_Spider.html - 55k -
Cached - Similar pages - Note this

Insects and **Spiders** for Beginners - A guide to Choosing an Insect ...
However, before deciding on an insect or spider as a pet, look at your reasons for wanting this kind of pet. If you are just looking for a pet that is ...
exoticpets.about.com/cs/insectsspiders/a/insectpider101.htm - 26k -
Cached - Similar pages - Note this

**Pet Arthropods: Insects, Tarantulas, Millipedes, Scorpions**
Some things to consider before committing to an insect or spider as a pet are discussed in our beginner's guide to these pets. Insects, **Spiders**, and More ...
exoticpets.about.com/od/insectsspiders/
Insects_Spiders_Scorpions_Millipedes_and_More.htm - 20k -
Cached - Similar pages - Note this

Man's moody **pet spider** turns on him - **Pet** Health - MSNBC.com
A New York man knew it was time to give up on his unusual pet when his Baboon **Spider** began to rear up on its hind legs and show its large fangs.
www.msnbc.msn.com/id/20321234/ - 47k - Cached - Similar pages - Note this

Eaten By His **Pet Spiders**
They devoured his body after he got a lethal bite from his favourite pet Bettina - a deadly Black Widow. More than 200 **spiders**, several snakes, ...
www.rense.com/general49/eaten.htm - 15k - Cached - Similar pages - Note this

The Sun Online - News: **Pet spider** kills its owner
A MAN who lived in his own "zoo" of lizards and insects was fatally bitten by a pet black widow **spider** — then eaten by the other creepy-crawlies.
www.thesun.co.uk/article/0,,2-2004092008,00.html - Similar pages - Note this

Digital Journal - Man Killed by **Pet Spider**, Eaten by Creepy Crawlies
Man Killed by Pet Spider, Eaten by Creepy Crawlies. Posted Aug 3, 2007 by

Google.

(continued)

**FIGURE 12.6**

(*continued*)

set before the search, the first three search results shown in the screenshot on page 357 would potentially yield useful information. The link to "Pet spider kills owner" and "Eaten by his pet spiders," however, would not offer very useful information.

**Read critically and synthesize information.** After a web page has been selected, critically evaluate the content for authenticity and relevancy. Teachers can provide children with guidelines for what to look for when reading a website: the author or institution associated with the website, the purpose for the website, the intended audience, the appropriate copyright data, and whether the information meets the needs of their intended audience.

The second screen shot, on this page (bottom), shows the web page of the second link from the search results: "Insects and Spiders for Beginners." The information answers many questions about spiders as pets, but how reliable is the information? A link on the page entitled "Our Story" leads to information on the purpose of About.com, the source of information, and the company who owns the site (the New York Times). This information leads the reader to believe it is a credible source of information. See the third screen shot, on page 359 (top).

**Cite your sources.** Documentation of sources used from the Internet is a necessary part of any research. Google Notebook is a free, easy-to-use online tool that allows students to clip and collect information in a central location as they browse the Web. Once Google Notebook has been installed, an icon in the shape of a notebook appears in the lower right-hand corner of the Google browser. When students find information they would like to keep, they simply highlight images, text, or links on the web page and click on the icon. The information is automatically stored in the student's notebook (see the screenshot above for an example of how the "insects and spiders for beginners" site was stored in Google Notebook). Site citations are created automatically, tracking where the student gathered information and allowing for organization and synthesis of information across online sources. Notebooks can be accessed from any computer and shared with other students.

Article on Insects and Spiders for Beginners

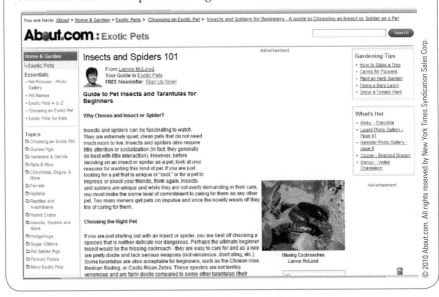

**FIGURE 12.6**

(*continued*)

Information About the Source of Insects and Spiders for Beginners. Is this a reliable source?

Storing Website Information in a Student's Online Notebook

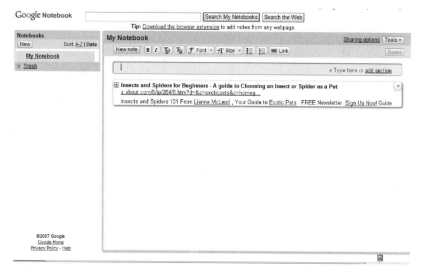

**How successful was your search?** Finally, students should reflect on the search process to identify the strategies they employed that were successful or unsuccessful and how they would approach the search task differently in the future.

The information needed to fulfill the goal of the search more than likely will come from several websites, and children then must synthesize the information into one response. Determining authenticity and relevancy of information from multiple websites, integrating that information into existing prior knowledge, and then synthesizing that information into a coherent response is a difficult task to say the least. Children initially will need a great deal of modeling and scaffolding by the teacher, who can then slowly release responsibility to them over time until they become independent (see Chapter 3 for a discussion of release of responsibility).

**Google Lit Trips.** Another way to enrich students' engagement with literature is by developing a depth of knowledge about the story's setting. Wouldn't it be great if students learning about Mem Fox could visit Australia and experience the places they read about in her books? Well, guess what? Now they can though Google lit trips! Google lit trips http://www.googlelittrips.com was created by Jerome Burg, a former English teacher who combined the excitement of a road trip with the interactive technology and satellite imagery of Google Earth http://earth.google.com to create the innovative experience of a journey similar to those taken by characters in literature.

The Google lit trip site has many "ready-made" lit trips for teachers and students to use that are categorized by grade level (K–2, 3–5, 6–8, and 9–12). Several lit trips have been created by Burg; however, teachers and students are taking his lead and creating their own virtual literary trips and sharing them with the online community. For example, the *Possum Magic* Google lit trip was created by Melanie Turner, an Instructional Technology Specialist for Colquitt County Schools in Georgia (see Figure 12.7). On this lit trip to

**FIGURE 12.7**

Google Lit Trip: *Possum Magic* Mem Fox
On this Google Lit Trip, students visit several cities in Australia to experience the setting of Possum Magic.

Australia, students will visit the cities of Adelaide, Melbourne, Sydney, Brisbane, Darwin, Perth and Tasmania. The Google lit trip *Marching for Freedom* was created by the book's author, Elizabeth Partridge.

After students become familiar with Google lit trips, teachers can engage them in the process of designing their own Google lit trips individually or in small groups. The power of students designing their own lit trip can provide an even deeper layer of understanding to a text. As students read, they can look for significant locations or information to add to their map.

**WebQuests.** A WebQuest facilitates the acquisition, integration, and extension of a vast amount of information. A WebQuest is designed by the teacher to specifically engage the learner in analysis and demonstration of understanding. According to Bernie Dodge (San Diego State University) and Tom March ozline.com, creators of the WebQuest, "A WebQuest is an inquiry-oriented activity in which most or all of the information used by learners is drawn from the Web. WebQuests are designed to use learners' time well, to focus on using information rather than looking for it, and to support learners' thinking at the levels of analysis, synthesis and evaluation" http://webquest.sdsu.edu/overview.htm. For an example of a WebQuest, see Figure 12.8.

A WebQuest creates an effective learning environment in which learners become oriented to an interesting and doable task with the resources and guidance to complete the task, including how they will be evaluated. WebQuests can be either long term or short term, depending on the instructional goal. Short-term WebQuests can take from one to three sessions and involve the learner in knowledge acquisition and integration of new information. Long-term WebQuests can take anywhere from one week to a month and involve the learner in extending and refining information through analysis and demonstrations.

**FIGURE 12.8**

Example of a WebQuest: *Chrysanthemum: What's in a Name?*

The design of a WebQuest is critical to its effectiveness as an instructional resource. WebQuests consist of the following critical attributes:

- **Introduction:** The purpose of this section is to both prepare and hook the reader. The introduction draws the reader into the learning situation by relating to the reader's interests or goals and/or engagingly describing a compelling question or problem. The introduction builds on the reader's prior knowledge by explicitly mentioning important concepts or principles, and it effectively prepares the learner for the lesson by foreshadowing new concepts and principles.

For example, *Chrysanthemum: What's in a Name?* is a WebQuest that is available in both Spanish and English, based on the picturebook *Chrysanthemum*, written and illustrated by Kevin Henkes. The WebQuest is designed to help children learn about author Kevin Henkes and learn about themselves along the way. The following is the introduction to the WebQuest:

*What **IS** a name? Is it just something that people call you? Does it have any meaning? We are going on a journey with Kevin Henkes to find out what your name is and who you are. Kevin Henkes is the author of great books that have friendly and funny little mice. These wonderful mice will be your guide. Your friends and family can't wait to learn more about you!*

The introduction immediately hooks students by indicating they will learn about their name, themselves, and author Kevin Henkes.

*(continued)*

**FIGURE 12.8**

(*continued*)

• **Task:** The task focuses learners on what they are going to do—specifically, the culminating performance or product that drives all of the learning activities. The task requires synthesis of multiple sources of information, and/or taking a position, and/or going beyond the data given and making a generalization or product. The task for the *Chrysanthemum* WebQuest follows:

**The Task**

*Your name is who you are. Anyone else with the same name is completely different. You are going on a journey to discover more about yourself. You will be working with your teacher, Kevin Henkes, family, and friends to help create a book and a life-size picture of yourself. Click on the books and learn about Kevin Henkes, and then click on the car and let's start our adventure!!*

The task requires students to synthesize information from Kevin Henkes books, family, and friends to create a book about themselves.

• **Process:** This section outlines how the learners will accomplish the task. Scaffolding includes clear steps, resources, and tools for organizing information. The steps readers must follow to complete the project are clearly outlined. The activities performed and/or the roles and perspectives to be taken on by the reader have a lot of variety. The process for the *Chrysanthemum* WebQuest leads students through ten clearly defined steps that culminate in a book about themselves. Here is Step 1:

*The first part of our "All About Me" book will have the story of your name. Read* Chrysanthemum *by Kevin Henkes with your class and discuss the story. Did you ever wonder where your name comes from? You can print out a form or ask your teacher or parent to print out the form for you. Once you have "the name form," you can ask different family members on how you got your name. Have a family member write out the story, or they can help you write it.*

• **Resources:** All links to web resources are pertinent to the task, make excellent use of the Web, and are working. Links for the *Chrysanthemum* WebQuest include information on Kevin Henkes and his books.

**FIGURE 12.8**
(*continued*)

- **Evaluation:** This section describes the evaluation criteria needed to meet performance and content standards. Explicit directions are included that tell how the readers will demonstrate their growth in knowledge. The "product" reflects this growth. Some evaluations include rubrics with clearly defined criteria, whereas others are more open-ended. The evaluation for the *Chrysanthemum* WebQuest asked students to reflect on the project by responding to the following questions:

  New things I learned about myself. . . .
  New things I would like to learn more about myself. . . .
  My favorite things about this project.
  Things I would make better about this project

In this way, students were given the opportunity to self-evaluate the process and product of the project.

**TABLE 12.5**

# Literature-Based WebQuests

- **WebQuests Based on Literature** http://webquest.sdsu.edu/literature-wq.htm. Choose WebQuests from a chart characterizing the different forms of these types of WebQuests, such as searching for information and connections about characters, settings, genres, or analyzing literature.

- **Literature-Based WebQuests** http://projects.edtech.sandi.net/projects/literature. html. WebQuests that incorporate literature and author studies. Divided by grade range. Some WebQuest projects include studying insects with Eric Carle (K–2), Kid's Court: Finding Justice in Fairy Tales (grades 3–5), and The Outsiders: Teens & Life Choices (grades 6–8).

- **Eduscape's WebQuest list** http://eduscapes.com/tap/topic4.htm. Contains information and links about WebQuests, including definition and creation as well as links to WebQuests.

Though WebQuests cross the curriculum, literature-based WebQuests center the experience on reading by using books as the focal point for activities. Tasks might involve children in exploration of the theme, characters, plot, or setting of the book being studied. Table 12.5 provides a list of literature-based WebQuests.

**Internet Projects: Connecting Children with the World.** An Internet project is a collaborative learning experience between two or more classrooms at different locations that takes place over the Internet. These projects can be initiated by individual teachers or coordinated through a website. For an example of a teacher-initiated Internet project, Susan Silverman, formerly a second-grade teacher and now a technology consultant, created many collaborative literature extension activities conducted between two or more classes around a book, genre, or topic, http://kids-learn.org. An example of a website Internet project, Journey North, http://www.learner.org/jnorth/index.html, engages students in a global study of wildlife migration and seasonal change. K–12 students share their own field observations with classmates across North America. They track the coming of spring through the migration patterns of monarch butterflies, bald eagles, robins, hummingbirds, whooping cranes, and other birds and mammals; the budding of plants; changing sunlight; and other natural events. Here are some websites that offer collaborative Internet projects:

- **Global Schoolhouse** http://www.globalschoolnet.org. Contains interactive projects designed so students worldwide can collaborate, communicate, and learn from each other. Teachers can sign up to participate in these projects.
- **Project Centre** http://www.2learn.ca/projects/projectcentre/projintro.html. Teachers can sign up for telecollaborative projects, which provide real-world contexts such as opportunities for students to interact with experts and other professionals.
- **Oz Projects** http://www.ozprojects.edu.au. Contains projects set around a concept or theme. The site can be searched for project by grade range, date, and subject.
- **iEarn** http://www.iearn.org. Over 150 projects are designed by teachers to help foster critical thinking and research skills, cultural awareness, and community involvement.
- **Flat Stanley: A Travel Buddy Project** http://eduscapes.com/tap/topic1h .htm. E-mail project based on the book *Flat Stanley* by Jeff Brown. Classrooms make their own Flat Stanleys and keep a journal that is then sent to other schools. Not limited to e-mail (snail mail can also be used).

## DIVERSITY OPPORTUNITIES

*New literacies permit new understanding and new appreciation of the diversity that exists in our world. The Internet is shrinking the world we inhabit in a significant way. Suddenly, without leaving our desks, we can visit a school or museum in Viet Nam or South Africa; instantly, without picking up a phone, we can communicate with students or experts in Helsinki or Brazilia. Our perception of how close we are to one another is fundamentally altered by this special technology and the new literacies we must acquire to use it.*

LEU, LEU, & COIRO, 2004, P. 356

Technology-supported instruction and projects can increase academic engagement among students of diverse backgrounds based on the extent to which two significant factors are present: (1) students are encouraged to explore and appreciate aspects of their own cultural and linguistic heritage, and (2) students come to see themselves as intelligent and capable human beings in the process of carrying out these projects (Cummins, Brown, & Sayers, 2007). Labbo (2005) states, "It is clear that when students gather and share cultural information for a cross-cultural Internet project, students engage in reading that is inherently meaningful, insightful, and motivating. The Internet opens up the world to students and helps them develop a respect for diversity" (p. 174).

**Internet Projects for Cultural and Language Diversity.** Teacher-created Internet projects can engage students in sharing cultural information that is relevant and meaningful. After reading the story, students engage in language arts, social studies, math, or science activities that are showcased on a website. For example, Susan Silverman and Patty Knox, two technology integration specialists, created Cinderella around the World http://www.northcanton.sparcc.org/~ptk1nc/Cinderella, (Figure 12.9), a global project that invited classes from around the world to read multicultural versions of *Cinderella* and share their learning. Students from 14 states in the United States and four countries participated, contributing their unique projects created around Cinderella stories and activities.

From the author information gained through the website, the children were able to make important connections to how the stories relate to Mem Fox's life and where she got ideas for writing many of her books.

Almost every author has a website or is part of the publisher's website. Author websites often offer a showcase of their works, appearances, interviews, speeches, and other news about the author. In addition, some authors include an online journal or blog that updates the audience on their daily lives, what they are currently writing,

**FIGURE 12.9**

Internet Project on Diversity: **Cinderella Around the World**
A teacher-created Internet project that features multicultural literature as an avenue for reader response and curriculum-related activities.

or their opinions on a variety of topics. Some have activity resources, such as worksheets, that go along with their books. Table 12.6 contains a few selected authors' websites.

Online resources such as the Global SchoolNet http://www.globalschoolnet.org are free services to help teachers link with partners in other cultures and countries for e-mail classroom penpals and other project exchanges. Teachers can involve students in creating personal technology-supported projects such as digital storytelling and biographies that provide authentic opportunities for students to bring their home culture into the classroom and share with other students around the world. This project is also good for English language learners and students with special learning needs.

**Options for Students with Special Needs.** Computers and other technologies allow students to work in multimodal ways, providing the opportunity to differentiate instruction. Supportive technology can be especially helpful in assisting students with learning disabilities and mental, physical, and emotional challenges to access and participate in reading online literature, projects, and research activities:

- **Accessibility options.** Microsoft http://www.microsoft.com/enable and Apple http://www.apple.com/education/accessibility have many accessibility options available as part of the software or browser functions. For visual impairments, the contrast, scroll bar, icon size, width, and speed of the cursor can be adjusted, and a magnifier that enlarges a portion of the screen where the cursor is placed and a voice recognition and text-to-speech screen reader can be turned on. For hearing impairments, SoundSentry provides a visual alert when the computer makes a sound, and ShowSounds displays captions for the speech and sound elements of various programs. Both can simply be switched on.
- **Specialized adaptive technology.** The adjustments to web browsers and software just mentioned may not meet the needs of all students with special needs to work around their areas of challenge. Alternative keyboards, such as IntelliKeys http://www.intellitools.com, can be customized in appearance and functions with special printed overlays; input devices, such as Kurzweil 3000 http://www.kurzweiledu.com/kurz3000.aspx, which allows any printed material to be scanned in and then read aloud or reads aloud a student's typed text; and high-powered screen magnifiers like ZoomText http://www.aisquared.com can be utilized.
- **Text-to-speech readers.** Text-to-speech readers such as ReadPlease http://www.readplease.com, a free download reads any text, including websites, e-mail, and files. The voice speed, word color, and background color can also be adjusted.
- **Online translators.** American Sign Language browser http://commtechlab.msu.edu/sites/aslWeb/browser.htm and Online Braille Translator http://pbskids.org/arthur/print/braille/index.html.
- **E-Buddies** http://www.ebuddies.org is dedicated to enhancing the lives of people with intellectual disabilities by providing opportunities for one-to-one friendships.
- **Internet inquiry.** Visit the Center for Applied Special Technology http://www.cast.org/teachingeverystudent/toolkits for an online toolkit and model lesson on Internet inquiry opportunities for students with special needs.

- **Kids' Quests** provide unique opportunities for students with and without special needs to build understanding and friendships with students with special needs. Kids' Quests http://www.cdc.gov/ncbddd/kids/kidhome. htm provides six WebQuests designed for students in fourth, fifth, and sixth grades that are intended to get kids to think about people with disabilities and some of the issues related to daily activities, health, and accessibility.
- **Ultralingua online dictionary** http://www.ultralingua.com/onlinedictionary. This online dictionary provides a word look-up in multiple languages and also turns any website into a dictionary. Just type in the Web address of any website, and it becomes dictionary enabled. The site also provides a grammar reference
- **The International Children's Digital Library** http://www.icdlbooks. org provides books and audiobooks in many languages. The Reading Is Fundamental site http://www.rif.org/readingplanet/content/read_aloud_ stories.mspx and Story Place http://www.storyplace.org have stories that are read aloud in Spanish and English.

## CONSIDERATIONS: SAFETY AND CENSORSHIP

The Internet is an open network in which anyone can post almost anything. Since Internet search engines find information based on key words that might appear in a variety of contexts, the search results might include content that is inappropriate for students. To prevent this from happening, schools require filtering software such as Net Nanny http://www.netnanny.com that blocks certain sites and keywords that are updated regularly. Blocked websites can be unblocked by a teacher. Students can also use search engines that are designed for them, such as Yahooligans, Ask Jeeves for Kids, and Kids Click. Teachers can also "bookmark" sites that are safe for students to access. Although parents and teachers must be cautious about students' Internet browsing, it is equally important to teach students how to protect themselves. Educators must discuss with students why some information is not appropriate for them and teach students how to evaluate websites for credibility and to never give out personal information on the Internet. Here are some resources for teachers and families on child Internet safety:

- **American Library Association: Online Safety Rules and Regulations** http://www.ala.org/ala/aboutala/offices/oif/iftoolkits/litoolkit/ onlineresources.cfm provides a list of websites on child Internet safety.
- **Net Smartz** http://www.netsmartz.org sponsored by the National Center for Missing & Exploited Children and Boys & Girls Clubs of America, this site provides educational resources for children ages 5 to 17, parents, and teachers on how to stay safer on the Internet.
- **SafeKids.com** http://safekids.com provides guidelines for parents and rules to ensure kids' online safety.

## Selecting and Evaluating Internet Sites

When selecting websites for students, a number of considerations must be made to ensure the site is a source of good information and is designed to support the emerging navigational skills of students rather than becoming a frustrating experience. The questions

**TABLE 12.6**

# Evaluating Internet Websites

**Accessibility**

- Does the page take a long time to load?

- Are the images big enough for children to see?

- Is there a picture on the page that you can use to choose links (site map)?

- If you go to another page, is there a way to get back to the first page?

**Usability**

- Does the title of the page tell you what it is about?

- Is there an introduction on the page telling you what is included?

- Are the facts on the page what you were looking for?

- Would you have gotten more information from an encyclopedia?

- Would the information have been better in the encyclopedia?

- Do the pictures and photographs on the page help you learn?

- Does the page lead you to some other good information (links)?

**Credibility**

- Was the site developed by a reputable company (.com or .net), educational institution (.edu), or organization (.org)?

- If the site is developed by an individual, is the author's name and e-mail address on the page?

- Is there a date that tells you when the page was created or updated?

- If there are photographs, do they look real?

- If there are sounds, do they sound real?

- Does the author of the page say some things you disagree with?

- Does the page include information you know is wrong?

Adapted from Kathy Schrock's web page: http://school.discovery.com/schrockguide/eval.html.

in Table 12.6 will guide your selection. These questions should also be shared with students so they can learn to judge the credibility and value of Internet sites.

# Opportunities for Reader Response

Internet communication can promote authentic interactions between students or a broader audience outside of the school. For example, children can communicate with astronauts, authors, historians, and scientists about topics being studied in class or events happening in the world. Writing is more conversational and brief (even one word) when using Internet communications, such as e-mail (Wollman-Bonilla, 2003), than traditional print. Wollman-Bonilla found that a six-year-old's e-mail messages were shorter and often more to the point compared to handwritten letters. Due to the speed of the communication, e-mail can become similar to conversation, which can also have an effect on the way e-mail is read. Wollman-Bonilla (2003) writes, "The notion that computers encourage superficial browsing rather than careful, extended attention to screen content suggests that writers might not attend to the details of e-mail messages as they would to printed (nonscreen) texts where reading is thought to be deeper and composing more deliberate" (p. 128). Although Internet communication differs from printed text in terms of writing and reading, it is an important tool of communication.

The following applications allow students to have meaningful, authentic responses to literature while providing an opportunity for teachers to scaffold their use of specific skills and strategies for reading and writing via Internet communication.

## ONLINE DISCUSSIONS, BLOGS, WIKIS, AND REVIEWS

The Internet makes it easier for children to discuss books with their peers locally, regionally, nationally, or internationally. Book discussions, sometimes called book raps or book chats, are online discussion groups about books that take place using e-mail, chat rooms, or discussion boards. Classes from different parts of the world can read and discuss books together. At the same time students can learn about culture and diversity (Leu et. al., 2004).

**Online Book Discussions.** Research has found that engagement in online literature discussions provides an opportunity for students to develop and verbalize ideas with others, promotes in-depth response and reflection and careful consideration of multiple perspectives and thoughts, encourages peer affirmation, and provides opportunities for more teacher-student and student-teacher interaction (English, 2007; Larson, 2009). Additionally, Zhang, Gao, Gail and Zhang (2007) found that online literature discussions influenced ESL students' writing skills and provoked critical thinking.

For online discussions to be meaningful conversations rather than superficial one-line responses, children must understand how to engage in meaningful face-to-face discussions about books. Online discussions should not replace in-class literature groups or book clubs but should be used as an important extension that allows children to connect with a broader audience with diverse perspectives, cultures, and experiences. When children understand how to participate in meaningful in-class discussions with other children and the teacher, it serves as a foundation for meaningful online discussions. Yet, online communication is different from face-to-face discussions, and it is important for teachers to scaffold students' understanding of how to read and respond to online communication. Table 12.7 contains online sources for finding classes for book discussions. Most will provide an overview of how the virtual book connection with another class works, when it will take place, how long it will last, and possibly the book that will be discussed. Teachers can also create their own online discussion communities in which students can discuss the books they are reading via collaborative online sites also listed in Table 12.7.

Software programs such as Skype allow real time video conferencing that can be used for face-to-face book discussions with other schools. For example, Clarence Fisher, a teacher in a remote area of Manitoba, Canada, used Skype with his students to discuss S. E. Hinton's *The Outsiders* with Barbara Barreda's eighth grade class in Los Angeles (Foote, 2008).

**Blogs.** Blogs are interactive online journals that are free, easy to create, and can be public or private. Teachers can create a class blog in which all students respond to an assignment or students can create individual blogs. Either way, all of the students can read and

---

**TABLE 12.7**

# Online Collaboration

- **Raps** http://www.learningplace.com.au/raps.asp?orgid=79&suborgid=497. Contains a variety of raps (discussions of a book, movie, piece of music, or game) in which teachers can register their classes to participate. Most raps last four to six weeks.

- **Book Raps** http://rite.ed.qut.edu.au/old_oz-teachernet/projects/book-rap/index1.html. Gives information about book raps, including definition, expected outcomes, and resources.

- **The Center for Interactive Learning and Collaboration** http://www.cilc.org CILC is the venue for educators to meet, create a collaborative project, and share their reflections.

- **E-pals** http://www.epals.com. K-12 online community that provides a way for educators and students to safely connect and collaborate. Options are available to connect via video conferencing.

**Social Networking Sites**
The following free online social networking resources allows users to create their own social network. Teachers can create book discussion forums and students can create their own profiles and pages. The sites can be public or private.

- **Ning** http://www.ning.com

- **Google Groups** http://groups.google.com

- **Moodle** http://moodle.org

- **ThinkQuest** http://www.thinkquest.org

*Read*

*Access a list of free blog providers and information on using blogs in the classroom.*

respond to each others' posts. If the blog is public, anyone anywhere can post a response to a student's blog post. This shift in audience from the teacher to the class or the world fundamentally changes the motivation for and engagement with written response for students (Thompson, 2009) and is a major reason for involving students in blogging.

However, if students' blogs are *only* used to respond online to assignments, then the full potential of blogs for promoting critical and analytical thinking will not be realized. Blogs allow students to create content in ways not possible in a traditional paper/pencil environment. Rather than simply using the blog as a context to post a response that could be written on paper, blogs allow students to link to and connect ideas (that can take the form of pictures, podcasts, videos and other multimedia), to make their thinking about ideas transparent and to have others link to their posts. To do this, students must engage in close reading and reflection, to think critically within and across sources of information, to form a clear and concise message for a real audience.

For example, if students are given an assignment to respond to a particular aspect of a book or poem, then the response could include links and connections to information from the author's blog, to book reviewers' blogs, other students' blogs, or other online resources. Students' responses would necessarily represent an analysis and synthesis of these multiple sources of information along with the students' own reflections or experiences that would ultimately articulate a deeper understanding of the content and response to the text. For an example of a classroom blog, visit Monica Edinger's blog site http://blogs.dalton.org/edinger in New York.

**Wikis.** A wiki is also a free, easy to create website that allows visitors to edit the content. The ease of interaction makes a wiki an effective tool for collaborative authoring, but it also creates potential for inaccurate, incomplete, or misleading information. Wikipedia, a popular wiki, is a free encyclopedia on the Web with over 1.5 million articles to which anyone can contribute. Although one might question the credibility of such an open-source encyclopedia, it is considered a viable alternative to commercial encyclopedias. One fourth-grade teacher used Wikipedia as a way to teach children about evaluating Internet resources and as a collaborative response to reading. The students had recently finished *Charlotte's Web* by E. B. White. The teacher displayed the Wikipedia entry for *Charlotte's Web* on a smart-board, a large interactive screen connected to a computer and projector. Unhappy with the inaccuracies in the entry, the teacher and children collaboratively edited the entry with the teacher as scribe on the smart-board. Table 12.8 is an example of the original text and how it was edited. The children had to use their critical thinking skills to assess the quality of the original entry and use their knowledge of the book and a good plot summary to edit and revise.

*Read*

*Access a list of free wiki providers and information on using wikis in the classroom.*

**Sharing Book Reviews Online.** Online book reviews are another way children can respond to reading. "The Child's Voice" on page 372 is an example of one fourth grader's online review of *Alabama Moon.*

Writing an online review creates an authentic audience. Potentially hundreds, even thousands of people could read the review, which in turn, may influence whether they decide to read the book. Some online booksellers offer readers the opportunity to post reviews of books, but several nonprofit sites also post children's book reviews such as The Spaghetti Book Club (http://www.spaghettibookclub.org), The World of Reading (http://www.worldreading.org), and Book Hooks (http://www.bookhooks.com).

Teachers can also use social networking sites such as Goodreads (http://www.goodreads.com) or LibraryThing (http://www.librarything.com) to provide virtual spaces for students to write and share book reviews. These sites allow members to recommend books, compare what they are reading, keep track of what they've read and would like to

*Read*

*Read Author Rodman Philbrick's writing tips, strategies, and challenges to help kids write a book review.*

**TABLE 12.8**

# Evaluating Internet Sources: Wikipedia's Entry About *Charlotte's Web*

**Wikipedia Entry on *Charlotte's Web***

Charlotte A. Cavatica, a spider, lives in the space above Wilbur's sty in the Zuckermans' barn; she befriends Wilbur and decides to help prevent him from being eaten. With the help of the other barn animals, including a rat named Templeton, she convinces the Zuckerman family that Wilbur is special by spelling out such descriptions as "Some Pig" in her web. Charlotte gives her full name as "Charlotte A. Cavatica," revealing her as a barn spider, an orb-weaver spider with the scientific name *Araneus cavaticus*.

**Students' Edited Version of the Wikipedia Entry**

"Where's Papa going with that ax?" asks eight-year-old Fern Arable to her mother one spring morning. It turns out that Mr. Arable is off to "do away with" a runty pig. Horrified, Fern softens him up and manages to save the pig. She names him Wilbur and tends to him as if she was his mother until he becomes too big and moves to Mr. Zuckerman's barn.

Charlotte, a spider, lives over the door near Wilbur's pen. She befriends him and, by weaving words such as "Terrific" and "Some Pig" in her web, tries to convince the Zuckerman family that Wilbur is so unique that he cannot ever be killed for food.

White's amazingly written, full-to-the-brim *Charlotte's Web* is a classic all-American children's book. Themes such as friendship, life and death, and nature make this book well worth reading.

## THE • CHILD'S • VOICE

*A Fourth Grader's Online Review of Alabama Moon*

This is a great book written by Watt Key about a young boy named Moon Blake. He is living with his father in a small house in the Alabama wilderness. Moon and his father are hiding from the government. But then his father dies and suddenly Moon is alone. Before his dad dies he tells Moon to head for Alaska, which he does, but he meets two other boys and they stay with him in the wild. I don't think I should tell you any more or you won't need to read the book. Thanks for reading.

—*In what ways has posting this review online influenced this child's response?*

*Read*

*Read a fourth grade teacher's blog on how she uses Goodreads in her classroom.*

read, and form book clubs. In order to become a member, students must have individual email accounts. However, if school email accounts are not available, teachers can receive free email accounts from e-pals.com.

Teachers can also create a blog and post reviews of books they have shared with their students as a way to keep their students' families informed and to share with others. "The Teacher's Voice" below is an example of one fourth-grade teacher's blog post.

**Book Trailers.** Another type of reading response that allows students to invoke multiple senses when conveying the heart of a story is creating a book trailer. VoiceThread http://voicethread.com is a free online program that gives students an easy way to share their passion for a book they've read. Students create a one to two-minute video using photos, transitions, special effects, voiceovers, and a soundtrack. The ability to use multimedia gives students the opportunity to share their learning in more powerful ways. Students must carefully select pictures, music, and narration that, in concert, convey the essence of

**THE · TEACHER'S · VOICE**

A Fourth Grade Teacher's Blog Review of *Henry's Freedom Box* by Ellen Levine, illustrated by Kadir Nelson

*Digital Literacy in the Classroom*

Blog by Amy Moser/Book cover used by permission of Scholastic, Inc.

—*How did access to the World Wide Web influence this teacher's response to* Henry's Freedom Box?

*Watch student-created book trailers.*

the story in a way that no one medium could. Showing students how to storyboard their ideas and work through the process of selecting, editing and revising for meaning and clarity will assist them with the process.

## LITERATURE EXTENSION ACTIVITIES

Literature extension activities allow children authentic ways to respond to reading. The Internet provides abundant choices for children to respond to literature with plays, retellings, poems, or stories. These responses can easily be shared with parents, grandparents, relatives, and other children around the world.

- **Collaborative and Interactive Online Projects** http://eduscapes.com/ladders/themes/interactive.htm. Provides information about collaborative projects, including the definition and how to create them. Also gives links to collaborative projects on the Web.
- **Literature Circles Resource Center** http://www.litcircles.org/Extension/extension.html. Gives steps for teachers to follow to plan and evaluate extension projects. Also contains examples that can be modified for several grade levels.
- **ePals Classroom Exchange Project** http://www.epals.com. Allows students to participate in projects with students from other cultures. Projects are divided into three age levels: 6–11, 12–14, and 15 and up.

## CREATING DIGITAL STORIES

*Story telling and listening not only helps the teller in the telling, it helps the listener in the hearing, even across great distances of space and time.*

**From the Center for Digital Storytelling** http://www.storycenter.org/index1.html. Children find themselves strongly connected to the books they enjoy. Many times books spark stories from children's own lives. With digital storytelling children take their written stories and incorporate illustrations and/or photographs and add voice recordings using Photo Story (a free download for Windows) that can be posted to the Internet. In addition to creating enthusiasm for writing, digital storytelling provides authentic opportunities for children to express themselves using multiple modes of communication and expression while also learning to use digital photography, audio, image, and video software. Furthermore, Sylvester and Greenidge (2009) found digital storytelling to be a promising tool for supporting struggling writers. Examples of K–12 digital stories can be found at the Center for Digital Storytelling http://www.storycenter.org.

## PUBLISHING STUDENT WRITING ON THE INTERNET

As with literature extension activities, publishing student writing on the Internet is motivating and expands the audience of readers. There are many websites that post student stories, poems, and art for other children to read and respond to. Several sites also offer support for young writers. Scholastic's Writing with Writers site http://teacher.scholastic.com/writewit provides an online opportunity for prominent children's authors to serve as mentors by offering tips and writing advice along with the author's biographical information, selected works, and recommended books (see Figure 12.10). The authors make explicit connections between the craft of writing and reading. This site also has students' stories posted at different age levels that children can read. Some of the students' stories have feedback from the author.

**FIGURE 12.10**

Writing with Writers: Poetry
Poetry writing workshop with Jack Prelutsky, Karla Kuskin, and Jean Marzollo.

When children's writing is posted on the Internet, their work becomes a part of the large network of stories and information on the World Wide Web, and they learn that they, too, can become published authors. Children's writing can be published on the Internet in many ways, such as a school or class homepage, but the following websites are also helpful:

- **CAST Universal Design for Learning (UDL) Book Builder** http://bookbuilder.cast.org. Use this site to create, share, publish, and read digital books that engage and support diverse learners according to their individual needs, interests, and skills.
- **Cyberkids** http://www.cyberkids.com/he/html/submit.html. Cyberkids publishes artwork, poetry, stories, and other creative projects submitted by kids.
- **Midlink Magazine** http://www.cs.ucf.edu/~MidLink. Contains learning activities that come directly from the classroom and where the technology used enhances the academics. It is geared toward students ages 8–18.
- **Kids' Pub** http://www.kidpub.org/kidpub. Collection of over 44,000 stories written by children. Kids can publish their own stories or read stories from other students. A fee for annual membership is charged that allows kids to post their stories.
- **Kids Space** http://www.kids-space.org. Provides a space for sharing student writing and collaborative projects.
- **Storybook Online** http://www.storybookonline.net. A collaborative writing site that allows students to write stories together.

## Making the Connection Across the Curriculum

The world of children's fiction and nonfiction can be enhanced by using the Internet to build experiences and knowledge around texts. For example, many children's books have been written about the Holocaust, but it is still difficult for children to imagine that such a horrific event ever happened. Wouldn't it be great if children could visit the Holocaust Museum in Washington, D.C.? (I live close to Washington, D.C., so I have had the opportunity to visit the museum, and it is truly a life-changing experience.) Most children, however, do not live close enough to visit the museum and cannot experience firsthand the many artifacts, videos, newspaper clippings, and audio recordings that make the events of the Holocaust real and understandable. Yet, a virtual visit to the Holocaust Museum http://www.ushmm.org is possible. Photo archives, online exhibits, and oral histories recorded by Holocaust survivors are accessible with the click of the mouse. The site has a special focus display on the rescue of Jews from Denmark, which pairs well with *Number the Stars* by Lois Lowry and *Darkness Over Denmark* by Ellen Levine. One can view photos of the boats that carried Danish refugees from German-occupied Denmark to neutral Sweden, a short biography of a Dane who helped Jews flee Denmark to Sweden, and a video of a Jewish survivor who made the trip from Denmark to Sweden http://www.ushmm.org/museum/exhibit/focus/Danish. An online exhibit houses photos and audio oral histories of what happened to Holocaust survivors after the war. Hearing a Holocaust survivor talk about her experience fleeing from Denmark or what happened to her after the war makes the events in *Number the Stars* real in a way that just studying about this period in a history book cannot. The following websites offer good information:

- **Virtual Free Sites** http://www.virtualfreesites.com/museums.museums.html. This site provides links to over 300 museums, exhibits, points of special interest, and real-time journeys that offer online multimedia guided tours on the Web.
- **Teachnology** http://www.teach-nology.com/teachers/ask_experts/science. This site provides links to various experts in the field of science who will answer students' questions.
- **TechnospudProjects** http://www.technospudprojects.com. This site hosts online collaborative projects, many of which are math related.

Integrating digital texts and tools in the classroom opens the door to a whole new world of stories, information, and collaborative opportunities to children. Further, it provides support for the development of the new literacies necessary for students to read, write, view, navigate, and communicate in a rapidly changing technological world. Technology in the classroom is motivating and engaging for students and provides them with access to information that enhances their educational opportunities.

# Top 10 Children's Literature Websites

1. **American Library Association (ALA)** http://www.ala.org. The ALA website houses an expansive amount of information and resources for teachers and librarians. ALA bestows some of the most prestigious awards in children's and young adult literature, so information on awards and noteworthy book lists are included along with information on intellectual freedom and diversity and equity.

2. **Barahona Center** http://www.csusm.edu/csb. Provided by California State University San Marcos, this site promotes literacy in English and Spanish. The Center endeavors to inform current and future educational decision makers about books about the Latino people and their culture and books in Spanish and their value in education of English-speaking and Spanish-speaking children and adolescents.

3. **The Cooperative Children's Book Center (CCBC)** http://www.education.wisc.edu/ccbc/books/default.asp. The CCBC is hosted by the School of Education at the University of Wisconsin-Madison and is committed to identifying excellent literature for children and adolescents. The site houses information and links on authors/illustrators, awards, bibliographies and book lists, intellectual freedom, and publications provided by the CCBC.

4. **Database of Award-Winning Children's Literature** http://www.dawcl.com. The purpose of this database is to create a tailored reading list of quality children's literature or to find out if a book has won one of the indexed awards. This site is geared toward librarians or teachers, but anyone can use it to find the best in children's literature, including parents, book store personnel, and children and young adults.

5. **Multicultural Children's Literature** http://www.multiculturalchildrenslit.com. This website contains links to annotated bibliographies of children's multicultural books appropriate for the elementary grades (kindergarten through grade six). Cultural groups currently listed include African Americans, Chinese Americans, Latino/Hispanic Americans, Japanese Americans, Jewish Americans, Native Americans, and Korean Americans. Books are categorized by genre, and each annotation includes an approximate grade level designation—for example, K–3, 4–6.

6. **ReadKiddoRead** http://www.readkiddoread.com. Inspired by the realization that his son didn't "exactly love books," renowned author James Patterson started ReadKiddoRead, a website dedicated to helping kids find books they love to read. Backed by a great board of children's literature experts, ReadKiddoRead offers a plethora of ways to find great books complete with reviews, interviews with authors/illustrators, reading guides, and advise.

7. **The Poetry Foundation's Children's Program** http://www.poetry-foundation.org/programs/children.html. The Poetry Foundation's Children's Program is the home of the Children's Poet Laureate and

*(continued)*

## Top 10 Children's Literature Websites (*continued*)

hosts many poetry resources such as videos, a poetry archive organized by theme, poetry book recommendations, featured children's poets such as Jack Prelutsky and Mary Ann Hoberman, and a curriculum for teaching essential African American poetry to students of all ages developed by Maya Angelou.

8. **Read.gov** http://read.gov. Read.gov is the Center for the Book's newest website for readers of all ages. The site offers pages specifically designed for kids and teens, as well as adults, educators and parents. Home of the National Ambassador for Young People's Literature, the read.gov site houses an impressive list of resources including: the *Exquisite Corpse Adventure* online story, access to 23 online classic children's books, the Letters About Literature contest, National Book Festival author webcasts, booklists and teaching resources.

9. **Reading Rockets** http://www.readingrockets.org. Reading Rockets is a comprehensive website that has something for everyone: parents, teachers, principals, librarians, and other professionals. The site, also available in Spanish, houses literacy resources, author interviews and videos, author studies and book lists,

10. **ReadWriteThink** http://www.readwritethink.org. ReadWriteThink is a partnership between the International Reading Association (IRA), the National Council of Teachers of English (NCTE), and the Verizon Foundation working together to provide educators and students with access to the highest-quality practices and resources in reading and language arts instruction through free, Internet-based content.

## Activities for Professional Development

### Think Critically About Children's Literature

1. As you can see from the information in this chapter, a whole world of online resources on children's literature is available. For students who are new to the field of children's literature and/or new to using online resources, I have created a professional development WebQuest on children's literature. Go to http://education. wm.edu/centers/childrenslit/webquest, and follow the instructions to complete the Web-Quest. It will take several weeks to complete. As a final product, you will create a resource notebook with the resources you find most valuable. Share your resource guide with other students in the class.

2. A listserv or mailing list is an electronic discussion group for people with similar interests. A message sent to the mailing list address is distributed to all member subscribers. Similarly, many teachers, librarians, and children's authors have blogs on which they post reviews of children's literature and other information related to children's books. Listservs and blogs are excellent ways to stay abreast of new books and current issues and trends in children's literature. Follow the directions on the website to subscribe to one or more of the listservs or blogs (select from the list of 100 Best Book Blogs listed under Online Resource below). Remain subscribed for at least a few weeks, and evaluate the information included in the

mailing list or blog. Did you find the resources valuable? Why or why not?

- **CHILD_LIT** http://email.rutgers. edu/mailman/listinfo/child_lit. An unmoderated discussion group convened for the express purpose of examining the theory and criticism of literature for children and young adults.
- **LM_NET** http://www.eduref.org/lm_net. A discussion group open to school library media specialists worldwide and to people involved with the school library media field. It is not for general librarians or educators.
- **CCBC-Net** http://www.education.wisc. edu/ccbc/ccbcnet/default.asp. A listserv that encourages awareness and discussion of ideas and issues critical to literature for children and young adults.

3. How has the Internet changed traditional views of literacy instruction? What reading strategies are necessary to comprehend text on the Internet? What challenges do teachers face in providing instruction in the new literacies in grades 3-5? In this professional development session, literacy expert Donald Leu addresses the reading and writing strategies required for using the Internet and how these new literacies are changing the way we teach. To view this session, go to the Annenberg Media video series, Teaching Reading 3-5 at http://www. learner.org/workshops/teachreading35/ session5/index.html. Click on "video summary" to read about the video you will be viewing, then watch the video. Afterward, click on "What did you learn?" under Reflect on Your Learning. Respond to the questions. Share your responses with your classmates.

### Learn About Authors and Illustrators

4. Author Jean Gralley not only writes and illustrates traditional print picturebooks (*The Moon Came Down on Milk Street, Hogula: Dread Pig of Night*) but also creates picture e-books. Visit her website at http://www.jeangralley. com, and read an enhanced version of her article that appeared in the January/February 2006 issue of *Horn Book Magazine* titled *Liftoff: When Books Leave the Page*. Then click on "Books Unbound" to view a digital animation that introduces and demonstrates the possibilities of digital picturebooks. You are in for a real treat! Share your thoughts about the article and digital picturebook with your classmates.

## Print and Online Resources

### Print Resources

Beach, R., Anson, C., Breuch, L., & Swiss, T. (2009). *Teaching writing using blogs, wikis, and other digital tools.* Norwood, MA: Christopher-Gordon.

Eagleton, M., & Dobler, E. (2006). *Reading the Web: Strategies for Internet inquiry.* New York: Guilford.

Hagood, M. (Ed.) (2009). *New literacies practices: Designing literacy learning.* New York: Lang.

Kist, W. (2010). *The socially networked classroom: Teaching in the new media age.* Thousand Oaks, CA: Corwin.

Labbo, L., Love, M., Prior, M., Hubbard, B., & Ryan, T. (2006). *Literature links: Thematic units linking read-alouds and computer activities.* Newark, DE: International Reading Association.

Moss, B., & Lapp, D. (Eds.) (2010). *Teaching new literacies in grades K-3: Resourcs for 21ˢᵗ century classrooms.* New York: Guilford.

Moss, B., & Lapp, D. (Eds.) (2010). *Teaching new literacies in grades 4-6: Resourcs for 21ˢᵗ century classrooms.* New York: Guilford.

Reissman, R. & Gura, M. (2010). *Teaching with author web sites K-8.* Thousand Oaks, CA: Corwin.

Watts-Taffe, S., & Gwinn, C. (2007). *Integrating literacy and technology: Effective practices for grades K–6.* New York: Guilford.

 **Online Resources**

*Center for Applied Special Technology (CAST)*
**http://www.cast.org**

CAST is a nonprofit organization that works to expand learning opportunities for all individuals, especially those with disabilities, through the research and development of innovative, technology-based educational resources and strategies.

*Integrating Literacy and Technology in the Curriculum*
**http://www.reading.org/General/AboutIRA/ PositionStatements/21stCenturyLiteracies.aspx**
A position statement by the International Reading Association.

*The International Reading Association's Resources in Technology*
**http://www.reading.org/Resources/Resources byTopic/Technology/Resources.aspx**
IRA's website has a listing of resources on the use of technology in literacy.

*The Literacy Project*
**http://www.google.com/literacy**
A search engine designed as a resource for teachers, literacy organizations, and anyone interested in reading and education. Find books, articles, and videos about literacy, or start your own literacy or reading group!

*Literacy & Technology Integration*
**http://www.literacy.uconn.edu/littech.htm**
Hosted by the University of Connecticut, this site provides an extensive annotated list of links to sites that provide examples of learning literacy with technology and sites devoted to integrating technology.

*100 Great Blogs That Young Writers Should Read*
**http://www.onlinedegreeshub.com/blog/2009/ 100-great-blogs-that-young-writers-should-read/**
This list of the best-of-the-best blogs about writing will provide young writers with valuable resources and information on writing.

*100 Best Book Blogs for Kids, Tweens, and Teens*
**http://www.onlineschools.org/2009/10/27/ 100-best-book-blogs-for-kids-tweens-and-teens/**
If you're looking for blogs about children's and young adult literature, no need to look any farther. This list features general to specialized blogs that will help you find the best books available.

*Electronic Books and Online Reading*
**http://eduscapes.com/tap/topic93.htm#1**

A comprehensive, annotated list of online books categorized by age. Icons indicate animation, audio, and interaction.

*Kids Reads*
**http://www.kidsreads.com**
Kidsreads provides a place on the web for kids to find information about their favorite books, series and authors. The site provides reviews of the newest titles, interviews with authors and special features on great books, trivia games, word scrambles and contests.

## CREATING YOUR CLASSROOM LIBRARY

In addition to the many online stories discussed in this chapter, here are a few more online books for your classroom library.

*The Exquisite Corpse Adventure*
**http://read.gov/exquisite-corpse**
A project of the Center for the Book and the National Children's Book and Literacy Alliance, the *Exquisite Corpse Adventure* is an episodic story game told by a series of renowned authors of children's literature. The first episode is written by Jon Scieszka and illustrated by Chris Van Dusen. Subsequent episodes are written by Katherine Paterson, Kate DiCamillo, Gregory Maguire, Fred and Patricia McKissack, Shannon Hale, Natalie Babbitt, Nikki Grimes, Megan McDonald, and Steven Kellogg. The *Exquisite Corpse Adventure* is an experiment in imagination and a must read for everyone.

*Brothers of the Night*
**http://www.kennedy-center.org/multimedia/ storytimeonline**
Based on the Grimms' fairy tale *The Twelve Dancing Princesses, Brothers of the Knight,* was written by Debbie Allen and illustrated by Kadir Nelson and is presented by the Kennedy Center's Storytime Online program. Brilliantly narrated by Debbie Allen, this fantastic story is not to be missed.

*Giggle Poetry*
**http://www.gigglepoetry.com**

*The Tale of Peter Rabbit*
**http://wiredforbooks.org/kids.htm**
Presented as a multimedia slide show and narrated by Karen Chan, this classic children's story continues to thrill students today.

*The Nightmare Room* by R. L. Stine
**http://www.thenightmareroom.com**

This site houses an online story *Dead of Night* by the master of scary books for children, R. L. Stine. Twelve-year-old David and his friends attempt to rescue their friend Keith from the hospital for one last night of total freedom, until night turns into nightmare.

*The Moonlit Road*
**http://www.themoonlitroad.com**
The Moonlit Road is a website that houses ghost stories and other strange Southern folktales, told by the region's best storytellers.

Visit the companion website at **www.cengage.com/education/johnson** to find links related to the Read/Watch/Listen icons noted throughout the chapter, as well as additional resources.

# References

Coiro, J. (2003). Reading comprehension on the Internet: Expanding our understanding of reading comprehension to encompass new literacies. *The Reading Teacher, 56*(5), 458–464.

Cummins, J., Brown, K., & Sayers, D. (2007). *Literacy, technology, and diversity: Teaching for success in changing times.* New York: Allyn & Bacon.

Danziger, P. (2000). *Snail mail no more.* New York: Scholastic.

English, C. (2007). Finding a voice in a threaded discussion group: Talking about literature online. *English Journal, 97*(1), 56–61.

Friedman, T. (2006). *The world is flat* (updated and expanded edition). New York: Farrar, Straus and Giroux.

Foote, C. (2008). *See me, hear me: Skype in the classroom.* Available at http://www.schoollibraryjournal.com/index.asp?layout=talkbackCommentsFull&talk_back_header_id=6497594&articleid=ca6515247.

Glasgow, J. N. (1996). It's my turn! Motivating young readers. *Learning and Leading with Technology, 24*(3), 20–23.

Henry, L. (2006). SEARCHing for an answer: The critical role of new literacies while reading on the Internet. *The Reading Teacher, 59*(7), 614–627.

Horrigan, J. (2007). A typology of information and communication technology users. Pew Internet & American Life Project, Washington, D.C. Available at http://www.pewinternet.org/PPF/r/213/report_display.asp.

Ito, M., Heather H., Bittanti, M., Boyd, D., Herr-Stephenson, B., Lange, P., …

Robinson, L. (with Baumer, S., Cody, R., Mahendran, D., Mart'nez, K., Perkel, D., Sims, C., & Tripp, L.) (2008). Living and learning with new media: Summary of findings from the Digital Youth Project. *Digital Youth Research and The John D. and Catherine T. MacArthur Foundation.* Retrieved from http://digitalyouth.ischool.berkeley.edu/files/report/digitalyouth-WhitePaper.pdf.

Johnson, D. (in press). Teaching with author's blogs: Connections, collaboration, creativity. *Journal of Adolescent and Adult Literacy.*

Labbo, L. (2005). Fundamental qualities of effective Internet literacy instruction: An exploration of worthwhile classroom practices. In R. Karchmer, M. Mallette, J. Kara-Soteriou, & D. Leu (Eds.), *Innovative approaches to literacy education: Using the Internet to support new literacies.* Newark, DE: International Reading Association.

Larson, L. (2009). Reader response meets new literacies: Empowering readers in online learning communities. *The Reading Teacher, 62*(8), 638–648.

Leu, D., Kinzer, C., Coiro, J., & Cammack, D. (2004). Toward a theory of new literacies emerging from the Internet and other information and communication technologies. In R. B. Ruddell & N. Unrau (Eds.), *Theoretical models and processes of reading* (5th ed.) (pp. 1570–1613). Newark, DE: International Reading Association.

National Council of Teachers of English (2008). *NCTE framework for 21st century curriculum and assessment.* Retrieved from: http://www.ncte.org/governance/literacies.

Kaiser Foundation (2010). *Generation M²: Media in the lives of 8-to18-year-olds*. Retrieved from http://www.kff.org/entmedia/8010.cfm.

Smith, F. (2006). *Ourselves: Why we are who we are*. Mahwah, NJ: Erlbaum.

Sylvester, R., & Greenidge, W. (2009). Digital storytelling: Extending the potential for struggling writers. *The Reading Teacher, 63*(4), 284–295.

Wollman-Bonilla, J. E. (2003). E-mail as genre: A beginning writer learns the conventions. *Language Arts, 81,* 126–134.

Zhang, T., Gao, T., Gail, R., & Zhang, W. (2007). Using online discussion forums to assist a traditional English class. *International Journal on E-Learning, 6*(4), 623–643.

# The Art of Children's Books:
# A Visual Discussion of Genre and Illustration

**1.** *JOHN HENRY* by Julius Lester, illustrated by Jerry Pinkney (Dial, 1994). 1995 Caldecott Honor.

**Traditional Literature.** *Julius Lester's retelling of the tall tale of John Henry, the African-American folk hero who was able to do more work with his sledgehammer than the steam power drill, is an excellent example of a traditional tale. A source note informs the reader that the retelling is true to the original ballad, while Lester's poetic language enhances and enriches the tale and contemporary details add humor. Pinkney's impressionistic illustrations are inextricably connected to the text.*

**2.** *YEH-SHEN: A CINDERELLA STORY FROM CHINA,* retold by Ai-Ling Louie, Illustrated by Ed Young (Philmel, 1982).

**Traditional Literature.** Yeh-Shen *is an example of a well-researched, written, and illustrated retelling of the Chinese folktale. Young's combination of innovative style and authentic Chinese art creates an imaginative interpretation of the story while maintaining an aesthetic feel of the Chinese culture. His use of simple page design consisting of panels and white space with misty, jewel illustrations uniquely balances the sparse text while also allowing the readers to bring their own interpretations and imagined details to the story.*

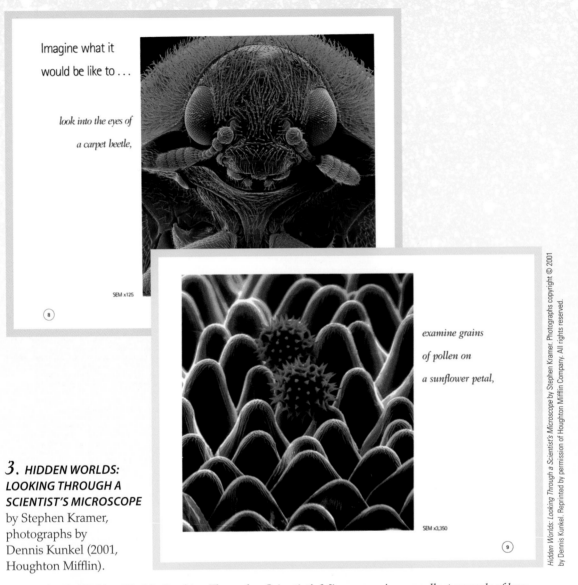

Imagine what it
would be like to . . .

*look into the eyes of*

*a carpet beetle,*

SEM x125

8

*examine grains*

*of pollen on*

*a sunflower petal,*

SEM x3,350

9

*3.* *HIDDEN WORLDS:*
*LOOKING THROUGH A*
*SCIENTIST'S MICROSCOPE*
by Stephen Kramer,
photographs by
Dennis Kunkel (2001,
Houghton Mifflin).

**Picturebook.** Hidden Worlds: Looking Through a Scientist's Microscope *is an excellent example of how technology has not only had a profound effect on the scientific community but also on the creation of children's books. Hidden Worlds combines the astonishingly beautiful photographs of microscopist Dennis Kunkel with the prosaic writing of Stephen Kramer to create a fascinating look into the world of a scientist. Kramer's use of accessible, clear writing brings Kunkel's work on the island of Oahu, Hawaii, up close—where and how he finds and captures his specimens and how he uses different microscopes to photograph them. Taken with dissecting, compound, and electron microscopes and magnified up to 12,000 times their original size, the photographs throughout the book provide a mesmerizing glimpse into a world most people don't even think about: the head of a tsetse fly, a butterfly's proboscis, a lacewing larva. Information on how to become a scientist and a list of further readings completes this insightful and informative book that will captivate children.*

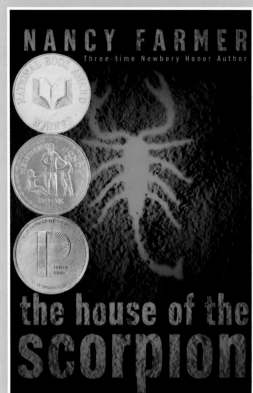

**4.** *THE HOUSE OF THE SCORPION* by Nancy Famer (Atheneum, 2002). 2003 Newbery Honor, National Book Award, 2003 Printz Honor.

**Science fiction.** The House of the Scorpion *explores the social implications of cloning. Farmer creates a fully realized, unique, and believable world. The House of Scorpion connects to current events but allows children to go beyond their everyday realities to contemplate questions about the meaning of life, death, and responsibility for others, thus nurturing their capacity for invention.*

**5.** *THE HIGHER POWER OF LUCKY* by Susan Patron, illustrated by Matt Phalen (Atheneum, 2006). 2007 Newbery Medal.

**Realistic fiction.** In The Higher Power of Lucky, *the author creates a careful balance between the well-developed, endearingly quirky characters, a fascinating desert setting, a succinct plot, use of interesting language, and a worthy theme of self-discovery. All of these qualities come together to address the difficult topics of death, absent parents, and addiction. Patron addresses these subjects with honesty and humor. Lucky, the main character, is a reflective decision maker and fits nicely among other characters from Newbery Medal winning realistic fiction books.*

**6. *THE THREE PIGS***, written and illustrated by David Wiesner (Houghton Mifflin, 2001). 2002 Caldecott Medal.

**Picturebook.** *This postmodern picturebook breaks from the traditional version of* The Three Pigs *both literally and figuratively as the pigs escape from the wolf by breaking out of the story. The double-page spread shown here is an excellent example of the use of point-of-view and framing in picturebook illustration.*

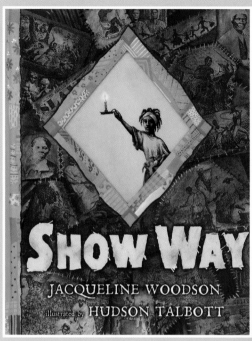

**7.** ***SHOW WAY*** by Jacqueline Woodson, illustrated by Hudson Talbott (Putnam, 2005). 2006 Newbery Honor.

**Historical Fiction.** *Show Way conveys the significance of quilts or Show Ways during the time of slavery and, over the passage of time, their importance to the author's family traditions. Woodson's use of poetic writing and Talbott's mixed media collages, including chalk, watercolors, and muslin, emphasize the importance of connections and courage through the story, making the difficult topic of slavery and the passage of time across eight generations accessible to children.* Show Way *is an excellent example of how historical fiction can help children understand that the present and future are linked to actions of the past.*

**8.** ***THE GAME OF SILENCE*** by Louise Erdrich (HarperCollins, 2005). 2006 Scott O'Dell Award for Outstanding Historical Fiction.

**Historical Fiction.** *The Game of Silence captures both the everyday life and devastating effect of the Westward Expansion on a Native American tribe, the Ojibwa. This meticulously researched novel warmly conveys the daily life of the Ojibwa—rich culture, traditions, language, values, and religious beliefs—while they prepare to move west due to the order from the U.S. president to remove Ojibwa from the area (Lake Superior) where they live.*

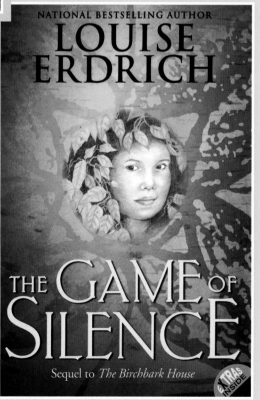

*9.* "Song of the Water Boatman and Backswimmer's Refrain" (unnumbered) from **SONG OF THE WATER BOATMAN AND OTHER POND POEMS** by Joyce Sidman, illustrated by Beckie Prange (Houghton Mifflin, 2005). 2006 Lee Bennett Hopkins Poetry Award, 2006 Caldecott Honor.

**Poetry.** *The collection of lively poems in* Song of the Water Boatman and Other Pond Poems *praises the diverse life in a northern pond across the seasons. Poems vary in structure and form from haiku to rhymed and unrhymed verse. Each poem is written from the author's keen sense of observation and humor, capturing fact and fantasy about pond life through captivating characterization and vivid imagery. Each poem is accompanied by a sidebar that provides more information about the bird, insect, or plant in the poem. Prangle's bold woodcut illustrations contrasted with pastel watercolors that change with the seasons give the reader a unique perspective on each poem.*

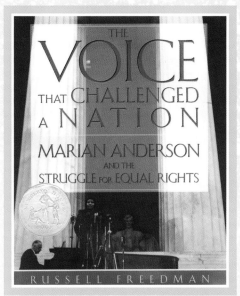

**10.** *THE VOICE THAT CHALLENGED A NATION: MARIAN ANDERSON AND THE STRUGGLE FOR EQUAL RIGHTS* by Russell Freedman (Houghton Mifflin, 2004). 2005 Sibert Medal for Outstanding Informational Book, 2005 Newbery Honor.

**Biography.** *In this engaging biography, Freedman captures the essence of Marian Anderson, an African-American contralto, whose career was affected by the racism of the 1930s. Freedman shows how her life was shaped by the social and cultural events of the time. Through careful research and clear, passionate writing, Freedman brings Anderson's voice and grace to life through quotations from her autobiography, papers, interviews and selected photographs, newspaper clippings, and concert programs. A bibliography, source notes, and a discography provide documentation for the biography and information for further research.*

**11.** *THE TARANTULA SCIENTIST* by Sy Montgomery, photographs by Nic Bishop (Houghton Mifflin, 2004). 2005 Sibert Honor for Outstanding Informational Book.

**Informational book.** *The Tarantula Scientist is a distinctive informational book that follows arachnologist Sam Marshall on a field expedition in search of tarantulas in the French Guiana rainforest and then back to his lab in Ohio. Montgomery uses conversational prose and clear, informative explanations to provide a personal account of the scientist's dedication and enthusiasm for his research. Integrated throughout the text are amazing color photos that provide close-up detail of tarantulas in their natural habitat. Montgomery effectively shows how the scientific process— observing, questioning, examining, testing—works in the real world.*

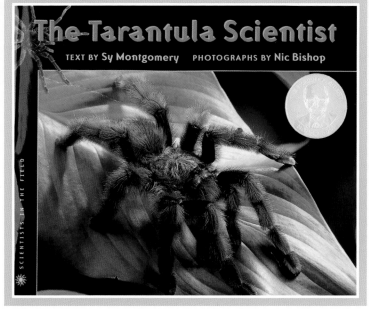

**12. *COMING TO AMERICA,*** written and illustrated by Bernard Wolf (Lee & Low, 2003).

**Multicultural literature.** *In the photo essay* Coming to America, *Wolf provides a broad perspective on a family emigrating from Egypt to America. Rather than focusing only on the family's Muslim religion, we see the family in their daily life—work, school, shopping, play—and learn how life in the United States is different from life in Egypt. Yet, the family maintains many customs from Egypt, such as their religious practices and meals. Wolf's use of personal accounts and photos of this loving family bring a sense of intimacy to the book, allowing readers to see the family as neighbors rather than strangers.*

**13. *THE PULL OF THE OCEAN*** by Jean-Claude Mourlevat (Delacorte, 2006). 2007 Batchelder Award.

**International literature.** The Pull of the Ocean, *translated from French to English, is a contemporary version of the Tom Thumb fable. The story is told from multiple first-person accounts with each character given a distinctive voice. As the story slowly unfolds, the reader is drawn into the plight of Yann as he leads his six siblings across the French countryside, away from their abusive parents, toward the sea. Blending realism and fantasy, Mourlevat provides details that are plausible and realistic, creating a challenging yet engaging tale.*

# Part III

# Children's Literature in the Classroom

# Teaching Literacy with Children's Literature

*Read*

*Regie Routman's website.*

The Optimal Learning Model in Figure 13.1 was constructed by Regie Routman in her book *Reading Essentials* (2003) and *Writing Essentials* (2005), and it offers a structure for teaching literacy with children's literature.

All of the theory and practical applications for using children's literature in the classroom—as presented in Parts I and II of this text—can be implemented using this framework. It is a flexible model that follows the gradual release of responsibility model presented in Chapter 3 and moves instruction from dependence on the teacher to student independence. It will help you organize instruction, structure teaching around the support your students need, and promote independence and the joy of reading and writing in your classroom. For a suggested schedule of daily reading, see Table 13.1.

When teachers think about teaching from the stance of students' needs and interests, they begin to make decisions that move children toward independence. Rather than concentrating on the teaching contexts, they concentrate on the level of support and explicitness the learner requires. Contexts for teaching, such as reading and writing aloud, shared reading and writing, guided reading, and independent reading and writing, allow teachers the opportunity to provide the supportive instruction students need. Chapter 13 discusses the contexts within the "reading to" and "reading with" sections of the Optimal Learning Model. Chapter 14 discusses the last section of the model, "reading by" learners.

**FIGURE 13.1**

Instructional Framework: Optimal Learning Model Across the Curriculum

| DEPENDENCE | | | INDEPENDENCE → |
|---|---|---|---|
| **To Learners** | **With Learners** | | **By Learners** |
| Demonstration | Shared Demonstration | Guided Practice | Independent Practice |
| *teacher* | *teacher* | *student* | *student* |
| • Initiates<br>• Models<br>• Explains<br>• Thinks aloud<br>• Shows how to do it | • Demonstrates<br>• Leads<br>• Negotiates<br>• Suggests<br>• Supports<br>• Explains<br>• Responds<br>• Acknowledges | • Applies learning<br>• Takes charge<br>• Practices<br>• Problem solves<br>• Approximates<br>• Self-corrects | • Initiates<br>• Self-monitors<br>• Self-directs<br>• Applies learning<br>• Problem solves<br>• Confirms<br>• Self-evaluates |
| *student* | *student* | *teacher* | *teacher* |
| • Listens<br>• Observes<br>• May participate on a limited basis | • Listens<br>• Interacts<br>• Collaborates<br>• Responds<br>• Approximates<br>• Participates as best he can | • Scaffolds<br>• Validates<br>• Teaches as necessary<br>• Evaluates<br>• Observes<br>• Encourages<br>• Clarifies | • Affirms<br>• Assists as needed<br>• Responds<br>• Acknowledges<br>• Evaluates<br>• Sets goals |
| *instructional context* | *instructional context* | *instructional context* | *instructional context* |
| • Reading and writing aloud<br>• Shared reading aloud<br>• Direct explanation | • Shared reading and writing<br>• Interactive reading<br>• Shared reading aloud | • Guided (silent) reading<br>• Reciprocal teaching<br>• Literature conversations<br>• Partner reading<br>• Guided writing experiences | • Independent reading and writing<br>• Informal conferences<br>• Partner reading |

HANDOVER OF RESPONSIBILITY

# 13

# Reading to and with Children: Reading Aloud, Shared and Guided Reading and Writing

Does reading aloud to students make a difference? Oh, you bet it does. When we read aloud to children, we fill the air and their ears with the sound of language. Reading aloud to students (of all ages) invites them to make meaning, create images, and linger with language—to become infatuated with words and simply fall into a story.

—*Laminack & Wadsworth, 2006, p. 1*

When teachers and children come together on a journey of words, something happens that transforms the "me" into "we." Shared characters, shared language, and shared experiences through the read aloud transport us in time and place to another world, one filled with excitement, anticipation, hope—a whole range of emotions that bonds us together—and we come out of the experience somehow changed. Maybe we know ourselves a little bit better, or maybe we know each other or the world a little bit better, but the experience has brought everyone just a little bit closer. According to Sipe (2002), "Making stories our own may be a powerful way—or perhaps the only way—for stories to affect our lives and to transform us" (p. 482).

**TABLE 13.1**

# Suggested Daily Reading Schedules

| Grade | Reading Activity | Time Frame |
|-------|-----------------|------------|
| 1–2 | Read aloud | 20–30 minutes |
| | Shared reading | 30–40 minutes |
| | Guided reading | 50–60 minutes (10–15 minutes per group) |
| | Independent reading | 20–30 minutes |
| 3–6 | Reading aloud | 20–30 minutes |
| | Shared reading | 15–20 minutes |
| | Guided reading, Literature circles | 20–30 minutes (2 or 3 times a week 10–15 minutes per group) |
| | Independent reading | 30–40 minutes |

Adapted from R. Routman (2003). *Reading essentials: The specifics you need to teach reading well* (p. 158). Portsmouth, NH: Heinemann.

## Reading Aloud

| To Learners | With Learners | | By Learners |
|-------------|---------------|--|-------------|
| Demonstration | Shared demonstration | Guided practice | Independent practice |

*Recently I received an e-mail message* from a fourth-grade teacher who had been one of my students in a reading methods course I taught several years ago. She reflected on how I read to the class every day:

> I still remember many of the books you shared with us! Thanks for making it such a big deal! It definitely made an impact with me. I [read aloud] every day! My kids LOVE it! They ask every day, "Are you going to read aloud?" Even though we do it at the same time every day! I incorporate picturebooks all the time and in every lesson I possibly can! Last year one of my students said, "When I read, it is kind of boring, but when you read to us, the story comes alive. It is really cool."

Of all the memories pre-service teachers have of their elementary school years, they hold most dearly those of being read to by their teachers. In the destined-to-be-a classic book, *Wondrous Words*, Katie Wood Ray (1999) said the following:

> Reading aloud has made countless children throughout time fall in love with a teacher who did it well and who did it often. And these teachers are never forgotten. Memories, some of them now decades old, of being read aloud to inhabit the dusty corners of so many of our minds, and though we may not remember any of the steps of mitosis, the positions of the planets, or the rest of our fourth-grade curriculum, we remember being read to. We recall the feeling of gazing up, gazing up at the teacher reading to us. (p. 67)

Indeed, it is passion and enthusiasm for reading that separates effective from ineffective teachers (Bohn, Roehrig, & Pressley, 2004). Harvey and Goudvis (2007) write, "There is nothing more powerful than a literacy teacher sharing her passion for reading, writing, and thinking" (p. 12). Passion is contagious. Kids will respond.

## BENEFITS OF READING ALOUD

Our own memories should be enough to convince and encourage us to read aloud to children, but ample research over the last two decades also supports reading aloud at all levels of education. In the early 1980s, a report from the Commission on Reading, *Becoming a Nation of Readers* (1984), found that "the single most important activity for building the knowledge required for eventual success in reading is reading aloud to children. There is no substitute for a teacher who reads children good stories. It is a practice that should continue throughout the grades" (Anderson, Hiebert, Scott, & Wilkinson, 1984, p. 51). In an extensive longitudinal study, Wells (1986) found that the number of stories children had heard read to them was the single greatest predictor of later success in reading. In a review of research of literature-based programs, Tunnell and Jacobs (1989) reported that "daily reading aloud from enjoyable books has been the key that unlocked literacy growth" (p. 475) for all students including English language learners and struggling readers.

Extensive research has shown that reading aloud aids the following:

- Increased motivation and positive attitude toward reading (Holdaway, 1979; Ivey & Broaddus, 2001; Palmer, Codling, & Gambrell, 1994).
- Language and literacy development in the understanding of story structure (Phillips & McNaughton, 1990; Sulzby, 1985).
- Conventions of print (Clay, 1991).
- Vocabulary development and listening comprehension (Dickinson & Smith, 1994; Elley, 1989; Feitelson, Kita, & Goldstein, 1986; Morrow, 1990).
- Decoding and reading comprehension (Rosenhouse, Feitelson, Kita, & Goldstein, 1997).
- Literary understanding (Sipe, 2000, 2008).

In addition to the preceding benefits, reading aloud provides a context for the cultivation of many tangential benefits that are difficult to measure through research but are still critical to the development of literacy and literary knowledge. Reading aloud does all of the following:

- Provides a context for teachers to demonstrate the nature, purpose, and act of reading and to model their own love of reading.
- Creates an environment in which all listeners have equal access to knowledge.
- Builds interest in language and provides models of language in use.
- Extends opportunities for the development of new insights and understandings and for building on existing knowledge.
- Provides a context for teachers to model fluent reading and how readers think in the process of reading.
- Builds interest and develops tastes in a range of genres available in written language.
- Improves listening skills and develops the use of imagery.
- Offers multiple perspectives and broadens a listener's worldview.

Although reading aloud to children is an important factor for providing motivation for reading, building critical concepts about reading, and developing an understanding of literature, this does not happen instantly. Just because a teacher pulls out a book and reads aloud does not mean that these benefits happen automatically. Meyer, Wardrop, Stahl, and Linn (1994) described negative effects on literacy development as a result of storybook reading. They reported that reading aloud is often not of sufficient quality to fully engage students and maximize literacy growth. Morrow and Brittain (2003) state, "Reading stories does not in itself necessarily promote literacy; however, the research suggests that certain methods, environmental influences, attitudes, and interactive behaviors apparently enhance the potential of the read aloud event for promoting literacy development" (p. 144).

Reading aloud must be an intentional act in which the teacher considers his or her goals and objectives based on student assessment and curriculum standards. Serafini and Giorgis (2003) write as follows:

> In our community of readers, our definition of what it means to read and be a reader is created by the way we read aloud with our students, the literature we choose to share, the demonstrations we provide as readers, the expectations we have for how our students respond to their readings, and the ways in which we encourage students to represent their understandings of the stories we read. In other words, we construct what it means to read, to make meanings with texts, and to be a successful reader in the context of our classroom by what we choose to attend to and by the expectations we set for our students. (p. 2)

Expectations are everything. If we expect read-alouds to make a difference, then with a few intentional decisions, they will. The effectiveness of a read-aloud depends on the amount of consideration given to how often to read aloud, what to read aloud, and how to read aloud.

### WHEN TO READ ALOUD

Deciding when to read aloud depends on students' strengths and needs and curricular goals. For example, reading the book *Nature's Green Umbrella: Tropical Rain Forests* by Gail Gibbons to a group of first graders might be a way of teaching a science objective while also fostering children's understanding of how nonfiction text structure works. In fifth grade, reading a chapter from the book *Dragonwings* by Laurence Yep might be a means of discussing a social studies objective of immigration at the turn of the twentieth century, while also building prior knowledge and vocabulary strategies necessary for reading and understanding historical fiction. The decisions to use these books, make these curricular connections, and teach these literacy strategies are based on the teacher's knowledge of her students and curricular objectives. The amount of time spent reading aloud will depend on how often the read aloud can serve as the most meaningful instructional agent for meeting students' needs and objectives across the curriculum. As a powerful method of demonstration used to model, explain, and "show kids how," the read aloud can serve as an instructional foundation for teaching concepts across the instructional day.

*Read an excerpt from Laminack and Wadsworth's book* Reading Aloud Across the Curriculum.

That said, there should also be a time every day when a book is read aloud just for fun. Laminack and Wadsworth (2006) recommend ceremonially starting and ending the day with a read aloud. Start the day with a book to build community; to bond with students; and to bond with authors, illustrators, and featured characters. Close the day with a read aloud that will have a lasting impression and leave students longing for more.

### WHAT TO READ ALOUD

*What* to read aloud is the million-dollar question. Many considerations have been discussed throughout this book: the importance of choosing a range of quality literature (Chapters 1 and 4–12); attending to the developmental levels and interests of students (Chapter 2); the standards and curriculum goals, classroom environment, and instructional needs of students (Chapter 3); and the cultural worlds of students (Chapters 2 and 11). This may seem like too many books to choose from and too many considerations to take into account. It can seem overwhelming, but a decision doesn't have to be made all at once. Choose from the many books mentioned in this text to begin the school year. Fill the air with the beautiful language from the books you choose, and send a message to your students that their teacher loves to read. Whet their appetite for what is to come as the school year progresses. Mary Hahn (2002), a fourth-grade teacher, chose *The Secret Knowledge of Grown-Ups* by David Wisniewski for the first read aloud of the school year "to give us an opportunity to laugh together at grown-ups and at the rules they impose on children" (p. 24).

After the first few weeks of school, you will have the opportunity to learn more about your students individually and instructionally. This will help with further book selection. As the year progressed, Mary Hahn read the following books:

*Watch*

*Watch an interview with David Wisniewski*

*Read/*

*Watch*

*Read or Watch interviews with most of these authors.*

- *Tales of a Fourth Grade Nothing* by Judy Blume because the characters are in the same grade as her students.
- *The Watsons Go to Birmingham—1963* by Christopher Paul Curtis, *Ramadan* by Suhaib Hamid Ghazi, *Fig Pudding* by Ralph Fletcher, *On My Honor* by Marion Dane Bauer, and *Just Juice* by Karen Hesse because they reflected the cultural, religious, gender, and social differences of her students.
- *Holes* by Louis Sachar because of the literary strategies she could teach about time and setting that allowed her students to move into more complex books.

Mary's choices reflected her knowledge of quality children's literature, a range of genres, and an in-depth understanding of her students individually and instructionally. Because of this, her students' engagement with and responses to these books were enhanced. See Table 13.2 for guidelines for choosing books to read aloud.

With the exception of quality series books, such as the *Ramona* books by Beverly Cleary, the *Fudge* books by Judy Blume, and the *Anastasia* books by Lois Lowry, it may be best to avoid series books. Although these books hold great appeal for children, their formulaic nature does not lend itself to thought-provoking literary analysis or the depth of response needed for the optimal read aloud experience.

Of course, picturebooks and chapter books are not the only choices for read alouds. Newspaper articles, magazine articles, Internet sites, short stories, brochures and pamphlets, and other "real world" literature are easily accessible, authentic, and allow for a variety of purposes for reading and responses to reading that can be modeled and shared in the classroom.

**TABLE 13.2**

## Choosing Books to Read Aloud

Choose books that have the following features:

- Are age appropriate and sustain readers emotionally and intellectually.
- Evoke a range of aesthetic responses and connect to children's lives.
- Are of high literary quality: memorable language, believable characters, engaging plots, and universal themes.
- Meet all of the preceding criteria and have relevant curricular connections.

## HOW TO READ ALOUD

*"The whole secret, Meggie," Mo had once told her, "is in the breathing. It gives your voice strength and fills it with your life. And not just yours. Sometimes it feels as if when you take a breath you are breathing in everything around you, everything that makes up the world and moves it, and then it all flows into the words."*

INKSPELL BY CORNELIA FUNKE, 2005, P. 477

*Watch*

Watch an interview with Cornelia Funke.

Every child deserves an Academy Award–winning read aloud! Adults who read aloud to children accept the opportunity and the responsibility for sharing a spectacular experience.

## THE READ ALOUD PROCESS

**Before the Read Aloud.** *Find the book's voice.* Laminack and Wadsworth (2006) contend that every book has a voice of its own and that we must listen to find that voice before reading it aloud to students. Read the book through silently and listen for the book's "voice" by interpreting the mood, rhythm, tone, intensity and pacing from signals such as punctuation, typeset changes (italics, capital letters, large or small words), shape words, line breaks, and so forth. Your understanding of the characters, setting, and the author's use of language will also affect the way you read. Then, read the book aloud to yourself, trying the voice on for size.

*Practice using tone, inflection, and voice variation.* The book's voice that you hear in your head as you read silently probably isn't a monotone. You can hear changes in pitch, tone, inflection, and voice variation to make the characters come to life, to create suspense, intrigue, exuberance, loneliness, or anticipation. Practice creating these sometimes subtle, sometimes outrageous voice changes to make the book come alive. Read with proper diction and clarity so children will be able to hear clearly and understand you.

*Find an appropriate pace.* The read aloud will have a certain rhythm that you must maintain that is in keeping with your interpretation of the book, but try not to read too fast.

*Think through intentional connections.* You have chosen the book you are planning to read aloud because it contains a particular connection you want to make to children's lives, literature, and/or the curriculum. Where are the best places to make these connections? Where are the appropriate places in the book to conduct demonstrations or model responses to reading? Where are the pivotal places in the book to stop and let children share their thoughts with each other?

*Watch*

Watch authors read aloud from their own books.

**During the Read Aloud.** *Make sure all students can see and hear.* This is critical. What's the point of reading aloud if everyone can't see or hear? Some teachers have children move to a carpeted area so they can position themselves in the best place to see and hear. When sharing a picturebook, be sure to pan the book around the entire viewing area.

*Hold up the book while you are reading.* If you are reading a picturebook, practice holding up the book with one hand while reading so children can see the illustrations. This is important for several reasons. First, as discussed in Chapter 4, the illustrations in picturebooks are critical to understanding the story, and the more time children have to look at the pictures, the better their understanding of the story. If you don't show the pictures until after you have finished reading the page, there is less time because you may rush at this point. The illustrations in most picturebooks are quite beautiful and deserve the extra time to be appreciated. Also, by holding up the book, you can occasionally look away from the text to make eye contact with students and observe their reactions to the illustrations and the story. Finally, you can use this time to think aloud and make connections from text to picture during the reading rather than afterward.

*Share the name of the author/illustrator.* If the author or illustrator is familiar, remind students of his or her other works and encourage predictions about this book.

*Give the children a preview.* The content of the book should not be a secret. Be sure the children understand your purpose for reading the book aloud, even if it's just for fun. By way of introducing the book, share the end papers, dedication, and title page of a picturebook, which all provide insight into the content of the book.

*Give children a chance to respond before, during, and after the reading.* Provide an opportunity for children to activate prior knowledge, ask questions, make predictions, and briefly discuss elements of the book throughout the read aloud. Research by Sipe (2000) suggests that young children may not be able to hold their responses until after the story, so it is important to pause throughout the story to give children the opportunity to make critical connections. Response time during the read aloud can be brief—for example, after you've read a page and are panning the picturebook in front of the students for a closer look. Ask students to "turn and talk" to a partner, dramatize their feelings about a character through facial expressions or to act out a word, or to stop and jot down their response to a question whenever they have a thought.

*Model rather than question.* Take the opportunity to model the joy of reading as well as the strategies that good readers employ while reading. Rather than using the read aloud as a time for an interrogation, ask just a few well-placed questions to nudge students to wonder, infer, or consider. Sometimes a "Hmmmm" or "I wonder . . ." is enough to get children thinking and is much more powerful than a grand inquisition.

**After the Read Aloud.** *Share any information at the end of the book, such as an author's note or source information.*

*Give children the opportunity to respond to the book.* Until this point, children have predicted based on prior knowledge, made connections, and had brief discussions. Now is the time to engage with the whole story. The shared reading experience provides a unique opportunity for an authentic conversation around a book: to agree or disagree with information in the text or ideas and thoughts of others, to pose questions, to make connections to others or to the world. Lucy Calkins, a professor at Teachers College Columbia, once stated in a speech that teachers should engage students in experiences that parallel adult reading experiences. She said, "When I'm curled up in bed and I finish a good book, I don't lean over to my husband and say, 'Please pass me the shoe box, scissors, and tape so I can do a diorama.'" Beware of assigning "activities" for children to complete after reading a book that are superficial and artificial. Many authentic response opportunities are included in each genre chapter in this book.

*Connect the book to other books, authors, genres, and content.* Build on previous classroom experiences that will lead to future experiences.

*Watch*

*Watch a think aloud modeled.*

## THINK ALOUDS

Throughout Part 2 of this text, reading aloud has been the first suggestion for immersing children in genre study, to provide opportunities for children to notice the structure of a genre and the author's craft, and for teachers to model comprehension strategies for understanding and promoting critical thinking. Thinking aloud during reading aloud can make the invisible processes of reading visible.

How does a good reader figure out unknown words while reading? How does a good reader make inferences between what the author states and what the reader knows? These are complex processes that take place "on the run" or while reading text that can't be adequately taught through de-contextualized, isolated skills worksheets. Thinking aloud is when the teacher models his thinking by voicing all the things he notices, sees, feels, or questions while processing the text. Wilhelm (2001a) explains, "Think alouds allow all students to hear how others sleuth out and make sense of all these text clues so that they can recognize and adopt these strategies as their own" (p. 19). According to Wilhelm, think alouds can be used to model the following:

- General processes of reading like predicting, monitoring, and summarizing
- Task-specific processes like symbolism, irony, or bar graphs
- Text-specific processes like understanding the structure of an argument and evaluating its effectiveness (p. 28)

Here are a few think-aloud prompts:

- I'm thinking . . .
- I'm picturing in my mind . . .
- I don't understand this part so I'm going to go back and reread.
- I'm connecting this part of the story to something that happened earlier in the story.
- I think this character is . . .

Think alouds can be conducted with a variety of genres and texts, including newspaper articles, magazines, and Internet sites, which are all primarily nonfiction. (See Figure 13.2 for an example of a think aloud.) Teachers can record think alouds on chart paper or overheads. This provides a record of the strategies modeled so students can refer to the charts later and make connections to other texts. Once students have observed the think-aloud process with a particular strategy numerous times, turn the process over for them to practice on their own. Children can use sticky notes to record their thinking to share with the teacher in conferences or with a peer. Wilhelm (2001b) relates, "After I modeled a few think alouds recently, one student asked me, 'Why didn't you tell us this before? If I had known what to do, I would have done it! Is it supposed to be a big secret or something?'" (p. 28). Teachers can help children unlock the secret to engaged reading by lending their expertise to students through think alouds. The think aloud process is also very effective for bringing attention to authors' writing craft and modeling the writing process, which will be discussed in the next sections.

## READ ALOUDS FOR WRITERS

> *I believe reading aloud is probably the single most important teaching tool I have at my disposal, particularly for the teaching of writing.*
>
> KATIE WOOD RAY, 2005, P. 1

*Read*

*Read a list of mentor texts.*

In her book *Wondrous Words*, Katie Wood Ray is a passionate advocate of authors as writing mentors for children by listening to the sound of well crafted text and analyzing the crafting technique the author used to create such a sound. Ray (1999) writes, "When we read aloud, often and well, we fill our classrooms with the sound of words, well placed and well written, and that sound wraps its arms around the work of young writers who are hard at work learning their craft" (p. 68).

The preceding benefits of reading aloud happen when children listen to the read aloud with their reading selves. But, as Ray points out, their writing selves are also present, listening in. When children "allow their writing selves to listen to the read aloud with the attention equal to that of their reading selves . . . they will open up for themselves vast storehouses of knowledge about, particularly, what good writing *sounds* like" (p. 70).

When reading aloud, pause to "sigh over" or notice powerful words or particularly beautiful-sounding phrases. Author studies allow time to think deeply about an author's craft. Provide opportunities for children to contribute what they think are well-crafted phrases and powerful words and document these on charts, as shown in Chapter 7. Later, these charts can be used to analyze the authors' techniques for creating such lovely language.

**FIGURE 13.2**

Sample of a
Think Aloud

When introducing the book *An Egg Is Quiet*, written by Dianna Aston and illustrated by Sylvia Long, the following think alouds could be used:

- *One of the good things readers do is* . . . use the title and cover illustrations to predict the content of a book.
- *From the title and cover illustration, I'm going to predict that* . . . this book is nonfiction because the illustrations are labeled like other nonfiction books I've read.
- *The illustrations help me to* . . . understand how many different kinds of eggs there are.
- *I'm connecting this to when* . . . my son found a nest with three eggs that had fallen from a tree in our backyard. We tried to figure out what kind of bird the eggs belonged to by looking at the size and color of the egg.

## Writing Aloud

The same process of thinking aloud while reading can be applied to writing. Writing *is* thinking. When we begin to compose on paper or the computer screen, we initially write down what we are thinking and then go back, reread to be sure it makes sense, and then add, change, or rearrange words, sentences, or paragraphs to clarify or organize the intended message. This is messy work that goes on silently in our mind (think about how a written rough draft looks before the final version). Reading involves these same silent processes, so reading and writing are reciprocal processes—they reinforce each other. What we know about reading can help us with writing and vice versa. Understanding the relationship between reading and writing can help teachers make powerful connections between reading and writing for children of all grade levels. Writing aloud can make the complicated, invisible process of composing visible to children so that they can recognize and adopt these strategies as their own. The primary goal is to demonstrate the importance of composing a meaningful, coherent message for a particular audience and a specific purpose. Routman (2005) explains as follows:

> Don't expect high-quality writing from your kids unless you're modeling what high-quality writing looks and sounds like. This is just as critical for kindergarteners as it is for older students. Many teachers find that when they do more and better modeling—writing for and with their students—everything improves: kids' engagement, abundance of ideas for writing, willingness to write and take risks, knowledge of how and what to write, and the quality and quantity of their writing. (p. 180)

## WHEN AND WHAT TO WRITE ALOUD

As with read alouds, when and what to write aloud will depend on the students' strengths and needs and curricular goals. Write alouds can be used with all genres and conducted on the chalkboard, overhead transparencies, or chart paper. The topic of the write aloud can emerge from read alouds, storytelling, hands-on experiences, shared readings, and content area instruction. Writing aloud can be used to model the following:

- Knowledge of letter/sound relationships and conventions of print
- Spelling strategies and grammar usage
- The importance of word choice and details
- The use of metaphor, simile, idioms, and so on to paint pictures in the reader's mind
- Rereading to check if writing makes sense and flows
- Different formats of writing, such as letter writing, poetry, compare/contrast, persuasive writing
- Creating a table of contents, index, or graph in nonfiction
- The use of crafting techniques from familiar authors
- Audience awareness

## HOW TO WRITE ALOUD

*Watch*

*Watch a write aloud modeled.*

As with reading aloud, the teacher is the primary scribe and discussant. The teacher vocalizes her thoughts as she composes text, inviting the children to contribute at selected points. The write aloud process includes interactions with students as described in Table 13.3.

When students see the multiple facets of the composing process in action, they are more likely to understand that writers don't produce perfect books the first time they write and that writing is a process that involves revisions, resources, and time.

**TABLE 13.3**

# The Write Aloud Process

1. Explain the purpose of the write aloud to students.

2. Explain that the first copy is a draft and that the main purpose is to put down thoughts on paper.

3. Explain that, at times, you will reread your writing to ensure the intended message is being communicated and to edit words or details.

4. Explain that while writing, you will model some ways to use effective strategies for figuring out how to write unknown words.

5. As you compose, ask students clarifying and extending questions that focus on building meaning.

6. Direct students to notice how you use classroom resources to help you compose text (anchor charts, word wall words, a personal dictionary or thesaurus).

7. Inform students that after you have completed the draft, you will reread to make sure it conveys the intended message and is clear to the intended audience.

8. Explain that after the draft is completed, you will reread to check for punctuation, capital letters, misspelled words, and grammar, and to be sure the intended message is communicated effectively.

## Shared Reading

| To Learners | With Learners | | By Learners |
|---|---|---|---|
| Demonstration | Shared demonstration | Guided practice | Independent practice |

Shared reading was developed by Don Holdaway (1979) in an effort to simulate the "lap reading" experience that some children have at home (remember Rachel in Chapter 2?). Yet, far from an experience for only very young children, this risk-free reading opportunity provides an apprenticeship environment for the teacher to support children at various levels of reading development. Whereas books read aloud to children by a teacher might be above their reading level, shared reading involves reading text with the teacher's support. In shared reading, the text is enlarged so children can see the words and illustrations. During the first reading, the teacher reads the text with fluency and expression. After the first reading, the children, who are sitting up close, are invited to read along. The text is then read and reread collaboratively several times over the next few days. By selecting an engaging text that is at an appropriate reading level for the students, teachers can model and demonstrate many of the same strategies for reading aloud but go further to involve students in reading the text that adds many additional benefits. After reading the text together several times, the teacher can delve deeper into parts of the text to explicitly teach basic concepts about print, phonemic awareness/alphabetic knowledge, word work, comprehension strategies, text structure, or understanding literary elements.

## BENEFITS OF SHARED READING

Eldredge, Reutzel, and Hollingsworth (1996) compared the effects of ten minutes of daily shared reading to ten minutes of round-robin reading practice on second-grade readers' fluency, accuracy, vocabulary acquisition, and comprehension. They found that the shared book experience produced statistically superior impacts on all measures of reading proficiency. In a survey of over 600 middle and high school students, Allen (2000) found that shared reading was cited as the reason for the greatest gains in reading achievement. Numerous studies have shown that a critical factor in shared book reading is the interactive talk that takes place between the teacher and the children (Crain-Thoreson & Dale, 1992; DeTemple, 2001; Dickinson, 2001a, 2001b; Dickinson & Smith, 1994; Wasik & Bond, 2001).

The effectiveness of shared reading depends on the selection of an appropriate text and modeling strategies based on the teacher's knowledge of students' reading strengths and needs and the teacher's ability to provide flexible scaffolding during students' reading.

## WHEN AND WHAT TO READ DURING SHARED READING

*Read*

*Read a list of big books for shared reading.*

Shared reading should be conducted as part of daily reading instruction, but it can also be used for content area instruction. Big books and other enlarged texts cross all topics and content subjects. For example, shared reading of nonfiction texts can serve as a way to learn about science, social studies, or math, as well as a way to learn to read a variety of informational text structures. Shared reading can be an excellent source of demonstration and collaborative reading across the curriculum.

Often, the enlarged text is a grade-appropriate "big book." Big books can be enlarged versions of fiction, nonfiction, and poetry trade books, or they can be created specifically for the purpose of shared reading. The guidelines in Table 13.4 can be used in the selection of big books for beginning and older readers.

Big books can be expensive, and many teachers pay for such instructional materials out of their own pockets. Teachers and students can create their own big books based on

*The teacher and students are actively engaged in reading an appropriate nonfiction book that has been carefully selected to meet the students' reading strengths and needs as well as the goals of the curriculum.*

© Susie Fitzhugh.

**TABLE 13.4**

# Guidelines for Selecting Big Books for Shared Reading

| Beginning Readers | Older Readers |
|---|---|
| • Quality literature | • Quality literature |
| • Highly engaging, informative, and meaningful | • Highly engaging, informative, and meaningful |
| • Connects to students' interests, needs, culture, and curriculum | • Connects to students' interests, needs, culture, and curriculum |
| • Print is large enough to read up to 15 feet away | • Print is large enough to read up to 15 feet away |
| • Words are well spaced, and font is familiar (the typeset *a* and *g* are known by students) | • Is close to the reading level of most of the students |
| • Predictable text with repeated patterns, refrains, pictures, and rhymes | • Contains elements that support fluent reading |
| • Contains easily understood concepts | • Contains elements that lend themselves to demonstration and deeper understanding, such as a table of contents, index, maps, diagrams, charts, a glossary, and illustrations with captions found in informational books |
| • Familiar vocabulary—the number of unknown words should be enough to read with support from the teacher and not overwhelming | |
| • Pictures should tell or support the reading of the story in sequence | • Lends itself to comprehension, higher-level thinking, and critical reading |
| • Print is consistently placed on the page rather than moving around from page to page | • Connects to other texts |
| • Connects to other texts | |
| • Lends itself to comprehension and student response | |

retellings of favorite read alouds or shared experiences. Poetry, chants, an alphabet chart, raps, songs, and rhymes can be written on chart paper or placed on overhead transparencies. Charts from writing aloud and shared writing can also be used as shared reading texts as well as multiple copies of a book.

Table 13.5 lists reading concepts, skills, and strategies that can be the instructional focus of shared reading for K–6 students, depending on their strengths, needs, and curricular goals.

**TABLE 13.5**

# Skills and Strategies to Teach During Shared Reading

- Book conventions, such as title, table of contents, author, illustrator, front/back of book

- Early concepts about print, alphabetical knowledge, and phonemic awareness

- Rereading for fluency and to monitor comprehension

- Learning new information and searching for additional information

- Author's craft (figures of speech, leads, endings)

- Text structure for fiction and nonfiction

- How to figure out unknown words

- Character motivation and behavior (how characters change)

- Comprehension strategies such as summarizing, predicting, questioning, inferring

- Enjoying reading

These reading concepts, skills, and strategies can be modeled and demonstrated for children during the first read-through by the teacher and then practiced in a supportive environment with the teacher as a scaffold on subsequent readings. Then, more explicit teaching with certain aspects of the text can take place.

*Watch*

*Watch a shared reading lesson.*

## HOW TO CONDUCT SHARED READING

As with read alouds, for shared reading to be effective, many intentional decisions must be made throughout the process—from text selection to follow-up experiences.

**Before the Shared Reading.** *Select an engaging, usually unfamiliar text, either nonfiction or fiction, that is at an appropriate level for your students to read with your support.*

*Think through intentional connections.* Although the text is at an appropriate level, does it provide you with the teaching opportunities to meet your students' needs? Carefully analyze the text for the connections you want to make to children's emotional and intellectual needs. Think through the think alouds you want to model and the explicit teaching opportunities you want to provide for students. Anticipate the parts of the text in which you will need to provide more or less support as students read the text collaboratively.

*Find the "voice" of the text, and practice reading aloud with expression as discussed in the read aloud section.*

*Choose several appropriate points at which to stop and discuss what has been read.* What questions will you ask?

**During the Shared Reading.** *Make sure all students can see and hear.* Big books are best placed on a big book stand constructed specifically for the purpose of shared reading.

*Share the name of the author/illustrator, and make connections to other books he or she may have written with which the children might be familiar.*

*Give the children a preview.* Share the purpose for reading. Activate students' prior knowledge of the topic. For big books, share the end papers, dedication page, and title page, as with a trade book. For younger children, this can be an opportunity to teach these aspects of books. Some teachers provide a brief picture walk of the illustrations in the text before the shared reading as a way to build on prior knowledge and create anticipation, predictions, and questions—all important to active engagement and comprehension. Incorporate a discussion of important vocabulary and concepts.

*Give children the chance to make predictions and ask questions based on their prior knowledge.*

*Give an award-winning read aloud!* Read the book all the way through the first time. Invite children to join in if there are repeating refrains with which they become familiar as you progress through the book. Teachers of younger children often use a pointer to direct students' attention to the words as they are read.

*Stop to think aloud,* demonstrating the aspects of reading important for children to observe in action such as making connections, inferring meaning, problem-solving vocabulary, confirming a prediction, rereading for meaning, and summarizing important events before reading on.

*Pose questions for discussion.* As mentioned earlier, a critical factor in shared book reading is the interactive talk that takes place between the teacher and the children. Children should also talk to one another. For instance, they can turn and talk to a peer for one or two minutes about a question posed by the teacher or by another student.

*Observe students' responses and behavior to determine appropriate next steps.*

**After the Shared Reading.** *Reread the text for fluency.* Young children especially enjoy rereading favorite books. Children can read collaboratively or chorally.

*Provide explicit teaching of certain reading concepts, skills, or strategies.*

*Use frames or highlighter tape to assist in bringing out certain features or characteristics of text.* For example, when reading a poem, a teacher might highlight the rime of several rhyming words (in the word *light* the rime is *ight*) that are the same to show students how if you know one word, it can sometimes help you read and write other words (*light, night, might,* etc.).

*Ask students to use their fingers or a frame to locate letters or words in the text.*

*Use correction tape or sticky notes* to serve as a cloze technique in which some letters or words are hidden and children must use their knowledge of words or context clues to problem-solve.

*Have older students use the index at the back of a nonfiction big book to find specific information or use their knowledge of word derivations to figure out content specific vocabulary.*

*If using a big book, place it in the classroom library for children to read later.* Copies of overhead transparencies can also be given to students to keep in a folder for reading independently at a later time. Charts can be also be copied down and placed in folders or hung around the room to be used as a resource and for partner reading.

*Follow-up experiences do not have to be provided for all shared reading texts* and should only be done if they are an authentic response to the book, such as writing a letter to the author, writing a response to the story in journals, creating a new version or innovation of the book, retelling the story through readers' theater, storyboard representations, or puppets.

# Shared Writing

In writing aloud, the teacher was the primary composer, but in shared writing, the teacher and students compose collaboratively. The teacher, serving as scribe, collaboratively constructs the text with students while focusing on the craft and conventions of a meaningful text. Primary grade teachers often write students' dictation based on their language and experiences. There are not expectations for correctness, as the teacher encourages all children's contributions. As children share their thoughts and ideas, teachers expand and paraphrase their thinking, modeling how written language looks and sounds. Upper-level teachers may take students' dictation when they record their prior knowledge, predictions, or questions on charts and create character maps, retellings, or collaborative poems. Routman (2005) explains, "One of the most powerful aspects of shared writing (or reading) is that it is here that many students begin to figure out how written language works. Much of that learning occurs through the collaborative opportunities and social interactions that take place, not just through our explicit teaching" (p. 84). The collaborative context supports authentic conversations around meaningful reading and writing for which teachers determine the amount of complexity and challenge based on their knowledge of students' emotional, instructional, and curricular needs. After creating shared writing texts, they can be used to conduct explicit teaching in phonics, word work, and more.

Shared writing benefits all students, including students from various cultures, students whose first language is not English, and students with differing levels of ability. These students contribute their own language and experiences and see them written in print. These co-constructed bilingual texts are motivating, and students can read them easily. The familiar texts can be revisited multiple times to focus on phonics, word work, fluency, and other reading skills.

## WHEN AND WHAT TO WRITE

As with shared reading, shared writing can take place during the language arts instructional block, as well as during content area subjects, since the topic of what is written can be anything. Texts can be short and completed in one session or long and written over several weeks, depending on the purpose and students' abilities. Following are some recommendations for shared writing activities:

- Retellings from read alouds and big books
- Original stories, poems, and book reviews
- Journal entries in response to reading
- Field trips, science experiments
- Class rules and the morning message
- Content area writing

*Watch*

*Watch a shared writing lesson.*

## HOW TO CONDUCT SHARED WRITING

Based on the students' strengths and needs and curricular goals, determine the purpose of the shared writing and convey that purpose to students. The topic may be predetermined by the teacher or collaboratively with students. Using chart paper or an overhead transparency, brainstorm possibilities for the content. Once the content has been decided, begin the shared writing using chart paper or a transparency. Table 13.6 gives some guidelines for conducting a shared writing.

**TABLE 13.6**

# Guidelines for Conducting a Shared Writing

1. You can start by writing a title or decide on the title once the piece is finished.

2. Solicit an opening sentence from students or suggest a beginning sentence.

3. Say the words while you write them.

4. Reread as you go, pointing to the words and checking to be sure what you've written is clear and makes sense and to determine what should come next.

5. Continue soliciting as much content as possible from as many students as possible. It may be necessary to shape students' language for clarity or conventions.

6. Advance as quickly as possible so students stay engaged, focusing on meaningful content and consistent organization. Model the process by asking, *Does this make sense? How can we say this in a way that's clear to the reader? What should we say next?*

7. Reread the entire text, checking to be sure the intended content has been effectively communicated, editing and refining as you go.

8. Shared writing can then be used for shared reading and guided reading, as a resource for writing conventions, and for extended word work.

## Guided Reading

| To Learners | With Learners | | By Learners |
|---|---|---|---|
| Demonstration | Shared demonstration | Guided practice | Independent practice |

*Guided reading is the heart of the literacy process.*

FOUNTAS & PINNELL, 2006, P. 27

Children must be given ample opportunities to apply reading strategies on their own in supported and independent contexts. Every day, children should be given time to read books they can read independently for an extended time and books that offer a challenge and can be read with teacher support. All children develop the skills and strategies of good readers at different rates, so it is important for all children to receive instruction within their zone of proximal development that builds on their particular strengths and needs. In guided reading, teachers meet with small groups of students who are similar in their reading behavior, their text-processing needs, and their reading strengths. Instruction focuses on specific aspects of the reading process and literary understanding that will assist the children in moving forward to independence. In their foundational book

*These first-grade children are reading independently during a guided reading lesson.*

Courtesy of Denise Johnson.

*Guided Reading: Good First Teaching for All Children,* Fountas and Pinnell (1996) provide the following definition of guided reading:

> Guided reading is a context in which a teacher supports each reader's development of effective strategies for processing novel texts at increasingly challenging levels of difficulty. The teacher works with a small group of children who use similar reading processes and are able to read similar levels of text with support. The teacher introduces a text to this small group, works briefly with individuals in the group as they read it, may select one or two teaching points to present to the group following the reading, and may ask the children to take part in an extension of their reading. (p. 2)

When teachers carefully plan for guided reading and model strategies, scaffold, and explicitly teach through reading/writing aloud and shared reading/writing, children receive the focused attention they need to become independent readers.

## BENEFITS OF GUIDED READING

Over the past two decades grouping for instruction nearly disappeared, replaced with whole group instruction. One reason for this is the plethora of research denouncing the prevalent practice of ability grouping. Groups designated by ability, usually according to standardized or criterion-referenced test scores, remain static throughout the year and are usually accompanied by the ineffective traditional teaching practices of round-robin reading, the use of one-size-fits-all texts, and a-story-a-week instruction. These are some of the negative outcomes of ability grouping:

- Students from minority groups are more likely to be assigned to low groups.
- Students who did not have preschool experience are more likely to be assigned to low groups.
- Students in low-ability groups received lower-quality instruction, spending more time doing round-robin reading and workbook assignments than students in high-ability groups.
- Students in low-ability groups are more likely to exhibit inattentive behaviors than students in high-ability groups.
- Students in low-ability groups have lower academic expectations and suffer damage to self-esteem and social relationships (as demonstrated by pre-service teachers' comments in Chapter 3).
- Teachers typically interrupt low readers more often during oral reading when they miscue.

Due to these negative effects, many schools and teachers stopped small-group instruction altogether, opting for only whole-group instruction. Although whole-group instruction certainly has its place in daily instruction, it should not be the only approach, since those students who need more interaction and closer contact with the teacher and a text to be successful are marginalized. Research has shown small-group instruction to be a critical component of effective instruction. Taylor, Pearson, Clark, and Walpole (2000) conducted a study of 70 first- through third-grade teachers from 14 low-income schools in four states and found that the teachers with high student achievement provided more small-group instruction. Allington and Johnston (2002) observed 30 fourth-grade teachers from five states and found that the most effective classrooms implemented small-group instruction. Yet, it is not simply the utilization of small groups that is the key to effective instruction.

Guided reading is based on dynamic grouping according to students' strengths and needs that change as students' strengths and needs change. Students read appropriate texts and instruction focuses on students' strengths and needs based on ongoing assessment. Students read a new book each time their group meets, and all students read simultaneously while receiving support from the teacher. Through the orchestration of instructional decisions based on ongoing assessment, students continually grow toward reading independence.

Effective guided reading depends on appropriate student grouping and then the selection of an appropriate text for the students in each group. Once initial groups have been designated and texts selected, the components of a guided reading lesson (described in the next section) must be implemented in such as way as to build on individual students' strengths while addressing their needs within the group.

The first and one of the most crucial aspects of guided reading is initial and ongoing dynamic—meaning temporary and fluid—grouping of students. Initial groups are formed based on running records and the teacher's observations of children's reading. Based on this information, small groups are convened around concept-based needs. According to Fountas and Pinnell (2001), "If the concept is one students can explore across several different levels of text, the group can be heterogeneous. If the concept is characteristic of a particular level of text or genre of text, the group should be homogeneous" (p. 219). As teachers continue to take running records and anecdotal notes, they will notice that some members of a group will move faster or slower than others, and the makeup of the group will change. Once initial groups are formed, appropriate leveled texts must be selected.

## WHAT CHILDREN READ DURING GUIDED READING

According to Fountas and Pinnell (2006), "Excellent teaching begins with matching books to readers, intentionally selecting books that will be accessible to the readers *with your help*" (p. 39). Several aspects of text must be taken into consideration to provide students with a book that is accessible. *Accessibility* means that a given reader can do the following:

- Process text well, using knowledge of what makes sense, sounds right, and looks right—simultaneously—in a smooth operating system.
- Read most of the time at a good rate with phrasing, appropriate stress, pausing, and intonation (that is, in oral reading, putting words together in groups or phrases so the reading sounds like talking).
- Know or rapidly solve most of the words and reads with a high level of accuracy.
- Interpret the full meaning of the text.

Texts that are accessible—within a readers' zone of proximal development or instructional level—are within the student's control (can be read with 90 percent accuracy) but provide a small challenge. A very important aspect of guided reading is that students read appropriate texts that help them build the reading strategies they need to read new books on their own. When a child reads a book that does not present even a few challenges, then his reading process is not moved forward. When a child attempts to read a book that is too difficult, his reading process shuts down because he does not have the strategies to problem solve. A text that offers minimal challenges is in the child's control and allows him to use the strategies he has but also to problem solve challenging aspects with the teacher's support.

*Read*

*Read a list of leveled guiding reading books.*

One way many teachers have found to match books to readers is by using "leveled books," or books that have been categorized according to certain characteristics. These characteristics include genre, formats (i.e., picturebooks, chapter books, diaries, and informational books), text structure, content, themes and ideas, language and literary features, sentence complexity, vocabulary, illustrations, and book and print features (i.e., length, size, layout). Many of these characteristics are discussed in the genre chapters of this text. Irene Fountas and Gay Su Pinnell (1996) created one of the first leveling systems for classroom teachers. Books are categorized according to a gradient of characteristics that gradually increase in difficulty from levels A to Z. Fountas and Pinnell (2001) said the following:

> Creating a gradient of text requires attention to a range of factors that research indicates contribute to the reading difficulty of a text. It means classifying books along a continuum based on the combination of variables that support and confirm readers' strategic actions and offer problem-solving opportunities that extend the reading process. (p. 228)

Using a leveling system allows teachers to match the reading behaviors of students to the supportive and challenging characteristics of books that will be accessible to the student with the teacher's support.

Leveled sets of books developed specifically for guided reading can be purchased, but any text can be analyzed for the level of difficulty and used for guided reading. Becoming familiar with the characteristics of texts that make reading more or less difficult can assist teachers in understanding the reading process and in ways children may need support during guided reading. Texts that can be used for guided reading include the following:

- Leveled stories within basal readers
- Sets of trade books
- Sets of leveled books
- *Weekly Reader, Scholastic News,* or other nonfiction magazines
- Internet sites
- Poetry
- Nonfiction texts including content area texts
- Writing aloud and shared writing texts

The decision to move a child from one level to another or to skip a level or to even move back a level will depend on the teacher's ongoing assessment and observations. A child will need to continue reading books within a particular level until she builds fluency and strategies for problem solving effectively and efficiently. When a child finds the books easy and there is nothing more to learn about processing text, then she is ready to move up.

- Children are not expected to read every book on a level.
- There is no prescribed "order" to the books at any given level.
- Students making fast progress will skip levels.
- You can always move up or down the gradient as you see the need for easier or more challenging texts for your students.
- For independent reading, students do not choose from books organized into levels.

*Watch*

*Watch a guided reading lesson.*

This last point is particularly important. Leveling is used for guided reading books and not books children self-select for independent reading. Books for independent reading should be categorized to reflect topics, genres, content, authors, and other aspects of students' interests.

## WHEN AND HOW TO CONDUCT GUIDED READING

The decision of when or how often to meet with guided reading groups should be based on students' needs and the time available in the literacy block. In the primary grades, it is important to meet with readers as often as possible to move them forward to independence. On page 387, a sample schedule is provided in which a 60-minute block of time is suggested for meeting with guided reading groups for 10 to 15 minutes per group. Holding guided reading groups at least four days a week, especially for struggling readers, is ideal. In the intermediate grades, many students will be independent readers, and you will not need to see them every day; two to three times a week is adequate. It is important for students to receive strong support through the other components of the literacy block—read aloud, shared reading, and independent reading—for students to continue to grow as readers.

Guided reading follows the gradual release of the responsibility model. The teacher selects an appropriate text based on students' strengths and needs and prepares an introduction to the text based on the support students will need to read the text easily. Responsibility is then turned over to the students to either "whisper read" or silently read the text individually. As the students read, the teacher observes and monitors their reading behaviors and provides support as necessary. After reading, the teacher engages the students in talking about the story, and, based on her observations of students' needs, the teacher may return to the text for one or two teaching opportunities. The lesson may include a follow-up activity. Table 13.7 provides an overview of the components of a guided reading lesson. By looking across the chart, you can see the shift in responsibility from the teacher to the students.

**TABLE 13.7**

# Components of a Guided Reading Lesson

| Before the Reading | During the Reading | After the Reading |
|---|---|---|
| • Teacher selects an appropriate text that will be supportive but with a few manageable challenges | • Teacher listens as the students read the whole text or a unified part to themselves (softly or silently) | • Teacher talks about the story with the children inviting personal response |
| • Teacher prepares an introduction to the story | • Teacher observes and documents individual reader's strategy use | • Teacher returns to the text for one or two teaching opportunities such as finding evidence or discussing problem-solving |
| • Teacher briefly introduces the story, keeping in mind the meaning, language, and visual information in the text, and the knowledge, experience, and skills of the reader | • Teacher interacts with individuals to assist with problem solving at point of difficulty (when appropriate) | • Teacher assesses children's understanding of what they read |
| • Teacher leaves some questions to be answered through the reading | • Students request help in problem solving when needed | • Teacher sometimes engages the children in extending the story through such activities as drama, writing, art, or more reading |
| • Students engage in a conversation about the story, raising questions, building expectations, and/or noticing information in the text | | • Teacher may engage students in rereading the story to a partner or independently |

Adapted from I. Fountas & G. Pinnell (1996). *Guided reading: Good first teaching for all children*. Portsmouth, NH: Heinemann, p. 7.

While meeting with a guided reading group, the other children may be engaged in learning centers or reading independently. It is critical for every minute of the brief 10 to 20 minutes you have with your guided reading groups to be spent engaged in purposeful activity with those students and not interrupted by other students in the class. During the first several weeks of school, when the teacher is assessing students prior to forming guided reading groups, teach the students what is expected when they participate in centers and independent reading. Model how to problem solve when the tape recorder doesn't work in the listening center, for example. Write the expectations on chart paper and post them next to each center activity so students can refer to them as necessary. It is important that the activities students are engaged in away from the teacher are as powerful as when they are with the teacher. The activities included in learning centers must be meaningful, engaging, and worthwhile. Several excellent books have been written about learning centers and are listed in the Print Resources section at the end of this chapter.

Reading and writing aloud, shared reading and writing, and guided reading are effective strategies teachers can use to address the many different needs of each of their students so that all kids can share in the joy of children's literature.

# Top 10 Read Alouds

## STORIES IN WHICH BOOKS COME TO LIFE

1. **The Book of Story Beginnings** by Kristin Kladstrup (2006, Candlewick). After moving with her parents to Iowa, 12-year-old Lucy discovers a mysterious notebook that can bring stories to life and that has a link to the 1914 disappearance of her great-uncle.

2. **Edward and the Pirates** by David McPhail (1997, Little, Brown). Once Edward has learned to read, books and his vivid imagination provide him with great adventures.

3. **The Great Good Thing** by Roderick Townley (2001, Atheneum). Nothing ever changes inside the storybook kingdom inhabited by 12-year-old Princess Sylvie, her parents, and many other characters until Sylvie discovers that by allying herself with the Reader, she can experience new adventures beyond the confines of the book.

4. **Inkheart** by Cornelia Funke (2003, Scholastic). Twelve-year-old Meggie learns that her father, who repairs and binds books for a living, can "read" fictional characters to life when one of those characters abducts them and tries to force him into service.

5. **Lionel and the Book of Beasts** by E. Nesbit, illustrated by M. Hague (2006, HarperCollins). As young King Lionel turns the pages of his magical book, a hungry red dragon and other creatures in the illustrations come to life.

6. **Magic by the Book** by Nina Bernstein, illustrated by Boris Kulikov (2005, Farrar, Straus and Giroux). After returning from a trip to the library, 11-year-old Anne and her younger brother and sister discover a magic book that sends them on adventures in which they meet Robin Hood, giant bugs, and a dark, sinister man with a wolfish face.

7. **My Book Box** by Will Hillenbrand (2006, Harcourt). A determined elephant creates his own book box and discovers all the magic and fun of books and reading.

8. **The Neverending Story** by Michael Ende (1997, Puffin). Shy, awkward Bastian is amazed to discover that he has become a character in the mysterious book he is reading and that he has an important mission to fulfill.

9. **The Red Book** by Barbara Lehman (2004, Houghton Mifflin). A magical red book without any words transports a girl across oceans and continents into a new world of possibility, where a friend she's never met is waiting. And the journey is not over.

10. **Who's Afraid of the Big Bad Book?** by Lauren Child (2003, Hyperion). A boy who loves books but has not always treated them well falls asleep and finds himself in his book of fairy tales, where his interaction with everyone from Goldilocks to Cinderella wreaks havoc.

# Activities for Professional Development

## Think Critically About Children's Books

1. Finding a book's "voice" and giving an "Academy Award–winning" performance can seem like a daunting task for anyone, especially pre-service teachers who may have not had as many opportunities to hear great read alouds or practice reading aloud. One way to fully understand the importance of using appropriate tone, inflection, voice variation, pacing, pauses, and silence to bring out a book's voice is by listening to audiobooks. Most audiobooks are recorded by actors or professional readers. Listen to several audiobooks from the local library. The American Library Association publishes an annual list of *Notable Children's Recordings* that can be found at http://www.ala.org. What characteristics does the narrator employ that influence how you interpret the story?

2. Select a picturebook to read aloud. Practice finding the book's voice by reading with appropriate tone, inflection, voice variation, pacing, pauses, and silence. Then record your reading of the story. You can easily record your voice directly on a computer. Go to the Start menu → all programs→ accessories → sound recorder. From there you can voice record yourself and then save it. Open the recording in Windows Media Player and burn the recording to a CD. The CD, along with a copy of the book, can be placed in the listening center of your classroom. Think about where you might stop to conduct think alouds if you were reading the story aloud to a group of students. How could you connect this read aloud to a write-aloud?

3. How can you use children's literature "touch-stone" and "mentor" texts in your writing instruction and teach students to look for writing strategies as they read? In the online video "Reading Like A Writer," you will learn how to immerse students in literary genres and use engaging texts to set the stage for writing. Go to: http://www.learner.org/workshops/writing35/session3/index.html Click on "Prepare for the workshop" from the left menu and read the information/access the resources provided. Then, click "Analyze the videos" from the left menu. Read the "Key Practices To Observe" and then watch videos 5 and 6. After viewing the videos, click on "Reflect on your learning" from the left menu and respond to the questions. Share your responses with your classmates.

4. The texts used for read alouds, shared reading, and guided reading serve different purposes in supporting children's literacy. Compare the texts of a picturebook, big book, and guided reading book. How are the writing, format, and content similar and different? Why is it important for children to have meaningful experiences engaging with all three types of books?

# Print and Online Resources

## Print Resources

Allen, J. (2002). *On the same page: Shared reading beyond the primary grades.* Portland, ME: Stenhouse.

Diller, D. (2005). *Practice with purpose: Literacy work stations for grades 3–6.* Portland, ME: Stenhouse.

Fountas, I., & Pinnell, G. (1996). *Guided reading.* Portsmouth, NH: Heinemann.

Fountas, I., & Pinnell, G. (2001). *Guiding readers and writers grades 3–6.* Portsmouth, NH: Heinemann.

Fox, M. (2008). *Reading magic: Why reading aloud to our children will change their lives forever.* NY: Mariner.

Laminack, L. (2009). *Unwrapping the read aloud: Making every read aloud intentional and instructional.* New York: Scholastic.

Laminack, L., & Wadsworth, R. (2006). *Learning under the influence of language and literature: Making the most of read-alouds across the day.* Portsmouth, NH: Heinemann.

Laminack, L., & Wadsworth, R. (2006). *Reading aloud across the curriculum: How to build bridges in language arts, math, science, and social studies.* Portsmouth, NH: Heinemann.

Owocki, G. (2005). *Time for literacy centers: How to organize and differentiate instruction.* Portsmouth, NH: Heinemann.

Ray, K. (1999). *Wondrous words: Writers and writing in the elementary classroom.* Urbana, IL: National Council of Teachers of English.

Routman, R. (2003). *Reading essentials: The specifics you need to teach reading well.* Portsmouth, NH: Heinemann.

Routman, R. (2005). *Writing essentials: Raising expectations and results while simplifying teaching.* Portsmouth, NH: Heinemann.

Sipe, L. (2008). *Storytime: Young children's literary understanding in the classroom.* New York: Teachers College Press.

Schulman, M. (2006). *Guided reading in grades 3–6.* New York: Scholastic.

Wilhelm, J. (2001). *Improving comprehension with think-aloud strategies.* New York: Scholastic.

 **Online Resources**

*Mem Fox: And Do It Like This*
**http://www.memfox.com/reading-magic-intro**
Mem Fox's website has a plethora of information and resources. You can learn more about Mem's life, the story behind her stories, you can hear her read aloud many of her books and you can hear her read aloud the "Do It Like This" section of her book, *Reading Magic* in which Mem gives her expert advice on how to read aloud.

*Jim Trelease on Reading*
**http://www.trelease-on-reading.com**
Jim Trelease, author of *Jim Trelease's Read-aloud Handbook* (now in the sixth edition), has long

been an advocate of reading aloud at home and in the classroom. His website has many valuable resources, including links to several chapters from his book.

*Reading Rockets: Reading Aloud*
**http://www.readingrockets.org/atoz/reading_aloud**
The Reading Rockets website has a wonderful set of resources on reading aloud including videos, webcasts, articles, and resources.

*Reading Is Fundamental: Reading Aloud*
**http://www.rif.org/parents/readingaloud/default
.mspx**
Reading Is Fundamental (RIF) prepares and motivates children to read by delivering free books and literacy resources to those children and families who need them most. The RIF website has many resources for educators and parents for reading aloud, creating a literacy-rich environment at home, lesson plans, and book selection.

*Literacy Connections: Reading Aloud*
**http://literacyconnections.com/ReadingAloud
.php**
Provides links to a variety of websites with resources on reading aloud.

*The National Writing Project: Mentor Texts*
**http://iuswp.com/mentor-texts**
The National Writing Project is a well-known, long-running program that provides educators with professional development on the teaching of writing. This site offers a list of children's literature that can be used as mentor texts for teaching the craft of writing.

Visit the companion website at **www.cengage.com/education/johnson** to find

links related to the Read/Watch/Listen icons noted throughout the chapter, as well as additional resources.

# References

Allen, J. (2000). *Yellow brick roads: Shared and guided paths to independent reading 4–12.* Portland, ME: Stenhouse.

Allington, R., & Johnston, P. (2002). *Reading to learn: Lessons from exemplary fourth-grade classrooms.* New York: Guilford.

Anderson, R., Hiebert, E., Scott, J., & Wilkinson, I. (1984). *Becoming a nation of readers.* Champaign-Urbana, IL: Center for the Study of Reading.

Bohn, C., Roehrig, A., & Pressley, M. (2004). The first days of school in the classrooms of two more effective and four less effective primary-grade teachers. *The Elementary School Journal, 104*(4), 269–287.

Clay, M. (1991). *Becoming literate: The construction of inner control*. Portsmouth, NH: Heinemann.

Crain-Thoreson, C., & Dale, P. (1992). Do early talkers become early readers? Linguistic precocity, preschool language, and emergent literacy. *Developmental Psychology, 28,* 421–429.

DeTemple, J. (2001). Parents and children reading books together. In. D. K. Dickinson & P. O. Tabors (Eds.), *Beginning literacy with language* (pp. 31–51). Baltimore: Paul H. Brookes.

Dickinson, D. (2001a). Book reading in preschool classrooms: Is recommended practice common? In D. K. Dickinson & P. O. Tabors (Eds.), *Beginning literacy with language* (pp. 175–203). Baltimore: Paul H. Brookes.

Dickinson, D. (2001b). Putting the pieces together: Impact of preschool on children's language and literacy development in kindergarten. In D. K. Dickinson & P. O. Tabors (Eds.), *Beginning literacy with language* (pp. 257–287). Baltimore: Paul H. Brookes.

Dickinson, D., & Smith, M. (1994). Long-term effects of preschool teachers' book readings on low-income children's vocabulary and story comprehension. *Reading Research Quarterly, 29,* 105–122.

Eldredge , J., Reutzel, D, & Hollingsworth, P. (1996). Comparing the effectiveness of two oral reading practices: Round-robin reading and the shared book experience. *Journal of Literacy Research, 28*(2), 201–225.

Elley, W. (1989). Vocabulary acquisition from listening to stories. *Reading Research Quarterly, 24,* 174–187.

Feitelson, D., Kita, B., & Goldstein, Z. (1986). Effects of listening to series stories on first graders' comprehension and use of language. *Research in the Teaching of English, 20,* 339–356.

Fountas, I., & Pinnell, G. (1996). *Guided reading.* Portsmouth, NH: Heinemann.

Fountas, I., & Pinnell, G. (2001). *Guiding readers and writers grades 3–6*. Portsmouth, NH: Heinemann.

Fountas, I., & Pinnell, G. (2006). *Leveled books K–8*. Portsmouth, NH: Heinemann.

Funke, C. (2005). *Inkspell*. New York: Scholastic.

Hahn, M. (2002). *Reconsidering read-aloud*. Portland, ME: Stenhouse.

Harvey, S., & Goudvis, A. (2007). *Strategies that work* (2nd ed.). Portland , ME: Stenhouse.

Holdaway, D. (1979). *The foundations of literacy*. Sydney: Ashton Scholastic.

Ivey, G., & Broaddus, K. (2001). "Just plain reading": A survey of what makes students want to read in middle school classrooms. *Reading Research Quarterly, 36,* 350–377.

Laminack, L., & Wadsworth, R. (2006). *Learning under the influence of language and literature: Making the most of read-alouds across the day*. Portsmouth, NH: Heinemann.

Meyer, L., Wardrop, J., Stahl, S., & Linn, R. (1994). Effects of reading storybooks aloud to children. *Journal of Educational Research, 88,* 69–85.

Morrow, L. (1990). Small group story readings: The effects on children's comprehension and responses to literature. *Reading Research and Instruction, 29,* 1–17.

Morrow, L., & Brittain, R. (2003). The nature of storybook reading in elementary school: Current practices. In A. van Kleeck, S. Stahl, & E. Bauer (Eds.), *On reading books to children: Parents and teachers* (pp. 140–158). Mahwah, NJ: Erlbaum.

Palmer, B. M., Codling, R. M., & Gambrell, L. B. (1994). In their own words: What elementary students have to say about motivation to read. *The Reading Teacher, 48*(2), 176–178.

Phillips, G., & McNaughton, S. (1990). The practice of storybook reading on preschoolers in mainstream New Zealand families. *Reading Research Quarterly, 25,* 196–212.

Ray, K. (1999). *Wondrous words: Writers and writing in the elementary classroom*. Urbana, IL: National Council of Teachers of English.

Ray, K. (2005). Read-aloud: Important teaching time. *School Talk, 10*(3), 1–6.

Rosenhouse, J., Feitelson, D., Kita, B., & Goldstein, Z. (1997). Interactive reading aloud to Israeli first graders: Its contribution to literacy development. *Reading Research Quarterly, 32,* 168–183.

Routman, R. (2003). *Reading essentials: The specifics you need to teach reading well*. Portsmouth, NH: Heinemann.

Routman, R. (2005). *Writing essentials: Raising expectations and results while simplifying teaching*. Portsmouth, NH: Heinemann.

Serafini, F., & Giorgis, C. (2003). *Reading aloud and beyond*. Portsmouth, NH: Heinemann.

Sipe, L. (2000). The construction of literary understanding by first and second graders in oral response to picture storybook read alouds. *Reading Research Quarterly, 35*(2), 252–275.

Sipe, L. (2002). Talking back and taking over: Young children's expressive engagement during storybook read alouds. *The Reading Teacher, 55*(5), 476–483.

Sulzby, E. (1985). Children's emergent reading of favorite storybooks: A developmental study. *Reading Research Quarterly, 20*(4), 458–481.

Taylor, B., Pearson, P. D., Clark, K., & Walpole, S. (2000). Effective schools and accomplished teachers: Lessons about primary grade reading instruction in low-income schools. *Elementary School Journal, 101*(2), 121–166.

Tunnell, M., & Jacobs, J. (1989). Using "real" books: Research findings on literature based reading instruction. *The Reading Teacher, 42*(7), 470–477.

Wasik, B., & Bond, M. (2001). Beyond the pages of a book: Interactive book reading and language development in preschool classrooms. *Journal of Educational Psychology, 93,* 243–250.

Wells, G. (1986). *The meaning makers: Children learning language and using language to learn.* Portsmouth, NH: Heinemann.

Wilhelm, J. (2001a). *Improving comprehension with think-aloud strategies.* New York: Scholastic.

Wilhelm, J. (2001b). Think-alouds: Boost reading comprehension. *Instructor, 111*(4), 26–28.

# Reading by Children: Independent Reading and Writing and Literature Circles

# 14

> "Sam!" said his mom, and held out her arms.
> "You can read!"
> "Yes!" Sam said. "I'm the Chief of wonderfulness!"
> "I still want you and Dad to read me stories," Sam told his mom as she took him up the stairs to bed.
> "Oh, of course," Mrs. Krupnik said. "We'll read you stories forever, if you let us. It's our favorite part of the day, when we read bedtime stories."
> "And I can read them to you now, too," Sam pointed out.
> —Lois Lowry, 1999, pp. 152–153

Sam, Anastasia's little brother in the Anastasia Krupnik series by Lois Lowry, has discovered the "wonderfulness" of reading, just like thousands of children across the country every day. As a mother and teacher, I have had the great honor of assisting children in becoming readers and writers and discovering the joy of children's literature. I also take pleasure in bringing that joy back into the lives of pre-service and inservice teachers, as many have not read children's literature since they were children. Over the course of a semester, they self-select books across the genres, read and write about the books they select, and share their thinking about these books in class book clubs. The opportunity to select, read, and discuss books with each other is a powerful motivator, not only for adults but for children. This chapter examines the ways children engage in reading on their own: independent reading, writing independently (often in response to their self-selected reading), and engaging in discussions of their reading (literature circles).

| To Learners | With Learners | | By Learners |
|---|---|---|---|
| Demonstration | Shared demonstration | Guided practice | Independent practice |

# Independent Reading

*Some schools set aside* a specific time each day for self-selected reading, sometimes called SSR (sustained silent reading) or DEAR time (drop everything and read). Although these schools value the importance of providing children with time to read every day, often the time is not used to its maximum benefit. Teachers find themselves frustrated by children who never find a book to read or never finish a book, or who use this time to sleep or do some other off-task activity. Teachers feel as if they are "the reading police"—ready to "catch" children who are not reading. With pressure for accountability from administrators and state and national testing, teachers feel the time could be better spent in other ways. Yet, research clearly shows there is a powerful relationship between volume of reading and reading achievement (Allington & Johnston, 2002; Pressley, Warton-McDonald, Allington, Block, & Morrow, 2001; Taylor, Pearson, Clark, & Walpole, 2000). Additionally, Allington's (2006) synthesis of research found that "a variety of studies provide reliable, replicated evidence that children whose reading development lags behind their peers engage in far less reading than other higher achieving peers" (p. 44).

To fully realize the benefits of self-selected reading time, independent reading cannot be only providing children with time to choose books and read. Allington (2002) found that in the classrooms of more effective teachers, independent reading was characterized by how effectively the time was allocated. Given one hour for reading instruction, 5 to 10 minutes was spent preparing children to read, 40 to 45 minutes was spent with children reading independently as the teacher conferenced individually with children, and 5 to 10 minutes was spent engaging children in follow-up activities related to their reading. During independent reading, children read self-selected books and respond to their reading in a journal. Teachers work with children in whole group, small group, and individual settings, providing essential scaffolding.

In the previous chapter, reading aloud, shared reading, and guided reading were presented as ways in which teachers share literature with children in structured and supported ways to promote engagement, model critical reading strategies, and provide opportunities for reading response. In each instructional setting, the teacher chose the book to be shared, decided what strategies were important to illustrate and teach, and determined how much support to provide for student success. These scaffolded instructional approaches are essential to student success, but students must also be given the opportunity to choose their own books and apply what they are learning, and assume responsibility for their own reading and writing independently.

Just as with reading aloud, shared reading, and guided reading, independent reading must be intentional—well thought through and informed by assessment and observation of children, and curricular goals. The next sections present important components of independent reading.

## PREPARING FOR INDEPENDENT READING

Jill Cole (2003), a second-grade teacher, conducted a classroom study of her students' motivations to read. Jill felt that her children had so much knowledge about their own education to share with her: "I decided that students' opinions, feelings, and choices were crucial to my understanding of their intrinsic motivation to read and that this information would enable me to be a more effective reading teacher" (p. 326). By conducting interviews and observations and reading students' reading logs and writing products, Jill found that "the students were motivated by very different books, activities, and other classroom components. They had their own beliefs, purposes, and reactions. In short, each one had a unique 'literacy personality'" (p. 326). When Jill discovered that her students were motivated to read by very different factors, she became more responsive by "providing a classroom culture that fostered their strengths, honored their voices, and met their needs" (p. 334). She accomplished this by incorporating many of the components of independent reading discussed here.

*Read*

*Read more about reading inventories.*

**Understanding Your Students' Literacy Personalities.** Like Jill, teachers can use a variety of methods to discover their children's literacy personalities. Many teachers have students respond to a reading inventory, such as the one constructed by a third-grade teacher in Figure 14.1. Observations of students during read/write aloud, shared reading/writing, guided reading, and one-on-one conferences reveal important information about how students interact with and respond to texts, other students, and the teacher during instructional and independent settings. Reading response journals and other written products provide insight into how children connect with texts. By using different sources of information, many facets of a student's personality can be discovered. As students change over the course of the school year, so will their personalities, and the classroom environment that supports their learning should change to accommodate them. With so many personalities in the classroom, teachers may feel overwhelmed at the thought of providing an environment that supports all of their learning needs. Yet, by providing a rich and evolving classroom library and providing a variety of supported and independent literacy contexts, all students can become motivated, engaged readers and writers.

*Read*

*Read more about classroom libraries.*

**Your Classroom Library.** When I was a little girl, I loved going to the public library. I would ride the bus downtown and spend hours browsing the shelves, looking through books on display, and lounging on the comfortable, kid-friendly furniture. I still love going to the public library, which now has videos, computer games, Internet access, magazines, audiobooks, and more. But it is much more convenient if I have books at home or in my office. So over the years I have collected hundreds of children's books for easy access. The books in my collection reflect my personal and professional interests and my course objectives. The well-stocked classroom library also allows easy access and must also reflect the range of student interests, preferences, and genres, and curricular resources.

Designing and stocking a classroom library around your students' literacy personalities takes time and careful consideration. For example, if you organize your library according to reading levels, as discussed in Chapter 13, children are only allowed to choose books within a certain level. Although you may have many books within each level, the topics, authors, and genres may not match the literacy personalities of your children. Moreover, how will they learn how to choose "just right" books on their

**FIGURE 14.1**

Third Grader's
Response to a
Reading Inventory

Name_____ Sean Shadle _____Date_____ 9/7 _____

How would you describe yourself as a reader?

"I'm an okay reader."

What are you currently reading?

John Henry

What kinds of things do you like to read?

Chapter books

What kinds of things do you not like to read?

"really small books with like 3 pages."

Do you have a favorite author? Who?

Mary Pope Osborne

What are you going to read next?

"My other Magic Tree House Book"

How do you choose the books you read?

"I look for books with a lot of words."

What do you do when you get stuck?

"I skip words I don't know and then I go back
and figure it out later."

What do you do when you start to read each day?

"I think about what the book is going to be like."

How do you keep track of the characters in the books you are reading?

"I look on the back to see if they are on there, or I will read back in the story
to figure it out."

What kind of reading is easy for you?

"really small books like Barney books."

What kind of reading is hard for you?

"really thick books with a lot of pages and
books with really long words."

own? If, instead, books are organized by authors, for instance, children will start to discuss authors, recommend books by various authors, and discover favorite authors. How you organize your classroom library sends a message about what you want children to learn about book choice. Sibberson and Szymusiak (2003, p. 14) offer a list of questions to ask when setting up a classroom library at the beginning of each year (Table 14.1).

Book baskets or tubs can be an effective and a flexible way to categorize books. They can be easily labeled and with the books facing out. Tubs create an attractive display that children can browse through. Tubs that are of medium size can be easily moved

**TABLE 14.1**

# Questions to Guide the Creation of Your Classroom Library

- How can the classroom library support good book-choice habits? How can it support children as they think about themselves as readers, find favorite authors, and read for different purposes?

- Will the entire classroom library be located in one area of the room, or will different sections be in different parts of the room?

- Will nonfiction be in a different area from fiction? How will this help children learn why they read different genres?

- What type of reading materials will students have access to during reading time? Will they be encouraged to read magazines, news articles, comic books, or poetry?

- How will I find space to display the books with the covers facing out?

- Which displays will be permanent? Which will include rotating titles?

- Will I use baskets to organize books with the same authors, topics, and genres?

- How will I highlight less popular books to make them appealing to students?

- How will I make room to highlight books throughout the year based on student need?

from shelves for browsing and replaced. Tubs make it convenient to display books in a variety of ways to maximize students' exposure to new authors, genres, and topics (see Table 14.2).

**Audiobooks in the Classroom.** Audiobooks have traditionally been used in schools by teachers of second-language learners, learning-disabled or impaired students, and struggling readers or nonreaders. In many cases, audiobooks have proven successful in providing a way for these students to access literature and enjoy books. But they have not been widely used with average, avid, or gifted readers. Varley (2002) writes, "Uncertain whether audiobooks belong to the respectable world of books or the more dubious world of entertainment, elementary and high school teachers have often cast a fishy eye at them, and many have opted for the safe course of avoidance" (p. 252).

It might be appropriate, then, to list the benefits of audiobooks for *all* students (Table 14.3).

Additionally, many audiobooks are read by the author or include commentary by the author. A recording of *The Fighting Ground* by Avi, for example, includes an author interview in which he explains how he came up with the idea for the book. *Joey Pigza Swallowed the Key* is read by author Jack Gantos and also includes commentary about why he wrote the book. This information can provide students with a connection to the author as well as insight into the author's thoughts and the writing process.

However, even with all the benefits of audiobooks, they are not for all students. For some, the pace may be too fast or too slow. For others, the narrator's voice can be

**TABLE 14.2**

# Suggestions for Categorizing Classroom Book Baskets

- Alphabet books
- Concept books
- Pop-up books
- Number books
- Wordless books
- Curriculum topics
- Authors
- Newspapers and magazines
- Comics and cartoons
- Genres and subgenres such as mysteries, sports, and memoirs
- Teachers'/students' recommendations
- Books written in a specific format, such as journals
- Favorite characters/series
- Award-winning books
- Books written by students in the class
- Books with memorable language
- Humorous books
- Books read aloud by the teacher

irritating or the use of cassette or CD players can be cumbersome when compared to the flexibility of the book. But the majority of students will find listening to well-narrated, quality literature to be a transformative experience. Varley (2002) states, "If one thing has struck me about the way people describe listening to audiobooks, it is the reported intensity of their absorption and the emotional grip of the experience. 'They go right to your soul,' says one listener" (p. 253).

It is important for librarians and teachers to do their homework before buying. Single-author unabridged audiobooks tend to be the best, although some dramatizations (such as Philip Pullman's *His Dark Materials* trilogy, read by the author with a cast of more than 40 British actors) can be excellent. There are many sources of audiobook reviews readily available online and in print. These reviews can be well worth the time in reading when making costly purchases and are also an excellent way of staying abreast of recently released titles. Articles are also available with suggestions for using audiobooks in the classroom, and some audiobooks are available for downloading free of charge (see Chapter 12).

**TABLE 14.3**

# Benefits of Audiobooks

- Introduce students to books above their reading level

- Model good interpretive reading

- Teach critical listening

- Highlight the humor in books

- Introduce new genres that students might not otherwise consider

- Introduce new vocabulary or difficult proper names or locales

- Sidestep unfamiliar dialects or accents, Old English, and old-fashioned literary styles

- Provide a read-aloud model

- Provide a bridge to important topics of discussion (this is a good suggestion for parents as well, who can listen with their children while commuting to sporting events, music lessons, or on vacations)

- Recapture "the essence and the delights of hearing stories beautifully told by extraordinarily talented storytellers"

Baskin & Harris, 1995, p. 376.

## STUDENTS' INDEPENDENT READING

The research provides clear evidence of a powerful role for providing students with choices in their reading materials. This makes sense when we think about our own reading. How excited were you to read some of your college textbooks? Yet, you might stay up all night to finish the latest bestselling thriller. We are much more likely to be motivated and engaged in reading something we choose to read. Hidi and Harackiewicz (2000) write, "Investigations focusing on individual interest have shown that children as well as adults who are interested in particular activities or topics pay closer attention, persist for longer periods of time, learn more, and enjoy their involvement to a greater degree than individuals without such interest" (p. 153).

**Self-Selection of Books.** As discussed in Chapter 2, if a reader has difficulty reading the text, is not interested or engaged in the text, or is distracted, or if the text is about situations, issues, or characters that are beyond the readers' experiences or development, he will not actively participate with the text. For independent reading to be beneficial for children, they must learn how to self-select books they can read. In the instructional contexts discussed in Chapter 13, the teacher carefully selects books to be read to and with children. But when do children learn to select books for themselves? What will they do if they go to the library and you're not there to help pick out books for them? There are two prominent methods teachers can use to teach children how to choose books: the Goldilocks method and the five-finger method.

One specific strategy geared toward the modeling process is what Ohlhausen and Jepson (1992) call the "Goldilocks Strategy." These educators have created an analogy that compares the experiences of Goldilocks to those of students attempting to find

**TABLE 14.4**

# Categories for the Goldilocks Strategy

| Category | Description |
| --- | --- |
| Too hard | A book you would like to read, but you do not have strategies for figuring out unfamiliar words and/or unfamiliar concepts. |
| Just right | A book you are interested in and you have strategies to figure out most unfamiliar words and/or unfamiliar concepts. |
| Too easy | Books you like to read for fun; books you've read before. |

"just right" books. Goldilocks made choices, so we can assume that because she made them, "she learned from her mistakes and deepened her understanding of what it means to be responsible for her own actions" (pp. 31–32). By taking advantage of the opportunity to make choices and to learn from them, Goldilocks takes a step forward toward self-discovery, and so, too, do students move toward an awareness of their needs by choosing their own literature.

Ohlhausen and Jepson (1992) offer specific models for mini-lessons to show students how to identify books that are "too hard," "just right," or "too easy." When introducing the Goldilocks Strategy, teachers must explain ways to identify these categories (see Table 14.4).

Another approach is the five-finger method. (This method is also called the "rule of thumb," "sticky palm," and "greasy fingers.") Students are instructed to open the book to any page and begin reading. As they read, the student puts up one finger for each word for which she is not familiar. If the student finishes the page and is holding up all five fingers, she will know that that particular selection is too difficult. If she is holding up no fingers, the book choice is too easy. If two or three fingers are held up, the selection is probably a "just right" book. The five-finger method is a fairly simple way to help students choose appropriate books.

Along with learning to select books is learning when to abandon a book. Requiring children to read a book from cover to cover regardless of whether they like it or not is likely to result in unengaged and unmotivated reading. If you think about your own reading, how long do you stick with a book that you find boring, too difficult, or uninteresting? Just as teachers can model how to choose a book, they can model when to abandon a book. "The Child's Voice" on page 421 is a chart created by students in which they have expressed how they choose "just right" books and why they abandon books or become distracted when reading. These charts provide a concrete representation of their thinking and can be used as reminders during independent reading.

Reading with persistence and stamina is also important for children to understand. Sometimes we have no choice but to read something we don't like or find difficult. A few years ago, I subscribed to *Time* magazine to stay current on national and international events. I read children's literature and professional journals and books but rarely step outside of those areas of interest. One day I realized that most of the *Time* magazines were stacked in the corner of the living room unread. Each time an issue arrived, I would browse the articles only to find them uninteresting or difficult to understand. Even though I am a good reader, my background knowledge on economy, politics, and international affairs is limited, and rather than push myself to read the articles, I put them aside. Of course, that defeats my purpose of staying current on world events, so I sat down and really thought through a few of the articles. As new issues arrived, I found the articles became easier to read as my background knowledge grew. Although I am far from an expert on national affairs, I accomplished my goal of becoming more knowledgeable about current events. Yet, without persistence and stamina, *Time* magazine would still be collecting dust in the corner.

Similarly, Franki Sibberson and Karen Szymusiak (2003) found that using *Time for Kids* could be used to teach kids about reading difficult text. After asking their fourth graders to read several issues to identify articles they found difficult and easy to read, they analyzed the articles to figure out what made them difficult or easy. The students found that articles on topics such as Iraq were long, filled with unknown vocabulary, and boring. Building on this information, Franki and Karen used one of the articles to conduct a think aloud and then identified what they learned from the article. From there they developed weekly lessons with *Time for Kids* articles on Iraq to build background knowledge and asked the students to continue to add to the list of information they learned. In an effort to get kids to think about the ways they worked through difficult text, Franki and Karen asked the students to use highlighters, sticky notes, two-column charts, and other strategies to identify easy or difficult reading and then to think about the strategies they used to help them understand. In this way, the students began to identify strategies they could use to persist and sustain their reading when it is not easy. This is important work for good readers.

*Read* **Time for Kids**
*online.*

## THE · CHILD'S · VOICE

How to Select "Just Right" Books and How to Sustain Reading

### What Is a "Just Right" Book?

- Something you are interested in
- The right length/number of pages
- Favorite authors
- Right level
- Can read most of the words
- Reminds you of something in your past
- Pictures/illustrations are good
- Funny

### What Distracts Us from Reading?

- Someone tries to show you something or asks you a question
- Someone asks you for help with a word
- Someone is reading too loud or is making noises
- People walking around
- Picking books that are not just right

**Book Talks.** The following book talk was shared enthusiastically by a student in a fourth-grade class that I was observing:

> *Love, Ruby Lavender* is a hilarious book by Deborah Wiles. This book is funny from the very beginning when nine-year-old Ruby and her grandmother, Miss Eula, steal chickens from Peterson's Egg Ranch. Miss Eula and Ruby write letters back and forth to each other throughout the book, which are very funny. This book is also about standing up for yourself, forgiveness, and friendship. So, don't be a chicken and read this book!

*Listen*

*Listen to an excerpt of Love, Ruby Lavender by Deborah Wiles.*

I was so inspired that I immediately went to the bookstore and purchased it. The student was right—it was hilarious and courageous and sad and heartwarming. Sometimes the best books come from recommendations by our friends and colleagues (young and old). That is why book talks in the classroom can be so powerful.

Book talks are brief "teasers" that, given enthusiastically by teachers or students, are a way to entice others to read a particular book. A book talk doesn't reveal the whole story but rather tells just enough to hook prospective readers. Book talks can be used to introduce students to books in the classroom library, books for literature circles, a text set of books for a unit, or books written by a particular author. During the one- to two-minute presentation, the presenter gives the title and author of the book and a brief summary and then explains why he liked it and why other students might like it, too. A short excerpt may be read aloud and a few illustrations shown. The book can then be displayed on a chalk tray or shelf to encourage students to read it.

*Listen*

*Listen to book talks available as podcasts.*

## TIME FOR READING

In *What Really Matters for Struggling Readers: Designing Research-Based Programs,* Richard Allington (2006) says the following:

> In learning to read it is true that reading practice—just reading—is a powerful contributor to the development of accurate, fluent, high comprehension reading. In fact, if I were required to select a single aspect of the instructional environment to change, my first choice would be creating a schedule that supported dramatically increased quantities of reading during the school day. (p. 35)

Allington recommends a minimum of 90 minutes of in-school reading per day. At first, this may seem impossible—there's *already* not enough time to teach everything! But take a careful look at how much of the school day is spent on non-instructional activities—opening and ending procedures, intercom announcements, and paperwork. With some improvements in organizational efficiency, it's possible to find 30 to 50 additional minutes for reading every day.

Independent reading time can be a time when all children read self-selected books individually, or other options can be included, such as buddy reading, author/genre study, inquiry research, reading the Internet, peer discussions, or listening to audiobooks.

## RESPONSES TO INDEPENDENT READING

Children's response to literature is discussed in Chapter 2 in terms of a complex transaction between the reader, the text, and the context in which the reader participates. A variety of reasons—text difficulty, lack of background knowledge, type of genre—affect

*During independent reading time, children can read self-selected books individually or engage in options such as buddy reading.*

Courtesy of Denise Johnson.

the breadth or depth of this transaction. Writing in response to literature can be a great way for children to develop meaning. Lucy Calkins (2001) writes the following:

> We write—we put our thinking onto the page—so we can hold onto our fleeting thoughts. When we write, we can hold our thoughts in our hand, we can put our thoughts in our pocket, and we can bring out yesterday's thoughts. When we write, we can give our thoughts to someone and combine our thoughts with someone else's thoughts, and *we can improve our thoughts* (Wells, 1999). When we write, we can look at our thinking and ask, "What's the really big idea here?" We can say, "What patterns do I see in my ideas?" We can ask, "How are your ideas like mine?" We can notice, "Things are changing!" (p. 372)

For "things to change" or for reflection on reading to take place through writing, children must integrate their text knowledge (message of the text), their strategic knowledge (cognitive strategies for problem solving such as monitoring comprehension), and their reflective knowledge (ability to analyze, synthesize, and critique information). In other words, reflection is "a reconstructive process, wherein the reader is able to create new meanings through the integration of his or her text and world experiences." (Dorn & Soffos, 2005, p. 17). The orchestration of these processes takes time and practice. Teachers must provide extensive modeling and scaffolding to assist children. The use of sticky notes, reading response journals, and individual conferences are discussed in the following sections as ways to promote reflection on reading.

**Sticky Notes.** Sticky notes can be an effective way to encourage children to think as they read. The notes actively involve the reader in monitoring her own thinking by serving as a way to question, predict, or talk back to the text. To understand this process, teachers must understand the process themselves. Therefore, I ask my children's litera-ture students to use sticky notes to document their thinking and to prepare for book club conversations. Many have never used this strategy and often comment on the usefulness of having the notes to remember their thinking and to make connections with other readers. For example, the students found the format of Paul Fleischman's *Seedfolks* par-ticularly challenging. *Seedfolks* is a novel told in a series of vignettes by different people of varying ages and backgrounds living in the inner-city who turned a trash-filled lot into a productive and beautiful garden and, in doing so, are themselves transformed. The multiple voices of the different characters provide a rich context for perspective tak-ing. It can also be a challenging book, since the reader must keep track of the different characters throughout the story to make important connections that tie the characters together. Several students found sticky notes very useful to keep track of the characters as they moved through the novel and then to talk about the characters in their book clubs. By understanding the effectiveness of a strategy at a personal level, we tier our experience and develop greater breadth and depth to draw on in our teaching.

*Read*

*Read an excerpt of Seedfolks.*

Children's understanding of how to use sticky notes will progress over time. Some children enjoy the novelty and use sticky notes abundantly. Modeling how to use sticky notes from your own reading will help children understand the types of things you might put on a sticky note. Sticky notes can be removed from texts when children are finished reading and placed in reading journals which can be referred to later. Reflection on all of their sticky notes can be a powerful way to engage students in the reconstructive process to create new meanings from their thinking across the text. One or two sticky notes can be left in the book for other students to read. It is like leaving tracks of thinking on the pages of books.

*Read*

*Discover more ideas for using sticky notes for reading instruction.*

**Reading Response Journals.** Reading response journals in which children write their thinking about the texts they read can be used to write reflections. Reading response journals can be constructed from composition notebooks or pocket folders fairly inex-pensively. One first-grade teacher divides a composition notebook into four sections (see Figure 14.2). A page is also attached to the inside front cover on which children re-cord the date, title, and genre of all of the books they read. This journal format provides the student with many ways to think about reading and provides the teacher with dif-ferent sources of information for assessing students' literary understandings. In addition to their notebooks, students also need other reading tools, such as pencils, sticky notes, highlighter pens, bookmarks, and page markers. These items can be kept in a pencil bag for easy access during independent reading.

It is important to establish guidelines for journal entries (Figure 14.3) and to model and demonstrate for students many examples of journal entries through writing aloud and shared writing over several weeks so they understand what you expect. Share your own reading notebook (discussed in Chapter 2) as a way of sharing your own literacy and model yourself as a reader inside and outside of school. Rubrics with scoring criteria that students use as guidelines when writing can be an effective way to provide children with criteria for reflective response.

Often, teachers write back a response in the journal, which can include questions or other comments that prompt the child to expand the breadth or depth of his or her thinking. Routman (2005) writes, "Many students, especially culturally and linguistically diverse students, substantially improve their writing—content, quantity, form, fluency— as a result of keeping these journals" (p. 125). Yet, Routman (2003) also cautions that writing back to students is extremely time consuming and isn't necessarily always the best indicator of the child's understanding of the text: "Some students respond with lots of written details and it looks like they are getting the meaning. However, when I

**FIGURE 14.2**

Sample Reading
Response Journal

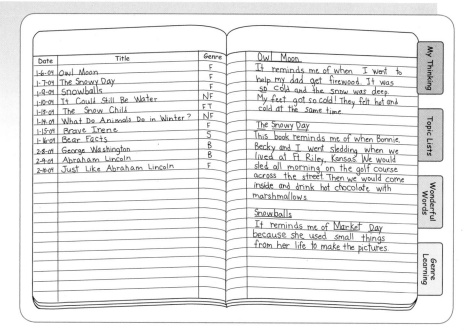

probe in depth, I sometimes find students have not understood after all—in fiction especially, things like character motivation, story resolution, or author's purpose" (p. 126). Therefore, it is important for teachers to confer with students on a regular basis. Rubrics can be used as a reference when conferring with individual students about their journal entries and provide a way for students to reflect on their own writing.

**One-on-One Reading Conferences.** While children are reading independently, the teacher works one-on-one with individual children every day in reading conferences to monitor their reading and provide specific feedback. By working with children individually, the teacher not only provides individualized feedback but also gains an understanding of how children are applying the skills and strategies previously taught, thus informing future instruction. During reading conferences, teachers should do the following:

- Have authentic conversations with the child about the texts they are reading
- Assist the child with understanding aspects of the routines of independent reading (i.e., self selecting "just right" books, reading for a sustained period of time)
- Teach the child effective reading skills and strategies
- Observe students' oral reading to ensure the use of fluency and phrasing
- Occasionally discuss students' journal responses

Routman (2003) offers a framework for informal reading conferences that encompass these roles within the context of working individually with a child (Table 14.5). Creating

**FIGURE 14.3**

Teacher-Created
Chart with Criteria
for Thoughtful
Journal Entries

## What Is a Thoughtful Journal Entry?

Making our thinking visible

ALWAYS USE EVIDENCE FROM THE TEXT!

Hmmm......

### Creates Mind Pictures/Visualizes
- How does the language (words, phrases) create visual or sensory images in my mind?
- How does the author use language to create the setting/s?
- How does the author use language to describe or create the character/s?
- How does the author use text features to help me learn more about the topic?

### Summarizes/Synthesizes
- What are the important things I am learning or have learned from my reading?
- What is the book mostly about?
- What is the character like so far?
- What do I think about what has happened so far?
- What is the author trying to teach me?

### Makes Connections
- Does any part of the book remind me of my own life?
- Does any part of the book remind me of the world and what is occuring or happened in the past?
- Does any event, character or theme/ message remind me of another book?
- Do I connect in any way with a character from the book?

### Offers Opinion
- Do I like or dislike the book?
- Who is my favorite or least favorite character and why?
- Will I read this book again? Why or why not?
- Will I recommend this book to a friend?
- Did this book teach me something?
- What is my favorite part of the book and why?

### Critiques
- What are the resources the author uses to provide me with accurate and current information?
- Did the author use text features to help me understand the information?
- Did the author follow the text structures for the genre?
- Do I agree or disagree with the way the author expressed meaning?

### Identifies Theme/Main Idea
- What is the author's message?
- What did the message teach me?
- How will the message change my life?
- What is the text really about?
- What did I learn from reading?
- What more do I need to learn?

### Wondering, Making Predictions Inferences
- I wonder…
- I think…
- I know…because…
- What does _____ mean?
- The mood in the book is _____ so far.

Adapted from L. Dorn & C. Soffos (2005). *Teaching for deep comprehension: A reading workshop approach* (p. 159). Portland, ME: Stenhouse.

*Watch*

*Watch one-on-one reading conferences.*

a system for organizing and maintaining documentation of each student's assessment information is essential when looking at students' progress over time and determining next steps in instruction.

In addition to deepening children's understanding of their reading, responses to reading discussed in this section and throughout the genre chapters of this book assist teachers with ways of knowing how children respond to the books they read in order to provide meaningful instruction that continues to extend and deepen their understanding of literacy and literature.

**TABLE 14.5**

# Framework for an Informal Reading Conference

| Say to Student | Assessment Information |
|---|---|
| Bring me a book that you can read pretty well. | • Is the child able to select books she can read and understand? |
| Why did you choose this book? | • Does the child take recommendations from peers? Is this a favorite author or series? |
| Is this an easy, just right, or too hard book for you? | • Does the child know how to select appropriate books?<br>• Is she over relying on being able to read all the words? |
| Tell me what the book is about so far. | • Can the child give an adequate retelling that shows she understands the gist and main ideas of the text? If not, check oral reading to be sure she can read the text. If oral reading is a problem, help her select an easier text. If not, probe to find out why she cannot say what the book is about. |
| Read this part of the book for me. | • Younger students who read orally will read aloud, and students who can read silently will read silently.<br>• Ask her to read two or three pages while you read along silently.<br>• Note the time she starts and finishes to approximate her reading rate per page.<br>• Jot down difficult vocabulary words so you can check to be sure she is figuring them out.<br>• Observe her as she reads silently. Does she subvocalize, reread, use illustrations and visuals, appreciate the humor, or seem to skip over hard vocabulary? |

*(continued)*

**TABLE 14.5**

(*continued*)

| Say to Student | Assessment Information |
|---|---|
| Tell me what you remember about what you just read. | • If the child is reading fiction, does she understand character motivation and behavior?<br>• If she is reading nonfiction, is she also using charts, photos, and graphs to get information?<br>• Check whether difficult vocabulary is understood.<br>• Is the student going beyond literal events in her retelling? |
| Let's discuss your strengths and what you need to work on. | • Always note first what the child has done successfully so she will continue to do it and be affirmed for her efforts.<br>• Strengths: Focus on what the child does well—selecting a "just right" book, retelling appropriately, figuring out vocabulary, inferring meaning, rereading when necessary.<br>• Goals: State, and have the student restate, one or two goals that have resulted from the conference. |
| How long do you think it will take you to complete this book? | • Has the student thought about it and set a realistic goal? For example, if there are 80 pages left to read, and she allots one hour a day for reading, 30 minutes at home and 30 minutes in school, at a rate of about one page a minute, she should easily be done with the book in one or two days. |

Adapted from R. Routman (2003). *Reading essentials*. Portsmouth, NH: Heinemann.

## GROUP SHARING

After independent reading time, it is important to bring the children together for a brief period to share their thinking about what and how they are reading and to evaluate how the group is working together during independent reading. During this time, the teacher invites individuals to share what they are reading with the whole class or asks students to discuss with each other in groups of twos or threes. Book sharing creates an environment in which children learn from each other, which is a strong influence and motivator. Children give and take book recommendations, reinforce strategy use or literary understandings, make connections to previous learning, and broaden perspectives.

This can also be a time for children to self-assess how effectively they used their independent reading time. This keeps children focused on the expectation that independent reading time must be purposeful, engaged, and active. After the teacher models the criteria and provides opportunities for guided practice, children can use a check sheet to self-assess individually or as a group (see Table 14.6).

**TABLE 14.6**

# Rubric for Self-Assessing Independent Reading Time

| 4 | 3 | 2 | 1 |
|---|---|---|---|
| I read the whole time. | I read most of the time. | I read some of the time. | I wasted precious reading time. |
| I stayed in one good reading spot the whole time. | I stayed in one good reading spot the whole time. | I changed reading spots. | I moved around a lot. |
| I picked just right books. | I picked just right books. | I had some just right books, but I could be more careful. | I was not very careful about my book choice. |
| I respected the readers around me. | I respected the readers around me. | I respected the readers around me. | I pretended to read. |
| I read way down deep. I was lost in the book. | My books made sense or I went back to reread. | I sort of understood what I read. | I got off track and even pulled other readers off track. |
| I read quietly. | I read quietly. | I got through some tricky spots, but I skipped some. | |
| I stopped and reread when it didn't make sense. | I tried certain strategies to figure out unknown words or parts I didn't understand. | | |
| I used sticky notes to help me with my thinking. | I used sticky notes to help me with my thinking at least once. | | |

Adapted from L. Calkins (2001). *The art of teaching reading.* Portsmouth, NH: Heinemann.

# Independent Writing

*To learn to read is to learn to walk. To learn to write is to learn to rise.*

JOSÉ MARTÍ

Children learn that their words matter by participating in a quality writing program that is based on the understanding that writing, like reading, is a process in which language is the foundation, thinking is the essence, and feeling is the energizer. Language, thinking, and feeling come together as students become intimately involved in the process of prewriting, drafting, revising, editing, and publishing. The process approach to writing instruction is based on how real writers write: They develop and redevelop content; play with word meanings, spelling, and sentence structure; expand and clarify ideas; reread; organize their thoughts; and share their writing with others. The process is not linear but recursive in nature. Teachers have modeled this process through writing aloud and supported and scaffolded children in shared writing. In independent writing, children get the opportunity to apply their learning during an uninterrupted time to write every day.

A quality writing program is also based on the understanding that writing contributes to the development of every aspect of reading comprehension and response. When students learn to control a particular aspect of writing, they are usually better able to negotiate that same aspect when reading. Thus, knowledge of decoding, vocabulary, grammar, language, literary patterns, and metacognition are all increased through development of writing abilities.

Independent writing can also bolster students' self-images. This happens as children learn that the details of their thoughts and experiences are important and worth writing about (Calkins, 2001). As children are given the time and strategies they need to write about their own experiences, their confidence and self-worth are developed. Block (2001) states that as students' writing is shared and appreciated by others, "their feelings of significance as people can also increase. Thus, through a well-constructed writing program, students can learn to use a tool to sculpt their initial thoughts into wise ideas that others can treasure" (p. 335).

A quality writing program also recognizes that strong reading and writing skills help prepare students for their futures outside of school. To become fully functional in today's world, students must become fully skilled in the use of word processors, web editors, presentation software, and e-mail. Effective writing programs integrate these technologies into writing instruction in order to prepare students for their literacy futures.

The next sections present important components of independent writing.

## PREPARING FOR INDEPENDENT WRITING

The information in the following sections will help you implement a writing workshop in your classroom.

### Know the Writing Process

*Understanding the writing process lies at the foundation of any writing workshop.*

FOUNTAS & PINNELL, 2001, P. 52

The writing process is based on what writers think and do as they write. The four stages of the writing process are exploring (prewriting), drafting (including revising), editing, and publishing (Figure 14.4). It is important to note that the stages of writing are recursive—writers do not necessarily progress through them linearly. Through writing aloud and shared writing, described in Chapter 13, the teacher models writing for a purpose and audience, the process of writing, and the recursive nature of the process. Through mini-lessons and individual conferences, teachers provide explicit instruction on specific writing skills and strategies. In this way, we go from the context of composing a whole piece of writing to looking at the parts and then connecting them back to the whole as children apply these strategies during independent writing. The quality writing in children's books can serve as a bridge to their own writing. Author Ralph Fletcher (2005), writes, "When kids come to know an author from the inside out, they

**FIGURE 14.4**

The Writing Process

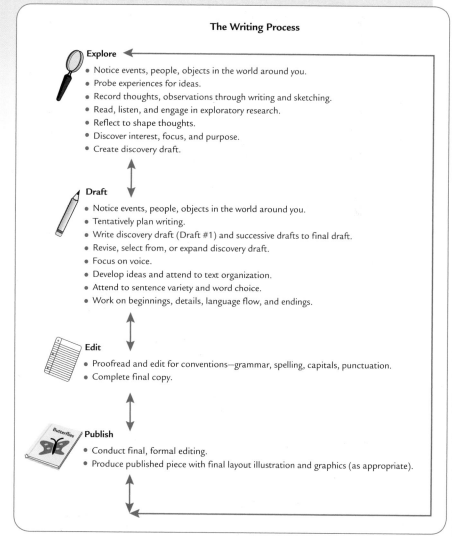

**The Writing Process**

**Explore**
- Notice events, people, objects in the world around you.
- Probe experiences for ideas.
- Record thoughts, observations through writing and sketching.
- Read, listen, and engage in exploratory research.
- Reflect to shape thoughts.
- Discover interest, focus, and purpose.
- Create discovery draft.

**Draft**
- Notice events, people, objects in the world around you.
- Tentatively plan writing.
- Write discovery draft (Draft #1) and successive drafts to final draft.
- Revise, select from, or expand discovery draft.
- Focus on voice.
- Develop ideas and attend to text organization.
- Attend to sentence variety and word choice.
- Work on beginnings, details, language flow, and endings.

**Edit**
- Proofread and edit for conventions—grammar, spelling, capitals, punctuation.
- Complete final copy.

**Publish**
- Conduct final, formal editing.
- Produce published piece with final layout illustration and graphics (as appropriate).

become insiders in the process, and this can have a transformative effect on them as writers, readers, and learners" (p. 1).

**Authors as Writing Mentors.** Authors have much to offer teachers in their quest to assist students on the journey to becoming good writers. To assist children with learning to write from authors, children must first see themselves as writers. Ray (1999) said, "Once students see themselves this way, they are able to lay their work down alongside that of other writers and see habits and crafts mirrored there, and also extend their own understandings of what it means to write. In order to gather a repertoire of craft possibilities that will help a writer write well, that writer first has to learn how to read differently, how to read with a sense of possibility, a sense of 'What do I see here that might work for me in my writing?'" (p. 14).

Lucy Calkins (1994) points out that for good books to play a strong role in improving the quality of writing, the reading-writing connection must be nurtured in classrooms. This can be accomplished by the following:

- Invite students to know a book or an author so well that the book or author stands a chance of affecting even their writing.
- Help students match their writing and their reading.
- Pay attention to the reading-writing connections our students are already making.
- Help students realize that the effects of literature are achieved because of an author's deliberate craftsmanship (p. 274).

*Read*

*Find lists of mentor texts online.*

The role of the teacher in each of the preceding actions serves as an important scaffold in the process of children learning to apprentice themselves to writers. An author inquiry chart (Table 14.7) can serve as a scaffold for looking closely at an author's crafting technique.

**Classroom Materials.** Just as there must be a variety of texts for independent reading, there must be a variety of materials for independent writing to support all of the purposes for writing in the classroom. The following materials will be for drafting, writing, research reports, book making, illustrating, and letter writing:

- Paper: construction paper, notepads and list pads, stationery, computer paper
- Pens, pencils, and markers, color markers
- Stapler, staple remover, scissors, tape, paper clips
- White out or cover-up tape, rulers, date stamp
- Envelopes, index cards, book binder
- Picturebooks
- Dictionaries, thesauruses, encyclopedias
- Anchor charts from mini-lessons

Some teachers use special lined paper for students' independent writing. The top of the paper might include a place for the student's name, date, the number of drafts, and the page number. Some teachers use different-colored paper for each draft. The final draft can be illustrated and bound and is sometimes typewritten on a word processor. Through management mini-lessons, children learn to take care of the materials in the writing center and to return items such as staplers and rulers when they are finished using them.

**TABLE 14.7**

# Inquiry Chart on an Author's Crafting Technique

| What is the author doing? | Why is the author doing this? | What can I call this crafting technique? | Have I ever seen another author craft this way? | Examples of this technique in my writing. |
|---|---|---|---|---|
| Short phrases from Chapter 1 of *Woodsong* by Gary Paulsen<br>• And learned nothing. (p. 1)<br>• Until a December morning … (p. 2)<br>• Wolves. (p. 4)<br>• And they were hunting the doe. (p. 4)<br>• And they were gaining on her. (p. 4)<br>• But it slowed her too much. (p. 5)<br>• On her. (p. 5)<br>• Spoke to the blood. (p. 6)<br>• There is horror in it. (p. 6)<br>• It was all in silence. (p. 7)<br>• And she sank. (p. 7)<br>• Leave her … (p. 7)<br>• But it did not frighten them. (p. 7)<br>• Just that. Look. (p. 7)<br>• They stopped and studied me. (p. 7)<br>• And it started with blood. (p. 8) | The author puts periods at the end of words that aren't sentences or uses one word as an entire paragraph to make a strong point or to emphasize a part. The author uses the word "and" over and over to create a sense of connectedness, things running together rather than separate. | Short sentences or one-word paragraphs "and" connectors | Cynthia Rylant<br>*In the Night Country*<br>"There are owls."<br>*The Relatives Came*<br>"We were so busy hugging and eating and breathing together." | |

Adapted from K. Ray (1999). *Wondrous words.* Urbana, IL: National Council of Teachers of English.

A writing folder or writer's notebook is also an essential tool for writers. The folder usually has multiple pockets for storing forms and writing pieces. Forms could include the following:

- A list of topic ideas
- A list of books that "spark" an idea
- A list of action words, describing words, or other word choices
- Writing rubrics, checklists, or guides

**Self-Selection of Writing Topics.** The use of writing prompts has a long history in elementary classrooms. With national and state testing at an all-time high, writing prompts are sometimes used exclusively to prepare students for the writing portion of the test. Yet, just as choice in reading books is a powerful motivator, so is choice in writing topics. It is difficult to read and write about topics for which you have limited prior knowledge or are disinterested. For the purposes of testing, however, children must learn to write to a prompt for something about which they have limited knowledge or interest, yet the majority of daily writing in the classroom should be self-selected topics. If we think about our own writing, it is always easier and more enjoyable if we are writing for our own purposes rather than someone else's.

On the other hand, some children just don't know what to write about. Here are several ways to suggest ideas for students that are broad enough for them to find their own place within the topic:

- Pull ideas from students' reading notebooks (reading response journal section: topic ideas).
- Brainstorm a list of ideas together as a class.
- Try genre or form writing.
- Talk with peers to get ideas.
- Look through students' writing notebooks.

English language learners should be given the opportunity to write in their first language as well as English to develop writing strategies as well as a sense of identity. Hubbard and Shorey (2003) write, "As these students learn to write in their native language using dialogue, paying attention to word choice, using detail and other strategies that are part of a writer's craft, they are adding skills that will serve them when they write in English" (p. 59).

Sometimes after a topic has been selected, it is obvious from the child's writing that it was not a good choice. The writing is forced, unengaged, or disconnected. Just as we teach children when to abandon books, we must teach them when to abandon a topic. Asking questions that serve as guidelines can be helpful: Do you care about the subject? Can you tell a lot about it? Can you include appropriate and interesting details (Routman, 2005, p. 178)?

Once students have decided on a topic about which they truly want to write, it's time to explore everything they know about the topic. During prewriting or discovery writing, children will consider the writing topic, purpose, audience, and form along with gathering and organizing ideas. Pulitzer Prize winning author and writing educator Donald Murray (1982) believes that 70% or more of writing time should be spent prewriting. For young writers, this often involves drawing a picture before writing. Older and more experienced writers may use graphic organizers or other frameworks to generate and organize their ideas. The time spent on prewriting activities, however, must remain flexible since the time needed depends on each individual child's writing personality.

As children engage in the writing process, they may start a piece and then for a variety of reasons leave it to start on a new piece. Thus, there are multiple pieces of writing in the students' writing folders at all times in various stages of the writing process.

## TIME FOR WRITING

Time for writing should constitute the majority of independent writing time. During this time the teacher confers with students, and children work individually or are peer conferencing. Modeling and providing clear expectations for behavior while the teacher is conferencing can be done at the beginning of the year through procedural mini-lessons. Additionally, peer conferencing is not a time for children to simply get together to participate in off-task conversations or to give each other poor advice. For this time to be productive, children must observe the teacher model conferencing to learn how to ask questions and give thoughtful feedback and then participate in peer conferences with the teacher's guidance before trying it out on their own.

**One-on-One Writing Conferences.** The individual student writing conference is a brief, focused opportunity to move the child forward as a writer. With this goal in mind, teachers ensure that the student learns something that will assist her with becoming a better writer in the future rather than "fixing" a piece of writing. Keeping records of what is taught during conferences is critical to the student's progress over time (see sample conference form in Table 14.8 and guidelines for a productive conference in Table 14.9). The teacher meets with every student over the course of a week.

Once a student has written and revised to the point of going as far as he can with the content, editing conferences can begin that focus on the clarity and correctness of the writing. Children can be taught to do much of their own editing prior to the conference through mini-lessons and editing check sheets.

*Watch*

*Watch one-on-one writing conferences.*

### GROUP SHARING

Group sharing, also known as the author's chair, occurs after independent writing time and is a brief period of time provided for students to share their work with each other. During group sharing children learn much about each other because they are also sharing their thinking. Writing always says something about the writer that makes sharing personal. After a child shares his or her writing with the class, the other children can give praise and ask clarifying questions. The teacher can also use this time as a way to provide the whole group with a chance to observe a conference in action, since the teacher's

**TABLE 14.8**

# Teacher Conference Form

| Student | Plan | Draft | Revise | Edit | Final | Teacher notes |
|---------|------|-------|--------|------|-------|---------------|
| Erica | ✓ | | | | | |
| Jason | | | ✓ | | | |
| Shanay | | | | ✓ | | |
| Ann | | ✓ | | | | |
| Bailey | ✓ | | | | | |
| Kadejiah | | ✓ | | | | |
| Sheridan | | | | | ✓ | |
| José | | | | | ✓ | |

**TABLE 14.9**

# Guidelines for a Productive One-on-One Writing Conference

- Have visible in front of you:
  - Established criteria for the piece of writing.
  - Essentials to look and listen for:
    - Organization.
    - Voice (one's personal style).
    - Enticing beginning.
    - Satisfying closing.
    - Evidence of rereading.
  - Use language of response:
    - Start with what the writing does. (I love the way . . . . I noticed that . . . .
    - Then move to what the writing has. (You tried out conversation. You spaced your words.)
    - Encourage your youngest writers and your developing writers. (I like how you were stretching your sounds as you write, I love the way your picture has lots of information.)
    - Use language that encourages and clarifies. (I really like how . . . . So you're saying . . . . Think about . . . . How about if you . . . ?)
  - Conference forms.
  - Writing tools (sticky notes, pencils, flip chart or whiteboard, scissors, tape, and extra paper).
- Sit side by side.
- Have the author (usually) read the piece twice.
- Listen for and focus on the writer's strengths and message.
- Focus on the overall meaning first of what the writer is trying to do (content).
- Narrow the teaching focus to one or two major points.
- Explain why editing is critical (so the reader can understand easily).
- Have the writer say back what he did, said, and will do.

interaction with the child during the group sharing would assist them in understanding the types of questions to ask and feedback to offer during peer conferences.

## PUBLISHING

The dictionary definition of *publish* is "to bring to the public attention; announce." When a student has completed his final draft, it is ready for publication, which takes many forms. For a book, publication might be a neatly handwritten bound text placed in the classroom library. A poem might be typewritten and hung on the wall. A letter might be mailed or given as a gift. A short story might be entered in a contest or published online. With the Internet, the audience becomes the world. Leu and Leu (1999) explain as follows:

> Publishing work on the Internet provides students with opportunities to write for an audience other than the teacher. It requires students to be precise and clear in their writing so that their readers understand their meaning. It moves students to naturally seek out opportunities for drafting, revision, and editing conferences as they seek to make meaning clear for their Internet audience. (p. 100)

There are many websites that allow students to publish their writing. Additionally, students can create individual portfolios via blogs or teachers can create a class anthology of student writing via a wiki. See Chapter 12 for websites and resources.

# Defining Literature Discussion

*I am committed to literature conversations because I have watched them change lives and perspectives. I've seen them build confidence and compassion. I truly believe that if all teachers committed to the conversation process, it would change the way in which students interact, both in and out of the classroom.*

Ardith Cole, 2003, p. xiii

I remember the night I finished reading *The Tale of Despereaux* by Kate DiCamillo. I closed the book and thought about whom I could call to talk to about it. But it was midnight, so I decided I'd better not. If I had called my friend Diane, and she, too, had read *The Tale of Despereaux* what do you think I might have said? "Diane, who were the main characters? What was the setting? Tell me about the plot? How did Despereaux solve the problem?" Diane would have hung up before long. We do not drill our friends on the story elements of the books they have read. We discuss books by engaging in conversations. If I had called Diane, the conversation would have started like this: "At first, I didn't like the way the narrator talked to the reader. It interrupted my thinking about the story. But, after a while I realized that the narrator's comments and questions brought new insight, and I began to look forward to it. What did you think?" Our conversation would have been in response to the book—both positive and negative. The nature of our responses is evaluative. We make judgments based on the connections we make to our experiences. I have not read many books in which the narrator spoke directly to the reader; this was a new experience for me, whereas other aspects, such as the fairy tale–like structure, were very familiar. Diane's response might have pushed me to think differently about the book, to pose questions, or to make a hypothesis about the author's intention. In short, our conversation would have confirmed, broadened, and deepened my understanding of *The Tale of Despereaux,* children's literature, my friend Diane, and the world in which we live.

Based on 30 years of teaching experience, Ardith Cole (2003) writes, "Literature conversations provide a platform for deep, rich comprehension of text. By developing these classroom structures for talk, teachers can help students collaborate, substantiate their ideas, and negotiate" (p. xiv). Calkin's (2001) affirms, "Talk, like reading and writing, is a major motor—I could even say *the* major motor—of intellectual thinking" (p. 226). Although several recent studies have found that in the classrooms of highly

*Students enjoy talking with peers about texts. These students are engaged in conversations about The Bee Tree as the teacher observes and enters into the conversations when appropriate.*

Courtesy of Denise Johnson.

effective teachers real conversations take place regularly between students and students and teachers (Allington, 2006), few teachers engage in classroom practices that promote such conversations or teach children how to talk about texts (Calkins, 2001; A. Cole, 2003; Ketch, 2005; Taylor & Pearson, 2002).

You might ask *why* teachers need to teach children how to talk about texts. Don't children participate in conversations at home and in their community? Family book sharing is not a universal practice across cultural, linguistic, and social lines; some homes do not have books; and some families are so busy rushing to soccer practice and dance class that they don't have time to discuss books. Of coursse, many parents do have conversations about books with their children. The bottom line is that many children come to school without knowing what a real conversation—deep, reflective talk—sounds like. Yet, with high expectations, time to read, teacher modeling, scaffolding, direct instruction, and a supportive classroom community, all children can learn to engage in deep, reflective conversations about books (Kong & Fitch, 2003).

Ketch (2005) writes, "Conversation is a basis for critical thinking. It is the thread that ties together cognitive strategies and provides students with the practice that becomes the foundation for reading, writing, and thinking" (p. 8). Students need opportunities to practice the use of cognitive strategies to internalize them and strengthen their comprehension. Students who engage in conversation in the classroom become intellectually engaged with text (Kucan & Beck, 2003). One way to engage students in conversation is through literature discussion groups—self-selected conversations about self-selected books.

## ESSENTIAL ELEMENTS OF LITERATURE DISCUSSION GROUPS

The sections that follow provide information on important aspects of literature discussion groups. Thinking through each of these essential aspects prior to engaging children in literature discussion will help you be prepared to promote conversations or teach children how to talk about texts.

**Providing a Model for Students.** The gradual release-of-responsibility model used throughout this book is the cornerstone of success for literature discussion groups. Since many children come to school without having models of what meaningful literature discussion looks like, it is important to provide them with a model. This can be done a couple of ways. If you have a colleague who implements literature discussion groups, ask if one of the groups could conduct a session in front of your class. This is sometimes called a fishbowl because the class outside of the discussion group is observing. As observers, students can jot down notes about what they noticed. Afterward, the teacher can conduct a mini-lesson on what the class noticed and how the actions observed supported the group discussion. Professional videos can also be used in the same way. The result might be a set of initial guidelines for conducting a good book discussion that the children can use as they start their own book clubs and find what works for them.

**Selecting Books for Literature Circles.** The selection of literature for discussion groups should be based on the teacher's knowledge of quality literature and of students' literary personalities, cultures, reading strengths and needs, independent reading levels, and cross-curricular goals. A set of four or five books for each title will be needed. Some of these books might be a part of the classroom library, and others might be borrowed from fellow teachers or the school and public libraries. Teachers can also send home a note requesting parents to donate titles. Having enough books is always a challenge, and collecting books takes time.

Although children should always have a choice when selecting books, the selection can be limited to a certain number of books ranging in reading levels that fall within a certain theme, content connection, author/illustrator study, or genre study. For example, if a fourth-grade teacher wanted her students to study historical fiction within the revolutionary war period, she might choose the following:

- *Revolutionary War on Wednesday* (Magic Tree House series) by Mary Pope Osborne
- *Hannah's Helping Hands* (Pioneer Daughters series) by Jean Van Leeuwen
- *Phoebe the Spy* by Judith Berry Griffin
- *George Washington's Socks* by Elvira Woodruff
- *Toliver's Secret* by Esther Wood-Brady
- *The Fighting Ground* by Avi

These books represent a range of reading levels, perspectives, and issues during the Revolutionary War that are developmentally appropriate for fourth graders. The teacher conducts a brief book talk on each of the books and then allows students to choose the book they want to read. A sign-up sheet can be used in which students indicate up to three different books they are interested in reading. Then the teacher decides who gets to read which books based on interest and reading level. The teacher should explain to students that not all students will get to read their first choice every time.

There are many other ways in which books might be selected:

- Student interests such as snakes
- Author/illustrator study
- Genre study
- Content connections
- Thematic study, such as friendship, appreciating differences, or taking responsibility
- Books with multiple character perspectives
- Books with global perspectives
- Student-suggested books

Interesting and relevant texts enhance discussions. Narrative and informational books should be used. Considerations should also be given to gender and cultural differences. Certain books may be more interesting to girls than boys and vice versa. Certain cultural groups may find certain perspectives in some books offensive. Considerations and guidelines presented in the genre chapters of this book for book selection should be taken into consideration before selecting books for literature discussion groups so that the best possible selections are made that promote rich conversations for all children.

**Forming Groups and Routines.** Literature discussion groups are heterogeneous, with no more than five or six members, based on books the students have chosen to read (although students who read different books on the same topic could also form a discussion group). In the preceding example, all students are reading books about the Revolutionary War. Students who have read each of the different books could form a group to talk about the different perspectives and issues discussed in the books. Students may have different reading abilities but still be able to engage in high-level discussion about topics they care about. Once a group has finished reading and discussing a book, it disbands, and children then join a different group when new groups are formed.

Once students have decided on a book and a group is formed, an initial meeting is held with the teacher. Although the teacher has given a brief book talk that provided enough information for students to decide if they were interested in the book, it is still necessary to build background knowledge, to set a purpose for reading, and to decide how much to read before the first group discussion. The teacher might create an anchor chart documenting students' prior knowledge, questions, and predictions that could be revisited during the first discussion group. Additionally, sometimes students get excited about reading a book and assign an unrealistic number of pages to be read before the first group meeting. The teacher can model how to judge an appropriate number of pages based on the number of days before the group meets and where a good stopping point might be in the book.

Over the next week students read the assigned pages during independent reading time. The students should be used to jotting down their thoughts on sticky notes and writing in response journals at this point, although students are reading with a new mindset—questions, thoughts, predictions, critiques—that will be shared with discussion group members, and this can open up a whole new way of thinking. The notes are critical to meaningful, thought-provoking discussion. Some children will read ahead or even complete the book before the first meeting. I know teachers who frown on reading ahead, but I think about my own reading. If I really love a book, I'll read all night to finish it. Do you really want to squelch that excitement and desire to read in your students?

During mini-lessons, the teacher can review the guidelines for literature discussions (Figure 14.5). The teacher meets with each group once a week—one group a day—during independent reading time. For example on Mondays, she meets with Group 1, Tuesdays Group 2, and so on. Fridays can be a group presentation day. Students in the group will know what day they meet and should come to the group prepared for the discussion with their book, reader's notebook, and tool bag.

**Talking About Texts.** Though research has shown peer-led discussion produces complex student responses and encourages higher-level thought processes than teacher-led groups, children may struggle to engage in good discussions on their own without at

**FIGURE 14.5**

Student/
Teacher-Created
Guidelines for
Literature Discussion
Groups

# Guidelines for Literature Discussion Groups

- Have places flagged for sharing.
- Have good log entries to share.
- Look at the person who is speaking.
- Listen carefully.
- Take turns talking.
- Participate in the discussion.
- Stay on task.
- Stick to the topic.
- Enjoy the discussion.

least initial teacher guidance. The teacher can serve as a coach, providing a level of scaffolding that will support readers in developing ways of engaging in conversation with each other that deepens their comprehension of the text. The following are ways the teacher can encourage productive discussions:

- **Building community and ensuring active involvement:** the teacher scaffolds students to invite and acknowledge each others' contributions and participation in the conversation (e.g., "Randy thinks the main character is jealous of his sister. What does everyone else think?").
- **Model discursive skills:** the teacher models ways to engage in productive discussion rather than off-topic discussion and redirects the discussion if needed (e.g., "Lin was saying that the book reminded her of . . . Does anyone want to talk more about . . . ?").
- **Model active listening:** the teacher models verbal and nonverbal ways of active engagement in conversation by nodding in agreement with another student's point, agreeing or disagreeing, saying, "I hadn't thought of that," or requesting clarification, evidence, or elaboration.
- **Facilitate deeper conversations:** the teacher prompts strategies such as making connections, finding evidence in the book, and making predictions and inferences before, during, and after the conversation that requires readers to think deeply about their reading rather than surface level thinking.

At first, the level of support may need to be high as the teacher supports text discussion and provides assistance to promote independent thinking. As she continues to monitor the students' engagement and comprehension over time, she gradually releases responsibility to the literature circle participants as they attain independence. Table 14.10 provides language prompts teachers can use as scaffolds to help students attain greater independence.

*Watch*

*Watch literature circles in action.*

**TABLE 14.10**

# Helping Children Talk About Books

| Goal: Help children internalize language that is used for discussing texts | | Teacher scaffolds: Prompting and offering assistance to help children achieve this goal |
|---|---|---|
| Restating | Repeats and adds to previous contribution | Can someone say that in a different way? |
| Inviting | Invites others to contribute | Do you want to invite anyone else to add to what you said? |
| Acknowledging | Confirms response without agreeing or disagreeing | Do you all get what _____ is trying to say here? |
| Focusing/ refocusing | Making a comment about the course of the conversation | I think we have lost track of the question we were trying to answer. Can anyone help us here? |
| Agreeing/ disagreeing | Confirming or disconfirming an opinion or thinking | Does everyone agree with ____? Does anyone want to disagree, or does anyone see it another way? |
| Elaborating | Building on someone else's thinking | Does anyone want to say something more about that? Can anyone think of another solution or another reason? |
| Providing evidence | Supporting one's own or another's thinking, examples can be inside or outside the text | Can anyone else give an example of ____ from the text? Has anything like this ever happened to you or someone you know? |
| Requesting clarification | Confused or need additional information for someone else's thinking or about this part | Does anyone want to raise any questions about ____'s thinking here? Did anyone find anything confusing in this part of the text? |
| Posing questions for the group | Questioning text information, their own thinking, or someone else's thinking about something | Does anyone have a question for the group? |
| **Goal: Children share and/or question their comprehending process before, during, and after reading** | | **Teacher scaffolds: Prompting and offering assistance. Helping children to share their thinking and learning with each other** |
| Making connections | Connecting text to a personal experience, to other texts, to the world, to the writer, or to other parts of the text | Did anyone make a connection to this part of the text? Does this text/part remind any of you of another text we've read? Would anyone like to discuss <br> • the theme of the text? <br> • what the text was mostly about? <br> • what the author was trying to convey? |

*(continued)*

**TABLE 14.10**

(*continued*)

| Goal: Children share and/or question their comprehending process before, during, and after reading | | Teacher scaffolds: Prompting and offering assistance. Helping children to share their thinking and learning with each other |
|---|---|---|
| Making predictions | Using background knowledge and text information to predict what the reader thinks is coming next or how the problem might be solved | Would anyone like to share their prediction or what they think might happen next? Would anyone like to predict how the problem might be solved? Why did the author put that part in the text? |
| Recalling | Paraphrasing or summarizing the text | Who would like to tell the group what the text was about? |
| Inferring | Using prior knowledge with new information gained from text in an effort to construct meaning | So, you think _____ because … |
| Visualizing | Using the author's language to create mind pictures—to feel, see, touch, taste, and/or hear | Would anyone like to share how the author created mind pictures here? |

Adapted from L. Dorn & C. Soffos. (2005). *Teaching for deep comprehension: A reading workshop approach.* Portland, ME: Stenhouse. © 2004, reproduced with permission of Stenhouse Publishers.

Special Topic:  Online Literature Discussions

Online environments create a learner-centered community in which peer support and collaboration are emphasized. Collaboration occurs when a group becomes interdependent on one another, formulating shared goals to achieve a deeper level of knowledge (Choi & Ho, 2002). Small communities of learners are created as a result of student feedback and interactions. Electronic discussion not only enables interaction and collaboration, but it also promotes reflection. Reading and responding to peers' comments compels us to think and to form and articulate ideas in a meaningful way. Reading peers' thoughts urges us to compare them with our own thoughts and ideas and, in turn, to examine our own understandings and interpretations. Online discussions share many characteristics of face-to-face interactions because they allow the sharing of ideas and opinions, allow individuals or groups to take risks, and encourage reflection. In online discussions, individuals sometimes take greater risks in the conversation because there is no face-to-face interaction, so gender, ethnicity, and other physical characteristics from which people tend to make judgments are no longer sources of bias.

There are three major advantages of using electronic dialoguing. First, the reason for writing is authentic and motivational because a real person is awaiting a communication. Second, planning and scheduling electronic dialoguing communications are extremely flexible on the part of both audiences because they respond at their own convenience.

Finally, it offers a real-world opportunity to use writing skills with an understanding audience. Online communication is also beneficial because it can be preserved for an outsider to consider or for the participants to look back and reflect on previous responses. The potential for online discussions is endless, allowing students to revisit their posting for reinterpretation or to challenge their ideas with new postings (Blackford, 2003).

Interviews with teachers conducted by Hemenway (2000) about the use of the Internet in their classrooms concluded that the use of the Internet engages students in literature. Teachers reported that when the students are excited about what they are doing, discussion in the classroom increases. Hemenway argued that the role of the teacher with the Internet is one of coach in which the students have guidelines and expectations but are also given the opportunity to explore on their own, learning about what interests them. Overall, Hemenway found that the use of the Internet improves the classroom atmosphere, and the students' attitudes toward learning became more positive.

Many resources on the Internet allow children to connect with other children to discuss literature. One such site is Book Raps, a project of oz-TeacherNet in Australia. Individuals or groups of students from across the country or around the world discuss books that have been selected and scheduled throughout the year. Some book raps may include exciting special events, such as author involvement, illustrators online, access to content area experts, and live chat sessions. Resources for finding online book discussions are provided in Chapter 12.

## Literature Extension Projects

*For too many years, kids in classrooms all over the United States have been asked to do a laundry list of activities when they finish reading books. You know the ones—dioramas, shadow boxes, word jumbles, word searches, and so on. Reading response is more than these.*

S. HARVEY & A. GOUDVIS, 2007, P. 52

As a parent, I have watched my son grudgingly write book reports, create mobiles, and complete countless worksheets after reading a book, none of which a real-life reader does after reading a great book. Extension projects are *not* contrived, complicated, or busy work that takes days away from independent reading to complete. A thoughtful extension project can provide readers with additional ways to revisit their reading and extend or broaden their thinking about concepts, themes, or characters. The following extension activities were discussed in the response sections of the genre chapters:

- Storytelling
- Reader's theater and drama
- Making books based on creative writing or research
- Choral reading
- Author/illustrator study
- Creating digital stories and publishing writing/projects on the Internet
- Online literature discussion

Good extension projects provide children with a diverse range of options to engage in meaningful learning that meets their needs as a learner and extends their joy of children's literature.

*Third-grade students engaged in a reader's theater production of* Rumplestiltskin. *The children worked together to decide on their costumes, character interpretations, and props, and to practice reading the text fluently before performing in front of the class.*

Courtesy of Denise Johnson.

# Top 10 Read Alouds

## BOOKS THAT CHANGE THE READER'S LIFE

1. **Aunt Chip and the Great Triple Creek Dam Affair** by Patricia Polacco (1996, Philomel). Aunt Chip saves the town of Triple Creek, where everyone has forgotten how to read because of the invasion of television.

2. **Endymion Spring** by Matthew Skelton (2006, Delecorte). Having reluctantly accompanied his academic mother and pesky younger sister to Oxford, 12-year-old Blake Winters is at loose ends until he stumbles across an ancient and magical book that was secretly brought to England in 1453 by Gutenberg's mute apprentice to save it from evil forces and that now draws Blake into a dangerous and life-threatening quest.

3. **Fly By Night** by Frances Hardinge (2006, HarperCollins). Mosca Mye and her homicidal goose, Saracen, travel to the city of Mandelion on the heels of smooth-talking conman, Eponymous Clent.

4. **The House of Wisdom** by Florence Parry Heide and J. Heide Gilliland, illustrated by Mary GrandPré (1999, Dorling Kindersley). Ishaq, the son of the chief translator to the Caliph of ancient Baghdad, travels the world in search of precious books and manuscripts and brings them back to the great library known as the House of Wisdom.

5. **The Library Card** by Jerry Spinelli (1997, Scholastic). The lives of four young people in different circumstances are changed by their encounters with books.

## Top 10 Read Alouds (*continued*)

6.  **Please Bury Me in the Library** by J. Patrick Lewis (2005, Gulliver). A collection of original poems about books and reading that range from sweet to silly to laugh-out-loud funny.

7.  **Read and Rise** by Sandra Pinkney, illustrated by Myles Pinkney (2006, Cartwheel Books). Photographs and poetic text celebrate reading as a means of encouraging African American children to pursue their dreams.

8.  **Richard Wright and the Library Card** by William Miller, illustrated by Gregory Christie (1997, Lee & Low). Based on a scene from Wright's autobiography *Black Boy*, in which the 17-year-old African American borrows a white man's library card and devours every book as a ticket to freedom.

9.  **Shelf Life: Stories by the Book** edited by Gary Paulsen (2003, Simon & Schuster). Ten short stories contributed by children's and young adult authors in which the lives of young people in different circumstances are changed by their encounters with books.

10. **The Tale of Despereaux** by Kate DiCamillo (2003, Candlewick). The adventures of Desperaux Tilling, a small mouse of unusual talents, the princess that he loves, the servant girl who longs to be a princess, and a devious rat determined to bring them all to ruin.

## Activities for Professional Development

### Think Critically About Children's Literature

1.  Create book talks for five of the books you are reading for class. To get an idea of what makes an enticing book talk, visit several online sources such as http://www.nancykeane.com. Share your book talks with your classmates.

### Bring Children's Literature into the Classroom

2.  Interview three children using the reading inventory in this chapter or one you create. After completing the interviews, write an analysis of each child's response to create a picture of his or her literacy personality. Based on each child's responses, what would you do to provide an environment that supports each child's learning needs?

3.  Create several text sets around a topic or theme for a particular grade level in the school curriculum or of interest to you. Be sure to include books on varied reading levels, and take into consideration gender and cultural differences.

### Learn About Authors and Illustrators

4.  Select a picturebook by an author whose writing you admire. Analyze the book for selections that would be good to use as examples of an author's craft. Create an inquiry chart following the example in this chapter. Share your chart with your classmates.

# Print and Online Resources

## Print Resources

Calkins, L. (2001). *The art of teaching reading.* Portsmouth, NH: Heinemann.

Calkins, L. (1994). *The art of teaching writing.* Portsmouth, NH: Heinemann.

Cole, A. (2003). *Knee to knee, eye to eye: Circling in on comprehension.* Portsmouth, NH: Heinemann.

Dorfman, L., & Cappelli, R. (2007). *Mentor texts: Teaching writing through children's literature, K–6.* Portland, ME: Stenhouse.

Dorfman, L., & Cappelli, R. (2009). *Nonfiction Mentor texts: Teaching informational writing through children's literature, K–8.* Portland, ME: Stenhouse.

Dorn, L., & Soffos, C. (2006). *Teaching for deep comprehension.* Portland, ME: Stenhouse.

Fountas, I., & Pinnell, G. (2006). *Teaching for comprehending and fluency: Thinking, talking, and writing about reading, K–8.* Portsmouth, NH: Heinemann.

Harvey, S., & Goudvis, A. (2007). *Strategies that work: Teaching comprehension for understanding and engagement.* Portland, ME: Stenhouse.

Hicks, T. (2009). *The digital writing workshop.* Portsmouth, NH: Heinemann.

Keene, E., & Zimmermann, S. (2007). *Mosaic of thought: The power of comprehension strategy instruction* (2nd ed.). Portland, ME: Stenhouse.

Leograndis, D. (2008). *Launching the writing workshop: A step-by-step guide in photographs.* New York: Scholastic.

Peterson, R., & Eeds, M. (2007). *Grand Conversations (Updated Edition): Literature Groups in Action.* New York: Scholastic.

Routman, R. (2003). *Reading essentials.* Portsmouth, NH: Heinemann.

Routman, R. (2005). *Writing essentials.* Portsmouth, NH: Heinemann.

 **Online Resources**

*Annenburg Media*
**http://www.learner.org**
The Annenburg site houses numerous videos on effective teaching, including *Teaching Reading K–2 Workshop, Teaching Reading 3–5 Workshop, Inside Writing Communities,* and *Developing Writers.*

*Literature Circles Resource Center*
**http://www.litcircles.org**
Hosted by the College of Education at Seattle University, this site houses information and resources for teachers and students K–8 for all aspects of literature circles from the initial structure to extension projects.

*Reading Rockets: Comprehension: Helping English Language Learners Grasp the Full Picture*
**http://www.readingrockets.org/webcasts/1005**
This 45-minute webcast offers practical information on how to teach English language learners effective comprehension skills.

*Reading Workshop*
**http://wblrd.sk.ca/~bestpractice/reader/process.html**
This site provides an overview of each step of the reading workshop with related lessons and links.

Visit the companion website at **www.cengage.com/education/johnson** to find links related to the Read/Watch/Listen icons noted throughout the chapter, as well as additional resources.

# References

Allington, R. (2002). What I've learned about effective reading instruction from a decade of studying exemplary elementary classroom teachers. *Phi Delta Kapan, 83,* 740–747.

Allington, R. (2006). *What really matters for struggling readers: Designing research-based programs* (2nd ed.). New York: Allyn & Bacon.

Allington, R., & Johnston, P. (Eds.). (2002). *Reading to learn: Lessons from exemplary 4th-grade classrooms*. Portland, ME: Stenhouse.

Baskin, B., & Harris, K. (1995). Heard any good books lately? The case for audiobooks in the secondary classroom. *Journal of Reading, 38*(5), 372–376.

Blackford, H. (2003). Adventures in virtualand: The challenges of teaching an online children's literature course. Commentary. Available at http://ts.mivu.org/default. asp?show=article&id=971.

Block, C. (2001). *Teaching the language arts* (3rd ed.). Needham Heights, MA: Allyn & Bacon.

Calkins, L. (1994). *The art of teaching writing*. Portsmouth, NH: Heinemann.

Calkins, L. (2001). *The art of teaching reading*. Portsmouth, NH: Heinemann.

Choi, C. & Ho, H. (2002). Exploring new literacies in online peer learning environments. *Reading Online 6*(1) Available at http://www .readingonline.org/newliteracies/lit_index. asp?HREF=choi/index.html.

Cole, A. (2003). *Knee to knee, eye to eye: Circling in on comprehension*. Portsmouth, NH: Heinemann.

Cole, J. (2003). What motivates students to read? Four literacy personalities. *The Reading Teacher, 56*(4), 326–336.

Dorn, L, & Soffos, C. (2005). *Teaching for deep comprehension*. Portland, ME: Stenhouse.

Fletcher, R. (2005). Author study: Knowing a writer from the inside out. *School Talk, 10*(4): 1–6.

Fountas, I., & Pinnell, G. (2001). *Guiding readers and writers grades 3–6*. Portsmouth, NH: Heinemann.

Harvey, S., & Goudvis, A. (2007). *Strategies that work: Teaching comprehension for understanding and engagement* (2nd ed.). Portland, ME: Stenhouse.

Hemenway, M. V. (2000, April). What effect does classroom use of the Internet have on the teacher-student relationships. *NASSP Bulletin, 84*, 114–119.

Hidi, S., & Harackiewicz, J. (2000). Motivating the academically unmotivated: A critical issue for the 21st century. *Review of Educational Research, 70*(2), 151–179.

Hubbard, R., & Shorey, V. (2003). Worlds beneath the words: Writing workshop with second language learners. *Language Arts, 81*(1), 52–61.

Ketch, A. (2005). Conversation: The comprehension connection. *The Reading Teacher, 59*(1), 8–13.

Kong, A., & Fitch, E. (2003). Using Book Club to engage culturally and linguistically diverse learners in reading, writing, and talking about books. *The Reading Teacher, 56*(4), 352–363.

Kucan, L., & Beck, I. (2003). Inviting students to talk about expository texts: A comparison of two discourse environments and their effects on comprehension. *Reading Research and Instruction, 42*, 1–29.

Leu, D., & Leu, D. (1999). *Teaching with the Internet: Lessons from the classroom.* Norwood, MA: Christopher Gordon.

Lowry, L. (1999). *Zooman Sam*. Boston: Houghton Mifflin.

Murry, D. (1982). *Learning by teaching*. Montclair, NJ: Boynton/Cook.

Ohlhausen, M., & Jepson, M. (1992). Lessons from Goldilocks: "Somebody's been choosing my books, but I can make my own choices now!" *The New Advocate, 5*, 31–46.

Pearson, P., & Duke, N. (2002). Comprehension instruction in the primary grades. In C. Block & M. Pressley (Eds.), *Comprehension instruction: Research-based best practices* (pp. 247–258). New York: Guilford.

Pressley, M., Warton-McDonald, R., Allington, R., Block, C., & Morrow, L. (2001). *Learning to read: Lessons from exemplary first-grade classrooms*. New York: Guilford.

Ray, K. (1999). *Wondrous words: Writers and writing in the elementary classroom*. Urbana, IL: National Council of Teachers of English.

Routman, R. (2003). *Reading essentials*. Portsmouth, NH: Heinemann.

Routman, R. (2005). *Writing essentials*. Portsmouth, NH: Heinemann.

Sibberson, F., & Szymusiak, K. (2003). *Still learning to read: Teaching students in grades 3–6*. Portland, ME: Stenhouse.

Taylor, B., Pearson, P., Clark, K., & Walpole, S. (2000). Effective schools and accomplished teachers: Lessons about primary grade reading instruction in low-income schools. *Elementary School Journal, 101*, 121–165.

Taylor, B., & Pearson, P. (2002). *Teaching reading: Effective schools, accomplished teachers*. Mahwah, NJ: Erlbaum.

Varley, P. (2002). As good as reading? Kids and the audiobook revolution. *Horn Book Magazine, 78*(3), 251–263.

# APPENDIX A: SELECTING CHILDREN'S LITERATURE

 Visit the companion website for all of the listings mentioned here.

## PROFESSIONAL ORGANIZATIONS

The following are professional organizations that provide information and/or services to support educators' knowledge of literacy and children's literature. The websites of these organizations house a wide variety of resources as well as information on membership and conferences.

*American Library Association* (www.ala.org)

*Children's Book Council* (www.cbcbooks.org)

*The Children's Book Guild* (www.childrensbookguild.org)

*Children's Literature Association* (www.childlitassn.org)

*The Foundation of Children's Books* (www.thefcb.org)

*International Reading Association* (www.reading.org)

*International Research Society of Children's Literature* (www.irscl.ac.uk)

*National Center for Research in Children's Literature* (www.roehampton.ac.uk/researchcentres/ncrcl)

*National Council of Teachers of English* (www.ncte.org)

*United States Board on Books for Young People* (www.usbby.org)

## PUBLICATIONS ABOUT CHILDREN'S LITERATURE

### Review Sources

The magazines listed below consist mainly of professional reviews of recently published or soon to be published children's books. They may also include annotated children's books and interviews with authors/illustrators.

*Booklist* (www.ala.org)

*The Bulletin of the Center for Children's Books* (http://bccb.lis.uiuc.edu)

*The Horn Book Magazine* (www.hbook.com)

*Publishers Weekly* (www.publishersweekly.com)

*School Library Journal* (www.schoollibraryjournal.com)

### Critical Analysis

These journals primarily print critical analyses of children's literature. They may also include annotated children's books and interviews with authors/illustrators.

*Bookbird: A Journal of International Children's Literature* is a quarterly journal of the International Board on Books for Young People (www.ibby.org).

*Children's Literature Association Quarterly* is the journal of the Children's Literature Association and is published four times per year (www.childlitassn.org).

*Children's Literature in Education: An International Quarterly* is published by Springer Publishing (www.springer.com).

*Dragon Lode* is the biannual journal of the Children's Literature and Reading Special Interest Group of the International Reading Association (www.tcnj.edu/~childlit).

*Journal of Children's Literature* is a biannual publication of the Children's Literature Assembly of the National Council of Teachers of English (www.childrensliteratureassembly.org).

## Teaching Research/Ideas

The magazines and journals on this list primarily consist of articles that report research on best teaching practices in literacy or brief articles on teaching ideas. They also have columns with annotated children's books and interviews with authors/illustrators.

*Book Links* (www.ala.org)

*Language Arts* (www.ncte.org)

*The Reading Teacher* (www.reading.org)

## Bibliographies

These books consist primarily of annotated lists of children's books. Compilations can be general or specific, but all use specific guidelines for selecting quality children's literature.

*A to Zoo: Subject Access to Children's Picture Books* (7th ed.) by Carolyn Lima (2005, Libraries Unlimited). A subject index to picturebooks for preschool through grade 2, covering approximately 28,000 in-print and out-of-print titles.

*A Broken Flute: The Native Experience in Books for Children* by Doris Seale and Beverly Slapin (Eds.) (2005, Altamira Press). An annotated bibliography of 600 books written between the early 1900s and 2003 arranged in alphabetical order and covering preschool through grade 12.

*Across Cultures: A Guide to Multicultural Literature for Children* by Kathy A. East and Rebecca L. Thomas (2007, Libraries Unlimited). Promotes cultural awareness and learning with 150 of the best multicultural children's literature titles.

*Adventuring with Books: A Booklist for Pre-K–Grade 6* (13th ed.) by Amy A. McClure and Janice Kristo (Eds.) (2002, NCTE). An annotated bibliography of 850 books in 24 general topics.

*Best Books for Children: Preschool Through Grade 6* (8th ed.) by Catherine Barr and John T. Gillespie (2005, Libraries Unlimited). An annotated bibliography of 26,958 in-print titles arranged thematically.

*The Essential Guide to Children's Books and Their Creators* by Anita Silvey (2002, Houghton Mifflin). Features 475 entries on children's authors and illustrators, essays on social and historical issues, and reading lists by category.

*Kaleidoscope: A Multicultural Booklist for Grades K–8* (4th ed.) by Nancy Hansen-Krening, Elaine Aoki, and Donald Mizokawa (Eds.) (2003, NCTE). An annotated bibliography of 242 fiction and nonfiction books published from 1999 to 2001 by and about people of color.

*Lesbian and Gay Voices: An Annotated Bibliography and Guide to Literature for Children and Young Adults* by Frances Ann Day (2000, Greenwood). An annotated bibliography of 275 books that feature both major and minor lesbian and gay characters.

*Subject Guide to Children's Books in Print* (2008, R. R. Bowker). A list of all children's books in print grouped into approximately 9,000 subject categories.

*Voices from the Margins: An Annotated Bibliography of Fiction on Disabilities and Differences for Young People* by Marilyn Ward (2002, Greenwood Press). An annotated bibliography of over 200 books for children and young adults published from 1990 to 2001.

*The World of Islam in Literature for Youth: A Selective Annotated Bibliography for K–12* by Garcha Rajinder (2006, Scarecrow). An annotated bibliography of more than 700 selected print and electronic resources.

*The World Through Children's Books* by Betsy Hearne (2002, Scarecrow). An annotated bibliography of international books published in the United States from 1996 through 2000, sponsored by the U.S. Board on Books for Young People (USBBY).

## Lists of Best Books/Notable Books

Several organizations select "best books" of the year based on criteria for quality children's books. These lists are both general and topic/genre specific.

*ALA's Notable Books for Children and Notable Books for Young Adults* (www.ala.org). Annotated lists for children and young adults selected by members of the Association for Library Service to Children (ALSC) and Young Adult Library Services Association (YALSA). Notable lists for children's recordings, videos, and computer software are also available.

*Bank Street College's Best Books of the Year* (www .bnkst.edu/bookcom). Annotated book lists for children aged infant to 14 selected by the staff of Bank Street College, New York.

*Children's Choices* (www.reading.org/Resources/ Booklists/ChildrensChoices.aspx). Annual list of best books selected by children for children K–8 sponsored by the International Reading Association with the Children's Book Council.

*Cooperative Children's Book Center Choices* (www.education.wisc.edu/ccbc/books/ choices.asp). Features annotated entries for 245 books for children and young adults published in the previous year and recommended by the CCBC staff.

*Great Graphic Novels for Teens* (www.ala.org). An annotated list of graphic novels selected by members of the Young Adult Library Services Association.

*Notable Books for a Global Society* (www.tcnj .edu/~childlit/proj/nbgs/intro-nbgs.html). Multicultural literature for readers ranging from kindergarten through high school selected by members of the Children's Literature and Reading Special Interest Group of the International Reading Association.

*Notable Trade Books for Social Studies* (www.social-studies.org/resources/notable). Annotated list of notable books for grades K–8 selected by the Book Review Committee appointed by National Council for the Social Studies.

*Outstanding Science Trade Books* (www.nsta.org/ publications/ostb). Annotated list of notable books for grades K–8 selected by a book review panel appointed by the National Science Teachers Association.

*Quick Picks for Reluctant Young Adult Readers* (www.ala.org). An annotated list of books selected by members of the Young Adult Library Services Association.

## Web Resources

The websites below offer book reviews, searchable databases for finding children's books, or lists of books organized by topic/theme.

*Africa Access Review* (www.africaaccessreview.org)

*Barahona Center for the Study of Books in Spanish for Children and Adolescents* (www.csusm.edu/csb/ english)

*Carol Hurst's Children's Literature Site* (www .booksintheclassroom.com/allreviewed.php)

*Children's Book Reviews* (http://childrensbookreviews.pbwiki.com)

*Children's Bookwatch Newsletter* (www .midwestbookreview.com/cbw/index.htm)

*Database of Award Winning Children's Literature* (www.dawcl.com)

*Guys Read* (www.guysread.com)

*Juvenile Series and Sequels* (www.mcpl.lib.mo.us/ readers/series/juv)

*Kids Momo* (www.kidsmomo.com)

*Kids Reads* (www.kidsreads.com/reviews)

*Multicultural Children's Literature* (www.multiculturalchildrenslit.com)

*New York Times* Children's Book Reviews (www.nytimes.com)

*Read Kiddo Read* (www.readkiddoread.com)

*Side Kicks: Graphic Novel Reviews* (www.noflying-notights.com/sidekicks/core.html)

*Through the Looking Glass Children's Book Reviews* (http://lookingglassreview.com)

*World of Words* (http://wowlit.org)

# APPENDIX B: AWARDS FOR CHILDREN'S LITERATURE

 Visit the companion website for all of the listings mentioned here.

## NEWBERY MEDAL WINNERS

The Newbery Medal was named for eighteenth-century British bookseller John Newbery. It is awarded annually by the Association for Library Service to Children, a division of the American Library Association, to the author of the most distinguished contribution to American literature for children.

2010 *When You Reach Me* by Rebecca Stead (Random House)

2009 *The Graveyard Book* by Neil Gaiman, illustrated by Dave McKean (HarperCollins)

2008 *Good Masters! Sweet Ladies! Voices from a Medieval Village* by Laura Schlitz (Candlewick)

2007 *The Higher Power of Lucky* by Susan Patron, illustrated by Matt Phelan (Simon & Schuster)

2006 *Criss Cross* by Lynne Rae Perkins (HarperCollins)

2005 *Kira-Kira* by Cynthia Kadohata (Simon & Schuster)

2004 *The Tale of Despereaux: Being the Story of a Mouse, a Princess, Some Soup, and a Spool of Thread* by Kate DiCamillo (Candlewick)

2003 *Crispin: The Cross of Lead* by Avi (Hyperion)

2002 *A Single Shard* by Linda Sue Park (Houghton Mifflin)

2001 *A Year Down Yonder* by Richard Peck (Dial)

2000 *Bud, Not Buddy* by Christopher Paul Curtis (Delacorte)

1999 *Holes* by Louis Sachar (Frances Foster)

1998 *Out of the Dust* by Karen Hesse (Scholastic)

1997 *The View from Saturday* by E. L. Konigsburg (Atheneum)

1996 *The Midwife's Apprentice* by Karen Cushman (Houghton Mifflin)

1995 *Walk Two Moons* by Sharon Creech (HarperCollins)

1994 *The Giver* by Lois Lowry (Houghton Mifflin)

1993 *Missing May* by Cynthia Rylant (Jackson/Orchard)

1992 *Shiloh* by Phyllis Reynolds Naylor (Atheneum)

1991 *Maniac Magee* by Jerry Spinelli (Little, Brown)

1990 *Number the Stars* by Lois Lowry (Houghton Mifflin)

1989 *Joyful Noise: Poems for Two Voices* by Paul Fleischman (Harper)

1988 *Lincoln: A Photobiography* by Russell Freedman (Clarion)

1987 *The Whipping Boy* by Sid Fleischman (Greenwillow)

1986 *Sarah, Plain and Tall* by Patricia MacLachlan (Harper)

1985 *The Hero and the Crown* by Robin McKinley (Greenwillow)

1984 *Dear Mr. Henshaw* by Beverly Cleary (Morrow)

1983 *Dicey's Song* by Cynthia Voigt (Atheneum)

1982 *A Visit to William Blake's Inn: Poems for Innocent and Experienced Travelers* by Nancy Willard (Harcourt)

1981 *Jacob Have I Loved* by Katherine Paterson (Crowell)

1980    *A Gathering of Days: A New England Girl's Journal, 1830–1832* by Joan W. Blos (Scribner)

1979    *The Westing Game* by Ellen Raskin (Dutton)

1978    *Bridge to Terabithia* by Katherine Paterson (Crowell)

1977    *Roll of Thunder, Hear My Cry* by Mildred D. Taylor (Dial)

1976    *The Grey King* by Susan Cooper (Atheneum)

1975    *M. C. Higgins, the Great* by Virginia Hamilton (Macmillan)

1974    *The Slave Dancer* by Paula Fox (Bradbury)

1973    *Julie of the Wolves* by Jean Craighead George (Harper)

1972    *Mrs. Frisby and the Rats of NIMH* by Robert C. O'Brien (Atheneum)

1971    *Summer of the Swans* by Betsy Byars (Viking)

1970    *Sounder* by William H. Armstrong (Harper)

1969    *The High King* by Lloyd Alexander (Holt)

1968    *From the Mixed-Up Files of Mrs. Basil E. Frankweiler* by E. L. Konigsburg (Atheneum)

1967    *Up a Road Slowly* by Irene Hunt (Follett)

1966    *I, Juan de Pareja* by Elizabeth Borton de Trevino (Farrar)

1965    *Shadow of a Bull* by Maia Wojciechowska (Atheneum)

1964    *It's Like This, Cat* by Emily Neville (Harper)

1963    *A Wrinkle in Time* by Madeleine L'Engle (Farrar)

1962    *The Bronze Bow* by Elizabeth George Speare (Houghton Mifflin)

1961    *Island of the Blue Dolphins* by Scott O'Dell (Houghton Mifflin)

1960    *Onion John* by Joseph Krumgold (Crowell)

1959    *The Witch of Blackbird Pond* by Elizabeth George Speare (Houghton Mifflin)

1958    *Rifles for Watie* by Harold Keith (Crowell)

1957    *Miracles on Maple Hill* by Virginia Sorensen (Harcourt)

1956    *Carry On, Mr. Bowditch* by Jean Lee Latham (Houghton Mifflin)

1955    *The Wheel on the School* by Meindert DeJong (Harper)

1954    *. . . And Now Miguel* by Joseph Krumgold (Crowell)

1953    *Secret of the Andes* by Ann Nolan Clark (Viking)

1952    *Ginger Pye* by Eleanor Estes (Harcourt)

1951    *Amos Fortune, Free Man* by Elizabeth Yates (Dutton)

1950    *The Door in the Wall* by Marguerite de Angeli (Doubleday)

1949    *King of the Wind* by Marguerite Henry (Rand McNally)

1948    *The Twenty-One Balloons* by William Pène du Bois (Viking)

1947    *Miss Hickory* by Carolyn Sherwin Bailey (Viking)

1946    *Strawberry Girl* by Lois Lenski (Lippincott)

1945    *Rabbit Hill* by Robert Lawson (Viking)

1944    *Johnny Tremain* by Esther Forbes (Houghton Mifflin)

1943    *Adam of the Road* by Elizabeth Janet Gray (Viking)

1942    *The Matchlock Gun* by Walter Edmonds (Dodd)

1941    *Call It Courage* by Armstrong Sperry (Macmillan)

1940    *Daniel Boone* by James Daugherty (Viking)

1939    *Thimble Summer* by Elizabeth Enright (Rinehart)

1938    *The White Stag* by Kate Seredy (Viking)

1937    *Roller Skates* by Ruth Sawyer (Viking)

1936    *Caddie Woodlawn* by Carol Ryrie Brink (Macmillan)

1935    *Dobry* by Monica Shannon (Viking)

1934    *Invincible Louisa: The Story of the Author of Little Women* by Cornelia Meigs (Little, Brown)

1933    *Young Fu of the Upper Yangtze* by Elizabeth Lewis (Winston)

1932    *Waterless Mountain* by Laura Adams Armer (Longmans)

1931    *The Cat Who Went to Heaven* by Elizabeth Coatsworth (Macmillan)

1930    *Hitty, Her First Hundred Years* by Rachel Field (Macmillan)

1929    *The Trumpeter of Krakow* by Eric P. Kelly (Macmillan)

1928    *Gay Neck, the Story of a Pigeon* by Dhan Gopal Mukerji (Dutton)

1927    *Smoky, the Cowhorse* by Will James (Scribner)

1926    *Shen of the Sea* by Arthur Bowie Chrisman (Dutton)

1925    *Tales from Silver Lands* by Charles Finger (Doubleday)

1924    *The Dark Frigate* by Charles Hawes (Little, Brown)

1923    *The Voyages of Doctor Dolittle* by Hugh Lofting (Stokes)

1922    *The Story of Mankind* by Hendrik Willem van Loon (Liveright)

## CALDECOTT MEDAL WINNERS

The Caldecott Medal was named in honor of nineteenth-century English illustrator, Randolph Caldecott. It is awarded annually by the Association for Library Service to Children, a division of the American Library Association, to the artist of the most distinguished American picturebook for children.

2010    *The Lion & the Mouse* illustrated and written by Jerry Pinkney (Little, Brown)

2009    *The House in the Night* illustrated by Beth Krommes, written by Susan Marie Swanson (Houghton Mifflin)

2008    *The Invention of Hugo Cabret* by Brian Selznick (Scholastic)

2007    *Flotsam* by David Wiesner (Clarion)

2006    *The Hello, Goodbye Window,* illustrated by Chris Raschka; text by Norton Juster (Michael di Capua/Hyperion)

2005    *Kitten's First Full Moon* by Kevin Henkes (Greenwillow Books/HarperCollins)

2004    *The Man Who Walked Between the Towers* by Mordicai Gerstein (Roaring Brook Press/ Millbrook Press)

2003    *My Friend Rabbit* by Eric Rohmann (Roaring Brook Press/Millbrook Press)

2002    *The Three Pigs* by David Wiesner (Clarion/ Houghton Mifflin)

2001    *So You Want to Be President?* illustrated by David Small; text by Judith St. George (Philomel Books)

2000    *Joseph Had a Little Overcoat* by Simms Taback (Viking)

1999    *Snowflake Bentley,* illustrated by Mary Azarian; text by Jacqueline Briggs Martin (Houghton Mifflin)

1998    *Rapunzel* by Paul O. Zelinsky (Dutton)

1997    *Golem* by David Wisniewski (Clarion)

1996    *Officer Buckle and Gloria* by Peggy Rathmann (Putnam)

1995    *Smoky Night,* illustrated by David Diaz; text by Eve Bunting (Harcourt)

1994    *Grandfather's Journey* by Allen Say; text and edited by Walter Lorraine (Houghton Mifflin)

1993    *Mirette on the High Wire* by Emily Arnold McCully (Putnam)

1992    *Tuesday* by David Wiesner (Clarion Books)

1991    *Black and White* by David Macaulay (Houghton Mifflin)

1990    *Lon Po Po: A Red-Riding Hood Story from China* by Ed Young (Philomel)

1989    *Song and Dance Man,* illustrated by Stephen Gammell; text by Karen Ackerman (Knopf)

1988    *Owl Moon,* illustrated by John Schoenherr; text by Jane Yolen (Philomel)

1987    *Hey, Al,* illustrated by Richard Egielski; text by Arthur Yorinks (Farrar)

1986    *The Polar Express* by Chris Van Allsburg (Houghton Mifflin)

1985    *Saint George and the Dragon,* illustrated by Trina Schart Hyman; retold by Margaret Hodges (Little, Brown)

1984    *The Glorious Flight: Across the Channel with Louis Bleriot* by Alice and Martin Provensen (Viking)

1983    *Shadow,* translated and illustrated by Marcia Brown; original text in French by Blaise Cendrars (Scribner)

# How to Use Children's Literature in the Classroom

© David Young-Wolff/PhotoEdit, Inc.

**Read to children.** *The teacher is sharing her passion and enthusiasm for reading while modeling important reading strategies as she reads aloud. It is one of the most important activities teachers can do throughout the grades to build the knowledge required for children's reading success.*

© Will Hart/PhotoEdit, Inc.

**Share reading with children.** *Shared reading provides supportive context for children at various levels of reading development. The teacher models reading the text with fluency and expression and then the children read the text together. The interactive talk between the teacher and the children is a critical factor in shared reading.*

**Write with children.** *When teachers model the writing process, the messy process of composing that goes on in the head is made visible. When students see the multiple facets of the composing process in action, they are more likely to understand that the writing process involves revisions, resources, and time.*

**Provide books for independent reading.** *Classroom libraries should include texts that match all students' literacy personalities in the classroom. Graphic novels, comics, magazines, and newspapers should be among the other genres in a well-stocked classroom library.*

© Susie Fitzhugh.

**Have children share reading.**
*This first-grade student is using the class book recommendation chart to recommend a book to another student in his classroom. This is just one way for children to share their joy and enthusiasm of reading with each other. Children should also be given regular opportunities to share the books they are reading with each other in small and large group settings.*

© Jeff Greenberg/PhotoEdit, Inc.

**Support children's reading with feedback.** *This teacher is providing individualized feedback to a student in a reading conference. Reading conferences provide a context for teachers to monitor students' reading while gaining an understanding of how children are applying the skills and strategies previously taught.*

**Have children share writing.**
*These children are participating in a peer conference where they ask each other questions about their writing and give thoughtful feedback. They will use the feedback they receive from each other to revise their writing.*

**Engage children in literature discussions.** *These children are participating in a literature discussion group. Literature discussion engages students in conversation that provides them with practice using cognitive strategies that strengthen and deepen comprehension.*

1982    *Jumanji* by Chris Van Allsburg (Houghton Mifflin)

1981    *Fables* by Arnold Lobel (Harper)

1980    *Ox-Cart Man*, illustrated by Barbara Cooney; text by Donald Hall (Viking)

1979    *The Girl Who Loved Wild Horses* by Paul Goble (Bradbury)

1978    *Noah's Ark* by Peter Spier (Doubleday)

1977    *Ashanti to Zulu: African Traditions*, illustrated by Leo and Diane Dillon; text by Margaret Musgrove (Dial)

1976    *Why Mosquitoes Buzz in People's Ears*, illustrated by Leo and Diane Dillon; retold by Verna Aardema (Dial)

1975    *Arrow to the Sun* by Gerald McDermott (Viking)

1974    *Duffy and the Devil*, illustrated by Margot Zemach; retold by Harve Zemach (Farrar)

1973    *The Funny Little Woman*, illustrated by Blair Lent; retold by Arlene Mosel (Dutton)

1972    *One Fine Day*, retold and illustrated by Nonny Hogrogian (Macmillan)

1971    *A Story A Story*, retold and illustrated by Gail E. Haley (Atheneum)

1970    *Sylvester and the Magic Pebble* by William Steig (Windmill Books)

1969    *The Fool of the World and the Flying Ship*, illustrated by Uri Shulevitz; retold by Arthur Ransome (Farrar)

1968    *Drummer Hoff*, illustrated by Ed Emberley; adapted by Barbara Emberley (Prentice-Hall)

1967    *Sam, Bangs & Moonshine* by Evaline Ness (Holt)

1966    *Always Room for One More*, illustrated by Nonny Hogrogian; text by Sorche Nic Leodhas, pseud. [Leclair Alger] (Holt)

1965    *May I Bring a Friend?* illustrated by Beni Montresor; text by Beatrice Schenk de Regniers (Atheneum)

1964    *Where the Wild Things Are* by Maurice Sendak (Harper)

1963    *The Snowy Day* by Ezra Jack Keats (Viking)

1962    *Once a Mouse*, retold and illustrated by Marcia Brown (Scribner)

1961    *Baboushka and the Three Kings*, illustrated by Nicolas Sidjakov; text by Ruth Robbins (Parnassus)

1960    *Nine Days to Christmas*, illustrated by Marie Hall Ets; text by Marie Hall Ets and Aurora Labastida (Viking)

1959    *Chanticleer and the Fox*, illustrated by Barbara Cooney; adapted from Chaucer's Canterbury Tales by Barbara Cooney (Crowell)

1958    *Time of Wonder* by Robert McCloskey (Viking)

1957    *A Tree Is Nice*, illustrated by Marc Simont; text by Janice Udry (Harper)

1956    *Frog Went A-Courtin'*, illustrated by Feodor Rojankovsky; retold by John Langstaff (Harcourt)

1955    *Cinderella, or the Little Glass Slipper*, illustrated by Marcia Brown; translated from Charles Perrault by Marcia Brown (Scribner)

1954    *Madeline's Rescue* by Ludwig Bemelmans (Viking)

1953    *The Biggest Bear* by Lynd Ward (Houghton Mifflin)

1952    *Finders Keepers*, illustrated by Nicolas, pseud. (Nicholas Mordvinoff); text by Will, pseud. [William Lipkind] (Harcourt)

1951    *The Egg Tree* by Katherine Milhous (Scribner)

1950    *Song of the Swallows* by Leo Politi (Scribner)

1949    *The Big Snow* by Berta and Elmer Hader (Macmillan)

1948    *White Snow, Bright Snow*, illustrated by Roger Duvoisin; text by Alvin Tresselt (Lothrop)

1947    *The Little Island*, illustrated by Leonard Weisgard; text by Golden MacDonald, pseud. [Margaret Wise Brown] (Doubleday)

1946    *The Rooster Crows* by Maud and Miska Petersham (Macmillan)

1945    *Prayer for a Child*, illustrated by Elizabeth Orton Jones; text by Rachel Field (Macmillan)

1944    *Many Moons*, illustrated by Louis Slobodkin; text by James Thurber (Harcourt)

1943    *The Little House* by Virginia Lee Burton (Houghton Mifflin)

1942   *Make Way for Ducklings* by Robert McCloskey (Viking)

1941   *They Were Strong and Good* by Robert Lawson (Viking)

1940   *Abraham Lincoln* by Ingri and Edgar Parin d'Aulaire (Doubleday)

1939   *Mei Li* by Thomas Handforth (Doubleday)

1938   *Animals of the Bible, A Picture Book,* illustrated by Dorothy P. Lathrop; text selected by Helen Dean Fish (Lippincott)

## CORETTA SCOTT KING AWARDS

Given to African-American authors and illustrators for outstanding inspirational and educational contributions, the Coretta Scott King Book Award titles promote understanding and appreciation of the culture of all peoples and their contribution to the realization of the American dream.

### Coretta Scott King Author Award

2010   *Bad News for Outlaws: The Remarkable Life of Bass Reeves, Deputy U.S. Marshal* by Vaunda Micheaux Nelson (Lerner)

2009   *We Are the Ship: The Story of Negro League Baseball* by Kadir Nelson (Disney)

2008   *Elijah of Buxton* by Christopher Paul Curtis (Scholastic)

2007   *Copper Sun* by Sharon Draper (Simon & Schuster)

2006   *Day of Tears: A Novel in Dialogue* by Julius Lester (Jump at the Sun)

2005   *Remember: The Journey to School Integration* by Toni Morrison (Houghton Mifflin)

2004   *The First Part Last* by Angela Johnson (Simon & Schuster)

2003   *Bronx Masquerade* by Nikki Grimes (Dial)

2002   *The Land* by Mildred Taylor (Putnam)

2001   *Miracle's Boys* by Jacqueline Woodson (Putnam)

2000   *Bud, Not Buddy* by Christopher Paul Curtis (Delacorte)

1999   *Heaven* by Angela Johnson (Simon & Schuster)

1998   *Forged by Fire* by Sharon M. Draper (Atheneum)

1997   *Slam* by Walter Dean Myers (Scholastic)

1996   *Her Stories* by Virginia Hamilton (Scholastic)

1995   *Christmas in the Big House, Christmas in the Quarters* by Patricia C. and Frederick L. McKissack (Scholastic)

1994   *Toning the Sweep* by Angela Johnson (Orchard)

1993   *Dark Thirty: Southern Tales of the Supernatural* by Patricia A. McKissack (Knopf)

1992   *Now Is Your Time: The African American Struggle for Freedom* by Walter Dean Myers (HarperCollins)

1991   *The Road to Memphis* by Mildred D. Taylor (Dial)

1990   *A Long Hard Journey: The Story of the Pullman Porter* by Patricia C. and Frederick L. McKissack (Walker)

1989   *Fallen Angels* by Walter Dean Myers (Scholastic)

1988   *The Friendship* by Mildred L. Taylor (Dial)

1987   *Justin and the Best Biscuits in the World* by Mildred Pitts Walter (Lothrop)

1986   *The People Could Fly: American Black Folktales* by Virginia Hamilton, illustrated by Leo and Diane Dillon (Knopf)

1985   *Motown and Didi* by Walter Dean Myers (Viking)

1984   *Everett Anderson's Good-bye* by Lucille Clifton (Holt)

1983   *Sweet Whispers, Brother Rush* by Virginia Hamilton (Philomel)

1982   *Let the Circle Be Unbroken* by Mildred D. Taylor (Dial)

1981   *This Life* by Sidney Poitier (Knopf)

1980   *The Young Landlords* by Walter Dean Myers (Viking)

1979   *Escape to Freedom* by Ossie Davis (Viking)

1978 *Africa Dream by Eloise Greenfield,* illustrated by Carole Bayard (Crowell)

1977 *The Story of Stevie Wonder* by James Haskins (Lothrop)

1976 *Duey's Tale* by Pearl Bailey (Harcourt)

1975 *The Legend of Africana* by Dorothy Robinson (Johnson Publishing)

1974 *Ray Charles* by Sharon Bell Mathis, illustrated by George Ford (Crowell)

1973 *I Never Had It Made: The Autobiography of Jackie Robinson,* as told to Alfred Duckett (Putnam)

1972 *17 Black Artists* by Elton C. Fax (Dodd)

1971 *Black Troubador: Langston Hughes* by Charlemae Rollins (Rand McNally)

1970 *Martin Luther King, Jr.: Man of Peace* by Lillie Patterson (Garrard)

## Coretta Scott King Illustrator Award

2010 *My People illustrated* by Charles R. Smith Jr., written by Langston Hughes (Atheneum)

2009 *The Blacker the Berry* by Floyd Cooper (HarperCollins)

2008 *Let It Shine* by Ashley Brian (Atheneum)

2007 *Moses: When Harriet Tubman Led Her People to Freedom,* illustrated by Kadir Nelson, written by Carole Boston Weatherford (Jump at the Sun)

2006 *Rosa,* illustrated by Bryan Collier; text by Nikki Giovanni (Holt)

2005 *Ellington Was Not a Street,* illustrated by Kadir A. Nelson; text by Ntozake Shange (Simon & Schuster)

2004 *Beautiful Blackbird* by Ashley Bryan (Atheneum)

2003 *Talkin' About Bessie: The Story of Aviator Elizabeth Coleman,* illustrated by E. B. Lewis; text by Nikki Grimes (Orchard Books/ Scholastic)

2002 *Goin' Someplace Special,* illustrated by Jerry Pinkney; text by Patricia McKissack (Anne Schwartz Book/Atheneum)

2001 *Uptown* by Bryan Collier (Henry Holt)

2000 *In the Time of the Drums,* illustrated by Brian Pinkney; text by Kim L. Siegelson (Jump at the Sun)

1999 *i see the rhythm,* illustrated by Michele Wood, text by Toyomi Igus (Children's Book Press)

1998 *In Daddy's Arms I Am Tall: African Americans Celebrating Fathers,* illustrated by Javaka Steptoe; text by Alan Schroeder (Lee & Low)

1997 *Minty: A Story of Young Harriet Tubman,* illustrated by Jerry Pinkney; text by Alan Schroeder (Dial Books for Young Readers)

1996 *The Middle Passage: White Ships Black Cargo* by Tom Feelings (Dial)

1995 *The Creation,* illustrated by James Ransome, text by James Weldon Johnson (Holiday House)

1994 *Soul Looks Back in Wonder,* illustrated by Tom Feelings; edited by Phyllis Fogelman (Dial)

1993 *The Origin of Life on Earth: An African Creation Myth,* illustrated by Kathleen Atkins Wilson, retold by David A. Anderson/ SANKOFA (Sights)

1992 *Tar Beach* by Faith Ringgold (Crown)

1991 *Aida,* illustrated by Leo and Diane Dillon; text by Leontyne Price (Harcourt)

1990 *Nathaniel Talking,* illustrated by Jan Spivey Gilchrist; text by Eloise Greenfield (Black Butterfly)

1989 *Mirandy and Brother Wind,* illustrated by Jerry Pinkney; text by Patricia McKissack (Knopf)

1988 *Mufaro's Beautiful Daughters: An African Tale* by John Steptoe (Lothrop)

1987 *Half a Moon and One Whole Star,* illustrated by Jerry Pinkney; text by Crescent Dragon-wagon (Macmillan)

1986 *The Patchwork Quilt,* illustrated by Jerry Pinkney; text by Valerie Flournoy (Dial)

1985 No award

1984 *My Mama Needs Me,* illustrated by Pat Cummings; text by Mildred Pitts Walter (Lothrop)

1983 *Black Child* by Peter Mugabane (Knopf)

1982 *Mother Crocodile: An Uncle Amadou Tale from Senegal,* illustrated by John Steptoe; text by Rosa Guy (Delacorte)

1981 *Beat the Story Drum, Pum-Pum* by Ashley Bryan (Atheneum)

1980 *Cornrows,* illustrated by Carole Byard; text by Camille Yarborough (Coward-McCann)

1979 *Something on My Mind,* illustrated by Tom Feelings; text by Nikki Grimes (Dial)

1978 *Africa Dream,* illustrated by Carole Bayard; text *by Eloise Greenfield* (Crowell)

1977 No award

1976 No award

1975 No award

1974 *Ray Charles,* illustrated by George Ford; text by Sharon Bell Mathis (Crowell)

## AWARDS FOR MULTICULTURAL AND INTERNATIONAL CHILDREN'S LITERATURE

*American Indian Youth Services Literature Award* (http://aila.library.sd.gov)

Annual award in the categories of illustration, children's books, and young adult books that honor the very best writing and illustrations by and about American Indians.

*Américas Award* (www.uwm.edu/Dept/CLACS/outreach/americas.html)

Annual award for children's books that engagingly portray Latin America, the Caribbean, or Latinos in the United States.

*Asian/Pacific American Award for Illustration and Youth Literature* (www.apalaweb.org)

Annual award in the categories of illustration and youth literature given to books that promote Asian/Pacific Americans' culture and their heritage.

*The Pura Belpré Award* (www.ala.org)

Annual award given to a Latino/Latina writer and illustrator whose work best portrays, affirms, and celebrates the Latino cultural experience.

*The Tomas Rivera Mexican American Children's Book Award* (www.education.txstate.edu/departments/Tomas-Rivera-Book-Award-Project-Link.html)

Annual award for an author/illustrator of the most distinguished book for children and young adults that authentically reflects the lives of Mexican-American children and young adults in the United States.

*Mildred L. Batchelder Award Winners* (www.ala.org)

This award, established in honor of Mildred Batchelder in 1966, is a citation awarded to an American publisher for a children's book considered to be the most outstanding of those books originally published in a foreign language in another country, and subsequently translated into English and published in the United States.

2010 *A Faraway Island* by Annika Thor, translated by Linda Schenck (Random House)

2009 *Moribito: Guardian of the Spirit* by Nahoko Uehashi, translated from the Japanese by Cathy Hirano (Scholastic)

2008 *Brave Story* by Miyaki Miyabe, translated from Japanese by Alexander Smith

2007 *The Pull of the Ocean* by Jean-Claude Mourlevat, translated from French by Y. Maudet (Delacorte)

2006 *An Innocent Soldier* by Josef Holub, translated from German by Michael Hofmann (Arthur A. Levine Books)

2005 *The Shadows of Ghadames* by Joëlle Stolz, translated from French by Catherine Temerson (Delacorte/Random House)

2004 *Run, Boy, Run* by Uri Orlev, translated from Hebrew by Hillel Halkin (Walter Lorraine Books/Houghton Mifflin)

2003 *The Thief Lord* by Cornelia Funke, translated by Oliver Latsch (The Chicken House/Scholastic)

2002 *How I Became an American* by Karin Gündisch, translated by James Skofield (Cricket Books/Carus)

2001 *Samir and Yonatan* by Daniella Carmi, translated from Hebrew by Yael Lotan (Arthur A. Levine/Scholastic)

2000 *The Baboon King* by Anton Quintana, translated from Dutch by John Nieuwenhuizen (Walker)

1999 *Thanks to My Mother* by Schoschana Rabinovici, translated from German by James Skofield (Dial)

1998   *The Robber and Me* by Josef Holub, edited by Mark Aronson and translated from German by Elizabeth D. Crawford (Henry Holt)

1997   *The Friends* by Kazumi Yumoto, translated from Japanese by Cathy Hirano (Farrar, Straus & Giroux)

1996   *The Lady with the Hat* by Uri Orlev, translated from Hebrew by Hillel Halkin (Houghton Mifflin)

1995   *The Boys from St. Petri* by Bjarne Reuter, translated from Danish by Anthea Bell (Dutton)

1994   *The Apprentice* by Pilar Molina Llorente, translated from Spanish by Robin Longshaw (Farrar, Straus & Giroux)

1993   No award

1992   *The Man from the Other Side* by Uri Orlev, translated from Hebrew by Hillel Halkin (Houghton Mifflin)

1991   *A Hand Full of Stars* by Rafik Schami, translated from German by Rika Lesser (Dutton)

1990   *Buster's World* by Bjarne Reuter, translated from Danish by Anthea Bell (Dutton)

1989   *Crutches* by Peter Härtling, translated from German by Elizabeth D. Crawford (Lothrop, Lee & Shepard)

1988   *If You Didn't Have Me* by Ulf Nilsson, translated from Swedish by Lone Thygesen -Clecher and George Blecher (McElderry Books)

1987   *No Hero for the Kaiser* by Rudolph Frank, translated from German by Patricia Crampton (Lothrop, Lee & Shepard)

1986   *Rose Blanche* by Christophe Gallaz and Robert Innocenti, translated from Italian by Martha Coventry and Richard Craglia (Creative Education)

1985   *The Island on Bird Street* by Uri Orlev, translated from Hebrew by Hillel Halkin (Houghton Mifflin)

1984   *Ronia, the Robber's Daughter* by Astrid Lindgren, translated from Swedish by Patricia Crampton (Viking Press)

1983   *Hiroshima No Pika* by Toshi Maruki, translated from Japanese through Kurita-Bando Literary Agency (Lothrop, Lee & Shepard)

1982   *The Battle Horse* by Harry Kullman, translated from Swedish by George Blecher and Lone Thygesen Blecher (Bradbury Press)

1981   *The Winter When Time Was Frozen* by Els Pelgrom, translated from Dutch by Maryka and Raphael Rudnik (Morrow)

1980   *The Sound of the Dragon's Feet* by Aliki Zei, translated from Greek by Edward Fenton (Dutton)

1979   Two awards given: *Rabbit Island* by Jörg Steiner, translated from German by Ann Conrad Lammers (Harcourt Brace Jovanovich); *Konrad* by Christine Nöstlinger, translated from German by Anthea Bell (Franklin Watts)

1978   No award

1977   *The Leopard* by Cecil Bødker, translated from Danish by Gunnar Poulsen (Atheneum)

1976   *The Cat and Mouse Who Shared a House* by Ruth Hürlimann, translated from German by Anthea Bell (Henry Z. Walck)

1975   *An Old Tale Carved Out of Stone* by A. Linevskii, translated from Russian by Maria Polushkin (Crown)

1974   *Petros' War* by Aliki Zei, translated from Greek by Edward Fenton (Dutton)

1973   *Pulga* by S. R. Van Iterson, translated from Dutch by Alexander and Alison Gode (Morrow)

1972   *Friedrich* by Hans Peter Richter, translated from German by Edite Kroll (Holt, Rinehart & Winston)

1971   *In the Land of Ur, the Discovery of Ancient Mesopotamia* by Hans Baumann, translated from German by Stella Humphries (Pantheon)

1970   *Wildcat Under Glass* by Aliki Zei, translated from Greek by Edward Fenton (Holt, Rinehart & Winston)

1969   *Don't Take Teddy* by Babbis Friis-Baastad, translated from Norwegian by Lise Sømme McKinnon (Scribner)

1968   *The Little Man* by Erich Kästner, translated from German by James Kirkup (Knopf)

# AWARDS FOR GENRE

## Nonfiction: Orbis Pictus Award

Established by the National Council of Teachers of English, the Orbis Pictus award recognizes excellence in the writing of nonfiction for children. The name *Orbis Pictus* commemorates the work of Johannes Amos Comenius, *Orbis Pictus—The World in Pictures* (1657), considered to be the first book actually planned for children.

2010    *The Secret World of Walter Anderson* by Hester Bass, illustrated by E. B. Lewis (Candlewick Press)

2009    *Amelia Earhart: The Legend of the Lost Aviator* by Shelley Tanaka, illustrated by David Craig (Abrams)

2008    *M.L.K.: Journey of a King* by Tonya Bolden (Abrams)

2007    *Quest for the Tree Kangaroo: An Expedition to the Cloud Forest of New Guinea* by Sy Montgomery, photographs by Nic Bishop (Houghton Mifflin)

2006    *Children of the Great Depression* by Russell Freedman (Houghton Mifflin)

2005    *York's Adventures with Lewis and Clark: An African-American's Part in the Great Expedition* by Rhoda Blumberg (HarperCollins)

2004    *The American Plague: The True and Terrible Story of the Epidemic of Yellow Fever 1793* by Jim Murphy (Houghton Mifflin)

2003    *When Marian Sang: The True Recital of Marian Anderson: The Voice of a Century* by Pam Munoz Ryan (Scholastic)

2002    *Black Potatoes: The Story of the Great Irish Famine, 1845–1850* by Susan Campbell Bartoletti (Houghton Mifflin)

2001    *Hurry Freedom: African Americans in Gold Rush California* by Jerry Stanley (Crown)

2000    *Through My Eyes* by Ruby Bridges, compiled and edited by Margo Lundell (Scholastic)

1999    *Shipwreck at the Bottom of the World: The Extraordinary True Story of Shackleton and the Endurance* by Jennifer Armstrong (Crown)

1998    *An Extraordinary Life: The Story of a Monarch Butterfly* by Laurence Pringle (Orchard)

1997    *Leonardo da Vinci* by Diane Stanley (Morrow)

1996    *The Great Fire* by Jim Murphy (Scholastic)

1995    *Safari Beneath the Sea: The Wonder World of the North Pacific Coast* by Diane Swanson (Sierra Club Books)

1994    *Across America on an Emigrant Train* by Jim Murphy (Houghton Mifflin)

1993    *Children of the Dust Bowl: The True Story of the School at Weedpatch Camp* by Jerry Stanley (Crown)

1992    *Flight: The Journey of Charles Lindbergh* by Robert Burleigh, illustrated by Mike Wimmer (Philomel Books)

1991    *Franklin Delano Roosevelt* by Russell Freedman (Houghton Mifflin)

1990    *The Great Little Madison* by Jean Fritz (Putnam)

*Nonfiction: Washington Post–Children's Book Guild Nonfiction Award* (www.childrensbookguild.org)

Annual award that honors an author or author-illustrator whose total work has contributed significantly to the quality of nonfiction for children.

## Historical Fiction: Scott O'Dell Award

Established in 1982, the Scott O'Dell Award is for a meritorious book of historical fiction published in the previous year for children or young adults. The award was established to increase the interest of young readers in the historical background that has helped to shape their country and their world.

2010    *The Storm in the Barn* by Matt Phelan (Candelwick)

2009    *Chains* by Laurie Halse Anderson (Simon and Schuster)

2008    *Elijah of Buxton* by Christopher Paul Curtis (Scholastic)

2007    *The Green Glass Sea* by Ellen Klages (Viking)

2006    *The Game of Silence* by Louise Erdrich (HarperCollins)

2005    *Worth* by A. LaFaye (Simon & Schuster)

2004    *The River Between Us* by Richard Peck (Dial)

2003    *Trouble Don't Last* by Shelly Pearsall (Knopf)

2002    *The Land* by Mildred Taylor (Phyllis Fogelman)

2001    *The Art of Keeping Cool* by Janet Lisle (Atheneum)

2000   *Two Suns in the Sky* by Miriam Bat-Ami (Front Street)

1999   *Forty Acres and Maybe a Mule* by Harriette Robinet (Atheneum)

1998   *Out of the Dust* by Karen Hesse (Scholastic)

1997   *Jip, His Story* by Katherine Paterson (Dutton)

1996   *The Bomb* by Theodore Taylor (Harcourt Brace)

1995   *Under the Blood-Red Sun* by Graham Salisbury (Delacorte)

1994   *Bull Run* by Paul Fleischman (HarperCollins)

1993   *Morning Girl* by Michael Dorris (Hyperion)

1992   *Stepping on the Cracks* by Mary Downing Hahn (Houghton Mifflin)

1991   *A Time of Troubles* by Pieter Van Raven (Scribner)

1990   *Shades of Gray* by Carolyn Reeder (Macmillan)

1989   *The Honorable Prison* by Lyll Becerra de Jenkins (Dutton)

1988   *Charley Skedaddle* by Patricia Beatty (Morrow)

1987   *Streams to the River, River to the Sea* by Scott O'Dell (Houghton Mifflin)

1986   *Sarah, Plain and Tall* by Patricia MacLachlan (Harper & Row)

1985   *The Fighting Ground* by Avi (Lippincott)

1984   *The Sign of the Beaver* by Elizabeth George Speare (Houghton Mifflin)

## Poetry: Lee Bennett Hopkins Award

Established in 1993, the Lee Bennett Hopkins Award is presented annually to an American poet or anthologist for the most outstanding new book of poetry for children published in the previous calendar year.

2010   *Button Up!* By Alice Schertle, illustrated by Petra Mathers (Houghton Mifflin Harcourt)

2009   *Diamond Willow* by Helen Frost (Farrar, Straus and Giroux)

2008   *Birmingham, 1963* by Carole Boston Weatherford (Wordsong)

2007   *Jazz* by Walter Dean Myers, illustrated by Christopher Myers (Holiday House)

2006   *Song of the Water Boatman & Other Pond Poems* by Joyce Sidman (Houghton Mifflin)

2005   *Here in Harlem* by Walter Dean Myers (Holiday House)

2004   *The Wishing Bone and Other Poems* by Stephen Mitchell (Candlewick)

2003   *Splash! Poems of Our Watery World* by Constance Levy, illustrated by David Soman (Orchard Books)

2002   *Pieces: A Year in Poems and Quilts* by Anna Grossnickle Hines (Greenwillow)

2001   *Light-Gathering Poems* by Liz Rosenberg (Holt)

2000   *What Have You Lost? selected* by Naomi Shihab Nye (Greenwillow)

1999   *The Other Side* by Angela Johnson (Orchard)

1998   *The Great Frog Race and Other Poems* by Kristine O'Connell George (Houghton Mifflin)

1997   *Voices from the Wild* by David Bouchard (Chronicle)

1996   *Dance With Me* by Barbara Juster Esbensen (HarperCollins)

1995   *Beast Feast* by Douglas Florian (Harcourt Brace)

1994   *Spirit Walker* by Nancy Wood (Doubleday)

1993   *Sing to the Sun* by Ashley Bryan (HarperCollins)

## Poetry: International Reading Association Promising Poet Award

(www.reading.org/association/awards/childrens_hopkins.html)

Given every three years to a promising new poet of children's poetry (for children and young adults up to grade 12) who has published no more than two books of children's poetry.

## Informational Books: Robert F. Sibert Informational Book Award

(www.ala.org)

Annual award given to the author and illustrator of the most distinguished informational book published in English during the preceding year.

## Mystery: The Edgar Award for Young Adult and Juvenile Mystery

(www.theedgars.com)

Annual award given to the best juvenile and young adult mystery book.

# ADDITIONAL AWARDS IN CHILDREN'S LITERATURE

*Jane Addams Book Award* (www.janeaddamspeace.org).

Annual award for children's books that effectively promote the cause of peace, social justice, world community, and the equality of the sexes and all races.

*ALA's Odyssey Award* (www.ala.org).

Established in 2008, the Odyssey Award is for excellence in audiobook production.

*Hans Christian Andersen Award* (www.ibby.org).

Biannual award given to a living author and illustrator whose complete works have made a lasting contribution to children's literature.

*Boston Globe—Horn Book Awards* (www.hbook .com).

Annual award for children's and young adult literature in three categories: Picture Book, Fiction and Poetry, and Nonfiction.

*Carnegie and Kate Greenaway Medals* (www .carnegiegreenaway.org.uk).

The Carnegie Medal is awarded annually to an outstanding book for children and young people. The Kate Greenaway Medal is awarded annually for distinguished illustration in a book for children. Both awards are given to books published or co-published in the UK the previous year.

*Margaret A. Edwards Award* (www.ala.org).

Annual award that honors an author of young adult literature, as well as a specific body of his or her work, that have been popular over a period of time.

*Theodor Geisel Award* (www.ala.org).

Annual award for the author and illustrator of the most distinguished American book for beginning readers published in English in the United States during the preceding year.

*Polly Gray Award for Children's Literature in Developmental Disabilities* (www.dddcec.org).

Sponsored by the Council for Exceptional Children, the Polly Gray Award recognizes children's books that appropriately portray individuals with developmental disabilities.

*Gryphon Award* (http://ccb.lis.illinois.edu/gryphon .html).

Annual award for a fiction or nonfiction book for which the primary audience is children in kindergarten through grade 4. The title chosen best exemplifies those qualities that successfully bridge the gap in difficulty between books for reading aloud to children and books for practiced readers.

*International Reading Association Children's Book Award* (www.reading.org/Resources/AwardsandGrants/ childrens_ira.aspx).

Annual awards given for an author's first or second published book written for children or young adults in the categories of fiction and nonfiction.

*Ezra Jack Keats New Writers Award* (www.ezra-jack-keats.org).

Annual award given to an outstanding new writer of picturebooks for children (age 9 and under).

*National Book Award for Young People's Literature* (www.nationalbook.org).

Annual award in the category of Young People's Literature.

*National Council of Teachers of English Award for Excellence in Poetry for Children* (http://www.ncte.org/awards/poetry/).

Given every three years to honor a living American poet for his or her aggregate work for children ages 3–13.

*Michael Printz Award for Excellence in Young Adult Literature* (www.ala.org).

Annual award for a book that exemplifies literary excellence in young adult literature.

*Laura Ingalls Wilder Award* (www.ala.org).

Annual award given to honor an author or illustrator whose books, published in the United States, have made, over a period of years, a substantial and lasting contribution to literature for children.

*Charlotte Zolotow Award* (www.education.wisc.edu/ ccbc/books/zolotow.asp).

Annual award for the author of the best picture book text published in the United States in the preceding year.

*Lambda Literary Award* (www.lambdaliterary.org/ awards).

The Lambda Literary Award in the category of children's and young adult literature seeks to recognize excellence in the field of lesbian, gay, bisexual, and transgender literature.

*Native Writers Circle of the Americas Award* (www .wordcraftcircle.org).

These are the only literature awards bestowed on Native American Indian writers by Native American Indian people. The awards are given in three categories: Lifetime Achievement Awards, First Book Awards for Poetry, and First Book Awards for Prose.

# CREDITS

Burleigh, Robert. Reprinted with the permission of Atheneum Books for Young Readers, an imprint of Simon & Schuster Children's Publishing Division from *Black Whiteness* by Robert Burleigh. Text copyright © 1998 Robert Burleigh.

Dickinson, Emily. Reprinted by permission of the publishers and the Trustees of Amherst College from *The Poems of Emily Dickinson*, Thomas H. Johnson, ed., Cambridge, MA: The Belknap Press of Harvard University Press, Copyright © 1951, 1955, 1979, 1983 by the President and Fellows of Harvard College.

Fisher, Aileen. "The Seed" from *Always Wondering: Some Favorite Poems of Aileen Fisher.* Copyright © 1991 by Aileen Fisher. Used by permission of Marian Reiner on behalf of the Boulder Public Library Foundation, Inc.

Fleischman, Paul. From *Joyful Noise* by Paul Fleischman. Text Copyright © 1988 by Paul Fleischman. Used by permission of HarperCollins Publishers.

Florian, Douglas. "The Daddy Longlegs" from *Insectlopedia*, copyright © 1998 by Douglas Florian, reprinted by permission of Houghton Mifflin Harcourt Publishing Company.

George, Kristine O'Connell. "Skating in the Wind" as found in *Poetry Speaks to Children*. Reprinted by permission of the author.

Gerstein, Mordecai. "Selected Quotes" from *The Man Who Walked Between The Towers* by Mordecai Gerstein. Copyright © 2003 by Mordecai Gerstein. Reprinted by arrangement with Roaring Brook Press/Henry Holt and Company, LLC.

Holbrook, Sara. From *Wham! It's a Poetry Jam* by Sara Holbrook. Copyright © 2002 by Sara Holbrook. Published by Wordsong, an imprint of Boyds Mills Press. Reprinted by permission.

Jacobsen, Rolf. "Look" from *Night Open* by Rolf Jacobsen, translated by Olav Grinde, published by White Pine Press. Reprinted by permission.

Lewis, J. Patrick. "Great, Good, Bad" from *Please Bury Me at the Library*, text copyright © 2005 by J. Patrick Lewis, reprinted by permission of Houghton Mifflin Harcourt Publishing Company.

Louie, Ai-Ling. From *Yeh-Shen: A Cinderella Story from China* by Ai-Ling Louie, copyright © 1982 by Ai-Long Louie. Used by permission of Philomel Books, A Division of Penguin Young Readers Group, A Member of Penguin Group (USA) Inc., 345 Hudson Street, New York, NY 10014. All rights reserved.

Nye, Naomi Shihib. From *A Maze Me: Poems for Girls* by Naomi Shihib Nye. Text copyright © 2005 by Naomi Shihab Nye. Reprinted by permission of HarperCollins Publishers.

O'Hara, Frank. "Autobiographia Literaria" copyright © 1971 by Maureen Granville-Smith, Administratix of the Estate of Frank O'Hara, from *The Collected Poems of Frank O'Hara* by Frank O'Hara, edited by Donald Allen. Used by permission of Alfred A. Knopf, a division of Random House, Inc.

Prelutsky, Jack. From *The New Kid on the Block*. Text Copyright © 1984 by Jack Prelutsky. Used by permission of HarperCollins Publishers, Inc.

Scieszka, Jon. "Mary Had a..." from *Science Verse* by Jon Scieszka, copyright © 2004 by Jon Scieszka, text. Used by permission of Viking Children's Books, A Division of Penguin Young Readers Group, A Member of Penguin Group (USA) Inc., 345 Hudson Street, New York, NY 10014. All rights reserved.

Sidman, Joyce. Backswimmer's Refrain from *Song of the Water Boatman and Other Pond Poems* by Joyce Sidman. Text copyright © 2005 by Joyce Sidman. Reprinted by permission of Houghton Mifflin Company. All rights reserved.

Van Allsburg, Chris. Excerpt from *The Polar Express* by Chris Van Allsburg. Copyright © 1985 by Chris Van Allsburg. Reprinted by permission of Houghton Mifflin Company. All rights reserved.

Wick, Walter. Excerpt from *A Drop of Water* by Walter Wick, Scholastic, Inc. Reprinted by permission.

Williams, William Carlos. "The Red Wheelbarrow" by William Carlos Williams, from *The Collected Poems: Volume I, 1909–1939*, copyright © 1938 by New Directions Publishing Corp. Reprinted by permission of New Directions Publishing Corp.

Wong, Janet. Speak Up is reprinted from *Good Luck Gold and Other Poems* by Janet S. Wong. Copyright © 1994 Janet S. Wong. Reprinted by permission of the author.

Woodson, Jacqueline. From *Locomotion* by Jacqueline Woodson, copyright © 2003 by Jacqueline Woodson. Used by permission of G.P. Putnam's Sons, A Division of Penguin Young Readers Group, A Member of Penguin Group (USA) Inc., 345 Hudson Street, New York, NY 10014. All rights reserved.

# TITLE/AUTHOR INDEX

# SUBJECT INDEX